Soft–Computing–Based Nonlinear Control Systems Design

Uday Pratap Singh
Madhav Institute of Technology and Science, India

Akhilesh Tiwari
Madhav Institute of Technology and Science, India

Rajeev Kumar Singh
Madhav Institute of Technology and Science, India

A volume in the Advances in Computer and
Electrical Engineering (ACEE) Book Series

Published in the United States of America by
   IGI Global
   Engineering Science Reference (an imprint of IGI Global)
   701 E. Chocolate Avenue
   Hershey PA, USA 17033
   Tel: 717-533-8845
   Fax: 717-533-8661
   E-mail: cust@igi-global.com
   Web site: http://www.igi-global.com

Library of Congress Cataloging-in-Publication Data

Names: Singh, Uday Pratap, 1979- editor. | Tiwari, Akhilesh, 1982- editor. |
   Singh, Rajeev Kumar, 1986- editor.
Title: Soft-computing-based nonlinear control systems design / Uday Pratap
   Singh, Akhilesh Tiwari, and Rajeev Kumar Singh, editors.
Description: Hershey, PA : Engineering Science Reference, [2018] | Includes
   bibliographical references.
Identifiers: LCCN 2017019872| ISBN 9781522535317 (hardcover) | ISBN
   9781522535324 (ebook)
Subjects: LCSH: Automatic control. | Nonlinear control theory. | Soft
   computing.
Classification: LCC TJ213 .S5176 2018 | DDC 629.8/9563--dc23 LC record available at https://lccn.loc.gov/2017019872

This book is published in the IGI Global book series Advances in Computer and Electrical Engineering (ACEE) (ISSN:
2327-039X; eISSN: 2327-0403)

British Cataloguing in Publication Data
A Cataloguing in Publication record for this book is available from the British Library.

For electronic access to this publication, please contact: eresources@igi-global.com.

Advances in Computer and Electrical Engineering (ACEE) Book Series

Srikanta Patnaik
SOA University, India

ISSN:2327-039X
EISSN:2327-0403

MISSION

The fields of computer engineering and electrical engineering encompass a broad range of interdisciplinary topics allowing for expansive research developments across multiple fields. Research in these areas continues to develop and become increasingly important as computer and electrical systems have become an integral part of everyday life.

The **Advances in Computer and Electrical Engineering (ACEE) Book Series** aims to publish research on diverse topics pertaining to computer engineering and electrical engineering. **ACEE** encourages scholarly discourse on the latest applications, tools, and methodologies being implemented in the field for the design and development of computer and electrical systems.

COVERAGE

- Applied Electromagnetics
- Electrical Power Conversion
- Digital Electronics
- Sensor Technologies
- Circuit Analysis
- Microprocessor Design
- Computer science
- Algorithms
- Power Electronics
- Chip Design

IGI Global is currently accepting manuscripts for publication within this series. To submit a proposal for a volume in this series, please contact our Acquisition Editors at Acquisitions@igi-global.com or visit: http://www.igi-global.com/publish/.

Titles in this Series

For a list of additional titles in this series, please visit: www.igi-global.com/book-series

Design and Use of Virtualization Technology in Cloud Computing
Prashanta Kumar Das (Government Industrial Training Institute Dhansiri, India) and Ganesh Chandra Deka (Government of India, India)
Engineering Science Reference • copyright 2018 • 315pp • H/C (ISBN: 9781522527855) • US $235.00 (our price)

Smart Grid Test Bed Using OPNET and Power Line Communication
Jun-Ho Huh (Catholic University of Pusan, South Korea)
Engineering Science Reference • copyright 2018 • 425pp • H/C (ISBN: 9781522527763) • US $225.00 (our price)

Transport of Information-Carriers in Semiconductors and Nanodevices
Muhammad El-Saba (Ain-Shams University, Egypt)
Engineering Science Reference • copyright 2017 • 677pp • H/C (ISBN: 9781522523123) • US $225.00 (our price)

Accelerating the Discovery of New Dielectric Properties in Polymer Insulation
Boxue Du (Tianjin University, China)
Engineering Science Reference • copyright 2017 • 388pp • H/C (ISBN: 9781522523093) • US $210.00 (our price)

Handbook of Research on Nanoelectronic Sensor Modeling and Applications
Mohammad Taghi Ahmadi (Urmia University, Iran) Razali Ismail (Universiti Teknologi Malaysia, Malaysia) and Sohail Anwar (Penn State University, USA)
Engineering Science Reference • copyright 2017 • 579pp • H/C (ISBN: 9781522507369) • US $245.00 (our price)

Field-Programmable Gate Array (FPGA) Technologies for High Performance Instrumentation
Julio Daniel Dondo Gazzano (University of Castilla-La Mancha, Spain) Maria Liz Crespo (International Centre for Theoretical Physics, Italy) Andres Cicuttin (International Centre for Theoretical Physics, Italy) and Fernando Rincon Calle (University of Castilla-La Mancha, Spain)
Engineering Science Reference • copyright 2016 • 306pp • H/C (ISBN: 9781522502999) • US $185.00 (our price)

Design and Modeling of Low Power VLSI Systems
Manoj Sharma (BVC, India) Ruchi Gautam (MyResearch Labs, Gr Noida, India) and Mohammad Ayoub Khan (Sharda University, India)
Engineering Science Reference • copyright 2016 • 386pp • H/C (ISBN: 9781522501909) • US $205.00 (our price)

Reliability in Power Electronics and Electrical Machines Industrial Applications and Performance Models
Shahriyar Kaboli (Sharif University of Technology, Iran) and Hashem Oraee (Sharif University of Technology, Iran)
Engineering Science Reference • copyright 2016 • 481pp • H/C (ISBN: 9781466694293) • US $255.00 (our price)

701 East Chocolate Avenue, Hershey, PA 17033, USA
Tel: 717-533-8845 x100 • Fax: 717-533-8661
E-Mail: cust@igi-global.com • www.igi-global.com

Table of Contents

Detailed Table of Contents

Chapter 1
Kanchan Bala, Birla Institute of Technology Mesra, India
Dilip Kumar Choubey, Birla Institute of Technology Mesra, India
Sanchita Paul, Birla Institute of Technology Mesra, India
Mili Ghosh Nee Lala, Birla Institute of Technology Mesra, India

Environmental disasters affect the economy, biodiversity, human life, and living organisms. Thunderstorms are one of such environmental disaster. By using proper methodology of forecasting thunderstorms, the adverse effects can be reduced. The prediction of thunderstorms is the most difficult task in weather forecasting due to their temporal and spatial extension either physically or dynamically. Lightning is associated with thunderstorms, which causes wildfires, kills people and other living organisms. Heavy rain from thunderstorms causes flash flooding. In this regard, several researchers have proposed different methodology such as statistical, numerical mode, data mining, soft computing, and machine learning for forecasting of severe weather to reduce the damages. This chapter focuses existing classification methods on thunderstorms and lightning prediction. This chapter includes suggestions on the future research directions.

Chapter 2
Monica Patrascu, University Politehnica of Bucharest, Romania

In the light of recent technological advances, semi-active structural damping systems for seismic vibration mitigation are considered part of the civil engineering design process. Various actuating devices have been integrated into structures along with specifically designed control strategies. Semi-active dampers are nonlinear switching systems that require enhanced controllers. In order to minimize instability risk, a cascaded fuzzy control system that integrates the switch behaviour is designed. The inner loop uses a PI (proportional-integral) controller that is tuned with evolutionary optimization. The case study uses an electrohydraulic damper and a three-story building. To anticipate robustness to real-world disturbances and equipment failure, an uncertainty effect analysis is included in which three control systems are compared. First, structural and actuator disturbances are considered. Then, the case of switch failure brings forth the high reliability of the fuzzy control system, in what concerns using semi-active dampers in the development of civil structures.

Chapter 3

Kamel Smiri, Université de Tunis El Manar, Tunisia
Nourhen Fourati, Université de Tunis El Manar, Tunisia

In this chapter, the authors explore the estimation of the performances in an earlier stage of (multi-processors system on chip) MPSoC design in which it is necessary to drive design space exploration and support important design decisions. Therefore, they address the co-design hardware/software with estimating performances in order to find an adequate solution, which consists in mapping the application on the components of architecture with respect the criteria of performance of the system defined from the beginning. The chapter provides a hybrid model for estimating performance in which cohabited simulation and analytical techniques are carried out via a link layer in order to reach an optimal architectural solution quickly. Thus, it allows faster performance estimation with better accuracy at different levels of abstraction.

Chapter 4

Saifullah Khalid, Independent Researcher, India

A novel adaptive blanket body cover algorithm (ABBC) has been presented, which has been used for the optimization of conventional control scheme used in shunt active power filter. The effectiveness of the proposed algorithm has been proven by applying this in aircraft system. The superiority of this algorithm over existing genetic algorithm results has been presented by analyzing the THD and compensation time of both the algorithms. The simulation results using the MATLAB model ratify that that algorithm has optimized the control technique, which unmistakably proves the usefulness of the proposed algorithm in 400 Hertz aircraft system.

Chapter 5

Constantin-Florin Caruntu, Gheorghe Asachi Technical University of Iasi, Romania

The problem considered in this chapter is to control a vehicle drivetrain in order to minimize its oscillations while coping with the time-varying delays introduced by the CAN communication network and the strict timing limitations. As such, two Lyapunov-based model predictive control design methodologies are presented: one based on modeling the network-induced time-varying delays using a polytopic approximation technique and the second one based on modeling the delays as disturbances. Several tests performed using an industry validated drivetrain model indicate that the proposed design methodologies can handle both the performance/physical constraints and the strict limitations on the computational complexity, while effectively coping with the time-varying delays. Moreover, a comparative analysis between the two Lyapunov-based model predictive control design methodologies in terms of computational complexity, number of optimization variables, and obtained performances is carried out.

Chapter 6

Maryam Shahriari-Kahkeshi, Shahrekord University, Iran

This chapter proposes a new modeling and control scheme for uncertain strict-feedback nonlinear systems based on adaptive fuzzy wavelet network (FWN) and dynamic surface control (DSC) approach. It designs adaptive FWN as a nonlinear-in-parameter approximator to approximate the uncertain dynamics of the system. Then, the proposed control scheme is developed by incorporating the DSC method to the adaptive FWN-based model. Stability analysis of the proposed scheme is provided and adaptive laws are designed to learn all linear and nonlinear parameters of the network. It is proven that all the signals of the closed-loop system are uniformly ultimately bounded and the tracking error can be made arbitrary small. The proposed scheme does not require any prior knowledge about dynamics of the system and offline learning. Furthermore, it eliminates the "explosion of complexity" problems and develops accurate model of the system and simple controller. Simulation results on the numerical example and permanent magnet synchronous motor are provided to show the effectiveness of the proposed scheme.

Chapter 7

Amit Kumar, Birla Institute of Technology Mesra, India
Bikash Kanti Sarkar, Birla Institute of Technology Mesra, India

Research in medical data prediction has become an important classification problem due to its domain specificity, voluminous, and class imbalanced nature. In this chapter, four well-known nature-inspired algorithms, namely genetic algorithms (GA), genetic programming (GP), particle swarm optimization (PSO), and ant colony optimization (ACO), are used for feature selection in order to enhance the classification performances of medical data using Bayesian classifier. Naïve Bayes is most widely used Bayesian classifier in automatic medical diagnostic tools. In total, 12 real-world medical domain data sets are selected from the University of California, Irvine (UCI repository) for conducting the experiment. The experimental results demonstrate that nature-inspired Bayesian model plays an effective role in undertaking medical data prediction.

Chapter 8

Deepika Singh Kushwah, Jaypee University of Engineering and Technology, India
Deepika Dubey, Uttarakhand Technical University, India

Wireless sensor networks are the evolutionary self-organizing multi-node networks. Due to dynamic network conditions and stochastically varying network environments, routing in WSNs is critically affected and needs to be optimized. The routing strategies developed for WSNs must be efficient to make it an operationally self-configurable network. For this we need to resort to near shortest path evaluation. Therefore, some soft computing approaches that can calculate the near shortest path available in an affordable computing time are required. WSNs have a high computational environment with limited and precise transmission range, processing, and limited energy sources. The sever power constraints strongly affect the existence of active nodes and hence the network lifetime. So, here, the authors use the power of soft computing because the potential features of soft-computing (SC) approach highly address their adaptability and compatibility to overwhelm the complex challenges in WSNs.

Chapter 9

Deepika Dubey, Uttarakhand Technical University, India
Deepika Singh Kushwah, Jaypee University of Engineering and Technology, India
Deepanshu Dubey, Indian Institute of Forest Management, India

An image may be mist full for the one or may be nostalgic for the other. But for a researcher, each image is distinguished on the basis of its low-level features like color, shape, size. Other features like edges, corner/interesting points, blobs/region of interest, ridges, etc. can also be used for computation purpose. Using these features distinctions, an image can be processed for the purpose of enhancing the images having same features, matching, and shortlisting of similar images from a random available image database. This could be done using soft computing techniques like neural networks, fuzzy logic, and evolutionary computation methods. Neural networks can participate effectively in image processing in several ways.

Chapter 10

Sowkarthika B, Madhav Institute of Technology and Science, India
Akhilesh Tiwari, Madhav Institute of Technology and Science, India
R. K. Gupta, Madhav Institute of Technology and Science, India
Uday Pratap Singh, Madhav Institute of Technology and Science, India

In this digital world, tremendous data are generated in every field. Useful information is inferred out of this data, which is valuable for effective decision making. Data mining extracts the interesting information from huge volumes of data. Association rule (AR) mining is one of the core areas of data mining where interesting information is extracted in the form of rules. Traditional AR mining is incapable of handling uncertain situations. In order to handle uncertainty, mathematical tools like vague theory can be utilized with AR mining methodologies for the development of novel vague theory based algorithms, which will be more suitable in effectively handling vague situations that helps framing effective selling strategy. Since an organization can't analyze the huge rule set obtained from these algorithms, every resultant rule should have a certain ratio of factors customized to the interest of the organization that can be achieved through optimization algorithms. This chapter explores the significance of vague theory and optimization means for effective uncertainty management.

Chapter 11

Abid Ali, Universiti Teknologi PETRONAS, Malaysia
Nursyarizal Mohd Nor, Universiti Teknologi PETRONAS, Malaysia
Taib Ibrahim, Universiti Teknologi PETRONAS, Malaysia
Mohd Fakhizan Romlie, Universiti Teknologi PETRONAS, Malaysia
Kishore Bingi, Universiti Teknologi PETRONAS, Malaysia

This chapter proposes a mixed-integer optimization using genetic algorithm (MIOGA) for determining the optimum sizes and placements of battery-sourced solar photovoltaic (B-SSPV) plants to reduce the total energy losses in distribution networks. Total energy loss index (TELI) is formulated as the main objective function and meanwhile bus voltage deviations and PV penetrations of B-SSPV plants are calculated. To deal the stochastic behavior of solar irradiance, 15 years of weather data is modeled by using beta probability density function (Beta-PDF). The proposed algorithm is applied on IEEE 33 bus and IEEE 69 bus test distribution networks and optimum results are acquired for different time varying voltage dependent load models. From the results, it is known that, compared to PV only, the integration of B-SSPV plants in the distribution networks resulted in higher penetration levels in distribution networks. The proposed algorithm was very effective in terms of determining the sizes of the PV plant and the battery storage, and for the charging and discharging of the battery storage.

Chapter 12

Shalini Stalin, Aisect University, India
Priti Maheshwary, Aisect University, India
Piyush Kumar Shukla, University Instituter of Technology RGPV, India
Akhilesh Tiwari, Madhav Institute of Technology, India
Ankur Khare, M. K. Ponda College of Business and Management, India

In last few decades, a lot of work has been done in the field of cryptography; it is being considered one of the safe methods to protect data. It was first used to protect communication by individuals, armies, and organizational companies. With the help encryption method, anyone can protect their data from a third-party attack. Images are used in various areas like biometric authentication, medical science, military, etc., where they are being stored or transferred over the network and the safety of such images are very important. The newest movement in encryption is chaos-based, which is a better encryption technique than AES, DES, RSA, etc. It consists of different property such as sensitive independence on original situation, non-periodicity, non-convergence, etc. In recent times, many chaos-based image encryption algorithms have been proposed, but most of them are not sufficient to provide full protection to data. In this chapter, a survey of different chaos-based image encryption techniques is discussed.

Chapter 13

K. Vinoth Kumar, Karunya University, India
Prawin Angel Michael, Karunya University, India

This chapter deals with the implementation of a PC-based monitoring and fault identification scheme for a three-phase induction motor using artificial neural networks (ANNs). To accomplish the task, a hardware system is designed and built to acquire three phase voltages and currents from a 3.3KW squirrel-cage, three-phase induction motor. A software program is written to read the voltages and currents, which are first used to train a feed-forward neural network structure. The trained network is placed in a Lab VIEW-based program formula node that monitors the voltages and currents online and displays the fault conditions and turns the motor. The complete system is successfully tested in real time by creating different faults on the motor.

In this chapter a review is done on the image segmentation techniques by using both traditional approaches and soft computing approaches. This chapter will figure out some soft computing approaches that can be used to solve the problem of identification of objects. Some traditional approaches for the extraction of objects are discussed along with their comparison with soft computing approaches. The chapter discusses various applications of image segmentation. The soft computing approaches are then analyzed and their performance is compared with the others by identifying the advantages and disadvantages of all.

Chapter 15

Due to growing demand of energy, green technologies are highly attractive among researchers because of their non-conventional nature. Energy harvesting is one of their best parts. Very low cost of maintenance and non-polluting nature are major reasons behind their growing demand. However, for ultra-low power applications, such as in wireless sensor devices, the energy scavenging from RF signal is another alternative. In the last few years, a great interest has been seen in microwave power scavenging for charging wireless devices. This chapter presents a RF energy harvesting circuit with tuned π-matching network that resonates at desired incident RF frequency to boost these signals. Various computer intelligent techniques have been used to optimize parameters value of matching circuit. The designed circuit has been analyzed for input power range from -30 dBm to 0 dBm. Approximately 80% maximum PCE is achieved at RF input of 0 dBm with 4 KΩ load. It is also demonstrated that better output power is produced for power range -15 dBm to 0 dBm at higher load values.

Preface

Soft computing approaches for nonlinear control systems have attracted a growing number of scientists, decision makers and practicing researchers in last few years. Since design of the exact mathematical model of the plant or industrial systems and find the solution of these models using traditional methods (hard computing methods) are not always possible. Due to uncertain nature of plants and industrial systems, soft computing techniques are employs to find the approximate solution of these systems. Soft computing methods are powerful intelligent computational techniques emerged for solving and control a vast number of nonlinear real-world problems. Neural network, fuzzy logic control and various hybrid methods including nature inspired metaheuristic techniques are examples of such soft computing techniques. Approximation or numerical solution of nonlinear model is much difficult in comparison to the linear model and these difficulties are increases in presence of external disturbances.

Nonlinear control system design serves as a new core perspective of the compendium and text book. It deals with approximation of numerical solution to the target and help a scientists, decision makers and researchers, in which each decision maker tries to optimize their objectives. Nonlinear control theory is a mathematical theory dealing with the modelling and the analysis of conflict and cooperation and has broad applicability in control theory, time-series prediction, economics, financial modelling, environmental management and pollution control etc.

With this book the editors aim as follows:

- To offer a compendium for all scientists, researchers, who will become able to familiarize with the nonlinear control systems, research subjects that are of common practical and methodological interest for representatives of nonlinear data predictions, industrial applications and engineering applications,
- To provide and create a platform and atmosphere in which scientist and researchers can grow knowledge to reading the book and developing them towards recognized experiments,
- To provide a dictionary and encyclopedia related to soft computing approaches which will enable scientists and practitioners to quickly access the key notions of their domains and, via suitable methods and references,
- Take initiate a momentum of excitement and encouragement on the way of preparing this book and of reading it later on, that will strongly support interdisciplinary science, the solution of striking real-world problems and a creative and fruitful collaboration between experts from all over the world,
- To further introduce IGI as a premium publisher in new regions and as a Center of Excellence.

This book provides a basic platform and an excellent reference to students of graduate, postgraduate level, scientists, researchers and decision makers in private/government sectors, universities, and industrialist in the field of various sciences, engineering and management such as mathematics/applied mathematics, control theory, physics, chemistry, computer engineering, mechanical engineering, electrical engineering, business management, economics and finance wherever one wants to model their uncertain practical and real-life problems. It is well known that predictability in a nonlinear environment is inevitable in every field of engineering, management and science. This book aims to become significant and to become very fruitful for humankind.

ORGANIZATION OF THE BOOK

The book is organized into 15 chapters, prepared by experts and scholars from all over the world. A brief description of each of the contents of the chapters is given as follows:

Chapter 1: Classification Techniques for Thunderstorms and Lightning Prediction – A Survey

In this chapter, the authors describe that a thunderstorm is a series of sudden electrical discharge resulting from atmospheric conditions. Electric discharged result in sudden flashes of light and rumbling sound wave, commonly known as thunder and lightning. The thunderstorm is a weather sensational phenomenon with few kilometers to 100 kilometers and time varying from an hour to several hours which occurs seasonally. A severe thunderstorm is a natural phenomenon that causes lots of damages to life, properties, animal and crops. Forecasting of severe thunderstorm and lightning is a challenge for researcher and scientists in world because such highly nonlinear and disorder phenomena may acquire significant consequences on the huge part of agricultural productivity. Now days, prediction of thunderstorm and lightning is challenging task. In this regard, several soft computing and data mining techniques have been applied for prediction and forecast. It is required a good technique for the predicting thunderstorm and lightning.

Chapter 2: Design of Semi-Active Seismic Vibration Controllers Using Fuzzy Logic and Evolutionary Optimization

This chapter presents the semi-active structural damping systems for seismic vibration mitigation are considered part of the civil engineering design process. Various actuating devices have been integrated into structures along with specifically designed control strategies. Semi-active dampers are nonlinear switching systems that require enhanced controllers. In order to minimize instability risk, a cascaded fuzzy control system that integrates the switch behaviour is designed. The inner loop uses a PI (proportional-integral) controller that is tuned with evolutionary optimization. The case study uses an electrohydraulic damper and a three-story building. To anticipate robustness to real world disturbances and equipment failure, an uncertainty effect analysis is included, in which three control systems are compared. First, structural and actuator disturbances are considered. Then, the case of switch failure brings forth the high reliability of the fuzzy control system, in what concerns using semi-active dampers in the development of civil structures.

Chapter 3: Hybrid Model to Performance Estimation in Co-Design Flow for Embedded Systems (MPSoC)

In this chapter, author's will speak about the estimation of the performances in an earlier stage of (Multi-Processors System on Chip) MPSoC design in which it is necessary to drive design space exploration and support important design decisions. So, we address to the co-design hardware/software with estimating performances in order to find an adequate solution, which consists in mapping the application on the components of architecture with respect the criteria of performance of the system defined from the beginning. Our contribution is to provide a hybrid model for estimating performance in which cohabited simulation and analytical techniques via a link layer in order to reach quickly an optimal architectural solution. Thus, it allows faster performance estimation with better accuracy at different levels of abstraction.

Chapter 4: Analysis of Shunt Active Power Filter Using Adaptive Blanket Body Cover Algorithm (ABBC) in Aircraft System

This chapter discusses, a novel Adaptive Blanket Body Cover Algorithm (ABBC) has been presented, which has been used for the optimization of conventional control scheme used in shunt active power filter. The effectiveness of the proposed algorithm has been proved by applying this in aircraft system. The superiority of this algorithm over existing Genetic Algorithm results has been presented by analyzing the THD and compensation time of both the algorithms. The simulation results using MATLAB model ratify that algorithm has optimized the control technique, which unmistakably prove the usefulness of the proposed algorithm in 400 Hertz Aircraft System.

Chapter 5: Lyapunov-Based Predictive Control Methodologies for Networked Control Systems

The problem considered in this chapter is to control a vehicle drivetrain in order to minimize its oscillations while coping with the time-varying delays introduced by the CAN communication network and the strict timing limitations. As such, two Lyapunov-based model predictive control design methodologies are presented: one based on modeling the network-induced time-varying delays using a polytopic approximation technique and the second one based on modeling the delays as disturbances. Several tests performed using an industry validated drivetrain model indicate that the proposed design methodologies can handle both the performance/physical constraints and the strict limitations on the computational complexity, while effectively coping with the time-varying delays. Moreover, a comparative analysis between the two Lyapunov-based model predictive control design methodologies in terms of computational complexity, number of optimization variables and obtained performances is carried out.

Chapter 6: Modeling and Dynamic Surface Control of Uncertain Strict-Feedback Nonlinear Systems Using Adaptive Fuzzy Wavelet Network

Author's present a new modeling and control scheme for uncertain strict-feedback nonlinear systems based on adaptive fuzzy wavelet network (FWN) and dynamic surface control (DSC) approach. It designs adaptive FWN as a nonlinear-in-parameter approximator to approximate the uncertain dynamics of the system. Then, the proposed control scheme is developed by incorporating the DSC method to the adaptive FWN-based model. Stability analysis of the proposed scheme is provided and adaptive laws are designed to learn all linear and nonlinear parameters of the network. It is proven that all the signals of the closed-loop system are uniformly ultimately bounded and the tracking error can be made arbitrary small. The proposed scheme does not require any prior knowledge about dynamics of the system and offline learning. Furthermore, it eliminates the "explosion of complexity" problems and develops accurate model of the system and simple controller. Simulation results on the numerical example and permanent magnet synchronous motor are provided to show the effectiveness of the proposed scheme.

Chapter 7: Performance Analysis of Nature-Inspired Algorithms-Based Bayesian Prediction Models for Medical Data Sets

This chapter deals about the research in medical data prediction has become an important classification problem due to its domain specificity, voluminous and class imbalanced nature. In this chapter four well known nature inspired algorithms namely Genetic Algorithms (GA), Genetic Programming (GP), Particle Swarm Optimization (PSO) and Ant Colony Optimization (ACO) are used for feature selection in order to enhance the classification performances of medical data using Bayesian classifier. Naïve Bayes is most widely used Bayesian classifier in automatic medical diagnostic tools. In total, 12 real world medical domain data sets are selected from the University of California, Irvine (UCI repository) for conducting the experiment. The experimental results demonstrate that nature inspired Bayesian model plays an effective role in undertaking medical data prediction.

Chapter 8: Routing in Wireless Sensor Networks Using Soft Computing

In this chapter author's presents, wireless sensor networks are the evolutionary self-organizing multi-node networks. Due to dynamic network conditions and stochastically varying network environments, routing in WSNs is critically affected, therefore needs to be optimized. The routing strategies developed for WSNs must be efficient to make it an operationally self-configurable network. For this we need to resort to near shortest path evaluation. Therefore the requirement of some soft computing approaches which can calculate the near shortest path available in an affordable computing time. WSNs high computational environment with limited and precise transmission range, processing and limited energy sources. The sever power constraints strongly affect the existence of active nodes and hence the network lifetime. So here we use the power of soft computing because the potential features of soft-computing (SC) approach highly addressed their adaptability and compatibility to overwhelm the complex challenges in WSNs.

Chapter 9: Study of Feature Apprehension Using Soft Computing Approaches

In this chapter, author's presents that each image is distinguished on the basis of its low level features like color, shape, size. Other features like Edges, Corner/ Interesting points, Blobs/ Region of Interest & Ridges etc. can also be used for computation purpose. Using these features distinctions, an image can be processed for the purpose of enhancing the images having same features, matching and shortlisting of similar images from a random available image database. This could be done using soft computing techniques like Neural Networks, Fuzzy Logic and Evolutionary computation methods. Neural Networks can be participate effectively in image processing in several ways.

Chapter 10: Utility and Significance of Vague Set Theory and Advanced Optimization Mechanisms for Uncertainty Management

In this digital world, tremendous data are generated in every field. Useful information is inferred out of this data, which is valuable for effective decision making. Data Mining extracts the interesting information from huge volumes of data. Association Rule (AR) mining is one of the core areas of Data Mining where interesting information is extracted in the form of rules. Traditional AR mining is incapable of handling uncertain situations. In order to handle uncertainty, mathematical tools like vague theory can be utilized with AR mining methodologies for the development of novel vague theory based algorithms, which will be more suitable in effectively handling vague situations that helps framing effective selling strategy. Since an organization can't analyze the huge rule set obtained from these algorithms, every resultant rule should have a certain ratio of factors customized to the interest of the organization, that can be achieved through optimization algorithms. This chapter explores the significance of vague theory and optimization means for effective uncertainty management.

Chapter 11: Sizing and Placement of Battery-Sourced Solar Photovoltaic (B-SSPV) Plants in Distribution Networks

This chapter proposes a Mixed Integer Optimization using Genetic Algorithm (MIOGA) for determining the optimum sizes and placements of Battery-Sourced Solar Photovoltaic (B-SSPV) plants to reduce the total energy losses in distribution networks. Total Energy Loss Index (TELI) is formulated as the main objective function and meanwhile bus voltage deviations and PV penetrations of B-SSPV plants are calculated. To deal the stochastic behavior of solar irradiance, 15 years of weather data is modeled by using Beta Probability Density Function (Beta-PDF). The proposed algorithm is applied on IEEE 33 bus and IEEE 69 bus test distribution networks and optimum results are acquired for different time varying voltage dependent load models. From the results, it is known that, compared to PV only, the integration of B-SSPV plants in the distribution networks resulted in higher penetration levels in distribution networks. The proposed algorithm was very effective in terms of determining the sizes of the PV plant and the battery storage, and for the charging and discharging of the battery storage.

Chapter 12: Fast Chaotic Encryption Using Circuits for Mobile and Cloud Computing: Investigations Under the Umbrella of Cryptography

In this chapter, the author describes and presents fast chaotic encryption using circuits for mobile and cloud computing. Cryptography being considered as one of the safe method to protect data. It was first used to protect communication by individuals, armies and organizational companies. These days it is assumed as a technique and application to secure the reliability and genuineness of information under different circumstances. Encryption is simple but it should be strong enough to protect data fully. In today's world security has become a very subject for communication and storage of images and maintaining the privacy one the important task. With the help encryption method anyone can protect its data from third party attack. Use of encryption method to safe digital contents has gained a lot of attention in recent era. One way to protect day is the method of encryption. Now day's images are used in various areas like biometric authentication, medical science, military etc where they are being stored or transferred over the network and the safety of such images are very important. The newest movement in encryption is chaos based which is a better encryption technique than AES, DES, RSA, etc. It consists of different property such as sensitive independence on original situation, non-periodicity, non-convergence, and etc. In recent times, many chaos-based image encryption algorithms have been proposed, but most of them are not sufficient enough to provide full protection to data. In this chapter survey of different chaos-based image encryption techniques has been discussed.

Chapter 13: Detection of Stator and Rotor Faults in Asynchronous Motor Using Artificial Intelligence Method

This chapter deals with the implementation of a PC based monitoring and fault identification scheme for a three-phase induction motor using artificial neural networks (ANNs). To accomplish the task, a hardware system is designed and built to acquire three phase voltages and currents from a 3.3KW squirrel-cage, three-phase induction motor. A software program is written to read the voltages and currents, which are first used to train a feed-forward neural network structure. The trained network is placed in a Lab VIEW based program formula node that monitors the voltages and currents online and displays the fault conditions and turns the motor. The complete system is successfully tested in real time by creating different faults on the motor.

Chapter 14: Soft Computing Approaches for Image Segmentation

In this chapter, the author presents a brief description for image segmentation techniques by using both traditional approaches and soft computing approaches. This chapter will figure out some soft computing approaches which can be used to solve the problem of identification of objects. Along with it some traditional approaches which being already have been applied for the extraction of objects has been discussed along with their comparison with soft computing approaches. At last will discuss various applications of image segmentation. The Soft computing approaches are then analyzed and their performance is compared with each other by identifying the advantages and disadvantages of all.

Chapter 15: An Innovative Design of RF Energy Harvester for Wireless Sensor Devices

This chapter presents that the energy harvesting is the most prominent solution to increase efficiency and battery life span of low power wireless devices. In the past few decades the application of wireless devices operated from ultra-low power sources have drastically increased in wireless communication system. With technological advancement, power requirement of various electrical and electronic devices has decreased, which encouraged researchers to move towards energy harvester to provide continuous power supply for ultra-low power devices like wireless sensors. The process of energy harvesting is to collect amounts of radiations from number of available natural and human made energy sources, converting them in to usable electrical energy and store it for charging up wireless sensor devices. Energy is available everywhere in the ambient around us and estimate the amount of power hitch can be harvested from various energy sources.

This book will be an excellent reference for the global research scholars across the planet in the research areas on design and control of Nonlinear System Using Soft-Computing techniques. Firstly, we would like to sincerely thank all the authors from Tunisia, Malaysia, Romania, USA, Turkey, India, and Iran etc. for their marvelous contribution to the book in submitting their valuable book chapters.

Secondly, we would like to thank and express our gratitude to the editorial and production staff at the IGI-Global. We would also like to thank Jordan Tepper and Joshua Herring who diligently worked with many aspects of the book. We would like to express my special thanks to Dr. Sanjeev Jain and Dr. R.K. Gupta for their encouragement and guidance in the preparation of the book. We found working with IGI, Jordan Tepper and Joshua Herring, a pleasant experience and an education into the many aspects of writing and publishing a book. I would also like to thank my students and colleagues, who encouraged and inspired me for editing this book. Lastly but not least, we would like to thank all the referees for their valuable time and great effort in reviewing all the book chapters.

Uday Pratap Singh
Madhav Institute of Technology and Science, India

Akhilesh Tiwari
Madhav Institute of Technology and Science, India

Rajeev Kumar Singh
Madhav Institute of Technology and Science, India

Acknowledgment

The theme and relevance of this book has attracted large number of researchers/ academicians around the globe, which enabled us to select good quality chapters and serve to demonstrate the popularity of this edited book titled "Soft Computing-Based Nonlinear Control Systems Design" for sharing ideas and research findings with truly national and international communities. Thanks to all who have contributed in producing such an ample edited book.

We would like to gratefully acknowledge the enthusiastic guidance and continuous support of Managing Editors of this book: Sanjeev Jain and R. K. Gupta.

It has been an honor for us to edit this book. We have enjoyed considerably working in cooperation with the IGI Global during the execution of all related aspects.

We express our sincere thanks to the benign reviewers for sparing their valuable time and effort in reviewing the chapters along with suggestions and appreciation in improvising the presentation, quality, and content of this book.

Last but not the least, the editorial members and officials of IGI Global deserve a special mention and our sincere thanks for not only making our dream come true in the shape of this edited book, but also for their valuable support, guidance, and timely publication of our book.

We hope, this book will serve as guiding media for the academia and research community to further open the new research dimensions and findings.

Uday Pratap Singh
Madhav Institute of Technology and Science, India

Akhilesh Tiwari
Madhav Institute of Technology and Science, India

Rajeev Kumar Singh
Madhav Institute of Technology and Science, India

Chapter 1
Classification Techniques for Thunderstorms and Lightning Prediction:
A Survey

Kanchan Bala
Birla Institute of Technology Mesra, India

Dilip Kumar Choubey
Birla Institute of Technology Mesra, India

Sanchita Paul
Birla Institute of Technology Mesra, India

Mili Ghosh Nee Lala
Birla Institute of Technology Mesra, India

ABSTRACT

Environmental disasters affect the economy, biodiversity, human life, and living organisms. Thunderstorms are one of such environmental disaster. By using proper methodology of forecasting thunderstorms, the adverse effects can be reduced. The prediction of thunderstorms is the most difficult task in weather forecasting due to their temporal and spatial extension either physically or dynamically. Lightning is associated with thunderstorms, which causes wildfires, kills people and other living organisms. Heavy rain from thunderstorms causes flash flooding. In this regard, several researchers have proposed different methodology such as statistical, numerical mode, data mining, soft computing, and machine learning for forecasting of severe weather to reduce the damages. This chapter focuses existing classification methods on thunderstorms and lightning prediction. This chapter includes suggestions on the future research directions.

DOI: 10.4018/978-1-5225-3531-7.ch001

INTRODUCTION

A thunderstorm is a series of sudden electrical discharge resulting from atmospheric conditions. Electric discharged result in sudden flashes of light and rumbling sound wave, commonly known as thunder and lightning. The thunderstorm is a weather sensational phenomenon with few kilometers to 100 kilometers and time varying from an hour to several hours which occurs seasonally. A severe thunderstorm is a natural phenomenon that causes lots of damages to life, properties, animal and crops. Forecasting of severe thunderstorm and lightning is a challenge for researcher and scientists in world because such highly nonlinear and disorder phenomena may acquire significant consequences on the huge part of agricultural productivity.

Moisture, unstable air and lifting mechanism are playing important role in the formation of thunderstorm. There are many causes that lead to uplifting of warm and humid air such as air-solar heating, two different air streams meet, vicinage of the low pressure channel, etc. When humid air is lifted upward and cooled then the moisture in the air is condensed and form clouds. Due to further lifting of humid air, the cloud would be extended larger and water droplets continue growing in the cloud and further freezes to form ice crystals. As soon as the water droplets are become so heavy, they are falling as hail. The hail acquires the negative charge due to rubbing against the ice crystals in clouds. Thus the negative charges are collected at the base of the cloud and positive charges are created at the top of the cloud. These negative charges are attracted by some other clouds, objects and earth. When the attraction extent to large, negative and positive charges are either discharge or come together to form lightning. Lightning is further heating and expanded the air, which produced the thunder. Thunderstorms are categorized on the basis of physical characteristic. Actually, thunderstorm type is a regular spectrum, but these can be broadly classified into four types- single cell storms, multicell cluster storms, multicell line storms and supercell storms. Single cell storms are not strong to produce dreadful weather and its life is 20-30 minutes. Due to poorly organized and occurred at arbitrary locations and time, it is challenging to forecast accurately where and when will happen. The multicell cluster storms are the most general type of thunderstorms. A group of cells and moving along as one unit can be considered as multicell cluster storms. Multicell cluster storms have stayed for several hours, but its cellular life is 20 minutes. It produces moderate size hail, downbursts heavy rain and occasionally weak tornadoes. Multicell cluster storm are more dangers than single cell storms, but less intense than supercell storms. The multicell line storms are also known as a squall line. Squall line consists of a long line of storms and well developed gust. It produces hail, heavy rainfall and weak tornadoes. Supercell storms are generally highly organized thunderstorm and poses high threat to life and properties. It consists of one main updraft and produces giant hail and strong to violent tornadoes. Every thunderstorm poses lightning. Lightning is generally classified into four broad categories: Inter-cloud, cloud to cloud, cloud to ground, cloud to air. Cloud to ground is more dangerous than the other types of lightning.

In the last two decades, the prediction of thunderstorm and lightning is an active area of research. Yet it is still a challenging work for researcher and forecasters due to its spatial and temporal extension. United Nation has stated that the lightning disasters are the most serious of ten natural disasters. According to the China Electrotechnical Commission, lightning disasters are major public hazardous in an electronic era. NCRB report of India reported 1, 95,745 total deaths in 45 years due to five major calamities. Out of which 39% were due to lightning, which is the most fatalities than other calamities. This leads to a lot of research work for prediction and forecasting of thunderstorm and lightning. Without electronic products, people's daily life, economic activities, development of social informationization can't be imagined. In such electronic era, the large scale forecast has been unable to meet the requirement. Therefore, development of small scale and sort term forecast research have practical and important significant. Soft computing and data mining have an aim to exploit the tolerance of uncertainty, approximation and imprecision to achieve the decision making. Several soft computing and data mining techniques are applied in the prediction of thunderstorm and lightning with the small scale and short term forecast. In this regard, the paper has been organized as follows: Literature review has been presented; summaries of some papers are presented next to literature review, the author also describes the different soft computing and data mining techniques which used in different research paper, introduces some software used in prediction of thunderstorm and lightning, last but not least devoted to the future direction.

LITERATURE REVIEW

Two methods are generally used to forecast weather phenomena: (a) Dynamical approach (b) empirical approach. In the first approach, equations and forward simulations of the atmosphere are used and it is generally referred to as computer modeling (Numerical Weather Prediction). Numerical Weather Prediction (NWP) is complement to interpretation of conventional observations. Simulation requires accurate knowledge about "when" and "where" storms will develop and evolve. Some of cases of thunderstorms are simulated by different type of numerical model (Zepka et.al., 2014), [23], [34]. The Second approach is analogous forecasting which uses past weather data to forecast the future events. Soft computing is an example of the second approach. In this regard, several data mining and soft computing techniques have been proposed for the prediction of thunderstorm and lightning.

Colquhoun (1987) used a decision tree to forecast thunderstorm, severe thunderstorm and tornadoes. Decision Tree produces forecasts of thunderstorms, no thunderstorms, thunderstorm with local floods, thunderstorms with dry microburst, thunderstorms with wet downburst or microburst, severe thunderstorms with wet downburst or tornadoes, etc. Decision tree includes 16 decisions on which discrimination between different types of thunderstorms and tornadoes are performed. The design of the decision tree is based on physical reasoning. Therefore, such decision tree design can be used in many countries for nowcasting and forecasting purpose. Supata Chaudhari (2011) proposed statistics and fuzzy logic to reveal a dependable quantitative range of CINE and CAPE for prevalence of severe thunderstorms. Z-Statistics of statistical hypothesis testing are used to determine the ranges of CINE (Convective Inhibition Energy) and CAPE (Convective Available Potential Energy) for the occurrences of thunderstorms. Fuzzy logic is used to define the membership functions for the linguistic variable "more" in relation to ranges of CINE and CAPE. Thus a statistical-fuzzy coupled method defined the CINE within the range of 0 to 150 J.kg-1 is more appropriate than the range of CAPE within 1000-3000 J.kg-1 for the occurrences of severe thunderstorms. Carlos Alberto Vasconcellos et. al. (2006) adopted K-means clustering. Electrical thunderstorm nowcasting is performed using lightning data. Lightning cluster is formed from parameters such as lightning location, time of occurrence, polarity and current intensity. Lightning cluster is tracked using K-means technique in 15 minutes time window and forecasted the lightning. Himadri Chakrabarty and Sonia Bhattacharya (2015) introduced K-Nearest Neighbor (K-NN) to predict severe thunderstorms. K-NN is an excellent classifier which classified two classes of 'storm day' and 'no storm day'. Dry adiabatic lapse rate, moisture difference and vertical wind shear are used as predictors. Predictors are considered at different geo-potential heights which contribute to total data set. The total data set is divided into testing and training data sets. Both training data and testing data sets have squall data and non squall data. K-NN is used to measure the similarity between each vector of training data and each vector of test data. Similarity measure is performed using cosine angle. Smaller angle of cosine reflects more similarity between test vector data and training vector data for thunderstorm prediction. Basak et al. (2012) worked on Artificial Neural Network (ANN) with back propagation algorithm to predict thunderstorms. Thunderstorm day is estimated using 20 parameters which are derived from dew-point temperature, pressure, wind speed and pressure at the lifting condensation level of radiosonde observations of 12 years. Thunderstorms or no thunderstorms are predicted by the ANN model using 3 years observation data. The ANN model predicted the thunderstorm separately for morning and afternoon. Efficiency of ANN model is estimated using nine skill score such as Percentage of correct result (PC), Correct Non-occurrences (C-NON), Miss Rate (MR), True Skill Score (TSS) Critical Success Index (CSI), Probability of Detection (POD), False Alarm Ratio (FAR) and Heidke Skill Score (HSS). Lee and Passner (1993) introduced an expert system to forecast the thunderstorm. Thunderstorm Intelligent Prediction System (TIPS) is an expert system which is based on a decision tree rule. Five stability indexes such as Showalter index, K index, total totals index (combination of vertical totals and cross totals), lift index and Severe Weather Threat Index (SWEAT) are used to describe a potential thunderstorm environment. Critical values of these stability indexes are exceeded which leads to favorable conditions for thunderstorm formation. The decision tree is used to develop initial logic of TIPS. The TIPS expert system is used as predictor of thunderstorm not as types of thunderstorm forecast. Juntian, et. al. (2014) used fuzzy C-means algorithm to develop real-time lightning warning system which is based on nephogram and lightning. Lightning flashes are clustered into different group. Each lightning flash group is tracked by improving clustering method instead of spatial clustering method. Nephogram is used to track the convective clouds. Nephogram uses remote sensing images for convective cloud. Image is preprocessed for eliminating noise and inferences. The fuzzy clustering algorithm is adopted after preprocessing of image to recognize convective regions. In this way, pixels of the image are classified into different convective clouds. These convective clouds are dynamically tracked the path using a neighbor cross-correlation method. CG-flashes and convective cloud tracking are integrated for improving the prediction performance. Anad, et. al. (2011) adopted ANN to predict and classify the thunderstorm in two geographical locations Wollemi National Park, New South Wales (Australia) and Paradeep, Orissa (India). ANN architecture design is supervised, feed-forward, multi-layer percentron network with back-propagation algorithm. Data are obtained from the Indian Meteorological Department (IMD) in the form of Gridded Binary (GRIB) archive data. GRIB data is decoded and enabled to access 234 parameters. Out of 234 parameters, only 8 parameters such as K-Index, Lifted index, amount of Precipitable water, Moisture, Precipitation rate, U (zonal) component of wind, V (meridional) component of wind and relative humidity are considered after quantitative analysis. Zepka, et. al. (2008) introduced Neural Network (NN) to forecast the Cloud-to-Ground (CG) lightning. This paper shows correlation between analysis field of meteorological parameters and CG lightning data. The proposed architecture of NN to forecast lightning is a back-propagation, feed forward, multilayer and fully connected network. Back-propagation with momentum and an axion as activation function with genetic algorithm is used by NN. Hourly number of lightning flashes, CAPE and best lifted index (BLI) are used as inputs in NN.

Result reveals 67% perchance of CG lightning forecast. Collins, W., & Tissot, P. proposed ANN to incorporate subgrid scale data and numeric model to improve the forecasting of Convective Initiation (CI) on both temporal and spatial scales. A grid of 14*23 equidistant points is developed which covers the County Warning and Forecast Area (CWFA) in Corpus Christi Texas (CRP). These points from 286 square regions. A framework is established to train 286 ANN in order to predict thunderstorm occurrences within 286 square regions. ANN architecture design is supervised, feed-forward, multi-layer percentron network with two layers- output layer and hidden layer. Logsig is used as a transfer function for both output layer and hidden layer. Only one hidden neuron is used for prediction purpose. Cloud-to-Ground (CTG) lightning and rainfall rate (R) are used for target criteria of the shower, no convection and thunderstorm. Total 23 parameters are used as input data. ANN model is evaluated using FAR, POD, HSS and Critical Success Index (CSI). Tang et. al. (2011) proposed particle swarm optimization algorithm which is based on Chaos searching (CPSO). CPSO is used to search the optimal parameters of SVM. In this way, the CPSO-SVM model is established for prediction of lightning. Ground data and upper air data are collected from Micaps system. The results reveal that proposed CPSO-SVM prediction model has better performance as compare with Chaos Particle swarm Optimization –Neural Network (CPSO-NN) and Least Squared Support Vector Machine (LS-SVM). (Choubey et al., Choubey & Paul) (2014, 2015, 2016, 2017) have implemented several classification techniques on Pima Indian Diabetes Dataset which has been obtained from UCI Repository of machine learning databases. They have also used feature selection with classification techniques to produce the good results and achieved. They have analyzed and compared several classification techniques on diabetes dataset and also have discussed on used tools and future work with existed work.

SUMMARY OF EXISTING WORKS

Here some papers are summarized on prediction of thunderstorm and lightning using soft computing and data mining techniques. Summarization is done in form of a table which includes dataset, tool and techniques along with advantages, issues and accuracy (Table 1).

SOFT COMPUTING AND DATA MINING TECHNIQUES

Different soft computing and data mining techniques are used in the aforementioned paper. Some of them are described below with advantages, disadvantages and application in the form of a table (Table 2).

SOFTWARE TOOLS

Some tools have been used in prediction of thunderstorms and lightning, which are discussed with some advantages, issues and application (Table 3).

Table 1. Summary of existing works

S.NO	Paper	Data Set	Techniques Used	Tool Used	Advantages	Issues	Accuracy
1	Artificial Neural Network Model for the Prediction of Thunderstorms over Kolkata (Litta, A. J. et. al., 2012)	Hourly weather data, such as wind speed, mean sea level pressure and relative humidity of 3 years data are collected from the Indian Meteorological Department (IMD) and used as training data and for test data as hourly surface temperature.	Artificial Neural Network (ANN) model with Levenberg Marquardt (LM) algorithm.	------	This paper investigates sensitivity of different learning algorithm of ANN. ANN with LM learning algorithm has been ability of predicting the hourly temperature in term of sudden temperature fall as compare to the other learning algorithms of ANN.	Accuracy of prediction is low as compare to other soft computing and data mining techniques. Nowcasting of thunderstorm is not mentioned.	76%
2	Application of Pattern Recognition Techniques to Predict Severe Thunderstorms (Chakrabarty, H. et. al., 2013 a)	Vertical moisture difference and dry adiabatic lapse rate at different heights of atmosphere of 40 years data are collected from the IMD. These data are recorded by radiosonde.	K-Nearest Neighbor(K-NN), Modified K-NN and Multi Layer Perceptron (MLP) model.	------	More than one techniques such as KNN, modified KNN and ANN are used and compared in this paper for prediction of thunderstorm. Simple modified K-NN model found as best classifier as compare to other algorithm.. Satisfactory result has been obtained using only five input variables through modified K-NN model.	Main disadvantage of this paper is that no satisfactory result can be obtained using modified K-NN with more than five input variables.	Modified K-NN model shows 82.02% prediction with around 10-14 hours lead time and MLP classify thunderstorms with 62.81%.
3	Probabilistic Forecasting for Isolated Thunderstorms using a Genetic Algorithm: The DC3 Campaign (Hanlon, C. J. et. al., 2014)	Relative Humidity (RH), Convective Available Potential Energy (CAPE), Bulk Richardson Number (BRN) and low level vertical velocity are predictors which drawn from WRF(Weather Research Forecast) system.	Genetic Algorithm, Fuzzy Logic and Logistic Regression.	MATLAB, WRF	Atmospheric variables are forecasted by numeric weather prediction model and then used for probability forecast. Automated forecasting scheme produces calibrated probabilities, unambiguous and consistent desired output on day with region scale .	Four criteria of thunderstorm are needed for experiment objective. Automated forecasting scheme showed not good Brier resolution than human forecasters.	Brier skill score of 32%
4	Identification of Significant Parameters for the Prediction of Pre-monsoon Thunderstorms at Calcutta, India (Ghosh, S. et. al., 1999)	Wind speed, convective instability (or stability), conditional instability (or stability) vertical shear of horizontal wind are contributing 20 parameters as input. These data are obtained through radiosonde of three years.	Correlation based Principal Component Analysis (PCA).	-------	Find out significant predictor by reduction from different predictor. Morning and evening have different structural difference is evaluated. Analysis is performed separately for morning and afternoon for thunderstorm days and fair-weather days, which indicates the structural difference between morning and afternoon.	This paper has not revealed that how much accurately predicts the occurrence of a thunderstorm. Now casting is also not find.	The result shows out of 20 parameters only 4 parameters in morning and 5 parameters in evening are found to be significant for occurrences and non-occurrences of thunderstorm.
5	Cumulonimbus Prediction using Artificial Neural Network Back Propagation with Radiosonde Indeces (Putra, A. W. & Lursinsap, C., 2014)	Radiosonde data are used as input and derived 52 atmospheric instability indices from these radiosonde data.	Back Propagation Neural Network (BPN), Self-Organizing Map (SOM) and PCA	-------	BPN-PCA achieves more accurate prediction of cumulonimbus clouds than BPN. Using PCA to reduce the dimensionality of input.	BPN-PCA have time consuming technique for prediction purpose.Data can be included from other sources like numerical weather prediction, synoptic surface, but here only radiosonde data are used for prediction purpose.	74.9% accuracy using BPN and 82.5% accuracy with BPN-PCA
6	An Efficient Approach towards Thunderstorm Detection using Saliency Map (Gawande, R. P. & Ghuse, N. D., 2015)	Satellite images are taken from the National Oceanic and Atmospheric Administration.	Saliency map, K-means clustering and Haar wavelet transform.	------	Segmentation is performed not only color basis, but also based on intensity, orientation, motion, scale, depth etc. Saliency map improved the prediction accuracy.	Lead time of forecasting is not mentioned.	Cloud-to-ground (CG) and cloud-to-cloud (CC) lightning predict with an accuracy of 94%.

continued on following page

Table 1. Continued

S.NO	Paper	Data Set	Techniques Used	Tool Used	Advantages	Issues	Accuracy
7	The Study on the Model of Thunderstorm Forecast Based on RS-SVM (Ping, L. et. al., 2013)	Laps analysis system provides wind analysis, temperature analysis, height analysis, cloud analysis, water analysis and derived analysis, There are 33 different type of derivative products provided by the analysis of quantity such as height field, wind field, temperature, vertical velocity, relative humidity, specific humidity, relative factor, cloud amount, cloud classification, cloud water content, cloud ice, content of snow, water content, cloud base height, cloud top height, precipitable water, liquid water content, lift index, convective available potential energy, convective inhibition of energy, showalter, k index, lifting condensation level.	Hauffman tree, Information Entropy, Rough Set (RS) and Support Vector Machine (SVM).	MATLAB 7.1, GrADS 1.9	Three classifiers are discussed such as RS, SVM, and RS-SVM. RS-SVM has been predicting the higher resolution nowcasting of lightning and thunderstorms than RS and SVM.	Only one year test data are used. Applicable for only regional forecast. RS-SVM classifier for non thunderstorm days has a lower forecasting accuracy than RS and SVM. Thunderstorm data are not collected enough which may lead to error in prediction.	An accuracy of 0.71 with 3 hours lead time prediction.
8	Application of Artificial Neural Network to Predict Squall-Thunderstorms using RAWIND Data (Chakrabarty, H. et. al., 2013 b)	Only one predictor wind shear is considered at four different geo-potential heights. Data are obtained from rawindsonde during the period of 18years from IMD.	MLP model.	------	MLP (4-3-2 configuration) network is an excellent classifier for the nowcasting of severe thunderstorm using only one upper air parameter.	Weather variables acquired from RSRW flight, which is constrained to a particular region.	98.34% accurately predicted with 10 to 12 hours lead time.
9	Analysis of a Statistically Initialized Fuzzy Logic Scheme for Classifying the Severity of Convective Storms in Finland (Rossi, P. j. et. al., 2014)	Composite Constant Altitude reflectivity PPI(Plan Position Indicator) (CAPPI), Composite echo-top altitudes with 45dBZ(ET45) and 20dBZ(ET20), CG flash density map, radar-derived rainfall accumulation, storm area, storm flash density, storm radar reflectivity factor are used as predictors.	Statistical approach, Fuzzy logic model with human oriented linguistic inference rules, clustering-based tracking algorithm and density based clustering algorithm.	------	Membership function has been initialized statistically which allows the algorithm to fit the local climate.	Large number of thunderstorms are produced which required the analysis laboriously and manually.	40000 storms are tracked.
10	Probabilistic Nowcasting of Severe Convection (Cintineo, J. L. et. al., 2012)	Four predictors are used such as the maximum rate of change in top of troposphere emissivity, maximum rate of change in ice cloud fraction, rate of change in area of the storm of top of troposphere emissivity, rate of change in the area of the storm of 0.65-μm optical depth	Naïve Bayesian.	------	Temporal trends of GOES-derived fields to proxy horizontal and vertical growth in convective clouds have an excellent differentiation capability between severe and non-severe thunderstorm.	The model is evaluated only by lead time. Lightning information and radar-derived fields have not yet incorporate to create a fused product for reliable prediction of severe weather.	65% of storm have at least 15 min of lead time prior to 1.5 in MESH (Maximum expected size of hail).
11	Application of Machine Learning Technique to Predict Severe Thunderstorms using upper Air Data (Chatterjee, D., & Chakrabarty, H., 2015)	Eight different types of upper air weather parameters such as Sunshine hour (SSH), Cloud coverage (Nh), Pressure at Freezing point (FRZ) and dry adiabatic lapse rates at different heights of the atmosphere are obtained through radiosonde and rawindsonde of 33 years from IMD.	K-Nearest Neighbor (K-NN).	------	K-NN is simple and flexible classifier for prediction purpose and uses the huge amount of data. Learning cost of K-NN is zero.	Nothing is learned from training and required large storage size.	72.16% accurately predicted with a lead time around 12 hours.

continued on following page

Table 1. Continued

S.NO	Paper	Data Set	Techniques Used	Tool Used	Advantages	Issues	Accuracy
12	Detection of Thunderstorms using Data Mining and Image Processing (Reddy C, K. K. et. al., 2014)	Satellite images	K-means clustering and Haar wavelet transform	MATLAB R2011a	The model improves the efficiency to great extent as compare to the other learning methods of MLP such as MOM, STP, LM, QKP etc.	Segmentation is performed using clustering technique which has not included motion, depth, orientation, etc for more detail data extraction. Nowcasting is not mentioned.	89.23%
13	Preferred Type of Cloud in the Genesis of Severe Thunderstorms- A Soft Computing Approach (Chaudhuri, S., 2007)	Low level clouds types and record of occurrences of thunderstorms are collected at 00 GMT, 03 GMT, 09 GMT and 12 GMT of ten years from IMD(Indian Meteorological Department) www.imd.ernet.in and National Data Centre www.imppune.org/nationaldata-center.html	Rough Set Theory	-------	The values of three factors certainty, coverage and strength are used for the decision rule with different condition for a particular decision.	Rough set theory is based on assumptions that have every object of discourse with some information associated with a decision rule.	Low level cloud and existence of cumulonimbus cloud at 06 GMT are more preferable for thunderstorm.
14	Lightning Forecasting using ANN-BP & Radiosonde (Weng, L. Y. et. al., 2010)	The data consists of four tables such as significant level temperature/ humidity, pressure, significant level wind Seed/ wind Direction, standard pressure level (PTU-Pressure, Temperature, Humidity), Standard pressure levels (wind). Only PTU table data and lightning data are used as input. Lightning data are collected from LLS (Lightning detection and Location System) of Malaysia Meteorological Department of the year 2006.	ANN-BP	C Language	ANN has been adopted which is simpler and more biased for the lightning days as compared to non-lightning days.	Not feasible for industry which is more sensible to lightning risk.	67%
15	A Real -Time Learning Technique to Predict Cloud -to- Ground Lightning (Lakshmanan, V., & Stumpf, G. J., n.d)	Following predictors are used. Reflectivity at constant temperature altitudes of 0^0C, -10^0C and -20^0C, echo top heights from multiple radars to minimize radar geometry problems, Vertically Integrated Liquid (VIL) estimated from multiple radars, cell echo areas at constant temperature altitudes, vertically integrated reflectivity related to constant temperature altitudes such as layer reflectivity differences(LDA), average layer reflectivity(LRA), maximum layer reflectivity(LRM).	RBF (Radial Basis function), K-Means clustering.	-------	The lightning density field is forecasted about 30 minutes lead time with actual CG lightning strike.	This paper has not mentioned about how much accurately predicts the occurrence of lightning	30 minutes lead time prediction
16	A Modular Neural Network Approach for Locating Cloud-to-Ground Lightning Strokes (Emamghoreishi, S. A. et.al., 2001)	Electromagnetic field	ANN-MLP feed forward with LM algorithm and MTLL model.	------	Modular ANN improves the prediction of locations CG lightning. Learning speed of ANN is improved using the LM algorithm.	An electromagnetic field is used as input, which obtained from only one radar station.	The relative error is less than 5% and an absolute error not greater than 1 km.

continued on following page

Table 1. Continued

S.NO	Paper	Data Set	Techniques Used	Tool Used	Advantages	Issues	Accuracy
17	Detection of Lightning Pattern Changes using Machine Learning Algorithms (Booysens A., & Viriri, S., 2014)	Data of four years from the Lightning Imaging Sensor (LIS) aboard the Tropical Rainfall Measuring Mission (TRMM) are used. The LIS TRMM measures all intra-cloud, inter cloud, cloud-to-air and cloud-to-ground flashes at every 90 second.	Decision Tree, Naïve Bayesian, K-Means clustering	R-Programming Language	The resultant information can be obtained in a variety of forms such as map, graph, and data. This paper helps in forecasting of future distribution of lightning.	Optimization of time complexity is needed through parallel computing	Global pattern detection rate achieves 73% for small datasets and 63% for larger data sets
18	A Lightning Motion Prediction Technology based on Spatial Clustering Method (Juntian, G. et. al., 2011)	Lightning data are collected from lightning database of Lightning Location System of State Grid Electric Power Research Institute (SGEPRI), China.	Spatial Clustering	------	The model predicts lightning every 5 minutes.	Only predict the linear-trend movement of lightning.	75%
19	Artificial Neural Network based Technique for Lightning Prediction (Johari, D. et. al., 2007)	Two types of data are used: meteorological data as input parameter and lightning data as target output. Meteorological parameters such as pressure, dew point, wind, humidity, temperature, cloud height and moisture difference of 50 years data are collected from Malaysian Meteorological Service and Tenaga National Research and Department.	ANN with back propagation	MATLAB	Season indicator and month indicator are introduced in input data which reduces the computational complexity in acquiring the converged solution. Learning speed of ANN is improved using the LM algorithm.	Post processing is needed for achieving perfection of developed network.	Rms error is 41% with R-value of 0.99997 along with four hour lead time prediction.
20	Application Study of Machine Learning in Lightning Forecasting (Qiu, T. et. al., 2013)	Laps data and other lightning positioning data are collected from the Jiangxi Meteorological Administration	RS and SVM with RBF kernel	MATLAB 7.1 and GrADS 1.9	The RS-SVM method has been adopted which achieves short time nowcasting and high resolution model for prediction of lightning.	The experiment has been conducted on data of one year.	An accuracy of 0.71 with short term nowcasting
21	A Logistic Regression Model for Prediction of Premonsoon Convective Development Over Kolkata (Dasgupta S. et al)	Saturated equivalent potential temperature, equivalent potential temperature, pressure at reference level, pressure at corresponding lifting condensation level and potential convective instability of the atmospheric layer	Logistic regression	SPSS	Logistic regression model makes prediction of premonsoon convective risk forecasting extremely handy and easy to use. This model can used locally as well as globly	Sample of data of experiment is considered only 87 days which is very low	80%
22	Prediction of Severe Thunderstorms Applying Neural Network using RSRW Data (Char)	Moisture dference, adiabatic laps rate wind shear as parameter at different geo-potential height from IMD of 18 years data	ANN-MLP	-----	ANN-MLP structure has minimum misclassification rate with respect to other MLP structure	Prior prediction time is not mention	70%
23	Lightning Severity Classification Utilizing the Meteorological Parameters: A Neural Network Approach	Data set consist of both meteorological data from Malaysian Meteorology Services and lightning data by Gobal Lightning Network from WSI	ANN with gradient descent with momentum backpropagation and scaled conjugated backpropagation algorithm	MATAB	Prediction of lightning is done in three categories such as hazardous, warning and low risk	Nowcasting is not mention	70%

Table 2. Brief description of Soft Computing and Data Mining Techniques

S.No	Methodologies	Advantages	Limitations	Applicability
1	ANN (Chakrabarty, H. et. al., 2013 a), (Chakrabarty, H. et. al. 2013 b), (Emamghoreishi, S. A. et. al., 2001), (Johari, D. et. al., 2007), (Litta, A. J. et. al., 2012), (Weng, L. Y. et. al., 2010)	Capable of parallel and high speed information processing, mapping capabilities, generalization and pattern association capability, fault tolerance, robustness, capable of training large amount of data sets, performance of output depends on the training parameters, reduces the processing time compared to other algorithms, it is self-adaptive and flexible computational tool, capable of capturing complex and nonlinear characteristic of any physical process.	Not simpler, the large neural network takes more time to process, they have no any explanation about their decisions, outcome of training depends on the initial choice of parameters, not probabilistic, required lots of tuning parameters, hard to train, not faster than the other techniques such as svm, decision tree, and regression.	Forecasting, image processing, pattern recognition, optimization, risk assessment, control system, constraint satisfaction, character recognition, image compression, stock market prediction, medicine, fraud detection, time series analysis, prediction and classification.
2	K-Nearest Neighbor (KNN) (Chakrabarty, H. et. al., 2013 a), (Chatterjee, D., & Chakrabarty, H., 2015).	Simple and easy to learn, simple classifier, effective for large training data and very flexible, training is fast, approximately optimized for large training data, local information is used, analytically tractable and robust to noisy training data, local approximation learning is used in complex concept using simple procedures, easy for parallel implementation, processes are transparent and easy to debug, the accuracy of classification is improved by using some reduction techniques, the cost of learning process is zero, simple in implementation.	Large training data have poor run time performance, large storage is required, the role of each predictor has no vision, data requirement is large, computationally rigorous for large value of K, optimum value of K is difficult to predict, large time is required in classification, there is no any explanation of learning concepts, performance is depended on dimensionality, sorted training data are needed at each prediction, lazy learner, there is no any explanation about which attributes and distance based learning methods are producing the best result, computationally complex and biased for K-value, K-NN is easily fooled by irrelevant attributes.	Stock market forecasting, weather generator model, agriculture and finance, text mining and optical character recognition, medicine and protein- protein interaction, 3D structure prediction.
3	Genetic Algorithm (GA) (Hanlon, C. J. et. al., 2014)	Problems can be solved with multiple solutions, solved the multi-dimensional, non-continuous, non-differential and non-parametric problems, easy to understand, practically does not need the knowledge of mathematics, easy to transfer into existing simulations and models.	No assurance of finding a global optimum, no assurance of constant optimal response time, limited to use in real time applications. the difference between longest and shortest optimization response time is much larger than conventional gradient methods.	State assignment problem, economics, computer –aided-design, scheduling, robotics, computer gaming, engineering design, encryption and code breaking.
4	Logistic Regression (Hanlon, C. J. et. al., 2014)	Unconstrained variables is not required to be unbounded and interval, no assumption is required for naturally distributed error, independent variables can be taken in any form, more robust, used for the classification accuracy, more than one quantified and explanatory values are included in the strength of association, power terms and explicit interaction can be added.	Large sample size is required, a combination of normal and binomial distribution leads to problematic, lots of data are required for meaningful and stable results, complicated explanatory variables must be planned.	Medical, engineering, health science, market, economics, social science, natural language processing.
5	Fuzzy Logic (Hanlon, C. J. et. al., 2014), (Rossi, P. j. et al., 2014)	They have a good explanation for their inherently robust, decisions, mimics the human control logic, vague and imprecise data are accepted for providing a decision, simple implementation and interpretation, no requirement of mathematical model.	An experience is required for the operators, complex system, updating and learning is not performed automatically, no formal methods are available for training, rules are not automatically acquired for the decision making.	Control system for washing machines, prediction system for prior recognition, bioinformatics, flight aid for helicopters.
6	Principle Component Analysis (PCA) (Ghose, S. et. al., 1999), (Putra, A. W., & Lursinsap, C., 2014)	Special case of factor analysis, data can be compressed without loss of information through the dimension reduction, useful in analysis of pattern movement and time series, highlights the differences and similarities in data, produces the orthogonal component in lacks of redundancy of data, parameters are not required, only projected training data are stored in the database, a few components can explain the large percentage of total variation, data are represented in simple and reduced form, complexity can be reduced through image grouping.	Linear, static and non-adaptive, standardization is one of the major drawbacks, simple invariance even does not capture unless explicitly provided the information on training data, not work well for complicated manifold data, covariance matrix is difficult to evaluate in an accurate manner, assumptions for the input data are continuous and real, some data sets are not effective, nonlinear processing is needed for dimension reduction of complex distribution, optimal linear features are bad for nonlinear problems.	Biology, psychology, neuroscience, genetics, image compression, economics, pattern recognition, artificial intelligence, finance, agriculture, chemistry, food research, climatology, demography, ecology, geology, oceanography, criminal investigation, linear regression analysis, process monitoring.
7	Self-Organizing Map (SOM) (Putra, A. W., & Lursinsap, C., 2014)	Easy to understand, work well, easy to interpreted, easy to observe the similarities in data by reduction of dimensionality and grid clustering, capable of handling a variety of classification problem.	Each and every SOM is different, problem in getting right data, a value is needed for each dimension of each member of the sample, lots of maps are needed to get final good map.	Meteorology and oceanography, project prioritization and selection.
8	K-Means Clustering (Booysens A., & Viriri, S. 2014), (Gawande, R. P., & Ghuse, N. D., 2015), (Lakshmanan, V., & Stumpf, G. J., n.d), (Reddy C, K. K. et. al., 2014),	Low complexity, robust and easier to understand, implementation is easy, simple and understandable, high speed performance and flexibility, automatically items or instances are assigned to clusters, terminated at local optima, globular cluster produces tighter cluster, faster than hierarchical clustering for large number of variables, the best result is produced from distinct and separated data, work faster for low dimensional data, this technique is efficient and measurable for large data.	Provides local optima, outliers are not identified, selection of number of optimal cluster is difficult for a given problem, total run time and the result are depended on initial partition, this technique is not work satisfactorily for different size, density and global cluster, sensible to change of coordinate and weight, quality of producing cluster is difficult to compare, noisy data are unable to handle, applicable only for defined mean, highly overlapped data are not resolved the cluster, this technique requires earlier value of the number of cluster centers.	Pattern recognition and image processing, data modeling and data compression, expression analysis and computer vision, market segmentation and agriculture, artificial intelligence and machine vision.

continued on following page

Table 2. Continued

S.No	Methodologies	Advantages	Limitations	Applicability
9	Haar Wavelet [6], [12] (Gawande, R. P., & Ghuse, N. D., 2015), (Reddy C, K. K. et. al., 2014)	Simple conceptual, fast and memory efficient, exactly reversible, low implementation cost.	Space limitation, not continuous and differentiable, fail to transform the original image in the range of 11- 12 element, shorter filter length is fail for detection of the large changes in input data.	Logic design, compressing digital image, speech Processing, control and communication, data coding, multiplexing and digital filtering, pattern recognition, robotic, military aero plane, geophysics.
10	Support Vector Machine (Ping, L. et. al., 2013), (Qiu, T. et. al., 2013)	The high dimensional data is well scaled, training is easy, prediction accuracy is high, robust, have a fast evaluation of the learned target function, error is handled explicitly.	Classification decisions are not justified, good Kernel functions are needed, takes a long training time, learned function is difficult to understand, lack of transparency of result.	Image classification, facial analysis, Pattern recognition, hypertext and text categorization, Handwriting analysis.
11	Rough Set (Chaudhuri, S., 2007), (Ping, L. et. al., 2013), (Qiu, T. et. al., 2013)	Dimensionality is reduced through elimination of redundant attributes, discovers minimal data sets and creates a decision rule from the resulting data, algorithms based on rough set the theory are suitable for parallel processing, characterizes and identify the uncertain systems.	Accurate analysis is not done efficiently, not applicable for noisy and dirty data, inefficient in computation, not suitable for large data set in real world application.	Forecasting. Signal and Image processing, finance, text mining, robotics, web and Text mining, multimedia mining, medicine, economics, bioinformatics.
12	Naive Bayes (Booysens A., & Viriri, S. (2014), (Cintineo, J. et. al., 2012),	Efficient to use, faster to classify and produces the stochastic classifier, simple learning algorithm and easy to compute, fast to train and handles real and discrete data, simple and easy to implement, handles huge amount of predictor, needed fewer amounts of training data, produced the probabilistic predictor, insensible to irrelevant features, performance of accuracy is high, good for numeric and texture data.	High computational cost and not perform regression. Over fitting or under fitting of data problem, problematic to handle the continuous feature, huge amount of data is required, continuous predictors needed to categorize, Naïve Bayesian classifier cannot model for dependencies existing among variables, Independence of a class condition leads to loss of accuracy, No vision about importance of each predictor, may arises zero condition probability problems.	Natural language processing, weather prediction, medical diagnosis, text classification, simple emotion modeling, hybrid recommender system, spam filtering.
13	Decision Tree (Booysens A., & Viriri, S., 2014), (Colquhoun, J. R., 1987), (Lee R. R., & Passner, J. E., 1993).	Easy to generate the rules, understandable, complexity of the problem can be reduced, variables are selected automatically and good handler for the missing values, previously not considered possibilities are highlight, state are recorded in memory, it can be learned and acceptable for noisy data, no requirement of distance function, compact and simpler representation, it is not expensive to construct all possible outcomes are created using tree, result is improved, easy to create and run.	Training time is expensive, many examples are required as possible and only probabilities are estimated, CPU cost is high and over fitting problem, tree is complex for numeric data, qualitative input is needed for complete picture, reliability of decision tree is determined due to accuracy of data, large pruning is required, any sub tree can be wrong due to mistake done at higher level, process can be unmanageable and time consuming for complex decision.	Remote sensing, biomedical engineering, molecular biology, control system, medicine, agriculture, financial analysis, object recognition, manufacturing and production, Power system, software development, text processing, astronomy, plant diseases, predicting library books..
14	Particle Swarm Optimization (Wang Q. & Fan W., 2011)	Derivative free and needed very few algorithmic parameters, faster convergence and have an efficient global search algorithm, concurrent process can be easily parallelized, simple in implementation with optimization ability, generates high quality solutions within shorter calculation time, less dependent on initial point set, less affected to objective function in comparison to conventional mathematical approaches, coding and concepts are easy as compare to the other heuristic optimization techniques, the calculations are simple.	Dearth of the solid mathematical foundation for analysis, less exact at speed and direction due to suffering from partial optimization, not worked well for the problem of optimization, scattering and non-coordinate system, variant of PSO has long computational time than mathematical approaches, premature and fast convergence for the mid optimum point, slow convergence of refined search, limitation for real time ED application, weak local search ability.	Power generation, metallurgy, biomedical, robotics, data mining, fuzzy system, neural network training, sensor network, prediction and forecasting, military and security, graphics and image, networking and optimization, signal processing and antenna design, modeling and design, electronic and electromagnetic.
15	Likelihood (Stern H, n.d)	Several popular statistical software packages are available, have lower variance than the other methods, statistically well understood and appropriate for the simple data, most accurately classified and evaluated the different tree topology, all sequence information is used, robust to the violation in many assumptions of evolutionary model, many explicit models of evaluation are available that fits the data, consistent approaches are available for the parameter estimation problem, methods have optimal mathematical properties.	Computationally intensive and slow, model of equation affects the result, covariance matrix is affected easily for large value, an assumption about the error distribution is required, complex models are difficult to evaluate, equations are required for distribution and estimation problems, philosophically less well established.	Image processing, classification of mammographic masses, structural refinement, Genetic analysis, estimation of linkage.

Table 3. Brief description of software tool

S. No	Tools	Advantages	Issues	Application
1	MatLab (Johari, D. et. al., 2007), (Ping, L., et al., 2013), (Reddy C, K. K. et. al., 2014).	Easy syntax and easy to use, beginner of computer programming can easily learn, manuals are easily available and well written, automatically generates the C code, available huge amount of free code, interpreted languages are available for numerical computation, graphical output can be optimized for interaction, functionalities can be enhanced using append the toolboxes, makes data analysis can easily perform due to matrix representation, performs vector operations, easily performs the numerical calculation and visualization without computer programming, problems are unambiguously solved and the code are effectively produce, integrated development environment (IDE) is powerful simple and, enrich with large support of multimedia format, logarithms are tested without recompilation, predefine function toolboxes and external libraries are called, contain the device automatic plotting ability.	Closed source and expensive, tough to integrate into standalone applications, time consuming for real time applications, consumes large amount of memory, poor programming practices lead to unacceptably slow down, syntax and development environment are complex, dynamic type and not object oriented, high price and slower than C++.	Physics, mathematics, medical science, robotic and engineering, control system and communication system, simulation and system modeling, image and video processing, test and measurement modeling, power system and quality control, time series and financial analysis, computational biology, and chemistry.
2	R-Studio (Booysens A., & Viriri, S., 2014)	Open source, easy to run the code, codes can be converted into reusable functions, easier to learn than ESS, support for version control, manipulates the packages for dynamically changing plot parameters, plots can be post-hoc exported, auto complete is fast, panels and windows are well organized, enough shortcut keys are available, Saving plots have a number of good options, sections of codes are highlighted.	Very large data sets are difficult to load, tiled display, use of R-studio is not marked as part of a product,, project, and services, name cannot paste during saving a file. formatting hasn't fine control over R-Studio,Help docs are not searchable, Graphing is quite slow.	Web application development, analytics warehouse services.
3	Weka (Vasconcellos, C. A. et. al., 2006)	Free availability and easy to use, preprocessing, portability capabilities and modeling techniques are provided with a comprehensive collection of data, provides a large collection of a data mining algorithm with access to SQL database, it can be integrated with any java apps. and applicable for real time application, covers the entire machine learning process with excellent interface with hardware, customization is possible, results of different implemented algorithm can be easily to compare, flexible APIs are provided for programmers with cross platform, The entire range of features selection, data preparation, and other data mining algorithm are integrated.	Memory bound, takes time to understand and learn, GUI have quite limited documentation, lacks of adequate and proper documentation, sequence of modeling is not included, multi-relational data mining are not possible, The system is constantly updated, The newest technology and technique implementations are not possible, uses specialized file format and need to know java, , data preparation and visualization techniques might not be enough, scaling problem, all the possible options are not implemented.	Machine learning, agriculture, education, bioinformatics, text classification. Visualization, data mining, sentimental analysis, big data, education and e3research, software project.
4	Java (Joe P. et al.)	Easy to learn and portable, easy to use and test, easy to write, compile and debug than the other programming language, allows modular programming using object-oriented paradigm, platform independent, secure and robust, easy to transition to C++, easy to test, Java is distributed due to networking capability, elimination of pointer, data can store and restore easily.	JVM is required. Slower than the other programming language, difficult to write perfect program, suffer from different types of problem due to the platform on which JVM run, single paradigm language, does not have enumeration type, takes more memory space than the other programming language.	Scientific application, commercial e-commerce website, android, game application, trading application, financial application, useful in development of software and tools
5	SPSS (Dasgupta, S., & De, U. K., 2004)	Easy to use and learn, data management is effective, statistical capabilities are deeply provided, provides complete presentation features, plotting and reporting, having a variety of options and good output organization.	Expensive and compatibility issues, simultaneous association between predictor (independent variables) and estimation of regression parameters and is not allowed, SPSS lags behind R, SAS for academic use, a license is not very a user friendly, structural equation modeling is not supported.	Text analysis, statistical analysis, higher education, banking finance and insurance, telecommunication and manufacturing, healthcare and retail, market research.
6	Oracle (Neill-Carrillo, E. O, et al., 2002)	Good performance and portability, scalable,, having declarative integrity, secure and reliable, easy to learn and use, market presence and version change, error handling capability, markup and recovery capability, control structures and cursor support, read consistency and code locking availability,, SQL dialect and multiple database support, define, retrieve and manipulates the data in the tables using SQL, transactional integrity and auditing with other data.	Setup takes longer time, specific expertise knowledge is required, an enterprise system cost has high, Customer Support Identifier (CSI) is required to join, role of privileges are treated non- consistently, no version control, overloading functionalities are restricted, does not allow constraints on views, staffs are required to maintain, hardware is required to run, bulky software, stored procedures of database can not overload.	Customer relationship management, Human resource management, product lifecycle management, supply chain management, warehouses management, financial software, call center services, E-Business Suite (EBS), Siebel.
7	Weather Research forecast (WRF) (Hanlon, C. J. et. al., 2014)	Single source of code is used by both research and operation, parallel computing environment, modular and offers numerous physics options, next generation mesoscale model, gives permit to real data and idealized simulation in same framework.	Takes more hours to compile, slower than the NN5 model, initialization problem, plug –in–architecture, software design is unintitutive for physical scientist, Netcdf files can be large.	Research simulation, operational forecasting, air chemistry, quality research, hurricane forecasting, regional climate studies.

Table 4. Summary of the existing works over the future works

S. No.	Paper with reference No.	Exiting Work	Future Work
1	Artificial Neural Network Model for the Prediction of Thunderstorms over Kolkata (Litta, A. J et al., 2012)	Hourly surface temperature is predicted by ANN with different learning algorithm during thunderstorm days, ANN with LM algorithm predicted more precisely than the other algorithm in terms of sudden fall of temperature.	Accuracy can further increased using other soft computing techniques, validation of thunderstorm can be further extended for few more days, experimental data of 3year can also increased.
2	Application of Pattern Recognition Techniques to Predict Severe Thunderstorms (Chakrabarty, H. et al., 2013 a)	Two parameters are moisture difference and dry adiabatic lapse rate at different geo- potential heights used to predict severe thunderstorms using machine learning tool such as K-NN, modified K-NN and MLP, Modified K-NN model produced more prominent result than K-NN and ANN with five input variables, modified K-NN predicts the thunderstorm with 0-14 hour lead time, experiment is done with 40 years data	Other data mining and soft computing techniques with more weather parameters can be applied to increase the accuracy of the result in future work, although K-NN with different K values and more than five parameters are experimented but not with modified K-NN, so experiment with more than five parameter can be done using modified K-NN.
3	The Study on the Model of Thunderstorm Forecast based on RS-SVM (Ping, L. et al., 2013)	This paper deals effective thunderstorm forecasting using RS-SVM with the short term and small scale, forecasting scale is 5km x 5km and short term is next 3 hour, SVM and RS are also discussed for nowcasting with high resolution model of lightning and thunderstorm on historic data with ignorance of regional geography and climate condition.	Regional geography and climate condition can also considered for further work to improve the accuracy of the model, RS-SVM can be further applied to real and huge amount of data sets, other soft computing or fusion method are also applied to improve the accuracy.
4	Application of Artificial Neural Network to Predict Squall-Thunderstorms using RAWIND Data (Chakrabarty, H. et al., 2013 b)	The thunderstorm associated with squall is predicted using MLP with one weather variable, vertical wind shears at different geo- potential heights with nowcasting of 12 hours, RSRW flight weather data are used which limited to a particular region, this paper used 4-3-2 MLP network structure.	Weather data can obtain globally in stead of RSRW flight data locally, nowcasting time can be reduce using other soft computing techniques.
5	Analysis of A Statistically Initialized Fuzzy Logic Scheme for Classifying the Severity of Convective Storms in Finland (Rossi, P. J. et. al., 2014)	This paper classified the severity of convective storm using lightning location data and real time weather radar data, fuzzy logic model based on statistical approach with human-oriented linguistic inference rules algorithm is used, density based spatial clustering algorithm is also used to classify the severity of the storm.	New parameters and sub model can be integrated into the existing model to improve an accuracy of the model, classification of severity can be also improved using dual-polarization radar.
6	Application of Machine Learning Technique to Predict Severe Thunderstorms using Upper Air Data (Chatterjee, D., et al., 2015)	This paper uses four weather parameter to classify no squall storm day and squall storm day using K-NN, one parameter dry adiabatic laps rate is taken at different geo-potential height, experiment is done using different value of K such as 5, 17, 21 in K-NN, for a similarity measure cosine angle is used in K-NN.	Experiment can be done on more amount of data, accuracy of prediction can be enhanced using other techniques such as machine learning tool, data mining techniques, soft computing techniques, nowcasting time can also reduced using other soft computing techniques.
7	Detection of Thunderstorms using Data Mining and Image Processing (Reddy C, K. K. et. al., 2014)	Thunderstorms is predicted using haar wavelet and K-means clustering techniques, here segmentation is done by K-means clustering technique which based on only color factor, statistical method is also applied in classification of thunderstorm.	Accuracy of prediction can further enhanced by other segmentation techniques, segmentation is not done only by color basis but can also considered motion, orientation, intensity not only on a color basis.
8	A Lightning Motion Prediction Technology based on Spatial Clustering Method (Juntian, G. et al., 2011)	Spatial clustering is used to predict the lightning motion using historical and real time lightning monitoring data, thunderstorm group is aggregated using discrete, independent, random flashes, position of lightning is predicted using speed, movement direction and tracking of thunderstorm group.	Prediction of a non-linear movement of thunderstorm cloud can be predicted in future work using some other techniques, electricity, density of lightning characteristics can be predicted in the future work also, accuracy of prediction can also be improved by other techniques such as soft computing, data mining, machine learning.
9	Application Study of Machine Learning in Lightning Forecasting (Qiu, T. et. al., 2013)	Short time nowcasting and high resolution of thunderstorm is forecasted by RS, SVM, and RS-SVM model with real data of one year, RS-SVM model is effective and acquires more precision in forecasting of thunderstorm.	Prediction accuracy can be increased by other soft computing, data mining, machine learning techniques, experiment can be done with more data not only for one year data, special model can be built for certain regional.
10	Lighting Severity Classification Utilizing the Meteorological Parameters: A Neural Network Approach (Omar M. A. et al., 2013)	Llightning severity are classified by ANN is used to classified the severity of lighting in hazardous, warning and low risks with two learning algorithms as Scaled Conjugated Gradient Back propagation (Trainscg) and Gradient Descent with Momentum Back propagation (Traingdm), seven parameter are used as input to ANN.	Accuracy of prediction can be improved using other fusion method of soft computing, data mining or machine learning in prediction of thunderstorm with huge amount of data.
11	Detection of Lightning Pattern Changes Using Machine Learning Algorithm (Booysens A. et al, 2014)	This paper presents the lightning distribution using different machine learning algorithm such as K-means, decision tree, Naïve Bayes, resultant information obtain in variety of form such as data, maps and graphs, different prediction accuracy of lightning distribution patterns are achieved with small data set and large data set.	Optimization of time complexity of this work can be achieved by parallel computing, accuracy of prediction can be enhanced using other data mining, soft computing, machine learning algorithm or fusion technology.

continued on following page

Table 4. Continued

S. No.	Paper with reference No.	Exiting Work	Future Work
12	Artificial Neural Network based Technique for Lightning Prediction (Johari, D. et. al., 2007)	Prediction of lightning is done using ANN with two layer back propagation based on meteorological data and historical lightning data, nowcasting of lightning is four hour, this paper does to test the several network structure of ANN, activation functions, training algorithms to acquire the most appropriate ANN with high prediction accuracy	Other techniques such as data mining, soft computing, machine learning can be applied for better result, deep learning can also be applied, learning rate of network can be enhanced
13	A Modular Neural Network Approach for Locating Cloud-to-Ground Lightning Strokes (Emamghoreishi, S. A. et.al., 2001)	This paper present modular neuro- based model to locate the cloud-to-ground lightning strokes, two stages are used in locating process, in first stage, obtaining the approximate value of lightning Return Stroke Channel (RSC) location range using ANN with feed forward network, for far (20-80 km), intermediate (10-20 km) and near (1-10km) zones, value of RSC determines the appropriate ANN network for far(20-80 km),intermediate (10-20 km) and near (1-10km) zones in the second stage, reduction of the relative error throughout the detecting range is also done in second stage, ANN with LM algorithm is employed in training to improve the learning speed	Other modular techniques can be applied, since now casting is not mention in the paper so, the time parameter as input parameter to the modular ANN can taken.
14	Lightning Forecasting using ANN-BP & Radiosonde (Weng, L. Y. et. al., 2010)	Cloud –to-ground lightning is predicted using ANN-BP, through using sensor lightning is detected, this paper uses three sensor, intersection point of these three sensors is location of occurrences of lightning	Accuracy of prediction is low, so need a such techniques which full fills the industries which make more sensible to lightning
15	A Logistic Regression Model for Prediction of Premonsoon Convective Development Over Kolkata (Dasgupta S. et al,2004)	Prediction of occurrence of convective development is achieved using logistic regression model with knowledge of value of significant parameter.	Nowcasting can achieved by inclusion of time parameter with soft computing techniques, experimental data can make large.

FUTURE DIRECTIONS

Now days, prediction of thunderstorm and lightning is challenging task. In this regard, several soft computing and data mining techniques have been applied for prediction and forecast. It is required a good technique for the predicting thunderstorm and lightning. So, the authors present the future directions of some papers, along with existing work which are summarized in Table 4.

For the future research work, the authors suggest developing an expert system of prediction of thunderstorm and lightning which will provide good prediction accuracy.

REFERENCES

Anad, S. M., Dash, A., Kumar, M. S. J., & Kesarkar, A. (2011). Prediction and Classification of Thunderstorms using Artificial Neural Network. *International Journal of Engineering Science and Technology*, *3*(5), 4031–4035.

Basak, P., Sarkar, D., & Mukhopadhyay, A. K. (2012). Estimation of Thunderstorm Days from the Radiosonde Observations at Kolkata (22.53⁰ N, 88.33⁰ E), India during Pre-monsoon Season: An ANN Based Approach. *Earth Science India*, *5*(4), 139–151.

Booysens, A., & Viriri, S. (2014). Detection of Lightning Pattern Changes using Machine Learning Algorithms. *Proceeding of International Conference on Communications, Signal Processing and Computers*.

Chakrabarty H. & Bhattacharya S. (2014). Prediction of Severe Thundestorms Applying Neural Network using RSRW Data. *International Journal of Computer Application, 89*(16).

Chakrabarty, H., & Bhattacharya, S. (2015). Application of K-Nearest Neighbor Technique to Predict Severe Thunderstorms. *International Journal of Computer Applications, 110*(10).

Chakrabarty, H., Murthy, C. A., Bhattacharya, S., & Gupta, A. D. (2013 b). Application of Artificial Neural Network to Predict Squall-Thunderstorms using RAWIND Data. *International Journal of Scientific & Engineering Research, 4*(5), 1313–1318.

Chakrabarty, H., Murthy, C. A., & Gupta, A. D. (2013 a). Application of Pattern Recognition Techniques to Predict Severe Thunderstorms. *International Journal of Computer Theory and Engineering, 5*(6), 850–855. doi:10.7763/IJCTE.2013.V5.810

Chatterjee, D., & Chakrabarty, H. (2015). Application of Machine Learning Technique to Predict Severe Thunderstorm using upper Air Data. *International Journal of Scientific and Engineering Research, 6*(7), 1527–1530.

Chatterjee, P., Pradhan, D., & De, U. K. (2008). Simulation of Local Severe Storm by Mesoscale Model MM5. *Indian Journal of Radio & Space Physics, 37*(6), 419–433.

Chaudhari, S. (2011). A Probe for Consistency in CAPE and CINE during the Prevalence of Severe Thunderstorms: Statistical-Fuzzy Coupled Approach. *Atmospheric and Climate Science, 01*(04), 197–205. doi:10.4236/acs.2011.14022

Chaudhuri, S. (2007). Preferred Type of Cloud in the Genesis of Severe Thunderstorms- A Soft Computing Approach. *Atmospheric Research, 88*(2), 149–156. doi:10.1016/j.atmosres.2007.10.008

Choubey, Paul, & Bhattacharjee. (2014). Soft Computing Approaches for Diabetes Disease Diagnosis: A Survey. *International Journal of Applied Engineering Research, 9*, 11715-11726.

Choubey & Paul. (2015). GA_J48graft DT: A Hybrid Intelligent System for Diabetes Disease Diagnosis. *International Journal of Bio-Science and Bio-Technology, 7*(5), 135–150.

Choubey & Paul. (2016). GA_MLP NN: A Hybrid Intelligent System for Diabetes Disease Diagnosis. *International Journal of Intelligent Systems and Applications, 8*(1), 49-59.

Choubey, & Paul. (2016). Classification Techniques for Diagnosis of Diabetes Disease: A Review. *International Journal of Biomedical Engineering and Technology, 21*(1), 15–39.

Choubey, & Paul. (2017). GA_RBF NN: A Classification System for Diabetes. *International Journal of Biomedical Engineering and Technology, 23*(1), 71–93.

Choubey, D. K., Paul, S., Kuamr, S., & Kumar, S. (2017). Classification of Pima Indian Diabetes Dataset using Naive Bayes with Genetic Algorithm as an Attribute Selection. *Proceedings of the International Conference on Communication and Computing Systems (ICCCS 2016)*, 451-455.

Choubey, D. K., & Paul, S. (2017). GA_SVM-A Classification System for Diagnosis of Diabetes. In *Handbook of Research on Nature Inspired Soft Computing and Algorithms.* IGI Global.

Cintineo, J. L., Pavolonis, M. J., Sieglaff, J. M., & Lindsey, D. T. (2012). Probabilistic Nowcasting of Severe Convection. *National Weather Association Annual Meeting*, Madison, WI.

Collins, W., & Tissot, P. (n.d.). Use of an Artificial Neural Network to Forecast Thunderstorm Location. *NOAA*.

Colquhoun, J. R. (1987). A Decision Tree Method of Forecasting Thunderstorms, Severe Thunderstorms and Tornadoes. American Meteorological Society.

Dasgupta, S., & De, U. K. (2004). A Logistic Regression Model for Prediction of Premonsoon Convective Development over Kolkata. *Indian Journal of Radio & Space Physics*, *33*, 252–255.

Emamghoreishi, S. A., Moini, R., & Sadeghi, S. H. H. (2001). *A Modular Neural Network Approach for Locating Cloud-To-Ground Lightning Strokes*. IEEE. doi:10.1109/ISEMC.2001.950547

Gawande, R. P., & Ghuse, N. D. (2015). An Efficient Approach towards Thunderstorm Detection using Saliency Map. *International Journal of Computer Science and Information Technologies*, *6*(3), 2429–2434.

Ghosh, S., Sen, P. K., & De, U. K. (1999). Identification of Significant Parameters for the Prediction of Pre-monsoon Thunderstorms at Calcutta, India. *International Journal of Climatology*, *19*(6), 673–681. doi:10.1002/(SICI)1097-0088(199905)19:6<673::AID-JOC384>3.0.CO;2-O

Hanlon, C. J., Young, G. S., Verlinde, J., Small, A. A., & Bose, S. (2014). Probabilistic Forecasting for Isolated Thunderstorms using a Genetic Algorithm: The DC3 Campaign. *Journal of Geophysical Research, D, Atmospheres*, *119*(1), 65–74. doi:10.1002/2013JD020195

Joe, P., Koppert, H. J., & Heizenreder, D. (n.d.). *Severe Weather Forecasting Tool in the Ninjo Workstation*. Meteorological Service of Canada.

Johari, D., Rahman, T. K. A., & Musirin, I. (2007). Artificial Neural Network based Technique for Lightning Prediction. In *Proceeding of Student Conference on Research and Development*. IEEE.

Juntian, G., Shanqiang, G., & Wanxing, F. (2011). A Lightning Motion Prediction Technology based on Spatial Clustering Method. In *Proceeding of International Conference on Lightning*. IEEE. doi:10.1109/APL.2011.6110234

Juntian, G., Shanqiang, G., Wanxing, F., Han, Z., & Yue, C. (2014). A Movement Prediction Method of CG Flashes based on Lightning and Convective Clouds Clustering and Tracking Technology. In *Proceeding of International Conference on Lightning Protection* (ICLP) (pp. 555-559). IEEE.

Lakshmanan, V., & Stumpf, G. J. (n.d.). A Real -Time Learning Technique to Predict Cloud -to- Ground Lightning. *NOAA*.

Lee, R. R., & Passner, J. E. (1993). *The Development and Verification of TIPS: An Expert System to Forecast Thunderstorm Occurrence*. Academic Press.

Litta, A. J., Idicula, S. M., & Francis, C. N. (2012). Artificial Neural Network for the Prediction of Thunderstorms over Kolkata. *International Journal of Computers and Applications*, *50*(11), 50–55. doi:10.5120/7819-1135

Neill-Carrillo, E. O., Arroyo, J., Rosado, J., Santiago, J., & Jimenez, I. (2002). The Atmospheric Phenomena Laboratory: Connecting Electrical and Computer Engineering Through Undergraduate Research. In *Proceeding of 32nd ASEE Frontiers in Education Conference*. IEEE doi:10.1109/FIE.2002.1158725

Omar, M. A., Hassan, M. K., Soh, A. Ch., & Kadir, M. Z. A. (2013). Lightning Severity Classification Utilizing the Meteorological Parameters: A Neural Network Approach. In *Proceeding of International Conference on Control System, Computing and Engineering*, (pp. 111-116). IEEE.

Ping, L., Tao-rong, Q., & Yu-yuan, L. (2013). The Study on the Model of Thunderstorm Forecast Based on RS-SVM. *Journal of Convergence Information Technology*, 8(10), 66–74. doi:10.4156/jcit.vol8.issue10.9

Putra, A. W., & Lursinsap, C. (2014). *Cumulonimbus Prediction using Artificial Neural Network Back Propagation with Radiosonde Indeces*. Academic Press.

Qiu, T., Zhang, S., Zhou, H., Bai, X., & Liu, P. (2013). Application Study of Machine Learning in Lightning Forecasting. *Information Technology Journal*, 12(21), 6031–6037. doi:10.3923/itj.2013.6031.6037

Reddy, C. Anisha, P. R., & Prasad, L. V. (2014). *Detection of Thunderstorms using Data Mining and Image Processing*. Academic Press.

Rossi, P. J., Hasu, V., Koistinen, J., Moisseev, D., Makela, A., & Saltikoff, E. (2014). Analysis of a Statistically Initialized Fuzzy Logic Scheme for Classifying the Severity of Convective Storms in Finland. Royal Meteorological Society.

Stern, H. (n.d.). *Using a Knowledge-Based System to Predict Thunderstorm*. Bureau of Meteorology, Australia.

Tang, X., Zhuang, L., & Gao, Y. (2011). Support Vector Based on Chaos Particle Swarm Optimization for Lightning Prediction. *CSISE*, 727-733.

Vasconcellos, C. A., Beneti, C., Sato, F., Pinheiro, L. C., & Curotto, C. L. (2006). Electrical Thunderstorm Nowcasting using Lightning Data Mining. *Proceeding of International Lightning Detection Conference*. doi:10.2495/DATA060161

Wang, Q., & Fan, W. (2011). Application of PSO in Thunderstorms Forecast. *Advanced Materials Research*, 171-172, 536–539. doi:10.4028/www.scientific.net/AMR.171-172.536

Weng, L. Y., Omar, J. B., Siah, Y. K., Ahmed, S. K., Abidin, I. B. Z., & Abdullah, N. (2010). Lightning Forecasting using ANN-BP & Radiosonde. In *Proceedings of International Conference on Intelligent Computing and Cognitive Informatics*. IEEE.

Zepka, G. S., & Pinto, O., Jr. (2008). A Forecast Cloud- to- Ground Lightning System Based on a Neural Network- Preliminary Results. *Proceedings of 20th International Lightning Detection Conference & 2nd International Lightning Meteorology Conference*.

Zepka, G. S., Pinto, O. Jr, & Saraiva, A. C. V. (2014). Lightning Forecasting in Southeastern Brazil using the WRF model. *Atmospheric Research*, 135-136, 344–362. doi:10.1016/j.atmosres.2013.01.008

Chapter 2
Design of Semi-Active Seismic Vibration Controllers Using Fuzzy Logic and Evolutionary Optimization

Monica Patrascu
University Politehnica of Bucharest, Romania

ABSTRACT

In the light of recent technological advances, semi-active structural damping systems for seismic vibration mitigation are considered part of the civil engineering design process. Various actuating devices have been integrated into structures along with specifically designed control strategies. Semi-active dampers are nonlinear switching systems that require enhanced controllers. In order to minimize instability risk, a cascaded fuzzy control system that integrates the switch behaviour is designed. The inner loop uses a PI (proportional-integral) controller that is tuned with evolutionary optimization. The case study uses an electrohydraulic damper and a three-story building. To anticipate robustness to real-world disturbances and equipment failure, an uncertainty effect analysis is included in which three control systems are compared. First, structural and actuator disturbances are considered. Then, the case of switch failure brings forth the high reliability of the fuzzy control system, in what concerns using semi-active dampers in the development of civil structures.

INTRODUCTION

During the lifetime of a structure located in seismically active geographical areas, high levels of ground acceleration can be observed. In recent years, special attention has been paid to the development of processes and structural vibration damping mechanisms to assess and mitigate the response of buildings and bridges to the action of winds and earthquakes. Notable results have been achieved in what concerns the damping of structural vibrations, with a wide variety of mechanisms, usually part of one in four categories: passive, active, hybrid, and semi-active. By adding damping devices, the natural frequencies

DOI: 10.4018/978-1-5225-3531-7.ch002

of a structure, its vibration modes, and its corresponding damping factors change during seismic motion. Some of these devices require the design of specialized control algorithms, supported by developments in the field of automation and control systems, incorporating both intelligent control strategies, and the necessary hardware and software support for their implementation.

This chapter discusses the design of control systems for semi-active seismic dampers, which are inherently nonlinear. These actuators have behaviours that cannot be linearized, approximated or reduced to linear models, so formal design of control systems, for those strategies that require the use of well identified models, is difficult. Although simulation validation is often successful, implementation requires further tuning or functioning modes that could not have been taken into account at an earlier design phase, as is the case in control engineering. With the development of computing power, the real world usage of more computationally expensive techniques has become practicable. Thus, controllers based on fuzzy systems or neural networks have started to enter the interdisciplinary field of control for civil engineering, while automated tuning or learning techniques have started to include meta-heuristic approaches like evolutionary computing or particle swarm optimization.

There are questions that arise, however, due to the highly uncertain nature of intelligent control systems design. Can these techniques be applied safely to systems as critical as seismic vibration mitigation? Does the control system retain robustness? Is the end result reliable? Or would it be better to consider combinations between formal and intelligent design, so that the advantages of both are used efficiently.

The main objective of the chapter is to analyse the robustness of fuzzy controllers for seismic vibration mitigation, when applied to semi-active dampers and tuned with genetic algorithms. Moreover, the discussion includes how conventional control systems (like the standard PID proportional-integral-derivative) can be enhanced for structural vibration and nonlinear actuators, with case-based robustness tests.

Ultimately, intelligent techniques can significantly improve the performance of conventional control systems, if used wisely. Implementation is already in progress for biological systems (such as drug regulation and heart rate control), and around the corner for seismic protection systems.

BACKGROUND

Seismic Damping Systems

Passive damping systems require no additional energy sources and use the response of the structure, measured at the location of the system, to synthesize the necessary control forces. They are currently based on two different techniques: base isolation and energy absorption/dissipation devices. Base isolation requires decoupling the structure from the horizontal components of the earthquake by interposing devices, between the foundation and superstructure, to ensure free movement of the foundation within the soil, while the superstructure remains at relative rest due to its inertia. For example, friction pendulum systems (Spencer and Sain, 1997; Ozbulut and Hurlebaus, 2010; Landi et al., 2016; Dhankot and Soni, 2017) offer this sort of flexible decoupling through which the earthquake induced energy is reduced. The second class of passive dampers dissipate or absorb the energy induced by earthquake or wind in the structure in terms of their dependence on natural frequencies, and are inserted into the structure in order to develop additional control forces depending on the structural displacement. Their types vary from tuned mass dampers TMD (Chen et al. 2007a; Johnson et al., 2015), to liquid mass dampers TLD (Li et al. 2004; Samanta and Banerji, 2010; Novo et al. 2014; Eswaran et al., 2017), to elasto-plastic hysteretic dampers (Pozo et al. 2006; Banisheikholeslami et al., 2016), to fluid viscous devices (Kelly, 2001; Zhou et al. 2014; Gidaris and Taflanidis, 2015). Passive damping systems have been initially preferred for their simplicity and reliability, remaining functional in the absence of external sources of energy and with a low risk of generating unstable situations. However, these devices are unable to adjust to any variations in the structure parameters, which has led to the development of active control systems, capable of handling more destructive seismic oscillations.

Active control systems usually require a considerable external power source for operation of the actuator elements that generate the required control forces, which are synthesized based on feedback signals from sensors measuring the structural response anywhere in the building. These systems are comprised of various types of actuators, from electrohydraulic to electromechanical, and driven by a control law in a closed loop configuration: active mass dampers AMD (Kobori, 1990; Liut et al. 2000; Yang et al. 2006; Teng et al., 2016), active tendon dampers ATD (Park et al. 2002; Preumont et al., 2016), electromagnetic (Nishimura et al. 1992; Jamshidi and Chang, 2017) and magnetostrictive (Flatau et al. 1993; Oates and Smith, 2008). Apart from conventional on/off or PID-class regulators, other control techniques applied to active dampers are neural networks (Rao and Datta, 2005; Khodabandolehlou et al., 2017), LQR (linear quadratic regulator) optimized with various metaheuristic methods (Chen et al. 2007b; Amini et al., 2013), or fuzzy controllers (Guclu and Yazici, 2007; Lakhani and Soni, 2017).

Subsequently, hybrid dampers have been designed in order to offset some of the disadvantages of passive systems, combining the use of active and passive elements throughout a structure (Kelly et al. 1987; Brodersen and Høgsberg, 2016). Symans et al. (1999) have addressed the limitations of passive damping systems, and thus semi-active strategies have emerged, for example in base isolation systems with controllable stiffness (Lu et al. 2008). Various configurations have been used, such as active isolation with electrohydraulic actuators and adaptive control (Zhang et al. 2005), or multiple semi-active TMD (Lin et al. 2010). In recent years some hybrid configurations no longer combine passive and active dampers. Instead, the active mechanisms are replaced with the more advantageous semi-active devices (Filip-Vacarescu et al., 2016; Heo et al., 2016), which are discussed in the following section. Thus, it becomes apparent why the need for technologies regarding semi-active damping systems is at the forefront of research, drawing together interdisciplinary efforts to design devices that are more efficient, safer, easier to control and use in real world implementations.

Semi-Active Control of Seismic Vibration

Semi-active damping systems require only a small external power source for operation. Control forces are synthesized based on feedback signals from sensors measuring the response of the structure, with the possibility of measurement at remote locations from the actual site of the control system. Semi-active systems can respond quickly to strong wind fronts and with enough precision to an earthquake, offering performance levels consistent with those of active systems, but without their high external energy needs. Because the system does not introduce extra mechanical energy in the structure, energy requirements are minimal, as are the risks of creating instability (in the systemic interpretation). Semi-active systems can work even on battery, remaining operational even in cases of electric grid failure. Semi-active damping devices have various configurations, ranging from electrohydraulic to smart fluid actuators. The major advantage is that, while semi-active dampers can not introduce energy into the structure, they are still able to change the stiffness and damping coefficients of a structure, as the mechanical properties of these systems can be continuously adjusted to the values of earthquake excitation, as well as the displacement, velocity and acceleration of structure, depending on the chosen control strategy. In addition, control forces in a semi-active system are always in the opposite direction of motion of the structural system, and thus promoting the overall (systemic) stability of the structure.

Figure 1 shows the general structure of a control system for a semi-active damper, whose behaviour is modelled using a switch that swaps between a passive command and an active type algorithm, depending, for example, on the earthquake induced ground velocity.

Semi-active control systems are classified into: electrohydraulic devices with servovalves, electrorheologic (ER) or magnetorheologic (MR) devices with controllable fluids, variable stiffness semi-active devices, tuned and liquid mass dampers (TMD, LMD), etc. For example, a semi-active pneumatic device is used by Rybakov (2009) for the seismic vibration control of a structure with multiple degrees of freedom, while Renzi and De Angelis (2005) present an optimal control algorithm for semi-active variable stiffness devices.

An energy dissipation semi-active electrohydraulic device is comprised of a hydraulic cylinder (figure 2) with a bypass controllable servovalve (usually proportional). Their damping characteristic can be controlled between two values (minimum damping for open valve, and maximum for closed) by varying the amount of fluid passing through the bypass between the cylinder chambers. Thus, for semi-active dampers with viscous fluid, energy dissipation occurs through the transformation of mechanical energy

Figure 1. Semi-active control principle

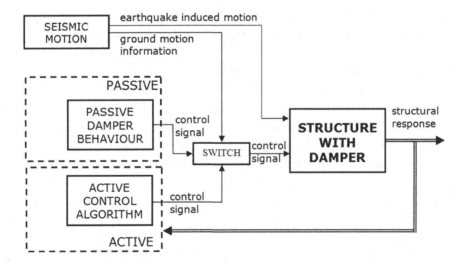

Figure 2. Electrohydraulic damper

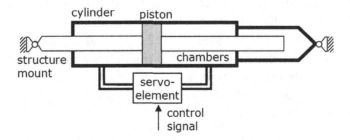

into heat. One of the first semi-active damping strategies was proposed by Symans and Constantinou (1997b). Using hydraulic dampers, the authors obtained structural response reductions comparable to those obtained using a passive control system. Experimental tests on a semi-active hydraulic damper were then presented in Symans and Constantinou (1997a), the authors focusing on the protection mechanisms needed to implement such a system in closed loop, while the subsequent control law has been in the form of biphasic command obtained from experimental data. On/off semi-active algorithms have been popular, Renzi and Serino (2003) addressing such a strategy for a steel structure equipped with magnetorheologic dampers, confirming that experimental semi-active algorithms not only reduce the maximum displacements, but also improve the time response of the entire structure.

For controllable fluid damping devices, the most important feature is the use of fluids that have the ability to modify, in a very short time of the order fractions of a second, in a reversible way, their viscous properties when exposed to an electric (ER fluid) or magnetic (MR fluid) field. During the absence of an electric or magnetic field, these fluids have low viscosity and thus a reduced damping factor. Recent research has shown that magnetorheologic fluids can be a viable alternative for the construction of controllable fluid dampers. The advantage of MR fluids compared with ER fluids is that they can operate at temperatures between -40 and 150 °C with small variations in flow resistance and they can be controlled with a small low voltage power source (12-24 V). Moreover, MR fluids are not sensitive to impurities and the dampers that would use these fluids would be much smaller than if ER fluids were to be used for the same dissipation capacity. For example, for a 1 m long device, with a piston displacement of $\pm$ 0.08 m, 250 kg weight and a capacity of 90 cc of fluid, the maximum generated damping force is 200 kN (Spencer and Sain, 1997).

The mounting procedures and distribution throughout the building of these damping devices is as important as their response time and the specifically designed control algorithms. Thus, through an analysis of seismic response of structures using MR and ER dampers, Hiemenz and Wereley (1999) demonstrate that the placement of actuators near the base of the structure vs. the higher stories will yield a better reduction of the structural vibrations. Hong and Choi (2005) present a hybrid combination of MR dampers and passive base isolation devices, together with an optimal control algorithm, while a sliding mode control law for multiple degrees of freedom scheme is tested by Neelakantan and Washington (2008). The performance of MR dampers in base isolation configurations is tested for near fault earthquakes in (Zhao and Li, 2015) relative to passive or optimal configurations, with improved results for a GA (genetic algorithm) tuned fuzzy supervisor. This issue is treated further in (Zamani et. al, 2017) where self-tuning and adaptive fuzzy controllers are designed for base isolation with a multi-objective cuckoo search algorithm.

Abdeddaim et. al (2016) address the mounting of MR dampers on the top floor of the building, with a control system comprised of fuzzy and on-off laws, in order to mitigate pounding hazard between buildings. Other control methods focus on lowering the power consumption of the damper (Wang and Liao, 2005), as others centre on performance criteria such as minimization of displacements, accelerations or inter-story drifts (Dyke et al. 1996a). In what concerns large scale structures (Rubió-Massegú et al., 2016), multiple-damper techniques are discussed, from 12-story seismic simulators with high robustness (Jing et al. 2004), to fuzzy controllers tuned with PSO (particle swarm optimization) techniques (Ali and Ramaswamy, 2009), inter-building multi-damper configurations with GA tuned fuzzy laws (Uz and Hadi, 2014), and cascaded structure-level modal controllers with genetically-tuned PID controllers in the inner loops (Patrascu, 2015).

A base isolation configuration using a fuzzy controller is analyzed by Kim and Roschke (2006), where a neuro-fuzzy model of the damper is simulated and genetic algorithms (GAs) are used to tune a fuzzy controller for seismic vibration mitigation, while a self-tuning fuzzy controller design over MR dampers is addressed by (Wilson and Abdullah, 2010). More evolutionary optimization methods are addressed in (Bitaraf et al. 2010) in order to determine the rulebase of a fuzzy controller for an MR damper, with results superior to those of an adaptive control scheme. Tuning fuzzy controllers with GAs is still a topic of interest (Ding et al., 2017); however, as the authors have shown, if the parameters of the genetic algorithm are not properly chosen, the run time can be as high as 10 hours, even though the results are promising.

Among other control techniques used for semi-active dampers are algorithms based on modal representation and supervision algorithms. Structural vibration adaptive control using modal coordinates is done by Rew et al. (2002), where the authors estimate online the natural frequencies of the modes. Fuzzy systems and modal design intersect in (Choi et al. 2005) as a vibration mitigation method in combination with electrohydraulic dampers, while a variant of modal space fuzzy controller is implemented by (Park et al. 2004) for a 6-story structure, and a fuzzy hierarchical sub-controller scheme is used by (Park et al. 2002) on a 3-story building.

The applications of synergic intelligent techniques for the design of vibration mitigation control systems do not stop here. In recent years, due partly to the rapid advances in computational power, the use of metaheuristics and intelligent methods has increased (Sahab et al., 2013; Yang et al., 2016). Thus, a geno-fuzzy supervisor is implemented on a test structure equipped with MR dampers (Kim and Roschke, 2007), the authors demonstrating the superiority of the algorithm compared to an optimal one, given a set of objectives that are tracked by the genetic algorithm in the choice of fuzzy sub-controllers organized in a hierarchical scheme. The same method is then applied to large-scale structures by (Shook et al. 2008), while multi-objective control algorithms that integrate genetic algorithms and fuzzy systems are used to minimize both displacements and accelerations (Yan and Zhou, 2006). In (Zafarani et al., 2016), the authors combine fuzzy control with a nondominated sorting genetic algorithm-II (NSGA-II), in order to compensate for the difficulties in designing a reliable genetic algorithm. The optimization of fuzzy controllers for seismic vibration is extended in adjacent fields, like neural computing (Braz-César and Barros, 2017) or even geno-neural techniques (Hashemi et al., 2016).

Limitations of Current Knowledge

The immersion of control systems design in neighbouring engineering fields is always limited by the interactions between terminology, technology, and specificity of processes to be controlled. Beside these inherent impediments, which are easily avoided by trading concepts between specialists, there are a few limitations caused by the novelty of intelligent systems. And it is, indeed, still a sort of newness to these fields, due to their continuous expansion through research that is still fertile, at the peak of implementation, applications, and design.

The limitations of control systems applied to semi-active dampers are specific to the type of controller, and some of the most important have been pointed out in the previous paragraphs as the development of seismic dampers has been outlined. Since this chapter deals with fuzzy controllers and genetic algorithm, it is more relevant to discuss their current disadvantages, while keeping in mind the specific nature of semi-active dampers as switching systems, which is presented in the next section.

In what concerns fuzzy systems, their main limitation resides in the very uncertain nature of their design process. Using expert knowledge in the construction of rulebases or the shape of membership functions is the attractive point of fuzzy systems. However, it also makes them very difficult to tune. For a simple controller with one input and one output, each with three triangular membership functions, and three rules in the rulebase, there are at least twenty seven controller parameters to take into account during tuning. The lack of formal models for the entire behaviour of the fuzzy controller (there are models for membership functions, relations, etc., but not for the knowledge itself, which is important) makes them impossible to tune with conventional optimizers, like least squares. This is why meta-heuristic methods are currently studied in combination with fuzzy systems.

In the case of genetic algorithms, the main limitation is tuning the GA parameters prior to running them. Otherwise, solutions might take too long to find, or even convergence might not be achieved. Due to their inclusion in the generative experiment (Patrascu et al., 2017), GAs might need several runs before providing a solution, thus at the moment these types of optimization algorithms are mainly used offline during the design phase.

SEMI-ACTIVE DAMPING: A NONLINEAR SWITCHING SYSTEM

There are three types of important nonlinearities to be considered when it comes to semi-active damping systems in structural vibration mitigation.

First, the issue of elasto-plastic behavior in buildings needs to be considered. In civil engineering, the response of a structure to external stimuli belongs to one of two domains (Patrascu and Ion, 2015). During the elastic phase of movement, deformation of the structure is distributed along the columns and beams. Once the deformation enters the plastic domain, a phenomenon known as "plastic hinge" (Kawai, 1977) will cause breaks in the beams or columns, leading to the ultimate collapse of the structure. This information is not new. More than that, civil engineering codes nowadays work toward the testing of the structure before implementation which includes seismic response in simulation/calculation, in this field known as earthquake engineering (Otani, 2004).

It is thus imperative that any damping or control system keeps the structure within the elastic domain. This is achieved by minimizing displacements, velocities, accelerations, and interstory drifts when under the action of seismic ground motion.

Second, the damper itself is a nonlinear actuator (Dangor et al. 2014), even when considered solely in active mode (Tubaldi etc al. 2015). Hydraulic class actuators are famously hysteretic (Zhang et al. 2015), output force presents saturation, command elements might have insensibility zones. In time, the type and quality of the fluids used within the cylinders can influence the behaviour of the damper. Of course, over time there have been efforts toward the linearization of such behaviour, some of which include soft computing techniques (Pedro et al. 2014), with various degrees of success (Dangor, 2014).

In this chapter, the focus is on managing the damper nonlinearities within the control system. Thus, when designing the controller for the damper output force, a series of stability constraints must be imposed. One of these is, for instance, eliminating command saturation. A well tuned controller would not compute commands that might cause the damper to develop forces outside the admissible domain. Such a control system would be extremely useful in keeping the behaviour of the damper within limits.

Therefore, including the damper in a stable control loop would linearize its behaviour without eliminating its natural nonlinearities. Moreover, this chapter proposes that structural vibration systems should be cascaded. There are two advantages to this approach:

- The command signals for the seismic vibration mitigation of the structure (from the outer loop controller) are as random as the earthquake signal, fast and quickly changing, as near to stochastic behaviour as ever there was an external stimulus;
- The inner control loop is designed solely for the damper, through which several requirements are met: avoiding saturation, making sure desired behaviour is acheived (command of outer loop is setpoint for the inner loop), avoid instabilities caused by damper, etc.

For the inner loop, this work proposes that the controller be a conventional one (PID class; proportional-integral-derivative). Due to significant nonlinearities, the controller parameters are obtained using evolutionary optimization, a soft computing technique more and more popular in the past few years.

Third, the switching system between the active and passive behaviours is another source of nonlinearity. Switching systems are highly sensitive and can lead to instability, even when designed carefully (Philippe et al. 2016). A switching system is, by definition, comprised of a series of subsystems and a switching signal (Xiong et al. 2013). In the case of seismic dampers, the switching signal is dependant on the earthquake ground motion, which is a random signal, in terms of control system design.

An important concern in switching systems is causing command shocks at transition. The issues of instability are undeniable in this case, and a cause of important risk in what concerns structural integrity. A switch failure that locks the damper in active mode while there is no seismic ground motion can force the structure into the plastic domain. The same effect can happen when the command varies widely and causes the damper to either generate massive forces at undesirable moments (when in passive mode, or when seismic motion is too small), or too small forces at large displacement amplitudes and critical points between the elastic and plastic domains.

In this chapter, the switching mechanism is introduced in the design of the fuzzy controller, thus assuring that its role can be covered even in case of failure, and the transition between subsystems is as smooth as possible.

CASE STUDY: CONTROL SYSTEM DESIGN

A Semi-Active Electrohydraulic Damper

The EH (electrohydraulic) damper (figure 2) taken into consideration in this case study has the following model (Patrascu et al., 2012):

$$\alpha_{EH} \cdot \frac{dp(r)}{dt} + \beta_{EH} \cdot \sqrt{p(t)} \cdot u(t) = A_{EH} \cdot v(t) \tag{1}$$

where $p(t)$ [kgm/s^2] is the pressure in the cylinder, $v(t)$ [m/s] is the ground velocity, A_{EH} [m^2] is the surface of the piston, α_{EH} [m^{4}s^2/kg] and β_{EH} [m^3/Vs(ms^2/kg)$^{1/2}$] are constants, and $u(t)$ [V] is the command voltage. To be noted the nonlinearity in the model, as described by the presence of the square root of pressure.

The hydraulic actuator is comprised of two chambers filled with viscous fluid, between which a piston moves freely. The two chambers are interconnected through a channel with variable opening. The opening of the connecting channel is controlled by the command voltage, generating higher or lower pressure in the cylinder chambers. The actuator receives a command voltage between 0 and 10V, for which: 0 means shutdown, 1 is the maximum command and 10 is the minimum (passive) command, so there is another dimension on nonlinearity introduced by the command inversion (specific to the construction of the servo-element in figure 2).

Structure Model

The motion equation of a three story structure, when equipped with a damper and under external earthquake disturbance is (Patrascu and Ion, 2015a):

$$M \cdot \ddot{x} + C \cdot \dot{x} + K \cdot x = -F_u - M \cdot a \tag{2}$$

where x is the displacement vector, while $\dot{x}$ and $\ddot{x}$ are the velocity and acceleration, respectively; M, C and K are mass, damping and stiffness coefficients, respectively; F_u is the control force; a is the earthquake induced ground acceleration.

In what follows two control strategies for the semi-active damper are designed. First, a PI controller is tuned and tested. Second, a fuzzy-logic controller is designed and analyzed, added into the outer loop of a cascaded control scheme with the PI controller governing the inner loop. The two strategies are implemented and tested in simulation, using the same damper and structure models.

PI Control

The conventional control loop for the semi-active damper consists of a proportional-integral algorithm (this choice was made following the results of the experimental studies developed in (Patrascu, 2011)). The control loop receives the earthquake induced ground velocity and sends it to a setpoint generator that establishes the active or passive mode, in accordance to the current seismic motion. The controlled output is the pressure (and hence, the force) generated by the hydraulic cylinder (figure 2).

The control structure is presented in figure 3, where: x is the displacement of the structure; $\dot{x}$ and $\ddot{x}$ are the velocity and acceleration of the structure, respectively; p is the output pressure of the damper, while p_d is the desired pressure; F is the control force; ε is the control deviation; u is the command voltage, u_P is the passive command voltage, u_A is the active command voltage; a and v are the earthquake induced ground acceleration and velocity, respectively.

The parameters of the PI controller for this damper were obtained using evolutionary optimization, more precisely a genetic algorithm (GA). Evolutionary computing is an umbrella term for the multitude of nature inspired metaheuristic optimizer algorithms that mimic natural evolution. Based on the Darwinian principle of survival, in genetic algorithms a population of problem solutions are artificially evolved. Through mechanisms of selection, recombination, and mutation, the genetic algorithm makes sure that, through each generation (until a given termination criterion is met), only the fittest solutions survive. The fitness of a solution is computed in accordance to its relevance to the problem and against given constraints.

Figure 3. PI control strategy of damper

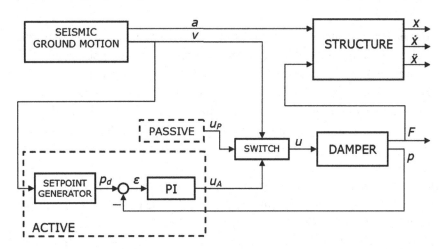

In what concerns tuning of controllers with GA optimization, the purpose is to find the set of controller parameters that fit the control loop requirements (figure 4). Thus, the population is comprised of individuals π that define various controllers, while the fitness function I describes the design requirements.

In the case of the electrohydraulic damper, the control loop requirement, beside stability, is to follow the setpoint precisely, without prior knowledge of its shape. This is a signal comprised of quick variations because it is computed based on earthquake motion (by the setpoint generator in this case, or by an outer controller if included in a cascaded scheme). For this purpose, a series of performance criteria are defined in (Patrascu and Ion, 2016): ISE, IAE, ITAE, and IEC. There, the authors applied the same procedure to design a PI controller for a magnetorheologic damper. A detailed description of the method is given in (Patrascu and Ion, 2016), while the source programs for the algorithm are included in a Matlab toolbox available for download (Patrascu and Ion, 2015b).

The most important concern over this type of control strategy is that the PI block is unable to directly control the displacements, velocities, and accelerations of the structure. Instead, the conventional algorithm is used to ensure a desired setpoint profile for the output pressure of the damper, and inherently the output force of this actuator, set by the control engineer together with the designing civil engineer expert while analyzing structural characteristics and maximum necessary force generated by the damper.

Figure 4. Principle of controller tuning with genetic algorithms

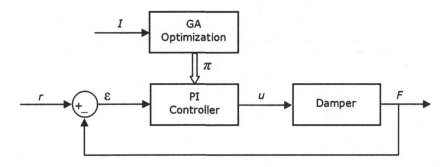

Cascaded Fuzzy Logic Control

Fuzzy logic control has the advantage of not requiring a strict mathematical model for design. The non-linearities of the plant are inherently included in the controller and little knowledge of the plant model is necessary. However, these controllers are usually based on human expertise.

Fuzzy logic is centred on linguistic terms and non-crisp coding of the process variables. Thus, each input and output variable is described in linguistic terms, as a human expert would. For the Mamdani fuzzy controller, the inputs need to pass through a fuzzification procedure, while the commands sent into the system need to be defuzzified, as the actuators currently used require numerical control signals (either discrete or continuous) .

The controller uses an inference mechanism to generate the control signal, as the consequence of a certain input and state. The entire rule set comprises the rulebase of the fuzzy logic controller (FLC). Every input and output of the FLC needs to be translated into a linguistic variable in order to be analyzed. Each linguistic variable is described by a set of membership functions: the linguistic terms and their distribution on the plant variable intervals.

The fuzzy controller designed in this chapter is Mamdani and it is part of the control strategy presented in figure 5, where: x is the displacement of the structure; $\dot{x}$ and $\ddot{x}$ are the velocity and acceleration of the structure, respectively; p is the output pressure of the damper, while p_d is the desired pressure; F is the control force, while F_d is the desired force; ε is the control deviation; u is the command voltage, u_P is the passive command voltage, u_A is the active command voltage; a and v are the earthquake induced ground acceleration and velocity, respectively. The setpoint generator, based on ground motion information and the fuzzy controller output, calculates the necessary pressure inside the cylinder so that the desired force will be applied to the structure.

In ideal conditions, the semi-active behaviour of the damper works in the classical sense: as long as external stimuli are under a given threshold, the damper works as a passive one. However, anticipating

Figure 5. Cascaded fuzzy control

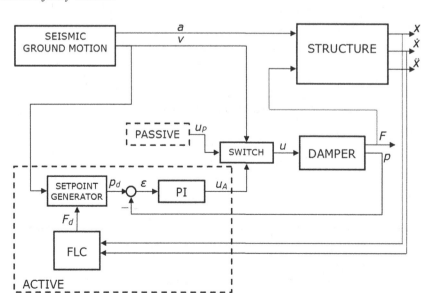

that the switch might fail, the fuzzy controller can generate such commands that keep the damper in passive or active mode even in the absence of the switch. There is, though, a reason to include the switch in the design: manual regimes, maintenance, structural evaluation, etc. The scope of the chapter is not to eliminate the switch, but to provide with a controller that can work with it, or compensate its absence.

The controller input variables are the displacement and velocity of the structure, while the output is the desired force that the elecrohydraulic damper needs to introduce into the structure. The discourse universes for each input variable are normalized to [-1, 1], while the output is generated in the normalized interval [0, 1]. The scaling factors used were obtained by analyzing the structure output.

The input and output variables are presented in table 1, along with the rulebase, in which all membership functions are triangular, with a 50% overlap. The linguistic terms are coded as follows: E - displacement (deviation from zero), D - velocity (derivative of first input), C - command (output), N - negative, P- positive, L - large, M - medium, S - small, Z - zero.

A second fuzzy controller was implemented in order to obtain better reduction of the structural displacement. While the triangular membership functions are widely used, they sometimes lack in precision. When the considered plant is sensible to small variations of input, then a higher resolution in generating the control signal is required. The second FLC in this paper was designed by assigning gaussian membership functions to the linguistic variables, while using the same rulebase.

Numerical Results and Uncertainty Analysis

The case study presented in this paper implements the two control strategies and compares the results in conditions of high modelling uncertainty and semi-active switch failure. The earthquake accelerogram is presented in figure 6, while the structure model used here has 3 stories and the damper is considered to be mounted in a base-isolation configuration (Patrascu, 2011).

Simulations consider structural displacement, velocity and acceleration as interest signals in this analysis. Figure 7 presents the results obtained in ideal working conditions with the PI controller, while figure 8 presents the results obtained using the fuzzy strategy. The following notations are used: TMF FLC for the triangular membership function FLC, GMF FLC for the gaussian membership function FLC. Using the GMF FLC, a decrease in structural displacement can be observed (figure 9).

The first simulation set is obtained by considering a 50% sinusoidal gain in one of the damper parameters (figure 10). Second, a white noise disturbance is considered in the structure model (figure 11),

Table 1. Rulebase of the fuzzy controller

Velocity	Displacement						
	ELN	**EMN**	**ESN**	**EZ**	**ESP**	**EMP**	**ELP**
DLN	CPL	CPL	CPL	CPS	CPS	CZ	CZ
DMN	CPL	CPL	CPM	CPS	CZ	CZ	CZ
DSN	CPL	CPL	CPM	CPS	CZ	CZ	CZ
DZ	CPM	CPM	CPS	CZ	CPS	CPM	CPM
DSP	CPM	CPS	CZ	CZ	CPS	CPM	CPL
DMP	CZ	CZ	CZ	CPS	CPM	CPL	CPL
DLP	CZ	CZ	CZ	CPS	CPM	CPL	CPL

Figure 6. Northridge 1994 earthquake accelerogram

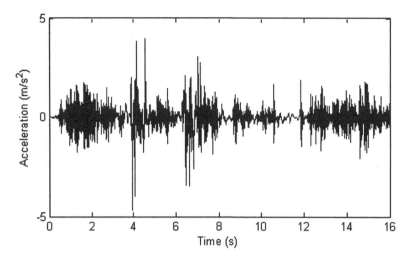

Figure 7. Ideal conditions PI response

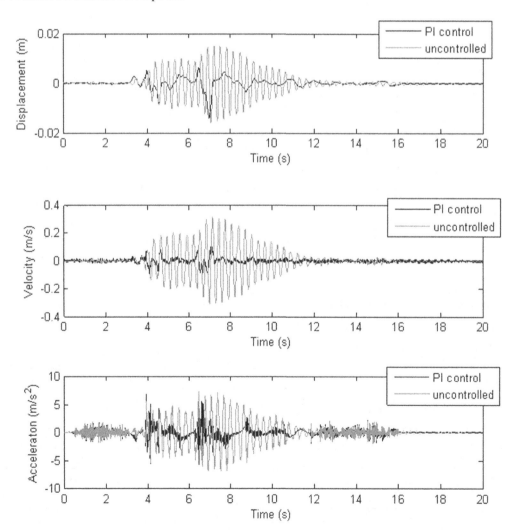

Figure 8. Ideal conditions TMF FLC response

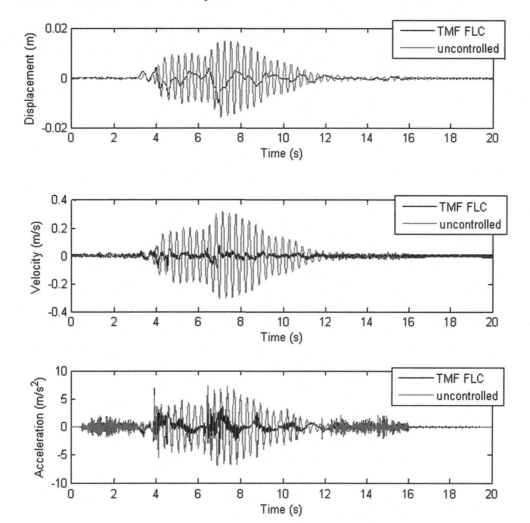

specifically at the velocity output. Figure 12 presents the response of the three systems in case of switch failure. In this case, the damper works only as an active actuator.

The system responses in ideal functioning conditions for the three controllers, show different damping: the PI controller brings a 10.8% damping in structure displacement, the TMF fuzzy controller generates 35% damping in structure displacement, while the GMF fuzzy controller shows a 45.2% damping in structure displacement. Table 2 presents the maximum displacements and accelerations in absolute value for all cases, as well as structural vibration reduction relative to the uncontrolled response.

Case 1 studies the effect of a sinusoidal disturbance in the damper model. This situation may arise from high levels of wear in the actuator, as well as from extreme temperature changes at the time of the earthquake vs. the time of set up. Results show 38.2% and 31.2% displacement reduction for the fuzzy strategies, while only 10.2% for the PI controller.

Case 2 models the appearance of a white noise disturbance in the structural response, either as a result of modelling uncertainties, or sensor failure or even incorrect data transmission from the sensor

Figure 9. Ideal conditions GMF FLC response

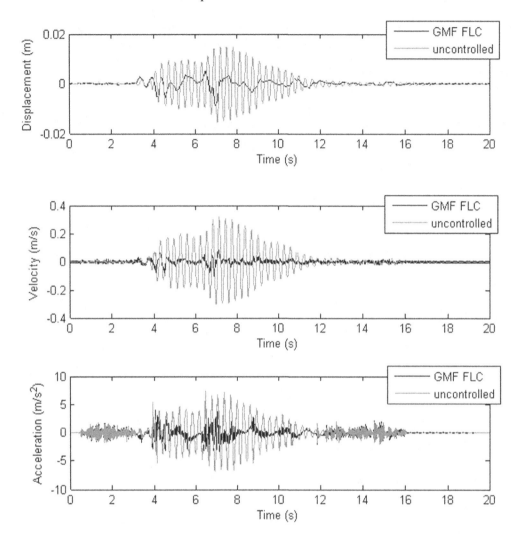

to the processing unit. An increase in displacement and acceleration of the structure was obtained in all cases. However, the GMF fuzzy controller offers the best combination of displacement and acceleration reduction.

Case 3 presents a switch failure scenario. The switch is an integrated part of the semi-active strategy control, making possible the shift from passive to active behaviour of the damper. While disconnecting this module, results show better performance for the two fuzzy controllers. The study brings forth the integration of the passive behaviour in the fuzzy rulebase, making the semi-active behaviour possible even in case of switch failure and thus excluding a risk factor from the vibration control loop.

For both displacement reduction and acceleration reduction, an increase in acceleration and displacement are observed for the PI controller in all cases vs. the ideal functioning conditions. It was observed that the GMF fuzzy strategy offers better performance than the conventional controller in all cases.

The presented results show better performance and higher reliability for the GMF fuzzy controller. Displacements and accelerations are significantly reduced when the GMF fuzzy controller is considered.

Figure 10. Case 1. Sinusoidal disturbance in the damper model

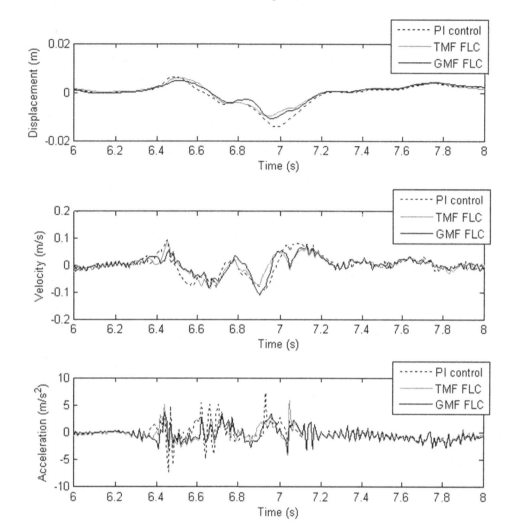

In case of switch failure, the fuzzy controllers are more reliable, since they incorporate the passive behaviour in their construction and directly consider the structural response, as opposed to the PI strategy, which only accounts for the active behaviour and only controls the output pressure of the damper.

Thus, the fuzzy controller integrates the passive behaviour of the semi-active damper, being able to compensate the absence of the switch.

CHALLENGES AND PERSPECTIVES

The study of nonlinear actuators inherently requires an interdisciplinary approach. Communication and knowledge transfer across fields form an ever-present challenge. Openness to alternative approaches must be cultivated in the engineering research community, in order to make use of the advantages brought forth by each and every field, and also to mitigate limitations in current technology. Moreover, new developments must be included in norms and regulations, especially when they concern critical domains.

Figure 11. Case 2. White noise disturbance in the structure model

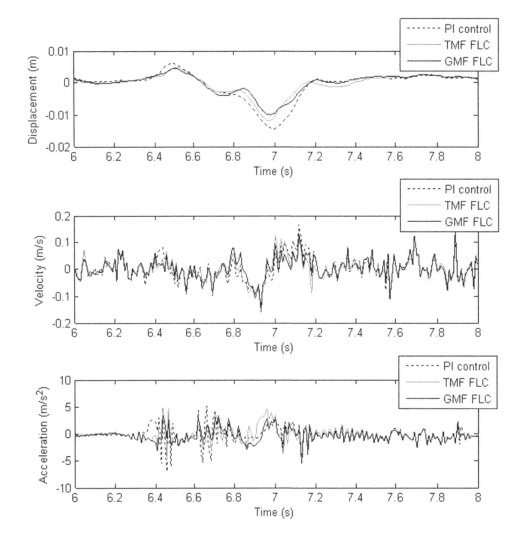

In particular, one of the most important challenges that intelligent techniques face in civil engineering is maintaining robustness even in case of component failure, while keeping in mind that the reliability of soft computing is still undergoing testing and development in other industrial applications as well. The intrinsic nature and design methodology of intelligent systems still raises questions of viability in what concerns their usage when human lives are involved. It is, however, a direction of research already tackled by other fields, like biology, sociology, sports sciences etc. with promising results.

Semi-active vibration control is not exclusive to civil engineering. There are plenty of domains that can benefit from specialized control algorithms to improve vibration mitigation, from aerospace engineering to the automotive industry, or even applications in which equipment needs to be isolated (biomedical machines, industrial lathes, manufacturing and precision robotics, etc.). The development of robust and fault-tolerant techniques for semi-active actuators is and will continue to be incredibly useful in these other areas as well, providing increased reliability and decreased energy consumption.

Figure 12. Case 3. Switch failure

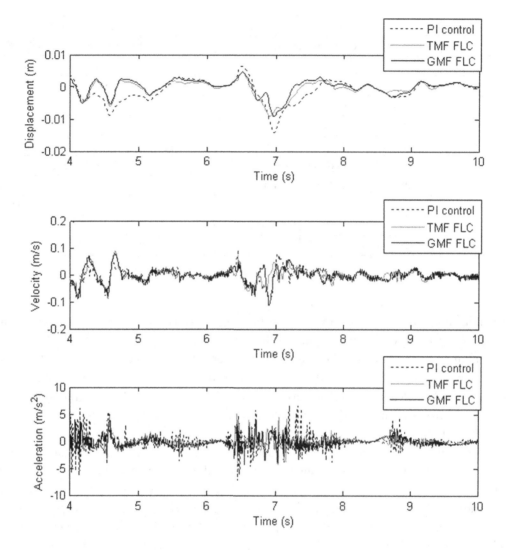

CONCLUSION

Semi-active damping systems for structural vibration mitigation are nonlinear switching systems. For such systems, robustness analysis is difficult; for a structural system with high modelling uncertainties, designing a robust control system is even more challenging. By comparing a PI control strategy obtained using evolutionary optimization with a cascaded fuzzy control strategy designed from human engineer experience, this chapter shows robustness of the cascaded fuzzy controller over the conventional one.

Considering the comparative results for three electrohydraulic damper control systems (one PI and two cascaded fuzzy schemes), it was shown that the fuzzy approach offers better performance. While taking into account equipment or sensor failure that led to full active control execution, the fuzzy control strategy offered higher reliability.

Results show that fuzzy controllers are more suitable for the semi-active damper. The nonlinear characteristics of the damper make the accurate design of a PI controller difficult. However, the fuzzy

Table 2. Response analysis

	Displacement [m]			Acceleration [m/s²]		
	PI	**TMF FLC**	**GMF FLC**	**PI**	**TMF FLC**	**GMF FLC**
Uncontrolled	0.0157			7.357		
Ideal conditions	0.014	0.0102	0.0086	6.784	6.870	4.122
Case 1	0.0141	0.0097	0.0108	7.306	7.476	6.238
Case 2	0.0144	0.0118	0.0099	7.389	7.108	5.576
Case 3	0.0142	0.009	0.009	7.200	6.089	4.144
	Displacement Reduction [%]			Acceleration Reduction [%]		
	PI	**TMF FLC**	**GMF FLC**	**PI**	**TMF FLC**	**GMF FLC**
Ideal conditions	10.8	35	45.2	7.8	6.6	44
Case 1	10.2	38.2	31.2	0.7	0	15.2
Case 2	8.3	24.9	36.9	-0.4	3.4	24.2
Case 3	9.6	42.7	42.7	2.1	17.2	43.7

strategy, making use of the available knowledge on the damper, and having a nonlinear character in itself, ensures adequate structural responses during earthquakes.

The essential and important contribution of this chapter is the introduction of the switching system (between active and passive behaviours) in the design of the fuzzy controller. Switching systems are highly sensitive and can lead to instability, even when designed carefully. By integrating the switching mechanism in the fuzzy controller, this work provides engineers with an alternative that minimizes the risk of destabilization.

One of the challenges that intelligent techniques face in civil engineering is maintaining robustness even in case of component failure. Their intrinsic nature and design methodology still raises questions of viability in what concerns their usage when human lives are involved. It is, however, a direction of research already tackled by other fields, like biology, sociology, sports sciences etc. with promising results.

The control of semi-active dampers is a hot topic in civil and structural engineering as well. Specialists in the field are always looking for interdisciplinary material that will ease their design efforts, especially when it comes to control and automation. Thus, this chapter provides an interesting and useful tool to civil engineers looking for insight into the design of fuzzy controllers for seismic vibration mitigation with semi-active dampers.

REFERENCES

Abdeddaim, M., Ounis, A., Djedoui, N., & Shrimali, M. K. (2016). Pounding hazard mitigation between adjacent planar buildings using coupling strategy. *Journal of Civil Structural Health Monitoring*, 6(3), 603–617. doi:10.1007/s13349-016-0177-4

Ali, S. F., & Ramaswamy, A. (2009). Optimal fuzzy logic control for MDOF structural systems using evolutionary algorithms. *Engineering Applications of Artificial Intelligence*, 22(3), 407–419. doi:10.1016/j.engappai.2008.09.004

Amini, F., Hazaveh, N. K., & Rad, A. A. (2013). Wavelet PSO-Based LQR Algorithm for Optimal Structural Control Using Active Tuned Mass Dampers. *Computer-Aided Civil and Infrastructure Engineering*, *28*(7), 542–557. doi:10.1111/mice.12017

Banisheikholeslami, A., Behnamfar, F., & Ghandil, M. (2016). A beam-to-column connection with viscoelastic and hysteretic dampers for seismic damage control. *Journal of Constructional Steel Research*, *117*, 185–195. doi:10.1016/j.jcsr.2015.10.016

Bitaraf, M., Ozbulut, O. E., Hurlebaus, S., & Barroso, L. (2010). Application of semi-active control strategies for seismic protection of buildings with MR dampers. *Engineering Structures*, *32*(10), 3040–3047. doi:10.1016/j.engstruct.2010.05.023

Braz-César, M., & Barros, R. (2017). Optimization of a Fuzzy Logic Controller for MR Dampers using an Adaptive Neuro-Fuzzy Procedure. *International Journal of Structural Stability and Dynamics*, *17*(05), 1740007. doi:10.1142/S0219455417400077

Brodersen, M. L., & Høgsberg, J. (2016). Hybrid damper with stroke amplification for damping of offshore wind turbines. *Wind Energy (Chichester, England)*, *19*(12), 2223–2238. doi:10.1002/we.1977

Chen, C.-W., Yeh, K., Chiang, W.-L., Chen, C.-Y., & Wu, D.-J. (2007a). Modeling, Hinf Control and Stability Analysis for Structural Systems Using Takagi-Sugeno Fuzzy Model. *Journal of Vibration and Control*, *13*(11), 1519–1534. doi:10.1177/1077546307073690

Chen, S.-H., Zheng, L.-A., & Chou, J.-H. (2007b). A Mixed Robust/Optimal Active Vibration Control for Uncertain Flexible Structural Systems with Nonlinear Actuators Using Genetic Algorithm. *Journal of Vibration and Control*, *13*(2), 185–201. doi:10.1177/1077546307070228

Choi, K.-M., Cho, S.-W., Kim, D.-O., & Lee, I.-W. (2005). Active control for seismic response reduction using modal-fuzzy approach. *International Journal of Solids and Structures*, *42*(16-17), 4779–4794. doi:10.1016/j.ijsolstr.2005.01.018

Dangor, M. (2014). *Dynamic neural network-based feedback linearization of electrohydraulic suspension systems* (Doctoral dissertation).

Dangor, M., Dahunsi, O. A., Pedro, J. O., & Ali, M. M. (2014). Evolutionary algorithm-based PID controller tuning for nonlinear quarter-car electrohydraulic vehicle suspensions. *Nonlinear Dynamics*, *78*(4), 2795–2810. doi:10.1007/s11071-014-1626-4

Dhankot, M. A., & Soni, D. P. (2017). Behaviour of Triple Friction Pendulum isolator under forward directivity and fling step effect. *KSCE Journal of Civil Engineering*, *21*(3), 872–881. doi:10.1007/s12205-016-0690-3

Ding, J., Sun, X., Zhang, L., & Xie, J. (2017). *Optimization of Fuzzy Control for Magnetorheological Damping Structures*. Shock and Vibration.

Dyke, S. J., Spencer, B. F., Jr., Sain, M. K., & Carlson, J. D. (1996). Experimental verification of semi-active structural control strategies using acceleration feedback. *Proceedings of the 3rd International Conference on Motion and Vibration Control*.

Eswaran, M., Athul, S., Niraj, P., Reddy, G. R., & Ramesh, M. R. (2017). Tuned liquid dampers for multi-storey structure: Numerical simulation using a partitioned FSI algorithm and experimental validation. *Sadhana*, *42*(4), 449–465.

Filip-Vacarescu, N., Vulcu, C., & Dubina, D. (2016). Numerical Model of a Hybrid Damping System Composed of a Buckling Restrained Brace with a Magneto Rheological Damper. *Mathematical Modelling in Civil Engineering*, *12*(1), 13–22.

Flatau, A. B., Hall, D. L., & Schlesselman, J. M. (1993). Magnetostrictive Vibration Control Systems. *Journal of Intelligent Material Systems and Structures*, *4*(4), 560–565. doi:10.1177/1045389X9300400419

Gidaris, I., & Taflanidis, A. A. (2015). Performance assessment and optimization of fluid viscous dampers through life-cycle cost criteria and comparison to alternative design approaches. *Bulletin of Earthquake Engineering*, *13*(4), 1003–1028. doi:10.1007/s10518-014-9646-5

Guclu, R., & Yazici, H. (2007). Fuzzy Logic Control of a Non-linear Structural System against Earthquake Induced Vibration. *Journal of Vibration and Control*, *13*(11), 1535–1551. doi:10.1177/1077546307077663

Hashemi, S. M. A., Haji Kazemi, H., & Karamodin, A. (2016). Localized genetically optimized wavelet neural network for semi-active control of buildings subjected to earthquake. *Structural Control and Health Monitoring*, *23*(8), 1074–1087. doi:10.1002/stc.1823

Heo, G., Kim, C., Jeon, S., Seo, S., & Jeon, J. (2016). Research on Hybrid Seismic Response Control System for Motion Control of Two Span Bridge. *Journal of Physics: Conference Series*, *744*(1), 1–12.

Hiemenz, G. J., & Wereley, N. M. (1999). Seismic Response of Civil Structures Utilizing Semi-Active MR and ER Bracing Systems. *Journal of Intelligent Material Systems and Structures*, *10*(8), 646–651. doi:10.1106/TTXP-20DM-G861-HU0M

Hong, S.-R., & Choi, S.-B. (2005). Vibration Control of a Structural System Using Magneto-Rheological Fluid Mount. *Journal of Intelligent Material Systems and Structures*, *16*(11-12), 931–936. doi:10.1177/1045389X05053917

Jamshidi, M., & Chang, C. C. (2017) A new self-powered electromagnetic damper for structural vibration control. *Proceedings SPIE Sensors and Smart Structures Technologies for Civil, Mechanical, and Aerospace Systems*.

Jing, C., Youlin, X., Weilian, Q., & Zhtlun, W. (2004). Seismic response control of a complex structure using multiple MR dampers: Experimental investigation. *Earthquake Engineering and Engineering Vibration*, *3*(2), 181–193. doi:10.1007/BF02858233

Johnson, J. G., Pantelides, C. P., & Reaveley, L. D. (2015). Nonlinear rooftop tuned mass damper frame for the seismic retrofit of buildings. *Earthquake Engineering & Structural Dynamics*, *44*(2), 299–316. doi:10.1002/eqe.2473

Kawai, T. (1977). New Element Models in Discrete Structural Analysis. *Journal of the Society of Naval Architects of Japan*, *141*(141), 174–180. doi:10.2534/jjasnaoe1968.1977.174

Kelly, J. M., Leitmann, G., & Soldatos, A. G. (1987). Robust Control of Base-Isolated Structures under Earthquake Excitation. *Journal of Optimization Theory and Applications*, *53*(2), 159–180. doi:10.1007/BF00939213

Kelly, T. E. (2001). *In-Structure Damping and Energy Dissipation Design Guidelines*. Holmes Consulting Group. Available on www.holmesgroup.com

Khodabandolehlou, H., Pekcan, G., Fadali, M. S., & Salem, M. (2017). Active neural predictive control of seismically isolated structures. *Structural Control and Health Monitoring*, e2061. doi:10.1002/stc.2061

Kim, H.-S., & Roschke, P. N. (2006). Design of fuzzy logic controller for smart base isolation system using genetic algorithm. *Engineering Structures*, *28*(1), 84–96. doi:10.1016/j.engstruct.2005.07.006

Kim, H.-S., & Roschke, P. N. (2007). GA-fuzzy control of smart base isolated benchmark building using supervisory control technique. *Advances in Engineering Software*, *38*(7), 453–465. doi:10.1016/j.advengsoft.2006.10.004

Kobori, T. (1990). Technology Development and Forecast of Dynamical Intelligent Building (D.I.B). *Journal of Intelligent Material Systems and Structures*, *1*(4), 391–407. doi:10.1177/1045389X9000100402

Lakhani, M. T., & Soni, D. P. (2017). Comparative Study of Smart Base-Isolation Using Fuzzy Control and Neural Network. *Procedia Engineering*, *173*, 1825–1832. doi:10.1016/j.proeng.2016.12.227

Landi, L., Grazi, G., & Diotallevi, P. P. (2016). Comparison of different models for friction pendulum isolators in structures subjected to horizontal and vertical ground motions. *Soil Dynamics and Earthquake Engineering*, *81*, 75–83. doi:10.1016/j.soildyn.2015.10.016

Li, H. N., Jia, Y., & Wang, S. Y. (2004). Theoretical and Experimental Studies on Reduction for Multi-Model Seismic Responses of High-Rise Structures by Tuned Liquid Dampers. *Journal of Vibration and Control*, *10*, 1041–1056.

Lin, C.-C., Lu, L.-Y., Lin, G.-L., & Yang, T.-W. (2010). Vibration control of seismic structures using semi-active friction multiple tuned mass dampers. *Engineering Structures*, *32*(10), 3404–3417. doi:10.1016/j.engstruct.2010.07.014

Liut, D. A., Matheu, E. E., Singh, M. P., & Mook, D. T. (2000). A Modified Gradient-Search Training Technique for Neural-Network Structural Control. *Journal of Vibration and Control*, *6*(8), 1243–1268. doi:10.1177/107754630000600807

Lu, L.-Y., Lin, G.-L., & Kuo, T.-C. (2008). Stiffness controllable isolation system for near-fault seismic isolation. *Engineering Structures*, *30*(3), 747–765. doi:10.1016/j.engstruct.2007.05.022

Neelakantan, V. A., & Washington, G. N. (2008). Vibration Control of Structural Systems using MR dampers and a Modified Sliding Mode Control Technique. *Journal of Intelligent Material Systems and Structures*, *19*(2), 211–223. doi:10.1177/1045389X06074509

Nishimura, I., Abdel-Ghaffar, A. M., Masri, S. F., Miller, R. K., Beck, J. L., Caughey, T. K., & Iwan, W. D. (1992). An Experimental Study of the Active Control of a Building Model. *Journal of Intelligent Material Systems and Structures*, *3*(1), 134–165. doi:10.1177/1045389X9200300108

Novo, T., Varum, H., Teixeira-Dias, F., Rodrigues, H., Silva, M. F., Costa, A. C., & Guerreiro, L. (2014). Tuned liquid dampers simulation for earthquake response control of buildings. *Bulletin of Earthquake Engineering*, *12*(2), 1007–1024. doi:10.1007/s10518-013-9528-2

Oates, W. S., & Smith, R. C. (2008). Nonlinear Optimal Control Techniques for Vibration Attenuation Using Magnetostrictive Actuators. *Journal of Intelligent Material Systems and Structures*, *19*(2), 193–209. doi:10.1177/1045389X06074159

Otani, S. (2004). Earthquake Resistant Design of Reinforced Concrete Buildings. *Journal of Advanced Concrete Technology*, *2*(1), 3–24. doi:10.3151/jact.2.3

Ozbulut, O. E., & Hurlebaus, S. (2010). Fuzzy control of piezoelectric friction dampers for seismic protection of smart base isolated buildings. *Bulletin of Earthquake Engineering*, *8*(6), 1435–1455. doi:10.1007/s10518-010-9187-5

Park, K.-S., Koh, H.-M., & Ok, S.-Y. (2002). Active control of earthquake excited structures using fuzzy supervisory technique. *Advances in Engineering Software*, *33*(11-12), 761–768. doi:10.1016/S0965-9978(02)00044-3

Park, K.-S., Koh, H.-M., & Seo, C.-W. (2004). Independent modal space fuzzy control of earthquake-excited structures. *Engineering Structures*, *26*(2), 279–289. doi:10.1016/j.engstruct.2003.10.005

Patrascu, M. (2011). *Advanced Techniques for Seismic Vibration Control* (PhD Thesis). Department of Automatic Control and Systems Engineering, University Politehnica of Bucharest.

Patrascu, M. (2015). Genetically enhanced modal controller design for seismic vibration in nonlinear multi-damper configuration. *Proceedings of the Institution of Mechanical Engineers. Part I, Journal of Systems and Control Engineering*, *229*(2), 158–168. doi:10.1177/0959651814550540

Patrascu, M., Dumitrache, I., & Patrut, P. (2012). A Comparative Study for Advanced Seismic Vibration Control Algorithms. *U.P.B. Scientific Bulletin, Series C*, *74*(4), 3–16.

Patrascu, M., & Ion, A. (2015a). *Seismic Vibration Control with Semi-Active Dampers*. Bucharest: MatrixRom.

Patrascu, M., & Ion, A. (2015b). *GAOT-ECM Seismic Vibration Case Study*. Available online: http://www.mathworks.com/matlabcentral/fileexchange/51131-gaot-ecm-seismic-vibration-case-study

Patrascu, M., & Ion, A. (2016). Evolutionary Modeling of Industrial Plants and Design of PID Controllers. In *Nature-Inspired Computing for Control Systems* (pp. 73–119). Springer International Publishing. doi:10.1007/978-3-319-26230-7_4

Patrascu, M., Patrascu, A., & Beres, I. (2017). An immune evolution mechanism for the study of stress factors in supervised and controlled systems. In *IEEE Evolving and Adaptive Intelligent Systems* (pp. 1–8). EAIS. doi:10.1109/EAIS.2017.7954823

Pedro, J. O., Dangor, M., Dahunsi, O. A., & Ali, M. M. (2014). Intelligent feedback linearization control of nonlinear electrohydraulic suspension systems using particle swarm optimization. *Applied Soft Computing*, *24*, 50–62. doi:10.1016/j.asoc.2014.05.013

Philippe, M., Essick, R., Dullerud, G. E., & Jungers, R. M. (2016). Stability of discrete-time switching systems with constrained switching sequences. *Automatica, 72*, 242–250. doi:10.1016/j.automatica.2016.05.015

Pozo, F., Ikhouane, F., Pujol, G., & Rodellar, J. (2006). Adaptive Backstepping Control of Hysteretic Base-Isolated Structures. *Journal of Vibration and Control, 12*(4), 373–393. doi:10.1177/1077546306063254

Preumont, A., Voltan, M., Sangiovanni, A., Mokrani, B., & Alaluf, D. (2016). Active tendon control of suspension bridges. *Smart Structures and Systems, 18*(1), 31–52. doi:10.12989/sss.2016.18.1.031

Rao, M. M., & Datta, T. K. (2005). Predictive Active Control of Building Frames with a Solo Neuro-controller. *Journal of Vibration and Control, 11*, 627–641.

Renzi, E., & De Angelis, M. (2005). Optimal Semi-active Control and Non-linear Dynamic Response of Variable Stiffness Structures. *Journal of Vibration and Control, 11*, 1253–1289.

Renzi, E., & Serino, G. (2003). Testing and modelling a semi-actively controlled steel frame structure equipped with MR dampers. *Structural Control and Health Monitoring, 11*(3), 189–221. doi:10.1002/stc.36

Rew, K.-H., Han, J.-H., & Lee, I. (2002). Multi-Modal Vibration Control Using Adaptive Positive Position Feedback. *Journal of Intelligent Material Systems and Structures, 13*(1), 13–22. doi:10.1177/1045389X02013001866

Ribakov, Y. (2009). Semi-active Pneumatic Devices for Control of MDOF Structures. *The Open Construction and Building Technology Journal, 3*(1), 141–145. doi:10.2174/1874836800903010141

Rubió-Massegú, J., Rossell, J. M., & Karimi, H. R. (2016). Vibration control strategy for large-scale structures with incomplete multi-actuator system and neighbouring state information. *IET Control Theory & Applications, 10*(4), 407–416. doi:10.1049/iet-cta.2015.0737

Sahab, M. G., Toropov, V. V., & Gandomi, A. H. (2013) A review on traditional and modern structural optimization: problems and techniques. *Metaheuristic Applications in Structures and Infrastructures*, 25-47.

Samanta, A., & Banerji, P. (2010). Structural vibration control using modified tuned liquid dampers. *The IES Journal Part A: Civil & Structural Engineering, 3*(1), 14–27.

Shook, D. A., Roschke, P. N., Lin, P.-Y., & Loh, C.-H. (2008). GA-optimized fuzzy logic control of a large-scale building for seismic loads. *Engineering Structures, 30*(2), 436–449. doi:10.1016/j.engstruct.2007.04.008

Spencer, B. F., Jr., & Sain, M. K. (1997). Controlling Buildings: A New Frontier in Feedback. IEEE Control Systems Magazine, 17(6), 19-35.

Symans, M. D., & Constantinou, M. C. (1997a). Experimental Testing and Analytical modeling of Semi-Active Fluid Dampers for Seismic Protection. *Journal of Intelligent Material Systems and Structures, 8*(8), 644–657. doi:10.1177/1045389X9700800802

Symans, M. D., & Costantinou, M. C. (1997b). Seismic testing of a building structure with a semiactive fluid damper control system. *Earthquake Engineering & Structural Dynamics*, *26*(7), 759–777. doi:10.1002/(SICI)1096-9845(199707)26:7<759::AID-EQE675>3.0.CO;2-E

Symans, M. D., Madden, G. J., & Wongprasert, N. (1999). Semi-Active Hybrid Seismic Isolation Systems: Addressing the Limitations of Passive Isolation Systems. *Proc. of Structures Congress 1999*.

Teng, J., Xing, H. B., Lu, W., Li, Z. H., & Chen, C. J. (2016). Influence analysis of time delay to active mass damper control system using pole assignment method. *Mechanical Systems and Signal Processing*, *80*, 99–116. doi:10.1016/j.ymssp.2016.04.008

Tubaldi, E., Ragni, L., & Dall'Asta, A. (2015). Probabilistic seismic response assessment of linear systems equipped with nonlinear viscous dampers. *Earthquake Engineering & Structural Dynamics*, *44*(1), 101–120. doi:10.1002/eqe.2461

Uz, M. E., & Hadi, M. N. (2014). Optimal design of semi active control for adjacent buildings connected by MR damper based on integrated fuzzy logic and multi-objective genetic algorithm. *Engineering Structures*, *69*, 135–148. doi:10.1016/j.engstruct.2014.03.006

Wang, D. H., & Liao, W. H. (2005). Semiactive Controllers for Magnetorheological Fluid Dampers. *Journal of Intelligent Material Systems and Structures*, *16*(11-12), 983–993. doi:10.1177/1045389X05055281

Wilson, C. M. D., & Abdullah, M. M. (2010). Structural vibration reduction using self-tuning fuzzy control of magnetorheological dampers. *Bulletin of Earthquake Engineering*, *8*(4), 1037–1054. doi:10.1007/s10518-010-9177-7

Xiong, J., Lam, J., Shu, Z., & Mao, X. (2014). Stability analysis of continuous-time switched systems with a random switching signal. *IEEE Transactions on Automatic Control*, *59*(1), 180–186. doi:10.1109/TAC.2013.2266751

Yan, G., & Zhou, L. L. (2006). Integrated fuzzy logic and genetic algorithms for multi-objective control of structures using MR dampers. *Journal of Sound and Vibration*, *296*(1-2), 368–382. doi:10.1016/j.jsv.2006.03.011

Yang, S. M., Chen, C. J., & Huang, W. L. (2006). Structural Vibration Suppression by a Neural-Network Controller with a Mass-Damper Actuator. *Journal of Vibration and Control*, *12*(5), 495–508. doi:10.1177/1077546306064269

Yang, X. S., Bekdaş, G., & Nigdeli, S. M. (2016). Review and applications of metaheuristic algorithms in civil engineering. In *Metaheuristics and Optimization in Civil Engineering* (pp. 1–24). Springer International Publishing. doi:10.1007/978-3-319-26245-1_1

Zafarani, M. M., Halabian, A. M., & Behbahani, S. (2016). Optimal coupled and uncoupled fuzzy logic control for magneto-rheological damper-equipped plan-asymmetric structural systems considering structural nonlinearities. *Journal of Vibration and Control*. doi:10.1177/1077546316660030

Zamani, A. A., Tavakoli, S., & Etedali, S. (2017). Control of piezoelectric friction dampers in smart base-isolated structures using self-tuning and adaptive fuzzy proportional–derivative controllers. *Journal of Intelligent Material Systems and Structures*, *28*(10), 1287–1302. doi:10.1177/1045389X16667561

Zhang, H., Wang, E., Zhang, N., Min, F., Subash, R., & Su, C. (2015). Semi-active sliding mode control of vehicle suspension with magneto-rheological damper. *Chinese Journal of Mechanical Engineering*, *28*(1), 63–75. doi:10.3901/CJME.2014.0918.152

Zhang, Y., Alleyne, A. G., & Zheng, D. (2005). A hybrid control strategy for active vibration isolation with electrohydraulic actuators. *Control Engineering Practice*, *13*(3), 279–289. doi:10.1016/j.conengprac.2004.03.009

Zhao, D., & Li, Y. (2015). Fuzzy control for seismic protection of semiactive base-isolated structures subjected to near-fault earthquakes. *Mathematical Problems in Engineering*.

Zhou, H., Sun, L., & Xing, F. (2014). Damping of full-scale stay cable with viscous damper: Experiment and analysis. *Advances in Structural Engineering*, *17*(2), 265–274. doi:10.1260/1369-4332.17.2.265

KEY TERMS AND DEFINITIONS

Control System: A set of control algorithms, actuators, sensors, and auxiliary elements that manages, commands, directs, or regulates the behaviour of other devices or systems.

Controller: A persistent systemic entity capable of sensing its environment and acting upon it, governed by internal rules.

Model: An abstract representation of a physical entity or process.

Seismic Damper: An actuator capable of developing large control forces in order to compensate or mitigate the seismic vibration of a structure.

Seismic Vibration: The response of a structure under the action of seismic ground motion.

Simulation: The representation of the behaviour or characteristics of one system or process through the use of a model.

Uncertainty: A state that involves imperfect or unknown information. In systemic interpretation, it refers to unknown behaviours, characteristics, or disturbances, especially in modelling, simulation, control system design, testing, and validation.

Chapter 3
Co–Design Flow for Embedded Systems (MPSoC):
Hybrid Model and Performance Estimation

Kamel Smiri
Université de Tunis El Manar, Tunisia

Nourhen Fourati
Université de Tunis El Manar, Tunisia

ABSTRACT

In this chapter, the authors explore the estimation of the performances in an earlier stage of (multi-processors system on chip) MPSoC design in which it is necessary to drive design space exploration and support important design decisions. Therefore, they address the co-design hardware/software with estimating performances in order to find an adequate solution, which consists in mapping the application on the components of architecture with respect the criteria of performance of the system defined from the beginning. The chapter provides a hybrid model for estimating performance in which cohabited simulation and analytical techniques are carried out via a link layer in order to reach an optimal architectural solution quickly. Thus, it allows faster performance estimation with better accuracy at different levels of abstraction.

INTRODUCTION

When one has a set of software and a set of hardware conceived for a specific application, one thus speaks an embedded system. Generally, this last system use microprocessors which necessarily very powerful but are not well adapted for each task. Often, the execution time of a task must be known and limited, and the system must be reliable and secure. The embedded systems are thus very often real time systems. Nowadays, the system micro-electronics is strongly directed towards the mobile and embedded applications such as; PDA (Staff DIGITAL Assistants), GPS (Total Positioning Systems), MPEG4, micro-satellites (Sergio et al., 2011). The multiprocessors systems on chip strongly emerged in this kind of applications (Rousseau et al., 2011), it is for that they become increasingly complex because of their functional constraints (energy consumption (Jayaram et al., 2012), computing power...) and nonfunc-

DOI: 10.4018/978-1-5225-3531-7.ch003

tional constraints (cost, reliability, Time to Market…) (Smiri et al., 2008) (Hocine et al., 2012) (Philippe et al., 2015). In order to answer the constraints and to find the best trade-offs among performance and cost, the design of system MPSoC should be based on a hybrid approach to performance estimation. Then, one will present initially system MPSoC and in second place, methodologies of MPSoC design by taking examples graphs SDF in analytical model and SoCLib in simulation model. Multi-core Systems-On-Chip MPSoC and Performance Estimation Modeling A multiprocessor system on chip MPSoC is a new generation of architectural System on Chip which makes it possible to raise the challenges of Mono-Processor System on Chip. This system integrates several heterogeneous components such as programmable calculating units and/or nonprogrammable (CPU, DSP, ASICIP, FPGA), components of the complex communication networks (Bus hierarchical on chip, network on chip), the components of memorizing, peripheral I/O, etc. These components integrate on only one silicon part.

Figure 1 illustrates a generic model of a heterogeneous MPSoC system with software and material parts:

- A material node is component which does not have the ability of programming.
- A communication network makes it possible to connect all the nodes together.
- The software nodes make it possible to provide the environment to execute the tasks of the applications.
- The embedded software is structured into layers:
  - *Application Layer:* This layer represents a set of tasks of the application which are carried out in parallel, in order to profit to the maximum of the parallelism offered by architecture multiprocessors. This layer communicates with the software node by calling on primitives of the operating system (OS).
  - *The Operating System OS:* The operating system makes it possible to provide an interface between hardware equipment and the application.
  - *Libraries:* The objective to use the library of communication is to call on the channels of communication and to use the various features of the library C standard and the library of mathematics.
  - *Hardware Abstraction Layer:* This layer makes it possible the operating system to interact with the material peripherals on a level abstract rather than on a detailed material level.

Figure 1. Typical architecture of a heterogeneous system multiprocessor (Smiri et al., 2008)

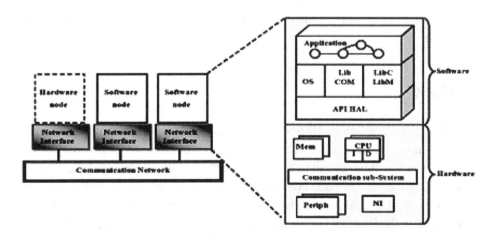

- Equipment is also cut out in two layers:
  - The lower layer contains the components of the calculation and memorizing.
  - The material layer of communication embedded on the chip made up of two under lays: structure of communication (links point-with-point, hierarchical bus, and network on chip) and communication adapters (Jordans et al., 2011).

1. Synchronous Data Flow Graphs SDFG

Now, we move to a short description of the state art on methodologies of MPSoC design flow. These methodologies contain the main stages of the design flow such as Cycle Static Data Flow CSDF, Scenario-Aware Data Flow SADF, and Synchronous Data Flow SDF3. This last tool is a particular case of the data flow and of the Petri network and it is based on graphs SDF to model the application and the target platform. Formalism SDF is often used for the entire predictable systems, in which the number of samples of data consumed and produced by each node with each execution, is specified a priori. Graphs SDF constitute the central element of modeling SDF (Smiri et al., 2009).

Moreover, SDF3 tool integrates several commands each one of it has a precise function. Indeed, the command *sdf3flow* is most interesting of tool SDF3 since it makes it possible to map a graph SDF of application with a constraint on graph architecture MPSoC (Ghamarian et al., 2007).

2. Graphs KPN in System on Chip Library SoCLib

The System on Chip Library (SoCLib) is an open framework for the virtual prototyping of MPSoC systems. This tool based on the simulation model and it respected the KPN formalism. In which, the SoCLib allows the development a software application in the form of a set of parallel (allow to deal the pipeline parallelism) and communicating tasks. These tasks can be implemented in hardware or software and use a Multi-Writer/Multi-Reader First-In/First-Out (MWMR FIFO) as a communication channel. Besides, SoCLib allows the simulation and the exploration of the hardware architecture via an open source library in two level abstractions (CABA and TLM) written in SystemC for the material components (SoCLib, 2017) (Kumar, 2003) (Kahn, 1974) (Youssef et al., 2007).

This paper is organized as follows. Section 2 presents the related work on performance estimation of MPSoC systems. Section 3 describes our approach of performance estimation of MPSoC systems with Hybrid model in which combine SDF3 tool and SoCLib simulation environment. Section 4 presents the experimentation of MJPEG Decoder. Finally, we will finish the article by the parties' discussion and conclusion in which we quote some perspectives.

RELATED WORK

The main aim of the tools of design of MPSoC is to evaluate and estimate profit in performance in order to fulfill the requirements of the market which it is always a question of estimating the performances of the applications which will be related to the target platforms, before the implementation. The methodology of estimate of the performance consists in checking if a modeled application can satisfy the constraints required with the application when it is carried out on architecture MPSoC, without losses financial and material in the implementation and the deployment of an application on a given platform.

Generally, the methods used for the evaluation of performances of systems MPSoC are analytical modeling, statistical models, models based on the trace and simulation platform. Simulation requires prohibitory computing times, while the models resulting from the analytical methods miss precision. Therefore, our approach consists in presenting a new hybrid model which combines the strong points of two tools; first is the analytical model SDF and the other is the simulation model SoCLib(Smiri et al., 2011)(Smiri et al., 2011).

The graphs of synchronous data flows (SDFG) are a very useful means for the modeling and the multimedia analysis of the applications. Certain indicators of performance, such as the latency time and the debit were studied ahead. In which this last is a very useful indicator of performance for the applications in real time simultaneously. So, in our work we interested in the estimation of the speed of execution (Smiri et al., 2009).

In 2007, Ghamarian and its team propose an algorithm to determine the realizable latency time minimal, by providing a system of execution to carry out a SDFG with this latency time, since this last cannot be tolerated in the most critical applications (Ghamarian et al., 2007).

Furthermore, we find the integration of the presentations by tool SDF3 of application, of material architecture and their Mapping of the software tasks on the platform given in the generation of the MPSoC systems for a platform FPGA Xilinx which have provided by tool MAMPS. This work is developed by Stuijk and his team whose objective is to carry out a design flow which gathers the forces of tool SDF3 and platform MAMPS (Ptolemy, 2013).

We cannot forget that tool SDF is one among the most known approaches for the estimate of the performance on the level of the migration of software tasks towards material tasks in the MPSoC systems. In this context, (Smiri et al., 2009) proposes an approach of performance estimation of migration software task to hardware component with SDF Graphs in order to study the problems of the estimate of the profit in the performance of the migration of one or more software tasks while composing material in the systems embedded MPSoC. As soon as the migration is made several changes concerning memorizing, the communication, etc. must be taken into account. The contribution of this work is in two essential points: modeling by graphs SDF of the software solutions with migration partial in material components and the improvement of the annotation of modeling to reach a more precise estimate (Smiri et al., 2009).

The major objective of this software-hardware migration is to accelerate the data processing of the multimedia applications in order to guarantee the performance.

Moreover, the Ptolemy environment was carried out by Edward Lee in the University of California. This environment makes it possible to jointly model, conceive and to simulate embedded systems which integrate several technologies such as software/hardware, analogical/digital, etc [25].

DIGITAL System Design Environment is an environment for the design of synchronous digital systems containing platform and it was developed by the laboratory LIP6-France, whose objective is to carry out the establishment of a software application written out of C on a modeled material architecture. This tool describes the problem of design in the shape of a triplet: architectural system (is a unit made up of a generic platform material and a micronucleus), application (is described in the form of a graph KPN and which understands at the same time the operating system), constraint (latency time, the silicon flow or surface used) (Buchmann et al., 2004).

In the project OSTRE, team INRIA developed methodology Algorithm Architecture Adequacy A3. This methodology uses the graph to conceive the application and material architecture. The interest principal to use the graph in the modeling of the algorithm, architecture and the mapping is to express it parallelism. As well as the context of adequacy presents itself in the selection of the originator among all the establishments (deployment of an algorithm on an architecture) possible, an establishment which to solve the problem of optimization (respects real time, minimizes the material resources, to satisfy the performances and etc). Methodology AAA is supported by the environment of Syndex implementation. This tool makes it possible to validate the establishment by simulation (Yves, 2014).

The Table 1 present a comparison between the various environments of co-design which are quoted at the beginning of this section by basing itself on the following criteria: the simplicity that is the manipulation of syntax of modeling is simple and easy, the rapidity it means that the hardware/software conception of a dedicated system does not set a lot of time to model and the precision it means that the obtained results will be more precise and nearest at the real results.

According to the results cleared from this overview table and according to the decision of the team and the availability of tools in the laboratory, we can choose both tools SoCLib and SDF to model our hybrid approach because these two tools can answer our objective that is to model architecture MPSoC by respecting given constraints, as well as to estimate performance in a fast and precise way.

HYBRID APPROACH FOR PERFORMANCE ESTIMATION

To meet performance requirements, video and multimedia applications have been mapped to MPSoC, but in the counterpart, the MPSoC design will be more complex (Senouci et al., 2007). So, the increase in the complexity of the design of MPSoC requires powerful development tools in order to conceive systems on chip in a short time and more effective way in material terms of exploitation of resources and deployment of the software application on the platform equipment. Our proposal consists with a hybrid methodology based on analytical models on the one hand and simulations on the other hand. The advantage of our approach is its ability to provide a tool-supported design flow for fault-tolerant embedded systems.

In the first place, we choose the analytical model in order to generate Mapping of software platform on the material platform, not only but also, to be aware the rate of use of material resource. Thereafter, due to the values and statistics generated in the file Output from the analytical model, we can use them in the model of the simulation in order to reduce the time of the tests.

Table 1. Comparison of design tools for embedded systems

Tools criteria	A3 (Yves, 2014)	SDF3 (Smiri., 2009)	SoCLib (Smiri., 2009)	Ptolemy (Ptolemy, 2013)
Analytic Model		+		+
Simulation Model	+		+	+
Hybrid Model				+
Simplicity of Modeling	+	++	-	-
Precision Performance	+	-	++	+
Execution Rapidity	+	++	+	-
Type of Communication Model	Data Flow	Synchronous Data Flow	Multi-Write Multi-Read	Process Networks, Discrete Events, SDF, Finite-State Machine…
Type of Computational Model	Data Flow Graph	Synchronous Data Flow Graph	Kahn Process Network Graph	Process Networks, Discrete Events, SDF, Finite-State Machine…

The figure 2 presents the global idea of the hybrid approach which is to group two techniques of estimation of performance and illustrates the initiative of the approach which begins with the analytical tool and we use the SDF tool (Synchronous Data Flow) and the second tool is based on the simulation and we opt SoCLib to make a prototype and simulate the resources materials of the platform architectural target, via of its library. We advance in the description of our hybrid approach proposed to detail more and explain three main clauses left in this hybrid model.

The figure 3 details the hybrid approach and present three main stages of the methodology of estimation of the performances: 1) Analytical Modeling, 2) Link layer and 3) Simulation Model.

Analytical Modeling

The analytical model used in this approach is a synchronous stream of data which is a particular case of the data flow and of the Petri network. The nodes of treatment (or tasks) are scheduled in a static way. The streams of synchronous data are analytical and predictive models in which the number of elements of data produced or consumed by a knot is known during the conception. The knots of treatment communicate through lines or arcs and can be statically organized according to the flow of E/S data (implicit synchronization by the data).

Figure 2. Hybrid Approach of estimation of the performances for the embedded systems

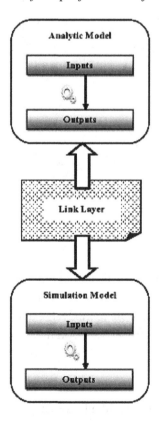

Figure 3. Detailed schema of the Hybrid Approach of estimation performance

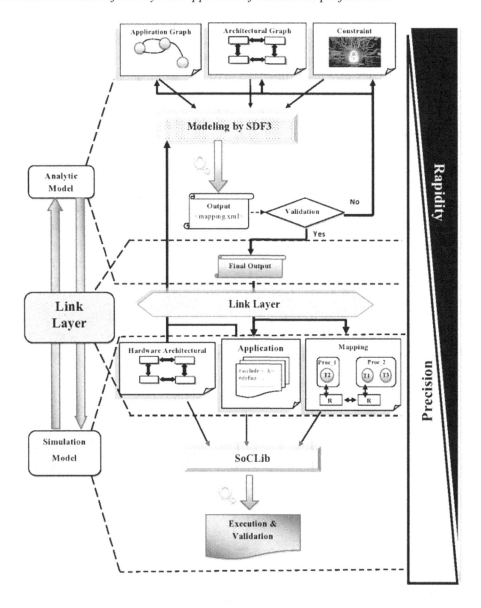

The first stage of our approach is analytical modeling. The latter consists in estimating the performances when designing MPSoC. In our methodology, analytical modeling is based on the exploitation of graph SDF, this formalism makes it possible to model the applications software and material, not only but also, the constraints to deploy the software tasks on the material resources, via SDF3 tool.

Modeling

The syntax of modeling in SDF3 tool will be like following:

- **Application Graph:** The software application or the graph of application is described in the form of an XML file. For each one actor must specify, with the first place, the ports input/output and their rates and then, on which processor must be also carried out the execution time as well as the memory size occupied by the pile of the actor who is expressed out of bits.
- **Architecture Graph:** Material architecture or the graph of architecture is described in an XML file. This file contains the material platform on which the application will be implemented. The graph of architecture is described in terms of nodes of execution, routers and links.
- **Constraint Debit:** The throughput of a graph SDF it is the number of activations of an actor per unit of time divided by the vector of repetition of the graph of the application. This information is very important to determine if material architecture is able to accommodate the application with acceptable performances.

Execution

After the modeling of graph of the application and the graph of architecture and to fix the constraint, we pass at the stage of execution. SDF3 tool offers several commands whose command sdf3flow are most interesting for the estimate of performance since, starting from a graph of application, from a group of architecture and a constraint of debit; it will construct the whole of the stages of the predictable design flow.

The procedure of execution is done via the following command line:

Sdf3flow-sdf --settings sdf3.opt --output output.xml --html

The file sdf3.opt it is a file of options described with XML beacons which contains the way of the graph of application, the way of the graph of architecture and the parameters of the algorithm of Mapping. For the moment, SDF3 offers an algorithm "load balance" which makes it possible to balance the loads between the nodes of execution. The parameter output indicates the file "output.xml" in which the data produced by the command will be written. The data produced by the order sdf3flow are:

- Application Graph,
- Architecture Graph,
- Mapping actors on processors,
- Allocation memory for actor,
- Allocation memory for channel,
- Scheduling actors on processors,
- Scheduling messages on NOC.

As well as the result of this command the satisfaction of the constraint indicates. But, we cannot say that modeled system MPSoC-NoC is validated, before checking and analyzing the statistics and the percentages of use of the material resources. Thus for the stage of validation, there exists a feedback with the graph of architecture in order to optimize the architectural platform, it means that when we notes the presence of the resources initialized, one will change the material platform to reach an optimal solution.

Link Layer

The kernel of our hybrid approach represents itself in the form of a link layer which allows combining the efforts of previous two models (analytics and simulation). This layer establishes an interaction during the conception of the embedded system by basing itself on the analytical model and the model based on the simulation. The features of this layer represent themselves in bi- directions; in the first sense, the exploitation of the measures of performance obtained by the analytical model and to integrate them into the environment of the simulation to limit the architectural solutions and accelerate the time of modeling and execution by the model of simulation. the second way, the link layer allows to migrating detailed data of a material resource of a target platform or specifications of a level of abstraction most low from a model based on the simulation towards the analytical model to reach more precise results.

The figure 4 the main objective of this middle layer is to mix the contribution of the analytical technique which consists in the speed of the modeling of platforms, desired constraints and estimation of performance on one hand and the contribution of the simulation which represents itself in the accuracy and the precision of the results due to the use of the models at the various levels of abstraction on the other hand.

We indicated in the previous stage that the data produced by the command of execution will be described in the file "output.xml". Therefore, this last cover all the necessary information or data which will be used by the tool for simulation. The tool for simulation used in our approach it is SoCLib which is based on SystemC. SoCLib offers a tool of design of space exploration DSX. Language DSX is API implemented using the language Python and which makes it possible for a designer to map a multi-thread software application on hardware architecture and to generate a final design description with the relevant precision (Huang et al., 2013; Sousa et al., 2013; Salehi et al., 2015).

In our approach, the deployment of a software application on the material resources will be carried out like already indicating in SDF3 tool. We know that the file "output.xml" contains Mapping or the deployment of the actors on the processors, but wait, it is necessary that the material platform modeled by tool SDF3 is the same one of material architecture modeled by the SoCLib tool.

Due to the parse of "xml.dom", we can analyze the file "output.xml" in the API Python. This parsing provides a module called "minidom". This last takes the argument (i.e. the file "output.xml") and turns over an analyzed presentation of XML documents.

And consequently, we can access the tag and their attributes of a file xml in order to show Mapping of the actors on the processors, not only but also, we can exploit other data in modeling of material architecture by the tool of simulation such as the allowances of memory capacity for actors and channels, this information enables us to fix the memory size according to the need for the software application in order to avoid the wasting of the material resources.

This parser is used in the first direction (of analytic towards simulation) to analyze and get back the information wished from file output, but, he cannot use this parser the other way (of simulation towards analytic) because the environment of simulation SoCLib uses the language SystemC.

In the second sense, we can use the tool Doxygen to optimize the analytical model by information more detailed from the library of SoCLib. And consequently, the fundamental objective of this link layer in this sense is to refine the analytical tool SDF3.

Figure 4. Detailed schema of Link Layer

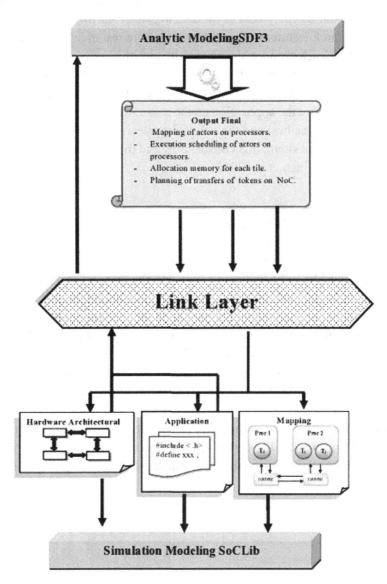

Simulation Model

In this stage, the designer must model by DSX/SoCLib the three following tasks (SoCLib, 2017):

- To define the structure of the multi-task software application, i.e. the graph of the tasks and communications (TCG).
- To define material architecture.
- To control the deployment of the software application on the material platform.

The file of mapping of the software application on the material platform it is the file of execution in which we will replace the static deployment of the data to extract starting from the file output.And even also in the file of material architecture, we can define or declare resources material such as the memory size, the space allocated for each channel, the bandwidth and etc.

The last stage of our hybrid approach is the execution and validation. This stage allows the execution and validation by the technique of simulation. After the modeling of the software application and the material platform, we will realize the application on the material platform modeled to level CABA. This execution is done on the machine host and the validation is carried out by the technique of simulation whose advantage is to accelerate simulation considerably and to validate the application, the communication and synchronization (Ehrlich et al., 2013).

EXPERIMENTATION: MJPEG DECODER

1. **Description of MJPEG Decoder:** The application used in the case study is decoder MJPEG. This code handles data per blocks of 8x8 pixels by using the technology of coding intra-screen. The decompression of an image JPEG is done in five most important stages: First actor VLD allows to analyze the input file and to decompress in blocks MCU "Minimum Coded Units". Then, each block passed through the opposite quantification and to reorder in ZIGZAG. The following task is the IDCT which makes it possible to transform the image starting from frequency field towards the space field. Finally, the conversion of the colors translates the colors of the blocks of components of an MCU to values of pixels; this task is carried out by actor LIBU (Smiri et al., 2008)(Smiri et al., 2011)(Karan et al., 2007).

2. **Validation of Approach:** We are going to try in this section to validate our hybrid model of estimation of the performances for the design of the embedded systems. We begin with the first part which is the analytical modeling and the data, which will be used by this model, can be obtained via tools of profiling

```
<actorProperties actor="iqzz">
    <processor type="mips0_0" default="true">
            <executionTime time="4464"/>
            <memory name="cram0_0">
                    <stateSize max="174763"/>
            </memory>
    </processor>
</actorProperties>
```

XML pseudo code describes the properties of an actor IQZZ either from the traces of a tool of simulation (we choose this method).

Analytical Modeling

The figure 5 represents the SDF model of the decoder MJPEG which is used during the estimations of performance. The actor VLD produces 36 tokens which correspond to 36 macros block of the image

Figure 5. Graph of the MJPEG decoder application

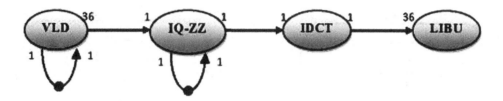

"plane.jpg" with a size of 48 pixels by 48. These are then transmitted to the actor IQ-ZZ, who reorganizes pixels according to the coding inverse zigzag then transmits it to the actor IQ-ZZ, who realizes the inverse quantification. The macro block is then treated by the actor IDCT who makes the inverse discreet transformed in cosine. Finally, the actor LIBU handles the pixels of the image to adapt them to the ring peripheral of exit, it is for it, he requires 36 macro blocks to reconstitute the whole image.

Auto-arcs on knots VLD and IQ-ZZ represents respectively the tables of Huffman and quantification auto-passed on executions after execution. Once the actors are modeled, it is necessary to determine the requirements in terms for memory and the execution times of the actors of the graph. These properties are also described in an XML file. This code makes it possible to carry out actor IQZZ on the processor mips0_0 with 174763 cycles like an execution time for this task.

We add the attribute name for the element memory to facilitate the assignment or the allowance of a segment of memory for each actor in the SoCLib simulation tool.

The latest information needed for the application description in its XML file is the throughput constraint which must be respectful when the decoder MJPEG mapped on the target platform. This following code presents how can define the throughput constraint in description file.

```
<timeConstraints>
        <throughput>0.0000005</throughput>
</ timeConstraints>
```

In this pseudo code, the objective of constraint is to reach a rate of 25 frames per second. So, the Application must be performed 25 iterations per second and the processor being clocked at 50 MHz (the time unit = 0.2 nanoseconds). We can deduct the constraint by multiplying the number of frames per second by the value of the unit time. For the platform targets will be modeled with two identical nodes of execution of topology torus and the type of communication system it is the NOC. The following figure (Figure 6) presents this platform.

The figure 7 illustrate for each action (mapping task on processor, initialization of Network Interface, link, connection and network) how defined by corresponding lines of code. At the second time, we will analyze the results of this modeling in order to validate the satisfaction constraint and the optimality of the material platform.

Question 1: Is That the Mapping Carried Respect the Throughput Constraint?

Figure 6. Synoptic diagram of the target platform

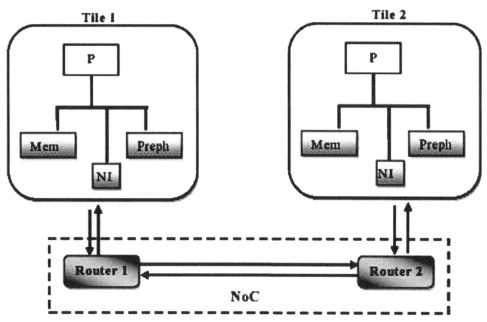

Figure 7. Screen shot for verifying throughput constraint

```
[INFO] Verifying throughput constraint
Throughput: 4.00047e-07
Constraint: 4e-07
Throughput constraint satisfied.
```

In this example, we fix the frequency of processor at 50 MHz and 20 frames per second as a throughput constraint. The following screen shot shows us that this mapping satisfied the throughput constraint (Figure 8).

Question 2: Is That Obtained Solution Optimal?

In this work, we are interested in the size memory allocated for each actor and Mapping of the tasks of the application on the processors of the modeled material platform. After each execution, the SDF3 tool checks the optimization of material architecture to leave the percentages use of the material resources. We note starting from this example execution the absence of wasting of material resource in terms of memorizing, the percentage of use of memory reaches to 78%. We cannot pass to modeling by simulation, so only if, we finished the checking, validation and the estimate of performance by the analytical model because this last enables us to optimize material architecture, on the other hand, the tool for SoCLib simulation does not indicate the percentage or the rate of use of material resources.

Figure 8. Mapping actor on processor and Initialization the Network

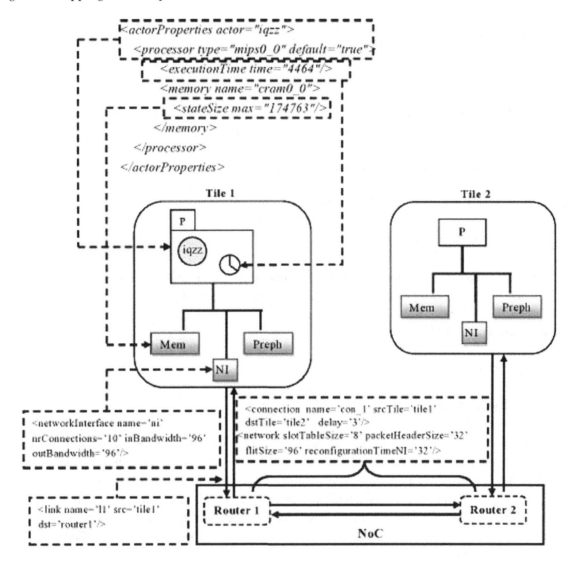

Link Layer

the main objective of the link layer is to combine the contribution of the analytic technique in which ensures the speed in modeling graphs, desired constraints and performance estimation in the one hand and combine the contribution of the technology based simulation shows that the accuracy of the results, using models at different levels of abstraction in the other hand. In this study case, we interested in the mapping carried by the SDF3 tool. Not only but also, we interested in allocation memory by tasks and channels. This information (Mapping + Allocations memory) will be analyzed, extracted and integrated in the simulation model. So, in this example, we use the link layer in the first sense (from analytic model to simulation model) and we use parser minidom for accessing, analyzing this information from the output file of the analytic model and integrating in the modeling file of the simulation model.

- *For accessing file*

xmldoc = minidom.parse('output.xml')

- *For extracting information*

We select the special element from the output file for extracting desired information ('actorProperties' for the mapping and 'memory' for the allocation memory).

actorlist=xmldoc.getElementsByTagName('actorProperties')

Mem = xmldoc.getElementsByTagName('memory')

- *For integrating information*

In this line of code, we show how integrated information; 'stack' defines a memory segment allocated by a task and 'run' defines a processor in which a task will be mapped on it.

stack = str(m.attributes['name'].value),

run = str (p.attributes['type'].value),

Modeling by Simulation

In the simulation environment SoCLib, the modeling of the software application is a set of classes coded in language C or C++ (for each class define a task). And for the modeling of material architecture, SoCLib provides a library (based on the SystemC language) for the material components simulation, these components use the protocol of interface VCI/OCP in order to guarantee interworking between the various components of the system. In our work, we have instantiated 2 clusters connected via a NoC. The first cluster includes a processor MIPS32, a coprocessor for the TG task and a RAM connected via Local Crossbar (Figure 9).

The second cluster is similar to the first cluster but it replaces a co-processor for the task TG by a co-processor for the task RAMDAC. This snippet of code (Fig 10) makes it possible to assign for each software task of the application MJPEG on the processor via the function 'mapper.map'.

According to the tests carried out during this work, we get the results which are presented in the following table, knowing that we take into account the feedback with the inputs/outputs of the model for optimizing the solution.

The sign (+) means that the tool takes a few time for modeling and the sign (-) means the reverse. We can conclude from this table which our hybrid approach makes it possible to reduce the time of design and optimizing for the SoCLib environment.

Figure 9. Architecture of the simulation platform SoCLib

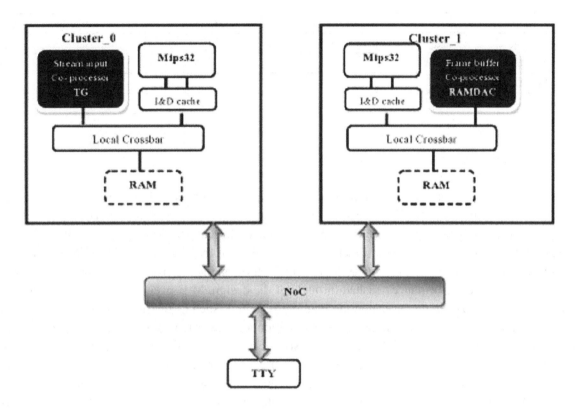

Figure 10. Description of Function "mapper.map'"

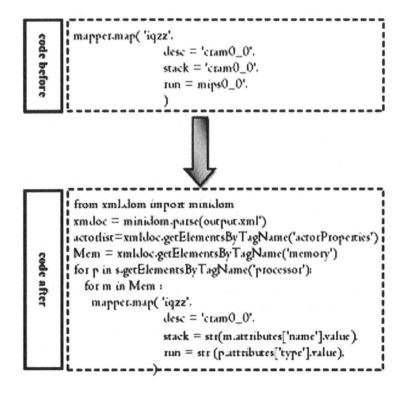

Table 2. Comparison of times for models

ApproachTime	SDF3	SoCLib	Hybrid
Modeling Time	++	− −	−
Execution Time	+++	+	++
Optimizing Time	++	− − −	++
Precision	− −	+++	+++

DISCUSSION

The contribution of this approach is to minimize the time of modeling and design of material architecture by the simulation tool SoCLib because this tool takes months to reach a platform which fulfills the requirements of the customer, but does not guarantee optimality (Smiri et al., 2009). It is for that, we start with the modeling and the estimate of performances of the NoC-MPSoC by SDF3 tool. This analytical tool enables us to deploy the tasks of an application on the material components, not only but also, to estimate the performances wished throughout the design. Moreover, tool SDF3 makes it possible to provide information concerning the material resources such as the number of processors and their types, arbitration, segments memory, number of connections, latency time…, and the structure of communication which is the NoC (many routers, size of package…). This information can be used in the environment of simulation. But, we always remain to speak with high level about abstraction and consequently, the error rate remains important. In our approach, the SoCLib tool of simulation is introduced of the second part of the approach in order to continue the objective of this hybrid model which is the precision. Moreover, SoCLib provides two types of models of simulation; the model of level CABA allows a precise evaluation of the performances and the model of level TLM-T allows a significant reduction of times of simulation but with a loss of precision (Smiri et al., 2009).

CONCLUSION

During this work, we interested in migration some data from SDF analytical tool towards the SoCLib tool of simulation such as Mapping of the actors on processors and the spaces of memory allocated for actors and channels. There is other information which can be migrated in the bidirectional (of SDF3 towards SoCLib or the opposite) such as; the distribution and the sequencing of execution of the actors and messages were transmitted between knots, these data seem the role of the operating system and when we integrate this information (generated by SDF3) in SoCLib, we thus speak about refinement of the system embedded at the transactional level. The integration of this information will be as a work in the future.

Not only but also, we have important information which will be integrated into the inverse direction (of SoCLib towards SDF3) such as the most detailed characteristic of a material component, because the tool SoCLib allows to simulate the material resources and the platform in a closer way in the realities due to the detailed information (such as: the size of memory cache for data, the size of memory cache for instructions and etc.) and when we integrate these data into the tool SDF3, the embedded system will be refine at the lower level and this work will also be as a prospect.

REFERENCES

Buchmann, R., Donnet, F., Gomez, P., Faure, E., Augé, I., & Pétrit, F. (2004). *Disydent: un environnement pour la conception.* Université Paris, VI.

Ehrlich, P., & Radke, S. (2013). Energy-aware software development for embeddedsystems in HW/SW co-design. *IEEE 16th International Symposium on Design and Diagnostics of Electronic Circuits & Systems (DDECS).*

Ghamarian, A. H., Stuijk, S., Basten, T., Geilen, M. G. W., & Theelen, B. D. (2007). *Latency Minimization for Synchronous Data Flow Graphs.* Digital System Design Architectures, Methods and Tools.

Hocine, R., Kalla, H., Kalla, S., & Arar, C. (2012). A methodology for verification of embedded systems based on systemc. *International Conference on Complex Systems (ICCS).* doi:10.1109/ICoCS.2012.6458557

Huang, J., Raabe, A., Hu, B. C., & Knoll, A. (2013). *A framework for reliability-aware design exploration on MPSoC based systems.* Springer Science and Business Media.

Jayaram, I., & Purdy, C. (2012). Using constraint graphs to improve embedded systemsdesign. *IEEE 55th International Midwest Symposium on Circuits and Systems (MWSCAS).*

Jordans, R., Siyoum, F., Stuijk, S., Kumar, A., & Corpal, H. (2011). *An Automated Flow to Map Throughput Constrained Application to a MPSoC.* Academic Press.

Kahn, G. (1974). The semantics of a simple language for parallel programming. *Information Processing, 74,* 471-475. doi:10.1109/MDSO.2007.28

Karan, S., Major, B., & Sally, A. M. (2009). Real Time Power Estimation and Thread Scheduling via Performance Counters. *SIGARCH Computer Architecture News, 37.*

Kumar, S. (2003). On Packet Switched Networks for on-Chip Communication. In *Networks on Chip.* Kluwer Academic.

Philippe, J.M., Carbon, A., Brousse, O., & Paindavoine, M. (2015). Exploration and design of embedded systems including neural algorithms. *Design, Automation & Test in Europe Conference & Exhibition (DATE).*

Prost-Boucle, A., Muller, O., & Rousseau, F. (2014). A Fast and Stand-alone HLS Methodology for Hardware Accelerator Generation Under Resource Constraints. *Journal of Systems Architecture.*

Rousseau, F., Sasongko, A., & Jerraya, A. (2005). *Shortening SoC Design Time with New Prototyping Flow on Reconfigurable Platform.* IEEE-NEWCAS Conference.

Salehi, M., & Ejlali, A. (2015). A Hardware Platform for Evaluating Low-Energy Multiprocessor Embedded Systems Based on COTS Devices. *Industrial Electronics, IEEE Transactions.*

Senouci, B., Bouchhima, A., Rousseau, F., Petrot, F., & Jerraya, A. (2007). *Prototyping Multiprocessor System-on-Chip Applications: A Platform-Based Approach.* IEEE Distributed Systems Online.

Sergio, C. A., Antonio, M. Á., Felipe, R., Francisco, R. P., & Hipólito, G. M., & Aguirre. (2011). Soft core based embedded Systems in critical aerospace applications. *Journal of Systems Architecture.*

Smiri, K., Ben Fadhel, A., Jemai, A., & Ammari, A-C. (2011). Automatic Generation of Software-Hardware Migration in MPSoC Systems. *Journal of Computer Technology and Application.*

Smiri, K., & Jemai, A. (2009). *Migration Methodology in MPSoC Based on Performance Analysis via SDF Graph.* Advances in Computational Sciences and Technology.

Smiri, K., & Jemai, A. (2011). NoC-MPSoC Performance Estimation with Synchronous Data Flow (SDF) Graphs. Autonomous and Intelligent Systems (AIS '2011), 406-415. doi:10.1007/978-3-642-21538-4_40

Smiri, K., Jemai, A., & Ammari, A-C. (2008). Evaluation of the Disydent Co-design Flow for an MJPEG Case Study. *International Review on Computers and Software.*

Sousa, L., Antao, S., & Germano, J. (2013). A Lab Project on the Design and Implementation of Programmable and Configurable Embedded Systems. *IEEE Transaction.*

Website Ptolemy. (2013). *Ptolemy project heterogeneous modeling and design.* Retrieved from http://www.ptolemy.eecs.berkeley.edu

Website SoCLib. (2017). Retrieved from http://www.soclib.fr

Youssef, A., & Zergainoh, N. E. (2007). Simulink-based MPSoC Design: New Approach to Bridge the Gap between Algorithm and Architecture Design. *IEEE Computer Society Annual Symposium.*

Yves, S. (2014). *The AAA methodology and syndex.* Retrieved from http://www.syndex.org

Chapter 4
Analysis of Shunt Active Power Filter Using Adaptive Blanket Body Cover Algorithm (ABBC) in Aircraft System

Saifullah Khalid
Independent Researcher, India

ABSTRACT

A novel adaptive blanket body cover algorithm (ABBC) has been presented, which has been used for the optimization of conventional control scheme used in shunt active power filter. The effectiveness of the proposed algorithm has been proven by applying this in aircraft system. The superiority of this algorithm over existing genetic algorithm results has been presented by analyzing the THD and compensation time of both the algorithms. The simulation results using the MATLAB model ratify that that algorithm has optimized the control technique, which unmistakably proves the usefulness of the proposed algorithm in 400 Hertz aircraft system.

INTRODUCTION

More advanced aircraft power systems have been needed due to increased use of electrical power on behalf of other alternate sources of energy (Chen Donghua, 2005) (Saifullah & Bharti, 2014) (Saifullah Khalid, Application of AI techniques in implementing Shunt APF in Aircraft Supply System, 2013). The subsystems like flight control, flight surface actuators, passenger entertainment, are driven by electric power, which flowingly increased the demand for creating aircraft power system more intelligent and advanced. These subsystems have extensive increased electrical loads i.e. power electronic devices, increased feeding of electric power, additional demand for power, and above to all of that great stability problems.

In peculiarity to standard supply system, the source frequency is 50 Hz, whereas, aircraft AC power system works on the source frequency of 400 Hz (Chen Donghua, 2005) (Saifullah & Bharti, 2014)

DOI: 10.4018/978-1-5225-3531-7.ch004

(Saifullah Khalid, Application of AI techniques in implementing Shunt APF in Aircraft Supply System, 2013). Aircraft power utility works on source voltage of 115/200V. The loads applicable to the plane a system differs from the loads used in 50 Hz system (Chen Donghua, 2005). When we deliberate the generation portion; aircraft power utility will remain AC driven from the engine for the plane primary power. Novel fuel cell technology can be used to produce a DC output for ground power, and its silence process would match up to suitably with the Auxiliary Power Unit (APU). Though when considering the dissemination of primary power, whether AC or DC; each approach has its merits. In DC distribution, HVDC power distribution systems permit the most resourceful employ of generated power by antithetical loss from skin effect. This allows paralleling and loads sharing amongst the generators. In AC distribution, AC Flogging is very clear-cut at high levels too. Due to its high dependence on HVDC system, a wide range of Contactors, Relays can be exploited.

While talking about Aircraft Power Systems we also need to consider increased power electronics application in aircraft which creates harmonics, large neutral currents, waveform distortion of both supply voltage and current, poor power factor, and excessive current demand. Besides if some non-linear loads is impressed upon a supply, their effects are additive. Due to these troubles, there may be nuisance tripping of circuit breakers or increased loss and thermal heating effects that may provoke early component failure. This is a prodigious problem to every motor loads on the system. Hence, decent power quality of the generation system is of scrupulous attention to the Aircraft manufacturer. We discern that aircraft systems work on high frequency so even on the higher frequencies in the range of 360 to 900Hz; these components would remain very significant.

Today, advanced soft computing techniques are used widely in the involuntary control system, and optimization of the system applied. Several of them are such as fuzzy logic (Guillermin, 1996) (Abdul Hasib, Hew Wooi, A, & F., 2002) (Jain, Agrawal, & Gupta, 2002), optimization of active power filter using GA (Chiewchitboon, Tipsuwanpom, Soonthomphisaj, & Piyarat, 2003) (Kumar & Mahajan, 2009) (Ismail, Abdeldjebar, Abdelkrim, Mazari, & Rahli, 2008), power loss reduction using particle swarm optimization (Thangaraj, Thanga, Pant, Ajit, & Grosan, 2010), Artificial neural network control (P, K, & Eduardo, 2001) (Rojas, 1996) (Rajasekaran, 2005) (Zerikat & Chekroun, 2008) (Seong-Hwan, Tae-Sik, YooJi-Yoon, & Gwi-Tae, 2001) (Saifullah Khalid, Comparison of Control Strategies for Shunt Active Power Filter under balanced, unbalanced and distorted supply conditions, 2013) (Mauricio Aredes, 1997) applied in together machinery and filter devices.

In this chapter, two totally different soft computing techniques i.e. adaptive Blanket Body cover algorithm and Genetic algorithm are applied for reduction of harmonics and others downside generated into aircraft system attributable to the nonlinear loads (Chen Donghua, 2005). The results obtained with each the algorithms are far better than those of typical strategies. ABBC algorithm has given the better results as compared to GA and traditional scheme. The effectiveness of the planned scheme has been evidenced by the simulation results mentioned. The result justified their effectiveness.

In this chapter, ABBC algorithm has been wont to search the optimum value of PI controller parameters. For the case of GA, an optimum value of filter inductor has been calculated. The controlling theme has been modeled on the idea of Constant instantaneous Power control Strategy. The chapter has been organized in the following manner. The Active Power Filter configuration and also the load into consideration are mentioned in Section II. The control algorithm for Active Power Filter is mentioned in Section III. MATLAB/ Simulink based mostly simulation results are mentioned in Section IV and at last Section V concludes the chapter.

SYSTEM DESCRIPTION

The aircraft power system is a three-phase power system with the frequency of 400 Hz. As exposed in Figure 1, Shunt Active Power Filter improves the power quality and compensates the harmonic currents in the system (Saifullah Khalid, Power Quality Issues, Problems, Standards & their Effects in Industry with Corrective Means, 2011) (R. C. Dugan, 1996) (Saifullah Khalid, Power Quality: An Important Aspect, 2010) (Ghosh & Ledwich, 2002) (S.Khalid, 2009). The shunt APF is comprehended by using one voltage source inverters (VSIs) connected at the point of common coupling (PCC) to a common DC link voltage (Khalid & Dwivedi, Power quality improvement of constant frequency aircraft electric power system using Fuzzy Logic, Genetic Algorithm and Neural network control based control scheme, 2013) (Khalid & Dwivedi, A Review of State of Art Techniques in Active Power Filters and Reactive Power Compensation, 2007).

The set of loads for aircraft system consist of three loads. The first load is a three-phase rectifier in parallel with an inductive load and an unbalanced load connected in a phase with the midpoint (Load 1). The second one is a three phase rectifier connects a pure resistance directly (Load 2). The third one is a three-phase inductive load linked with the ground point (Load 3). Finally, a combination of all three loads connected with system together at a different time interval to study the effectiveness of the control schemes has been used to verify the functionality of the active filter in its ability to compensate for current harmonics. For the case of all three load connected, Load 1 is always connected, Load 2 is initially connected and is disconnected after every 2.5 cycles, Load 3 is connected and disconnected after every half cycle. All the simulations have been done for 15 cycles. The circuit parameters are given in Appendix.

CONTROL THEORY

The projected control of APF depends on Constant instantaneous Power control Strategy optimized with soft computing techniques like adaptive Blanket Body cover algorithm/ Genetic algorithm (Ahmed & E. Z Nahla., 2009) (Abdul Hasib, Hew Wooi, A, & F., 2002) (Seong-Hwan, Tae-Sik, YooJi-Yoon, & Gwi-Tae, 2001). Overall control theme using constant instantaneous power control strategy with the application of adaptive Blanket Body cover algorithm/Genetic algorithm has been dealt in following sections (Saifullah Khalid, Comparison of Control Strategies for Shunt Active Power Filter under balanced, unbalanced and distorted supply conditions, 2013) (Khalid & Dwivedi, Power quality improvement of constant frequency aircraft electric power system using Fuzzy Logic, Genetic Algorithm and Neural network control based control scheme, 2013) (Ghosh & Ledwich, 2002).

Figure 1. Aircraft system using Shunt Active Power Filter

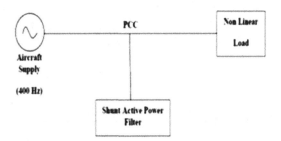

Constant Instantaneous Power Control Strategy (C.I.P.C.)

Figure 2 shows the control diagram of the shunt active filter using constant instantaneous power control strategy. We can see that four low pass filters have been shown in the control block; in which, three with cut off of 6.4 KHz has been applied to filter the voltages and one for the power p_0. Due to instability quandary, direct application of the phase voltages cannot be used in the control. There may be resonance among source impedance and the small passive filter. Low pass filters have been applied to the system to block the voltage harmonics at the resonance frequency that are higher than 6.4 KHz. P, q,p_0, v_α, and v_β are attained after the calculation from α-β-0 transformations and send to the α-β current reference block, which calculates I'$_{c\alpha}$ and i'c$_\beta$. Finally, α-β-0 inverse transformation block computes the current references and applies it to the PWM current control i.e. hysteresis band controller.

Design Using Genetic Algorithm

GA could also be a search technique that's used from generation to generation for optimizing performs. In fact, GA works on the rule of survival of the fittest. For the selecting the parameters used in the controller using GA, the analysis methodology wants a check, performed on-line on the particular plant or off-line with simulations on the computer. Every on-line and offline methodology are having advantages and disadvantages each. If we've got a bent to means on-line approach, the foremost advantage is that the consistency of the final word answer, as a results of it's chosen on the idea of its real performances, whereas if we have a tendency to predict concerning its disadvantage, it always involves thousands of tests to attain an even result i.e. this optimization methodology will take long run for experiments to run on the real system. Simply just in case of the off-line approach, GA improvement relies on a so much plenty of precise model of the system in conjunction with all elements, all nonlinearities, and limits of the controllers. It has to be compelled to, however, be well-known that a negotiation must be met in terms

Figure 2. Control block diagram of the shunt active filter using constant instantaneous power control strategy

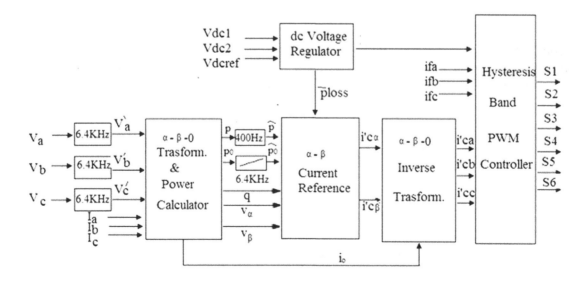

of simulation accuracy and optimization time. Offline, computer simulation using MATLAB Simulink has been applied to hunt out the optimum value.

In this chapter, the GA is applied to figure out the appropriate APF parameters i.e. device filter (Lf). The boundary and limits of parameters inside the filter have been outlined and a program using genetic algorithm has been written to return up with the foremost effective value of the filter device.

For the program, the limits, inequality and bounds need to be defined. This research work has attempted to develop a single GA code program for optimizing the objective function. $x0 = [V_{dc}; V_s; I_c; t; L_f]$;

$lb = [V_{dcmin}; V_{smin}; I_{cmin}; t_{min}; L_{fmin}]$;

$ub = [V_{dcmax}; V_{smax}; I_{cmax}; t_{max}; L_{fmax}]$;

Aeq = [];

beq = [];

A = [1 -1 1 -1 1; 1 1 -1 1 -1; 0 0 1 1 1; 1 1 -0 0 -1; 1 1 0 1 0];

$b = [$Values of $V_{dc}; V_s; I_c; t; L_f$ depending upon the equations$]$;

[x,fval,exitflag]=fmincon(@myobj,x0,A,b,Aeq,beq,lb,ub)

Design Using Novel Adaptive Blanket Body Cover Algorithm (ABBC)

Adaptive Blanket Body cover algorithm (ABBC) is proposed for combinatorial optimization issues. Non-linear continuous optimization issues need a robust search methodology to resolve them and this new adaptive Blanket Body blanket algorithm (ABBC) has been developed for them.

In the ABBC algorithm, an eternal search space has been discretized and back-tracking and adaptive radius features are utilized to lift the performance of the search method.

In this chapter, the proposed ABBC algorithm searches the optimum value of the proportional integral controller parameters i.e. Kp and Ki and therefore the objective function (OB) is determined such as to give their optimum value with the conditions of % overshoot, rise time and settling time. Objective function has an equation that has 3 variables i.e. % overshoot, rise time and settling time. Initially, the Boundary of Kp and Ki, their higher limits and lower limits, then radius value, conditions for ABBC backtracking, objective function and stop criteria has been outlined.

The shape of the blanket is supposed to be rectangular. We have assumed that the size of the blanket is such that it can be folded maximum twenty times solely. We have outlined some random values of Kp & Ki, which will be within the range of predefined initial values. As shown in figure 1, the folds are named as X1, X2,............X20. Each fold has different values of Kp & Ki.

This comparison direction has been inspired from the human nature of using the blanket to cover the body during chilled winter. The blanket has been initially folded to cover upper body. When the body senses the cold in the lower portion, the upper fold will be opened. Thereafter, the lower portion of the blanket will be folded to cover the body. When the full body senses the cold, only lower or upper portion fold alone cannot cover the whole body. So, the full blanket will be folded such that the layer of the blanket will be doubled.

The comparison will move downward direction up to the tenth fold, thereafter it will start from the twentieth fold in the upward direction up to eleventh fold. In the last step, the blanket will be folded half for a complete check of optimum values. Best value of each blanket fold will be compared with the initial value of next blanket fold. Then the best outcome will be saved and will be compared to next one. This process will repeat itself and will stop when stopping criteria fulfills.

We have observed that comparison of each blanket fold values goes through forty times as shown in figure 3 and that is that the reason for selecting maximum searching iteration (40 iterations) for ABBC as the stop criterion. There's a predefined list named as Blanket fold list, which contains the values which are distributed over the folds of the blanket.

Figure 4 shows the flow chart for the search of parameters using the adaptive body blanket cover (ABBC) algorithm. The values initially used for Kp and Ki were 0.1 and 45 respectively. After the calcu-

Figure 3. Blanket folds Used for Optimization

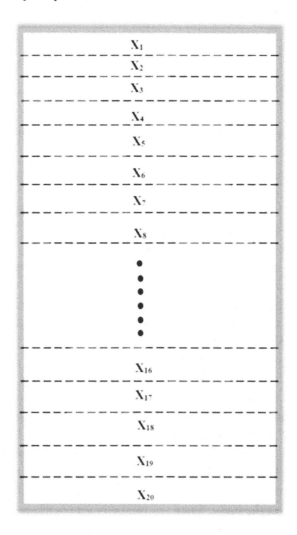

Figure 4. Flow chart for finding the parameters Using ABBC

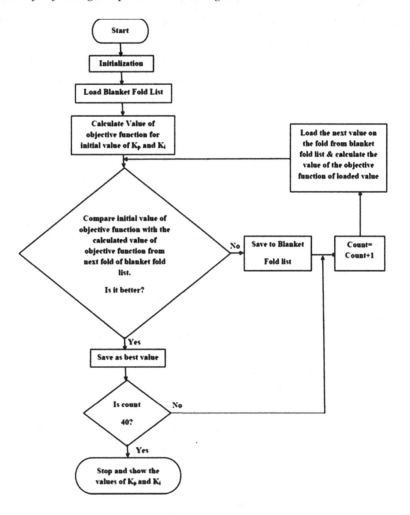

lation, ABBC algorithm gives the value 0.184 and 14.32. it's been ascertained that whereas using these ABBC calculated values of Kp and Ki, the THD of supply current and voltage are reduced staggeringly that proves that the values are optimum.

Function evaluations: since this chapter relies on the critical analysis supported THD of the supply it's been seen that the objective function taken has shown its effectiveness, which may be seen from the reduction of THD.

Computational time has conjointly been seen terribly less i.e. within seconds, all iterations are over and optimum values of Kp and Ki are often seen on MATLAB/Simulink complier. We will see that this method is extremely stable since it's been calculated offline and so are often used to replace the present values. Robustness of this algorithm is often understood by the great results and less computational time. Convergence analysis has been done offline. The range of iterations with variation in Kp and Ki values has been taken to prove the pliability of the algorithm. This algorithm is extremely convenient to use because of the programming and fewer computational time. The feasibleness and good thing about the algorithm are proved by the simulation results. It's in no time. The parameters i.e. Kp and Ki have been set at random at first and so it has been tuned by using this algorithm offline. Standard equations of Kp and Ki using settling time (T-$_{Settling}$), rise time (T$_{Rise}$) and percent overshoot (P.O.) are used for locating the objective function within the program.

There has been a counter used, which will count the number of iterations and therefore the program will stop automatically once the count is up to forty i.e. stopping criteria is forty iterations. Objective function (OB) is defined by

$$OB \text{ (settling time, rise time and percent overshoot)} = E + G + O \tag{1}$$

$$E + G + O = 1 \tag{2}$$

E, G, and O are the priority coefficients of settling time, rise time and percent overshoot respectively.

In this chapter, the values of (E, G, and O are set to 0.33, 0.33, and 0.34, respectively. The ABBC search will try to find the best controller parameters to achieve the minimum OB value.

Step 1: Blanket fold list having values of Kp and Ki have been loaded and the counter has been made zero, which will check the number of iteration.

Step 2: The value of the objective function has been calculated for initial values of Kp and Ki.

Step 3: Resultant of step 2 has been compared with the calculated value of the objective function of Blanket fold list i.e. first comparison from upward to downward, then downward to upward, thereafter half fold of the blanket, and comparison from upward to the downward direction.

Step 4: If the results are not better, it will be saved in blanket fold list and then the counter will automatically increase and there will be a change in Kp and Ki values from the blanket fold list. These values will replace the previous values. The objective function for these values will be calculated and then again go to step 3.

Step 5: If the results are better than blanket fold list solutions, it will be saved as the best solution.

Step 6: If number of iteration i.e. count value is 40, the results with the optimum value of Kp and Ki will be shown otherwise it will check the counter value and change the Kp and Ki values from the blanket fold list and these value will replace the previous value and then objective function for these values will be calculated and then again go to step 3.

It will be seen in Figure four that ABBC can search the voltage controller parameters Kp and KI and the objective function is set like to provide their optimum value with the conditions of minimum overshoot, rise time and settling time.

Initially, we have a tendency to define the boundary of Kp and Ki, their higher limits and lower limits, then radius value, conditions for ABBC backtracking, objective function and stop criteria. Maximum searching iteration (40 rounds) for ABBC has been set as stop criterion.

Control Scheme

In this chapter, Constant instantaneous Power control Strategy [19], [20], [23] has been used for active power filter with the appliance of soft computing algorithms as shown in the Figure five. The soft computing techniques like ABBC & GA are accustomed provide the most effective optimized values

Figure 5. Block diagram of the optimized active filter using GA, ABBC Techniques

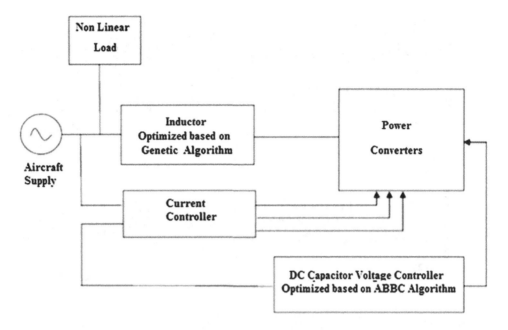

of the essential parts of the system so the system can provide the most effective performance below all conditions. The controller has been modeled using MATLAB/Simulink and it's been simulated below balanced, unbalanced and distorted supply conditions.

SIMULATION RESULTS AND DISCUSSIONS

The proposed scheme of APF is simulated in MATLAB environment to estimate its performance. Three loads have been applied together at a different time interval to check the affectivity of the control schemes for the reduction of harmonics. A small amount of inductance is also connected to the terminals of the load to get the most effective compensation. The simulation results clearly reveal that the scheme can successfully reduce the significant amount of THD in source current and voltage within limits.

Uncompensated System

Figure 6 shows the waveforms obtained after the simulation of an uncompensated system. It has been observed that the THD of source current calculated when loads connected with the system is 9.5% and THD of source Voltage were 1.55%. By observing these data, we can easily recognize supply has been polluted when loads have been connected and is obviously not within the limit of the international standard.

Compensated System

The performance of APF under different loads connected has been discussed below for the control strategy given below.

Figure 6. Source Voltage and source current waveforms of uncompensated system

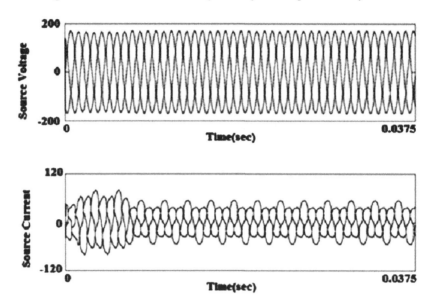

Simulation Results and Discussion of Shunt APF for Constant Instantaneous Power Control Strategy

From Figure 7 it has been empiric that that the THDs of source current and source voltage were 2.84% and 1.88% respectively. The compensation time was 0.0147 sec. At t=0.0147 sec, it is apparent that the waveforms for source voltage and source current have become sinusoidal. Fig. 7 shows the waveforms of compensation current, DC capacitor voltage, and load current.

The aberration in dc voltage can be acutely apparent in the waveforms. As per claim for accretion the compensation current for accomplishing the load current demand, it releases the energy, and after that, it accuses and tries to achieve its set value. If we carefully observe, we can acquisition out that the compensation current is, in fact, accomplishing the appeal of load current, and afterward, the active filtering the source current and voltage is affected to be sinusoidal.

Simulation Results and Discussion of Shunt APF Using Genetic Algorithm

From the simulation results shown in figure eight, it's been ascertained that the THD of supply current & supply voltage was 2.12% and 1.87% severally. The compensation time was 0.0066 sec. At t=0.0066 sec, we are able to see that the waveforms for supply voltage and supply current became sinusoidal.

From figure 8, we will see the waveforms of compensation current, dc capacitor voltage and load current. The variation in dc voltage is clearly seen within the waveforms. As per demand for increasing the compensation current for fulfilling the load current demand, it releases the energy and thenceforth it charges and tries to regain its set value. If we tend to closely observe, we will conclude that the compensation current is really fulfilling the demand of load current and when the active filtering the supply current and voltage are forced to be sinusoidal.

Figure 7. Source Voltage, source current, compensation current (phase b), DC link Voltage and load current waveforms of Active power filter using constant instantaneous power control strategy

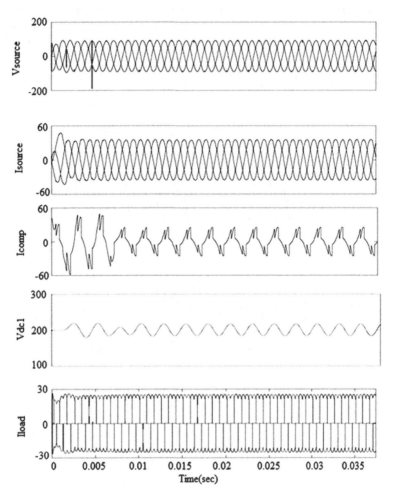

Simulation Results and Discussion of Shunt APF Using ABBC Algorithm

From the simulation results shown in figure nine, it's been ascertained that the THD of supply current & supply voltage was 2.10% and 1.05% severally. The compensation time was 0.0064 sec. At t=0.0064 sec, we are able to see that the waveforms for supply voltage and supply current became sinusoidal.

From figure 9, we will see the waveforms of compensation current, dc capacitor voltage and load current. The variation in dc voltage is clearly seen within the waveforms. As per demand for increasing the compensation current for fulfilling the load current demand, it releases the energy and thenceforth it charges and tries to regain its set value. If we tend to closely observe, we will conclude that the compensation current is really fulfilling the demand of load current and when the active filtering the supply current and voltage are forced to be sinusoidal.

Figure 8. Source Voltage, source current, compensation current (phase b), DC link Voltage and load current waveforms of Active power filter using Constant Instantaneous Power Control Strategy using Genetic Algorithm with all three loads connected together at different time interval

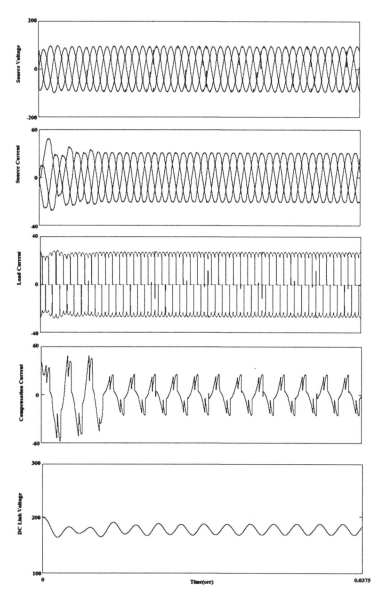

Comparative Analysis of the Simulation Results

From the Table 1, we can easily say that novel ABBC algorithm has been found best for current and voltage harmonic reduction. When these results have been compared based on compensation time, it has been also found that ABBC algorithm is also fastest one. It clearly proves its dynamic ability and superiority over typical constant instantaneous power control current management technique and its optimized version using GA technique by perceptive its least THD and less compensation time.

Figure 9. Source Voltage, source current, compensation current (phase b), DC link Voltage and load current waveforms of Active power filter using Constant Instantaneous Power Control Strategy using ABBC Algorithm with all three loads connected together at different time interval

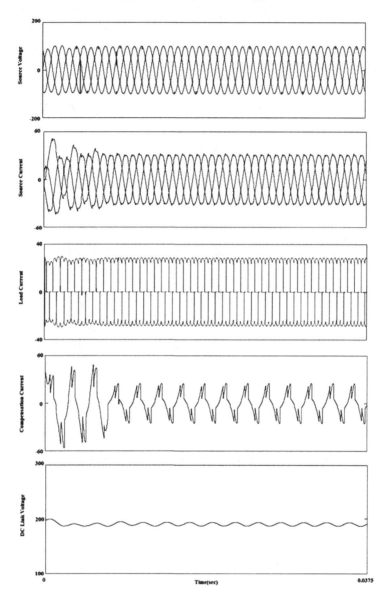

Figure 10 and figure 11 present the graphical illustration of Table 1. We are able to observe clearly that ABBC is best yet as quickest, that proves its superiority over GA and traditional control technique.

CONCLUSION

A novel improved algorithm i.e. adaptive Blanket Body cover (ABBC) algorithm applied in shunt active power filter has been conferred, that works effectively under the aircraft supply system. System optimiza-

Table 1. Summary of Simulation Results

Strategy	THD-I (%)	THD-V (%)	Compensation Time (sec)
CIPC	2.84	1.88	0.0147
CIPC-GA	2.12	1.87	0.0066
CIPC-ABBC	2.10	1.05	0.0064

Figure 10. Bar diagram of THD-I & THD-V for Different Control Algorithm Used in APF

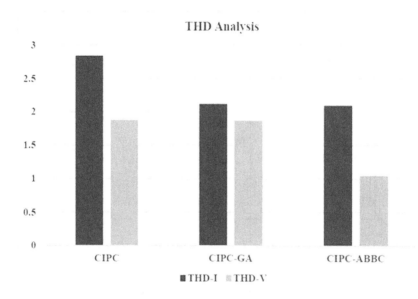

Figure 11. Line Diagram of Compensation Time for Different Control Algorithm Used in APF

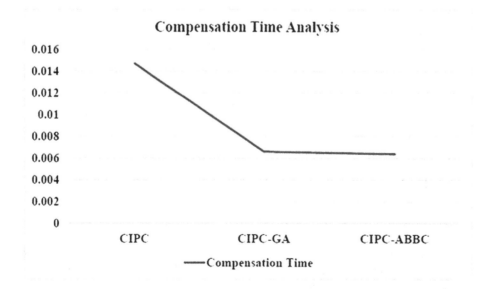

tion by using adaptive Blanket Body cover algorithm has well worked for the model using conventional constant instantaneous power control Technique. ABBC has effectively compensated the system. THD for source current and source voltage has been reduced significantly over a very little time of few seconds. While comparing with the conventional as well as advanced GA technique, it can be clearly said that ABBC is better as well as faster than both techniques. The simulation results clearly prove ABBC superiority over GA and conventional control technique.

REFERENCES

Abdul Hasib, A., & Hew Wooi, P. (2002). Fuzzy Logic Control of a three phase Induction Motor using Field Oriented Control Method. *Society of Instrument and Control Engineers, SICE Annual Conference*, 264-267.

Afonso, J. L., F. J. (1998). Genetic Algorithm Techniques Applied to the Control of a Three-Phase Induction Motor. *UK Mechatronics Forum International Conference*, 142-146.

Ahmed, A. H., & Nahla, E. Z. G. Y. (2009). Fuzzy Logic Controlled Shunt Active Power Filter for Three-phase Four-wire Systems with Balanced and Unbalanced Loads. World Academy of Science, Engineering and Technology, 58, 621-626.

Chen, D., T. G. (2005). Shunt Active Power Filters Applied in the Aircraft Power Utility. In *36th Power Electronics Specialists Conference, PESC '05* (pp. 59-63). IEEE. doi:10.1109/PESC.2005.1581602

Chiewchitboon, T., Soonthomphisaj, & Piyarat. (2003). Speed Control of Three-phase Induction Motor Online Tuning by Genetic Algorithm. *Fifth International Conference on Power Electronics and Drive Systems, PEDS 2003*, 184-188. doi:10.1109/PEDS.2003.1282751

Dugan, R. C. M. F. (1996). Electrical Power Systems Quality. New York: McGraw-Hill.

Eid, A., El-Kishky, H., Abdel-Salam, M., & El-Mohandes, T. (2010). VSCF Aircraft Electric Power System Performance with Active Power Filters. *42nd South Eastern Symposium on System Theory University of Texas at Tyler*, 182-187. doi:10.1109/SSST.2010.5442838

Ghosh, A., & Ledwich, G. (2002). *Power Quality Enhancement Using Custom Power Devices*. Boston, MA: Kluwer. doi:10.1007/978-1-4615-1153-3

Guillermin, P. (1996). Fuzzy logic Applied to Motor Control. *IEEE Transactions on Industry Applications*, *32*(1), 51–56. doi:10.1109/28.485812

IEEE(1992*IEEE Recommended Practices and Requirements for Harmonic Control in Electrical Power Systems, IEEE Standard 519-1992*. IEEE.

Ismail, B., Abdeldjebar, H., Abdelkrim, B., Mazari, B., & Rahli, M. (2008). Optimal Fuzzy Self-Tuning of PI Controller Using Genetic Algorithm for Induction Motor Speed Control. *International Journal of Automotive Technology*, *2*(2), 85–95. doi:10.20965/ijat.2008.p0085

Jain, S., Agrawal, P., & Gupta, H. (2002). Fuzzy logic controlled shunt active power filter for power quality improvement. *IEE Proceedings. Electric Power Applications*, *149*(5), 317–328. doi:10.1049/ip-epa:20020511

Khalid, S. N. (2009). Application of Power Electronics to Power System. New Delhi: University Science Press.

Khalid, S., & Dwivedi, B. (2007). A Review of State of Art Techniques in Active Power Filters and Reactive Power Compensation. *National Journal of Technology*, *3*(1), 10–18.

Khalid, S., & Dwivedi, B. (2013). Power quality improvement of constant frequency aircraft electric power system using Fuzzy Logic, Genetic Algorithm and Neural network control based control scheme. *International Electrical Engineering Journal*, *4*(3), 1098–1104.

Kumar, P., & Mahajan, A. (2009). Soft Computing Techniques for the Control of an Active Power Filter. *IEEE Transactions on Power Delivery*, *24*(1), 452–461. doi:10.1109/TPWRD.2008.2005881

Lavopa, E., Zanchetta, P., Sumner, M., & Cupertino, F. (2009). Real-time estimation of Fundamental Frequency and harmonics for active shunt power filters in aircraft Electrical Systems. *IEEE Transactions on Industrial Electronics*, *56*(8), 412–416. doi:10.1109/TIE.2009.2015292

Luo, Y. Z. C. (2011). A cascaded shunt active power filter with high performance for aircraft electric power system. In Energy Conversion Congress and Exposition (ECCE) (pp. 1143 – 1149). IEEE.

Mauricio Aredes, J. H. (1997). Three-Phase Four-Wire Shunt Active Filter Control Strategies. *IEEE Transactions on Power Electronics*, *12*(2), 311–318. doi:10.1109/63.558748

Norman, M., Samsul, B., Mohd, N., & Jasronita, J., & B., O. S. (2004). A Fuzzy logic Controller for an Indirect vector Controlled Three Phase Induction. *Proceedings of Analog And Digital Techniques In Electrical Engineering*, 1–4.

P, P. J., K, B. B., & Eduardo, B. d. (2001). A Stator-Flux-Oriented Vector-Controlled Induction Motor Drive with Space-Vector PWM and Flux-Vector Synthesis by Neural Networks. *IEEE Transaction on Industry Applications*, *37*(5), 1308-1318.

Rajasekaran, S. P. (2005). *Neural Networks, Fuzzy Logic and Genetic Algorithm: Synthesis and Applications*. New Delhi: Prentice Hall of India.

Rojas, R. (1996). *Neural Network- A Systematic Introduction*. Berlin: Spriger-Verlag.

Saifullah, K., & Bharti, D. (2014). Comparative Evaluation of Various Control Strategies for Shunt Active Power Filters in Aircraft Power Utility of 400 Hz. *Majlesi Journal of Mechatronic Systems*, *3*(2), 1–5.

Saifullah Khalid, B. D. (2010). Power Quality: An Important Aspect. *International Journal of Engineering Science and Technology*, *2*(11), 6485–6490.

Saifullah Khalid, B. D. (2011). Power Quality Issues, Problems, Standards & their Effects in Industry with Corrective Means. *International Journal of Advances in Engineering and Technology*, *1*(2), 1–11.

Saifullah Khalid, B. D. (2013). Application of AI techniques in implementing Shunt APF in Aircraft Supply System. In *SOCROPROS Conference on Dec 26-28* (pp. 333-341). Roorkee, India: Springer Lecture Notes.

Saifullah Khalid, B. D. (2013). Comparison of Control Strategies for Shunt Active Power Filter under balanced, unbalanced and distorted supply conditions. *IEEE Sponsored National Conference on Advances in Electrical Power and Energy Systems (AEPES-2013)*, 37-41.

Saifullah Khalid, B. D. (2013). Comparative critical analysis of SAF using soft computing and conventional control techniques for high frequency (400 Hz) aircraft system. In *IEEE 1st International Conference on Condition Assessment Techniques in Electrical Systems (CATCON)* (pp. 100-110). Kolkata, India: IEEE.

Seong-Hwan, K., & Tae-Sik, P. (2001). Speed-Sensorless Vector Control of an Induction Motor Using Neural Network Speed Estimation. *IEEE Transactions on Industrial Electronics*, *48*(3), 609–614. doi:10.1109/41.925588

Thangaraj, R., Thanga, R. C., Pant, M., Ajit, A., & Grosan, C. (2010). Optimal gain tuning of PI speed controller in induction motor drives using particle swarm optimization. *Logic Journal of IGPL Advance Access*, 1-4.

Wang, G., & Zhang, M., XinheXu, & Jiang, C. (2006). Optimization of Controller Parameters based on the Improved Genetic Algorithms. *IEEE Proceedings of the 6th World Congress on Intelligent Control and Automation*, 3695-3698.

Woods, E. J. (1990). Aircraft Electrical System computer Simulation. *Proceedings of the 25th Intersociety Energy Conversion Engineering Conference, IECEC-90*, 84-89. doi:10.1109/IECEC.1990.716551

Zerikat, M., & Chekroun, S. (2008). Adaptation Learning Speed Control for a High-Performance Induction Motor using Neural Networks. Proceedings of World Academy of Science, Engineering and Technology, 294-299.

Zhong Chen, Y. L., Yingpeng Luo, , & Miao Chen, . (2012). Control and Performance of a Cascaded Shunt Active Power Filter for Aircraft Electric Power System. *IEEE Transactions on Industrial Electronics*, *59*(9), 3614–3623. doi:10.1109/TIE.2011.2166231

APPENDIX

The aircraft system parameters are:
Three-phase source voltage: 115V/400 Hz
Filter capacitor: 5 μF,
Filter inductor=0.25m H
Dc capacitor: 4700μF
Dc voltage reference: 400 V

Chapter 5

Lyapunov–Based Predictive Control Methodologies for Networked Control Systems

Constantin-Florin Caruntu
Gheorghe Asachi Technical University of Iasi, Romania

ABSTRACT

The problem considered in this chapter is to control a vehicle drivetrain in order to minimize its oscillations while coping with the time-varying delays introduced by the CAN communication network and the strict timing limitations. As such, two Lyapunov-based model predictive control design methodologies are presented: one based on modeling the network-induced time-varying delays using a polytopic approximation technique and the second one based on modeling the delays as disturbances. Several tests performed using an industry validated drivetrain model indicate that the proposed design methodologies can handle both the performance/physical constraints and the strict limitations on the computational complexity, while effectively coping with the time-varying delays. Moreover, a comparative analysis between the two Lyapunov-based model predictive control design methodologies in terms of computational complexity, number of optimization variables, and obtained performances is carried out.

INTRODUCTION

Feedback control systems over real-time communication networks, also called networked control systems, are now widely used in different industries, ranging from automated manufacturing plants to automotive and aero-spatial applications. This evolution of standalone control systems to networked control systems (NCSs) brought many attractive advantages, which include low cost, simple installation and maintenance, increased system agility, higher reliability and greater flexibility. In most cases, introducing a communication network does not significantly affect the control system performances. Nevertheless, for certain physical plants which are time-restricted, implementing a networked control system must be realized taking into account the fact that a communication network is not perfect. For such systems, implementing a communication network for closed-loop control leads to introducing an

DOI: 10.4018/978-1-5225-3531-7.ch005

additional delay, either constant, or time-varying, which makes system analysis and controller design much more complex. Existing constant time-delay control methodologies may not be directly suitable for such applications, e.g., controlling a system over a communication network, since network delays are usually unpredictable and time-varying. Therefore, to handle network delays in a closed-loop control system over a communication network, an advanced technique is required, a significant emphasis being on developing control methodologies to handle the network delay effect in NCSs. Another consequence of introducing communication networks in the control loop is represented by the possibility of data packet dropout. These two problems can seriously affect the control performances and can even destabilize the closed-loop control system if they are not taken into account in the design phase of the controllers.

Regarding the application considered in this chapter, the vehicle drivetrains are characterized by fast dynamics, subject to physical and control constraints, which make controller design for driveline oscillations damping a challenging problem. When a vehicle is subjected to acceleration, the elasticity of the various components in the driveline may cause torsional vibrations or disturbances. The focus of this chapter is on vibrational comfort, which is recognized as the most important factor for passenger comfort. The torsional vibrations can result in driveline or vehicle speed oscillations, also known as shuffle mode, which are low-frequency oscillations corresponding to the first resonance frequency of the driveline. These oscillations give rise, apart from material stress, to noticeable reduced driveability.

As such, motivated by the shortcomings of the existing controller design methods for drivetrain oscillation damping using networked control, the problem considered in this chapter is to minimize these oscillations while coping with the time-varying delays introduced by the communication network and the strict timing limitations. Two Lyapunov-based model predictive control design methodologies are presented: one based on modeling the network-induced time-varying delays using a polytopic approximation technique and the second one based on modeling the delays as disturbances.

BACKGROUND

The evolution of standalone control systems to networked control systems brought many attractive advantages, but the use of communication networks makes it necessaryto deal with the effects of the network-induced imperfections and constraints. These are categorised into fivetypes in (Heemels et al., 2010), but, usually, the available literature considers only some of them in the analysis of NCS: (1) quantisation errors in the signals transmitted over the network; (2) packet dropouts caused by the unreliability of the network (Cloosterman et al., 2010; Munoz de la Pena and Christofides, 2008); (3) variable sampling/transmission intervals (Cloosterman et al., 2010); (4) time-varying network-induced delays, which can be smaller than the sampling period (Huang et al., 2010) or larger than the sampling period (Li et al., 2008; Cloosterman et al., 2009; Cloosterman et al., 2010); and (5) communication constraints caused by the sharing of the network (Liu et al., 2010). Moreover, an analysis of different aspects of the limitations imposed by the use of communication channels to connect the elements of NCSs is given in (Hespanha et al., 2007).

Nowadays, different research results were reported on model predictive control (MPC) for NCS. In (Onat et al., 2008) a plant model is kept inside the controller node, which is used to predict the plant states into the future to generate corresponding control outputs. In (Li et al., 2008) two predictive observer-based controllers are designed, which are used when the full state vector is not available. A

Lyapunov-based model predictive controller is designed in (Munoz de la Pena and Christofides, 2008) for nonlinear uncertain systems, which takes data losses explicitly into account. Another recent approach is to consider the communication delays (Natori et al., 2008) or the data-packet dropouts (Li and Shi, 2013) as disturbances and to use a communication delay observer (CDOB) to compensate the effect of the time-varying delays as in (Natori et al., 2008) or to incorporate them in external disturbancesand design a robust output feedback MPC to compensatethe effects of disturbances and measurement losses as in (Li and Shi, 2013).

Moreover, the delays introduced by the communication network are time-varying and unpredictable and maydeteriorate the closed-loop system performance and even reduce the system's stability region. Several methods havebeen proposed to improve the stability of NCSs with time-varying delays: a Lyapunov-based stability criterion in terms of linear matrix inequalities for discrete-time NCS models is given in (Cloosterman et al., 2009; Huang et al., 2010) and for continuous-time models in (Yue et al., 2009); in (Zhao et al., 2010) a stabilized controller design method obtained using time delay switched theory is proposed; in (Liu et al., 2007) a networked predictive control (NPC) scheme is proposed to overcome the effects of network delay and data dropout, while it is shown that a closed-loop NPC system with bounded random network delay is stable if its corresponding switched system is stable; the work in (Shi and Yu, 2011) is concerned with the two-mode-dependent robust control synthesis of NCSs where random delays exist in both forward and feedback communication links; in (Yu et al., 2011) the authors consider the design of NCSs using the modified generalised predictive control method while taking into account both forward and feedbackchannel delays and deriving a sufficient and necessarycondition to guarantee the stochastic stability.

Recently, the greater demand for increased driveability and passenger comfort, which requires a reduction of the noise and vibration characteristics of vehicles, has led to the design of proper models for vehicle drivetrains and to the development of different control strategies to minimize the effects of drivetrain oscillations: robust pole placement (Stewart et al., 2005), linear quadratic Gaussian control design with loop transfer recovery (Berriri et al., 2008) and MPC (Rostalski et al., 2007; Caruntu et al., 2011b). Although the majority of the control strategies that are implemented on real vehicles are based on standard PID loops and look-up tables, it was shown that MPC has a large potential for control of automotive subsystemssubsystems, e.g., semi-active suspensions (Canale et al., 2006), brakes (ABS) (Yoo and Wang, 2007), mechatronic actuators (Di Cairano et al., 2007; Hermans et al., 2009), driveline (Saerens et al., 2008), rear active differential (Canale et al., 2010), and engine (Di Cairano et al., 2010). This is supported by the increased power of electronic control units that enable the implementation of more complex real-time control algorithms. However, all of these solutions assume that the sensors, controllers and actuators are directly connected, which is not realistic. Rather, in modern vehicles, the control signals from the controllers and the measurements from the sensors are exchanged using a communication network, i.e., controller area network (CAN), among control system components (Herpel et al., 2009). This brings up a new challenge on how to deal with theeffects of the CAN-induced time-varying delays in the controlloop, knowing that these delays may be unknown andtime-varying and may degrade the performances of controlsystems designed without considering them and can evendestabilize the closed-loop system.

MAIN FOCUS OF THE CHAPTER

Issues, Controversies, Problems

The problem considered in this chapter is the minimization of the oscillations in a vehicle drivetrain while coping with the time-varyingdelays introduced by the CAN communication network andthe strict timing limitations. It is important to point out thatsuppressing drivetrain oscillations is equivalent with fast asymptoticstabilization of the torsion in the driveshaft. This explainsthe poor behavior, in this respect, obtained by standard outputfeedback controllers, such as PID, which only regulate the vehicle velocity. Therefore, it is important to design a controller with a stability guarantee. While MPC is increasingly seen as an attractive methodology for automotive applications, standard MPC strategies (Maciejowski, 2002; Rawlings and Mayne, 2009), which typically require a sufficientlylong prediction horizon to assure stability and performance,are likely to yield solutions that are too complex for driveline oscillations damping, even when delays are not present. Notice that the previously mentioned MPC solutions (Rostalski et al., 2007) do not offer an a priori closed-loopstability guarantee. For closed-loop MPC systems in anexplicit piecewise affine form, stability can be checked a posteriori,but such an explicit form cannot be obtained for models withtime-varying delays.

Motivated by the shortcomings of the existing controllerdesign methods for drivetrain oscillation damping, the contributionof this chapteris twofold: firstly, two methods of modeling the network-induced delays are presented, i.e., one based on polytopic inclusions and one based on disturbances; secondly, two advanced control techniques (based on model predictive control) for damping the drivetrain oscillations are designed starting from a typical two inertia drivetrain model and the two network-induced time-varying delay modeling methods.

Considering that there is a need to know the upper bound of the network-induced delays in order to apply the two modeling methods, a technique for estimating the maximum delay that can be introduced by a CAN is presented. This further enables the usage of the polytopic approximations modeling technique developed in (Gielen et al., 2010) for general networked control systems as a first modeling method. The second modeling method considers the errorcaused by the network-induced time-varying delays as a disturbance and a method of finding thebounds of the disturbance is proposed.

Please note that an affine model of a vehicle drivetrain with network-induced time-varying delays, poses serious challenges to existing MPC design methodologies. For example, depending on the complexity of the polytopic approximation, long horizon MPC schemes typically lead to a computationally unfeasible solution due to the matrix uncertainty. State-of-the-art explicit MPC approaches, which may be able to cope with uncertain linear systems and can result in a computationally feasible solution, are not applicable due to the presence of time-varying delays. Lyapunov based predictive control provides an attractive alternative, as it results in a low-complexity problem due to a unitary horizon and offers a stability guarantee. Still, the presence of hard constraints and time-varying delays makes standard Lyapunov MPC approaches over conservative. Recently, a relaxation of the conventional notion of a Lyapunov function was proposed, the so-called flexible Lyapunov function. A first application of flexible Lyapunov functions in automotive control problems was on electromagnetic actuators (Hermans et al., 2009) and it was indicated that flexible Lyapunov functions can be used to design stabilizing MPC schemes with a single step horizon, without introducing excessive conservatism. As such, in this chapter two flexible

Lyapunov function MPC schemes are designed and it is demonstrated that such approaches are able to deal with time-varying delays in a non-conservative and computationally tractable way.

As such, a non-conservative stabilizing predictive control scheme is designed for the model of the closed-loop CAN system based on the polytopic approximations technique using the concept of a flexible control Lyapunov function. Moreover, a robust one step ahead MPC scheme is designed using the concept of flexible control Lyapunov functions (CLFs) that explicitly accounts for rejection of disturbances introduced by the time-varying delay in the communication network and guarantees also the input-to-state stability (ISS) of the system in a non-conservative way. The resulting control algorithms have the potential to satisfy the chronometric requirements, as they can be implemented as low-complexity linear programs (LPs), while they offer a non-conservative solution to stabilization due to the flexibility of the Lyapunov function.

Several tests performed using an industry validated drivetrain model indicate that the proposed design methodologies can handle both the performance/physical constraints and the strict limitations on the computational complexity, while effectively coping with the time-varying delays. Moreover, a comparative analysis between the two Lyapunov-based model predictive control design methodologies in terms of computational complexity, number of optimization variables and obtained performances is carried out and the results are discussed.

Notation and Basic Definitions

$\mathbb{R}, \mathbb{R}_+, \mathbb{Z}$ and $\mathbb{Z}_+$ are the real, non-negative real, integer and non-negative integer numbers, respectively. For $\Pi \subseteq \mathbb{R}$ the notations $\Pi_{\geq c_1}$ and $\Pi_{\geq (c_1, c_2]}$ are used to denote the sets $\{k \in \Pi \mid k \geq c_1\}$ and $\{k \in \Pi \mid c_1 < k \leq c_2\}$, respectively, for some $c_1, c_2 \in \mathbb{Z}_+$ and similarly $\Pi_{\leq c_1}$, $\mathbb{R}_\Pi := \Pi$ and $\mathbb{Z}_\Pi := \mathbb{Z} \cap \Pi$. For a vector $x \in \mathbb{R}^n$, let $\| \bullet \|$ denote an arbitrary p-norm and let $[x]_i$, $i \in \mathbb{Z}_{[1,n]}$ denote the ith component of x. Let $\|x\|_\infty := \max_{i \in \mathbb{Z}_{[1,n]}} |[x]_i|$, where $|\bullet|$ denotes the absolute value. For a matrix $Z \in \mathbb{R}^{m \times n}$, let Z^{T} denote its transpose. Let $\mathbf{z} := \{z_l\}_{l \in \mathbb{Z}_+}$ with $z_l \in \mathbb{R}^n$ for all $l \in \mathbb{Z}_+$ denote an arbitrary sequence. Define $\|\mathbf{z}\| := \sup\{\|z_l\| \mid l \in \mathbb{Z}_+\}$ and $\mathbf{z}_{[0,k]} := \{z_l\}_{l \in \mathbb{Z}_{[0,k]}}$. A polyhedron, or a polyhedral set, in $\mathbb{R}^n$ is a set obtained at the intersection of a finite number of open and/or closed half-spaces. A polytope is a compact (closed and bounded) polyhedron. A function $\varphi : \mathbb{R}_+ \to \mathbb{R}_+$ belongs to class $\mathcal{K}$ if it is continuous, strictly increasing and $\varphi(0) = 0$. A function $\varphi : \mathbb{R}_+ \to \mathbb{R}_+$ is said to belong to class $\mathcal{K}_\infty$ if it is of class $\mathcal{K}$ and $\lim_{s \to \infty} \varphi(s) = \infty$. Let $S_1 \subseteq \mathbb{R}^n$ and $S_2 \subseteq \mathbb{R}^n$ denote arbitrary sets. $S_1 \oplus S_2 := \{x + y \mid x \in S_1, y \in S_2\}$ denotes the Minkowski addition of S_1 and S_2. Let $\mathrm{Co}(\bullet)$ denote the convex hull and let $\mathrm{int}(S)$ denote the interior of an arbitrary set S.

SOLUTIONS AND RECOMMENDATIONS

Network Delay Modeling

In this section, a general framework will be established to show how to model the network-induced time-varying delays using polytopic inclusions or as disturbances for controller design purposes.

Consider the standard NCS illustrated in Figure 1, which is composed of five parts: a communication network, where it is assumed that delay occurs completely randomly, a physical plant, one sensor node (S), one controller node and one actuator node (A). The delays introduced by the network, which can be smaller and larger than a sampling period, are represented as τ^{ca} for the delay in the forward channel and as τ^{sc} for the delay in the feedback channel. In the same figure, $u(t)$ and $y(t)$ represent the control signal and the output of the system, respectively.

Please note that for a linear physical plant, the feedback channel (from sensor to controller) induced delays can be considered as forward channel (from controller to actuator) induced delays from the controller point of view, Figures 1 and 2 are equivalent. In the following please consider the continuous time delay only in the forward channel $\tau = \tau^{ca} + \tau^{sc}$.

In what follows it is assumed that the time-varying delays induced by the communication network are bounded and this bound is known. A generic method for establishing such a bound is provided in the next subsection (Caruntu et al., 2013). Under this assumption, the task is to obtain a discrete-time model of the network-controlled architecture that accounts for time-varying delays within the provided bound. To this end, consider that the continuous-time model of the physical plant with input delay is given by

$$
\dot{x}\left(t\right) = A_c x\left(t\right) + b_c u^*\left(t\right),
$$
$$
u^*\left(t\right) = u_k, \forall t \in \left[t_k + \tau_k, t_{k+1} + \tau_{k+1}\right],
$$

(1)

Figure 1. Control system with network-induced time delays

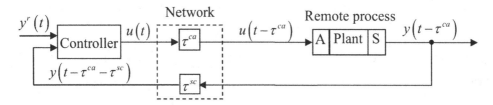

Figure 2. Control system with grouped network-induced time delays

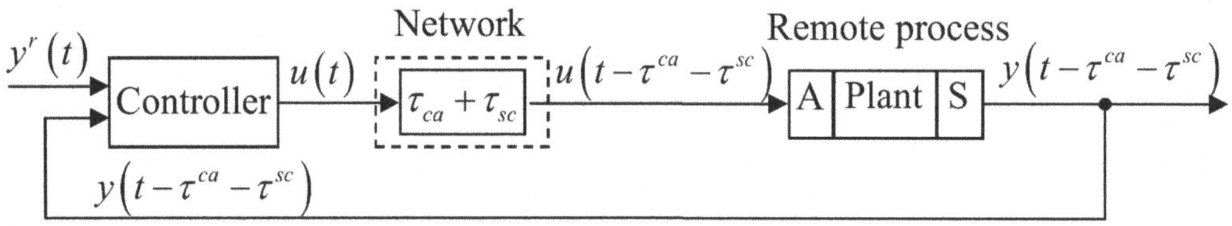

where $t_k = kT_s, k \in \mathbb{Z}_+$, $T_s \in \mathbb{R}_+$ denotes the sampling period and assume that $u^*(t) = u_0$ for all $t \in [0, \tau_0]$ with $u_0 \in \mathbb{R}$ some predetermined constant. Above, $u_k \in \mathbb{R}$ is the control action generated at time $t = t_k$, $\tau_k \in \mathbb{R}_{[0,\tau^{\text{large}}]}$ denotes the delay induced by the network at time $k \in \mathbb{Z}_+$ and $\tau^{\text{large}} \in \mathbb{R}_+$ is the maximal possible delay.

The maximum delay can be expressed as $\tau^{\text{large}} = (\Upsilon + \upsilon)T_s$, where $\Upsilon \in \mathbb{Z}_+$ and $\upsilon \in \mathbb{R}_{[0,1)}$. Assuming that u_k is known for all $k \in \mathbb{Z}_{[-\Upsilon-1,-1]}$ with $\psi_{[-\Upsilon-1,-1]}$ some predetermined vector, the discretized model is

$$x_{k+1} = A_d x_k + b_d u_k + \Delta_0(\tau_k)(u_{k-1} - u_k) + \Delta_1(\tau_k)(u_{k-2} - u_{k-1}) + \cdots + \Delta_\Upsilon(\tau_k)(u_{k-\Upsilon-1} - u_{k-\Upsilon}) =$$
$$= A_d x_k + b_d u_k + \sum_{i=0}^{\Upsilon} \Delta_i(\tau_k)(u_{k-i-1} - u_{k-i})$$

$$(2)$$

where $A_d := e^{A_c T_s}, b_d := \int_0^{T_s} e^{A_c(T_s - \theta)} d\theta b_c$,

$$\Delta_i(\tau_k) := \begin{cases} 0, & \tau_{k-i} - iT_s \leq 0 \\ \int_0^{\tau_{k-i} - iT_s} e^{A_c(T_s - \theta)} d\theta b_c, & 0 < \tau_{k-i} - iT_s < T_s \\ \int_0^{T_s} e^{A_c(T_s - \theta)} d\theta b_c, & T_s \leq \tau_{k-i} - iT_s \end{cases}$$

$$(3)$$

for all $k \in \mathbb{Z}_+$ and $i \in \mathbb{Z}_{[0,\Upsilon]}$.

An Upper Bound on CAN-Induced Delays

To obtain the model for controller design purposes, as described in the previous subsection, an upper bound on the CAN-induced delays is necessary. In what follows, the results presented in (Herpel et al., 2009), which aim at providing a method for calculating the worst-case response time of each message sent on CAN in automotive applications, is used to determine such an upper bound. The result is based on Network Calculus (Le Boudec and Thiran, 2001), which is a theoretical framework for deterministic queuing systems, based on min-plus algebra. Its main focus is on determination of bounds on worst case performance. One aim is to determine lower and upper bounds for end-to-end delays of nodes or collections of nodes within a network, for traffic backlog and for output limitations. The Network Calculus technique requires only the statically assigned CAN identifiers and the specific cycle times at which each message is sent as input data. There is no need to know the global bus-wide schedule of traffic to obtain reasonable upper bounds on the delay for each priority class.

Let $x_j(t)$ denote the input data and $y_j(t)$ the output data at time t per node of priority $j = 0, \ldots, N$. The procedure starts with input $x_0(t)$ and output $y_0(t)$. Then, the delay for the first priority class yields:

$$\tau_0^{\text{large}} \leq \sup_{t \geq 0} \left\{ \inf_{\tau \geq 0} \{ \alpha_0(t) \leq \beta_0(t + \tau) \} \right\}, \tag{4}$$

where $\alpha_0(t)$ is a step-function-type arrival curve of input $x_0(t)$ and the rate-latency service curve $\beta_0(t) = \beta_{R,T}(t) = 500\text{kbps} \cdot [t - 0.000272s]^+$, with $[t - T]^+ := \max\{0, t - T\}$. The maximum delay for frames of priority 1 is

$$\tau_1^{\text{large}} \leq \sup_{t \geq 0} \left\{ \inf_{\tau \geq 0} \{ \alpha_1(t) \leq \beta_1(t + \tau) \} \right\}, \tag{5}$$

where $\beta_1(t + \tau) = \beta_0(t + \tau) - \bar{\alpha}_1(t + \tau)$, $\beta_1(t)$ is the service curve for the nodes of priority 1 and $\bar{\alpha}_1(t)$ is the upper bound for the cumulative higher priority arrivals. Using the same reasoning several times, one obtains

$$\tau_j^{\text{large}} \leq \sup_{t \geq 0} \left\{ \inf_{\tau \geq 0} \{ \alpha_j(t) \leq \beta_j(t + \tau) \} \right\}, \tag{6}$$

where $\alpha_j(t)$ and $\beta_j(t)$ are the arrival curve and, respectively, the service curve for the nodes of priority j. As demonstrated in (Herpel et al., 2009) the above sup-inf problem can be solved geometrically, which yields the following explicit expression for the upper bound on the delays of j-th priority:

$$\tau_j^{\text{large}} \leq \frac{(j + 2)l}{R - \sum_{i=0}^{j-1} \dfrac{l}{c_i}}, \tag{7}$$

where $l = 136$ [bits] denotes the maximum frame length, $R = 500$ [kbps] is the rate of a high-speed CAN and c_i is the cycle length of the i-th priority message. A cycle length c_n, corresponding to a message of priority n, represents the period after which the message is repeated.

This completes the determination of the upper bound of the CAN-induced delays. Next, the two network-induced time-varying delays methods (the one based on polytopic approximations and the one based on disturbances) are presented.

Modeling Delays Using Polytopic Inclusions

Note that the matrices $\Delta_i\left(\tau_k\right)$ given in (3) are uncertain and time-varying due to their (non-linear) dependence on the uncertain time-varying delays $\tau_{k-i} \in \mathbb{R}_{\left[0, \tau^{\text{large}}\right]}, k \in \mathbb{Z}_+$ and $i \in \mathbb{Z}_{[0, \Upsilon]}$. In (Gielen et al., 2010) several methods to transform the nonlinear matrix expression (3) into a sum of nonlinear scalar functions multiplied by fixed matrices, were considered. Based on this transformation and by computing upper and lower bounds for the nonlinear scalar function, a polytopic over-approximation of (3) can be obtained. Therefore, let

$$\Delta^{\bar{\tau}} := \mathrm{Co}\left(\left\{\bar{\Delta}_l\right\}_{l\in\mathbb{Z}[1,L]}\right) \subset \mathbb{R}^{n\times m},$$ (8)

with $\bar{\tau} \in \mathbb{R}_{[0,T_s]}$, $\bar{\Delta}_l \in \mathbb{R}^{n\times m}$ the vertices (generators) of the convex parameter set $\Delta^{\bar{\tau}}$, $\Delta^{\bar{\tau}}$ be a matix polytope such that $\Delta_i\left(\tau_k\right) \in \Delta^{\bar{\tau}}$ for all $\tau_{k-i} \in \mathbb{R}_{[0,\tau^{\text{large}}]}$ and $L \in \mathbb{Z}_{\geq 1}$ is the finite number of generators. For the remainder of this chapter it is assumed that the polytopic set (8) is known, while additional details regarding its construction can be found in (Gielen et al., 2010).

As $\Delta_i\left(\tau_k\right) \in \Delta^{T_s}$ for all $i \in \mathbb{Z}_{[0,\Upsilon-1]}$ and $\Delta_\Upsilon\left(\tau_k\right) \in \Delta^{vT_s}$, it results that irrespective of the actual delay realization the trajectories of system (2) are a subset of the trajectories of the polytopic difference inclusion (Caruntu et al., 2011b; Caruntu et al., 2013)

$$x_{k+1} = \phi\left(x_k, \mathbf{u}_{[k-\Upsilon-1,k]}\right), k \in \mathbb{Z}_+,$$ (9)

where the inputs $\mathbf{u}_{[-\Upsilon-1,0]}$ are equal to some fixed, predetermined values and

$$\phi\left(x_k, \mathbf{u}_{[k-\Upsilon-1,k]}\right) :=$$
$$:= \left\{A_d x_k + b_d u_k + \sum_{i=0}^{\Upsilon} \Delta_i\left(\tau_k\right)\left(u_{k-i-1} - u_{k-i}\right) \mid \Delta_i\left(\tau_k\right) \in \Delta^{T_s}, i \in \mathbb{Z}_{[0,\Upsilon-1]}, \Delta_\Upsilon\left(\tau_k\right) \in \Delta^{vT_s}\right\}.$$ (10)

Note that the past input vectors within $\mathbf{u}_{[k-\Upsilon-1,k]}$ are known at time $k \in \mathbb{Z}_+$.

The computational complexity of virtually all existing controller synthesis algorithms for polytopic delay difference inclusions increases exponentially with the maximum value of the delay, i.e., $\tau^{\text{large}} \in \mathbb{R}_+$. This increase is mainly due to the fact that all possible combinations of the matrix vertices of the sets Δ^{T_s} and Δ^{vT_s} have to be taken into account. Still, for the proposed method, as detailed in (Gielen and Lazar, 2011), if the delays are larger than two sampling periods, Minkowski additions can be performed to reduce the number of vertices spanning the original polytopes, which makes the control of the reduced system far simpler than of the original one. However, determining an exact upper bound on the number of vertices spanning a polytope resulting from a Minkowski addition is a non-trivial problem that has attracted much interest.

Modeling Delays as Disturbances

For this modeling methodology please consider that the delays introduced by the communication network (considered only in the forward channel) are multiples of the sampling period $T_s \in \mathbb{R}_+$, i.e., $\tau_k / T_s \in \mathbb{Z}_{\geq 0}$.

Notation: Let a_k denote the delay in the forward channel at discrete-time instant $k \in \mathbb{Z}_+$, expressed as a number of sampling periods: $a_k = \lceil \tau_k / T_s \rceil \in \mathbb{N}$. Moreover, let $\bar{a}$ denote the maximum delay that can be introduced by the communication network in the forward channel, expressed as a number of sampling periods: $\bar{a} = \left\lceil \tau^{\text{large}}/T_s \right\rceil = \Upsilon T_s \in \mathbb{N}$, i.e., $a_k \in \mathbb{Z}_{[0,\bar{a}]}$.

Consider the continuous-time model of the physical plant with input delay (1) where

$$u^*\left(t\right) = u_k, \forall t \in \left[t_k + a_k, t_{k+1} + a_{k+1}\right],$$ (11)

Now, (3) becomes

$$\Delta_i\left(\tau_k\right) := \begin{cases} 0, & a_{k-i} - i \leq 0 \\ \int_0^{T_s} e^{A_c\left(T_s - \theta\right)} d\theta b_c, & 1 \leq a_{k-i} - i \end{cases}$$ (12)

for all $k \in \mathbb{Z}_+$, $i \in \mathbb{Z}_{[0,\Upsilon]}$.

The discrete-time forward channel disturbance representation is given by (Caruntu and Lazar, 2012; Caruntu and Lazar, 2014)

$$u_k^d = u_{k-a_k} - u_k$$ (13)

and the goal is to find a bounded set W_u in which to include all possible disturbances that can appear due to the time-varying delays introduced in the forward channel, knowing that the input of the physical plant is bounded.

Consider that the control signal is bounded by lower and upper bounds

$$u^{\min} \leq u_k \leq u^{\max},$$ (14)

where $u^{\min}$ and $u^{\max}$ are the minimum and the maximum control signal values, respectively, that can be given as input to the physical process. Then, the disturbance can be bounded as

$$u^{\min} - u^{\max} \leq u_k^d \leq u^{\max} - u^{\min}.$$ (15)

Furthermore, if the discrete control signal is also restricted by an incremental bound

$$-u^{\Delta} \leq \Delta u_k \leq u^{\Delta},$$ (16)

where $\Delta u_k = u_k - u_{k-1}$, for all $k \in \mathbb{Z}_{\geq 1}$, with u_0 some predetermined value and u^{Δ} is the maximum incremental/decremental value of the control signal at each sampling time instant $k \in \mathbb{Z}_{\geq 1}$, the disturbance can be rebounded as

$$-\bar{a}u^{\Delta} \leq u_k^d \leq \bar{a}u^{\Delta}. \tag{17}$$

Now, from the controller point of view, the model of the physical plant affected by input disturbances yields as

$$x_{k+1} = A_d x_k + b_d u_k + b_d u_k^d, \tag{18}$$

this model being used in the design phase of the predictive controller.

Even though the time-varying delay generates a time-varying disturbance, the set

$$\mathbb{W}_u = \left\{ b_d u_k^d \in \mathbb{R}^n \mid -\bar{a}u^{\Delta} \leq u_k^d \leq \bar{a}u^{\Delta} \right\} \tag{19}$$

remains fixed since the delays are substituted by their bounds, so this modeling technique is suitable for the use of the results presented in (Lazar and Heemels, 2008), in which the disturbances are explicitly taken into account during the design phase of the predictive controller, which will be accomplished in the next subsection.

Lyapunov-Based Model Predictive Control

State-of-the-art explicit MPC approaches, which may be able to cope with uncertain linear systems and can result in a computationally feasible solution, are not applicable for the problem considered in this chapter due to the presence of time-varying delays. Lyapunov based model predictive control (LMPC) provides an attractive alternative, as it results in a low-complexity problem due to a unitary horizon and offers a stability guarantee. Still, the presence of hard constraints and time-varying delays makes standard Lyapunov MPC approaches over conservative.

Recently, a relaxation of the conventional notion of a Lyapunov function was proposed in (Lazar, 2009), which resulted in a so-called flexible Lyapunov function. A first application of flexible Lyapunov functions in automotive control problems was presented in (Hermans et al., 2009). Therein it was indicated that flexible Lyapunov functions can be used to design stabilizing MPC schemes with a single step horizon, without introducing excessive conservatism.

LMPC Based on Polytopic Inclusions

In this subsection a flexible Lyapunov function MPC scheme is designed for the system (9) with $\Delta_i\left(\tau_k\right)$ from (3) and it is demonstrated that such an approach isable to deal with time-varying delays in a non-conservative andcomputationally tractable way.

Consider the discrete-time constrained non-autonomous system (9) with $\Delta_i\left(\tau_k\right)$ from (3) where $x_k \in \mathbb{X} \subseteq \mathbb{R}^n$ is the state at discrete-time instant k and $\mathbf{u}_{[k-\Upsilon-1,k]} \in \mathbb{U}^{\Upsilon+2} := \mathbb{U} \times \cdots \times \mathbb{U} \subseteq \mathbb{R}^m \times \cdots \times \mathbb{R}^m$ are the control inputs starting with discrete-time instant $k - \Upsilon - 1$ up to and including k. The mapping

$\phi : \mathbb{R}^n \times \mathbb{R}^m \times \cdots \times \mathbb{R}^m \rightrightarrows \mathbb{R}^n$ is a continuous set-valued function with $\phi(0, \mathbf{0}_{[-\Upsilon-1,0]}) = \{0\}$. Assume that $0 \in \text{int}(\mathbb{X})$ and $0 \in \text{int}(\mathbb{U})$. Next, let $\alpha_1, \alpha_2 \in \mathcal{K}_\infty$ and let $\rho \in \mathbb{R}_{[0,1)}$.

Definition 1: A function $V : \mathbb{R}^n \to \mathbb{R}_+$ that satisfies

$$\alpha_1(\ x\ ) \le V(x) \le \alpha_2(\ x\ ), \quad \forall x \in \mathbb{R}^n, \tag{20}$$

and for which there exists a control law, possibly set valued, $\pi : \mathbb{R}^n \rightrightarrows \mathbb{U}$ such that $x^+ \in \mathbb{X}$ and that

$$V(x^+) \le \rho \max_{\theta \in \mathbb{Z}_{[-\Upsilon-1,0]}} V(x_\theta), \tag{21}$$

for all $x_\theta \in \mathbb{X}$, $u_\theta \in \pi(x_\theta)$, $\theta \in \mathbb{Z}_{[-\Upsilon-1,0]}$ and all $x^+ \in \phi\left(x, \mathbf{u}_{[-\Upsilon-1,0]}\right)$ is called a *control Lyapunov-Razumikhin function (CLRF)* for the difference inclusion (9).

Consider the following inequality correponding to (21)

$$V(x_{k+1}) \le \rho \max_{\theta \in \mathbb{Z}_{[-\Upsilon-1,0]}} V(x_{k+\theta}) + \lambda_k, \tag{22}$$

for all $k \in \mathbb{Z}_+$ and all $x_{k+1} \in \phi\left(x_k, \mathbf{u}_{[k-\Upsilon-1,k]}\right)$. Here λ_k is a variable which allows for additional freedom in the evolution of the CLRF, i.e., it can increase if (21) is too conservative at time instant $k \in \mathbb{Z}_+$, possibly due to active state/input constraints. Based on (22) the following optimization problem is formulated.

Let $\alpha_3, \alpha_4 \in \mathcal{K}_\infty$ and $J : \mathbb{R} \to \mathbb{R}_+$ be an arbitrary function such that $\alpha_3(|\lambda|) \le J(\lambda) \le \alpha_4(|\lambda|)$ for all $\lambda \in \mathbb{R}$. Let V be a candidate CLRF for system (9).

Problem 1: Assume that at time $k \in \mathbb{Z}_+$, x_k and $\mathbf{u}_{[k-\Upsilon-1,k]}$ are known and minimize the cost $J(\lambda_k)$ over u_k and λ_k subject to

$$u_k \in \mathbb{U}, \ \phi(x_k, \mathbf{u}_{[k-\Upsilon-1,k]}) \subseteq \mathbb{X}, \ \lambda_k \ge 0, \qquad \text{(a)}$$
$$V(x_{k+1}) \le \rho \max_{\theta \in \mathbb{Z}_{[-\Upsilon-1,0]}} V(x_{k+\theta}) + \lambda_k, \quad \text{(b)} \tag{23}$$

for all $x_{k+1} \in \phi(x_k, \mathbf{u}_{[k-\Upsilon-1,k]})$ with $\rho \in \mathbb{R}_{[0,1)}$.

Let $\pi(x_k) := \{u_k \in \mathbb{R}^m \mid \exists \lambda_k \in \mathbb{R} \text{ s.t. (23a) holds}\}$ and let $\phi_{cl}(x_k, \mathbf{u}_{[k-\Upsilon-1,k-1]}, \pi(x_k)) := \{\phi(x_k, \mathbf{u}_{[k-\Upsilon-1,k-1]}, u) \mid u \in \pi(x_k)\}$. Furthermore, let $\mathcal{V}_\Gamma := \{x \in \mathbb{R}^n \mid V(x) \le \Gamma\}$ for any $\Gamma \in \mathbb{R}_+$. Let λ_k^* denote the optimum in Problem 1 for all $k \in \mathbb{Z}_+$. Next, the main stability result is stated.

Theorem 1: *Suppose that V is a function that satisfies (20) and that $\mathbb{X}$ and $\mathbb{U}$ are bounded. Furthermore, suppose that Problem 1 is feasible for all $\left(x_0, \mathbf{u}_{[-\Upsilon-1,0]}\right) \in \mathbb{X} \times \mathbb{U}^{\Upsilon+2}$ and that $\lim\limits_{k\to\infty} \lambda_k^* = 0$. Then, the origin of the difference inclusion*

$$x_{k+1} \in \phi_{cl}(x_k, \mathbf{u}_{[k-\Upsilon-1,k-1]}, \pi(x_k)), k \in \mathbb{Z}_+, \tag{24}$$

is attractive. Moreover, if $\exists \Gamma \in \mathbb{R}_{>0}$ such that V is a cLRF for initial conditions in $\mathcal{V}_\Gamma$ for system (9), the system (24) is asymptotically stable in $\mathbb{X}$.

The Proof of Theorem 1 follows from standard arguments employed in proving input-to-state stability and Lyapunov stability and consideration of the time-delay setting, and is therefore omitted here. The interested reader is referred to (Lazar, 2009) and (Gielen et al., 2009) for more details. The crux of the stability proof is the limiting condition $\lim\limits_{k\to\infty} \lambda_k^* = 0$, which is enforced via the following lemma.

Lemma 1: *Let $\Omega \in \mathbb{R}_+$ be a fixed constant to be chosen a priori and let $\rho \in \mathbb{R}_{[0,1)}$. If*

$$0 \leq \lambda_k \leq \rho(\lambda_{k-1}^* + \rho^{k-1}\Omega), \forall k \in \mathbb{Z}_{\geq 1}, \tag{25}$$

then $\lim\limits_{k\to\infty} \lambda_k = 0$.

Lemma 1 is proven in (Caruntu et al., 2013) and is omitted here for brevity.

By augmenting Problem 1 with constraint (25) the property $\lim\limits_{k\to\infty} \lambda_k^* = 0$ is thus guaranteed, which is sufficient for asymptotic stability under the hypothesis of Theorem 1. Note that, in constraint (25) $\rho^{k-1}\Omega$ gives a decreasing ramp envelope and λ_{k-1}^* dictates with what value the ramp is allowed to be violated in order to maintain the feasibility of the closed-loop control system. It is worth to mention that the proposed limiting condition is less conservative than the solution presented in (Lazar, 2009) and (Gielen et al., 2009), which corresponds to setting $\Omega = 0$.

Next, consider the following infinity-norm based candidate cLRF, i.e.,

$$V(x) = \|Px\|_\infty, \tag{26}$$

where $P \in \mathbb{R}^{p \times n}$, $p \geq n$, is a full-column rank matrix to be determined. Function (26) satisfies (20) with $\alpha_1(s) = \underline{\sigma}/\sqrt{p} \cdot s$, where $\underline{\sigma}$ is the smallest singular value of P, and with $\alpha_2(s) = \|P\|_\infty s$. In order to implement the proposed MPC algorithm, P must be computed off-line as a local cLRF for system (9), which can be done as follows.

Lemma 2: *Suppose there exist $\rho \in \mathbb{R}_{[0,1)}$, a full column-rank $P \in \mathbb{R}^{p \times n}$, for some $p \in \mathbb{Z}_{\geq n}$ and $K \in \mathbb{R}^{m \times n}$ such that*

$$\left\| \left[P(A_d + (b_d - \bar{\Delta}_l)K \quad P\bar{\Delta}_l K) \right] \begin{bmatrix} P & 0 \\ 0 & P \end{bmatrix}_{.}^{-L} \right\|_\infty - \rho \leq 0, \tag{27}$$

for all $l \in \mathbb{Z}_{[1,L]}$. *Then* (9) *in closed loop with the controller* $u_k = Kx_k$ *is asymptotically stable and* $V(x) = \| Px \|_\infty$ *is a (local) cLRF for system* (9).

The proof of Lemma 2 is similar to the proof in (Lazar et al., 2006), Theorem IV.2, and is therefore omitted here. Matrices P and K can be obtained by solving a nonlinear optimization problem (Lazar et al., 2006). Notice that the resulting explicit state-feedback controller Kx_k, $K \in \mathbb{R}^{m \times n}$, is never to be used on-line in the actual control input u_k calculation. However, knowledge of this feedback is useful to determine the set $\mathcal{V}_\Gamma$ and thus verify the hypothesis of Theorem 1, which in turn is crucial for guaranteeing stability. As explained before, asymptotic stability is equivalent with effective driveline oscillation damping for the considered model.

Additionally, a one-step performance cost can be added to Problem 1 without affecting feasibility and thus, asymptotic stability, as follows. Consider the following cost function to be minimized

$$J_1(x_k, \mathbf{u}_{[k-Y-1,k]}, \lambda_k) = J_{\mathrm{MPC}}(x_k, \mathbf{u}_{[k-Y-1,k]}) + J(\lambda_k) := \| Qx_{k+1} \|_\infty + \| Ru_k \|_\infty + G\lambda_k, \tag{28}$$

where $x_{k+1} \in \phi(x_k, \mathbf{u}_{[k-Y-1,k]})$ and the matrices Q and R are pre-determined full-column rank matrices of appropriate dimensions and $G \in \mathbb{R}_{>0}$.

The fact that the developed networked Lyapunov-based model predictive control scheme for the constrained system (9) with $\Delta_i(\tau_k)$ from (3) can be implemented by solving a single LP during each control cycle using an infinity-norm based candidate cLRF is shown in (Caruntu et al., 2013) and is omitted here.

LMPC Based on Disturbances

In this subsection, a robust one step ahead MPC scheme is designed for the system (18). It employs a flexible Lyapunov function (Lazar, 2009) to attain stability and performance, in which the disturbances are explicitly taken into account during the design phase by using ISS concepts (see, e.g., Jiang and Wang, 2001; Sontag and Wang, 1995).

Consider the perturbed discrete-time system (18), where $x_k \in \mathbb{X} \subseteq \mathbb{R}^n$ is the state at discrete-time instant k and $u_k \in \mathbb{U} \subseteq \mathbb{R}^m$ is the control input and $w_k := b_d u_k^d \in \mathbb{W} \subseteq \mathbb{R}^n$ is an unknown disturbance at the discrete-time instant k. Naturally, it is assumed that the set of feasible states $\mathbb{X}$, the set of feasible inputs $\mathbb{U}$ and the disturbance set $\mathbb{W}$ are bounded polyhedra with non-empty interiors containing the origin. Next, let $\alpha_1, \alpha_2, \alpha_3 \in \mathcal{K}_\infty$ and let $\sigma \in \mathcal{K}$.

Definition 2: A function $V : \mathbb{R}^n \to \mathbb{R}_+$ that satisfies

$$\alpha_1(\| x \|) \leq V(x) \leq \alpha_2(\| x \|), \quad \forall x \in \mathbb{R}^n, \tag{29}$$

and for which there exists a control law, possibly set valued, $\pi : \mathbb{R}^n \rightrightarrows \mathbb{U}$ such that $x^+ \in \mathbb{X}$ and that

$$V(x^+) - V(x) \leq -\alpha_3\left(\|x\|\right) + \sigma\left(\|w\|\right), \tag{30}$$

for all $x \in \mathbb{X}$, $u \in \pi(x)$ and $w \in \mathbb{W}$ is called an *input-to-state stabilitycontrol Lyapunov function (ISS-CLF)* system (18) and disturbances in $\mathbb{W}$.

ISS theory (Jiang and Wang, 2001; Sontag and Wang, 1995) can be used to derive an input-to-state stabilizing predictive control scheme with improved disturbance rejection, as done in (Lazar and Heemels, 2008), where this property is refereed to as *optimized ISS*.

As such, let $\mathbb{W}$ be a convex hull of vertices $w^e, e = 1, \dots, E$ and let λ_k^e, $k \in \mathbb{Z}_+$ be optimization variables associated with each vertex w^e. Let $J(\lambda^1, \dots, \lambda^E, \lambda) : \mathbb{R}_+^E \times \mathbb{R}_+ \to \mathbb{R}_+$ be a strictly convex, radially unbounded function (i.e., $J(\cdot)$ tends to infinity when its arguments tend to infinity) and let $J(\lambda^1, \dots, \lambda^E, \lambda) \to 0 \Rightarrow \lambda^e \to 0$ for all $e = 1, \dots, E$, $\lambda \to 0$ and $J(0, \dots, 0, 0) = 0$.

Choose offline a CLF $V(\cdot)$ for system (18) without disturbances and let $\alpha_3 \in \mathcal{K}_\infty$ and $x_k \in \mathbb{X}$ be given. At each control sampling instant $k \in \mathbb{Z}_+$ the one step ahead ISS MPC controller solves the following problem.

Problem 2: At time $k \in \mathbb{Z}_+$ measure the state x_k and minimize the cost $J(\lambda_k^1, \dots, \lambda_k^E, \lambda_k)$ over $u_k, \lambda_k^1, \dots, \lambda_k^E$ and λ_k subject to the constraints

$$
\begin{aligned}
&u_k \in \mathbb{U}, \, x_{k+1} \in \mathbb{X}, \lambda_k^e \geq 0, \lambda_k \geq 0, &&\text{(a)} \\
&V(x_{k+1}) - V(x_k) + \alpha_3\left(\|x_k\|\right) \leq \lambda_k, &&\text{(b)} \\
&V(x_{k+1} + w^e) - V(x_k) + \alpha_3\left(\|x_k\|\right) \leq \lambda_k^e, &&\text{(c)}
\end{aligned} \tag{31}
$$

for all $e = 1, \dots, E$.

Note that in (31b) λ_k is a variable which allows for additional freedom in the evolution of the CLF, i.e., it can increase if (30) is too conservative at time instant $k \in \mathbb{Z}_+$, possibly due to active state/input constraints.

Let

$$\pi(x_k) := \{u_k \in \mathbb{R}^m \, \big| \, \exists \lambda_k, \lambda_k^e, e \in \mathbb{Z}_{[1,E]} \text{ s.t. (31) holds}\}$$

and let $\phi_{cl}(x_k, \pi(x_k), w_k) := \{x_{k+1} + w_k \, \big| \, u \in \pi(x_k)\}$ denote the difference inclusion corresponding to system (18) in closed loop with the set of feasible solutions obtained by solving Problem 2 at each sampling instant $k \in \mathbb{Z}_+$. Let λ_k^* denote the optimum in Problem 2 for all $k \in \mathbb{Z}_+$. Next, the main robust stability result in terms of ISS is stated.

Theorem 2: Let $\alpha_1, \alpha_2, \alpha_3 \in \mathcal{K}_\infty$, a continuous and convex CLF $V(\cdot)$ and a cost $J(\cdot)$ be given. Suppose that Problem 2 is feasible for all states $x \in \mathbb{X}$ and assume that $\lim_{k \to \infty} \lambda_k^* = 0$. Then, the trajectories generated by the difference inclusion

$$x_{k+1} \in \phi_{cl}(x_k, \pi(x_k), w_k), k \in \mathbb{Z}_+, \tag{32}$$

with initial state $x_0 \in \mathbb{X}$ converge in finite time to a robustly positively invariant subset of $\mathbb{X}$, in which the difference inclusion is ISS for disturbances in $\mathbb{W}$.

The proof of Theorem 2 follows from standard arguments employed in proving input-to-state stability and Lyapunov stability and is therefore omitted here. The interested reader is referred to (Lazar and Heemels, 2008) and (Lazar, 2009) for more details. Advantageous properties of the proposed robust controller are that ISS is guaranteed for any (feasible) solution of the optimization problem, state and input constraints can be explicitly accounted for, and feedback to disturbances is provided actively, on-line. The key of the stability proof is the limiting condition $\lim_{k \to \infty} \lambda_k^* = 0$. In what follows a non-conservative solution for guaranteeing this condition is provided.

Lemma 3: Let $\Delta \in \mathbb{R}_+$ be a fixed constant to be chosen a priori and let $\rho \in \mathbb{R}_{[0,1)}$ and $M \in \mathbb{Z}_{>0}$. If

$$0 \leq \lambda_k \leq \rho^{\frac{1}{M}} (\lambda_{k-1}^* + \rho^{\frac{k-1}{M}} \Omega), \forall k \in \mathbb{Z}_{\geq 1}, \tag{33}$$

then $\lim_{k \to \infty} \lambda_k = 0$.

Lemma 3 is proven in (Caruntu et al., 2011a) and is omitted here for brevity. By augmenting Problem 2 with constraint (33) the property $\lim_{k \to \infty} \lambda_k^* = 0$ is thus guaranteed, which is sufficient for asymptotic stability under the hypothesis of Theorem 2.

A similar infinity-norm based candidate CLF as described by (26) which satisfies (29) was considered for the constrained system afected by disturbances (18).

Additionally, a one-step performance cost can be added to Problem 1 without affecting feasibility and thus, asymptotic stability, as follows. Consider the following cost function to be minimized

$$J_1(x_k, u_k, \bar{\lambda}_k, \lambda_k) := J_{\text{MPC}}(x_k, u_k) + J(\bar{\lambda}_k, \lambda_k) := \| Qx_{k+1} \|_\infty + \| Ru_k \|_\infty + J(\bar{\lambda}_k, \lambda_k), \tag{34}$$

where the cost on the optimization variables $\bar{\lambda}_k := [\lambda_k^1, \dots, \lambda_k^E]^{\text{T}}$ and λ_k is defined as $J(\bar{\lambda}_k, \lambda_k) := \| \bar{\Lambda}\bar{\lambda}_k \|_\infty + | \Lambda\lambda |$, where $\bar{\Lambda}$ is a full-column rank matrix of appropriate dimensions and $\Lambda \in \mathbb{R}_{>0}$. The cost $J(\cdot)$ is chosen as required in Problem 2 and the matrices P_x, Q_x and R are known full-column rank matrices of appropriate dimensions.

The fact that the developed networked Lyapunov-based model predictive control scheme for the constrained system (14) can be implemented by solving a single LP during each control cycle using an infinity-norm based candidate CLF is shown in (Caruntu and Lazar, 2014) and is omitted here.

Vehicle Drivetrain Model and Control Architecture

The automotive drivetrain is the mechanical system that transmits the engine power to the driving wheels. The aim is to increase the comfort by reducing the vibrational oscillations, which can be achieved by proper control of the power transmission. To this end, a suitable model of the drivetrain is required for controller design. Numerous models of conventional powertrains were proposed in the literature during the last years, such as: two inertias models, one inertia corresponding to the engine and the other inertia to the vehicle mass and the wheels (Rostalski et al., 2007; Saerens et al., 2008; Templin, 2008), and three inertias models, one representing the engine, the second representing the gearbox and the final reduction gear and the third inertia corresponding to the vehicle mass and the wheels (Van Der Heijden et al., 2007; Naus, 2010). The complexity of the numerous models reported in the literature varies (Hrovat et al., 2000), but the two inertias models are most commonly used, and this fact is justified in Pettersson (1997), where it is shown that this model is able to capture the first torsional vibrational mode.

The model suitable for the control problem considered in this chapter should satisfy two requirements. Firstly, it should be complex enough to capture the essential dynamics of the drivetrain. Secondly, it should result in a tractable problem when delays are included in the model of the vehicle drivetrain.

The considered model is graphically illustrated in Figure 3 (dashed box). Therein, a schematic representation of a simplified drivetrain is given, which consists of two inertias, one for the engine, gearbox and final reduction gear (FRG), i.e., J_{eg}, and the other one representing the contributions from the vehicle and from the driving wheels, i.e., J_v, connected through a flexible driveshaft. The engine generates a torque, i.e., T_e, which is transmitted towards the wheels through the driveline. The engine torque is used as the control signal and assumed to be available on demand, e.g., engine torque is requested from the engine electronic control unit (ECU).

A fundamental requirement for model-based control is a model that captures the main characteristics of the plant. In this case the oscillations originating from driveline flexibilities are of interest. The drive-

Figure 3. Drivetrain schematic representation and control architecture

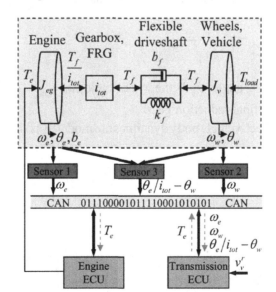

train flexibility is given by the driveshaft and the half-shafts, which transmit the received torque from the gearbox to the wheels. The driving wheels are the final components of the drivetrain converting rotation into traction used to defeat the vehicle load torque given by rolling resistance and aerodynamic drag.

Networked Control Architecture

The complete networked control architecture considered in this chapter, schematically depicted in Figure 3, performs the following tasks at each control cycle:

- The time-driven sensor nodes (e.g., Sensor 1) execute periodically the following tasks: measure the outputs of the system and send the samples to the Transmission ECU via CAN.
- The transmission ECU, which contains an event-driven task that is triggered each time a measurement data arrives via CAN, receives the measurements from the sensor nodes and the desired velocity reference $v_v^r = r_w \omega_w^r$ and computes the required torque, while handling the physical/control constraints and the delays; r_w is the effective wheel radius and or ω_w^r is the desired wheel speed.
- The control signal, i.e., the torque computed by the transmission controller, is sent to the Engine ECU via CAN.
- The Engine ECU, which contains an event-driven task that is triggered each time a measurement data arrives via CAN, receives the control signal and actuates the spark timing and airflow as requested for driveline control.

In Figure 3 the dashed arrows represent the direction of the messages sent to and from the controllers.

Continuous-Time Drivetrain Model

Consider as state variables the engine speed ω_e, the wheel speed ω_w and the torsion in the driveshaft, also called axle wrap, and as control input, the engine torque

$$x_1^m = \omega_e, x_2^m = \omega_w, x_3^m = \theta_e \big/ i_{tot} - \theta_w, u^m = T_e, \tag{35}$$

where θ_e is the engine's outgoing angle, θ_w is the wheel angle and $i_{tot} = i_g i_f$ is the overall transmission ratio from the gearbox and the final reduction gear.

The engine-gearbox and wheel-vehicle body dynamics are modeled as single inertial systems (Kiencke & Nielsen, 2005), i.e.,

$$\begin{aligned} J_{eg} \dot{\omega}_e &= T_e - b_e \omega_e - T_f \big/ i_{tot}, \\ J_v \dot{\omega}_w &= T_f - T_{load}, \end{aligned} \tag{36}$$

where $J_{eg} = J_e + J_g \big/ i_{tot}^2$ is the equivalent inertia of the engine-gearbox system, with J_e the engine inertia and J_g the gearbox inertia, b_e is the damping coefficient of the engine, T_f is the torque in the flexible driveshaft and T_{load} is the load torque. The vehicle inertia can be obtained by adding the wheels inertia J_w to the equivalent inertia of the vehicle mass, i.e.,

$$J_v = J_w + m_w r_w^2, \tag{37}$$

where m_w is the mass of the vehicle and r_w is the effective wheel radius.

The torque in the driveshaft, which is modeled as a spring and damper system, can be expressed as

$$T_f = b_f \left(\omega_e / i_{tot} - \omega_w \right) + k_f \left(\theta_e / i_{tot} - \theta_w \right), \tag{38}$$

where b_f is the damping coefficient and k_f is the elasticity factor of the flexible driveshaft. Since the vehicle driveability depends primarily on reduced driveshaft torque oscillations, this part will be used as a criterion to determine the driver's and passenger's comfort.

The load torque is modeled as

$$T_{load} = T_{airdrag} + T_{roll} + T_{grade}, \tag{39}$$

where $T_{airdrag}$ is the aerodynamic torque of the vehicle body, T_{roll} is the rolling torque of the tires and T_{grade} is the torque due to road grade

$$\begin{aligned}
T_{airdrag} &= 0.5 \rho_{air} A_f c_d \omega_w^2 r_w^3, \\
T_{roll} &= c_r m_v g \cos\left(\chi_{road}\right) r_w, \\
T_{grade} &= m_v g \sin\left(\chi_{road}\right) r_w,
\end{aligned} \tag{40}$$

where ρ_{air} is the air density, A_f is the frontal area of the vehicle, c_d is the airdrag coefficient, c_r is the coefficient of rolling resistance, g is the gravitational acceleration and χ_{road} is the road grade. Please observe that $T_{airdrag}$ is a nonlinear function of ω_w, but instead of this function, a linear approximation will be used, i.e.,

$$T_{airdrag} = b_a \omega_w, \tag{41}$$

where b_a is an approximation parameter. This approach provides a valid approximation for vehicle velocities up to 40 km/h and it can be extended to higher velocities by considering a piecewise affine approximation.

Thus, the following drivetrain state-space model is obtained

$$\dot{x}^m\left(t\right) = A_c^m x^m\left(t\right) + b_c^m u^m\left(t\right) + f_c^m, t \in \mathbb{R}_+, \tag{42}$$

where $x^m\left(t\right) = \left(x_1^m\left(t\right) \quad x_2^m\left(t\right) \quad x_3^m\left(t\right)\right)^{\mathrm{T}} \in \mathbb{R}^3$ is the system state, $u^m\left(t\right) \in \mathbb{R}$ is the system input (engine torque), $A_c^m \in \mathbb{R}^{3\times3}$ and $b_c^m \in \mathbb{R}^{3\times1}$ are the system matrices and $f_c^m \in \mathbb{R}^{3\times1}$ is the affine term obtained from the previous equations as follows:

$$A_c^m = \begin{pmatrix} -\dfrac{b_e}{J_{eg}} - \dfrac{b_f}{i_{tot}^2 J_{eg}} & \dfrac{b_f}{i_{tot} J_{eg}} & -\dfrac{k_f}{i_{tot} J_{eg}} \\[3ex] \dfrac{b_f}{i_{tot} J_v} & -\dfrac{b_a + b_f}{J_v} & \dfrac{k_f}{J_v} \\[3ex] \dfrac{1}{i_{tot}} & -1 & 0 \end{pmatrix}, b_c^m = \begin{pmatrix} \dfrac{1}{J_{eg}} \\[2ex] 0 \\[1ex] 0 \end{pmatrix}, f_c^m = -\begin{pmatrix} 0 \\[1ex] \dfrac{T_{roll} + T_{grade}}{J_v} \\[1ex] 0 \end{pmatrix}. \tag{43}$$

The engine torque (control input) is restricted by lower and upper bounds and by a torque rate constraint, i.e.,

$$0 \leq u^m(t) \leq T_e^{\max}, T_e^m \leq \dot{u}^m(t) \leq T_e^M, \tag{44}$$

where $T_e^{\max}$ is the maximum torque that can be generated by the internal combustion engine, and T_e^m, T_e^M are torque rate bounds.

The engine and wheel speeds are bounded, i.e.,

$$\omega_e^{\min} \leq x_1^m\left(t\right) \leq \omega_e^{\max}, \omega_w^{\min} \leq x_2^m\left(t\right) \leq \omega_w^{\max}, \tag{45}$$

where $\omega_e^{\min}$ and $\omega_e^{\max}$ are the idle speed and the engine limiter speed, respectively, and $\omega_w^{\min}$ and $\omega_w^{\max}$ are the minimum and the maximum speeds of the wheels, respectively.

Note that for a desired wheel speed value, i.e., x_2^{ss}, it is straightforward to obtain the corresponding steady-state engine speed, axle wrap and engine torque as follows:

$$x_1^{ss} = i_{tot} x_2^{ss}, x_3^{ss} = \frac{b_a}{k_f} x_2^{ss} + \frac{T_{roll} + T_{grade}}{k_f}, u^{ss} = b_e i_{tot} x_2^{ss} + \frac{b_a}{i_{tot}} x_2^{ss} + \frac{T_{roll} + T_{grade}}{i_{tot}}. \tag{46}$$

Hence, using the following change of coordinates in (), i.e.,

$$x(t) = x^m(t) - x^{ss}(t), u(t) = u^m(t) - u^{ss}(t), \tag{47}$$

where $x^{ss} = \left(x_1^{ss} \quad x_2^{ss} \quad x_3^{ss}\right)^{\mathrm{T}}$ yields the following equivalent linear system description

$$\dot{x}(t) = A_c x(t) + b_c u(t), \tag{48}$$

where A_c and b_c are equal to A_c^m and b_c^m, respectively.

Simulation Results

The continuous-time model (42) was implemented in Matlab/Simulink and three different control strategies were applied to damp driveline oscillations: a PID controller and the two networked predictive controllers proposed in this chapter. The sampling period of the system was chosen as $T_s = 0.01\,\mathrm{s}$ and the values of the parameters used in simulations were obtained with the help of Ford Research and Advanced Engineering, US, and are given in (Caruntu et al., 2013).

The upper bound of the delays that are introduced by CAN was calculated using equation (7) given by the methodology described in a previous subsection, which resulted in $\tau^{\text{large}} = 1.7T_s = 0.017s$ s. The delays are time-varying and uniformly distributed in the interval $[0, \tau^{\text{large}}]$. The polytopic over-approximation of the nonlinear functions $\Delta_{i,k}$ was found using the Cayley-Hamilton theorem as in (Gielen et al., 2010).

The delays were considered in the design phase for both the networked predictive controllers proposed in this chapter, but they were introduced in simulations for all the strategies (including the PID controller). The purpose for applying the control strategies that do not take delay into account is to illustrate that these network-induced time-varying delays can have adverse effects on the controllers performances as it is shown in what follows.

The control objective is to reach a desired speed reference in a short time, but, at the same time, to increase the passenger comfort by reducing the oscillations that occur when tip-in and tip-out maneuvers are performed. The axle wrap rate ($\dot{x}_3$) is calculated as the difference between the engine speed (divided by the total transmission ratio) and the wheel speed, and it is used as a measure of the driveline oscillations. Also, the driveshaft torque is calculated and it is used as a measure of driveline oscillations.

PID

A PID controller was designed based on (O'Dwyer, 2006) and it was tuned to have a fast response, which yielded the proportional, integral and derivative terms $K_R = 17$, $T_i = 0.01$ and $T_d = 0.0015$, respectively.Clearly, no stability guarantee can be obtained for the affine system in closed-loop with the PID controller.

Note that, although the PID controller does not enforce constraints on the control command, its output was saturated in order to enforce the engine limitations, i.e., the torque limit $T_e^{\max}$, and the limitation on the control input increment.

The worst case time needed for computation of the controlinput for the PID controller was lessthan 0.1ms on a personal computer (PC) running MATLAB/Simulink, which meets the imposed timing constraints.

LMPC Based on Polytopic Inclusions

The Lyapunov-based model predictive controller based on polytopic inclusions was designed using the following weight matrices of the cost (28):

$$Q = \begin{pmatrix} 11 & 0 & 0 \\ 0 & 11 & 0 \\ 0 & 0 & 20 \end{pmatrix}, R = 0.5 \text{ and } G = 1. \tag{49}$$

Lemma 2 was used for the off-line computation of the infinity norm based cLRF $V(x) = \parallel Px \parallel_\infty$ for $\rho = 0.99$ and the affine model of the drivetrain in closed-loop with $u_k := Kx_k$. The following matrices were obtained:

$$P = \begin{pmatrix} 2.8334 & 64.8108 & 1892.5781 \\ 5.0452 & -143.6492 & -726.0745 \\ 2.4102 & 160.7912 & 1483.0628 \end{pmatrix},$$

$$K = \begin{pmatrix} -8.7959 & 89.1542 & -459.5117 \end{pmatrix}. \tag{50}$$

Note that the control law $u_k := Kx_k$ was only employed off-line, to calculate the weight matrix P of the cLRF V, and it was never used for controlling the system. The larger number for the third state in the matrix Q of the performance cost is meant to suppress the drivetrain oscillations by fast asymptotic stabilization of the torsion in the driveshaft.

For the proposed networked predictive control scheme, recursive feasibility implies asymptotic stability, as guaranteed by Theorem 1. However, recursive feasibility is not a priori guaranteed and hinges mainly on the constraint (25) on the future evolution of λ_k^*. For the considered case study, through extensive simulations, the employed $\rho = 0.99$, $\lambda_0^* \approx 100$ and $\Omega = 550$ proved to be large enough to guarantee recursive feasibility for a wide range of operating scenarios.

For the considered drivetrain model, which has 3 states, 1 input, $1.7T_s$ delay dimension, 12 generators for both Δ^{T_s} and Δ^{vT_s} sets, $Q \in \mathbb{R}^{3\times3}$, $R \in \mathbb{R}$ and $G \in \mathbb{R}$, the LP corresponding to Problem 1 has 1163 constraints and 5 variables. Although the number of constraints and variables depends polynomially on the dimension of the system, the resulting LP is low-complexity and it fits the stringent timing requirements.

The worst case time needed for computation of the controlinput for the proposed predictive controller was lessthan 9ms on a PC running MATLAB/Simulink, which meets the imposed timing constraints.

LMPC Based on Disturbances

The Lyapunov-based model predictive controller based on disturbances was designed using the following weight matrices of the cost (34):

$$Q = \begin{pmatrix} 11 & 0 & 0 \\ 0 & 11 & 0 \\ 0 & 0 & 20 \end{pmatrix}, R = 0.5, \overline{\Lambda} = 0.01 \text{ and } \Lambda = 1. \tag{51}$$

The technique presented in (Lazar, 2006) was used for the off-line computation of the infinity norm based local LRF $V(x) = \| Px \|_\infty$ for $\rho = 0.99$ and the affine model of the drivetrain in closed-loop with $u_k := Kx_k$. The following matrices were obtained:

$$P = \begin{pmatrix} 2.2669 & 32.1093 & 946.2197 \\ 2.5314 & -71.6993 & -363.0408 \\ 2.4062 & 81.7867 & 741.4772 \end{pmatrix},$$

$$K = \begin{pmatrix} -6.3471 & 45.7387 & -229.6221 \end{pmatrix}.$$

(52)

As for the previous controller design method, the control law $u_k := Kx_k$ was only employed off-line, to calculate the weight matrix P of the CLF V, and it was never used for controlling the system. Again, the larger number for the third state in the matrix Q of the performance cost is meant to suppress the drivetrain oscillations by fast asymptotic stabilization of the torsion in the driveshaft.

For the proposed networked predictive control scheme, recursive feasibility implies asymptotic stability, as guaranteed by Theorem 2. However, recursive feasibility is not a priori guaranteed and hinges mainly on the constraint (33) on the future evolution of λ_k^*. For the considered case study the values for $\rho = 0.99$, $\lambda_0^* \approx 100$ and $\Omega = 550$ were chosen equal to the ones used in the previous control design method for comparison purposes and $M = 5$.

For the considered drivetrain model, which has 3 states, 1 input, $1.7T_s$ delay dimension, 2 generators for the disturbance set $\mathbb{W}_u$, $Q \in \mathbb{R}^{3\times3}$, $R \in \mathbb{R}$, $\overline{\Lambda} \in \mathbb{R}$ and $\Lambda \in \mathbb{R}$, the LP corresponding to Problem 2 has 43 constraints and 7 variables, which is much less than the number of constraints imposed in Problem 1.

The worst case time needed for computation of the control input for the proposed predictive controller was less than 2ms on a PC running MATLAB/Simulink, which meets the imposed timing constraints.

Illustrative Results

A simulation test is performed in Matlab/Simulink on an acceleration scenario where the vehicle has to accelerate from 7 km/h to 30 km/h. In what follows the performance of the resulting closed-loop systems for each technique is analyzed using the plotted trajectories.

The evolution of the cLRF relaxation variable λ_k^* and the corresponding upper bound for the Lyapunov based model predictive control technique based on polytopic inclusions is shown in Figure 4, for this particular simulation. Therein, it can be observed that λ_k^* may be small or even 0 for some time after which it is allowed to increase again, as long as this does not violate the upper bound. However as $k \to \infty$, λ_k^* is forced to converge to 0 using (25), which in turn implies asymptotic stability as guaranteed by Theorem 1.

The evolution of the CLF relaxation variable λ_k^* and the corresponding upper bound for the Lyapunov based model predictive control technique based on disturbances is shown in Figure 5, for this particular simulation. Therein, it can be observed that λ_k^* may be small or even 0 for some time after which it is

Figure 4. History of λ_k^* throughout the simulation – polytopic inclusions technique

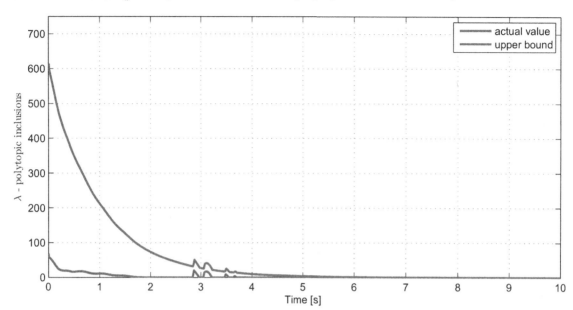

Figure 5. History of λ_k^* throughout the simulation – disturbances technique

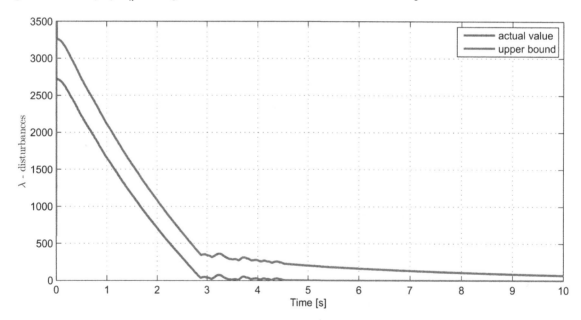

allowed to increase again, as long as this does not violate the upper bound. However as $k \to \infty$, λ_k^* is forced to converge to 0 using (33), which in turn implies asymptotic stability as guaranteed by Theorem 2.

The delays introduced by CAN for this simulation scenario are represented in Figure 6, where it can be seen that they are time-varying and uniformly distributed in the interval $[0, \tau^{\text{large}}]$.

Figure 6. Delays induced by CAN

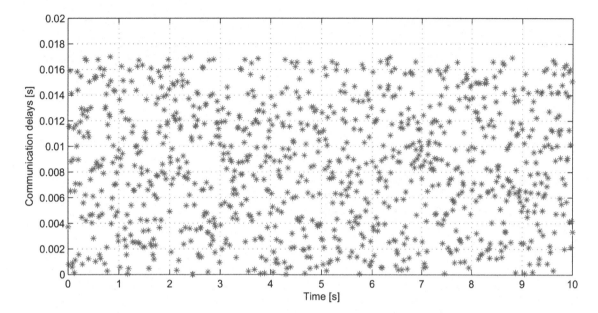

In Figure 7 a), the vehicle velocity is represented, as obtained by the three controllers, and it is seen that in terms of rising time all the controllers have almost the same response and the PID controller has a slight overshoot.

In Figure 7 b) one can see that for the first 3 seconds the difference between the engine speed divided by the total gear ratio i_{tot} and the wheel speed (axle wrap rate) is the same for the three controllers. After that, the driveline oscillations go to 0 for the two networked predictive controllers proposed in this chapter and this difference in speeds keeps on oscillating further for the PID controller. Note that the axle wrap rate is proportional to the torque rate and hence to the jerking (acceleration derivative). These increased oscillations frequency are undesirable because they can produce excessive wear to the driveline components and reduced vehicle driveability.

The engine torque is represented in Figure 7 c), where one can see that the constraint on the upper bound of the control signal is satisfied by all tested control strategies.

The oscillations of the drivetrain obtained using the PID controller can also be seen in Figure 7 d), where the driveshaft torque is presented; the longitudinal oscillations produced by the PID controller are quite severe and they can be easily felt by the passengers of the vehicle.

Although the response is a little more oscillating for the Lyapunov-based model predictive control technique based on modeling the time-varying delays as disturbances, the fact that the computational time is shorter makes it applicable to physical plants with even faster dynamics.

FUTURE RESEARCH DIRECTIONS

In this chapter two modeling techniques for the network-induced time-varying delays are proposed,but it is assumed that the delays introduced by the communication network are boundedand the bounds are

Figure 7. Simulation results

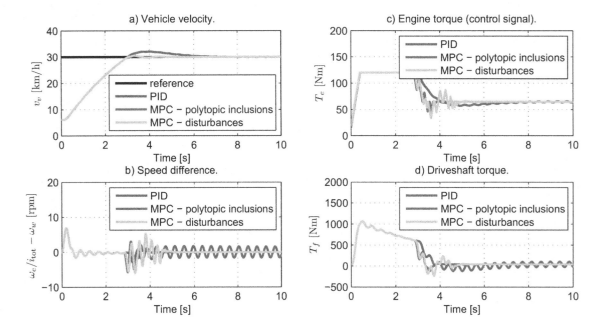

used in the controller design. The remaining questions are how to predict the delaywithout a model and how to design a controller without knowing the bounds of the time-varying delays?

Moreover, in this chapter the delays on the feedback channel are considered as delays in the forward channel and this can be used when the physical plant can be modeled as a linear system. So, the task will be to consider output delays inusing the polytopic over-approximation technique (Gielen et al., 2010). Regarding the second modeling technique, in (Caruntu and Lazar, 2014) a method is proposed to model the feedback channel delays as disturbances and to obtain the bound of this disturbance to be taken into account in the design phase of a model predictive controller.

Furthermore, there are many network-induced imperfections and constraints which are categorized in five types in (Heemels et al., 2010), but, usually, the available literature on NCS considersonly some of them in the analysis of NCS. Throughout this chapter, only network-inducedtime-varying delays are considered in the controller design. It would be also useful toconsider data-packet dropouts, quantization errors, variable sampling/transmission intervalsand the network load (limited communication) in the controller design.

CONCLUSION

In this chaptertwo methods of modeling the network-induced time-varying delays were discussed: one based on modeling the delays using polytopic approximations and one based on modeling the delays as disturbances. For each modeling method, a Lyapunov-based model predictive control technique was designed to minimize the drivetrain oscillations and to handle both the performance/physical constraints and the variable time-delays. The concept of flexible control Lyapunov functions was employed to obtain a non-conservative stability guarantee for the developedMPC schemes.

A simulation experiment validated the proposed approaches and indicated that the developed schemes have the potential to meet the required real-time control specifications. The results obtained with the proposed methods were compared with the results obtained with a classical controller (PID) and the comparison illustrates that the proposed controller has an overall superior performance and it meets the required timing constraints.

REFERENCES

Berriri, M., Chevrel, P., & Lefebvre, D. (2008). Active damping of automotive powertrain oscillation by a partial torque compensator. *Control Engineering Practice*, *16*(7), 874–883. doi:10.1016/j.conengprac.2007.10.010

Canale, M., Fagiano, L., & Novara, C. (2006). Semiactive suspension control using "fast" model predictive techniques. *IEEE Transactions on Control Systems Technology*, *14*(6), 1034–1046. doi:10.1109/TCST.2006.880196

Canale, M., Fagiano, L., & Razza, V. (2010). Approximate NMPC for vehicle stability: Design, implementation and SIL testing. *Control Engineering Practice*, *18*(6), 630–639. doi:10.1016/j.conengprac.2010.03.002

Caruntu, C. F., Balau, A. E., Lazar, M., van den Bosch, P. P. J., & Di Cairano, S. (2011). A predictive control solution for driveline oscillations damping. In Hybrid systems: Computation and Control (pp. 181-190). Chicago, IL: Academic Press. doi:10.1145/1967701.1967728

Caruntu, C. F., & Lazar, C. (2012). Robustly stabilising model predictive control design for networked control systems with an application to direct current motors. *IET Control Theory & Applications*, *6*(7), 943–952. doi:10.1049/iet-cta.2011.0103

Caruntu, C. F., & Lazar, C. (2014). Network delay predictive compensation based on time-delay modelling as disturbance. *International Journal of Control*, *87*(10), 2012–2026.

Caruntu, C. F., Lazar, M., Di Cairano, S., Gielen, R. H., & van den Bosch, P. P. J. (2011). Horizon-1 predictive control of networked controlled vehicle drivetrains. *18th IFAC World Congress*, 3824-3830. doi:10.3182/20110828-6-IT-1002.02780

Caruntu, C. F., Lazar, M., Gielen, R. H., van den Bosch, P. P. J., & Di Cairano, S. (2013). Lyapunov based predictive control of vehicle drivetrains over CAN. *Control Engineering Practice*, *21*(12), 1881–1898. doi:10.1016/j.conengprac.2012.05.012

Cloosterman, M. B. G., Hetel, L., van de Wouw, N., Heemels, W. P. M. H., Daafouz, J., & Nijmeijer, H. (2010). Controller synthesis for networked control systems. *Automatica*, *46*(10), 1584–1594. doi:10.1016/j.automatica.2010.06.017

Cloosterman, M. B. G., van de Wouw, N., Heemels, W. P. M. H., & Nijmeijer, H. (2009). Stability of networked control systems with uncertain time-varying delays. *IEEE Transactions on Automatic Control*, *54*(7), 1575–1580. doi:10.1109/TAC.2009.2015543

Di Cairano, S., Bemporad, A., Kolmanovsky, I. V., & Hrovat, D. (2007). Model predictive control of magnetically actuated mass spring dampers for automotive applications. *International Journal of Control*, *80*(11), 1701–1716. doi:10.1080/00207170701379804

Di Cairano, S., Yanakiev, D., Bemporad, A., Kolmanovsky, I., & Hrovat, D. (2010). Model predictive powertrain control: An application to idle speed regulation. In L. del Re et al. (Eds.), Automotive Model Predictive Control (pp. 183-194). Springer-Verlag Berlin Heidelberg.

Gielen, R. H., & Lazar, M. (2009a). Stabilization of networked control systems via non-monotone control Lyapunov functions. In *48th IEEE Conference on Decision and Control* (pp. 7942-7948). Shanghai, China: IEEE. doi:10.1109/CDC.2009.5400139

Gielen, R. H., & Lazar, M. (2011). Stabilization of polytopic delay difference inclusions via the Razumikhin approach. *Automatica*, *47*(12), 2562–2570. doi:10.1016/j.automatica.2011.08.046

Gielen, R. H., Olaru, S., Lazar, M., Heemels, W. P. M. H., van de Wouw, N., & Niculescu, S.-I. (2010). On polytopic inclusions as a modeling framework for systems with time-varying delays. *Automatica*, *46*(3), 615–619. doi:10.1016/j.automatica.2010.01.002

Heemels, W. P. M. H., Teel, A. R., van de Wouw, N., & Nesic, D. (2010). Networked control systems with communication constraints: Tradeoffs between transmission intervals, delays and performance. *IEEE Transactions on Automatic Control*, *55*(8), 1781–1796. doi:10.1109/TAC.2010.2042352

Hermans, R. M., Lazar, M., Di Cairano, S., & Kolmanovsky, I. V. (2009). Low complexity model predictive control of electromagnetic actuators with a stability guarantee. In *28th American Control Conference* (pp. 2708-2713). St. Louis, MO: Academic Press. doi:10.1109/ACC.2009.5160328

Herpel, T., Hielscher, K. S., Klehmet, U., & German, R. (2009). Stochastic and deterministic performance evaluation of automotive CAN communication. *Computer Networks*, *53*(8), 1171–1185. doi:10.1016/j.comnet.2009.02.008

Hespanha, J., Naghshtabrizi, P., & Xu, Y. (2007). A survey of recent results in networked control systems. *Proceedings of the IEEE - Special Issue on Technology of Networked Control Systems, 95*(1), 138-162. doi:10.1109/JPROC.2006.887288

Hrovat, D., Asgari, J., & Fodor, M. (2000). Automotive mechatronic systems. In C. T. Leondes (Ed.), *Mechatronic Systems Techniques and Applications* (Vol. 2, pp. 1–98). CRC Press.

Huang, C., Bai, Y., & Liu, X. (2010). H-infinity state feedback control for a class of networked cascade control systems with uncertain delay. *IEEE Transactions on Industrial Informatics*, *6*(1), 62–72. doi:10.1109/TII.2009.2033589

Jiang, Z. P., & Wang, Y. (2001). Input-to-state stability for discrete-time nonlinear systems. *Automatica*, *37*(6), 857–869. doi:10.1016/S0005-1098(01)00028-0

Kiencke, U., & Nielsen, L. (2005). *Automotive control systems: For engine, driveline, and vehicle*. Springer-Verlag Berlin. doi:10.1007/b137654

Lazar, M. (2006). *Model predictive control of hybrid systems: Stability and robustness* (PhD thesis). Eindhoven University of Technology, The Netherlands.

Lazar, M. (2009). Flexible control Lyapunov functions. In *28th American Control Conference* (pp. 102-107). St. Louis, MO: Academic Press.

Lazar, M., & Heemels, W. P. M. H. (2008). Optimized input-to-state stabilization of discrete-time non-linear systems with bounded inputs. In *27th American Control Conference* (pp. 2310-2315). Seattle, WA: Academic Press. doi:10.1109/ACC.2008.4586836

Lazar, M., Heemels, W. P. M. H., Weiland, S., & Bemporad, A. (2006). Stabilizing model predictive control of hybrid systems. *IEEE Transactions on Automatic Control, 51*(11), 1813–1818. doi:10.1109/TAC.2006.883059

Le Boudec, J.-Y., & Thiran, P. (2001). *Network calculus*. Springer-Verlag Berlin. doi:10.1007/3-540-45318-0

Li, H., & Shi, Y. (2013). Output feedback predictive control for constrained linear systems with inter-mittent measurements. *Systems & Control Letters, 62*(4), 345–354. doi:10.1016/j.sysconle.2013.01.003

Li, H., Sun, Z., Liu, H., & Chow, M. Y. (2008). Predictive observer-based control for networked control systems with network-induced delay and packet dropout. *Asian Journal of Control, 10*(6), 638–650. doi:10.1002/asjc.65

Liu, G. P., Xia, Y., Chen, J., Rees, D., & Hu, W. (2007). Networked predictive control of systems with random network delays in both forward and feedback channels. *IEEE Transactions on Industrial Electronics, 54*(3), 1282–1297. doi:10.1109/TIE.2007.893073

Liu, X., Xia, Y., Mahmoud, M. S., & Deng, Z. (2010). Modeling and stabilization of MIMO networked control systems with network constraints. *International Journal of Innovative Computing, Information, & Control, 6*(10), 4409–4419.

Maciejowski, J. M. (2002). *Predictive control with constraints*. Harlow: Prentice Hall.

Munoz de la Pena, D., & Christofides, P. D. (2008). Lyapunov-based model predictive control of nonlinear systems subject to data losses. *IEEE Transactions on Automatic Control, 53*(9), 2076–2089. doi:10.1109/TAC.2008.929401

Natori, K., Oboe, R., & Ohnishi, K. (2008). Stability analysis and practical design procedure of time delayed control systems with communication disturbance observer. *IEEE Transactions on Industrial Informatics, 4*(3), 185–197. doi:10.1109/TII.2008.2002705

Naus, G. (2010). *Model-based control for automotive applications* (PhD Thesis). Eindhoven University of Technology, The Netherlands.

O'Dwyer, A. (2006). *Handbook of PI and PID controller tuning rules*. London: Imperial College Press. doi:10.1142/p424

Onat, A., Naskali, A. T., & Parlakay, E. (2008). Model based predictive networked control systems. In *17th IFAC World Congress* (pp. 13000-13005). Seoul, Korea: Academic Press.

Pettersson, M. (1997). *Driveline modeling and control* (PhD Thesis). Linkoping University, Sweden.

Rawlings, J. B., & Mayne, D. Q. (2009). *Model predictive control: Theory and design.* Nob Hill Publishing.

Rostalski, P., Besselmann, T., Maric, M., Van Belsen, F., & Morari, M. (2007). A hybrid approach to modelling control and state estimation of mechanical, systems with backlash. *International Journal of Control, 80*(11), 1729–1740. doi:10.1080/00207170701493985

Saerens, B., Diehl, M., Swevers, J., & Van den Bulck, E. (2008). Model predictive control of automotive powertrains—First experimental results. In *47th IEEE Conference on Decision and Control* (pp. 5692-5697). Cancun, Mexico: Academic Press. doi:10.1109/CDC.2008.4738740

Shi, Y., & Yu, B. (2011). Robust mixed *H2/H∞* control of networked control systems with random time delays in both forward and backward communication links. *Automatica, 47*(4), 754–760. doi:10.1016/j. automatica.2011.01.022

Sontag, E. D., & Wang, Y. (1995). On characterizations of the input-to-state stability property. *Systems & Control Letters, 24*(5), 351–359. doi:10.1016/0167-6911(94)00050-6

Stewart, P., Zavala, J., & Flemming, P. (2005). Automotive drive by wire controller design by multi-objectives techniques. *Control Engineering Practice, 13*(2), 257–264. doi:10.1016/j.conengprac.2004.03.010

Templin, P. (2008). Simultaneous estimation of driveline dynamics and backlash size for control design. In *IEEE International Conference on Control Applications* (pp. 13-18). San Antonio, TX: IEEE. doi:10.1109/CCA.2008.4629642

Van Der Heijden, A., Serrarens, F., Camlibel, M., & Nijmeijer, H. (2007). Hybrid optimal control of dry clutch engagement. *International Journal of Control, 80*(11), 1717–1728. doi:10.1080/00207170701473995

Yoo, D. K., & Wang, L. (2007). Model based wheel slip control via constrained optimal algorithm. In *IEEE International Conference on Control Applications* (pp. 1239-1246). Singapore: IEEE.

Yu, B., Shi, Y., & Huang, J. (2011). Modified generalized predictive control of networked systems with application to a hydraulic position control system. *ASME Journal of Dynamic Systems, Measurement, and Control, 133*(3), 031009-1, 031009–9. doi:10.1115/1.4003385

Yue, D., Tian, E., Zhang, Y., & Peng, C. (2009). Delay-distribution-dependent robust stability of uncertain systems with time-varying delay. *International Journal of Robust and Nonlinear Control, 19*(4), 377–393. doi:10.1002/rnc.1314

Zhao, Y. B., Liu, G. P., & Rees, D. (2010). Packet-based dead-band control for internet-based networked control systems. *IEEE Transactions on Control Systems Technology, 18*(5), 1057–1067. doi:10.1109/TCST.2009.2033118

KEY TERMS AND DEFINITIONS

Control Lyapunov Function: A Lyapunov function for a system with control inputs.

Controller Area Network: A vehicle bus standard designed to allow microcontrollers and devices to communicate with each other in applications without a host computer.

Flexible Control Lyapunov Function: A Lyapunov function for a system with control inputs that is time-variant and trajectory-dependent.

Model Predictive Control: An advanced method of process control based on using a model of the process to predict at each sampling instant the future evolution of the system from the current state along a given prediction horizon.

Network Disturbance: A method through which the network-induced imperfections are modeled as disturbances.

Network-Induced Delay: A time-delay introduced in sending data from one node of the networked control system to another.

Networked Control System: A spatially distributed control system in which its components (controller, actuator, sensor) exchange information through a real-time communication network.

Polytopic Approximation: A method for reachable set computation that gives anover-approximation of the exact reachable set which is computationally efficient.

Vehicle Drivetrain: The mechanical system that transmits the engine power to the driving wheels.

Chapter 6

Modeling and Dynamic Surface Control of Uncertain Strict–Feedback Nonlinear Systems Using Adaptive Fuzzy Wavelet Network

Maryam Shahriari-Kahkeshi
Shahrekord University, Iran

ABSTRACT

This chapter proposes a new modeling and control scheme for uncertain strict-feedback nonlinear systems based on adaptive fuzzy wavelet network (FWN) and dynamic surface control (DSC) approach. It designs adaptive FWN as a nonlinear-in-parameter approximator to approximate the uncertain dynamics of the system. Then, the proposed control scheme is developed by incorporating the DSC method to the adaptive FWN-based model. Stability analysis of the proposed scheme is provided and adaptive laws are designed to learn all linear and nonlinear parameters of the network. It is proven that all the signals of the closed-loop system are uniformly ultimately bounded and the tracking error can be made arbitrary small. The proposed scheme does not require any prior knowledge about dynamics of the system and offline learning. Furthermore, it eliminates the "explosion of complexity" problems and develops accurate model of the system and simple controller. Simulation results on the numerical example and permanent magnet synchronous motor are provided to show the effectiveness of the proposed scheme.

1. INTRODUCTION

Recently, approximator-based adaptive backstepping control approaches have been widely applied for the control of a wide class of uncertain nonlinear systems in (Yang and Zhou, 2005, Wang, Chen, and Dai, 2007, Tong, C. Li, and Y. Li, 2009, Tong and Li, 2009, Chen and Zhang, 2010 and Wang, Liu, Zhang, X. Chen and C.L.P. Chen, 2015). In these studies, many approximators such as neural networks (NNs),

DOI: 10.4018/978-1-5225-3531-7.ch006

fuzzy systems (FSs) and wavelet functions are used to approximate the unknown nonlinear dynamics of the system and then adaptive backstepping technique is applied to provide a systematic framework for the controller design. The developed approaches handle wide class of uncertain nonlinear systems. For example, they can apply to the uncertain nonlinear systems that their uncertainty does not satisfy the matching condition, or their uncertainty cannot be linearly parameterized, or their uncertainty is completely unknown. However, they suffer the "explosion of complexity" problem which is caused by the repeated differentiations of virtual control inputs in the backstepping control design.

To overcome this problem, Swaroop, Hedrick, Yip, and Gerdes (2000) proposed a dynamic surface control (DSC) approach that introduces a first-order low-pass filter at each step of the backstepping design procedure to eliminate the "explosion of complexity" problem. After (Swaroop et al. 2000), several adaptive approximator-based DSC schemes have been developed in (Wang and Huang, 2005, Zhang and Ge, 2008, Xu, Shi, Yang, and Sun 2014, Tong, Y-M. Li, Feng, and T-S Li 2011a and Tong, Yu. Li, Yo. Li, and Liu, 2011b).

Wang and Huang (2005) developed a radial basis function NN-based adaptive tracking control scheme for a class of uncertain nonlinear systems. Then, the adaptive NN-based DSC scheme of Wang and Huang (2005) was extended to a general class of pure feedback SISO systems in (Zhang and Ge, 2008). Composite adaptive tracking control for a class of uncertain nonlinear systems in strict feedback form was studied by (Xu et al. 2014). The authors of Tong et al. (2011a) and Tong et al. (2011b) developed an adaptive fuzzy backstepping dynamic surface control approach for a class of MIMO nonlinear systems and uncertain stochastic nonlinear strict-feedback systems. Adaptive fuzzy output feedback control was designed for uncertain nonlinear systems with unmodeled dynamics using DSC technique by Liu, Tong, and Chen (2013). Some extensions and applications of approximator-based DSC scheme can be found in (Li, Tong, and Feng, 2010a, Li, Wang, Feng, and Tong, 2010b, Yu, Shi, Dong, Chen, Lin, 2015, H. Wang, D. Wang, and Peng, 2014; Y. Li, Tong, T. Li, 2015 and Chang and Chen, 2014).

The aforementioned control schemes suffer the "explosion of learning parameters" or "curse of dimensionality" problem. This problem is caused due to applications of NN or FLS approximator as a linear-in-parameter approximator to handle uncertain systems. To achieve a better approximation result in the NN or FS approximators-based adaptive schemes, the number of parameters to be tuned online is very large, especially for high-dimensional systems, so the learning time tends to become unacceptably long when implemented. Therefore, the complexity of the controller drastically grows as the order of the system increases.

In this work, to overcome the mentioned problems and achieve better learning performance, an adaptive fuzzy wavelet network-based control scheme, which is performed by incorporating the DSC approach and adaptive FWN, is developed for uncertain nonlinear systems in the strict-feedback form. The FWN preserves ability of wavelet transform for analyzing nonstationary signals to present their local details, ability of FLSs for reducing the complexity and uncertainty of the system and learning ability of NNs. Therefore, it has fast learning capability and high computational strength, which made it as a powerful tool for approximation purposes. Some applications of the FWN can be found in the works of Zekri, Sheikholeslam, and Sadri (2008), Mousavi, Noroozi, Safavi, and Ebadat (2011), Lu (2011), Shahriari-kahkeshi, and Sheikholeslam (2014) and Loussifi, Nourim, and Braiek (2016).

In this work, to overcome the mentioned problems and achieve better learning performance, a new modeling and control scheme is developed for uncertain strict-feedback nonlinear systems. It designs adaptive FWN to represent the model of the uncertain dynamics of the system and then incorporates the DSC technique into the developed adaptive FWN-based model. It proposes a systematic design procedure to develop the control scheme and develops adaptive learning laws to tune all parameters of the AFWN approximator for modeling uncertain dynamics of the system. Furthermore, it guarantees that for any sufficiently smooth desired input, all the signals of the closed-loop systems are uniformly ultimately bounded and the tracking error can be made arbitrary small.

The main advantages of the proposed schemes can be summarized as follows: (i) both problems of "explosion of complexity" and "explosion of learning parameters" are omitted simultaneously, which lead to a simple controller with less computational cost. (ii) Design of adaptive FWN to model the uncertain dynamics of the system during real time operation, without requiring any prior knowledge about uncertainty, offline learning phase and computational cost. (iii) Development of adaptive laws to learn the weights of the network and dilation and translation parameters of the wavelet functions based on Lyapunov stability theorem. (iv) Furthermore, unlike the backstepping-based schemes, the proposed scheme does not require the availability and boundedness of all derivatives of the reference trajectory for controller design.

The reminder of this chapter is organized as follows. A class of uncertain nonlinear systems and control objectives are first described in section 2. The proposed modeling and control scheme and stability analysis of the closed-loop system are provided in section 3. To show the effectiveness of the proposed scheme, some simulation results are presented in section 4. Finally, some conclusions are given in section 5.

2. PROBLEM FORMULATION

Consider a class of nonlinear uncertain systems that are described by the following differential equation:

$$
\begin{aligned}
\dot{x}_1 &= f_1(x_1) + g_1(x_1)x_2 \\
\dot{x}_2 &= f_2(x_1, x_2) + g_2(x_1, x_2)x_3 \\
&\vdots \\
\dot{x}_i &= f_i(x_1, x_2, \ldots, x_i) + g_i(x_1, x_2, \ldots, x_i)x_{i+1} \\
&\vdots \\
\dot{x}_n &= f_n(\mathbf{x}_n) + g_n(\mathbf{x}_n)u \\
y &= x_1
\end{aligned}
\tag{1}
$$

where x_i, $i = 1, 2, \ldots, n$, is the state variable, $\mathbf{x}_n = [x_1, x_2, \ldots, x_n]^T \in R^n$ is the state vector, $u \in R$ is the control input and $y \in R$ is the system output. Terms $f_i(\mathbf{x}_i)$ for $i = 1, 2, \ldots, n$, $\mathbf{x}_i = [x_1, x_2, \ldots, x_i]^T \in R^i$, represents the unknown smooth nonlinear function and $g_i(\mathbf{x}_i)$ for $i = 1, 2, \ldots, n$ denotes the known smooth virtual control gain functions.

The control objective is to design a new modeling and control scheme based on the adaptive FWN and DSC approach for uncertain nonlinear system (1) such that all the signals of the resulting closed-loop system be uniformly ultimately bounded and the tracking error can be made arbitrary small. Since system is uncertain and its nonlinear functions $f_i(\mathbf{x}_i)$, $i = 1, 2, \ldots, n$ are unknown, adaptive FWN as a nonlinear-in-parameter approximator is designed to represent the model of unknown functions of the system. Then, DSC controller is designed based on the presented model; also, adaptive learning laws are developed to tune the weights of the network and dilation and translation parameters of the wavelet functions, on-line. Throughout the paper, following Assumptions are made:

Assumption 1: It is assumed that the desired command $y_d(t)$ is a sufficiently smooth function of t and y_d, $\dot{y}_d$ and $\ddot{y}_d$ are bounded, i.e., there exists a positive constant B such that $\Pi := \{(y_d, \dot{y}_d, \ddot{y}_d) : y_d^2 + \dot{y}_d^2 + \ddot{y}_d^2 \leq B\}$ (Swaroop et al., 2000).

Assumption 2: There exist some constants $\overline{g}_{li} > 0$, $\overline{g}_{hi} > 0$ for $i = 1, 2, ..., n$ such that $\overline{g}_{il} \leq |g_i(x_1, x_2, ..., x_n)| \leq \overline{g}_{hi}$.

3. THE PROPOSED MODELING AND CONTROL SCHEME AND STABILITY ANALYSIS OF THE CLOSED-LOOP SYSTEM

In this section, at first, adaptive FWN is designed to model the uncertain dynamics of the system. Then, the proposed control scheme is developed based on the adaptive FWN model. In the following, a brief description of FWN is provided.

3.1 Brief Description of the Fuzzy Wavelet Network

The fuzzy wavelet network has been composed of N fuzzy rule in the following form (Lin, 2006):

R^j : If x_1 is A_1^j, x_2 is A_2^j, ... and x_n is A_n^j, Then $f_1^j = \theta_{1j}\psi(d_{1j}(x_1 - t_{1j}))$ ... $f_2^j = \theta_{2j}\prod_{i=1}^{2}\psi(d_{ij}(x_i - t_{ij}))$ ...

and $f_n^j = \theta_{nj}\prod_{i=1}^{n}\psi(d_{ij}(x_i - t_{ij}))$ (2)

where x_1, x_2, ..., x_n are the input variables of the network, f_i^j ($i = 1, 2, ..., n$, $j = 1, 2, ..., N$) is the output variable of the network, $\theta_{ij} \in R$ is the weight of the output layer, $\psi(d_{ij}(x_i - t_{ij}))$ is a wavelet family that is obtained from a single mother wavelet function by translation and dilation parameters (t_{ij}, d_{ij}) and A_i^j denotes the linguistic term characterized by the Gaussian type fuzzy membership function as follows:

$$A_i^j(x_i) = \exp\left[-d_{ij}^2\left(x_i - t_{ij}\right)^2\right]$$ (3)

where d_{ij} and t_{ij} determine the inverse of width and center of the corresponding membership function that are chosen as the same as the dilation and translation parameters of wavelet functions. Using the well-known TSK fuzzy inference system, the output of the FWN is calculated as:

$$f_i(\mathbf{x}_i) = \sum_{j=1}^{N} \theta_{ij} \varphi_j(\mathbf{x}_i, \mathbf{d}_i, \mathbf{t}_i) \tag{4}$$

where $i = 1, 2, ..., n$ and $\varphi_j(\mathbf{x}_i, \mathbf{d}_i, \mathbf{t}_i)$ is the multidimensional fuzzy wavelet basis function which is represented by the product of the one dimensional fuzzy wavelet basis functions as follows:

$$\varphi_j(\mathbf{x}_i, d_{ij}, t_i) = \varphi_j(x_1, d_{1j}, t_{1j}) \varphi_j(x_2, d_{2j}, t_{2j}) ... \varphi_j(x_i, d_{ij}, t_{ij}) \tag{5}$$

where $\varphi_j(x_i, d_{ij}, t_{ij}) = \left[1 - d_{ij}^2 \left(x_i - c_{ij}\right)^2\right] \exp\left[-d_{ij}^2 \left(x_i - c_{ij}\right)^2\right]$. For notation simplicity, the output of the FWN model in (5) is written as:

$$f_i(\mathbf{x}_i; \boldsymbol{\theta}_i, \mathbf{d}_i, \mathbf{t}_i) = \boldsymbol{\theta}_i^T \boldsymbol{\varphi}(\mathbf{x}_i, \mathbf{d}_i, \mathbf{t}_i) \tag{6}$$

where $i = 1, 2, ..., n$, $\mathbf{x}_i = [x_1, x_2, ..., x_i]^T \in R^i$, $\boldsymbol{\theta}_i \in R^{N \times 1}$ denotes the weight vector and $\boldsymbol{\varphi} = [\varphi_1, \varphi_2, ..., \varphi_N]^T \in R^{N \times 1}$ is the vector of fuzzy wavelet basis functions. $\mathbf{d}_i = [d_{i1}, d_{i1} \ ... \ d_{iN}]^T \in R^{Ni}$ and $\mathbf{t}_i = [t_{i1}, t_{i2} \ ... \ t_{iN}]^T \in R^{N \times 1}$ represent the vector of dilation and translation parameters, respectively. According to the approximation property of the FWN in Lin (2006), there exists an optimal parameter vectors $\boldsymbol{\theta}_i^*$, $\mathbf{d}_i^*$ and $\mathbf{t}_i^*$ such that the FWN can approximate any continues real value function $f_i(\mathbf{x}_i)$ as:

$$f_i(\mathbf{x}_i) = \boldsymbol{\theta}_i^{*T} \boldsymbol{\varphi}(\mathbf{x}_i, \mathbf{d}_i^*, \mathbf{t}_i^*) + \delta_i^*(\mathbf{x}_i) \tag{7}$$

where δ_i^* is the approximation error which is unknown bout bounded, i.e. $\left\| \delta_i^* \right\| < \bar{\delta}_i$; also, ideal parameter vectors are norm bounded; i.e., $\boldsymbol{\theta}_i^{*T} \boldsymbol{\theta}_i^* \leq \bar{\theta}$, $\mathbf{d}_i^{*T} \mathbf{d}_i^* \leq \bar{d}$ and $\mathbf{t}_i^{*T} \mathbf{t}_i^* \leq \bar{t}$. However, the optimal parameter vectors are unknown; so, it is necessary to adjust them. Define the approximation of the uncertain function $f_i(\mathbf{x}_i)$ as follows:

$$\hat{f}_i(\mathbf{x}_i; \hat{\boldsymbol{\theta}}_i, \hat{\mathbf{d}}_i, \hat{\mathbf{t}}_i) = \hat{\boldsymbol{\theta}}_i^T \boldsymbol{\varphi}(\mathbf{x}_i, \hat{\mathbf{d}}_i, \hat{\mathbf{t}}_i) \tag{8}$$

where $\hat{\boldsymbol{\theta}}_i$, $\hat{\mathbf{d}}_i$ and $\hat{\mathbf{t}}_i$ are the estimation of the $\boldsymbol{\theta}_i^*$, $\mathbf{d}_i^*$ and $\mathbf{t}_i^*$, respectively. The structure of the FWN as a nonlinear-in-parameter approximator for modeling purpose is shown in Figure 1.

In the following, for ease of notation simplicity, φ^* and $\hat{\varphi}$ are used to denote the ideal and estimated fuzzy wavelet basis function $\varphi^* = \varphi(\mathbf{x}_i, \mathbf{d}_i^*, \mathbf{t}_i^*)$ and $\hat{\varphi} = \varphi(\mathbf{x}_i, \hat{\mathbf{d}}_i, \hat{\mathbf{t}}_i)$, respectively.

Figure 1. Structure of the adaptive FWN for modeling

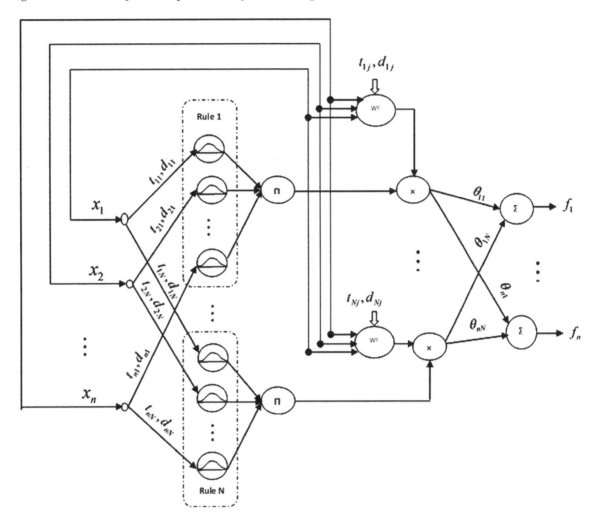

3.2 Design of the Proposed Control Scheme

In this section, the proposed control scheme is designed based on the adaptive FWN. The recursive design procedure of the DSC-based control scheme contains n steps (Swaroop et al., 2000). From step 1 to n-1, the virtual control v_{i+1}, $i = 1, 2, ..., n-1$, are designed at each step. Finally, an overall control input u is constructed at step n. The design procedure is as follows:

Step 1: The first error surface is defined as

$$S_1 = y - y_d \tag{9}$$

Considering (1) and (7), the time derivative of S_1 is obtained as:

$$\dot{S}_1 = g_1 x_2 + \boldsymbol{\theta}_1^{*T} \boldsymbol{\varphi}_1^* + \delta_1^* - \dot{y}_d \tag{10}$$

Choose a virtual control v_2 as:

$$v_2 = g_1^{-1} \left(-\hat{\boldsymbol{\theta}}_1^T \hat{\boldsymbol{\varphi}}_1 - k_1 S_1 + \dot{y}_d \right) \tag{11}$$

where $k_1 > 0$ is a design parameter. In order to avoid the repeated differentiations which cause "explosion complexity" problem in the backstepping approach, virtual input v_2 is passed through the first-order filter with time constant τ_2 to obtain v_{2f}

$$\tau_2 \dot{v}_{2f} + v_{2f} = v_2, \quad v_{2f}(0) = v_2(0) \tag{12}$$

Step i ($2 \leq i \leq n - 1$): Analogous to the step 1, the ith error surface is defined as:

$$s_i = x_i - v_{if} \tag{13}$$

where $v_{if} \in R$ is the filtered virtual control input. Considering (1), (7) and (13), the dynamics of the ith error surface is obtained as:

$$\dot{s}_i = g_i x_{i+1} + \boldsymbol{\theta}_i^{*T} \boldsymbol{\varphi}_i^* + \delta_i^* - \dot{v}_{if} \tag{14}$$

Now, the ith virtual control is chosen as:

$$v_{i+1} = g_i^{-1} \left(-\hat{\boldsymbol{\theta}}_i^T \hat{\boldsymbol{\varphi}}_i - k_i s_i + \dot{v}_{if} \right) \tag{15}$$

where $k_i > 0$, $i = 2, \ldots, n - 1$ is a design parameters.

Let v_{i+1} pass through the first-order filter with time constant τ_{i+1} to obtain the ith filtered virtual control $v_{(i+1)f}$, that is:

$$\tau_{i+1} \dot{v}_{(i+1)f} + v_{(i+1)f} = v_{i+1}, \quad i = 2, \ldots, n - 1 \tag{16}$$

Step n: At the final design step, similar to the above procedure, the *n*th error surface is defined as:

$$s_n = x_n - v_{nf} \tag{17}$$

Considering (1), (7) and (17), the time derivative of s_n is obtained as

$$\dot{s}_n = g_n u + \boldsymbol{\theta}_n^{*T} \boldsymbol{\varphi}_n^* + \delta_n^* - \dot{v}_{nf} \tag{18}$$

and the actual control input u is proposed as:

$$u = g_n^{-1} \left(-\hat{\boldsymbol{\theta}}_n^T \hat{\boldsymbol{\varphi}}_n - k_n s_n + \dot{v}_{nf} \right) \tag{19}$$

where $k_n > 0$ is a design parameter. For the stability analysis, the following boundary layer error is defined:

$$\boldsymbol{\varpi}_{i+1} = v_{(i+1)f} - v_{(i+1)} \quad , \quad i = 1, \ldots, n-1 \tag{20}$$

So, the derivative of each error surface is written as:

$$\begin{aligned}
\dot{S}_1 &= g_1 S_2 - k_1 S_1 + g_1 \boldsymbol{\varpi}_2 + \boldsymbol{\theta}_1^{*T} \boldsymbol{\varphi}_1^* + \delta_1^* - \hat{\boldsymbol{\theta}}_1^T \hat{\boldsymbol{\varphi}}_1 \\
\dot{S}_2 &= g_2 S_3 - k_2 S_2 + g_2 \boldsymbol{\varpi}_3 + \boldsymbol{\theta}_2^{*T} \boldsymbol{\varphi}_2^* + \delta_2^* - \hat{\boldsymbol{\theta}}_2^T \hat{\boldsymbol{\varphi}}_2 \\
&\vdots \\
\dot{S}_i &= g_i S_{i+1} - k_i S_i + g_i \boldsymbol{\varpi}_{i+1} + \boldsymbol{\theta}_i^{*T} \boldsymbol{\varphi}_i^* + \delta_i^* - \hat{\boldsymbol{\theta}}_i^T \hat{\boldsymbol{\varphi}}_i \\
&\vdots \\
\dot{S}_n &= -k_n S_n + \boldsymbol{\theta}_n^{*T} \boldsymbol{\varphi}_n^* + \delta_n^* - \hat{\boldsymbol{\theta}}_n^T \hat{\boldsymbol{\varphi}}_n
\end{aligned} \tag{21}$$

Now, differentiating (20), results

$$\dot{\boldsymbol{\varpi}}_{i+1} = -\frac{\boldsymbol{\varpi}_{i+1}}{\tau_{i+1}} + B_{i+1}(s_1, \ldots, s_n, \boldsymbol{\varpi}_2, \ldots, \boldsymbol{\varpi}_n, \hat{\boldsymbol{\theta}}_1^T, \ldots, \hat{\boldsymbol{\theta}}_n^T, y_d, \dot{y}_d, \ddot{y}_d) \quad , \quad i = 1, \ldots, n-1 \tag{22}$$

where

$$B_2 = \frac{1}{\left(g_1\right)^2} \left[\left(\dot{\hat{\boldsymbol{\theta}}}_1^T \hat{\boldsymbol{\varphi}}_1 + \hat{\boldsymbol{\theta}}_1^T \dot{\hat{\boldsymbol{\varphi}}}_1 + k_1 \dot{S}_1 - \ddot{y}_d \right) g_1 - \dot{g}_1 \left(\hat{\boldsymbol{\theta}}_1^T \hat{\boldsymbol{\varphi}}_1 + k_1 S_1 - \dot{y}_d \right) \right]$$

and

$$B_{i+1} = \frac{1}{\left(g_i\right)^2} \left[\left(\dot{\hat{\boldsymbol{\theta}}}_i^T \hat{\boldsymbol{\varphi}}_i + \hat{\boldsymbol{\theta}}_i^T \dot{\hat{\boldsymbol{\varphi}}}_i + k_i \dot{s}_i + \frac{\dot{\boldsymbol{\varpi}}_i}{\tau_i} \right) g_i - \dot{g}_i \left(\hat{\boldsymbol{\theta}}_i^T \hat{\boldsymbol{\varphi}}_i + k_i S_i + \frac{\boldsymbol{\varpi}_i}{\tau_i} \right) \right]$$

for $i = 2, \ldots, n-1$ is a continuous function (Wang & Huang, 2005).

Theorem 1

Consider the nonlinear system (1). Under Assumption 1 and 2, for any initial conditions satisfying $V(0) \leq \alpha$, where α is a positive constant, the control law (19), the intermediate virtual control (11), (15) and the following adaptive laws guarantee that all signals of the resulting closed-loop system are uniformly ultimately bounded. Moreover, the tracking error can be made arbitrary small by choosing appropriate design parameters.

$$\dot{\hat{\mathbf{d}}}_i = \gamma_1 \left(S_i \boldsymbol{\varphi}_{id}'^{T} \hat{\boldsymbol{\theta}}_i - \sigma \hat{\mathbf{d}}_i \right) \tag{23}$$

$$\dot{\hat{\mathbf{t}}}_i = \gamma_2 \left(S_i \boldsymbol{\varphi}_{i\hat{c}}'^{T} \hat{\boldsymbol{\theta}}_i - \sigma \hat{\mathbf{t}}_i \right) \tag{24}$$

$$\dot{\hat{\boldsymbol{\theta}}}_i = \gamma_3 \left[S_i \left(\hat{\boldsymbol{\varphi}}_i^{T} - \hat{\mathbf{t}}_i^{T} \boldsymbol{\varphi}_{i\hat{t}}' - \hat{\mathbf{d}}_i^{T} \boldsymbol{\varphi}_{id}' \right) - \sigma \hat{\boldsymbol{\theta}}_i \right] \tag{25}$$

where $\boldsymbol{\varphi}_{i\hat{t}}' = \partial \tilde{\boldsymbol{\varphi}}_i / \partial \mathbf{t}_i \big|_{\mathbf{t}_i = \hat{\mathbf{t}}_i}$, $\boldsymbol{\varphi}_{id}' = \partial \tilde{\boldsymbol{\varphi}}_i / \partial \mathbf{d}_i \big|_{\mathbf{d}_i = \hat{\mathbf{d}}_i}$, γ_1, γ_2 and γ_3 are positive design parameters and $\sigma > 0$ is a small constant that denotes the fixed σ-modification term.

Proof

Consider the Lyapunov function candidate

$$V = \frac{1}{2} \sum_{i=1}^{n} S_i^2 + \frac{1}{2} \sum_{i=1}^{n-1} \varpi_{i+1}^2 + \frac{1}{2\gamma_1} \sum_{i=1}^{n} \tilde{\mathbf{d}}_i^T \tilde{\mathbf{d}}_i + \frac{1}{2\gamma_2} \sum_{i=1}^{n} \tilde{\mathbf{t}}_i^T \tilde{\mathbf{t}}_i + \frac{1}{2\gamma_3} \sum_{i=1}^{n} \left(\tilde{\boldsymbol{\theta}}_i^T \tilde{\boldsymbol{\theta}}_i \right)^2 \tag{26}$$

where $\tilde{\mathbf{d}}_i = \mathbf{d}_i^* - \hat{\mathbf{d}}_i$, $\tilde{\mathbf{t}}_i = \mathbf{t}_i^* - \hat{\mathbf{t}}_i$ and $\tilde{\mathbf{w}}_i = \mathbf{w}_i^* - \hat{\mathbf{w}}_i$ are the parameter estimation error. The derivative of the Lyapunov function is found as:

$$
\begin{aligned}
V &= \sum_{i=1}^{n} S_i \dot{S}_i + \sum_{i=1}^{n-1} \varpi_{i+1} \dot{\varpi}_{i+1} - \frac{1}{\gamma_1} \sum_{i=1}^{n} \tilde{\mathbf{d}}_i^T \dot{\hat{\mathbf{d}}}_i - \frac{1}{\gamma_2} \sum_{i=1}^{n} \tilde{\mathbf{t}}_i^T \dot{\hat{\mathbf{t}}}_i - \frac{1}{\gamma_3} \sum_{i=1}^{n} \tilde{\boldsymbol{\theta}}_i^T \dot{\hat{\boldsymbol{\theta}}}_i \\
&= \sum_{i=1}^{n-1} g_i S_i S_{i+1} - \sum_{i=1}^{n} k_i S_i^2 + \sum_{i=1}^{n-1} g_i S_i \varpi_{i+1} + \sum_{i=1}^{n} S_i \left(\boldsymbol{\theta}_i^* \boldsymbol{\varphi}_i^* - \hat{\boldsymbol{\theta}}_i \hat{\boldsymbol{\varphi}}_i + \delta_i^* \right) \\
&\quad + \sum_{i=1}^{n-1} \left(-\frac{\varpi_{i+1}^2}{\tau_{i+1}} + B_{i+1} \varpi_{i+1} \right) - \frac{1}{\gamma_1} \sum_{i=1}^{n} \tilde{\mathbf{d}}_i^T \dot{\hat{\mathbf{d}}}_i - \frac{1}{\gamma_2} \sum_{i=1}^{n} \tilde{\mathbf{t}}_i^T \dot{\hat{\mathbf{t}}}_i - \frac{1}{\gamma_3} \sum_{i=1}^{n} \tilde{\boldsymbol{\theta}}_i^T \dot{\hat{\boldsymbol{\theta}}}_i
\end{aligned} \tag{27}
$$

Let define the estimation error as $\tilde{f}_i = \boldsymbol{\theta}_i^{*T} \boldsymbol{\varphi}_i^* - \hat{\boldsymbol{\theta}}_i^T \hat{\boldsymbol{\varphi}}_i + \delta_i^*$, it can be written as:

$$\tilde{f}_i = \hat{\boldsymbol{\theta}}_i^T \tilde{\boldsymbol{\varphi}}_i + \tilde{\boldsymbol{\theta}}_i^T \hat{\boldsymbol{\varphi}}_i + \tilde{\boldsymbol{\theta}}_i^T \tilde{\boldsymbol{\varphi}}_i + \delta_i^* \tag{28}$$

where $\tilde{\boldsymbol{\varphi}}_i = \boldsymbol{\varphi}_i^* - \hat{\boldsymbol{\varphi}}_i$. By applying Taylor series expansion linearization to $\tilde{\boldsymbol{\varphi}}_i$, we have:

$$\tilde{\boldsymbol{\varphi}}_i = \boldsymbol{\varphi}_{i\mathbf{t}}' \tilde{\mathbf{t}}_i + \boldsymbol{\varphi}_{i\hat{\mathbf{d}}}' \tilde{\mathbf{d}}_i + \mathbf{h}_i(.) \tag{29}$$

where $\boldsymbol{\varphi}_{i\mathbf{t}}' = \partial \tilde{\boldsymbol{\varphi}}_i / \partial \mathbf{t}_i \big|_{\mathbf{t}_i = \hat{\mathbf{t}}_i}$, $\boldsymbol{\varphi}_{i\hat{\mathbf{d}}}' = \partial \tilde{\boldsymbol{\varphi}}_i / \partial \mathbf{d}_i \big|_{\mathbf{d}_i = \hat{\mathbf{d}}_i}$, and $\mathbf{h}_i(.)$ is a vector of high order terms; Substituting (29) into (28) and (27), results

$$\begin{aligned}
\dot{V} = &\sum_{i=1}^{n-1} g_i S_i S_{i+1} - \sum_{i=1}^{n} k_i S_i^2 + \sum_{i=1}^{n-1} g_i S_i \boldsymbol{\varpi}_{i+1} + \sum_{i=1}^{n-1} \left(-\frac{\boldsymbol{\varpi}_{i+1}^2}{\tau_{i+1}} + B_{i+1} \boldsymbol{\varpi}_{i+1} \right) \\
&+ \sum_{i=1}^{n} \left[S_i \hat{\boldsymbol{\theta}}_i^T \boldsymbol{\varphi}_{i\mathbf{t}}' \tilde{\mathbf{t}}_i + S_i \hat{\boldsymbol{\theta}}_i^T \boldsymbol{\varphi}_{i\mathbf{d}}' \tilde{\mathbf{d}}_i + S_i \hat{\boldsymbol{\theta}}_i^T h_i + S_i \tilde{\boldsymbol{\theta}}_i^T \hat{\boldsymbol{\varphi}}_i + S_i \tilde{\boldsymbol{\theta}}_i^T \left(\boldsymbol{\varphi}_{i\mathbf{t}}' \tilde{\mathbf{t}}_i + \boldsymbol{\varphi}_{i\mathbf{d}}' \tilde{\mathbf{d}}_i + h_i(.) \right) + S_i \delta_i^* \right] \\
&- \frac{1}{\gamma_1} \sum_{i=1}^{n} \tilde{\mathbf{d}}_i^T \dot{\hat{\mathbf{d}}}_i - \frac{1}{\gamma_2} \sum_{i=1}^{n} \tilde{\mathbf{t}}_i^T \dot{\hat{\mathbf{t}}}_i - \frac{1}{\gamma_3} \sum_{i=1}^{n} \tilde{\boldsymbol{\theta}}_i^T \dot{\hat{\boldsymbol{\theta}}}_i
\end{aligned} \tag{30}$$

Equation (30) can be written as:

$$\begin{aligned}
\dot{V} \leq &\sum_{i=1}^{n-1} g_i S_i S_{i+1} - \sum_{i=1}^{n} k_i S_i^2 + \sum_{i=1}^{n-1} g_i S_i \boldsymbol{\varpi}_{i+1} + \sum_{i=1}^{n-1} \left(-\frac{\boldsymbol{\varpi}_{i+1}^2}{\tau_{i+1}} + \left| B_{i+1} \boldsymbol{\varpi}_{i+1} \right| \right) \\
&+ \frac{1}{\gamma_1} \sum_{i=1}^{n} \left(-\tilde{\mathbf{d}}_i^T \dot{\hat{\mathbf{d}}}_i + S_i \tilde{\mathbf{d}}_i^T \boldsymbol{\varphi}_{i\mathbf{d}}'^T \hat{\boldsymbol{\theta}}_i \right) + \frac{1}{\gamma_2} \sum_{i=1}^{n} \left(-\tilde{\mathbf{t}}_i^T \dot{\hat{\mathbf{t}}}_i + S_i \tilde{\mathbf{t}}_i^T \boldsymbol{\varphi}_{i\mathbf{t}}'^T \hat{\boldsymbol{\theta}}_i \right) + \sum_{i=1}^{n} S_i \Delta_i \\
&+ \frac{1}{\gamma_3} \sum_{i=1}^{n} \tilde{\boldsymbol{\theta}}_i^T \left(-\dot{\hat{\boldsymbol{\theta}}}_i + \hat{\boldsymbol{\varphi}}_i^T - S_i \hat{\mathbf{t}}_i^T \boldsymbol{\varphi}_{i\mathbf{t}}' - S_i \hat{\mathbf{d}}_i^T \boldsymbol{\varphi}_{i\mathbf{d}}' \right)
\end{aligned} \tag{31}$$

where $\Delta_i = \tilde{\boldsymbol{\theta}}_i^T \boldsymbol{\varphi}_{i\mathbf{t}}' \mathbf{t}_i^* + \tilde{\boldsymbol{\theta}}_i^T \boldsymbol{\varphi}_{i\mathbf{d}}' \mathbf{d}_i^* + \boldsymbol{\theta}_i^{*T} h_i + \delta_i^*$. Using the facts

$$\begin{aligned}
S_i S_{i+1} &\leq S_i^2 + \frac{1}{4} S_{i+1}^2 \\
S_i \boldsymbol{\varpi}_{i+1} &\leq S_i^2 + \frac{1}{4} \boldsymbol{\varpi}_{i+1}^2 \quad , \quad i = 1, 2, ..., n-1 \\
S_i \Delta_i &\leq S_i^2 + \frac{1}{4} \Delta_i^2
\end{aligned} \tag{32}$$

Considering (32), the adaptive learning laws (23)-(25) and Assumption 2, we have:

$$
\begin{aligned}
\dot{V} \leq & \sum_{i=1}^{n-1}\left(\overline{g}_{hi}S_i^2 + \frac{1}{4}\overline{g}_{hi}S_{i+1}^2\right) - \sum_{i=1}^{n}k_iS_i^2 + \sum_{i=1}^{n-1}\left(\overline{g}_{hi}S_i^2 + \frac{1}{4}\overline{g}_{hi}\varpi_{i+1}^2\right) + \sum_{i=1}^{n-1}\left(-\frac{\varpi_{i+1}^2}{\tau_{i+1}} + \left|B_{i+1}\varpi_{i+1}\right|\right) \\
& + \sum_{i=1}^{n}\left(S_i^2 + \frac{1}{4}\Delta_i^2\right) + \sigma\sum_{i=1}^{n}\tilde{\mathbf{t}}_i^T\hat{\mathbf{t}}_i + \sigma\sum_{i=1}^{n}\tilde{\mathbf{d}}_i^T\hat{\mathbf{d}}_i + \sigma\sum_{i=1}^{n}\tilde{\boldsymbol{\theta}}_i^T\hat{\boldsymbol{\theta}}_i \\
\leq & \sum_{i=1}^{n-1}\left(-k_iS_i^2 + 2\overline{g}_{hi}S_i^2 + S_i^2 + \frac{1}{4}\overline{g}_{hi}S_{i+1}^2 + \frac{1}{4}\overline{g}_{hi}\varpi_{i+1}^2 + \frac{1}{4}\Delta_i^2\right) - k_nS_n^2 + \sum_{i=1}^{n-1}\left(-\frac{\varpi_{i+1}^2}{\tau_{i+1}} + \left|B_{i+1}\varpi_{i+1}\right|\right) \\
& + S_n^2 + \frac{1}{4}\Delta_n^2 + \sigma\sum_{i=1}^{n}\tilde{\mathbf{t}}_i^T\hat{\mathbf{t}}_i + \sigma\sum_{i=1}^{n}\tilde{\mathbf{d}}_i^T\hat{\mathbf{d}}_i + \sigma\sum_{i=1}^{n}\tilde{\boldsymbol{\theta}}_i^T\hat{\boldsymbol{\theta}}_i
\end{aligned}
$$

(33)

Using $\tilde{\mathbf{d}}_i^T\hat{\mathbf{d}}_i \leq \frac{1}{2}\left(\left\|\mathbf{d}_i^*\right\|^2 - \left\|\tilde{\mathbf{d}}_i\right\|^2\right)$, $\tilde{\mathbf{t}}_i^T\hat{\mathbf{t}}_i \leq \frac{1}{2}\left(\left\|\mathbf{t}_i^*\right\|^2 - \left\|\tilde{\mathbf{t}}_i\right\|^2\right)$, $\tilde{\boldsymbol{\theta}}_i^T\hat{\boldsymbol{\theta}}_i \leq \frac{1}{2}\left(\left\|\boldsymbol{\theta}_i^*\right\|^2 - \left\|\tilde{\boldsymbol{\theta}}_i\right\|^2\right)$ gives:

$$
\begin{aligned}
\dot{V} \leq & \sum_{i=1}^{n-1}\left(-k_iS_i^2 + 2\overline{g}_{hi}S_i^2 + S_i^2 + \frac{1}{4}\overline{g}_{hi}S_{i+1}^2 + \frac{1}{4}\overline{g}_{hi}\varpi_{i+1}^2 + \frac{1}{4}\Delta_i^2\right) - k_nS_n^2 + \sum_{i=1}^{n-1}\left(-\frac{\varpi_{i+1}^2}{\tau_{i+1}} + \left|B_{i+1}\varpi_{i+1}\right|\right) \\
& + S_n^2 + \frac{1}{4}\Delta_n^2 + \frac{\sigma}{2}\sum_{i=1}^{n}\left(\mathbf{t}_i^{*T}\mathbf{t}_i^* - \tilde{\mathbf{t}}_i^T\tilde{\mathbf{t}}_i\right) + \frac{\sigma}{2}\sum_{i=1}^{n}\left(\mathbf{d}_i^{*T}\mathbf{d}_i^* - \tilde{\mathbf{d}}_i^T\tilde{\mathbf{d}}_i\right) + \frac{\sigma}{2}\sum_{i=1}^{n}\left(\boldsymbol{\theta}_i^{*T}\boldsymbol{\theta}_i^* - \tilde{\boldsymbol{\theta}}_i^T\tilde{\boldsymbol{\theta}}_i\right)
\end{aligned}
$$

(34)

Choose

$$
\begin{aligned}
k_1 &= 2\overline{g}_{h1} + 1 + \lambda \\
k_i &= 2\overline{g}_{hi} + 1 + \frac{1}{4}\overline{g}_{h(i-1)} + \lambda, \quad i = 2,\ldots, n-1 \\
k_n &= 1 + \frac{1}{4}\overline{g}_{h(n-1)} + \lambda
\end{aligned}
$$

(35)

where λ is a positive constant. Also, for any positive number β, we have $\left|B_{i+1}\varpi_{i+1}\right| \leq \left(B_{i+1}^2\varpi_{i+1}^2/2\beta\right) + \left(\beta/2\right)$. So, inequality (34) is written as:

$$
\begin{aligned}
\dot{V} \leq & \sum_{i=1}^{n}\left(-\lambda S_i^2 + \frac{1}{4}\overline{g}_{hi}\varpi_{i+1}^2 + \frac{1}{4}\Delta_i^2\right) + \sum_{i=1}^{n-1}\left(-\frac{\varpi_{i+1}^2}{\tau_{i+1}} + \left(B_{i+1}^2\varpi_{i+1}^2/2\beta\right) + \left(\beta/2\right)\right) \\
& + \frac{\sigma}{2}\sum_{i=1}^{n}\left(\mathbf{t}_i^{*T}\mathbf{t}_i^* - \tilde{\mathbf{t}}_i^T\tilde{\mathbf{t}}_i\right) + \frac{\sigma}{2}\sum_{i=1}^{n}\left(\mathbf{d}_i^{*T}\mathbf{d}_i^* - \tilde{\mathbf{d}}_i^T\tilde{\mathbf{d}}_i\right) + \frac{\sigma}{2}\sum_{i=1}^{n}\left(\boldsymbol{\theta}_i^{*T}\boldsymbol{\theta}_i^* - \tilde{\boldsymbol{\theta}}_i^T\tilde{\boldsymbol{\theta}}_i\right)
\end{aligned}
$$

(36)

From Assumption 1, it is concluded that for a positive constant B_0, the set $\Pi := \{(y_d, \dot{y}_d, \ddot{y}_d) : y_d^2 + \dot{y}_d^2 + \ddot{y}_d^2 \leq B_0\}$ is compact in R^3, also $V(0) \leq \alpha$ results that for a positive constant α, the set $\Pi_i := \{\sum_{j=1}^{i} s_j^2 + \sum_{j=1}^{i-1} \varpi_{j+1}^2 + \frac{1}{\gamma_1}\sum_{i=1}^{j} \tilde{\mathbf{d}}_i^T \tilde{\mathbf{d}}_i + \frac{1}{\gamma_2}\sum_{i=1}^{j} \tilde{\mathbf{t}}_i^T \tilde{\mathbf{t}}_i + \frac{1}{\gamma_3}\sum_{i=1}^{j} \left(\tilde{\boldsymbol{\theta}}_i \tilde{\boldsymbol{\theta}}_i^T\right)^2 \} \leq 2\alpha$ for $i = 1, ..., n$ is compact in $R^{\left(\sum_{j=1}^{i} 2i-1+3nN_j\right)}$. Compactness of Π and Π_i results that B_{i+1} is bounded on the set $\Pi \times \Pi_i$ in $R^{\left(\sum_{j=1}^{i} 2i+2+3nN_j\right)}$, i.e., there exists a maximum $R_{i+1} > 0$ such that $\left|B_{i+1}\right| \leq R_{i+1}$. Choose $\frac{1}{\tau_{i+1}} = \frac{1}{4}\bar{g}_{hi} + \frac{R_{i+1}^2}{2\beta} + \lambda^*$, eq. (37) can be written as:

$$\begin{aligned}
\dot{V} &\leq -\sum_{i=1}^{n} \lambda S_i^2 - \sum_{i=1}^{n-1} \lambda^* \varpi_{i+1}^2 - \frac{\gamma_1^*}{\gamma_1}\sum_{i=1}^{n} \tilde{\mathbf{t}}_i^T \tilde{\mathbf{t}}_i - \frac{\gamma_2^*}{\gamma_2}\sum_{i=1}^{n} \tilde{\mathbf{d}}_i^T \tilde{\mathbf{d}}_i - \frac{\gamma_3^*}{\gamma_3}\sum_{i=1}^{n} \tilde{\boldsymbol{\theta}}_i^T \tilde{\boldsymbol{\theta}}_i + \Delta^* \\
&\leq -2\xi V + \Delta^*
\end{aligned} \tag{37}$$

where $0 < \xi < \min[\lambda, \lambda^*, \gamma_1', \gamma_2', \gamma_3']$ and $\Delta^* = \frac{\sigma(n-1)}{2}(\bar{\theta}^2 + \bar{d}^2 + \bar{t}^2) + \frac{1}{4}\sum_{j=1}^{n} \Delta_j^2 + \frac{n-1}{2}\beta$. From (37), the following inequality is obtained:

$$0 \leq V(t) \leq e^{-2\xi t}V(0) + \frac{\Delta^*}{2\xi}(1 - e^{-2\xi t}) \tag{38}$$

Equation (38) implies that $V(t)$ is bounded by $\Delta^*/2\xi$. Thus, all signals of the resulting closed-loop system are uniformly ultimately bounded. Moreover, by increasing the values of k_i, $i = 1, 2, ..., n$, γ_1', γ_2' and γ_3', the quantity $\Delta^*/2\xi$ can be made arbitrary small. Thus, the tracking error can be made small arbitrary.

4. SIMULATION RESULTS

To show the effectiveness of the proposed approach, simulation results on a numerical example and the permanent-magnet synchronous motor are presented.

4.1 Numerical Example

Consider the following third-order nonlinear system described by the following form in the work of Wang and Huang (2005) and Sun, D. Wang, Li, Peng, and H. Wang (2013):

$$\dot{x}_1 = x_2 + f_1(x_1)$$
$$\dot{x}_2 = x_3 + f_2(x_1, x_2)$$
$$\dot{x}_3 = u + f_3(x_1, x_2, x_3)$$
$$y = x_1$$

(39)

where $f_1(x_1)$, $f_2(x_1, x_2)$ and $f_3(x_1, x_2, x_3)$ are unknown smooth functions. For simulation purpose, the unknown dynamics of the system f_i for $i = 1, 2, 3$ are assumed as:

$$f_1(x_1) = x_1^3$$
$$f_2(x_1, x_2) = x_1^2 + x_2^2$$
$$f_2(x_1, x_2, x_3) = 0$$

(40)

Figure 2. Output of the closed-loop system and desired command

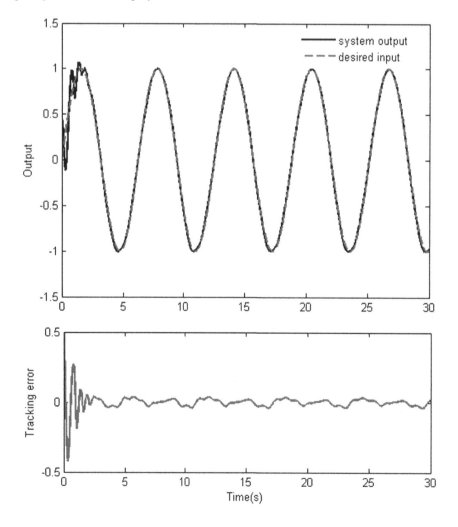

The simulation is carried out under the zero initial condition. The desired command is taken as $y_d(t) = \sin(t)$. Also, "Mexican hat" wavelet function is chosen as a mother wavelet function and adaptive FWN containing two fuzzy rules is constructed to approximate the unknown dynamics of the system. Initial values of $\hat{d}$, $\hat{t}$ and $\hat{\theta}$ are set to 1, 0.01 and 1, respectively, then adaptive learning laws (23)-(25) are applied to tune them. The control parameters are chosen as $k_1 = 4$, $k_2 = 4.5$ and $k_3 = 2.5$. Also, learning rates are set to $\gamma_1 = 1$, $\gamma_2 = 2$ and $\gamma_3 = 10$.

Simulation results are shown in Figures 2 and 3. The tracking result can be observed from Figure 2, it shows that the tracking performance is satisfactory despite the unknown systems dynamics. The output of the FWN for estimating the unknown dynamics of the system is shown in Figure 3. It is clear

Figure 3. Learning performance of the proposed scheme (a): $f_1(x_1)$ and its estimation, (b): $f_2(x_1, x_2)$ and its estimation

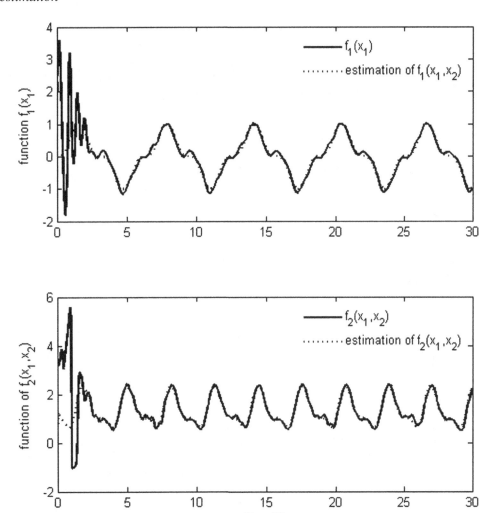

that after a short transient process the output of the FWN matches to the real dynamics. In fact, without any off-line learning phase and prior knowledge, the proposed scheme is able to model the unknown dynamics of the system using less computation.

4.2 Permanent-Magnet Synchronous Motors

This class of motors has attracted considerable attention in a wide range of drive applications because of their high power density, large torque to inertia density and high efficiency, for example see Carroll and Dawson (1995), Yang, Feng, and Ren (2004) and Yu, Shi, Dong, Chen, and Lin (2015). In Leonhard (1995), the state-space model of the PMSM in dq framework is described as

Figure 4. (a) Output response and desired output; (b) tracking error

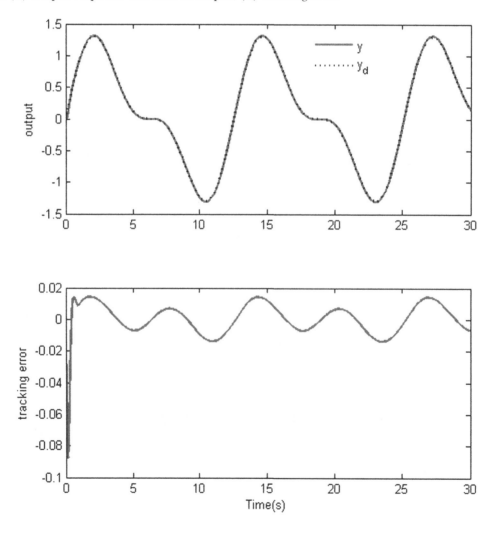

$$\dot{x}_1 = x_2$$

$$\dot{x}_2 = -\frac{P}{J}\Big[\big(L_d - L_q\big)x_4 + \phi_f\Big]x_3 - \frac{f_v}{J}x_2 - \frac{T_L}{J}$$

$$\dot{x}_3 = -P\frac{\phi_f}{L_q}x_2 - P\frac{L_d}{L_q}x_2x_4 - \frac{R_s}{L_q}x_3 + \frac{1}{L_q}u_q \tag{41}$$

$$\dot{x}_4 = -\frac{R_s}{L_d}x_4 + P\frac{L_q}{L_d}x_2x_3 + \frac{1}{L_d}u_d$$

$$y = x_1$$

where x_1 and x_2 is the angular position and angular velocity of the motor shaft, respectively, x_3 is the quadrature current and x_4 is the direct current, u_q is the quadrature voltage and u_d is the direct voltage.

Figure 5. (a) quadrature voltage u_q ; (b) direct voltage u_d

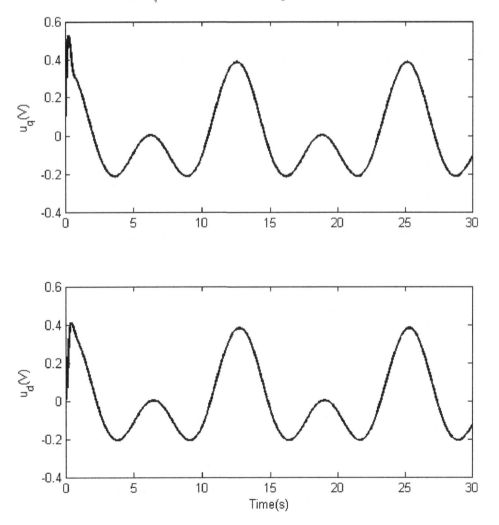

J is the rotor moment of inertia, P is the number of pole pair, ϕ_f is the flux of the permanent magnet, L_d and L_q are the direct and quadrature stator inductances, respectively. f_v represents the viscous damping coefficient and T_L is the load torque. The nominal values of the parameters were chosen similar to Yu et al. (2015).

The simulation is carried out for zero initial condition. The desired command is taken as $y_d(t) = 0.5\sin(t) + \sin(0.5t)$. The adaptive FWN composed of two fuzzy rules was constructed to approximate the unknown dynamics of the system. For this, "Mexican hat" wavelet function and "Gaussian" type fuzzy membership function were chosen to construct the fuzzy wavelet basis function. Initial values of the translation, dilation and weights were set to 1, 0.1 and 1, respectively, and then adaptive learning laws (23)-(25) were applied to adjust all parameters of the network.

Simulation results are shown in Figures 4-9. The output response and the tracking error are shown in Figure 4. The results show that the tracking performance is satisfactory despite the unknown systems dynamics. Figure 5 shows the quadrature voltage and direct voltage. Also, state variables x_3 and x_4

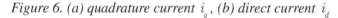

Figure 6. (a) quadrature current i_q, (b) direct current i_d

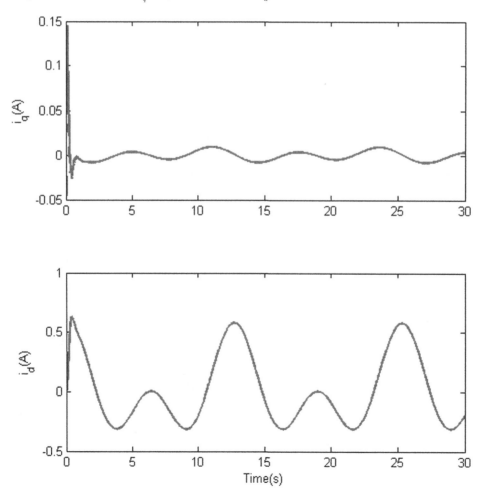

Time(s)

that represent the quadrature and direct current, respectively, are shown in Figure 6. Finally, the output of the adaptive FWN for modeling the unknown dynamics of the system is shown in Figures 7-9. It is clear that after a short transient process the output of the FWN matches to the real dynamics. Presented results verify the ability of the FWN for approximation of unknown dynamics of the system without any offline learning or prior knowledge.

5. CONCLUSION

In this chapter, the modeling and dynamics surface control problem has been considered for a class of strict-feedback uncertain nonlinear systems. It is assumed that uncertainty is not linearly parametrized and no prior knowledge is available. Inspiring from the DSC approach and FWN approximator, an adaptive FWN-based modeling and control scheme has been designed. The proposed scheme guarantees that all the signals of the closed-loop system are uniformly ultimately bounded and the tracking error can be made arbitrary small. The main feature of the proposed scheme is the elimination both of the "explosion of complexity" problem and "explosion of learning parameters" problem. So, it proposes simple controller with low computation load. Simulation results on a numerical example and PMSM verify the effectiveness of the proposed scheme.

Figure 7. Unknown function f_2 and its approximation

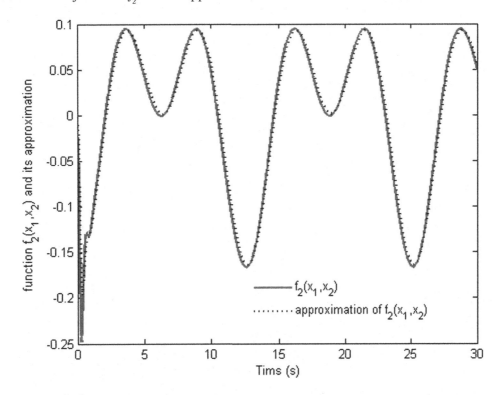

Figure 8. Unknown function f_3 *and its approximation*

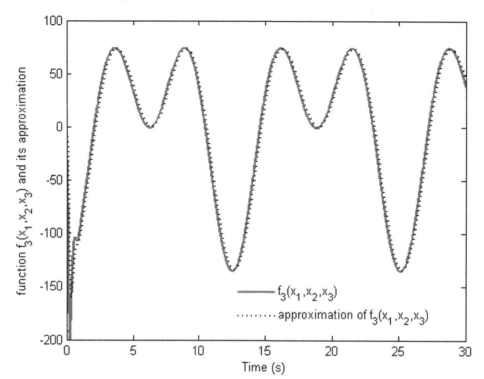

Figure 9. Unknown function f_4 *and its approximation*

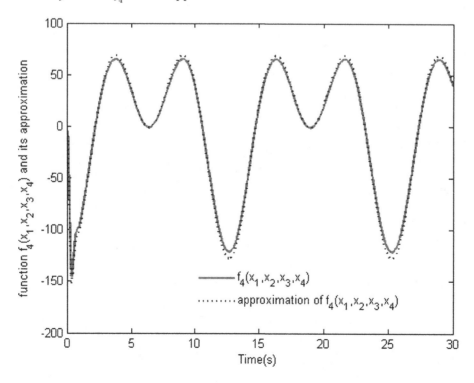

REFERENCES

Carroll, J., & Dawson, D. M. (1995). Integrator backstepping techniques for the tracking control of permanent magnet brush DC motors. *IEEE Transactions on Industry Applications*, *55*(2), 248–255. doi:10.1109/28.370270

Chang, Y.-H., & Chan, W.-S. (2014). Adaptive dynamic surface control for uncertain nonlinear systems with interval type-2 fuzzy neural networks. *IEEE Transactions on Cybernetics*, *44*(2), 293–304. doi:10.1109/TCYB.2013.2253548 PMID:23757550

Chen, W., & Zhang, Z. (2010). Globally stable adaptive backstepping fuzzy control for output-feedback systems with unknown high-frequency gain sign. *Fuzzy Sets and Systems*, *161*(6), 821–836. doi:10.1016/j.fss.2009.10.026

Leonhard, W. (1985). *Control of electrical drives*. New York: Springer-Verlag. doi:10.1007/978-3-662-11371-4

Li, T.-S., Tong, S.-C., & Feng, G. (2010a). A novel robust adaptive-fuzzy-tracking control for a class of nonlinear multi-input/multi-output systems. *IEEE Transactions on Fuzzy Systems*, *18*(1), 150–160. doi:10.1109/TFUZZ.2009.2038277

Li, T.-S., Wang, D., Feng, G., & Tong, S.-C. (2010b). A DSC approach to robust adaptive NN tracking control for strict-feedback nonlinear systems. *IEEE Transactions on Systems, Man, and Cybernetics. Part B, Cybernetics*, *40*(3), 915–927. doi:10.1109/TSMCB.2009.2033563 PMID:19887321

Li, Y., Tong, S., & Li, T. (2015). Adaptive fuzzy output feedback dynamic surface control of interconnected nonlinear pure-feedback systems. *IEEE Transactions on Cybernetics*, *45*(1), 138–149. doi:10.1109/TCYB.2014.2333738 PMID:25051573

Lin, C.-K. (2006). Nonsingular terminal sliding mode control of robot manipulators using fuzzy wavelet networks. *IEEE Transactions on Fuzzy Systems*, *14*(6), 849–859. doi:10.1109/TFUZZ.2006.879982

Liu, Y.-J., Tong, S., & Chen, C. P. (2013). Adaptive fuzzy control via observer design for uncertain nonlinear systems with unmodeled dynamics. *IEEE Transactions on Fuzzy Systems*, *21*(2), 275–288. doi:10.1109/TFUZZ.2012.2212200

Loussifi, H., Nourim, K., & Braiek, N. B. (2016). A new efficient hybrid intelligent method for nonlinear dynamical systems identification: The Wavelet Kernel Fuzzy Neural Network. *Communications in Nonlinear Science and Numerical Simulation*, *32*, 10–30. doi:10.1016/j.cnsns.2015.08.010

Lu, C.-H. (2011). Wavelet fuzzy neural networks for identification and predictive control of dynamic systems. *IEEE Transactions on Industrial Electronics*, *58*(7), 3046–3058. doi:10.1109/TIE.2010.2076415

Mousavi, S. H., Noroozi, N., Safavi, A. A., & Ebadat, A. (2011). Modeling and control of nonlinear systems using novel fuzzy wavelet networks: The output adaptive control approach. *Communications in Nonlinear Science and Numerical Simulation*, *16*(9), 3798–3814. doi:10.1016/j.cnsns.2010.12.041

Shahriari-kahkeshi, M., & Sheikholeslam, F. (2014). Adaptive fuzzy wavelet network for robust fault detection and diagnosis in non-linear systems. *IET Control Theory & Applications, 8*(15), 1487–1498. doi:10.1049/iet-cta.2013.0960

Sun, G., Wang, D., Li, T., Peng, Z., & Wang, H. (2013). Single neural network approximation based adaptive control for a class of uncertain strict-feedback nonlinear systems. *Nonlinear Dynamics, 72*(1-2), 175–184. doi:10.1007/s11071-012-0701-y

Swaroop, D., Hedrick, J. K., Yip, P. P., & Gerdes, J. C. (2000). Dynamic surface control for a class of nonlinear systems. *IEEE Transactions on Automatic Control, 45*(10), 1893–1899. doi:10.1109/TAC.2000.880994

Tong, S., Li, C., & Li, Y. (2009). Fuzzy adaptive observer backstepping control for MIMO nonlinear systems. *Fuzzy Sets and Systems, 160*, 2755–2775. doi:10.1016/j.fss.2008.09.004

Tong, S., Li, Yu., & Li, Y. (2011b). Observer-based adaptive fuzzy backstepping control for a class of stochastic nonlinear strict-feedback systems. *IEEE Transactions on Systems, Man, and Cybernetics. Part B, Cybernetics, 41*(6), 1693–1704. doi:10.1109/TSMCB.2011.2159264 PMID:21788195

Tong, S. C., & Li, Y. M. (2009). Observer-based fuzzy adaptive control for strict-feedback nonlinear systems. *Fuzzy Sets and Systems, 160*(12), 1749–1764. doi:10.1016/j.fss.2008.09.004

Tong, S.-C., Li, Y.-M., Feng, G., & Li, T.-S. (2011a). Observer-based adaptive fuzzy backstepping dynamic surface control for a class of MIMO nonlinear systems. *IEEE Transactions on Systems, Man, and Cybernetics. Part B, Cybernetics, 41*(4), 1124–1135. doi:10.1109/TSMCB.2011.2108283 PMID:21317084

Wang, D., & Huang, J. (2005). Neural network-based adaptive dynamic surface control for a class of uncertain nonlinear systems in strict-feedback form. *IEEE Transactions on Neural Networks, 16*(1), 195–202. doi:10.1109/TNN.2004.839354 PMID:15732399

Wang, F., Liu, Z., Zhang, Y., Chen, X., & Chen, C. L. P. (2015). Adaptive fuzzy dynamic surface control for a class of nonlinear systems with fuzzy dead zone and dynamic uncertainties. *Nonlinear Dynamics, 79*(3), 1693–1709. doi:10.1007/s11071-014-1768-4

Wang, H., Wang, D., & Peng, Z. (2014). Neural network based adaptive dynamic surface control for cooperative path following of marine surface vehicles via state and output feedback. *Neurocomputing, 133*, 170–178. doi:10.1016/j.neucom.2013.11.019

Wang, M., Chen, B., & Dai, S.-L. (2007). Direct adaptive fuzzy tracking control for a class of perturbed stric-feedback nonlinear systems. *Fuzzy Sets and Systems, 158*(24), 2655–2670. doi:10.1016/j.fss.2007.06.001

Xu, B., Shi, Z., Yang, C., & Sun, F. (2014). Composite neural dynamic surface control of a class of uncertain nonlinear systems in strict-feedback form. *IEEE Transactions on Cybernetics, 44*(12), 2626–2634. doi:10.1109/TCYB.2014.2311824 PMID:24718583

Yang, Y., Feng, G., & Ren, J. (2004). A combined backstepping and small-gain approach to robust adaptive fuzzy control for strict-feedback nonlinear systems. *IEEE Transactions on Systems, Man, and Cybernetics. Part A, Systems and Humans*, *34*(3), 406–420. doi:10.1109/TSMCA.2004.824870

Yang, Y., & Zhou, C. (2005). Adaptive fuzzy H_∞ stabilization for strict-feedback canonical nonlinear systems via backstepping and small-gain approach. *IEEE Transactions on Fuzzy Systems*, *13*(1), 104–112. doi:10.1109/TFUZZ.2004.839663

Yu, J., Shi, P., Dong, W., Chen, B., & Lin, C. (2015). Neural network-based adaptive dynamic surface control for permanent magnet synchronous motors. *IEEE Transactions on Neural Networks and Learning Systems*, *26*(3), 640–645. doi:10.1109/TNNLS.2014.2316289 PMID:25720014

Zekri, M., Sheikholeslam, F., & Sadri, S. (2008). Adaptive fuzzy wavelet network control design for nonlinear systems. *Fuzzy Sets and Systems*, *159*(20), 2668–2695. doi:10.1016/j.fss.2008.02.008

Zhang, T. P., & Ge, S. S. (2008). Adaptive dynamic surface control of nonlinear systems with unknown dead zone in pure feedback form. *Automatica*, *44*(7), 1895–1903. doi:10.1016/j.automatica.2007.11.025

Chapter 7
Performance Analysis of Nature-Inspired Algorithms-Based Bayesian Prediction Models for Medical Data Sets

Amit Kumar
Birla Institute of Technology Mesra, India

Bikash Kanti Sarkar
Birla Institute of Technology Mesra, India

ABSTRACT

Research in medical data prediction has become an important classification problem due to its domain specificity, voluminous, and class imbalanced nature. In this chapter, four well-known nature-inspired algorithms, namely genetic algorithms (GA), genetic programming (GP), particle swarm optimization (PSO), and ant colony optimization (ACO), are used for feature selection in order to enhance the classification performances of medical data using Bayesian classifier. Naïve Bayes is most widely used Bayesian classifier in automatic medical diagnostic tools. In total, 12 real-world medical domain data sets are selected from the University of California, Irvine (UCI repository) for conducting the experiment. The experimental results demonstrate that nature-inspired Bayesian model plays an effective role in undertaking medical data prediction.

INTRODUCTION

Medical data prediction is one of the most challenging tasks in data mining. At the present date, data mining in medical domain greatly contributes in discovery of disease diagnosis, and provides the domain users (i.e., medical practitioners) with valuable and previously unavailable knowledge to enhance diagnosis and treatment procedures for various diseases. A number of tools have been proposed to assist medical practitioners in their clinical decisions. The trend says that these tools have widely been used in clinical diagnosis, prediction and risk forecasting for different diseases. Although, several clinical models have been introduced but each of these is suffering from one or more of the identified deficiencies as pointed out below.

DOI: 10.4018/978-1-5225-3531-7.ch007

- No generalized model is designed for showing better or on an average disease prediction *accuracy* over all medical data sets. In other words, each of these is well-suited for a specific data set. Some literature reviews are cited here for the references (Chen, & Tan, 2012; Kensaku, Caitlin, Houlihan, Andrew, & David, 2005; Narasingarao, Manda, Sridhar, Madhu & Rao, 2009; Ye, Yang, Geng, Zhou, & Chen, 2002; Srimani, & Koti, 2014; Komorowski, & Ohrn, 1999; Shanker, 1996; Lekkas, & Mikhailov, 2010; Aslam, Zhu, & Nandi, 2013; Temurtas, Yumusak, & Temurtas, 2009).
- Most of the present diagnostic methods are black-box models, that is, they have no explanation power in terms of understandablity of rules (Kensaku et al., 2005; Narasingarao et al., 2009; Azar, & EI-Metwally, 2013; Hall, & Frank, 2008). Consequently, the models are unable to provide the reasons underlying diagnosis to physicians; therefore, further insight are needed for those algorithms.
- In general, each of the existing systems has deficiency for handling high dimensional, inconsistencies and vagueness (uncertainty) issues of clinical data.
- Most of the existing approaches suffer from generating *accurate rules* which are highly desired by CDSS (clinical decision support systems).
- The models are generally dependent on the hypothesis of statistical techniques.

Obviously, constructing a suitable generalized and accurate disease predictive model (model with highly accurate rules) is a complex and challenging task. Existence of *missing values* is also a vital problem for natural domain data sets. That is why the present study priorities in medical domain research.

In any classification problem, datasets usually consist of a large number of features. Likewise, it is true that medical data sets contain large number of features but all the features do not necessarily contribute to the classification performance. The existence of irrelevant and redundant features may hamper the classification performance. Also, adopting less number of features reduces the construction time of any learning model. Further, in diagnosis point of view, using less number of excellent features assists greatly the medical professionals. Obviously, good feature selection scheme is the essential solution in this respect.

Therefore, selection of appropriate features has become an important task in mining medical data. A number of feature selection techniques have been proposed in this respect. For the last few decades the evolutionary computation algorithms owe their popularity as solutions in various search and optimization problems due to their global applicability. Recently, nature inspired computation algorithms have become a popular mechanism for feature selection with great success. These algorithms include GA, GP, PSO and ACO. These algorithms is used to select an optimal set of features and optimize the learners. Each of the algorithms has their own characteristics, like, algorithms based on GA are able to preserve a few set of features due to their genetic operators during the process of evolutionary. The simplicity in updates mechanism, makes PSO better and computationally cheap than the other algorithms. GP performs better feature selection using feature construction. ACO incrementally include features due to the graphic representation. Although nature-inspired methods for feature selection have reached some success, there exist challenges in their potential. A comprehensive comparative study on nature-inspired algorithms on medical data sets may help to develop a novel efficient approach.

The present study focuses on conducting a comparison study showing performances of four well-known nature inspired approaches over medical data sets. In this purpose, the study adopts GA, GP, PSO and ACO algorithms over each data set to select a minimal set of features, and then a Bayesian learner, naïve Bayes is applied to train the data sets. Finally, the learned knowledge is applied over test data for final evaluation of the classifiers.

The paper is organized as follows. *INTRODUCTION* section describes the importance of nature inspired mining algorithms for *classification tasks* in a medical domain. *BACKGROUND* section briefly discusses the introduction of *feature selection*, GAs, GPs, PSOs, ACOs and widely used n*aïve Bayesian* classifier. The *METHODOLOGY* section describes the proposed nature inspired based hybrid model, whereas the experimental results and discussions are presented in the *RESULTS AND ANALYSIS* section. Finally, conclusions are summarized in *CONCLUSION* section.

BACKGROUND

A brief discussion on *feature selection, nature inspired evolutionary approaches* adopted in this study and *naïve Bayes* learner is presented in this section.

Feature Selection

Feature selection is a process of *extracting* a subset of the original attributes by discarding the *irrelevant* and *redundant* attributes as possible. The main purpose is to *maximize* the classification accuracy of the learners.

The main advantage of nature-inspired feature selection methods is that they do not need to have domain knowledge and any assumption about search space as compared to other traditional search methods. The population based mechanism of nature inspired techniques generate multiple solutions in a single run. This mechanism is very useful for multi-objective feature selection problems in finding a set of non-dominated solutions with the trade-off between number of features and classification performance. However, they require high computational cost due to large number of evaluations. There exist four well-known feature selection approaches: (i) GA, (ii) GP (iii) PSO and (iv) ACO. For better understanding these techniques, Figure-1 is depicted below.

Figure 1. Some well-known nature-inspired algorithms

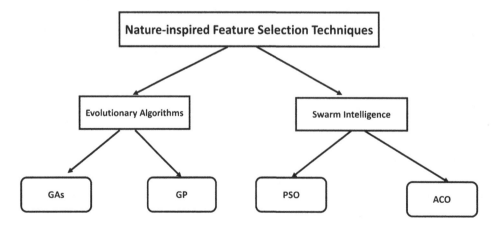

Feature selection using GA is the most widely used technique for investigating the effect of population size, selection, crossover and mutation operators. GP is mostly applied in the feature extraction rather than feature selection due to its flexible representation. It does not perform well in large population size. PSO is the swarm based simplest nature-inspired algorithm. It has fewer parameters, less expensive and can converge more quickly than GA and GP. ACO based feature selection technique focuses mostly on relatively small scale problems. Certainly, each method initially takes all the given features and then it makes an analysis of the classifier to discuss the utility of the features.

Undoubtedly, feature selection is an important part of data mining algorithms. For better understanding the process, *Figure-2* is depicted below.

One may note that the stopping criterion is either a *fixed number* of iterations or a particular *threshold value* that is to be achieved.

Genetic Algorithm (GA)

Genetic algorithm is a *probabilistic search algorithm* and also an *optimization technique* based on the principles of evolution and natural genetic systems (Goldberg, 1989). During the last decade, the *GA* has become increasingly popular in science and engineering applications. It is also being applied to a wide range of *optimization* and *learning* problems. The simplicity of the algorithm and returning fairly accurate results is the main advantages of *GA* formulation. Certainly, *GA* uses a *fitness function* as a judge for repeated attempts.

The GA-based problem solving strategy was first introduced by Prof. John Holland of the *University of Michigan* in 1975 (Holland, 1975), but it gradually gained its popularity as solution spaces in different search and optimization problems to its global acceptance and wide range of applicability. In particular, GA associates nature inspired phenomenon like *genetic inheritance* and *survival of the fittest*. Some very basic steps of a simple GA are pointed out below.

Figure 2. Steps for feature selection

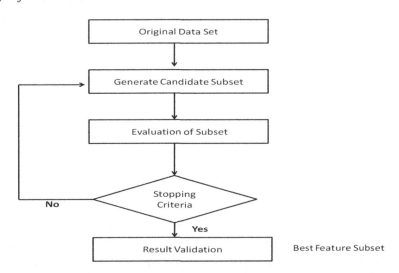

Step 1: Initialize a set of population of *n* chromosomes (solutions) for a problem P and decide a fitness function f(x) for the problem, where x is a solution of P.

Step 2: Determine the fitness value for each of the chromosomes (x).

Step 3: Select two solutions and encode them.

Step 4: Apply crossover and mutation over these two to generate two new offsprings (o_1 and o_2).

Step 5: Compute f (o_1) and f (o_2). Discard or keep one or both depending on the fitness value.

Step 6: If the terminating condition reaches, then stop else go to *Step 3*.

GA Components

Genetic algorithm consists of the following important components.

Encoding Techniques

Genetic algorithms starts with the *chromosomal* representation of a population set encoded as a finite size string so that computer can understand. The important encoding schemes are respectively binary *encoding, permutation encoding, value encoding, tree encoding*, etc.

Evaluation Technique

In genetic algorithms, feasible solution set follows the concept of *'survival of the fittest'* to obtain an optimal solution. Therefore, they use a fitness function as an objective function in order to select the *fittest* string that will generate new and probably better population set of strings. Actually, the fitness function takes a string as an input and assigns a corresponding fitness value to the string. These values are subsequently used for selecting the fittest strings to result ultimately an improved solution set.

Selection

According to *selection* or *reproduction* operator, the chromosomes are selected as parents to perform *crossover* and produce *offspring* usually from the population set. In this process, individual strings are copied into a provisional new population known as *mating pool*, for genetic operations. The number of copies that an individual receives for the next generation is usually based on Darwin's evolution theory *'Survival of the fittest'*, i.e., the best one should survive and generate new offspring thereby mimicking the natural evaluation. The strategy is commonly known as the *proportionate selection strategy*. The most frequently used selection procedures are respectively *Roulette wheel selection, Rank Selection, Steady-State Selection* and *Elitism*. It is important to note that the *elitist* selection scheme of *GAs* assists to retain the best *chromosome* of the previous generation.

Crossover

The main objective of *crossover* operation is to combine (mate) two parent chromosomes to produce two new chromosomes (also known as offspring). It is true that new chromosomes may be better than both the parents if they inherit the *best characteristics* from the parents. Crossover occurs during evolution according to a user defined *probability*. The most commonly used techniques are *single point crossover*, *two point crossover, uniform crossover, arithmetic crossover* and *tree crossover*.

Mutation

Mutation takes place after a crossover operation. It is, indeed, used as a genetic operator that maintains *genetic diversity* from one generation of a population to the next generation. It occurs during evolution according to a user defined *mutation probability*. Actually, mutation *alters* one or more *gene* values in a chromosome from its initial state. Hence, it results *entirely* new gene values being added to the gene pool. With the new gene values, the genetic algorithm may be able to produce a *better* solution than previous one.

Genetic Algorithm as Feature Selection

This sub-section presents a short review to show the importance of GA in selecting features for medical data sets. A GA based image segmentation optimization system is proposed to determine the best parameter set that maximizes the segmentation quality criteria in terms of changes in environmental conditions (Bhanu, Lee, & Ming, 1995). A GA based feature selection approach using multi-criteria fitness functions is introduced to minimize the number of features in order to achieve high classification accuracy (Emmanouilidis, Hunter, MacIntyre, & Cox, 1999). Estevez and Caballero (1998) presented GA for features selection with neural network classifiers by introducing a new mutation operator. To improve the classification performance of tissues in MRI segmentation problem through neural networks, GA is applied to find the optimal set of features (Matsui, Suganami, & Kosugi, 1999). A medical image segmentation has been also discussed using GA (Maulik, 2009).

The short literature review of GA says about the trend of feature selection in the field of medical service.

Genetic Programming (GP)

GP is an important evolutionary algorithm that is used to evolve as a computer program to solve a given problem. It was introduced by Koza as the programming of computers by means of natural selection (Koza, 1992). It is a highly flexible and automated tool for building an objective function based mathematical model. GP is an optimization technique for a given population set of computer programs based on fitness function which determines the ability of a program to perform a certain computational task. The search space of GP is computed by exploring genetic operators like GA. Similar to GA, GP also associates nature inspired phenomenon like *genetic operators* and *survival of the fittest*. Some very basic steps of a simple GP are as follows.

Step 1: Initialize a set of population of individual programs as solutions.
Step 2: Determine the fitness value for each of the individual programs.
Step 3: Select some individuals by applying a selection method and encode them.
Step 4: Apply crossover and mutation operators over any two individuals to generate new individuals.
Step 5: Replace these new individuals with the population of next generation.
Step 6: Compute a fitness value for each individual program according to fitness function.

Step 7: Return the program with highest fitness value as the best solution and discard the rest.
Step 8: If the terminating condition reaches, then stop else go to *Step* 3.

GP Components

Genetic programming consists of the following important components.

Encoding Techniques

GP initialize with the *program* representation of a population set. The program is generally executed by a program interpreter. The important encoding schemes are respectively using a *tree structure*, *linear GP*, *Cartesian GP* and *grammatical GP*.

Evaluation Technique

Like GA, GP feasible solution set follows the concept of *'survival of the fittest'* to obtain an optimal solution. Therefore, they use a fitness function as an objective function to determine the goodness of an individual program. Actually, the better fitness of a program, the probability of its selection and survival is more. These values are subsequently used for selecting the fittest individual to result ultimately an improved solution set.

Selection

According to *selection* or *reproduction* operator, the programs are selected as parents to perform *crossover* and produce new program usually from the population set. In this process, individual programs are copied into a provisional new population known as *mating pool*, for genetic operations. The reproduction operator is applied in two cases. (a) For random preservation of genetic characteristics, some programs are randomly selected and copied to the next generation population. (b) For elitism selection scheme, the best performing programs are retained for the next generation to ensure that the performance does not degrade during evolution. The most frequently used selection procedure is *tournament selection.*

Crossover

The main objective of the *crossover* operation is to share genetic characteristics between individuals in the population set. Generally, this operator combines (mate) two parent individuals to produce two new individuals (also known as children). It is true that new chromosomes may be better than both the parents if they inherit the *best characteristics* from the parents. Crossover occurs during evolution according to a user defined *probability*. The most commonly used technique for GP is *tree crossover*.

Mutation

Mutation takes place after a crossover operation. It is, indeed, used as a genetic operator that brings new genetic *characteristics* from one generation of a population to the next generation. It occurs during evolution to one individual at a time. Actually, it is performed by randomly selecting a node from a tree and then the subtree at that node is replaced with a new randomly created subtree. Hence, it results *entirely* new individual values being added to the pool. With the new individual values, the GP may be able to produce a *better* solution than the previous one.

Genetic Programming as Feature Selection

GP have very less work done as feature selection compared to other evolutionary techniques. GP is used to enhance feature selection for biomarker detection in LC-MS data, mass spectrometry data and proteomics mass spectrometry data (Ahmed, Zhang, & Peng, 2012; 2013; 2014). Dimensionality reduction in face detection is also done by a genetic programming approach (Neshatian & Zhang, 2009). A novel feature selection method using two stage GP for metabolomic 1H NMR data is proposed (Davis, Charlton, Oehlschlager, & Wilson, 2006).

The short literature review of GP says about the trends of feature selection in the field of medical domain services.

Particle Swarm Optimization (PSO)

PSO is a well-known bionic algorithm motivated by social behaviour of bird flocking for solving optimization as well as feature selection problems. It was firstly introduced by Kennedy and Eberhart (Kennedy, & Eberhart, 1995). PSO algorithm can be easily implemented with less parameters to solve feature selection problem in comparison to GA.

In PSO starts with the random initialisation of a population set of candidate solutions also known as swarm. They all are encoded as particles in the search space. Each particle in the whole swarm moves in the search space to search for the best solution by updating its position based on own experience and interacting its neighbouring particles. During movement every particle has its own memory. The current position of each particle i is denoted by a vector p_i which may also be represented as $p_i = (p_{i1}, p_{i2, ...}, p_{in.})$, where n represents the dimensionality of the search space. Similarly, velocity vector for each particle i is denoted by $v_i = (v_{i1}, v_{i2, ...}, v_{in})$. The velocity of the particle is limited by its maximum value, v_{max} and $v^t_{in} \in [-v_{max}, v_{max}]$. During movement, each particle has its best position so far is recorded as *pbest*. At the same time, the best position obtained by the swarm so far is also recorded as *gbest*. On the basis of *pbest* and *gbest* values, PSO updates the position and velocity of each particle to find the optimal solution according to the following objective functions:

$$x^{t+1}_{in} = x^t_{in} + v^{t+1}_{in}$$

$$v^{t+1}_{in} = w_* v^t_{in} + a_{1*} r_{1i*} (pbest - x^t_{in}) + a_{2*} r_{2i*} (gbest - x^t_{in})$$

Here, *t* represents the tth iteration and *n* represents the nth dimension in the search process. Similarly, w denotes the inertia term, a_1 and a_2 denotes acceleration constants and r_{1i}, r_{2i} denotes random numbers uniformly distributed in [0,1].

PSO algorithm is generally used for finding feature subsets over a large and complex search space. The main constraints of PSO in feature selection are that the particle moves up to certain velocity within the feature space.

Particle Swarm Optimization (PSO) as Feature Selection

This sub-section presents a short reviews to show the importance of PSO in selecting features for medical data sets. Recently, a PSO based approach is proposed in which a brain response pattern based on connectivity of the selected voxels is examined for Haxby's data set with improved classification accuracy as compared to state-of- art feature selection algorithms (Ma, Chou, Sayama, & Chaovalitwongse, 1916). Some new supervised feature selection methods using hybridized PSOs are investigated for medical disease diagnosis and found good results over the existing feature selection techniques (Inbarani, Azar, & Jothi, 2014). A modified binary PSO (MBPSO) for feature selection using SVM applied to mortality prediction of septic patients (Mendonca, Farinha, & Sousa, 2013). This method is tested over several data sets and achieved better classification accuracy over GA and PSO based algorithms.

The brief review of PSO presented above claims its importance in context of medical science (especially for feature selection purpose).

Ant Colony Optimization (ACO)

ACO is another important nature-inspired meta heuristic optimization technique based on real ants. It was investigated to solve the problems of combinatorial optimization such as TSP (Travelling Salesman Problem) problem (Dorigo, & Stutzle, 2004). The foraging behaviour of real ants is the basic inspiring source for ACO. ACO algorithms are based on the computation paradigm obtained by real ant colonies and the way ants function.

The ACO paradigm evolved from the observations made by the ethnologists about ability to find the optimal path followed by a swarm of ants to communicate their information to reach the food source from their nests. While walking from food sources to their nest and vice versa, ants deposit a chemical substance called pheromone on the ground, forming a path using pheromone trail. When an isolated ant practically moves at random, it encounters a previously laid trail (pheromone) and decides with high probability to follow that path with its own pheromone. Such a repeating process is categorized by a positive feedback loop.

1. Specifying how many ants follow the previously constructed path or modify a path.
2. Updating the pheromone trail.

The construction or modification of a solution path is performed in a probabilistic way. The pheromone trails are updated considering the evaporation rate and the quality of current solution.

Ant Colony Optimization (ACO) as Feature Selection

This sub-section presents a review to show the importance of ACO in selecting features for medical data sets. An ACO based feature selection algorithm with back propagation neural network (BPNN) that improves the classification accuracy for 6-channel pre-treatment electroencephalogram (EEG) data from theta and delta frequency bands for measure depressive disorder (Erguzel, Ozekes, Gultekin, & Tarhan, 2014). An ACO based selected features for predicting post synaptic activity in protein data set (Basiri, Ghasem-Aghaee, & Aghdam, 2008). Recently, a hybrid support vector machine is proposed using ACO based prediction accuracy of hepatitis specific drug activity by 94 percent (Mishra, Ananth, Shelke, Sshgal, &Valadi, 2016).

The short review of ACO presented above claims its applications in context of medical science (especially for feature selection purpose).

Naïve Bayes

The *naïve bayes classifier* is an example of Bayesian classifier. It has been studied extensively since the 1950s. In the purpose of classification, the approach calculates probabilities of different classes given some observed evidence. An illustration on this classifier is given bellow.

Let T be a training set of tuples and their corresponding class labels. Each tuple is represented by n-dimensional attribute vector, $X = (x_1, x_2, x_3, \ldots, x_n)$, associated with n attributes $A_1, A_2, A_3 \ldots A_n$.

Let us consider that there are m classes, $C_1, C_2, C_3, \ldots C_m$.

The Naïve Bayesian classifier predicts X belongs to the class C_i if and only if

$P(C_i/X) > P(C_j/X)$ for $1 \le j \le m, j \ne i$.

The training data can be used to determine P(X), $P(X/C_i)$ and $P(C_i)$. Here, $P(C_i)$ is the prior probability for each class estimated by counting how often each class occurs in the training data. Similarly, $P(X/C_i)$ can be evaluated by counting how often each attribute value occurs in the class in the training data. Using these values, Bayes theorem can be applied to calculate the posterior probability as

$$P(C_i/X) = \frac{P(X/C_i)P(C_i)}{P(X)}$$

If the data set contains a large number of attributes, then it becomes extremely expensive to compute $P(X/C_i)$. Therefore, to reduce computation cost, class conditional independence concept is introduced.

$$P(X/C_i) = \prod_{k=1}^{n} P(x_k/C_i) = P(x_1/C_i) \times P(x_2/C_i) \times \ldots \times P(x_k/C_i)$$

It shows that there does not exist dependent relationships among the attributes and individual probabilities of the training tuples can be easily estimated. Here, x_k denotes the attribute value for A_k.

It is called naïve because it assumes that all attributes are independent of each other. Such a method is particularly suites in high dimensional inputs. Naive Bayes models use the method of maximum likelihood for parameter estimation. Although, there is no complicated iterative parameter estimation for naïve Bayes. Generally, it performs better in many complex and real world situations. The classifier is the most successful known method for classification over almost all domains like *natural, artificial* etc.

Naïve Bayes Classifier and Classification Tasks

Naïve Bayes is very much useful in text and image categorization and network intrusion detection. It is also being widely used in automatic medical diagnosis. Naïve Bayesian Classifier (*NBC*) is applied as an important supporting tool for the assessment of individual risk of *relapse* or *progression* in patients diagnosed with brain tumor undergoing radiotherapy postoperatively (Kazmierska, & Malicki, 2008). A classification technique for public health data using naïve Bayes classifier was proposed (Hickey, 2013). In this technique, he used greedy approach for relevant feature selection. An investigation on personalized cancer treatment was also done by using naïve Bayes classifier (Karlik, & Oztopark, 2012). This study supports the use of personalized drug therapy in clinical diagnosis. In healthcare applications, a semi supervised naive Bayesian classification system is developed by applying weighted kernel density estimation (Chen, Li, Nie, Hu, Wang, Chua, & Zhang, 2012). The naïve Bayes classifier is also applied with kernel density estimation to the prediction of protein-protein interaction sites (Murakami, & Mizuguchi, 2010). Recently, a new privacy preserving patient centric clinical decision support system is proposed based on naïve Bayesian classification technique (Liu, Lu, Ma, Chen, & Qin, 2016).

The presented literature review ensures the application of naïve Bayes learner in medical domain.

METHODOLOGY

In order to study the performance evaluations of the nature-inspired algorithms based Bayesian prediction model, a hybrid model is constructed. Four well-known nature-inspired GA, GP, PSO and ACO algorithms are used for feature subset selection and naïve Bayes learner is applied on selected features to evaluate the classification in terms of accuracy.

Anyway, the exact model is built, consisting of *two* phases (in sequence). The first phase is responsible for extracting more relevant features from each data set drawn from UCI (University of California) machine learning repository using *GA, GP, PSO* or *ACO*. Next, the data set (with reduced but excellent features) is passed to naïve Bayes learner to train. For better understanding the hybrid approach, one may refer Figure- 3.

Data Sets Discussion

Note that all the selected data sets are drawn from UCI, a *machine learning repository* [3]. They all belong to real world *medical* domains. Their features are *summarized* in Table 3. The problem names are arranged in *alphabetical order* in the Table 3. The first five columns in the table represent respectively problem *name, non-target attributes, number of classes, number of instances* and presence of *missing values*. On the other hand, the last three columns show detail about *class imbalance* of the data sets. The imbalance ratio of each data set has been calculated by the following mathematical formula (Tanwani, & Farooq, 2009).

$$\text{Imbalance ratio}(I_r) = \frac{N_c - 1}{N_c} \sum_{i=1}^{N_c} \frac{I_i}{I_n - I_i} \text{ where } I_i \text{ denotes the number of instances of } i^{th} \text{ class,}$$

whereas I_n represents the total number of instances. On the other hand, N_c denotes the number of class-

Figure 3. Hybrid Model

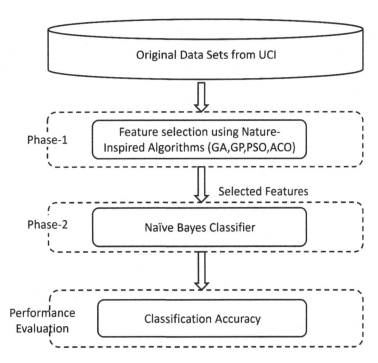

es present in the data set. The value of I_r (imbalance ratio) lies between the range: $1 \leq I_r < \infty$ and $I_r = 1$ implies that the data set is completely balanced having equal instances of all classes. More specifically, the last two columns represent the percentage of minority and majority class instances of each data set.

Performance Matrices

The well-known 10-fold cross validation scheme is used in the present study to measure the performances (in terms of mean accuracy) of the nature inspired based proposed hybrid Bayesian classifiers. A 10-fold cross validation takes a set of n numbers of examples of a given data set and divides them into 10 sub-sets (folds), each of size n/10, where n is the total number of instances. For each fold, a classifier is initially trained on the other folds and then it gets tested. Further, the average trained accuracies are calculated over all 10 outcomes. Several matrices are proposed for evaluation of classifier systems (i.e., for assessing how good or how accurate a classifier is predicting the class level of tuples). These include respectively, accuracy (also known as the recognition rate), error rate (or misclassification rate), precision, sensitivity (or recall) and F-measure. In addition to the accuracy-based measures, classifiers can also be compared with respect to speed, robustness, scalability and interpretability. For easy understanding of several measures, a simple confusion matrix is shown below.

As illustration of the matrix, assume that an example possesses class-level positive (true). Now, if it is predicted as positive, then it is termed as a *true positive*. However, if it is predicted as negative then it is *false negative* (i.e., actually it is positive but predicted as negative). Similarly, if it is negative but predicted as positive, then it is termed as *false positive*, however, if it is predicted as negative then it is termed as true negative.

Table 1. Data sets summary drawn from UCI

Problem Name	Number of Non-Target Attributes	Number of Classes	Number of Examples	Missing Values	Imbalance Ratio	%of Minority Class With Minimum Instances	%of Majority Class With Majority Instances
Breast Cancer (Wisconsin)	10	2	699	Yes	1.2133	34.47	65.52
Dermatology	34	6	366	Yes	1.0526	5.4	30.60
Ecoli	8	8	336	No	1.2495	0.5	42.55
Heart (Hungarian)	13	5	294	Yes	1.7389	5.1	63.94
Heart (Swiss)	13	5	123	Yes	1.1409	4.06	39.02
Heart (Cleveland)	13	5	303	Yes	1.3693	4.29	54.12
Hepatitis	19	2	155	Yes	2.051	20.64	79.35
Lung Cancer	56	3	32	Yes	1.02	28.12	40.62
Lymphography	18	4	148	No	1.46	1.35	54.72
New-thyroid	5	3	215	No	1.7673	13.95	69.76
Pima-Indians	8	2	768	Yes	1.2008	34.89	65.94
Primary Tumor	17	22	339	Yes	1.3334	0.5	24.77

Let us consider a binary classification problem with a number of positive and negative examples respectively P and N. Suppose that TP, TN, FP and FN refer respectively the number of true positive, true negative false positive and false negative. It may be noted that, in case of multi-class problem, the tuples of the *main class* of interest, are considered as positives tuples and all other tuples of different classes are termed as negative tuples. In general, *rare class* tuples are taken as the positive class. Now, the evaluation measures are described and formulated as below.

1. *Accuracy*: The accuracy of a classifier on a given test set is the *percentage* of test tuples that are correctly classified by the classifier. It may be defined as:

    a. $Accuracy = \dfrac{TP + TN}{P + N} \times 100$

    b.   In fact, accuracy is the overall *recognition rate* of the classifier over various classes.

2. *Error rate* or *misclassification rate* of a classifier is simply (1- *accuracy*). This can also computed as *error rate* (e) $= \dfrac{FP + FN}{P + N}$.

3. *Precision* =TP/(TP+FP), i.e., *Measure of exactness*. What percentage of tuples labeled as positive are actually such. More specifically, it shows the measure of telling exactly true.

4. *Sensitivity* or *Recall* = *TP/P* = *TP/(TP+FN)*, i.e., *true positive rate* or *Measure of completeness*. This is actually the *portion* of positive tuples that are correctly identified. Clearly, the number of positive examples is P. Out of P, TP are correctly classified, whereas FN= P-TP are incorrectly classified. In other words, this measure tells the chance of *sensing* the exact class.

5.   *F-Measure* = It shows the preciseness and robustness of the classifier. The F-measure of the system may be defined as the weighted harmonic mean of its precision and recall. It can be calculated as follows: $F - Measure = \dfrac{2 \times \text{Re}\,cal \times \text{Pr}\,ecision}{\text{Re}\,cal + \text{Pr}\,ecision}$

Note that sensitivity is related to prediction accuracy over a *particular* class (namely positive class), whereas accuracy is the prediction accuracy over all classes. Further, recall and precision are, in fact, the relevance measures (i.e., they are related to an individual).

Parameter Settings

Note that, all the experiments are performed using WEKA 3.7.2 package, an open software implementation tool for data mining. For GA, the correlation coefficient is used to estimate correlation between subsets of features and the target class label. Finally, to evaluate best feature subset *CFS* (Correlation Based Feature Selection) is combined with genetic search strategy. The parameter setting for GA is as follows: Population size = 20, No. of generations = 20, crossover probability = 0.6 and mutation probability = 0.033.

Notably, there exist a number of parameters in GP that have to be controlled by the user. Some such widely used parameters include *population size*, *genetic operators* and *stopping criteria*. Note that there are no specific guidelines for their choice of such parameter exists in the literature.

In PSO, the wrapper approach with *k*-NN algorithm is used to evaluate the goodness of the selected features. The parameter setting for PSO is as follows: population size = 100, maximum generation =50, acceleration constants a_1 = 1.0 and a_2 = 2.0.

Similarly, ACO is combined with *CFS* base subset evaluator to generate best feature subset. The parameter setting for ACO is as follows: population size = 10, maximum generation = 10, α = 1.0 and β = 2.0. Rest settings are kept as default.

Finally, the classification performance of the proposed hybrid model using selected feature subsets is evaluated by 10-fold cross-validation scheme for each nature-inspired algorithm.

RESULTS AND ANALYSIS

This section discusses about the conducted experiments, experimental results and their analysis.

Experimental results of the naïve Bayes classifier and its hybridized combination with three well-known natured-inspired algorithms are shown in Table-2 to Table-5. The performance measures of the classifiers are shown in terms of mean percentage accuracies, absolute mean square error, precision, recall and f-measure. Finally, a comparative study is conducted with nature-inspired feature selection techniques over 12 real world medical data drawn from UCI repository.

Table 2. Experimental results of GA_NB based hybrid classifier

Problem Name	Number of Original Features	Number of Selected Features	Accuracy (%)	Mean Error	Precision	Recall	F-Measure
Breast Cancer (Wisconsin)	10	5	72.37	0.324	0.713	0.724	0.717
Dermatology	34	21	98.08	0.009	0.981	0.981	0.981
Ecoli	8	6	85.41	0.043	0.861	0.854	0.854
Heart (Cleveland)	13	8	84.15	0.071	0.842	0.842	0.841
Heart (Hungarian)	13	6	83.67	0.077	0.835	0.837	0.835
Heart (Swiss)	13	1	39.02	0.286	0.152	0.391	0.219
Hepatitis	19	9	86.45	0.151	0.871	0.865	0.867
Lung Cancer	56	17	75	0.285	0.751	0.751	0.751
Lymphography	18	10	80.40	0.109	0.811	0.804	0.803
New-thyroid	5	5	97.20	0.024	0.972	0.972	0.972
Pima-Indians	8	4	77.47	0.298	0.771	0.775	0.769
Primary Tumor	17	12	47.78	0.401	0.401	0.478	0.428

Results Analysis Using GA-Naïve Bayes Learner

According to the Table-4, GA based naïve Bayes classifier shows better results in *heart* (*Hungarian*) and *hepatitis* data sets in terms of accuracy percentage and mean precision value in comparison to other nature inspired based hybrid learners. However, it shows good performances in *dermatology, ecoli, heart* (*Cleveland*), *new-thyroid, pima-Indians* and *primary tumor* data sets. The reliability of this classifier increases as the mean absolute errors are low in these data sets. Therefore, naïve Bayes with GA based classifier can be recommended for better performance in most of the medical data sets.

Results Analysis Using GP-Naïve Bayes Learner

Here, GP based naïve Bayes learner remarkably outperforms in *lung-cancer* and *lymphography* data sets compared to other selected hybrid learners. It shows good results in *dermatology, heart (Swiss)* and *pima-Indians* data sets. However, breast cancer and primary tumor data sets show poor results with this hybrid learner.

Results Analysis Using PSO-Naïve Bayes Learner

Likewise, it can also be observed that the PSO based proposed hybrid model performs better prediction results in four cases (namely, *breast cancer, dermatology, ecoli* and *new-thyroid* data sets in comparison to other hybrid models under consideration in this study. However, it shows poor results in the case of *lung cancer* and *pima-Indians* data sets.

Table 3. Experimental results of GP_NB based hybrid classifier

Problem Name	Number of Original Features	Number of Selected Features	Accuracy (%)	Mean Error	Precision	Recall	F-Measure
Breast Cancer (Wisconsin)	10	2	69.93	0.379	0.674	0.699	0.679
Dermatology	34	12	97.52	0.017	0.975	0.975	0.975
Ecoli	8	4	83.63	0.052	0.842	0.836	0.837
Heart (Cleveland)	13	9	79.86	0.088	0.801	0.799	0.799
Heart (Hungarian)	13	5	80.95	0.091	0.807	0.811	0.805
Heart (Swiss)	13	6	41.46	0.269	0.401	0.415	0.399
Hepatitis	19	1	79.35	0.310	0.631	0.794	0.702
Lung Cancer	56	6	90.62	0.145	0.877	0.906	0.891
Lymphography	18	7	85.81	0.113	0.861	0.858	0.857
New-thyroid	5	4	94.41	0.041	0.945	0.944	0.943
Pima-Indians	8	4	77.47	0.298	0.771	0.775	0.769
Primary Tumor	17	8	34.51	0.069	0.229	0.345	0.268

Table 4. Experimental results of PSO_NB based hybrid classifier

Problem Name	Number of Original Features	Number of Selected Features	Accuracy (%)	Mean Error	Precision	Recall	F-Measure
Breast Cancer (Wisconsin)	10	4	74.82	0.343	0.732	0.748	0.733
Dermatology	34	15	98.36	0.011	0.984	0.984	0.984
Ecoli	8	6	86.01	0.044	0.861	0.861	0.859
Heart (Cleveland)	13	3	82.50	0.104	0.825	0.825	0.825
Heart (Hungarian)	13	3	80.95	0.089	0.807	0.811	0.807
Heart (Swiss)	13	6	38.21	0.278	0.335	0.382	0.345
Hepatitis	19	10	83.87	0.176	0.845	0.839	0.841
Lung Cancer	56	12	59.37	0.269	0.571	0.594	0.582
Lymphography	18	13	83.10	0.107	0.838	0.831	0.833
New-thyroid	5	3	97.20	0.027	0.972	0.972	0.972
Pima-Indians	8	3	74.08	0.316	0.735	0.741	0.736
Primary Tumor	17	10	44.24	0.062	0.366	0.442	0.383

Results Analysis Using ACO-Naïve Bayes Learner

Based on Table – 4, Bayesian classifier shows better performance on *heart* (*Cleveland*), *heart* (*Swiss*) and *primary tumor* data sets on applying feature selection approach using ACO. However, the performance is good on rest of the data sets except *dermatology* and *lymphography*.

Table 5. Experimental results of ACO_NB based hybrid classifier

Problem Name	Number of Original Features	Number of Selected Features	Accuracy (%)	Mean Error	Precision	Recall	F-Measure
Breast Cancer (Wisconsin)	10	3	73.42	0.351	0.721	0.734	0.724
Dermatology	34	17	96.99	0.015	0.971	0.971	0.971
Ecoli	8	6	85.41	0.043	0.861	0.854	0.854
Heart (Cleveland)	13	7	84.48	0.075	0.846	0.845	0.844
Heart (Hungarian)	13	4	78.91	0.116	0.786	0.789	0.786
Heart (Swiss)	13	2	42.27	0.269	0.375	0.423	0.359
Hepatitis	19	10	84.51	0.161	0.853	0.845	0.848
Lung Cancer	56	7	71.87	0.313	0.694	0.719	0.699
Lymphography	18	11	79.72	0.101	0.804	0.797	0.798
New-thyroid	5	5	97.20	0.024	0.972	0.972	0.972
Pima-Indians	8	4	77.47	0.298	0.771	0.775	0.769
Primary Tumor	17	14	49.26	0.057	0.431	0.493	0.448

The present study shows that the GA, GP, PSO and ACO approaches are applied to select features and simultaneously optimize the Bayesian classifier. Since all the approaches have their own characteristics, therefore, the performance varies from problem to problem. The overall performance of the proposed hybrid models in terms of mean percentage accuracies is shown in Figure 4.

One may note that all the *experiments* discussed in this section are performed on an *ACER ASPIRE* notebook computer with *P6200* @ 2.13 *GHZ CPU* running Microsoft Windows 7 and 2 *GB RAM*.

Figure 4. Confusion matrix of size m x m, here m=2

Class	Predicted Positive ⇓	Predictive Negative ⇓
Actual Positive ⟹	True Positive (TP)	False Negative (FN)
Actual Negative ⟹	False Positive (FP)	True Negative (TN)

Figure 5. Comparative mean accuracy percentage chart for proposed nature inspired hybrid models with given data sets

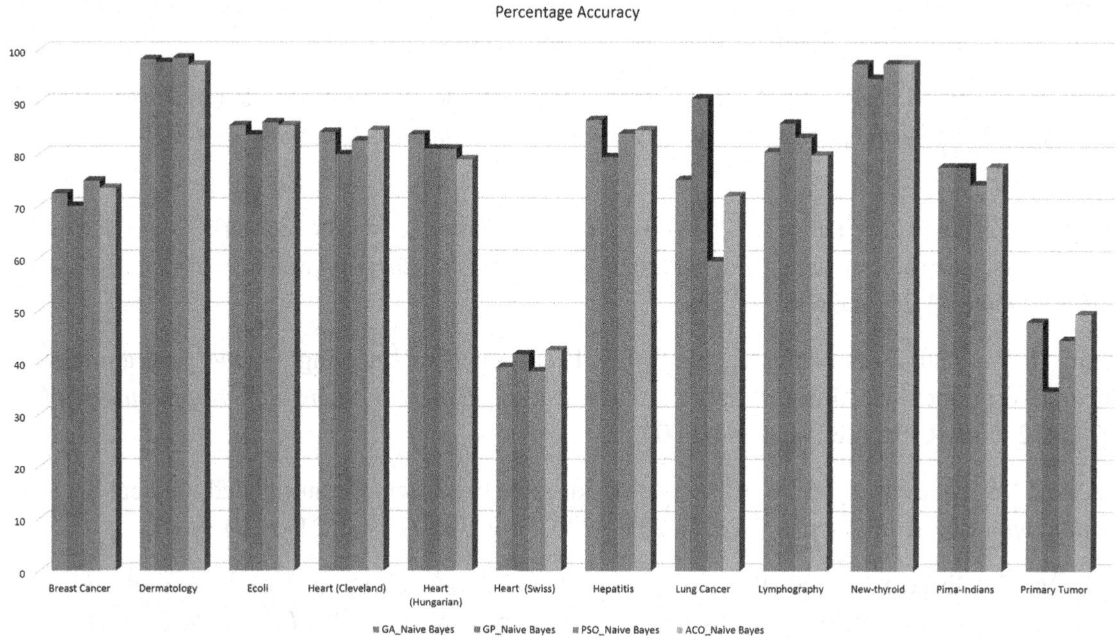

For a more accurate representation see the electronic version.

CONCLUSION

Many classification approaches for medical data mining have been proposed in the past decades but they have drawbacks like, disease *specificity* of model and *vagueness* of patient's data. Therefore, feature selection using nature-inspired algorithms is analysed with naïve Bayes classifier in this study. On the basis of statistical analysis of the obtained results, it may be concluded that individual hybrid model constructed in this article claims to improve accuracy that may help in *diagnosis* and treatment strategies of distinct diseases. However, some specific conclusions are summarized below.

- *GA*-based hybrid model with relevant feature selection performs better results in four cases.
- *GP*-based hybrid model with relevant feature selection performs better results in three cases.
- *PSO*-based hybrid model with relevant feature selection performs better results in four cases.
- *ACO*-based hybrid model with relevant feature selection performs better results in five cases.
- Among the four learners, GA and ACO based Bayesian hybrid models outperform over most of the given data sets. Hence, they may be recommended for most of the medical data sets.

However, the proposed hybrid approach with naïve Bayes learner, could not improve on all the data sets in the present study. The reason is that these data sets are very much complex and problem specific in nature. Our future research is to be extended to it.

REFERENCES

Ahmed, S., Zhang, M., & Peng, L., (2012). Genetic programming for biomarker detection in mass spectrometry data. *Advances in Artificial Intelligence*, *7691*, 266-278.

Ahmed, S., Zhang, M., & Peng, L. (2013). Enhanced feature selection for biomarker discovery in LC-MS data using GP. *Proceedings on IEEE Congress on Evolutionary Computation*, 584-591. doi:10.1109/CEC.2013.6557621

Ahmed, S., Zhang, M., & Peng, L. (2014). Improving feature ranking for biomarker discovery in proteomics mass spectrometry data using genetic programming. *Connection Science*, *26*(3), 215–243. doi:10.1080/09540091.2014.906388

Aslam, M. W., Zhu, Z., & Nandi, A. K. (2013). Feature generation using genetic programming with comparative partner selection for diabetes classification. *Expert Systems with Applications*, *40*(13), 5402–5412. doi:10.1016/j.eswa.2013.04.003

Azar, A. T., & El-Metwally, S. M. (2013). Decision Tree classifiers for automated medical diagnoses. *Neural Computing & Applications*, *23*(7), 2387–2403. doi:10.1007/s00521-012-1196-7

Basiri, M. E., Ghasem-Aghaee, N., & Aghdam, M. H. (2008). Using ant colony optimization-based selected features for predicting post-synaptic activity in proteins. *EvoBIO, LNCS*, *4973*, 12–23.

Bhanu, B., Lee, S., & Ming, J. (1995). Adaptive image segmentation using a genetic algorithm. *IEEE Transactions on Systems, Man, and Cybernetics*, *25*(12), 1543–1567. doi:10.1109/21.478444

Blake, C., Koegh, E., & Mertz, C. J. (1999). *Repository of Machine Learning*. University of California at Irvine. Retrieved from http://www.mlearn.ics.uci.edu/MLRepository.html

Chen, H., & Tan, C. (2012). Prediction of type- 2 diabetes based on several element levels in blood and chemo metrics. *Biological Trace Element Research*, *147*(1-3), 67–74. doi:10.1007/s12011-011-9306-4 PMID:22201046

Chen, Y., Li, Z., Nie, L., Hu, X., Wang, X., Chua, T. S., & Zhang, X. (2012). A Semi-Supervised Bayesian Network Model for Microblog Topic Classification. In Coling, 561-576.

Davis, R. A., Charlton, A. J., Oehlschlager, S., & Wilson, J. C. (2006). Novel feature selection method for genetic programming using metabolomic ^{1}H NMR data. *Chemometrics and Intelligent Laboratory Systems*, *81*(1), 50–59. doi:10.1016/j.chemolab.2005.09.006

Dorigo, M., & Stutzle, T. (2004). *Ant Colony Optimization*. MIT Press.

Eberhart, R., & Kennedy, J. (1995). A new optimizer using particle swarm theory. *Micro Machine and Human Science, 1995. MHS'95, Proceedings of the Sixth International Symposium*, 39-43. doi:10.1109/MHS.1995.494215

Emmanouilidis, C., Hunter, A., MacIntyre, J., & Cox, C. (1999). Multiple-criteria genetic algorithms for feature selection in neuro-fuzzy modeling. *International Joint Conference on Neural Networks (IJCNN'99)*, *6*, 4387-4392. doi:10.1109/IJCNN.1999.830875

Erguzel, T. T., Ozekes, S., Gultekin, S., & Tarhan, N. (2014). Ant Colony Optimization Based Feature Selection Method for QEEG Data Classification. *Psychiatry Investigation*, *11*(3), 243–250. doi:10.4306/pi.2014.11.3.243 PMID:25110496

Estevez, P. A., & Caballero, R. E. (1998) A niching genetic algorithm for selecting features for neural classifiers. *Proceedings of 8th International Conference on Artificial Neural Networks*, 311-316. doi:10.1007/978-1-4471-1599-1_45

Goldberg, D. E. (1989). *Genetic Algorithms in Search, Optimization, and Machine Learning*. Reading, MA: Addison-Wesley Professional.

Hickey, S. J. (2013). Naive Bayes Classification of Public Health Data with Greedy Feature Selection. *Communications of the IIMA*, *13*(2), 87–97.

Holland, J. H. (1975). *Adaptation in Natural and Artificial Systems: an introductory analysis with applications to biology, control, and artificial intelligence*. University of Michigan Press.

Inbarani, H. H., Azar, A. T., & Jothi, G. (2014). Supervised hybrid feature selection based on PSO and Rough sets for medical diagnosis. *Computer Methods and Programs in Biomedicine*, *113*(1), 175–185. doi:10.1016/j.cmpb.2013.10.007 PMID:24210167

Karlik, B., & Oztoprak, E. (2012). Personalized cancer treatment by using Naïve Bayes Classifier. *International Journal of Machine Learning and Computing*, *2*(3), 339–344. doi:10.7763/IJMLC.2012.V2.141

Kazmierska, J., & Malicki, J. (2008). Application of the Naïve Bayesian Classifier to optimize treatment decisions. *Radiotherapy and Oncology: Journal of the European Society for Therapeutic Radiology and Oncology*, *86*(2), 211–216. doi:10.1016/j.radonc.2007.10.019 PMID:18022719

Kensaku, K., Caitlin, A., Houlihan, E., Andrew, B., & David, F. L. (2005). Improving clinical practice using clinical decision support systems: a systematic review of trials to identify features critical to success. BMJ (Clinical Research Ed.), 330(7494), 765.

Komorowski, J., & Ohrn, A. (1999). Modelling prognostic power of cardiac tests using rough sets. *Artificial Intelligence in Medicine*, *15*(2), 167–191. doi:10.1016/S0933-3657(98)00051-7 PMID:10082180

Koza, J. R. (1992). *Genetic Programming: On the Programming of Computers by Means of Natural Selection*. Cambridge, MA: MIT Press.

Lekkas, S., & Mikhailov, L. (2010). Evolving fuzzy medical diagnosis of Pima Indians diabetes and of dermatological disease. *Artificial Intelligence in Medicine*, *50*(2), 117–126. doi:10.1016/j.artmed.2010.05.007 PMID:20566274

Liu, X., Lu, R., Ma, J., Chen, L., & Qin, B. (2016). Privacy-preserving patient centric clinical decision support system on naïve Bayesian classification. *IEEE Journal of Biomedical and Health Informatics*, *20*(2), 655–668. doi:10.1109/JBHI.2015.2407157 PMID:26960216

Ma, X., Chou, C.-A., Sayama, H., & Chaovalitwongse, W. A. (2016). Brain response pattern identification of fMRI data using a particle swarm optimization-based approach. *Brain Informatics*, *3*(3), 181–192. doi:10.1007/s40708-016-0049-z PMID:27747594

Matsui, K., Suganami, Y., & Kosugi, Y. (1999). Feature selection by genetic algorithm for MRI segmentation. *Systems and Computers in Japan, 30*(7), 69–78. doi:10.1002/(SICI)1520-684X(19990630)30:7<69::AID-SCJ8>3.0.CO;2-U

Maulik, U. (2009). Medical image segmentation using genetic algorithms. *IEEE Transactions on Information Technology in Biomedicine, 13*(2), 166–173. doi:10.1109/TITB.2008.2007301 PMID:19272859

Mendonca, L. F., Farinha, G. J., & Sousa, J. M. C. (2013). Modified binary PSO for feature selection using SVM applied to mortality prediction of septic patients. *Applied Soft Computing, 13*(8), 3494–3504. doi:10.1016/j.asoc.2013.03.021

Mishra, G., Ananth, V., Shelke, K., Sehgal, D., & Valadi, J. (2016). Classification of anti- hepatitis peptides using Support Vector Machine with hybrid Ant Colony Optimization: The Luxembourg database of trichothecene type B *F. graminearum* and *F. culmorum producers. Bioinformation, 12*(1), 12–14. doi:10.6026/97320630012012 PMID:27212838

Murakami, Y., & Mizuguchi, K. (2010). Applying the Naïve Bayes classifier with kernel density estimation to the prediction of protein-protein interaction sites. *Bioinformatics (Oxford, England), 26*(15), 1841–1848. doi:10.1093/bioinformatics/btq302 PMID:20529890

Narasingarao, M., Manda, R., Sridhar, G., Madhu, K., & Rao, A. (2009). A clinical decision support system using multilayer perceptron neural network to assess well-being in diabetes. *The Journal of the Association of Physicians of India, 57*, 127–133. PMID:19582980

Neshatian, K., & Zhang, M. (2009). Dimensionality reduction in face detection: A genetic programming approach. *Proc. 24ᵗʰ International Conference Image Vis. Comput. New Zealand (IVCNZ)*, 391-396.

Robbins, K. R., Zhang, W., & Bertrand, J. K. (2008). The Ant Colony Algorithm for Feature Selection in High-Dimension Gene Expression Data for Disease Classification. *Journal of Mathematical Medicine and Biology*, 1-14.

Shanker, M. S. (1996). Using neural networks to predict the onset of diabetes mellitus. *Journal of Chemical Information and Computer Sciences, 36*(1), 35–41. doi:10.1021/ci950063e PMID:8576289

Srimani, P.K. & Koti, M.S. (2012). Cost sensitivity analysis and the prediction of optimal rules for medical data by using rough set theory. *International Journal of Industrial and Manufacturing Engineering*, 74-80.

Tanwani, A. K., & Farooq, M. (2009). The role of biomedical dataset in classification. *Conference on Artificial Intelligence in Medicine in Europe*, 370-374. doi:10.1007/978-3-642-02976-9_51

Temurtas, H., Yumusak, N., & Temurtas, F. (2009). A comparative study on diabetes disease diagnosis using neural networks. *Expert Systems with Applications, 36*(4), 8610–8615. doi:10.1016/j.eswa.2008.10.032

Ye, C. Z., Yang, J., Geng, D. Y., Zhou, Y., & Chen, N. Y. (2002). Fuzzy rules to predict degree of malignancy in brain glioma. *Medical & Biological Engineering & Computing, 40*(2), 145–152. doi:10.1007/BF02348118 PMID:12043794

KEY TERMS AND DEFINITIONS

Conflicting Data Set: Data set that possesses instances with different class values for identical non-target attribute values, is termed as conflicting data set. More specifically, such instances are, indeed, inconsistent instances.

Imbalanced Data Set: A data set in which the number(s) of instances of some class(es) is/are very less in comparison to other classes, is termed as imbalanced data set. Classes with very less examples are known as rare cases.

Incomplete Data Set: A data set in which any information is either missing or incomplete, is known as incomplete data set.

Vagueness (or Complex) Data Set: If drawing any conclusion is very difficult for a data set, then it is called as vagueness (or complex) data set.

Voluminous Data Set: Data set that consists of a large number of instances or large number of attributes (i.e., high defensibility) or both, are usually called as voluminous data set.

Chapter 8
Routing in Wireless Sensor Networks Using Soft Computing

Deepika Singh Kushwah
Jaypee University of Engineering and Technology, India

Deepika Dubey
Uttarakhand Technical University, India

ABSTRACT

Wireless sensor networks are the evolutionary self-organizing multi-node networks. Due to dynamic network conditions and stochastically varying network environments, routing in WSNs is critically affected and needs to be optimized. The routing strategies developed for WSNs must be efficient to make it an operationally self-configurable network. For this we need to resort to near shortest path evaluation. Therefore, some soft computing approaches that can calculate the near shortest path available in an affordable computing time are required. WSNs have a high computational environment with limited and precise transmission range, processing, and limited energy sources. The sever power constraints strongly affect the existence of active nodes and hence the network lifetime. So, here, the authors use the power of soft computing because the potential features of soft-computing (SC) approach highly address their adaptability and compatibility to overwhelm the complex challenges in WSNs.

WIRELESS SENSOR NETWORK

Wireless Sensor Network (WSN) is a network of distributed autonomous devices that are called sensors or nodes that are performs sensing, computing and wirelessly communicating with each other. Nodes in this Network have constrained like power, memory and their computations. The lifetime of Wireless Sensor Network mainly depends on the battery power. A Wireless Sensor Network is based on ad-hoc networks, where each node transfers data to and from an Access Point that is connected to the Internet by a wired or wireless network. Also, the network is flexible i.e. the size of nodes are adding & deleting of nodes so the network size is unpredictable. The Access Points need not be in the reach of all the nodes in the network. Nodes around the Access Points forward the data from the faraway nodes to the Access Point.

DOI: 10.4018/978-1-5225-3531-7.ch008

If there are many nodes in the network, distant nodes can send data with the help of Access Point. Apart from mobility, Wireless Networks have some advantages that they can work in a distributed fashion & are cheap with minimum investment for initial infrastructure, more reliable, scalable and can easily increased coverage therefore they are widely used in campus networks, metropolitan area networks, transportation system, security. Therefore works better than traditional networks. Different routing approaches have been used by these networks called multi constraint routing. These constraints are a path which may contains many hops to reach to a destination. Also there are so many issues related to multicast routing approach like scalability in wireless networks, overall optimal performance and cross network routing etc.

Selecting the shortest path between source and sink is not always mean optimal routing in WSNs. The scarce power in sensors challenges the routing protocol in WSNs. Mainly the lifetime of a wireless network is dependent on the power of nodes, Therefore a power awareness based routing algorithms should be introduced to increasing WSN power and hence extend the network life time. Because of WSNs constrains and limitations, design of routing protocols for WSNs is challenging.

ROUTING IN WIRELESS NETWORKS

Traditional WSN routing protocol works in three types:

1. Flat-Based Routing,
2. Hierarchical-Based Routing
3. Location-Based Routing

In the above approaches, which one to opt is totally depend on the network structure.

Routing protocols can be classified into proactive and reactive. Proactive protocols need to maintain routes between all node pairs all the time, while reactive routing protocols only build and maintain routes on demand. Studies have shown that reactive routing protocols perform better in terms of packet delivery ratio and incur lower routing overhead especially in the presence of high mobility. In Wireless Network, transfer of data takes place to and from the AP. Each node sends route requests to its neighbours. When the requests reach the different APs, they send back a route reply. The sending node receives all these replies and decides which route and AP to use based on different conditions. Since transfer of data in

Figure 1. Wireless Sensor Network

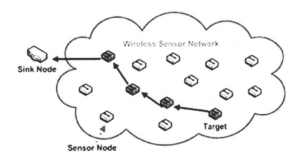

ad-hoc networks is similar to this, the existing ad-hoc routing protocols like DSR and AODV were used. But these protocols assume some properties of adhoc networks that are no longer true for Wireless Network. In the case of ad-hoc networks, most of the transfer might be among the different computers in the network itself and the network usage is spread over different routes. Unlike ad-hoc networks, in Wireless Network most of the data transfer is between the nodes and a few APs. Moreover, most of these ad-hoc protocols choose the shortest route to the destination. Some of the paths in the network are more utilized compared to others. Hence, when these protocols are used in Wireless Network it leads to congested routes. Some of the APs are over used while others have a low traffic. This might lead to busy nodes in some routes, while others are rarely used. Presence of overloaded nodes in a route may lead to high collision rates, packet drops in the queue and long delays in waiting at the queues. Also this leads to wastage of the bandwidth. Hence, there is a great demand for an efficient routing protocol for Wireless Networks.

Hence by using that rule, traffic serviced by the overloaded node in route 1 is 5G. In route 2, the traffic at the two overloaded nodes is G and 2G respectively. Sending such high traffic to an already overloaded node, the average delay spent in this overloaded node may increase and packets may be dropped at a high rate. Also, it may lead to failure of this node. It is better to use route 2 in this case rather than further loading the overloaded node in route 1 by sending 5G through it.

CHALLENGES IN WIRELESS SENSOR ROUTING

Practically WSN face a number of great challenges that needs focus of researchers on it so as to reach an optimal performance of WSN, we discuss some general challenges that have been faced in different WSNs applications.

- **Hardware Constraint:** Since WSNs depend on battery based power devices; power Supply is the most important part in the sensor nodes. The less energy consumption done by devices in WSN is the most efficient and long lasting network. The characteristic of sensor nodes; such as the computational approach and storage capacity; will also affect the performance and life time of WSN as they may increase the energy consumption and data redundancy. The size, processing, cost and the amount of the sensors in the applied environment should be focused while we are developing WSNs.
- **Power Used:** The limitation of power resources in WSNs vice versa the high energy consumption direct the researchers attentions to power conservation and power management approaches that is directly proportional to the WSN lifetime.
- **Deployment of Nodes:** A WSN's size is less randomly deployed network as it consists of small autonomously distributed systems. The network deployment can be densely by a huge number of sensors in applied area of application or dense network with a few and limited number of sensors. Communication in WSNs is achieved by single or multi transmission mode of hops between sensors. The importance of application as well as the cost of deployment controls the class of WSN deployment.
- **Scalability:** WSNs should be able to support variety of routing protocols, huge nodes number and wide area of application as well as the frequent increases of network expansion. The scale of performance and workload of WSN should not be anticipated during the initial network design stage.

- **Flexibility:** Due to the wide diverse of WSN application, as well as the network constraints and scarcity of resources, some sort of flexibility are needed such as different network deployment schemes and topologies, routing protocols, power management methods and so on.
- **Reliability:** A WSN should be able to adapt and manage the corruption of the network in case of node failure. The functionality and performance to WSNs should not be affected negatively. Some fault tolerance techniques ensure reliability in WSNs.
- **Connectivity:** Maintain connectivity among all sensor nodes through the network life time is a very challenging issue. The importance of each sensor node as well as the importance of sensed data and routing route that each sensor may take urges the network to preserve the life of each node. Some sleep modes can be practiced by some nodes in order to reduce the rate of harvested energy.
- **Lifetime:** The longevity and coverage of the WSN should be guaranteed. The main emphasis is to prolong the network lifetime. Sensor nodes are finite life time devices as they are battery powered. Some adapting mechanisms such as power management techniques and adaptive routing protocols are used to overcome the limited resources efficiently and to ensure the maximum network lifetime.

SOFT COMPUTING TECHNIQUE

Soft computing is the fusion of some components that make possible to solve real world problems which are not modelled or too complex for mathematical modelling. Its ambition is to exploit the tolerance for some hazier elements given.

- **Approximation:** It indicates the features that are similar to the real ones but not the same.
- **Uncertainty:** It indicates a situation which involves imperfect and/or unknown information.
- **Imprecision:** It indicates the features that quantities are not same as real ones but close to them.
- **Partial Truth:** It indicates close to truth but not exact truth. Its value between true and false. The controlling theory of soft computing is to use these tolerances to accomplish, robustness tractability and low solution cost. It based of natural as well as artificial ideas. It is referred as a computational intelligence was originally coined. It gives low solution cost, and better understanding with reality.

CONSTITUENT ELEMENTS OF SOFT COMPUTING

The basic components of soft computing are Fuzzy Logic (FL), Genetic Algorithm (GA), Artificial Neural Network (ANN) and its inherent component.

ROUTING USING SOFT COMPUTING APPROACH

To overcome many challenges of the wireless networks, the idea and approaches of soft computing are used, so as to remove the redundancy and uncertainty of the data in harsh environment has attract

Figure 2. Constituents of soft computing

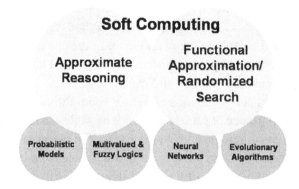

Figure 3. Soft Computing Approach

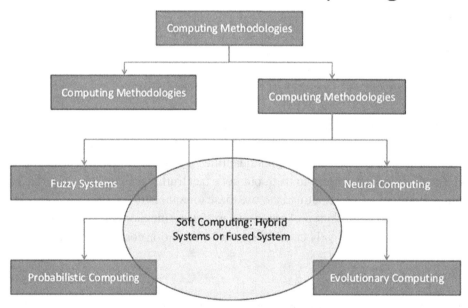

researches attentions to the idea of employing embedded soft computing methods in Wireless Networks after deployment. The characteristics of soft computing gives great analogy and compatibility in wireless sensor networks especially in energy management approaches, self-decision making techniques are knowledge-based routing and node processing routing.

First, we will outline the characteristics, design objectives and problems faced in Wireless Networks. This will secondly followed by a comprehensive survey of the different categories of Wireless Networks routing protocols. Now thirdly introduce, analyse and sort the usability of different Soft Computing paradigms in routing Wireless Networks.

Fuzzy Routing

In a network like the WMN, the various constraints like collisions, traffic level, buffer occupancy, battery power, etc. need to be considered. It is not enough if only one constraint is considered. This is because of the complex relationship existing between the different constraints. Multi-constrained routing is a NP complete problem and does not have a polynomial.

Routing for Wireless Mesh Networks With Multiple Constraints Using Fuzzy Logic

A Fuzzy system is best suited in making optimal routing decisions in a network involving multiple constraints and multiple objectives. There are several studies of fuzzy multi-objective routing where a fuzzy system is implemented over classical methods like DSR to do multi-objective routing. A fuzzy system is considered over classical DSR. Routes are decided based on the metrics Node Delay, Node loss and node speed. A fuzzy routing algorithm based on several metrics for a mobile ad-hoc network is proposed. A fuzzy logic system where unnecessary routes are eliminated by removing links not accepted by the system is considered. An adaptive algorithm based on fuzzy logic to change the security level of the mobile node is proposed. A possible solution is, we consider that a fuzzy system is designed for making routing decisions in Wireless Network where the destination AP is common for several users. Here it is necessary that the traffic gets spread across the system for maximum bandwidth usage. Various constraints that are considered are buffer occupancy, residual energy of nodes and the distance of source (hops) from the AP.

ROUTING WITH FUZZY LOGIC

In this routing, the constraints first undergo fuzzification and are mapped into sets using membership functions. Then the inference engine with the help of the rule base computes the fuzzy output. This fuzzy output is sent back after defuzzification.

- **Fuzzifier and Membership Function**

The membership function of a fuzzy set represents the degree of truth. Fuzzy truth represents membership in vaguely defined sets, not likelihood of some event or condition. Membership functions on any fuzzy input X represent fuzzy subsets of X. In the membership function under consideration, the fuzzy inputs buffer occupancy and hop count have been divided into three fuzzy subsets - low, medium and high. Fuzzifier is the mechanism that is used to map the real-world fuzzy inputs to the range [0, 1]. Triangular membership functions as shown in Figure 4 have been extensively used for fuzzification of inputs Sharad Sharma, Shakti Kumar, Brahmjit Singh (2014) and for real-time operations as they provide simple formulae and computational efficiency. Then the, Triangular membership function for buffer occupancy, residual node energy and hop count over a normalized range.

- **Inference Engine and Fuzzy Rule Base**

The fuzzy inference engine takes the value of fuzzy inputs at each node and scans through the fuzzy rule base to find the appropriate entry corresponding to the fuzzy inputs to calculate the fuzzy output cost for each node.

- **Defuzzifier**

Defuzzifier produces a quantifiable result in fuzzy logic. Thus, defuzzifier produces a real-world output from the fuzzy outputs which are in the range [0, 1] by using defuzzification techniques. Since the objective of our system is to choose the paths with the best fuzzy cost, it doesn't require the fuzzy outputs to be defuzzified and results can be derived by comparing the fuzzy costs itself. As an example, consider two paths P1 and P2.The better path can be derived as follows without further defuzzifying the fuzzy outputs:

If Fuzzy (P1) < Fuzzy (P2) Better path= P1

Else

Better path = P2.

- **Fuzzy applied with different protocols:**

A fuzzy system is built over the AODV protocol with the following constraints:

1. **Buffer Occupancy:** The length of buffer is an important indicator of the load serviced by the route. Since nodes in ad-hoc networks are expected to serve traffic for others also, it is expected that they have bigger buffers. For optimal usage of network resources, the buffers should be uniformly used and several nodes alone shouldn't be overused.
2. **Node Residual Energy:** Energy is spent by each node for transmitting and receiving packets. Energy might not be a big issue for fixed hardware like APs as they might have plugged power supply. But it is very crucial in the case of laptops and handheld devices where the battery capacity will be a few thousand joules. Hence, the routing protocol should ensure that the energy of nodes are uniformly used up and not that of specific users.
3. **Hop Count:** As the length of the route increases, the throughput achieved also reduces. So, it is required to ensure that the number of hops is not too high and the route chosen is also not much congested. These two constraints are very important in WMN since here traffic is mainly directed towards the APs.

Implementation of Fuzzy Multi Constraint Routing

There are 3 phases involved in the implementation of proposed multi constraint routing using fuzzy logic:

- *Phase 1: Sending route requests.* Whenever a node wants to discover a new route, it sends Route REQuest (RREQ) packets to its neighbors. It starts a time window as soon as it sends this RREQ. This is the time till which it will receive the route replies sent back from the destination node. At each node on the path, the routing constraints are measured. Then the fuzzy system works as follows:
  - The constraints are divided into sets of low, medium and high based on the membership function for that constraint which is decided by repeated trials and expert analysis.
  - The fuzzy inputs are then fed into the inference engine which decides the fuzzy grade of that node with the help of the rule.
- *Phase 2: Route reply phase.* When the RREQ packets arrive at the destination node, it sends back a Route REPly Packet (RREP) to the source node, through that given route with the fuzzy grade value in its packet header.
- *Phase 3: Route decision phase.* The source node accepts all RREP packets which arrive within the time frame. It then compares the value of fuzzy grade to the route already available in its routing table. If the current route has a better value, then this route replaces the one present in the routing table else this RREP is simply dropped.

ROUTING IN MOBILE ADHOC NETWORK

Mobile adhoc network (MANET) is a "on the fly" network of mobile nodes. Packets are routed through mobile nodes instead of any fixed base station. In a typical ad hoc network, mobile nodes come together for a period of time to exchange information. While exchanging information, the nodes may continue to move, and so the network must be prepared to adapt continually. In the applications we are interested in, networking infrastructure such as repeaters or base stations will frequently be either undesirable or not directly reachable, so the nodes must be prepared to organize themselves into a network and establish routes among themselves without any outside support. The idea of ad hoc networking is sometimes also called infrastructure-less networking, since the mobile nodes in the network dynamically establish routing among themselves to form their own network "on the fly".

The basic routing problem is that of finding an ordered series of intermediate nodes that can transport a packet across a network from its source to its destination by forwarding the packet along this series of intermediate nodes. In traditional hop-by-hop solutions to the routing problem, each node in the network maintains a routing table: for each known destination, the routing table lists the next node to which a packet for that destination should be sent. The routing

table at each node can be thought of as a view into part of a distributed data structure that, when taken together, describes the topology of the network. The goal of the routing protocol is to ensure that the overall data structure contains a consistent and correct view of the actual network topology. If the routing tables at some nodes were to become inconsistent, then packets can loop in the network. If the routing tables were to contain incorrect information, then packets can be dropped. The problem of maintaining a consistent and correct view becomes harder as there is an increase in the number of nodes whose information must be consistent, and as the rate of change in the actual topology increases.

The challenge in creating a routing protocol for ad hoc networks is to design a single protocol that can adapt to the wide variety of conditions that can be present in any ad hoc network over time. The routing protocol must perform efficiently in environments in which nodes are stationary and bandwidth is not a limiting factor. Yet, the same protocol must still function efficiently when the bandwidth available between nodes is low and the level of mobility and topology change is high. Because it is often impossible to know *a priori* what environment the protocol will find itself in, and because the environment can change unpredictably, the routing protocol must be able to adapt automatically. Most routing protocols include at least some *periodic* behaviors, meaning that there are protocol operations that are performed regularly at some interval regardless of outside events. These periodic behaviors typically limit the ability of the protocols to adapt to changing environments. If the periodic interval is set too short, the protocol will be inefficient as it performs its activities more often than required to react to changes in the network topology. If the periodic interval is set too long, the protocol will not react sufficiently quickly to changes in the network topology, and packets will be lost This concentrates on achieving high-performance multicast routing in multi-hop wireless ad hoc networks.

The Dynamic Source Routing protocol (DSR) is based on source routing, which means that the originator of each packet determines an ordered list of nodes through which the packet must pass while traveling to the destination. The key advantage of a source routing design is that intermediate nodes do not need to maintain up-to-date routing information in order to route the packets that they forward, since the packet's source has already made all of the routing decisions. This fact, coupled with the entirely on-demand nature of the protocol, eliminates the need for any type of periodic route advertisement or neighbor detection packets. The DSR protocol consists of two basic mechanisms: Route Discovery and Route Maintenance. Route Discovery is the mechanism by which a node S wishing to send a packet to a destination D obtains a source route to D. To reduce the cost of Route Discovery, each node maintains a Route Cache of source routes it has learned or overheard. Route Maintenance is the mechanism by which a packet's originator S detects if the network topology has changed such that it can no longer use its route to the destination D because some of the nodes listed on the route have moved out of range of each other.

SOURCE ROUTING

The routes that DSR discovers and uses are *source routes*. That is, the sender learns the complete, ordered sequence of network hops necessary to reach the destination, and, at a conceptual level, each packet to be routed carries this list of hops in its header. The key advantage of a source routing design is that intermediate nodes do not need to maintain up-to-date routing information in order to route the packets that they forward, since the packets themselves already contain all the routing decisions. Aggregating information about the network topology at the source of each packet allows the node that cares most about the packet, namely its source, to expend the appropriate amount of effort to deliver the packet. It also enables the explicit management of the resources in the ad hoc network. In some sense, DSR has an even stronger "end-to-end philosophy" than the Internet itself. Intermediate nodes in a DSR network maintain even less state than nodes in the core of the Internet, which must maintain up-to-date routing tables for all destinations in the network. Basing the routing protocol on source routes also has two additional benefits. First, the protocol can be trivially proved to be loop-free, since the source route used to control the routing of a packet is, by definition, of finite length, and it can be trivially checked for loops. Second, each source route is a statement that a particular path is believed to exist through the network. As source routes travel through the network riding on control packets, such as ROUTE REQUESTs or ROUTE REPLYs, or the data packets whose forwarding they control, any node overhearing a source route can incorporate the information it contains into its Route Cache. At the cost of no overhead above that used to carry out the normal operation of the protocol, the protocol itself spreads topology information among the nodes in the network. The information carried by a source route on a data packet also has the useful property that the more frequently heard routes and the most recently heard routes are the most likely to contain accurate information, since those routes are currently being tested by the packets flowing along them [Mala Chelliah, Siddhartha Sankaran, Shishir Prasad, Nagamaputhur Gopalan, and Balasubramanian Sivaselvan (2014) and [Marwa Sharawi, Imane Aly Saroit, Hesham El-Mahdy, Eid Emary (2013). Although DSR uses source routes, and each packet is routed based on a discovered source route, recent improvements to DSR have made it so that most packets do not need to incur the overhead of carrying an explicit source route header.

ROUTE DISCOVERY

Route Discovery works by flooding a request through the network in a controlled manner, seeking a route to some target destination. In its simplest form, a source node A attempting to discover a route to a destination node D broadcasts a ROUTE REQUEST packet that is re-broadcast by intermediate nodes until it reaches D, which then answers by returning a ROUTE REPLY packet to A. Many optimizations to this basic mechanism are used to limit the frequency and spread of Route Discovery attempts. The controlled flood approach used by DSR works well in wired networks, but it is particularly well-suited to the nature of many wireless networks, where the communication channel between nodes is often inherently broadcast. A single transmission of a ROUTE REQUEST is all that is needed to re-propagate the REQUEST to all of a node's neighbors. *Route Maintenance-* When sending or forwarding a packet to some destination D, Route Maintenance is used to detect if the network topology has changed such that the route used by this packet has broken. Each node along the route, when transmitting the packet to the next hop, is responsible for detecting if its link to the next hop has broken. In many wireless MAC protocols, such as IEEE 802.11, the MAC protocol retransmits each packet until a link-layer acknowledgment is received, or until a maximum number of transmission attempts have been made. Alternatively, DSR may make use of a *passive acknowledgment* or may request an explicit network-layer acknowledgment. When the retransmission and acknowledgment mechanism detects that the next link is broken, the detecting node returns a ROUTE ERROR packet to the original sender A of the packet. The sender A can then attempt to use any other route to D that is already in its route cache, or can invoke Route Discovery again to find a new route for subsequent packets. ROUTE CACHE All the routing information needed by a node participating in an ad hoc network using DSR is stored in a Route Cache. Each node in the network maintains its own Route Cache, to which it adds information as it learns of new links between nodes in the ad hoc network, for example through packets carrying either a ROUTE REPLY or a source route. Likewise, the node removes information from the cache as it learns previously existing links in the ad hoc network have broken, for example through packets carrying a ROUTE ERROR or through the link-layer retransmission mechanism reporting a failure in forwarding a packet to its next-hop destination.

There is tremendous room for innovation inside the interface defined for the Route Cache, and this is intentional. An implementation of DSR may choose for its Route Cache whatever cache replacement and cache search strategy are most appropriate for its particular network environment.

Shortest route to a node (the shortest sequence of hops), while others may select an alternate metric for the Get() operation. I have experimented with many different types of Route Cache, and found that several general principles are helpful. The Route Cache should support storing more than one source route for each destination. If a node **S** is using a source route to some destination D that includes intermediate node N, S should shorten the route to destination D when it learns of a shorter route to node N than the one that is listed as the prefix of its current route to D. However, the cache should still retain the ability to revert to the older, longer route to N if the shorter one does not work. The Route Cache replacement policy should allow routes to be categorized based upon "preference", where routes with higher preferences are less likely to be removed from the cache. For example, a node could prefer routes for which it initiated a Route Discovery over routes that it learned as the result of promiscuous snooping on other packets. In particular, a node should prefer routes that it is presently using over those that it is not.

During the past decades, the use of soft computational approaches has been extended to a large variety of software engineering applications. Soft computational methods, such as fuzzy systems, neural networks, evolutionary computation, and probability models including Bayesian network and chaos theory, are currently attractive topics in the extensive software engineering research problems. This special issue provides a platform for the dissemination of knowledge on both the empirical research and applied research in the field of soft computing. The objective of the special issue is to facilitate a forum to a wide spectrum of articles that cover the state-of-the-art techniques and recent results in the research of soft computational approaches. In particular, the special issue focuses on publishing the highly technical articles describing the software development topics: advanced software engineering, computational intelligence, and wireless sensor networks. This special issue has received overwhelming responses from researchers, and it has received a total of 28 high-quality submissions from various countries around the world. All the submitted papers have been evaluated by at least three independent reviewers. However, due to focused scope of the special issue, only a few manuscripts are published. Inevitably, hard editorial decisions had to be made, and some high-quality articles could not even be included. We believe that this special issue presents cohesive information related to the applications of soft computing methods in software development, and it also provides stimulations for future research.

An algorithm for the wireless sensor network (WSN) is there, in which the clustering and clustering head selection are done by using the Particle Swarm Optimization (PSO) algorithm with respect to minimizing the power consumption in the WSN. The results obtained have been compared and evaluated on the basis of energy efficiency.

Y. Rastegari and F. Shams presents a method to decompose service level objectives to web service policy assertions. Transformation of Web Service Choreography Description Language (WS-CDL) to Web Service Business Process Execution Language (WSBPEL) has been addressed in some related works, but neither of them considers quality aspects of transformation or run-time adaptation. In this paper, in conformity with web services standards, the authors proposed an optimal decomposition method to make a set of WS-policy assertions. Assertions applied to WSBPEL elements and affect their run-time behaviors. The decomposition method achieves the best outcome for a performance indicator. It also guarantees the lowest adaptation overhead by reducing the number of service reselections. This research considered securities settlement case study to prototype and evaluated the decomposition method. The results show an acceptable threshold between customer satisfaction, the targeted performance indicator through the case study, and adaptation overhead.

In modern era, application of Mobile Ad-hoc Network (MANET) increases rapidly. It used in various sector of life such as E-commerce, Multi-media, Disaster management etc. is composed of more than one mobile nodes which can move freely in an infrastructure-less environment. It does not have centralized controllers, which makes it different from traditional wireless networks. Mobile nodes can typically move in any direction they want due to its dynamic nature. The main role of this node is not only responsible for network traffic but also has to forward packet. Therefore, dynamic topology, unstable links and limited energy are special features for MANET when compared to wired networks. But a vital problem in MANET is finding an energy efficient route between source and destination node.

The framework of the proposed protocol in based on intelligent system that control by fuzzy logic system. This intelligent system takes three parameters such as hop count, packet and energy to resolve energy efficiency issue in routing. The main advantage of this protocol is that intelligent system divide entire route in two categories A and B. Category A contains the routes those having same linguistic behavior and Category B contains the routes those having different linguistic behavior. Finally, it assigns priority to each route based on some priority scale. The range of all priorities is divided between 0 and 1. This priority statistic helps to determine energy efficient route.

All hard computing approaches modelled with accurate solution which are achieved very quickly. Resultant solution having exactness and full truth. But when these problems comes with incomplete knowledge than its fails to achieve the goal. Thus, soft computing techniques are easily applied in this situation with its variety of components. The research community has investigated and explored this techniques over traditional techniques. However, recently, there have been numerous efforts toward making use of soft computing techniques as engineering problems and the optimization solver for science, based on their distinctive characteristics and appropriate use for imprecision, uncertainty, partial truth, and approximation scenarios to achieve practicability and robustness as a low-cost solution, e.g., evolutionary and swarm intelligence-based algorithms as well as bio-inspired computation, which are applicable for real-world scenarios.

HARD COMPUTING TECHNIQUE

Hard computing is a conventional method. It requires a precisely stated analytical model and often a lot computation complexity. Various analytical models are useful in many cases but maximum are invalid in the case of hesitate environment. In hard computing, first problem is defined, then based on the problem mathematical model is designed and data are collected Abhishek Kumar (2017). It solve the problem by using mathematical model and collect data to get final output. If output of the final solution is valid, then model implemented in real world otherwise modify the model by remodelling and re-collection of data. The several features of hard computing are given below:

- Real-time constraints.
- Need of accuracy and precision in calculations and outcomes.
- Useful in critical systems.

DIFFERENCE BETWEEN HARD COMPUTING AND SOFT COMPUTING TECHNIQUES

Hard computing based on precision and accuracy whereas soft computing based on approximation. In hard computing, imprecision and uncertainty are undesirable properties, but in soft computing the tolerance for imprecision and uncertainty is exploited to achieve tractability, lower cost solution. There are various dissimilarities between them due to contradiction natures. But some solutions are depend on the traditional approach (i.e. hard computing technique) approach as well as modern (soft computing technique) approach. So, in this situation hybrid computing relation between hard computing and soft computing techniques. Table 1 illustrates the differences between them.

SEVERAL INNOVATIONS IN DIFFERENT AREAS BASED ON SOFT COMPUTING TECHNIQUES

Innovation is the development of new principles through explanations that meet new requirements, inarticulate needs, and market needs. This is accomplished through more effective products, processes, services, technologies, or ideas that are readily available to markets, governments, and society. In daily life, human directly or indirectly attached with different types e-commerce services such as Consumer to Consumer (C2C), Consumer to Business (C2B), Business to Business (B2B), Business to Consumer (B2C) etc. and face different uncertainty problems. In last few decades, soft computing play key role of innovation in various areas. The fusion of soft computing techniques increases rapidly. It has been used considerably in human-related fields (e.g. aircraft, cloud computing, robotics, image processing, e-commerce etc.).

The effective applications of soft computing over hard computing suggest that it has important role in engineering and science. It represents a significant paradigm in modern era. It gives greater impact in present as well as future. Its integrated components inspires to deals with uncertainty and vagueness information. It can be extended with computing not only from human thinking aspects but also from artificial intelligence techniques. It is already a major area of academic research but nowadays it becomes academic as well as industrial. It much more effective in a real-world problem which is not evaluated by the helps of traditional hard computing techniques. It will gives greater impact in the coming years in the fields of science and engineering. Future scope includes, selecting any real world problem and solving with the help of soft computing techniques. Then implement it by the help of simulator and wish to compare the analytical results with simulation results.

Table 1.

S.No.	Soft Computing	Hard Computing
1	Real time constraints	Artificial constraints
2	Need of accuracy and precision	Need of robustness rather than accuracy
3	It requires, programs to be written	It requires, its own programs
4	It follows two-valued logic	It follows multi-valued logic
5	It requires exact input data	It requires inexact input data
6	It is strictly sequential in computation	It is parallel in computations
7	It produce precise answers	It produce approximate answers
8	It is deterministic	It is non-deterministic

REFERENCES

Chakraborty, Sharma, & Tewari. (2017). Application of soft computing techniques over hard computing techniques: A survey. *International Journal of Indestructible Mathematics & Computing, 1*(1), 8-17.

Chelliah, M., Sankaran, S., Prasad, S., Gopalan, N., & Sivaselvan, B. (2012, January). Routing for Wireless Mesh Networks with Multiple Constraints Using Fuzzy Logic. *The International Arab Journal of Information Technology, 9*(1).

Giri, P. K. (2012). A Survey on Soft Computing Techniques for Multi-Constrained QoS Routing in MANET. *IJCIT, 3*(2).

Kumar, A. (2017). Intelligent and efficient routing for manet: A soft computing technique. *International Journal of Research in Computer Applications and Robotics, 5*(1).

Patearia. (2011). Performance analysis of dynamic routing protocol in mobile ad hoc network. *Journal of Global Research in Computer Science, 2*(10).

Sharawi, Saroit, El-Mahdy, & Emary. (2013). Routing wireless sensor networks based on soft computing paradigms: Survey. *International Journal on Soft Computing, Artificial Intelligence and Applications, 2*(4).

Sharawi, M., Elmahdy, H., & Emary, E. (n.d.). *Routing Wireless Sensor Networks based on Soft Computing Paradigms: Survey.* Retrieved from https://www.researchgate.net/publication/255754336

Sharma, S., Kumar, S., & Singh, B. (2014). Hybrid Intelligent Routing in Wireless Mesh Networks: Soft Computing Based Approaches. *Intelligent Systems and Applications, 1*, 45-57. Retrieved from http://www.mecs -press.org/

Siddesh, Muralidhara, & Harihar. (n.d.). Routing in Ad Hoc Wireless Networks using Soft Computing techniques and performance evaluation using Hypernet simulator. *International Journal of Soft Computing and Engineering.*

Chapter 9
Study of Feature Apprehension Using Soft Computing Approaches

Deepika Dubey
Uttarakhand Technical University, India

Deepika Singh Kushwah
Jaypee University of Engineering and Technology, India

Deepanshu Dubey
Indian Institute of Forest Management, India

ABSTRACT

An image may be mist full for the one or may be nostalgic for the other. But for a researcher, each image is distinguished on the basis of its low-level features like color, shape, size. Other features like edges, corner/ interesting points, blobs/region of interest, ridges, etc. can also be used for computation purpose. Using these features distinctions, an image can be processed for the purpose of enhancing the images having same features, matching, and shortlisting of similar images from a random available image database. This could be done using soft computing techniques like neural networks, fuzzy logic, and evolutionary computation methods. Neural networks can participate effectively in image processing in several ways.

INTRODUCTION

Soft computing is a phenomenon, which allows the computer for a collective use of multiple computational applications like fuzzy logics, probabilistic reasoning, neural computing, evolutionary computation and many more, which aims to harvest the low cost solutions of complex problems. It focuses on analyzing, studying, modeling and testing very complex phenomenon, which could not be handle by conventional methods. Zargarzadeh et al. (2014)

It is the Juncture of the application of multiple fields, which collectively works to equip the computer to handle more complex and unconventional problems under a specific discipline.

DOI: 10.4018/978-1-5225-3531-7.ch009

OVERVIEW

This is the starting of the virtual system in which we merge two different techniques Modares et al. (2013) to solve task smoothly and easily. In this section we are discussing about what feature detection is? And how it is helpful in computer vision. How the pictorial representation of data is being calculated and how a computer process an image. In overview of this chapter you will find out you will final a general introduction about the facts and knowledge about the topic. There is no references used in this section all the references used in the mid and end of it.

The Human Vision

A computer vision is a techniques in which system process an image which is captured by camera like electronic camera, digital camera or by using mobile phone camera, which is same compared by the human vision. The whole working is inspired by human vision working like and image captured by an eye and send it to the brain and with the help of brain neuron we will process that image for further applications. This is very interesting topic on which researcher and scientist are working. Liu et al. (2014) .Now a day it is used and form a commercial fortune. There are so many vision system which check software part as well as mechanical parts to fetch the features.

Main use of this type of technologies are forensic studies and in biometric using human vision as well as computer vision which included face recognition, finger print recognition and handwriting recognition. These study also helpful in field of biologist and physiologist who compare it with human vision system that how human vision system work and how the whole processing is helpful to recognize objects. Haykin (1994) An image is selected after selection of image set of points called feature (pixel) excluded with the help of it we analysis the shape, feature color and texture of the image. These all analysis is done with the use of human vision system.

Human vision is a knowledgeable system that aware and take action on visual boost. Rani et al. (2013) & Wang et al. (2015). Computer and human vision work as same or we can say that the computer vision is inspired from human vision system. The purpose of both the system action on the spatial data. Function of both the system are same, we cannot distinguished the main difference is human vision system use human eye for input and computer vision uses the scanner or camera for an image as input after that the whole processing is same.

Neural System

Neural system is the processes which is done by the neurons present in the human brain. Artificially we are using the concept of ANN (Artificial Neural Network) Modares et al. (2013) .Neurons sends the neural signals provided by the eye which is depend on the wavelength of the object. Shojaei (2015) the weight factor is also consider that control response of particular regions. Weighting factor help in filtering of the features. More detail about neural system explained below in this chapter.

Processing

The neural signals are transmitted in the brain in two parts for further processing are associative cortex (link between the objects) and occipital cortex (pattern processing). The input is captured by the eyes Melingui et al. (2015) & Yan (2012) and forwarded it to the brain next processing is done by the brain with the help of biological neuron by sending neural signals by operating the brain. Human vision system uses edges, boundaries of the objects to achieve the tasks.

BASIC IMAGE PROCESSING APPLICATIONS

Image processing is the process of image by using some operations related mathematically Pan (2015) with the help of signal processing. In image processing large data sets required to processing purpose. And the output of the image is either an image or parameter of the image. Image processing related to the digital image processing. Image processing closely related to computer graphics and computer vision.

Overview

In this topic, we discuss the basic theory about image processing and its formation. In this we explore about an image and its looks having different point in the image. Images having different representation called as frequency domain. Liu (2016) we consider that image is a collection of frequency components. To generate the features from the image so many transformation is applied on the image this is beneficial for further processing and to develop the new techniques also give the fast processing.

Histogram

A histogram is a graphical representation of the numerical data of the image. Author Hsu (2013) introduced by Karl Pearson say it is kind of bar graph. In this first divide an image into parts (intervals). Histogram is the graphical representation of image brightness levels shown by the image, image contrast is measured by range of its level of brightness Narendra (1996) & Antsaklis (1995). Number of pixel with that brightness level. It shows all lowest and highest level shown together. Histogram shows dark and light portion of the image counted number of the pixel. Main concept of histogram is dark portion in image the histogram thicken concentrated area, but with low contrast, histogram shows thinner. Wang & Hill (2006) It will become thinner a low contrast in image.

Histogram Normalization

Histogram normalization is the method of histogram used for magnify the concentrate of the images. In this original image histogram is convert with the help of normalized cumulative sum of that image. The intensity value of the main image is depict to new intensity to generate a uniform histogram. So many method used to work with this task interpolation techniques is one of them. In Histogram normalization interpolation is done with its closest contrast values. Displayed result is combination of both the image intensities. Fock (2014) it is used to adjust contrast of the images simultaneously. It is useful in image background as well as in main ground of the image treated with both brightness as well as darkness part in image. Histogram equalization generate unrealistic effects in photographs. Main application of histogram normalization are; satellite or x-ray image.

Histogram Equalization

Histogram is a graphical representation of the intensity sharing of the image it is totally depend on number of the pixel in the image. Contrast of the image increased using histogram stretching. Histogram equalization mainly used two concepts are known as PMF (probability mass function) for all pixels and CDF (cumulative distributive function). Histogram equalization improves the image contrast by stretching method of intensity value. Equalization is a mapping of uniform distribution of intensity values in whole range.

Feature Detection Level

Feature detection are divided into three parts low Level Feature Detection, mid-Level Feature Detection, high Level Feature Detection. According to these categories features is to be detected and fix it according to algorithms used. All are mentioned below in detail.

Low Level Feature Detection

Low-level features is the features which is indicating by the reality that the inputs and outputs of the system are the images. They included primitive operations like image preprocessing to decreases the noise, contrast enhancement and image sharpening.

Mid-Level Feature Detection

Mid-level features is the features which is indicating by the reality that the system uses two things input and output in which inputs basically are images, and the outputs are attributes of that images features which is extracted from input images like, edges, contours, and the identity of individual objects. Farrell (1998) Mid-level processing features on images merge with tasks segmentation, description of objects make them a form suitable for computer processing, and classification (recognition) of individual objects.

High Level Feature Detection

High-level feature which introduced to deduce a recognized objects, from analysis of the images to performing the function which is cognitive in nature always associated with vision.

SOFT COMPUTING APPROACHES

Soft computing is a technique basically used in computing some calculations is done on concepts or techniques but it is a combination of different methods having different ways to solve the problems, Wang et al. (2012) basic aim of soft computing is to situate the tolerance for implications and uncertainty to achieve traceability.

Soft computing based on, methods and combination of different algorithms like Fuzzy Logics, Dai et al. (2014) Nero-computing, supervised and unsupervised learning, Genetic Algorithms, Machine Learning, Neural Networks and Evolutionary Computing, Support Vector Machine, Ant Colony Optimization, Practical Swan Optimization, Swarm Intelligence, Bayesian network, Brief Propagation etc.

So computing treated as a series of methods and techniques, which is applied on real situation practically. We treated soft computing same as human think and behave which is based on human mind there intelligence, experience, their approaches, and there common sense in every situations. If we conclude soft computing we can say that it is a problem solution methods, which is based on searching as well as area of intelligent system called AI (Artificial Intelligence). So Soft computing is now a days a developing and growing topic as AI.

These all methods are to be explained in the given figure 1.

Basic Soft Computing Tools

The components of soft computing include: machine learning, fuzzy logics (FL), Neural networks (NN), Support Vector Machines (SVM), Evolutionary computation (EC), Genetic algorithms, Evolutionary algorithms, Differential evolution, Swarm Intelligence, Ant colony optimization, Particle swarm optimization, Perceptron etc. we can also called it as a tools of soft computing techniques.

Soft computing is used to exploit tolerance, probabilistic reasoning and uncertainty to achieve close similarity with human behavior like decision making. So soft computing is working on new generation of algorithms and work on principal similar to an AI Known as Computational Intelligence. Soft computing is used to construct intelligent machine like AI working. Main applications of this computing is

Figure 1. Different approaches of soft computing techniques

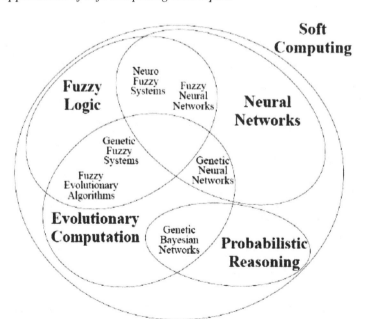

1.   This computing basically used to solve non-linear problems in which mathematical calculations are not entertained by the systems.
2.   It will work on human knowledge such as recognition, understanding and learning and make the system intelligent.

.   Hard computing, also called as conventional computing, based on previous methods which requires a precisely stated analytic model and takes a lot of computation calculation time. Soft computing is different from conventional or hard computing, Gorinevsky (1995) soft computing is based on the human mind working it is the role model of human brain uses neural network concepts.

Hard computing is treated with precision having perfect and accurate answer and soft computing is based on approximations only assumptions is done in this methods in soft computing the tolerance is done to avoid imprecision and uncertainty to achieve submission, having lower cost, and communication is completed economically.

Hard computing in which binary logic is used for calculations means the whole working is based on 0 & 1, crisp systems software, numerical analysis but on the other hand soft computing based on fuzzy logic that is working on assumptions principles, neural nets and probabilistic reasoning.

In Hard computing programs to be written for further processing, uses two-valued logic, it is deterministic in nature, requires exact input data, is strictly in a sequential, follow set of rules produces accurate answers; Kurdila et al. (1995) soft computing can make its own programs for next working, can use multi valued logics or fuzzy logic, it deal with ambiguous and noisy data with full of disturbance, it allows parallel computations, fast in working but results is not accurate. Problem solving techniques are shown in figure 2.

Figure 2. Problem solving techniques- hard computing vs soft computing

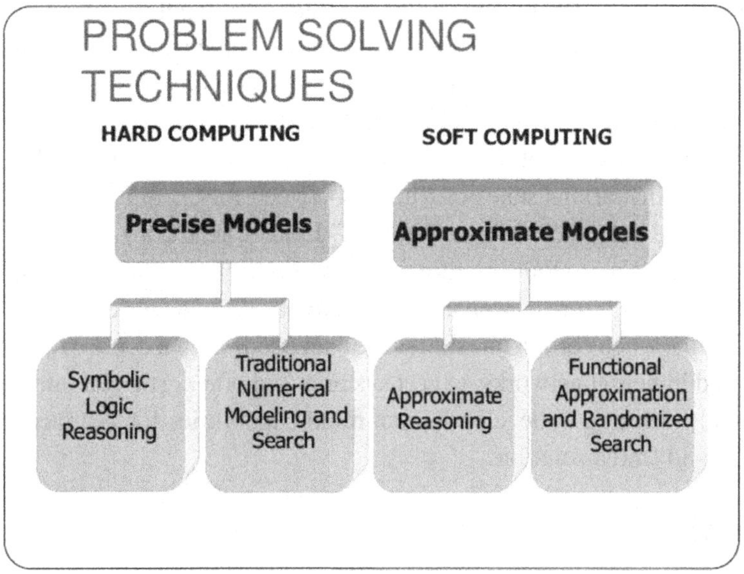

Fuzzy Logic

The invention of fuzzy set is done due to because of represent the real world applications with its fuzzy data sets having uncertainty. The linguistic variables are changes in fuzzy data sets.

BASIC DEFINITIONS AND OPERATIONS

The Fuzzy Logic (FL) was introduced by Professor Lotfi Zadeh, from the University of California at Berkley, FL not to control methodology, but use to processing data by working in partial set membership compare to crisp set membership or non-membership. Fuzzy logic was not used to control the system due to insufficient capability of the computers having small processing units.

FL is a problem-solving system methodology to control that is used to implementations in systems from simple, small, multi uses micro-controllers used to large, networked workstation which is based on data acquisition and control systems. These can be implemented in hardware, software or used in combination of both. Fuzzy logic gives a perfect result in which data is ambiguous, noisy and partial information is used. Fuzzy logic totally based on human mind work but faster than human brain. Khemaissia and Morris (1998)

Fuzzy logic work on numeric data to find the accurate result it is work on critical values but the result is not critical. Fetched result is very useful having very responsive in performance. Fuzzy logics is basically used for sorting of data and for data handling purpose mainly used to control system. These type of systems are designed for the small system but executed the large datasets. It is very robust in nature

Fuzzy Logic Relations

The idea of fuzzy logic working on the concept of problem of computer understandable language also called machine language (natural language) Natural is only a simple language which is not based on true or false or 0 & 1 not easily translated into the absolute terms. It will help to solve fuzzy logic in such a way really works and binary or Boolean logic is simply a special case of it.

Fuzzy logic introduced the concept of 0 and 1 as extreme cases of truth (or "the state of matters" or "fact") but also includes the various states of truth in between for example, the result of a comparison between two data could be not "one" or "zero" but ".5" Lam et al. (2006).

Fuzzy logic looks like closer to the structure of our brains working. In which working and decisions takes on the basis of facts and figure as well as current situations data aggregates is calculated and form a number of partial truths, when certain thresholds are exceeded, shown certain further results. A similar kind of concept is used in neural networks, expert systems and other artificial intelligence applications. Fuzzy logic is basically working to develop human mind capabilities for AI: faced with an unfamiliar task, the AI system could find a solution.

Fuzzy Logic Rules

Union

The union of two sets A and B is

A U B = { x | x ∈ A or x ∈ B }

The union of two fuzzy sets of membership function A and B is μ_A and μ_B respectively is defined as the higher of the two individual membership functions. This is called the *maximum* criterion.

$$\mu A_{\cup B} = max\ (\mu A,\ \mu B)$$

Intersection

The intersection of two sets A and B is

A ∩ B = { x | x ∈ A and x ∈ B }

The intersection of two fuzzy sets of membership function A and B is μ_A and μ_B respectively is defined as the higher of the two individual membership functions. This is called the minimum criterion.

$$\mu A_{\cap B} = min\ (\mu A,\ \mu B)$$

Compliment

It is denoted by Ã and is

Ã = { x | x does not belongs A and x ∈ X }

Figure 3. Union fuzzy set operations

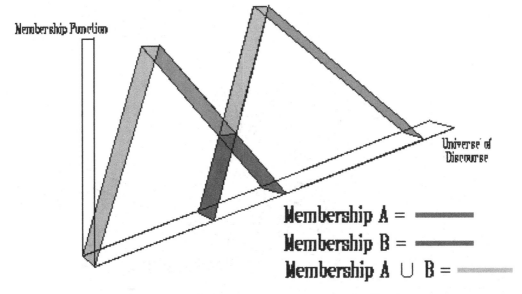

*For a more accurate representation see the electronic version.

Figure 4. Intersection fuzzy set operations

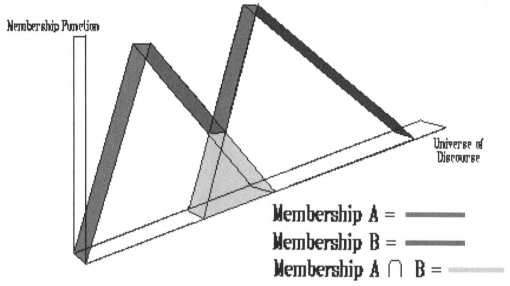

For a more accurate representation see the electronic version.

The Complement of membership function a Fuzzy set A with membership function μ_A is defined as negation or just inverse of function.

$$\mu_A = 1 - \mu_A$$

Figure 5. Compliment of fuzzy set operations

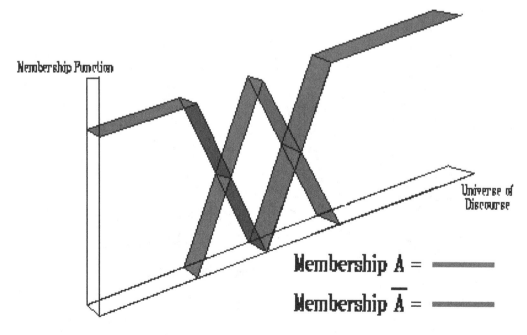

For a more accurate representation see the electronic version.

Associativity

A' is the set that contains everything in the universal set that is not in *A*:

A' = {*x* | *x* **U** and *xA*}.

De Morgan's Law

De Morgan stated two laws about sets.
   If A and B are any two sets then,

$(A \cup B)' = A' \cap B'$

The complement of A union B equals the complement of A intersected with the complement of B.

$(A \cap B)' = A' \cup B'$

The complement of A intersected with B is equal to the complement of A union to the complement of B.

Commutative Law

For any two finite sets A and B;

$A \cup B = B \cup A$

$A \cap B = B \cap A$

Distributive Law

For any three finite sets A, B and C;

$A \cup (B \cap C) = (A \cup B) \cap (A \cup C)$

$A \cap (B \cup C) = (A \cap B) \cup (A \cap C)$

Thus, union and intersection are distributive over intersection and union respectively.

FUZZY LOGIC INFERENCE

Fuzzy interface is the main process in mapping between given input and output using fuzzy logic concepts in fuzzy logic interface the basic terms used are: membership function, if then else rules and fuzzy logic operators. Lee and Terzopoulos (2006).

Figure 6. Elementary Fuzzy Logics

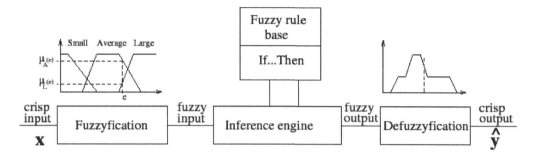

Main applications of fuzzy logic interface are data classification, decision analysis, expert system and computer vision etc. because of its interdisciplinary nature, fuzzy interface having many names such as fuzzy-rule-based system, fuzzy expert system, fuzzy model, fuzzy associative memory, fuzzy logic controller, and simply fuzzy system.

The steps of Fuzzy logic Inference

1. Compare the input variable with its membership functions on linguistic level.
2. Combine all the multiplicative values for getting fulfilment of all the results.
3. Generate all crisp sets of each rules
4. Defuzzification is done after producing crisp output

FUZZIFIER AND DEFUZZIFIER

Fuzzification is the initial step in interfacing process of fuzzy system. In this method transformation is applied where crisp sets take as input and transformed into fuzzy inputs. Crisp having a properties calculate exact input measured by the sensors and that inputs are passed for processing to control system best example of fuzzification are temperature and pressure. Wagner and Smith (2008). Main aim of fuzzification is to coordinate the inputs with the help of sensors having value of 0 & 1. Inputs are mapped with fuzzy numbers.

Defuzzification is the method used to generate results in crisp logic having quantifiable in nature, in this process calculating the fuzzy sets to a crisp set. It is totally based on fuzzy control system. Defuzzification is based on the set of rule that transform the variable into fuzzy as results gets in fuzzy sets. Center of gravity is a common defuzzification technique. Common methods of Defuzzification are COA (center of area), COG (center of gravity), AI (adaptive integration) and QM (quality method).

Defuzzification is the method in which translation of fuzzy sets into fixed quantities and fuzzification is just opposite to it in fuzzification fixed quantities converted into fuzzy quantities.

NEURAL NETWORK

Neural network is a network whose working is based on neuron in brain of human works. In neural network having a large number interrelated processing elements called neurons Hsu (2013) and Pan

Figure 7. Fuzzy logic model with its fundamental input- output relationship

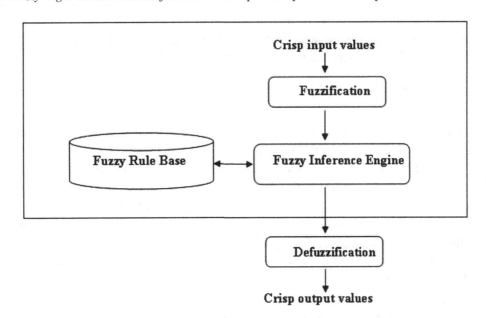

(2013) they all are working together in parallel mode to solve the problems. In neural network not a tuned programed is perform for specific tasks. Neural Network having so many approach to solve the problems as compare to conventional methods. In past conventional computers algorithms techniques are used follows sets of instructions. Conventional computers use cognitive approach to resolve the problem. Ambiguous instructions are used by the Neural Network. Basically in conventional methods computer knows what the problem how to solve is done by neural network.

Introduction and History

Neural Network is also a part of Artificial Neural Network, is recent area of research, which is also a rapid growing area of development, which attracting researchers as well as users related to this discipline. It will cover all other methods with terms of their capabilities pros and cons. An Artificial Neural Network (ANN) is fully based on the concept of biological nervous systems, such as brain, highly interconnected processing elements called neurons working to solve the problems.

A neural network is the network in which neurons are take parts to send information in a network. An ANN (Artificial Neural Network) is a computational model that's working is based on human mind to process any task. ANN is important for the machine learning approaches also used in speech recognition, computer vision and text and data recognition. In this article we explain type of ANN with their history and background details. An ANN having many types like Single neuron, Feed forward Neural Network, Multi-Layer Perceptron, Back-Propagation neural network, Deep Neural Networks.

A simplest definition of Neural Network defined by developer of NN Dr. Robert Hecht-Nielsen. He defines as:

...a computing system made up of a number of simple, highly interconnected processing elements, which process information by their dynamic state response to external inputs.

Neural Network basically work in layers are having so many layers connected through number of neurons each nodes are interconnected with each other having so many layers: input layer is the first layer after that so many intermediate layers and the last layer called an output layer. ANN having so many hidden layers. ANN work according to learning rules.

Biological Neural Network

Concept of computer starting from human brain both working in the common ways. Human brains having so many cells called neurons with so many connection called dendrites which carry information for cell body. Pan and Yu (2008) in neural network there is so many neuron send information from one neuron to another with so many layers with lots of hidden layers. And axon are the cell output which carry information axons are very tiny particle having more than 100 of cell bodies in a millimeter.

Human body neural system consists of three sections receptors, a neural network, and effectors. The receptors are the receiver which receives the signals from inside the body or from outer most world, after receiving the signal it passes that signals to the neurons in electrical impulses forms. Inside neurons forms a network called biological neural network that process the input then and after the whole processing is completed after a proper result as decision displayed. Finally, the effectors convert electrical impulses with the help neural network. Figure (9) shows the communication of neural system.

The main element of the whole biological neural system is neuron. Neurons are also divided into parts these parts are dendrites, soma, and axon. Dendrites are tree like fashion that getting the informa-

Figure 8. A neuron: the basic structure of a brain cell, cell body, the dendrites and the axon

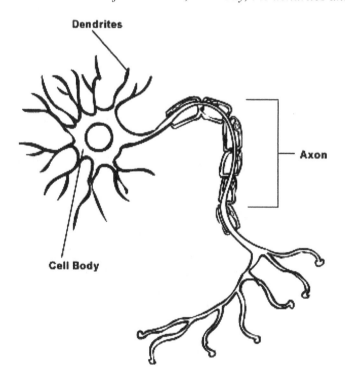

Figure 9. Biological Neural System

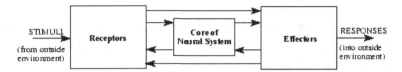

tion from neighbor neurons where each neuron are connected into another and working in several layers. Farrell and Polycarpou (2006) the axon are main unit of neural system, able to transfer the signals many of them are divided into sub branches, they convey the information in different ways. Last but not the least soma is the cell body. Figure (10) shows the whole structure of single biological neuron.

Brain handle both the tasks parallel as well as serial ways. It is totally depend the mechanism of the brain nervous system. Parallel and serial processing easily find out to perform related tasks.

Components of Artificial Neural Network

Artificial neural networks (ANNs) also called as connection system are the computational model in computer science and other application fields which uses the large data sets working as human brain with the help of neurons called artificial neurons, they are loosely coupled with each other like a biological brain functions. Connection in between neurons send the information in form of signals and that signals travels along the neurons and send the information from inner to outer cell. Zhang (1999) typically neurons are working in layers and the signal travels along the layers from the first layer called input layer some intermediate layers are there after that last layer called outer layer in which result is to be displayed. Now a days millions of neural projects uses this concept to solve particular task more easily with in short duration of time like speech recognition and computer vision.

Artificial neural network are of many types as mentioned below

Figure 10. Structure of a biological neuron

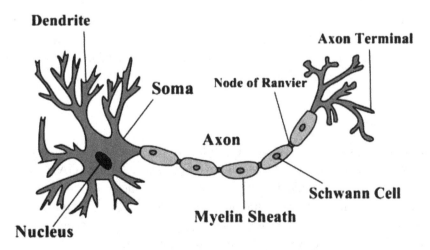

Single Layer Feed Forward Network

In single layer feed forward network the information is forwarded to the next layers but not vice versa. Only forward options is available to send information to next layers in between two layers only. One is input layer and next is output layer.

Multilayer Feed Forward Network

In multi-layer feed forward network the information is forwarded to the next layers but not vice versa. Which having so many hidden layers in between input and output layers only forward options is available to send information to next layers in between number of the layers. One is input layer and next layer is intermediate layer and last layer is called output layer.

Recurrent Network

In this type of network basically work as feed forward network but there is at least a backward network is also available for sending information back to the previous layer called recurrent network.

Hopfield Network

A Hopfield network is a type of recurrent ANN having work as feed forward network but there is at least one backward network is also available for sending information back to the previous layer called recurrent network which is discovered by John Hopfield in 1982, describe earlier by Little in 1974 having addressable memory with binary nodes using threshold. Sastry and Bodson (2002). It is working on converge to a local minimum. Hopfield network same working as to understand the model of human memory.

Genetic Algorithms

Genetic algorithms (GA) is the adaptive heuristic search algorithm based on the idea of automatic selection and genetic order in human body. It is based on intelligent unplanned search to solve many problems like optimization. Unplanned doesn't mean that totally unplanned it is basically depend upon the previous data and historical information to categorical search for best performance. Genetic algorithms (GA) is based on natural selection and process in human body. It is basically used in Artificial Intelligent system but totally differ from conventional AI system.

Overview

Genetic algorithms (GA) is used to solve constrained as well as unconstrained optimization problems that is based on random selection or called as naturally Genetic algorithms (GA) continuously work for betterment of the population of individual solutions. The process which is followed by Genetic algorithms (GA) is step processing. In first step select individuals un-sequentially for individual solution. Working on a principle for individual principle consider current population is parents and produced the children for next generations. Mainly it is used to solve optimization problem.

It is based on three rules

1. *Selection rules* select the individuals.
2. *Crossover rules* join parents to get children to the next generation.
3. *Mutation rules* used unplanned conversion to single parents to form children.

Genetic algorithm reproduced the endurance of the fittest in dispersion of individuals over connective generation to solve the problem. Each generation based on the population of string characters that are related to the chromosomes that are shown in our DNA. DNA of the parents cross together and results children the same searching process is used in genetic algorithm. Shown figure explain the processing. Haykin (1994)

Genetic algorithms (GA) are based on the concept having generic structure and chromosomes behavior to generate the individual child. Genetic algorithm are based biological genetic system. Which is used to solve variety of problems which given the bunch of solution. And find the possible best solution fit for reproduction from all possible solution to get a new solution.

APPLICATION OF SOFT COMPUTING TECHNIQUES

1. **Script Recognition:** In this application handwriting of the individual is to be recognized with the help of soft computing techniques. It is the ability of the computer to recognize handwriting by using handwritten input as source by optical scanner also called as word recognition. It also handle formatting, with the help of segmentation techniques.
2. **Data Compression:** Data compression is the method to compress the large amount of data info small size help to send the data from sender to receiver. And at the receiver end data is decompressed for use. Data compression is method of encoding information uses the concept of bits. Compression is important because it reduces resources to store and transmit the data.

Figure 11. Process of Genetic Algorithm

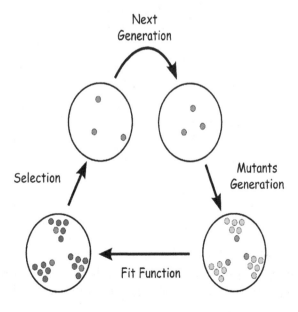

3. **Automotive Systems and fabrication:** Automotive Systems is very useful now a days in the world. It help to produced, harvest and distribution of food to the appropriate centers. Requirement of this type of system is due to because of regularly increment in the population.

4. **Architecture of Soft Computing:** Soft computing is a technique used usually in computer science. Basically computing means some calculations it is not only means concepts or techniques but it is a combination of different methods having different ways to solve the problems, main aim of soft computing is to exploit the tolerance for implications and uncertainty to achieve traceability.

5. **Decision-support Systems:** A bunch of computer program help to any organization for decision making in all of related field of that organization in theoretical as well as in technical issues. It helps to any organization in their foundation and implementation purpose.

6. **Consumer applications:** Application which are related to consumers like AC refrigerator heater, washing machines in all day to day useable device use the concept of soft computing.

7. **Robotic engineering:** It is the creativity by the humans for the human like the human i.e the concept of robot which help to perform task easier with using the man power. It is very important invention of the century. It is invented by the engineers which is relate to mechanical, electrical as well as software engineering discipline. Robot used in every field where the man power is required. It is working by using concept of soft computing.

8. **Food preparations appliances:** Food preparations appliances like microwave, rice cooker or any other device which uses the timer soft computing technique is used.

9. **Game playing:** In game playing by the computer or with the computer soft computing is required for decision making purpose.

Soft Computing Based Feature Detection

Feature detection is the concept used in image processing is a type of computing which extract the information of the image based on their features by taking decisions at every point in the image called an image features. The output features are the parts of the image having considered as a single separated point divided into categories. Application of feature extraction decided which features required as output. Bhartiya and Whiteley (2001) Different algorithms are used according to the variation in their application. Overall algorithms will offer best feature detection techniques. Main property of feature detection is repeatability.

Feature detection is considered as a low level feature in image processing. It is the initial operation which is applied on an image and consider and treated with every pixel in which feature is too extracted. Sometimes when feature detection is quite expensive in computation time then we consider high level algorithms to process the feature detection of the image. It is basically considered as initial step of image and main used in computer vision. Dufour (2005) Due to initial step large number of features developed which help for applying in soft computing techniques for classification purpose.

SUMMARY

Soft computing is the techniques which solve the variety of application. In this chapter mainly we are focusing on feature extraction techniques and that feature is to be classified with the help of soft computing techniques. Soft computing having so many algorithms for each applications. In this chapter we are basically focused on Introduction to Soft Computing with Fuzzy logic systems which explains the basic definitions of fuzzy set theory, i.e., the basic notions, the properties of fuzzy sets and operations on fuzzy sets. Some popular constructions of fuzzy systems are presented Neural networks gives a short introduction to neural networks. The basic concepts are presented Unified form of soft computing methods chapter describes soft computing methods in neural networks Training of soft computing methods chapter gives more detail describes of soft computing training methods in neural networks

REFERENCES

Antsaklis, P. J. (1995, June). Intelligent learning control. *IEEE Control Syst.*, *15*(3), 5–7. doi:10.1109/MCS.1995.594467

Bhartiya, S., & Whiteley, J. R. (2001, September). Development of inferential measurements using neural networks. *ISA Transactions*, *40*(4), 307–323. doi:10.1016/S0019-0578(01)00004-0 PMID:11577819

Dai, S.-L., Wang, C., & Wang, M. (2014, January). Dynamic learning from adaptive neural network control of a class of nonaffine nonlinear systems. *IEEE Transactions on Neural Networks and Learning Systems*, *25*(1), 111–123. doi:10.1109/TNNLS.2013.2257843 PMID:24806648

Dufour, P., Bhartiya, S., Dhurjati, P. S., & Doyle, F. J. III. (2005). Neural network-based software sensor: Training set design and application to a continuous pulp digester. *Control Engineering Practice*, *13*(2), 135–143. doi:10.1016/j.conengprac.2004.02.013

Farrell, J. A. (1998, September). Stability and approximator convergence in nonparametric nonlinear adaptive control. *IEEE Transactions on Neural Networks*, *9*(5), 1008–1020. doi:10.1109/72.712182 PMID:18255784

Farrell, J. A., & Polycarpou, M. M. (2006). *Adaptive Approximation Based Control: Unifying Neural, Fuzzy and Traditional Adaptive Approximation Approaches*. Hoboken, NJ: Wiley. doi:10.1002/0471781819

Fock, E. (2014, August). Global sensitivity analysis approach for input selection and system identification purposes—A new framework for feedforward neural networks. *IEEE Transactions on Neural Networks and Learning Systems*, *25*(8), 1484–1495. doi:10.1109/TNNLS.2013.2294437 PMID:25050946

Gorinevsky, D. (1995, September). On the persistency of excitation in radial basis function network identification of nonlinear systems. *IEEE Transactions on Neural Networks*, *6*(5), 1237–1244. doi:10.1109/72.410365 PMID:18263411

Haykin, S. (1994). *Neural Networks: A Comprehensive Foundation*. Upper Saddle River, NJ: Prentice-Hall.

Hsu, C.-F. (2013, April). Adaptive neural complementary sliding-mode control via functional-linked wavelet neural network. *Engineering Applications of Artificial Intelligence*, *26*(4), 1221–1229. doi:10.1016/j.engappai.2012.11.012

Khalil. (2002). *Nonlinear Systems* (3rd ed.). Upper Saddle River, NJ: Prentice-Hall.

Khemaissia, S., & Morris, A. (1998, June). Use of an artificial neuroadaptive robot model to describe adaptive and learning motor mechanisms in the central nervous system. *IEEE Transactions on Systems, Man, and Cybernetics. Part B, Cybernetics, 28*(3), 404–416. doi:10.1109/3477.678635 PMID:18255956

Kurdila, A. J., Narcowich, F. J., & Ward, J. D. (1995, March). Persistency of excitation in identification using radial basis function approximants. *SIAM Journal on Control and Optimization, 33*(2), 625–642. doi:10.1137/S0363012992232555

Lam, T., Anderschitz, M., & Dietz, V. (2006, February). Contribution of feedback and feedforward strategies to locomotor adaptations. *Journal of Neurophysiology, 95*(2), 766–773. doi:10.1152/jn.00473.2005 PMID:16424453

Lee, S.-H., & Terzopoulos, D. (2006, July). Heads up! Biomechanical modeling and neuromuscular control of the neck. *ACM Transactions on Graphics, 25*(3), 1188–1198. doi:10.1145/1141911.1142013

Liu, D., Wang, D., & Li, H. (2014, February). Decentralized stabilization for a class of continuous-time nonlinear interconnected systems using online learning optimal control approach. *IEEE Transactions on Neural Networks and Learning Systems, 25*(2), 418–428. doi:10.1109/TNNLS.2013.2280013 PMID:24807039

Liu, G. P. (2001). *Nonlinear Identification and Control: A Neural Network Approach.* London, UK: Springer. doi:10.1007/978-1-4471-0345-5

Liu, T., Wang, C., & Hill, D. J. (2009, September). Learning from neural control of nonlinear systems in normal form. *Systems & Control Letters, 58*(9), 633–638. doi:10.1016/j.sysconle.2009.04.001

Liu, Y.-J., Gao, Y., Tong, S., & Li, Y. (2016, February). Fuzzy approximation-based adaptive backstepping optimal control for a class of nonlinear discretetime systems with dead-zone. *IEEE Transactions on Fuzzy Systems, 24*(1), 16–28. doi:10.1109/TFUZZ.2015.2418000

Liu, Y.-J., & Tong, S. (2014, October). Adaptive fuzzy control for a class of nonlinear discrete-time systems with backlash. *IEEE Transactions on Fuzzy Systems, 22*(5), 1359–1365. doi:10.1109/TFUZZ.2013.2286837

Lu, S., & Ba¸sar, T. (1998, May). Robust nonlinear system identification using neuralnetwork models. *IEEE Transactions on Neural Networks, 9*(3), 407–429. doi:10.1109/72.668883 PMID:18252465

Melingui, A., Lakhal, O., Daachi, B., Mbede, J. B., & Merzouki, R. (2015, December). andR. Merzouki,"Adaptive neural network control of a compact bionic handling arm. *IEEE/ASME Transactions on Mechatronics, 20*(6), 2862–2875. doi:10.1109/TMECH.2015.2396114

Modares, H., Lewis, F. L., & Naghibi Sistani, M.-B. (2013, October). Adaptive optimal control of unknown constrained-input systems using policy iteration and neural networks. *IEEE Transactions on Neural Networks and Learning Systems, 24*(10), 1513–1525. doi:10.1109/TNNLS.2013.2276571 PMID:24808590

Narendra, K. S. (1996, October). Neural networks for control theory and practice. *Proceedings of the IEEE, 84*(10), 1385–1406. doi:10.1109/5.537106

Pan, Y., Liu, Y., Xu, B., & Yu, H. (2016, April). Hybrid feedback feedforward: An efficient design of adaptive neural network control. *Neural Networks*, *76*, 122–134. doi:10.1016/j.neunet.2015.12.009 PMID:26890657

Pan, Y., Sun, T., & Yu, H. (2015, December). Peaking-free output-feedback adaptive neural control under a nonseparation principle. *IEEE Transactions on Neural Networks and Learning Systems*, *26*(12), 3097–3108. doi:10.1109/TNNLS.2015.2403712 PMID:25794400

Pan, Y., & Yu, H. (2014). Biomimetic hybrid feedback feedforword adaptive neural control of robotic arms. *Proc. IEEE Symp. Comput. Intell. Control Autom.*, 1–7. doi:10.1109/CICA.2014.7013254

Pan, Y., Zhou, Y., Sun, T., & Er, M. J. (2013, January). Composite adaptive fuzzy H∞ tracking control of uncertain nonlinear systems. *Neurocomputing*, *99*(1), 15–24. doi:10.1016/j.neucom.2012.05.011

Rani, A., Singh, V., & Gupta, J. R. P. (2013). Development of soft sensor for neural network based control of distillation column. *ISA Transactions*, *52*(3), 438–449. doi:10.1016/j.isatra.2012.12.009 PMID:23375672

Sastry, S., & Bodson, M. (1989). *Adaptive Control: Stability, Convergence and Robustness*. Englewood Cliffs, NJ: Prentice-Hall.

Shojaei, K. (2015, July). Neural adaptive robust output feedback control of wheeled mobile robots with saturating actuators. *International Journal of Adaptive Control and Signal Processing*, *29*(7), 855–876. doi:10.1002/acs.2509

Wagner, M. J., & Smith, M. A. (2008, October). Shared internal models for feedforward and feedback control. *The Journal of Neuroscience*, *28*(42), 10663–10673. doi:10.1523/JNEUROSCI.5479-07.2008 PMID:18923042

Wang, C., & Hill, D. J. (2006, January). Learning from neural control. *IEEE Transactions on Neural Networks*, *17*(1), 130–146. doi:10.1109/TNN.2005.860843 PMID:16526482

Wang, C., Wang, M., Liu, T., & Hill, D. J. (2012, October). Learning from ISS-modular adaptive NN control of nonlinear strict-feedback systems. *IEEE Transactions on Neural Networks and Learning Systems*, *23*(10), 1539–1550. doi:10.1109/TNNLS.2012.2205702 PMID:24808000

Wang, M., Wang, C., & Liu, X. (2014, September). Dynamic learning from adaptive neural control with predefined performance for a class of nonlinear systems. *Inf. Sci.*, *279*, 874–888. doi:10.1016/j.ins.2014.04.038

Wang, Y.-C., Chien, C.-J., Chi, R., & Hou, Z. (2015, September). A fuzzy-neural adaptive terminal iterative learning control for fed-batch fermentation processes. *International Journal of Fuzzy Systems*, *17*(3), 423–433. doi:10.1007/s40815-015-0059-7

Xu, B., Yang, C., & Shi, Z. (2014, March). Reinforcement learning output feedback NN control using deterministic learning technique. *IEEE Transactions on Neural Networks and Learning Systems*, *25*(3), 635–641. doi:10.1109/TNNLS.2013.2292704 PMID:24807456

Yan, W. (2012, July). Toward automatic time-series forecasting using neural networks. *IEEE Transactions on Neural Networks and Learning Systems, 23*(7), 1028–1039. doi:10.1109/TNNLS.2012.2198074 PMID:24807130

Zargarzadeh, Dierks, & Jagannathan. (2014). Adaptive neural network-based optimal control of nonlinear continuous-time systems in strict-feedback form. *Int. J. Adapt. Control Signal Process, 28*(3-5), 305–324.

Zhang, J. (1999). Inferential estimation of polymer quality using bootstrap aggregated neural networks. *Neural Networks, 12*(6), 927–938. doi:10.1016/S0893-6080(99)00037-4 PMID:12662667

Chapter 10
Utility and Significance of Vague Set Theory and Advanced Optimization Mechanisms for Uncertainty Management

Sowkarthika B
Madhav Institute of Technology and Science, India

Akhilesh Tiwari
Madhav Institute of Technology and Science, India

R. K. Gupta
Madhav Institute of Technology and Science, India

Uday Pratap Singh
Madhav Institute of Technology and Science, India

ABSTRACT

In this digital world, tremendous data are generated in every field. Useful information is inferred out of this data, which is valuable for effective decision making. Data mining extracts the interesting information from huge volumes of data. Association rule (AR) mining is one of the core areas of data mining where interesting information is extracted in the form of rules. Traditional AR mining is incapable of handling uncertain situations. In order to handle uncertainty, mathematical tools like vague theory can be utilized with AR mining methodologies for the development of novel vague theory based algorithms, which will be more suitable in effectively handling vague situations that helps framing effective selling strategy. Since an organization can't analyze the huge rule set obtained from these algorithms, every resultant rule should have a certain ratio of factors customized to the interest of the organization that can be achieved through optimization algorithms. This chapter explores the significance of vague theory and optimization means for effective uncertainty management.

DOI: 10.4018/978-1-5225-3531-7.ch010

INTRODUCTION

Data is being generated and gathered in every field which results in an increase in the size of the data. Any organization is not in need of data. It needs information that is inferred out of data. That is, the data is useless until and unless it is converted to useful information. Since manual examination is entirely incomprehensible with huge volume of data, automated tools came into the picture. Data Mining is an automated tool which helps in extracting useful or interesting patterns or information from huge volumes of data like database or other data repositories. There are various tasks pertaining to data mining. Some of the essential tasks are Association Rule mining (AR mining), Classification and Clustering. Since classification and clustering need AR mining to be performed, and AR mining has direct relevance with real-life scenarios, the authors focus more on AR mining.

AR mining is useful in examining and analyzing the customer's behavior. Association in retail store refers to the patterns that contain items that are frequently purchased together. It gives the frequently occurring patterns in the transaction data. This basically gives the relationship between the products that is useful in strategic business decisions and product marketing. The problem of AR mining is defined by Agrawal (Han & Kamber, 2006) as:

Let $I = \{i_1, i_2, \ldots i_n\}$ {\displaystyle I=\{i_{1},i_{2},\ldots,i_{n}\}\} be a set of n {\displaystyle n}nnnbinary attributes called items.

Let $D = \{t_1, t_2, \ldots, t_n\}$ {\displaystyle D=\{t_{1},t_{2},\ldots, t_{m}\}\} be a set of transactions called the database.

Each transaction in *{\displaystyle D}DDD* has a unique transaction identifier *TID* and contains a subset of the items in *I*. IA rule is defined as an implication of the form *{\displaystyle X\Rightarrow Y}* $A \Rightarrow B$ where *A, B* are the set of items i.e., $A, B \subseteq I$. Also, $A \cap B = \phi$. For example, from *Bread* $\Rightarrow$ *Jam*, the retailer could get an idea that whenever *Bread* is purchased, *Jam* is also purchased. Based on the rule generated, some discount could be offered or the store layout could be changed accordingly thereby boosting the sales. Association rules are represented by 'if-then' rules. In $A \Rightarrow B$, *A* is the antecedent and *B* is the consequent and it implies 'if *A* is purchased, then *B* is more likely to be purchased'. Antecedent is the set of items in the database and consequent is the set of items that are in relationship with the antecedent. The two important criteria in identifying a relationship and making a rule interesting are support and confidence. AR is considered interesting only when it satisfies minimum support and minimum confidence thresholds. The thresholds are set by the domain experts or users who have rich knowledge of the system. These play a key role in making any business decisions. A strong association rule is generated if the support and confidence of a rule are greater than minimum support and minimum confidence thresholds.

Support gives how frequent *A* and *B* occur in the database of transactions *D*. Support of the rule is the probability of the occurrence of items *A* and *B* in the database *D*.

$$support(A \rightarrow B) = P(A \cup B) = \frac{|A \cup B|}{|D|}$$

Confidence is measured as the fraction of the transactions containing *A* also contain *B*. This is the conditional probability.

$$confidence(A \rightarrow B) = P(\frac{B}{A}) = \frac{support(A \cup B)}{support(A)}$$

Here, the domain under discussion is market-basket analysis where, for a given database of customer transactions with each transaction containing set of items, the goal is to find groups of items which are frequently purchased together. A set of items is referred to as itemset. A rule that contains *k*-items and these items are occurring frequently together in the given set of transactions is referred to as k-frequent itemset. It is represented by L_k.

Conventional AR mining proposed so far is unequipped in handling uncertain and vague situations. Real – world data has vague values. Crisp set fails to represent approximate values. But, a real world entity contains approximate values (redundant, missed, inconsistent, uncertain data). There is always an uncertainty in knowledge. Though the traditional algorithms fail to address the uncertainty, some algorithms on fuzzy, rough and vague set try to address these concerns. This chapter briefs the existing models used for mining and its failure in addressing uncertainty. It also provides a detailed discussion on the capability of fuzzy, rough and vague theories in handling uncertain situations. It also analyzes the need for the optimization algorithms in AR mining.

ASSOCIATION RULE MINING

Generating interesting rules is the core idea of data mining. Hence, the authors consider the AR mining on the large database of sales transactions. Various research papers have been proposed in affiliation with AR mining involving crisp data. Numerous modifications have been made in the newly evolved algorithms to make AR mining more efficient, scalable and to have low CPU and I/O overheads. This section discusses the modifications made in the traditional algorithms to improve efficiency and also summarizes the failure of these algorithms in addressing the uncertain situations.

AIS

The items that have been brought frequently are the ones that interest the retailers since it can help framing good strategy that helps in boosting the sales. Mining applied to these items is frequent pattern mining. Frequent pattern mining was initially proposed by (Agarwal, Imielinski & Swami, 1993, 207-216) for market basket analysis. The algorithm proposed is AIS. It helps in finding the relationship between items that are placed in the basket by the customer. Scanning the database, L_k is generated from L_{k-1}. That is, *k*-frequent itemset are generated from *k*-1 frequent itemset simply by scanning the database for the frequency of the occurrence of items in the rule. Though support and confidence is applied for achieving *k*-frequent itemsets where *k*=1... *n* for '*n*' is the number of items, the rules generated at the end of each *k*-frequent itemset is huge and most of them are found to be not frequent. Also, no proper structure has been proposed for AIS.

SETM

Then SETM was proposed by (Agrawal & Srikant, 1994, pp.487-499) which has a proper structure represented by *<TID, itemset>* where *TID* is the unique transaction identifier. In spite of addressing the issue of data structure, it fails to reduce the number of passes at each level which was also a problem in AIS. Also, each candidate itemset needs its transaction information to be stored which increases the space occupied thereby making it inefficient.

Apriori

Apriori was proposed by (Agrawal & Srikant, 1994, pp.487-499) to counter the problems faced by AIS and SETM. Apriori has the structure of the form <TID,itemset> and it mines the frequent itemset for Boolean ARs. This algorithm uses the prior or previous knowledge to generate the rules containing frequent itemset. It follows level-wise approach of exploring k-itemset to extract $(k+1)$ -itemset. Apriori property has been introduced which states that all non-empty subsets of a frequent itemset must be frequent, thereby reducing the search space and the scans to a considerable extent. That is, if $P(K) <$ *minimum Support* where 'K' is the set of items, then $P(K \cup X) <$ *minimum Support* where 'X' can be any item i.e., $X \subseteq I$ where 'I' is the set of items in the transactional database. This property is anti monotone property which says if a set fails a test, then any superset formed out of this will fail the same test. On finding L_k from L_{k-1}, Apriori property is applied with the help of two processes (Prune and Join). In Join operation, if I_1 and I_2 are the itemsets in L_{k-1} and $I_i(j)$ denotes j^{th} item in I_i, the join $L_{k-1 \bowtie} L_{k-1}$ is performed if and only if their first $(k-2)$ items are in common. That is,

$$[I_1(1)=I_2(1)] \wedge [I_1(2)=I_2(2)] \wedge \ldots \wedge [I_1(k-2)=I_2(k-2)] \wedge [I_1(k-1) < I_2(k-1)].$$

The resultant itemset is $I_1(1) I_1(2).. I_1(k-1) I_2(k-1)$. Prune step follows Apriori anti monotone property. If *AB* is not frequent and *AC, BC* are frequent, then *ABC* cannot be considered as frequent. This subset testing is done by maintaining a hash tree of all frequent items.

For the above set of transactions, maximum frequent itemset is calculated with the minimum support count assumed as 2. Tables in figure 1 illustrate the extraction of frequent itemsets from the transactional database in table 1.

Though Apriori has reduced the candidate itemset to a considerable extent, still the numbers are huge. It also involves too much scanning of the database. In order to improve the efficiency of Apriori, various variations on Apriori has been proposed. These variations are briefly summarized in the following sections.

Variants of Apriori

Partitioning

Partitioning was proposed by (Savasere, Omiecinski & Navathe, 1995, pp.432-444). The partition technique has two phases. In Phase I, the transactional database are divided or partitioned into 'n' pieces where no two partitions contain the same transaction. Then the minimum support count is evaluated as *min_sup* × *Number of transactions in that partition* and frequent itemset is generated for each partition which is

Table 1. Transactional database

TID	List of item_IDs
T1	I1,I2,I5
T2	I2,I4
T3	I2,I3
T4	I1,I2,I4
T5	I1,I3
T6	I2,I3
T7	I1,I3
T8	I1,I2,I3,I5
T9	I1,I2,I3

Figure 1. Generation of candidate itemsets and frequent itemsets, where the min. support= 2

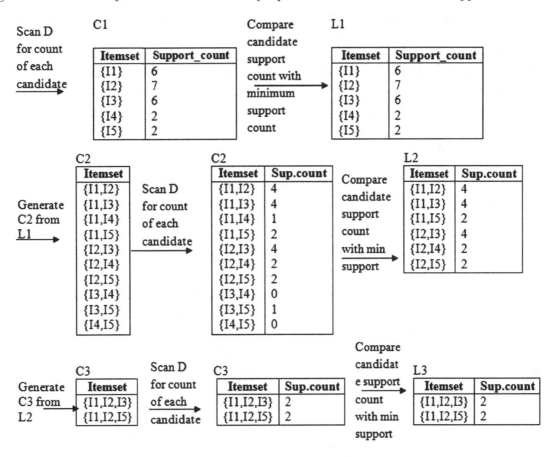

referred to as *local frequent itemsets*. Combine all the local frequent itemsets to form a global frequent itemset. In Phase II, a second scan of *D* is done where the actual support of each candidate is analyzed to determine the global frequent itemsets. This helps in parallel execution and reduces the overhead.

Sampling

Sampling was proposed by (Toivonen, 1996, pp.134-145). The basic idea behind sampling approach is to pick some random sample consisting of a set of transactions from the database D instead of taking the entire transaction D and find the frequent itemset in that sample. But in this case, some tradeoff is needed between degree of accuracy and the efficiency. This is particularly useful in the case of very large database D. Since some frequent itemsets might be missed, the minimum support threshold is also reduced accordingly. The rest of the database is then checked to see whether the frequent itemset obtained from the sample is frequent in the whole database D as well. Eventually, only those itemsets that are frequent in the D are considered to be frequent. This method is really helpful only when the frequent itemsets are extracted from large database on a frequent basis.

Dynamic Itemset Counting

Dynamic itemset counting was proposed by (Brin, Motwani, Ullman & Tsur, 1997, pp.207-216). In this technique, the frequent itemset is updated dynamically with the addition of each new transaction in the database. The database D is partitioned into blocks that are marked with start points. Here the new candidate itemsets are added at any start point that helps in determining new candidate itemset prior to each database scan. It calculates the support count of all itemsets that has been estimated till now and the itemsets that have been newly added, which requires only few scans. But it suffers from the problem of taking each and every tuple in the calculation.

Transaction Reduction

It is based on the idea that any transaction that does not contain k-frequent itemset cannot contain $(k+1)$-frequent itemset as well. So those transactions are eliminated in the future, thereby reducing the number of scanning actually required.

Hashing

Hashing technique was proposed by (Park, Chen & Yu, 1995, ppp.175-186). The hash based technique is used basically to reduce the size of the candidate itemset. On scanning each transaction in the database to generate the frequent 1-itemsets, 2-frequent itemsets can also be generated for each transaction by hashing them into the buckets. The hash table structure is used and a hash function is defined. For the transactions given in table 1, the hash table is given in table 2

Figure 2. Mining by partitioning the data

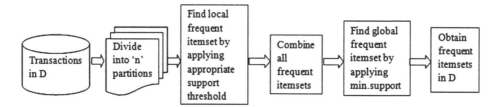

Table 2. Mining using Hashing technique

Bucket Address	0	1	2	3	4	5	6
Bucket count	2	2	4	2	2	4	4
Bucket contents	{I1,I4} {I3,I5}	{I1,I5} {I1,I5}	{I2,I3} {I2,I3} {I2,I3} {I2,I3}	{I2,I4} {I2,I4}	{I2,I5} {I2,I5}	{I1,I2} {I1,I2} {I1,I2} {I1,I2}	{I1,I3} {I1,I3} {I1,I3} {I1,I3}

The hash table is obtained by scanning the set of transactions in the transactions table used in Apriori algorithm. The hash table in table 2 gives candidate 2-itemsets where the order of items $I1$, $I2$, $I3$, $I4$, $I5$ are given by 1,2,3,4,5 respectively, and their hash function is defined as $h(x, y) = ((order\ of\ x) \times 10 + (order\ of\ y))\ mod\ 7$. If minimum support is 3, then the itemsets in window 0,1,3,4 cannot be frequent and they are not included as frequent itemset.

CARMA

CARMA (Continuous Association Rule Mining Algorithm) was proposed by (Hidber et al., 1999). This algorithm gives the frequent itemsets online. It shows the current association rule and allows changes to the parameters (minimum support and confidence) during the first scan of the database. It is a 2-scan algorithm. The feedback is obtained continuously. The interestingness parameters are user-controllable since the values can be changed by the user at any point of time. CARMA yields deterministic and accurate results. CARMA is more memory efficient and it computes association rules which are sometimes intractable for Apriori.

Few alternative algorithms have been proposed in mining Boolean association rule to reduce the number of scans and size of the candidate itemset. Some of the algorithms are FP-growth, Pincer and vertical data layout.

FP-Growth Algorithm

FP (Frequent Pattern) -growth is proposed by (Han, Liu, Pan & Wang, 2002). This method removes the candidate generation in order to extract the frequent itemsets. It uses highly compact data structure called FP-tree which compresses the original database. It adopts divide and conquer strategy. Though it compresses the database table, it also retains the necessary information. The compressed information is then divided into a set of conditional databases where each database contains one frequent item.

After creating an FP-tree, for mining the FP, start from frequent length-1 patterns as an initial suffix pattern and construct a conditional database for every path, and construct the conditional FP-tree and perform mining recursively on that tree. Pattern growth is obtained by the concatenation of the suffix pattern with the frequent patterns generated from the conditional FP-tree. This method reduces the search costs substantially. There is a problem with this method when the size of the database is huge, because FP-tree cannot fit in main memory. This algorithm is about an order of magnitude faster than Apriori.

Mining Using Vertical Data Format (ECLAT)

(Zaki, n.d) proposed vertical data mining. This method transforms the dataset of format *<TID, Itemset>* to *<Item, TIDset>* where *TIDset* contains the transaction IDs that are involved in the purchase of the particular item. In the vertical case, the item is unique. It mines the transformed data by analyzing the *TIDset* intersections for each item and calculating its frequency count. It then follows Apriori property. Tables in table 3 and table 4 demonstrate the extraction of 2-frequent itemsets from the transactional database in table 1.

Frequent k-itemset are useful in constructing $(k+1)$ –itemset. This method doesn't scan the database since the frequency is evaluated based on the intersection count of transaction IDs. If there are too many *TID*s, then this method takes substantial memory space as well as computation time. To reduce the cost of registering *TID*s, diffsets have been proposed by (Zaki & Gouda et al., n.d) which stores only the difference between two *TID*s of $(k+1)$ -itemset and k-itemset.

Pincer Algorithm

Pincer Search Algorithm was proposed by, (Lin & Kedem, 1997). Typical AR mining algorithms operate in bottom-up breadth-first search in finding the frequent itemset. In Pincer algorithm, the main search direction is bottom-up (which is very much similar to Apriori) except the fact that this algorithm conducts simultaneous a restricted top-down search, which is done to maintain a data structure called Maximum Frequent Candidate Set (MFCS). It yields Maximum Frequent Set as output i.e. the set containing all maximal frequent itemsets. The algorithm deals with large size maximal frequent itemsets. This algorithm improves the performance in several orders of magnitude. This performs well even if the maximum frequent itemsets are long.

Table 3. Extraction of 2-candidate itemsets in vertical format

Itemset	TID
{I1,I2}	{T1,T4,T8,T9}
{I1,I3}	{T5,T7,T8,T9}
{I1,I4}	{T4}
{I1,I5}	{T1,T8}
{I2,I3}	{T3,T6,T8,T9}
{I2,I4}	{T2,T4}
{I2,I5}	{T1,T8}
{I3,I5}	{T8}

Table 4. Extraction of 2-frequent itemsets in vertical format

Itemset	TID
{I1,I2}	{T1,T4,T8,T9}
{I1,I3}	{T5,T7,T8,T9}
{I2,I3}	{T3,T6,T8,T9}

Challenges Associated With Simple AR Mining Methodologies

Representation and Analysis of the uncertain situation are impractical with Boolean association rules (i.e., with the crisp set) since it takes only two values '0' and '1'. The algorithms proposed so far operate on Boolean values and generate Boolean association rules. But the real world data does not essentially comprise of Boolean values. The approximate values fall in [0, 1] which couldn't be represented by crisp or Boolean set.

Algorithms for Handling Uncertainty

In shopping applications, algorithms dealt so far estimate the relationship between items that are placed in the basket. But, these algorithms fail to analyze some items that are 'almost bought' by customers. This hesitation information cannot be represented by '0' and '1'. This leads to the need for evolution of a different tool in handling this adverse situation. So, usage of fuzzy, rough or vague set theories in AR Mining is done to address the uncertain or vague situation.

UNCERTAINTY WITH FUZZY SET

According to (Zadeh, 1965), Fuzzy set was defined as "Let X be a set of points and $X = \{x\}$. A fuzzy set A in X is characterized by a membership function $f_A(x)$ which associates with each point in X a real number in the interval [0,1] that gives the "grade of membership" of x in A".

Example: U= Set of ages of a person and $A=Youth$

$f_A(x) = 0$ if $x<=14$ and $x>=40$

$f_A(x) = 1$ if $20<= x <=30$

$f_A(x) = (0,1)$ if $14<= x <=20$ and $30<= x <=40$. This is represented diagrammatically in figure 3.

In order to represent and analyze approximate values, few algorithms were proposed on fuzzy AR mining. This section deals with the algorithms and models proposed on fuzzy AR mining.

Boolean transformation of quantitative attributes leads to sharp partitioning of the dataset. So, there was a need for fuzzy Association Rule Mining (FARM). Fuzzy gives a more precise representation of

Figure 3. Age vs. Fuzzy Membership function

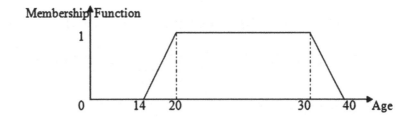

quantitative attributes. For example, replace the quantitative attribute age by values young, middle-aged and old corresponding to intervals [0,35],[35,65],[65,100] of binary attributes. Suppose a person reaches 36, then his status changes abruptly from young to middle-aged. Be, that is as it may, transition is a gradual phenomenon. This problem is referred as sharp boundary problem and thus, there comes a requirement for fuzzy set.

Fuzzy Apriori

(Verlinde, Cock & Boute, 2006, pp. 679-683) described how a fuzzy version of Apriori aides in generating fuzzy association rules and eliminates sharp boundary problem. Fuzzy Apriori, initially uses fuzzy c-means clustering (FCM) as a preprocessing technique to retrieve fuzzy attributes from numerical attributes. Fuzzy partition of each numerical attribute is selected by finding the maximum value of the sum of each partition. Then it follows an approach similar to Apriori and uses a record-by-record counting approach. The major difference between Apriori and Fuzzy Apriori is that, for each record, the latter takes the fuzzy membership function of each item in the itemset into account.

Fast and Efficient Method for Fuzzy AR

Fuzzy version of Apriori is slow and inefficient in handling large data sets. (Mangalampalli & Pudi, 2009, pp. 1163-1168) proposed a new fuzzy association rule mining algorithm, which is more efficient. This is a two step process. In the first step, c-means clustering is done where the dataset is partitioned into c-clusters. If every item belongs to every cluster with a certain degree $\mu \varepsilon [0,1]$, then algorithm need to minimize $\sum_{i=1}^{N} \sum_{j=1}^{c} \mu_{ij}^{m} \left\| x_i - c_j \right\|^2$ where μ_{ij}=degree of membership of x_i in cluster j and c_j is the center of the cluster j. In the next step, quantitative items might be the member of more than one cluster is processed. In other cases, the membership function uniquely belongs to a cluster. Based on this, the items are assigned and processed by fuzzy version of Apriori. The bit vector representation for a cluster with 5 partitions is given in figure 4.

The support and confidence values are given by

$$support(A \rightarrow B) = \sum_{x \in D} \frac{(A \cap B)(x)}{|X|}$$

Figure 4. Frequent itemset generation in fuzzy clustering

0.05	0.23	0.00	0.12	0.54	**ABC**

0.12	0.52	0.23	0.00	0.03	**BCD**

0.05	0.23	0.00	0.00	0.03	**ABCD=ABC ∩ BCD**

$$confidence(A \rightarrow B) = \frac{\sum_{x \in D}(A \cap B)(x)}{\sum_{x \in D}A(x)}$$

$A \cap B = \min\{A(x), B(x)\}$ for all $x \in X$

Since bit vector representation may take huge space in memory, compression algorithms are employed which reduces the space occupied. Here, the authors have used US Census raw set data in which there were 10 million transactions with 8 quantitative and 4 binary attributes. This algorithm is 10 times faster than the fuzzy Apriori algorithm.

Challenges Associated With Fuzzy AR Mining Methodologies

Though fuzzy set resolves the sharp boundary problem with quantitative attributes, fuzzy set needs preliminary knowledge of data which is quite impossible in real time scenarios. Also, it is point based. i.e., every member in the membership function has a particular concrete value, based on the knowledge of the user on the member in the set. An approximate or uncertain value for a member is needed to be represented as a particular interval in the membership function which lies entirely within [0, 1], which is impractical with fuzzy set. This resulted in the search for an alternative approach which gives rise to rough set association rule mining.

UNCERTAINTY WITH ROUGH SET

Rough set (Pawlak, 1982, pp.341-356) (Pawlak, Grazymala-Busse, Slowinski & Ziarko, 1995) is used to represent vagueness, and it is embedded in classical set theory. While imprecision in fuzzy is represented as partial membership, imprecision in rough set is expressed as boundary region of a set.

Let the set of objects be the universe U and the lack of knowledge about the elements of U represented as an indiscernibility equivalence relation $R \subseteq U \times U$. Let $X \subseteq U$. X can be characterized with respect to R as.

- The lower approximation which are the most certain member of X. *POSITIVE (B)* = B_*= {$Y\varepsilon$ $U/B:Y\subseteq X$}
- The upper approximation (B^*) which cannot be classified for certain as X. *NEGATIVE (B) = U-B** where B^*= {$\varepsilon U/B: Y \cap X \neq\phi$ }
- The boundary region contains the set of all objects which can neither be classified as X nor as $\neg X$. *BOUNDARY (B) = B* - B_{*}*

Few algorithms were proposed on Rough set AR mining where the class association rule set is generated. This section deals with the algorithms and models on rough set AR mining.

Figure 5. Representation of Rough set

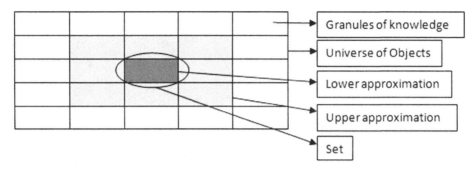

Rough Set Theory for Generating Class Association Rule Set

Class association rule set (CAR) is generated (Slimani, 2013, pp.1-10) [12] where classes are specified as consequences. This method is used when available information is not sufficient in deriving AR. A CAR is represented by $A{\rightarrow}B$ where $A{\subseteq}I$ where I is the set of items in the transaction in the given database and $B{\subseteq}Y$ where Y is the class label and $I{\cap}Y{=}\phi$. The support and confidence remain same as normal AR mining, but consequence has only a single item that does not belong to I. The main objective is to find a proper association between I and Y. The support and confidence are given by

$$support = \frac{|B_*(i) \cup B_*(y)|}{|U|}$$

$$confidence = \frac{|B_*(i) \cup B_*(y)|}{|B_*(i)|} \text{ where } i{\subseteq}I, y{\subseteq}Y$$

This is followed by applying the Apriori algorithm where candidate 1-itemset is represented by $C_0 = \{(\{I\}, y)$ where $i{\varepsilon}I$ and $y{\varepsilon}Y\}$. Thin $(k-1)$ -frequent itemset is used in deriving k-frequent itemset. The support for both condition rule and rule are updated together and minimum support and confidence are checked at each step. Joining and pruning are done at each step. Joining is done same as Apriori except that the class (consequent) should be the same for both the rules that are to be joined.

Rough Set for AR Mining

(Grzymala & Busse, 1997, pp.27-39) proposed three representative rule induction methods. The rule takes the form *if (attribute-1, value-1) and (attribute-2, value-2) and... (attribute-n, value-n), then (decision, value)*. Here, the antecedents are attributes and consequent variable is labeled as decision. A set of cases labeled with the same decision value is called a concept. Any numerical attributes have to be converted to symbolic attributes before the occurrence of rule induction. This process is called discretization or quantization. The input data could be incomplete or inconsistent. A case 'x' is covered by a rule 'r' if every condition of the rule is satisfied by attribute value of 'x'. A rule set is complete if every concept is covered by the rules.

For example, in the decision table shown in table 5,

The rule (*H, Yes*) → (*F, Yes*) does not entirely covers the concept {1,2,4,5}. It covers only {1,2,4}. But it is consistent. The rule (*H, No*) → (*F, No*) covers the concept {3,6,7} but it is not consistent.

In order to obtain rule set, many rule induction algorithms were proposed. Among them is LEM1 (Learning from Examples Module, version 1) and LEM2 (Learning from Examples Module, version 2).

LEM1

LEM1 is a global rule induction algorithm where the search space is set of all attribute values. The indiscernibility relation *IND* (*B*) on *U* for *x, y* ε *U* is for *x, y* every value of attribute is identical in *B*. For example *IND* {*H, W*} = {{1,4}, {2}, {3,6}, {5}, {7}}. Global covering (relative reduct) B^* of decision {*d*} is the subset of *B* such that *B* is the minimal cover. If consistency is not violated and the minimal cover is quite enough to represent the whole, then some attributes can be dropped (i.e., *U- B^** could be dropped).

{*T,H,W,N*} →*F* could be written as {*T,W,N*} →*F* since both gives the same indiscernibility relation of {{1}, {2}, {3}, {4}, {5}, {6}, {7}}. Taking case 1, the rule based on the indiscernibility relation is given by

(*T, Very High*) and (*W, yes*) and (*N, No*) →*Flu* (*yes*)

If (*T, Very High*) is removed in the rule, it leads to inconsistency with case 7. If (*W, Yes*) is removed, then there is no inconsistency. So, the rule becomes,

(*T, Very High*) and (*N, No*) →*Flu* (*yes*)

If (*N, No*) is removed, the rule still successfully represents case 1 and has no inconsistency.

(*T, Very High*) →*Flu* (*yes*)

By using the same way, others rules of induction are obtained as well.

Table 5. Sample Decision Table

Case	Attributes				Decision
	Temperature T	Headache H	Weakness W	Nausea N	Flu F
1	Very High	Yes	Yes	No	Yes
2	High	Yes	No	Yes	Yes
3	Normal	No	No	No	No
4	Normal	Yes	Yes	Yes	Yes
5	High	No	Yes	No	Yes
6	High	No	No	No	No
7	Normal	No	Yes	No	No

LEM2

LEM2 is a rule induction algorithm which uses blocks of attribute-value pairs. Since the input data file is always lower or upper approximation of the concept, it is always consistent. Local covering is done here where the search space is a set of attribute-value (a, v) pairs. If $(a, v) = t$, then set of t, $[t]$ set of cases where attribute 'a' has a value 'v' and B is upper or lower approximation represented by decision—value pair (d, w) and T is the minimal complex of B which is set of attribute-value pair is the local covering of B if each member T of τ is minimal complex of B and $\bigcup_{t \in \tau} [T] = B$.

- For example, attribute-value pairs are formed. $B = G = \{1, 2, 4, 5\}$
- $T(G) = \{(T, Very\ High), (T, High), (T, Normal), (H, Yes), (H, No), (W, Yes), (W, No), (N, Yes), (N, No)\}$.
- Now identify (a, v) with largest $|(a, v) \cap G|$. Here, $|(H, Yes)| = |(W, Yes)| = 3$
- On considering the size of attribute-value pair block, $|(H, Yes)| < |(W, Yes)|$. So (H, Yes) is taken.
- $G = B - (H, Yes) = \{1, 2, 4, 5\} - \{1, 2, 4\} = \{5\}$. Now, $T(G) =$ concept that represent case 5 = $\{(T, High), (H, No), (W, Yes), (N, No)\}$.
- On repeating the same procedure, $(T, High) = \{2, 5, 6\} \nsubseteq B$. So $(T, High) \cap (H, No) = \{5, 6\} \nsubseteq B$. On adding (W, Yes), $(T, High) \cap (H, No) \cap (W, Yes) = \{5\}$ rule is estimated $\subseteq B = \{1, 2, 4, 5\}$. So, the minimal complex set is given by $(T, High) \cap (H, No) \cap (W, Yes)$.
- By LEM2 algorithm,

For each $t \in T$ do

If $T - \{t\} \subseteq B$, then $T = T - \{t\}$

So, the next minimal complex is given by $(T, High) \cap (W, Yes)$ which gives rise to the rule $(T, High) \cap (W, Yes) \rightarrow (F, Yes)$. Other rules are obtained in the same way.

Challenges Associated With Rough Set AR Mining Methodologies

The problem with rough set is redundancy. After eliminating the redundant attribute in a rule, the addition of a new row in the database table may lead to inconsistency. This inconsistency is because of the discrimination between criteria and hesitation on the part of the decision maker. These inconsistencies can't be considered as a basic blunder as they can pass on critical data that ought to be considered in the development of the decision maker's preference model. Additionally, construction and maintenance of decision table are costly. So, there was a need for the evolution of vague set in AR mining.

UNCERTAINTY WITH VAGUE SET

In order to represent uncertainty or vagueness, specialized algorithm is needed which will handle these circumstances. It is therefore required to have some mathematical tools such as vague set theory that can be utilized with AR mining methodologies. Vague set based algorithms will be more suitable in effectively handling vague in uncertain situations.

The definition for vague set is as follows: A vague set V in a universe of discourse U is characterized by a true membership function, α_v and a false membership function, β_v, as follows:

$$\alpha_v: \rightarrow [0, 1],$$

$$\beta_v: \rightarrow [0, 1], \text{ and}$$

$$\alpha_v(x) + \beta_v(x) \leq 1,$$

where $\alpha_v(x)$ is a lower bound on the grade of membership of x derived from the evidence for x, and $\beta_v(x)$ is a lower bound on negation of x derived from the evidence against x.

Vague Association Rule Mining

The uncertainty or vague information can be processed by vague theory and rules extracted are termed as Vague Association Rule. This was proposed by (Lu, Ke, Cheng & Ng, 2007). The user might hesitate to buy an item online. This hesitation is the vague information that is being captured from the web log. Information is extracted out of it by applying vague set theory. For any transaction id, the item that is being bought is taken as $\alpha(x)$ and the item that is not bought is considered as $\beta(x)$. $\sum h(x)$ gives the overall hesitation in buying an item 'x'. Also, $\alpha(x) + \beta(x) + \sum h(x) \leq 1$. The hesitation region is in between the lower and upper bound. i.e., $\alpha(x) < region < 1 - \beta(x)$. This vague gives the interval based membership. In this case, the hesitation region is within the interval of $[\alpha(x), 1-\beta(x)]$ which gives the customer's intent.

Hesitation and Attractiveness of an item are the things that interest the organization and assist in boosting sales. The attractiveness of x, $AT(x)$ is defined as the median membership of x. The hesitation of x, $H(x)$ is defined as the difference of $1 - \beta(x)$ and $\alpha(x)$.

$$AT(x) = (\alpha(x) + 1 - \beta(x)) / 2, AT(x) \, \varepsilon \, [0,1].$$

Figure 6. The true (α) and False (β) Membership Functions of a Vague set

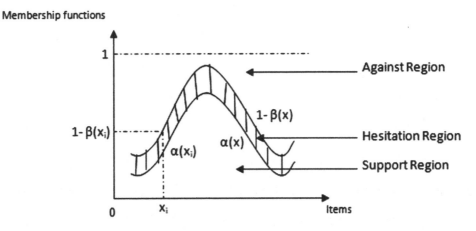

$H(x) = \{1 - \beta(x)\} - \alpha(x)$

A Vague Association Rule (VAR), $r = (X \rightarrow Y)$ obtained based on the AH (Attraction-Hesitation) pair values. Based on the attractiveness and hesitation of an item, various types of confidence and support of a VAR have been proposed.

For support of a given AH-pair database D, four support-types and confidence-types for VAR $r = X \rightarrow Y$ where $Z = X \cup Y$ are

- When both X and Y are Attractive (being bought), A-support of Z and A-confidence of r are given by,

$$A_{supp}(Z) = \frac{\sum\limits_{T \in D} \Pi_{z \in Z} M_A(Z)}{|D|}$$

$$A_{conf}(r) = \frac{A_{supp}(Z)}{A_{supp}(X)}$$

- When both X and Y are being Hesitated to buy, H-support of Z and H-confidence of r are given by,

$$H(Z) = \frac{\sum\limits_{T \in D} \Pi_{z \in Z} M_H(Z)}{|D|}$$

$$H_{conf}(r) = \frac{H_{supp}(Z)}{H_{supp}(X)}$$

- When X is bought and Y is being hesitated to buy, AH-support of Z and AH-confidence of r are given by,

$$AH(Z) = \frac{\sum\limits_{T \in D} \Pi_{x \in X, y \in Y} M_A(X) M_H(Y)}{|D|}$$

$$AH_{conf}(r) = \frac{AH_{supp}(Z)}{A_{supp}(X)}$$

- When Y is bought and X is being hesitated to buy, HA-support of Z and HA-confidence of r are given by,

$$HA(Z) = \frac{\sum_{T \in D} \Pi_{x \in X, y \in Y} M_H(X) M_A(Y)}{|D|}$$

$$HA_{conf}(r) = \frac{HA_{supp}(Z)}{A_{supp}(X)}$$

(Lu, Ke, Cheng & Ng, 2007) proposed the mining of vague data through vague association rule. In a market basket analysis, the hesitation at different stages of buying a product is analyzed by vague theory. Then AR mining is carried out. This step of applying vague theory and generating rules is called Vague Association Rule mining (VAR). The vague theory helps in calculating the intent, attraction and hesitation of a particular item. Apriori is applied for AR mining.

VAR for Mining Course Information

(Pandey & Pardasani, 2012, pp.1-5) proposed a model for mining the course information based on the vague theory. The courses containing different topics are taken and the most preferred topic is estimated to analyze the interests of the students in particular topic, so that it could be added to other courses in order to make them interesting as well. The attendance of students is viewed which gives the hesitation status of a student in attending the topic. Each course contains different topics. The topics with full attendance are considered as most preferred topics while the ones with almost full attendance are considered as hesitated topics. For example, the hesitation status is captured as $s1$ for 0-20% attendance, $s2$ for 0-40% and $s3$ for 0-60% attendance and the criteria $s1 \leq s2 \leq s3$ exists. VAR is applied over this data.

Here, 'attended the class' and 'not attended the class' corresponds to $\alpha(x)$ and $\beta(x)$ (i.e., evidence of support and against with respect to the class). Here $\alpha(x)$ refers to the topic 'x' is well attended and has the high probability of attending it again while $h(x)$ refers to topic 'x' is being hesitated by students and it might have a high probability of attending if the issue is sorted out. The intent is then calculated and AH-pairs are generated. The study is made in the Data Structure course of IT department in UIT-RGPV Bhopal. The hesitation information is mined by vague theory in this model.

(Pandey & Pardasani, 2013, pp. 063-074) proposed a model for mining VAR for making courses effective at any point of time. From time to time, the interestingness in the course varies. So a temporal database is taken and VAR is applied over that to mine the hesitation status at that instant.

Vague Set Theory for Profit Pattern Mining

(Badhe, R.S.Thakur & G.S.Thakur, 2015, pp.182-186) proposed profit pattern mining on vague data. The traditional methods have used statistical measures like support and confidence as their interesting measurers. So, to reduce the gap between statistical measure and value based measure, profit mining is done.

Variable table or Matrix is calculated which contains N rows and M columns where N=number of transactions and M=number of items. Here, the database is given by $|D|=V_t+V_f+V_p \leq 1$ where V_t and V_f corresponds to true and false membership function and V_p corresponds to vague percentage. Here, true support which is true membership of an item is the ratio of true membership to the sum of true and false membership is calculated.

$$Support_{true} = \frac{\{V_t + [\frac{V_p * V_t}{V_t + V_f}]\}}{|D|}$$

And true confidence is calculated as the ratio of true support of two itemsets to true support of either of the itemsets (*A* or *B* in rule *A→B*).

$$Confidence_{true} = \frac{Support_{true}(A \cup B)}{Support_{true}(A)} for\ rule\ A{\to}B$$

This helps in generating rules that yield certain profit by eliminating the vagueness. From the variable matrix, true and false membership of each item is calculated and the vague table is constructed. For any vague item, the true membership is calculated and this is done iteratively and necessary pruning operations are done. The experiment was conducted on FMCG database that consist of daily inventory of products purchased by customers. Here, the algorithm generates rules of profit significance that were ruled out because of statistical violation caused by vagueness in ordinary cases of association mining.

From the study, it is evident that vague theory is more capable of handling the uncertain situations. The resultant rules of type A-H and H-A have products that are hesitated, and by framing appropriate strategy, these products could be sold thereby increasing the profit. Although hesitation of the product is removed with the help of these algorithms, they failed to do justice by producing a huge rule set rather than concentrating on the interesting ones. The retrieval of interesting rules from the huge rule set is done by optimization algorithms.

The differences in characteristics of fuzzy, rough and vague set are detailed in the table 6.

Table 6. The differences in characteristics of fuzzy, rough and vague set

Characteristic	Fuzzy set	Rough set	Vague set
Reason for evolution	To deal with uncertainty in knowledge where the user knows how uncertain each member is.	To deal with uncertainty in knowledge where the user has no idea on how uncertain each member is. It also gives fastest convergence once the decision table is identified.	To eliminate the cost of decision table and inconsistency, vague set theory has been introduced.
Applicational use	Fuzzy set can be used in approximate reasoning where the users have detailed knowledge on the members of the function. It could be useful where quantitative attributes are used and sharp boundary problem exists.	Rough set can be used in places where hidden patterns are found. It identifies partial or total dependencies (i.e. cause-effect relations) in data bases, dynamic data and others. It is used in classification and decision rule mining.	Vague can be used in places where hidden patterns are found. It can be used in places where data is not clean(missing data, null values)
Disadvantage	Fuzzy has a point based membership function where the estimation of membership value is not possible in all real-time scenarios.	The redundancy, inconsistency, decision table maintenance lead to the need for evolution of alternate theory.	More parameters cannot be added. Convergence of a rule takes some time.

OPTIMIZATION ALGORITHMS IN MINING

Although many modifications have been done in processing association rule mining, the number of rules generated is still huge. In an organization point of view, this is still considered to be high. The interesting rules are only needed. So, optimization of rules is needed, which eliminates the uninteresting or less interesting rules and gives the optimal rules for the organization. The fitness function is formulated accordingly so that the demands of the organization are met. Few optimization algorithms like genetic, PSO and ant colony optimization are discussed here.

Genetic Algorithm

Genetic Algorithm (Deepa & Sivanandam, 2007) is a heuristic search algorithm based on the Darwin's theory of evolution. It is based on the natural selection. Darwin suggested that the fittest individual among the group survives. In genetic algorithm, particular number of random solutions is selected from the search space and the fittest among the solutions are taken as a parent, to get the children who are more likely to be fitter than the parents. Genetic algorithm is purely based on 'preservation of favorable variations and the rejection of unfavorable variations'. Variation refers to the differences between the parents and offspring. It is a stochastic algorithm since randomness is part and parcel of genetic algorithm.

The space consisting of all possible solutions is referred to as search space. Each member in this search space is an individual solution. The individual is represented as chromosome, which is a collection of genes. The fitness function gives the value of the objective function. Collection of individuals that are assumed to be solution is called population.

Genetic Operators

- **Selection:** Selection involves choosing two parents from the population for crossing. Choosing better individuals yields better offspring.
- **Crossover:** Crossover involves producing offspring from the parents chosen by selection process. It involves choosing a random point and exchanging all bits after that by the parents.
- **Mutation:** Mutation involves either recovering any lost genetic material from its parent or random modification of genetic information. This prevents the GA to be trapped in local maxima or minima and extend the search as widely as possible.

Few algorithms were proposed on genetic algorithm for optimizing the resultant rules from AR mining. Resolving sharp boundary problem and mining the negative AR through genetic algorithm have been discussed in the following sections. These algorithms enlighten the use of intelligence techniques in AR mining methodologies. Appropriate changes in fitness function can be made in the following algorithms in order to get optimal rule set that meets any requirement of the organization.

Optimization Through Genetic Using Fitness

(Haldulakar & Agrawal, 2011, pp.1252-1259) proposed genetic algorithm for optimization of rules where condition attributes and decision attributes are differentiated in order to reduce the overhead in time and space. Classification of attributes helps in reducing the candidate itemset thereby improving efficiency.

Figure 7. Flow chart of Genetic Algorithm

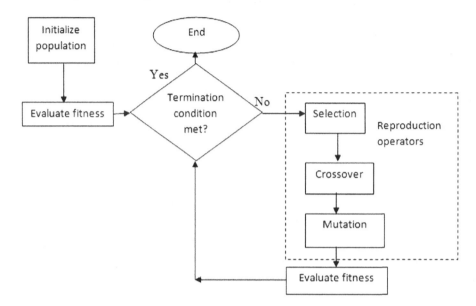

The continuous attributes are discretized by dividing them at selected cut-points to intervals. The rules are initially generated by Apriori.

Abolan Dataset which is generally used for classification is used for study where 8 attributes are continuous. Genetic Algorithm cannot work on directly on the raw data. So binary encoding (0s and 1s) is done. The parameter settings are size of the population N=100, crossover rate=0.006, mutation rate=0.001. The fitness function is given by

$$f(x) = \frac{Support(x)}{minsupport} = \{p(support(x) > minsupport), q(support(x) < minsupport)\}$$

$q(support(x))$ is normally rejected since the value is less than the minimum support, but the values very close to the minimum support could be considered. So q is divided into two parts, $C1$ and $C2$.

$$q = C1 = dataWithMinSupport < 0.5$$

$$q = C2 = dataWithMinSupport > 0.5$$

$$f(q) = \frac{support(C2)}{minsupport} = \{\alpha = support(C2) > C1\} \, or \, \{\beta = support(C2) = C1\}$$

The selection is based on the individual fitness.

$$Pi = \frac{f(xi)}{\sum\limits_{1}^{M} f(xj)} e^{-\alpha f(\alpha)} \text{ Where } \alpha \text{ is the adjustment factor}$$

Pi consist of individuals whose fitness > 1 and *f* (*α*) whose fitness < 1, but close to 1. *Pi* is calculated for each individual in the population. Crossover divides the domain of each attribute in a group and inserts cut points for the continuous attributes. This is followed my mutation. The obtained rules are checked to see whether the minimum confidence threshold is satisfied. The resulting rules obtained through genetic are found to be interesting.

Optimization of Positive and Negative Attributes in Rules Through Genetic

(Saggar, Lad & Agrawal, 2004) The rules generated by Apriori do not consider the negative occurrence of attributes. But, GA helps in obtaining rules that contains negative attributes (Researchers have always considered rule of type $A{\rightarrow}B$ and not of $A{\rightarrow}_{\neg} B$ or $\neg A{\rightarrow}B$ or $\neg A{\rightarrow}\neg B$). GA is used in AR mining since they perform global search and avoid the algorithmic complexity which increases many fold with the increase in the number of attributes (or items in case of market-basket scenario) and the need for finding interesting rules from the existing rules.

Initially binary encoding is done to each rule. There are totally 8 subjects. Each subject is represented by 00 or 01 (00-not choosing and 01-choosing the subject). Here, there is no boundary for the number of antecedents, but there should be only one consequent (A rule $A, D{\rightarrow}B, C$ can be represented as two separate rules $A, D{\rightarrow}B$ and $A, D{\rightarrow}C$). Later genetic operators (Selection, Crossover, Mutation) are applied. Two fit parents are chosen by selection (Roulette Wheel selection is used. Here, a linear search through a wheel with the slots in the wheel weighted in proportion to the individual's fitness values is done. Individuals with high fitness make them the natural choice for crossover/mutation) and new rules are evolved with the help of crossover and mutation operators. The fitness function is estimated such that it has a high predictive accuracy, and it should be comprehensible as well as interesting.

For a rule $A{\rightarrow}B$, the confusion matrix, which is a 2*2 matrix, summarize the predictive performance. Here *A* is the conjugate of conditions and *B* is the predictive class or decision attribute.

The rule is better if *TP* and *TN* values are higher while *FP* and *FN* values are lower. The fitness function is given by *Fitness=CF * Comp* where

$$confidence factor, CF = \frac{TP}{TP + FP}$$

Figure 8. Optimization through genetic using fitness

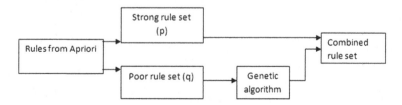

$$Completeness, Comp = \frac{TP}{TP + FN}$$

The completeness gives what portions of *C* are actually covered by the rule. In order to improve the comprehensibility, the fitness function is given by

$$Fitness = w1 * CF * Comp + w2 * Simp$$

$$Simp = \frac{1}{No.ofConditionInAntecedent}$$

Simp gives the rule simplicity. *w*1 and *w*2 are user-defined weights. Synthetic database consisting of the selection procedure of electives in 3rd year B.Tech course is taken in this case. The crossover prob-

Table 7. Positive and Negative antecedent and consequent for rule A→B

Actual Class		A	¬*A*
Predicted class			
B		TP	FP
¬B		FN	TN

Where *TP*=True Positives = Number of samples in *D* satisfying both *A* and *B*.
FP=False Positives= Number of samples in *D* satisfying *B*, but not *A*.
TN=True Negative= Number of samples in *D* not satisfying both *A* and *B*.
FN=False Negative= Number of samples in *D* satisfying *A*, but not *B*.

Figure 9. Optimization through genetic using fitness for Negative AR mining

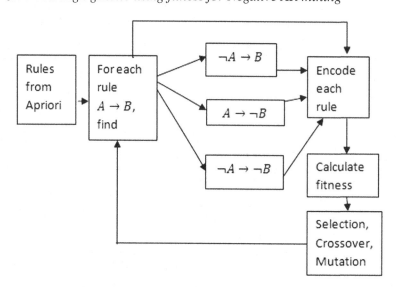

ability of 0.1 and mutation probability of 0.005 is chosen. Thus the rules containing positive as well as negative attributes are generated.

Optimization of AR With Positive and Negative Attributes Using Genetic

(Anandhavalli, Sudhanshu, Kumar & Ghose, 2009, pp. 01-04) proposed an algorithm where the negative attribute in the rules is being considered along with more than one attribute in the consequent part. Suppose, for the given rules p $(x \rightarrow y)$ and p $(x \rightarrow z)$, the rule p $(x \rightarrow yz)$ is generated by the intersection of both the association rules and a new rule is achieved p $(x \rightarrow yz) = p$ (xyz) $/p$ (x).

In case of encoding, for a rule A, $B \rightarrow \neg C$ the representation can either be 1 1 0 (positive and negative attributes represented by 1 and 0 respectively) or 00 1 01 1 10 0 (00-A, 01-B, 10-C with 1-positive and 0-negative attribute). The first method needs only n bits, whereas in the second method, 1 extra bit is needed to represent the presence or absence of an item, $p * (\log_2 n + 1)$ bits are totally needed where n=number of bits and p=number of items.

The selection is done with the help of roulette wheel selection which is followed by crossover and mutation. Here, Lens database is used. The crossover and mutation probabilities are taken as 0.1 and 0.005 respectively. The complexity of the algorithm is high.

PSO (Particle Swarm Optimization)

PSO [29] is a stochastic optimization technique inspired from the social behavior of flocking of birds or schooling of fishes. This is stochastic since the initial population is taken randomly from the set of possible solution. Based on the personal best and global best solution, the next possible solution is updated. Bird is called a particle which is the solution in the search space. After finding the two best values, the particle updates its velocity and positions with following equations

$$v(t+1) = w * v(t) + c1 * rand(0,1) * (pbest - present) + c2 * rand(0,1) * (gbest - present)$$

$$x = x + v$$

'v' is the particle velocity, 'w' is the inertia that controls the magnitude of old velocity $v(t)$, 'x' is the current solution. pbest and gbest are personal best and global best respectively, rand ε (0,1) is a random number between (0,1), $c1$, $c2$ are learning factors. Usually $c1 = c2 = 2$.

Few modifications to the existing algorithms are done in order to increase the efficiency in mining to generate the optimal rule set. These algorithms give a concrete idea of generating optimal rules according to the emerging demands of the organization.

Optimization Using PSO

Generating frequent itemset from large dataset using association rule mining is inefficient. PSO based meta-heuristic algorithm (Deepa & Kalimuthu, 2012, pp.80-85) generates not only frequent itemsets

Figure 10. Flow chart of PSO Algorithm

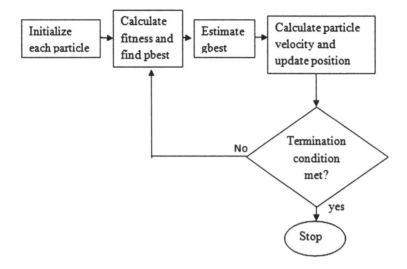

but also rules containing negative attributes. Here, it is considered that the number of consequents in any rule is one.

Following are assumptions are made in PSO.

- Homogeneity: Every bird in the flock has the same behavior.
- Locality: Movement of each bird is influenced by its neighbors.
- Collision avoidance: Avoiding collision with nearest neighbors.
- Velocity matching: Match velocity with nearby neighbors.
- Flock Centering: Each bird tries to stay close to the flock.

The encoding used here is string encoding. The fitness function is given by particle velocity and particle position. The standard Dataset of American Lottery System is taken and the results are found to be promising. The number of rules generated is comparatively reduced.

Optimization Using Weighted Quantum Based PSO

The problem with the existing PSO is that items have the same implication without considering the items/ attributes in the transaction or item space. So, weighted quantum particle swarm optimization algorithm (WQPSO) (Gokila & Rajalakshmi, 2014, pp.680-686) is proposed with weighted mean position based on their fitness value that leads to faster convergence. WQPSO is comparatively efficient than PSO for many benchmark functions. Also WQPSO is independent of all the problems faced by Genetic and ACO.

Initially, preprocessing is done where the missing, inconsistent and incomplete data is removed and the data are changed to binary format. Itemset Range (*IR* value) is then calculated. This involves front and back partition points of every chromosome and the range determined by these points is *IR*.

$$IR = [\log(mTransnum(m)) + \log(nTransnum(n))] * \frac{Trans(m,n)}{TotalTrans}$$

Where $m \neq n$, $m < n$ and m, n=length of the itemset, *Transnum* (*I*) =No. of transactions containing '*i*' items, *Trans(m,n)*= No. of transaction records obtaining m to n products, *TotalTrans*= total number of transactions. Encoding is done, which is followed by calculating the fitness value to each and every chromosome.

$$Fitness(k) = confidence(k) * \log[support(k) * length(k) + 1]$$

The particle with high fitness value is taken and their support and confidence values are considered as the minimum support and confidence values respectively. Here weights are assigned to each particle that has high fitness value. The fitness is calculated and rank is assigned to each particle based on their fitness (higher fitness particles have lower rank and vice versa). Then association rule mining is applied and frequent itemsets are calculated by Apriori algorithm.

ACO

Ant Colony Optimization (Patel, Chaudhari, Vijay, Rajneesh & Rana, 2011, 24-26) (Blum, 2005, pp.353-373) is inspired from the foraging behavior of ants. This optimization provides solution for routing and load balancing. This algorithm is inspired from the social behavior of ants in searching shortest paths between their food source and nest. Ants initially start in random manner and leave a chemical substance called pheromone along their path. If the concentration of pheromone is high along a path, then it implies the path is the most used one. During their return trip from food source to the nest, the ant leaves pheromone on their path and this quantity determines the quantity and quality of food found.

For a graph G (V, E) where V consist of two vertices v_s=ant nest and v_d=food source. Let E consist of two links e_1 and e_2 between v_d and v_s of length l_1 and l_2 where $l_2 > l_1$. Let τ_i represents the strength of the pheromone trail for e_i. Let n_a be the number of ants. Each ant chooses a path with probability,

$$Pi = \frac{\tau_i}{\tau_1 + \tau_2} \text{ where } \tau_i = \tau_1, \tau_2$$

If $\tau_1 > \tau_2$, then the probability of choosing 1st path is higher. On returning, the ant changes the τ_i value as

$$\tau_i \leftarrow \tau_i + \frac{Q}{l_i} \text{ where Q>0 is the parameter that is based on the length of the path}$$

All pheromones are evaporated at some point of time. This is given by

$\tau_i \leftarrow (1 - p) * \tau_i$ where pϵ(0,1] regulates phermone evaporation

In case of AR mining, this system (Patel, Chaudhari, Karan & Rana, 2011) follows a rough set approach and assumes two things. The unnecessary or irrelevant attributes are removed. Decision table is taken which contains conditional attributes and decision attributes. In this approach, by using ACO, partial solution is formed at each step and it incrementally constructs a solution until a complete solution is obtained. Trail evaporation is there which removes trails over time. Deamon action invokes local optimization procedure and updates global components. The probability of moving from one state to another is determined by the profit out of the move in the past and the probabilistic desirability of the move.

Here ACO is used to reduce the number of rules being generated and makes sure that the rules are interesting. The rules generated by Apriori might be weak. The confidence value is taken as the pheromone (p) value. The path updating value is calculated as $p = p + \Delta t$ where $\Delta t = \dfrac{2^{d+1} - 1}{d}$ where d=number of transaction set. By using this, optimized association rule is generated.

Table 8 illustrates the difference in the nature of the 3 reputed optimization algorithms.

ISSUES AND CHALLENGES

Various algorithms have been summarized on uncertainty management and the application of AR mining methodologies in intelligence techniques. It is evident that the algorithms discussed lacks major enhancements (optimization means for uncertainty management, profitable hesitation pattern mining, occasional hesitation pattern mining), although the uncertain situation is handled. The major concerns pertaining to the existing models are discussed in this section.

Table 8. Difference in nature of the Genetic, PSO and ACO algorithms

Algorithm	Genetic	PSO (Particle Swarm Optimization)	ACO (Ant Colony Optimization)
Based On	Darwin's theory of Evolution of organisms	Social behavior of bird flocking or fish schooling	Social behavior of ants
Characteristic	Find the optimal ones by 'fittest individual survives' and performing crossover and mutation to get the best individuals.	Finding the optimal path by updating each individual with respect to its local and global best values.	Finding the optimal path from ant nest to food source by calculating the pheromone trail.
Application feasibility	• Can be used in eliminating sharp boundary problems. • Can be used where negative attributes are needed. • Can be used where some other interesting parameters are needed.	• Can be used where rules containing negative attributes are used. • Weighted PSO is used for faster convergence since weights are assigned proportional to the fitness function.	• Used in classification. • Useful in place where Decision table with conditional and decision attributes are found.
Drawback	It is slow, parameters are more stochastic, presence of noise affects optimization, involves more parameters, difficulty in generating optimal solution though it produces best solution.	It may fall into local optimum value if high-dimensional space is present. It has low convergence. So, WPSO came into picture.	Theoretical analysis is difficult and probability distribution changes in every iteration.

- The key for any association rule is support and confidence threshold. This basically prunes the uninteresting rules. The support threshold can be used only when the items that are frequently bought together are considered interesting. The existing parameters like support and confidence gives the statistical significance while the value-based significance is being expected by the customer and the organization. So, appropriate changes in parameter settings are needed. In market-basket analysis, the frequently bought items might produce less profit while the high profit items may not be bought frequently. If the support threshold is too high, then the highly profitable products are removed out of the picture. This results in the rare item problem which is not good in a business organization point of view. On the other hand, if the support threshold is set too low, too many meaningless uninteresting patterns will be generated that will overload the decision makers.

- Sometimes, large numbers of rules are obtained where an organization can't spare time to look at each and every rule. So, the rules have to be generated in such a way that will meet the interest of the customer as well as the organization.

- Interestingness varies over time. Different set of items might be of interest at different point of time. The algorithms discussed so far do not generate rules that interest the organization on some special occasion or event.

- The traditional AR fails to capture uncertain or vague information. It always uses crisp set for generating rules. In order to represent uncertainty or vagueness, approximation theories like vague set is needed. These can be utilized with AR mining methodologies. Vague set based algorithms will be more suitable in effectively handling vague in uncertain situations.

CONCLUSION

Discussion under previous section reveals that researchers have developed different algorithms for mining regular association rules. It has been observed that these algorithms are varying in different aspects such as the way of handling database, search strategy, candidate generation mechanism and pruning. Further, it has also been observed that there are only a few algorithms which are available for addressing uncertain and vague situations. The authors have performed a critical analysis on these vague association rule mining algorithms and realized that there is a need to further enhance these algorithms by considering currently available issues and challenges pertaining to profitability concern and optimization.

REFERENCES

Agarwal, R., Imielinski, T., & Swami, A. (1993) Mining association rules between sets of items in large databases. *Proceedings of the 1993 ACM SIGMOD International Conference on Management of Data*, 207–216. doi:10.1145/170035.170072

Agarwal, R., & Srikant, R. (1994). Fast Algorithms for Mining Association Rules in Large Databases. *VLDB '94 Proceedings of the 20th International Conference on Very Large Data Bases*, 487-499.

Badhe, V., Thakur, R.S., & Thakur, G.S. (2015). Vague Set Theory for Profit Pattern and Decision Making in Uncertain Data. *International Journal of Advanced Computer Science and Applications*, 6(6), 182–186. doi:10.14569/IJACSA.2015.060625

Blum, C. (2005). Ant colony optimization: Introduction and recent trends. *Science Direct*, 353–373.

Brin, S., Motwani, R., Ullman, J., & Tsur, S. (1997). Dynamic Itemset Counting and Implication Rules for Market basket data. *Proceedings of the 1997 ACM SIGMOD International Conference on Management of Data*, 207-216. doi:10.1145/253260.253325

Deepa, S. N., & Sivanandam. (2007). *Principles of Soft Computing*. John Wiley & Sons India Pvt. Ltd.

Deepa, S., & Kalimuthu, M. (2012). An Optimization of Association Rule Mining Algorithm using Weighted Quantum behaved PSO. *International Journal of Power Control Signal and Computation*, *3*(1), 80-85.

Gokila, D., & Rajalakshmi, S. (2014). Weighted Quantum Particle Swarm Optimization To Association Rule Mining And PSO To Clustering. *Journal of Theoretical and Applied Information Technology*, *65*(3), 680–686.

Grzymala Busse, J. W. (1997). A new version of the rule induction system. *Fundamenta Informaticae*, *31*, 27–39.

Haldulakar, R., & Agrawal, J. (2011). Optimization of Association Rule Mining through Genetic Algorithm. *International Journal on Computer Science and Engineering*, *3*(3), 1252-1259.

Han, J., & Kamber, M. (2006). Data Mining: Concepts and Techniques. Morgan Kaufmann.

Jafarzadeh, H., & Sadeghzadeh, M. (2014). Improved Apriori algorithm using fuzzy logic. *IJARCSSE*, *4*(6), 439-447.

Lu, A., Ke, Y., Cheng, J., & Ng, W. (2007). *Mining Vague Association Rules*. Springer.

M, A., Sudhanshu, S., Kumar, A., & Ghose, M.K. (2009). Optimized association rule mining using genetic algorithm. *Advances in Information Mining*, *1*(2), 01-04.

Mangalampalli, A. (2009). *Pudi, Vikram*. Fuzzy Association Rule Mining Algorithm for Fast and Efficient Performance on Very Large Datasets.

Pandey, A., & Pardasani, K. R. (2012). A Model for Mining Course Information using Vague Association Rule. *International Journal of Computers and Applications*, *58*(20), 1–5. doi:10.5120/9395-7825

Pandey, A., & Pardasani, K. R. (2013). A Model for Vague Association Rule Mining in Temporal Databases. *Journal of Information and Computer Science*, *8*(1), 63–74.

Park, J. S., Chen, & Yu, P. S. (1995). An Effective Hash-Based Algorithm for Mining Association Rule. *Proceedings of the 1995 ACM SIGMOD International Conference on Management of Data*, 175-186. doi:10.1145/223784.223813

Patel, B., Chaudhari, V. K., Karan, R. K., & Rana, Y. K. (2011). Optimization of Association Rule Mining Apriori Algorithm Using ACO. *International Journal of Soft Computing and Engineering*, *1*(1), 24–26.

Pawlak, Z. (1982). Rough Sets. *International Journal of. Computer and Information Sciences*, *11*(5), 341–356. doi:10.1007/BF01001956

Pawlak, Z., Grazymala-Busse, J. W., Slowinski, R., & Ziarko, W. (1995). Rough sets. *Communications of the ACM, 38*(11), 88–95. doi:10.1145/219717.219791

Saggar, M., Agrawal, A., & Lad, A. (2004). Optimization of Association Rule Mining using Improved Genetic Algorithms. *IEEE International Conference on Systems, Man and Cybernetics*. doi:10.1109/ICSMC.2004.1400923

Savasere, A., Omiecinski, E., & Navathe, S. (1995). An Efficient Algorithm for Mining Association Rules in Large Databases. *Proceedings of the 21ˢᵗ VLDB Conference*, 432-444.

Shrivastava, S., & Rajput, V. (2015). Particle Swarm Optimization Based Association Rule Mining. *International Journal of Computers and Applications, 5*(5), 105–114.

Slimani, T. (2013). Class Association Rules Mining based Rough Set Method. *International Journal of Computer Science & Network Solutions, 1*(3), 1-10.

Toivonen, H. (1996) Sampling large databases for Association rules. *Proceedings of the 22nd VLDB Conference*, 134-145.

Verlinde, H., De Cock, M., & Boute, R. (2006). Fuzzy Versus Quantitative Association Rules: A Fair Data-Driven Comparison. *IEEE Transactions on Systems, Man, and Cybernetics, 36*(3), 679–683. doi:10.1109/TSMCB.2005.860134 PMID:16761820

Chapter 11
Sizing and Placement of Battery–Sourced Solar Photovoltaic (B–SSPV) Plants in Distribution Networks

Abid Ali
Universiti Teknologi PETRONAS, Malaysia

Nursyarizal Mohd Nor
Universiti Teknologi PETRONAS, Malaysia

Taib Ibrahim
Universiti Teknologi PETRONAS, Malaysia

Mohd Fakhizan Romlie
Universiti Teknologi PETRONAS, Malaysia

Kishore Bingi
Universiti Teknologi PETRONAS, Malaysia

ABSTRACT

This chapter proposes a mixed-integer optimization using genetic algorithm (MIOGA) for determining the optimum sizes and placements of battery-sourced solar photovoltaic (B-SSPV) plants to reduce the total energy losses in distribution networks. Total energy loss index (TELI) is formulated as the main objective function and meanwhile bus voltage deviations and PV penetrations of B-SSPV plants are calculated. To deal the stochastic behavior of solar irradiance, 15 years of weather data is modeled by using beta probability density function (Beta-PDF). The proposed algorithm is applied on IEEE 33 bus and IEEE 69 bus test distribution networks and optimum results are acquired for different time varying voltage dependent load models. From the results, it is known that, compared to PV only, the integration of B-SSPV plants in the distribution networks resulted in higher penetration levels in distribution networks. The proposed algorithm was very effective in terms of determining the sizes of the PV plant and the battery storage, and for the charging and discharging of the battery storage.

DOI: 10.4018/978-1-5225-3531-7.ch011

INTRODUCTION

Due to the inadequate fuel reserves, the power producers are considering to use renewable energy sources for the development of new power plants. Unlike the conventional large scale power stations, the new small and medium sized power stations are considered suitable to be installed at nearer to distribution stations, also known as distribution generation (DG) (Liu, Wu, Tu, Huang, & Lou, 2008). The concept of using renewable energy resources for producing the electricity, has been globally accepted and according to reports (Lee et al., 2012), electricity production in coming years will mainly depend on the renewable sources such as solar and wind energy. The major advantages of using renewable energy sources over the traditional power producing technologies are reflected as the environment friendly and the fuel free sources. Some of these sources especially wind and solar energy, are rapidly growing and have become more competitive, because per unit cost of electricity produced through wind turbines and solar photovoltaic (PV) modules, is much cheaper than the cost of electricity produced by the fossil-fuel based power plants. During the recent years, several studies have covered the technical possibility of an electrical network that can be powered through renewable energy sources (Gökçek, Bayülken, & Bekdemir, 2007; Plebmann, Erdmann, Hlusiak, & Breyer, 2014). Furthermore, the research also suggests that in 2050, 80% of total U.S. electricity demand could be supplied by using existing renewable electricity technologies (Bazilian et al., 2014).

Among the other renewable energy sources, solar PV technology is getting more mature and popular (Tyagi, Rahim, Rahim, Jeyraj, & Selvaraj, 2013). This is mainly due to the availability of good solar irradiance levels in many countries, ease of operation & maintenance (O&M), environmental benefits, increasing efficiency and reduced cost of PV panels (Aman et al., 2015; Devabhaktuni et al., 2013). The Photovoltaic (PV) technology converts the sunlight directly into the electricity without using any fuel. The upper surface of the atmosphere of the earth receives 174 Peta Watts (PW) of solar energy and it is naturally available across many parts of the world. Most PV modules come with 15 - 25 years warranties on their rated power outputs and these modules require virtually no maintenance during their life. The efficiency of commercial silicon modules has dramatically seen improvement during the last decade and in recent days, some manufacturers are claiming to have prototypes of PV modules, which can convert the sunlight into the electricity with an efficiency of 22.5% (Panasonic, 2015). The good thing with utilizing the PV technology is that the maintenance required for solar PV systems is mostly the cleaning of the PV modules.

The output of the PV modules mainly depends on the solar irradiations, but however, this is also affected by the temperature. Surface irradiations of the solar lights are measured as Watt/m^2. The ideal irradiation required for a PV module to produce the maximum power output is 1000 Watt/m^2 at temperature of 25 ^{0}C (Al Riza & Gilani, 2014). A 1 kWp solar PV system installed in a location with good solar irradiations can produce about 5-6 kilowatt/m^2/day. Besides the technical systems constraints, the output power of the solar PV modules, is a function of sun light and mainly depends on the levels of solar irradiation and temperature, therefore, the changes in weather conditions will affect the power output of the PV modules. In order to cope with the uncertainties associated with solar irradiations, the solar weather data is modeled by using Beta Probability Density Function (Beta-PDF). (Atwa, El-Saadany, Salama, & Seethapathy, 2010; Fan, Vittal, Heydt, & Ayyanar, 2012; Hung, Mithulananthan, & Lee, 2014; Khatod, Pant, & Sharma, 2013; Tan, Hassan, Majid, & Rahman, 2013)

In addition to the supply of electricity, distributed generators or generation (DGs) are considered beneficial for reducing system losses, voltage improvement, system load-ability enhancement, and network upgradability. However, one should not expect these benefits if installation of DG is done without any planning. If not properly designed, the installation of oversized DGs in distribution network will increase the overall system losses (Passey, Spooner, MacGill, Watt, & Syngellakis, 2011). The negative effects of improper sizing and locating of DGs in distribution networks were identified by (Acharya, Mahat, & Mithulananthan, 2006), which necessitates toward the studies for proper sizing and planning of future power plants. During the 10-15 years, the sizing and locating of DGs has become one of the most important topics in power system planning. The sizing and location have much influence on the quality of grid. By the review of literature it is known, that sizing and placement of DGs is done by considering the various network constraints i.e. reduction in system losses and improvement in system voltage profile. Some detailed reviews on DG sizing and placement methods is available in (Georgilakis & Hatziargyriou, 2013) and (Tan et al., 2013). Tools and programs which are deployed for the sizing and placement of DGs, use complex iterative mathematical algorithms such as Genetic Algorithm (GA) (Whitley, 1994). By the review of literature, it is also known that system losses in distribution networks can be reduced to the minimum level, if the installation of DGs in distribution networks is done through determining the optimum sizes and locations of DGs. Any deviation in optimum sizes and locations of DGs will result to increase the total network losses. From this it is identified that, by increasing the sizes of DGs, the network losses starts to increase again, On other hand, this also forbids from using the maximum utilization of energy from renewable resources. For a case, if the size of the DG is higher than the optimum size, then in order to fix the rate of reduction of system losses, a huge amount of energy will be required to waste during a specific period, when the power from DG is higher than the power required by the network. In order to utilize the electricity from renewable sourced power plant more efficiently, identification of the appropriate methods has become one of the main objectives for power plant planners and researchers.

On other hand, to avoid wasting the excessive energy, Battery Energy Storage Systems (BESS) can be used to support the PV plants by storing the unused electricity and later by supplying it back when it is required by the network (Bhargava & Dishaw, 1998). Since the last decade, ESSs are continuously gaining more importance due to commence of renewable energy sources in electricity markets. In addition to supply of bulk electricity, BESS are considered suitable for many power system applications, such as increasing the penetration of intermittent sources, enhancement network reliability by increasing transmission line capacities and improving power quality by alleviating voltage oscillations (Jamali, Nor, & Ibrahim, 2015). Compared to other energy storage technologies, the battery is a mature technology that has been utilized in the past many years for the needs of various applications. Batteries have been used for lighting, automation in industries, automotive applications and electronic gadgets. It is also considered as a heart of standalone PV and electric vehicle (EV) systems (Daud, Mohamed, & Hannan, 2013; Teleke, Baran, Bhattacharya, & Huang, 2010). A typical Battery-Sourced Solar Photovoltaic (B-SSPV) plants, with addition of its auxiliary parts is shown in Figure 1 (Jamali, Nor, Ibrahim, & Romlie, 2016). During the last few years, the rate of installation of grid-scaled PV plants worldwide was observed much higher, mainly due to reduction in cost of PV modules. Further it is expected that power from PV plants will contribute more than 40% of global energy demand by year 2050 (Mekhilef, Saidur, & Safari, 2011). Some sources (Jamali et al., 2016) are indicating that cost of electricity produced by a PV-Battery system could be much competitive to the cost of electricity produced through PV only. It is expected that in addition to reduction of cost of PV modules, cost of batteries will also reduce in the coming years.

Figure 1. A typical Battery-Sourced Solar Photovoltaic (B-SSPV) plant

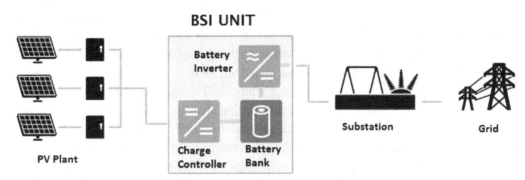

CHALLENGES

In order to reduce the production of greenhouse gases from fossil fuel based power plants, the utilization of renewable energy at higher scale is being promoted through various global institutes. However, the technical constraints associated with the optimum sizes and placement of DGs in distribution networks, have limited the utilization of renewable energy sources to a short scale. BESS can be used to store the energy during a specific period, when the excessive power from DGs is causing to increase the system losses. Later, during the period, when output from solar PV is less than the power required by the network, battery banks can be discharged and this way the energy from the battery bank can be released more efficiently. This method will not only help to increase the penetration of power from PV plants, but also help to reduce more system losses. Since the life and cost of battery system is highly crucial when choosing the sizes of energy storage systems, therefore the size of battery system must also be determined optimally. Additionally, in order to provide maximum benefits to distribution network; such as reduction of network losses, the charging and discharging timings of the battery system must also be determined intelligently.

STUDY OBJECTIVE AND METHODOLOGY

The objective of this book chapter is to determine the optimum sizes and placements of Battery-Sourced Solar Photovoltaic (B-SSPV) plants in distribution networks by using Mixed Integer Optimization using Genetic Algorithm (MIOGA) in order to reduce the total energy losses. An optimization framework is to be developed to determine the sizes of the PV plant and the battery storage, and to determine the optimum levels of energy requirements for scheduling the charging and discharging of the battery storage. The main objective of this research study is to reduce total energy losses, however, the study shall also monitors the impact of PV-Battery power on the voltage deviations and PV penetration levels. To estimate the PV plant yields, solar site's historical satellite's 15 years hourly weather data from the years 2000 - 2014 shall be used. For handling of that much data, the yearly data shall be partitioned into four seasons. Furthermore, in order to calculate the probability of solar PV power outputs, the seasonal data shall be modeled by using Beta Probability Density Function (Beta-PDF) and a 24 hour solar curve for each season shall be generated. To test the effectiveness of the proposed method, the study shall adopt four time varying voltage dependent load models, which include constant load model, industrial load model, residential load model and commercial load model. The proposed method shall be tested on IEEE 33 bus and IEEE 69 bus test distribution networks. For investigating the impact of the BESS unit, two cases shall be considered. In the first case, study shall consider the output of PV plant without any storage. During this, the simulation work shall be carried out for determining the optimum sizes of solar PV plant without the BESS unit. In the second case, study shall consider the BESS units for calculating the output of PV plant. In the second case, the optimization shall be done for determining the sizes of solar PV plant and the BESS unit. During the optimization in second case, the optimum levels of energy requirements shall also be determined for scheduling the charging and discharging of the battery storage. The optimum levels of energy requirements will help to decide to charge or discharge the battery storage during the each hour. The simulation code of the proposed algorithm is developed in MATLAB R2015a (Matlab, 2015). Furthermore, the structure of this chapter is described as follows.

The section 2 consists of the modeling of system parameters, which includes the modeling of weather data, the modeling of PV module power output, the modeling of load flow equations, the modeling of PV plant & B-SSPV plant power outputs, and finally the modeling of load models takes place. The section 3 consists of the problem formulations that include the mathematical expressions of Total Energy Loss Index (TELI), bus voltage deviations and the penetrations of PV and B-SSPV plants. The system and network constraints are also defined in section 3. The explanation and flowchart of the proposed algorithm is provided in section 4. In section 5, the simulation results of the proposed study are discussed in detail and are also provided in form of tables and graphical plots. And finally, the conclusion of the work and future study considerations are provided in section 6.

MODELING OF THE SYSTEM PARAMETERS

Weather Data Modelling

The 15 year time series hourly weather data of the site at coordinates (29°19'25.6"N, 71°49'11.8"E) is acquired through the National Solar Radiation Database (NSRDB, 2016). The time series weather data consists of the hourly solar irradiations and the temperature. For the ease to handling of that big data, the yearly data is partitioned into 4 seasons namely Winter, Spring, Summer and Autumn. Each of these seasons consists of three months weather data. The three months of each season include January, February & March, April, May & June, July, August & September, and October, November & December, for Winter, Spring, Summer and Autumn, respectively.

The seasonal data is then modeled by using Beta Probability Density Function (Beta-PDF) and a 24 hour solar curve for each season is generated. So from the 15 years of weather data, only four-24 hours solar curves are calculated and by summing these four 24 hours curves, finally a 96 sample curve is produced. The Beta Probability Density Function (Beta-PDF) has widely been used and accepted in many studies for the modeling of solar irradiance by using historical weather data. The Beta-PDF is used for modeling the solar weather data in (Atwa et al., 2010; Fan et al., 2012; Hung, Mithulananthan, & Lee, 2014; Khatod et al., 2013; Teng, Luan, Lee, & Huang, 2013). The Beta-PDF uses the hourly historical weather data as the input and calculates the probability of occurrence of a range of possible values during the each hour.

The Beta-PDF for solar irradiance for any hour can be expressed as follows.

$$
beta(s) = \begin{cases} \dfrac{\Gamma(\alpha+\beta)}{\Gamma(\alpha)\Gamma(\beta)} s^{(\alpha-1)}(1-s)^{(\beta-1)}, 0 \leq s \leq 1, \alpha, \beta \geq 0 \\ 0 \qquad\qquad\qquad\qquad\qquad\qquad otherwise \end{cases}
\tag{1}
$$

where s is the irradiance of solar light in kW/m², whereas α and β are two input parameters of the Beta-PDF, which are calculated with the help of Mean (μ) and Standard Deviation (σ) of solar irradiance. The α and β can be calculated by using following equations.

$$
\beta = (1-\mu)\left(\frac{\mu(1+\mu)}{\sigma^2} - 1 \right)
\tag{2}
$$

$$
\alpha = \frac{\mu X \beta}{1-\mu}
\tag{3}
$$

The probability of the solar irradiance state during any specific hour can be calculated as follows (Atwa et al., 2010; Hung, Mithulananthan, & Lee, 2014).

$$
p(s) = \int_{s1}^{s2} beta(s) ds
\tag{4}
$$

where s1 and s2 are the two solar irradiance limits, in which the probability of s has to be determined.

Output From PV Module

The peak power of a PV module is measured in Watts and it is equal to the maximum power of module's output under the standard test conditions. Normally the characteristics of PV modules are provided in the form of following parameters (Atwa et al., 2010; Hung, Mithulananthan, & Lee, 2014).

- Isc (Short circuit current in A)
- Voc (Open-circuit voltage in V)
- IMPP (Current at maximum power point in A)
- VMPP (Voltage at maximum power point in V)
- NOTC (Nominal operating temperature of cell in °C)
- Kv (Voltage temperature coefficients in V/°C)
- Ki (Current temperature coefficients in A/°C)

The short circuit current is directly proportional to the solar radiations, whereas the voltage is inversely proportional to the temperature. The power output of PV module during a time segment (h), can be measured by using following equations.

$$PV_{OUT}\left(h\right) = \int_0^1 PV_{NET}\, p\left(s\right) ds \qquad (5)$$

$$PV_{NET} = FF\, x\, V_{NET}\, x\, I_{NET}$$

$$FF = \frac{V_{MPP}\, x\, I_{MPP}}{V_{OC}\, x\, I_{SC}}$$

$$V_{NET} = V_{OC} - K_V\, x\, T_C$$

$$I_{NET} = s\left[I_{SC} + K_i x\left(T_C - 25\right)\right]$$

$$T_C = T_A + s\left(\frac{\left(NOCT - 20\right)}{0.8}\right)$$

where T_C and T_A are cell and ambient temperatures (^{0}C), respectively, whereas the FF is known as fill factor.

Power Flow Equations

Due to the presence of high R/X ratios in Radial Distribution System (RDS), the traditionally used load flow methods that have been used in transmission systems, such as Newton Raphson Load Flow method, are considered unsuitable for solving the power flows equations in distribution networks. As an alternative, for load flow analysis in RDS, some other computational methods, such as Backward Forward Sweep Load Flow methods are used (Bompard, Carpaneto, Chicco, & Napoli, 2000). Backward Forward Sweep load flow methods is an iterative method and consists of two sets of equations; one set is used to calculate the power flows in each branch of the network, while in the second iteration, voltage magnitude and voltage angle of each bus is calculated. This process is carried out from root bus to last bus; meanwhile two sets of equations are solved.

Figure 2 shows the single line diagram of a section of a distribution network, showing two buses; k and k+1, connected through a branch line i. The power flows in this section can be computed through following sets of equations (Jamil & Anees, 2016).

Figure 2. One-line diagram of a two-bus section in a Radial Distributed Network

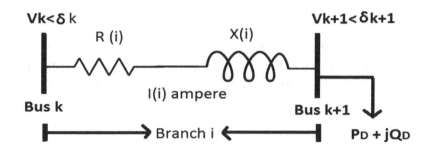

$$P_{(i)} = P_{(k+1)} + P_{loss(i)} \tag{6}$$

$$Q_{(i)} = Q_{(k+1)} + Q_{loss(i)} \tag{7}$$

$$V_{(k+1)} = V_{(k)} - I_{(i)}\left(R_{(i)} + jX_{(i)}\right) \tag{8}$$

P(i) and Q(i) are the active and reactive power that flow across the branch i. $P_{D(k+1)}$ and $Q_{D(k+1)}$ are active and reactive loads, connected at bus k+1.

Total power injections at bus k+1 is the sum of total loads connected at bus k+1 and the effective power which is flowing towards bus k+1 from the other buses. Therefore, the equations (6) and (7) can be written as followings (Prabha & Jayabarathi, 2016).

$$P_{(i)} = P_{(k+1),eff} + P_{D(k+1)} + P_{loss(i)} \tag{9}$$

$$Q_{(i)} = Q_{(k+1),eff} + Q_{D(k+1)} + Q_{loss(i)} \tag{10}$$

Resistance and reactance of the branch i are represented by Ri and Xi, respectively, whereas I(i) is the current that is flowing through the branch i. The power losses across the branch i can be calculated by using following equations (Hung, Mithulananthan, & Lee, 2014)

$$P_{loss(i)} = R_{(i)} * \frac{P_{k+1}^{~2} + Q_{k+1}^{~2}}{\left|V_{k+1}\right|^2} \tag{11}$$

$$Q_{loss(i)} = X_{(i)} * \frac{P_{k+1}^2 + Q_{k+1}^2}{|V_{k+1}|^2} \tag{12}$$

where, Ploss(i) and Qloss(i) are the active and reactive power losses across the branch i. The total power losses in distribution network can be calculated by summing the active and reactive power losses of all the branches in the network. Mathematically, the following equation can be used to calculate the total system losses (Rao, Ravindra, Satish, & Narasimham, 2013).

$$P_{loss\_total} = \sum_{i=1}^{no.of\ branches} P_{loss(i)} + jQ_{loss(i)} \tag{13}$$

PV Plants Model

The output power from the solar PV plants can be used as a negative power load (Shaker, Zareipour, & Wood, 2016). Assuming if the PV plant is going to be installed at bus k+1, then hourly total active and reactive power injections for bus k+1 can be calculated by using followings equations (Hung, Mithula-nanthan, & Lee, 2014).

$$P_{(i)}(t) = P_{(k+1),eff}(t) + P_{D(k+1)}(t) + P_{loss(i)}(t) - P_{PV}(t) \tag{14}$$

$$Q_{(i)}(t) = Q_{(k+1),eff}(t) + Q_{D(k+1)}(t) + Q_{loss(i)}(t) - Q_{PV}(t) \tag{15}$$

Since Q_{PV} is a function of P_{PV} with a fixed power factor, therefore:

$$Q_{PV} = aP_{PV}$$

And,

$$a = \pm tan\left(cos^{-1}\left(pf\left(P_{PV}\right)\right)\right)$$

When sign = +1: the inverter is injecting reactive power, sign = −1: the inverter is consuming reactive power, where pf is the operating power factor of the inverter. With no reactive power capability, the power factor of solar PV invertor is unity. After connecting PV plant, the new power losses across the branch i can be calculated by using following equations.

$$P^{PV}_{loss(i)} = R_{(i)} * \frac{(P_{k+1} - P_{PV})^2 + (Q_{k+1} - Q_{PV})^2}{\left|V_{k+1}\right|^2} \tag{16}$$

$$Q^{PV}_{loss(i)} = X_{(i)} * \frac{(P_{k+1} - P_{PV})^2 + (Q_{k+1} - Q_{PV})^2}{\left|V_{k+1}\right|^2} \tag{17}$$

Similarly, to calculate the total power losses with the addition of PV plant, the following equation can be used(Rao et al., 2013)..

$$P^{PV}_{loss\_total} = \sum_{i=1}^{no.\,of\,branches} P^{PV}_{loss(i)} + jQ^{PV}_{loss(i)} \tag{18}$$

The conversion efficiencies and performance of the inverters highly affect the overall system operation and outputs of PV modules. Normally, inverters are chosen based on the rating of system demand or maximum outputs that a solar PV plant can produce. From the typical inverter's conversion efficiency curve as provided in (SMA, 2016), the inverter's conversion efficiency from DC-to-AC is not constant and this efficiency is less if the input DC power from solar PV modules is less than the rated DC values of inverter. In that case, the size of inverter should also be chosen based on predicted yields from PV plants. However, the size of the inverters in this study is considered 120% of the maximum power that the solar PV farm can produce under the optimum PV plant size. The study uses the typical inverter's conversion efficiency curve as provided in (SMA, 2016).

Battery-Sourced PV Plants Model

The idea of developing the Battery-Sourced PV plants (B-SSPV) is convert the non-dispatchable PV power into dispatchable generator (Chen, Kwan, & Tan, 2014). The B-SSPV is considered as dispatchable source of energy; the output power from batteries can be adjusted at any time according the network energy requirements and depending on the availability of stored in batteries. The times when batteries are needed to get discharged, they are treated as generators, and the times when batteries are needed to get charged, they are treated as loads. The inverters with battery backup are capable of injecting or absorbing the reactive power as well. During the charging and discharging conditions, the power factor of the battery inverters can be adjusted according to the system requirements (Hung, Mithulananthan, & Bansal, 2014).

Similar to the solar PV plants, output power from the Battery-Sourced Solar Photovoltaic (B-SSPV) plant shall be used as negative load. To avoid putting additional burden on existing on existing generators, the batteries shall be charged only from the electricity produced through the solar PV plant. However, the time to charge and discharge the battery storage in this study is dynamic and is not pre-determined. The charging and discharging of battery storage during the each hour shall depend on the percentage of peak load, which is chosen by using a simulation parameter "Load_multiplier". The explanations of "Load_multiplier" are provided later. Assuming if the B-SSPV plant is going to be installed at bus k+1, depending on the output of B-SSPV plant, the hourly total active and reactive power injections for bus k+1 can be calculated by using followings equations.

$$P_{(i)}\left(t\right) = P_{(k+1),eff}\left(t\right) + P_{D(k+1)}\left(t\right) + P_{loss\,(i)}\left(t\right) - P_{B-SSPV}\left(t\right) \tag{19}$$

$$Q_{(i)}\left(t\right) = Q_{(k+1),eff}\left(t\right) + Q_{D(k+1)}\left(t\right) + Q_{loss\,(i)}\left(t\right) - Q_{B-SSPV}\left(t\right) \tag{20}$$

Since Q_{PV} is a function of P_{PV} with a fixed power factor, therefore:

$$Q_{PV} = aP_{B-SSPV}$$

And,

$$a = \pm tan(cos^{-1}\left(pf\left(P_{B-SSPV}\right)\right)$$

Inverters with battery backup can provide reactive power (Monteiro et al., 2012). However, this study does not consider the supplying of reactive power, and in that case, the power factor of B-SSPV plant invertor is unity. After connecting B-SSPV plant, the new power losses across the branch i can be calculated by using following equations.

$$P^{B-SSPVG}{}_{loss(i)} = R_{(i)} * \frac{(P_{k+1} - P_{B-SSPV})^2 + (Q_{k+1} - Q_{B-SSPV})^2}{\left|V_{k+1}\right|^2} \tag{21}$$

$$Q^{B-SSPV}{}_{loss(i)} = X_{(i)} * \frac{(P_{k+1} - P_{B-SSPV})^2 + (Q_{k+1} - Q_{B-SSPV})^2}{\left|V_{k+1}\right|^2} \tag{22}$$

Similarly, to calculate the total power losses with the addition of B-SSPV plant, the following equation can be used.

$$P^{B-SSPV}{}_{loss\_total} = \sum_{i=1}^{no.\,of\,branches} P^{B-SSPV}{}_{loss(i)} + jQ^{B-SSPV}{}_{loss(i)} \tag{23}$$

Load Model

In practical distribution networks, the load can be classified as constant, industrial, residential and commercial load (Hung, Mithulananthan, & Lee, 2014; Devender Singh & Misra, 2007; Deependra Singh & Verma, 2009). These types of loads are also referred to as voltage-dependent load models. Depending on the type of loads, the new loads P_{Dnew} for every bus are calculated by using following equations (Price et al., 1995).

$$P_{Dnew(k)} = P_{Da(k)} * V_{(k)}^{v\alpha} \tag{24}$$

$$Q_{Dnew(k)} = Q_{Da(k)} * V_{(k)}^{vr} \tag{25}$$

where P_{Da} and Q_{Da} are the actual active and reactive loads connected at bus k, and V(k) is the voltage magnitude of kth bus which is calculated under the base load conditions. The two parameters $v\alpha$ and vr are known as voltage coefficients for active and reactive power loads. The values of $v\alpha$ and vr are provided in Table 1.

Similarly, the hourly total loads of the network can be calculated as following.

$$P_{DTotal}(t) = \sum_{k=2}^{number\ of\ buses} P_{Dnew(k)}(t) \tag{26}$$

$$Q_{DTotal}(t) = \sum_{k=2}^{number\ of\ buses} Q_{Dnew(k)}(t) \tag{27}$$

The objective of using time varying voltage dependent load models is because the output from PV farm is also time varying. For each season, the study considers the seasonal time varying load magnitudes using IEEE-RTS load data as in (Chairman, Bhavaraju, & Biggerstaff, 1979). For calculating, time varying loads models at time t, the equations (24) and (25) can be rewritten as followings.

Table 1. Voltage coefficients for active and reactive power loads

Type of load	vα	vr
Constant	0	0
Industrial	0.18	6.00
Residential	0.92	4.04
Commercial	1.51	3.40

$$P_{Dnew(k)}\left(t\right) = P_{Da(k)}\left(t\right) * V_{(k)}^{v\alpha}\left(t\right) \tag{28}$$

$$Q_{Dnew(k)}\left(t\right) = Q_{Da(k)}\left(t\right) * V_{(k)}^{vr}\left(t\right) \tag{29}$$

PROBLEM FORMULATION

In addition to the supplying of electrical power, distributed generations (DGs) are considered useful for reducing system losses and enhancing the bus voltages. However, the main objective of this study is the reduction of total energy losses. For time varying voltage-dependent load models, the hourly total power losses in distribution network can be calculated by summing the hourly active and reactive power losses of the all branches in the network. Mathematically, to calculate the total system losses, the following equation can be used.

$$P_{loss\_total}\left(t\right) = \sum_{i=1}^{no.\,of\,branches} P_{loss(i)}\left(t\right) + jQ_{loss(i)}\left(t\right) \tag{30}$$

For a time varying voltage-dependent load model, to calculate the total power losses with the addition of solar PV only, the following equation can be used.

$$P^{PV}_{loss\_total}\left(t\right) = \sum_{i=1}^{no.\,of\,branches} P^{PV}_{loss(i)}\left(t\right) + jQ^{PV}_{loss(i)}\left(t\right) \tag{31}$$

Similarly, for a time varying voltage-dependent load model, to calculate the total power losses with the addition of B-SSPV, the following equation can be used.

$$P^{B-SSPV}_{loss\_total}\left(t\right) = \sum_{i=1}^{no.\,of\,branches} P^{B-SSPV}_{loss(i)}\left(t\right) + jQ^{B-SSPV}_{loss(i)}\left(t\right) \tag{32}$$

Since the main objective of this study is to minimize the sum of hourly total real power losses of the whole network, however, the study will also observe the impact of solar PV farm outputs on bus voltages profile. Any deviation in network losses due to the installation of DG (say PV only or B-SSPV), can be observed by dividing the real parts of equation (30) with the real parts of equation (31). This method is also termed as Total Energy Loss Index (TELI) and mathematically can be expressed as following (Deependra Singh & Verma, 2009).

$$Total\,Power\,loss\,index\left(PLI\right) = \sum \frac{real\left(P^{DG}_{loss\_total}\left(t\right)\right)}{real\left(P_{loss\_total}\left(t\right)\right)} \tag{33}$$

The minimization of the equation (33) is actually the main objective of this study. This can be expressed as following.

$$Min\, f = Total\, Energy\, Loss\, Index\left(TELI\right)$$
(34)

In addition to reduce the network power losses, the addition of DGs in distribution network improves the bus voltage profile. The change in bus voltage magnitude is measured as deviation in bus voltages and hourly voltage deviation of each bus can be calculated as following (Jamil & Anees, 2016).

$$VDev_k\left(t\right) = \left|1 - V_k\right|^2\left(t\right)$$
(35)

In time varying voltage-dependent load model, the bus voltages starts to decrease with the increase in loads values and system will experience the minimum voltages during the peak hours. Using the equation (35), the bus with lowest voltage magnitude will give maximum voltage deviation ($VDev_{max}$). Then the bus with maximum voltage deviation ($VDev_{max}$) will be given more importance as the voltage deviation of this bus will indicate the status of whole network. So, in addition to reduce the network losses, the study will put continuous monitoring on the $VDev_{max}$. The maximum voltage deviation ($VDev_{max}$) can be calculated by using following equation (Kowsalya, 2014).

$$VDev_{max} = \max(\left|1 - V_k\right|^2\left(t\right))$$
(36)

Penetration level of PV power is known as the ratio of total energy of PV farm supplied to the electric network and the total energy consumption of the network (Hung, Mithulananthan, & Bansal, 2013). For a DG (say PV only or B-SSPV) plant with no reactive power capabilities, the plant's penetration level can be calculated through following equation (Hung, Mithulananthan, & Lee, 2014).

$$PV\, penetration\left(\%\right) = \frac{\sum_{t=1}^{96} P_{DG}\left(t\right)}{\sum_{t=1}^{96} P_{DTotal}\left(t\right)} * 100$$
(37)

NETWORK CONSTRAINTS

To acquire the main objective of reducing the network losses, the simulation of the proposed algorithm must fulfill the following constraints.

Distributed Generation Capacity

$$P^{min}_{DG} < P_{DG} < P^{max}_{DG}$$
(38)

whereas P^{min}_{DG} is equal to 0 and P^{max}_{DG} is equal to the peak active power load of each voltage-dependent load. Therefore, P^{max}_{DG} for each type of load type will not be the same.

BESS Capacity

$$0 < BESS < P^{max}_{DG} * BESS\_multiplier \tag{39}$$

whereas the BESS_multiplier is factor which determines the value of BESS as percentage of the size PV plant. Since the cost of battery is comparatively high, therefore the maximum value of multiplier, considered in this study is 200%. For example, for a 1 MW_p sized PV plant, the maximum BESS size that can be used is 2 MWh throughout the study. But since size of the PV plant is randomly chosen, therefore the size of BESS will keep changing throughout the simulation with the changing of size of the PV plant.

Hourly Energy Requirements Factor

$$0 < Hourly\,Energy\,Requirements\,Factor < Eop * E\_multiplier \tag{40}$$

whereas the Eop is the optimum energy requirement needed to bring the network losses to minimum. Say if the load of the current hour is at peak (3715kW) and if the randomly chosen bus number is 6, then the Eop of the current hour will be 2.59 MWh. (Acharya et al., 2006). E_multiplier is factor which determines the value of energy requirements for the current hour as a percentage of the peak energy requirements of the current hour. The values of the E_multiplier are ranging in 0 and 1. With a randomly chosen value E-multiplier=0.5, the system will consider to arrange only 50% of the total energy requirement during the each hour. In example as mentioned above, Say if the load of the current hour is at peak (3715kW) and if the randomly chosen bus number is 6, then the Eop of the current hour with E_multiplier = 0.5, will be 1.25 MWh. And in that case, if the output of PV plant is higher than the 1.25 MW, then the remaining amount of power shall be considered to charge the batteries. And, if the output of PV plant is less than 1.25 MW, the remaining energy shall be arranged from the BESS by discharging the batteries. This way, the value of E_multiplier helps to decide whether to charge or discharge the battery storage.

Charge/Discharge Factor

The charge discharge factor is also similar to "Hourly Energy Requirements Factor", but the charge/discharge factor here is used to choose a percentage of hourly load in which the batteries will be considered for the charging or discharging.

$$0 < Charge\,/\,Discharge\,Factor < hourly\,load * Load\_multiplier$$

where, the Load_multiplier is the load multiplier and its value ranges in between 0 to 1. For example if the value of the L-multiplier is randomly chosen 0.7, then the simulation will only consider to charge or discharge the batteries if the load of the current hour is approx. 0.7 p.u. of the peak system load. In that case, for hourly loads other than 0.7 p.u., the output of PV plant will be dispatched directly to network without looking for the options to charge or discharge the batteries.

Network Power Balance

$$P_{substation(t)} + P_{DG}\left(t\right) = P_{DTotal}\left(t\right) + P_{loss\_total}\left(t\right) \tag{41}$$

$$Q_{substation(t)} + Q_{DG}\left(t\right) = Q_{DTotal}\left(t\right) + Q_{loss\_Total}\left(t\right) \tag{42}$$

where $P_{substation}$ and $Q_{substation,}$ are respectively the active and reactive power supplies to distribution network from the substation.

DG Placement

As previously mentioned, the bus no.1 in the distributed network is considered as slack bus, therefore, the DGs can be connected to any bus excluding the bus no.1.

$$2 \leq DG_{location} \leq max\left(number\,of\,buses\right) \tag{43}$$

Bus Voltage Limits

$$V_{min} \leq V \leq V_{max} \tag{44}$$

In order to maintain the power quality of distribution network, the bus voltage magnitude will remain under a Vmax of 1.0 p.u.

GENETIC ALGORITHM

The Genetic Algorithm (GA) is a programming optimization technique to solve constrained and unconstrained problems. Inspired by Darwinian's principle, to solve the real world problem, this optimization technique follows biological growth process. GA optimizes by using an evolution and a natural selection. GA consists of a data structure similar to chromosomes and these chromosomes are changed by using selection, crossover and mutation operators. The details of working mechanism of GA and functions of its parameters are provided in (Boor & Hosseini, 2012; Moradi & Abedini, 2012). The optimization process flowchart of GA is provided in Figure 3. The Genetic Algorithm (GA) is also capable of solving problems if the unknown value is integer. Since the location of the DG in distribution network is actually the number of a bus, whereas the size is a percentage of system's peak demand. The mix of DG location as integer and DG size as non-integer creates a need of optimization of mixed integer variables. In order to solve this, Mixed Integer Optimization using Genetic Algorithm (MIOGA) is adopted.

Figure 3. Flowchart of Genetic Algorithm for solar PV and B-SSPV sizing and placement

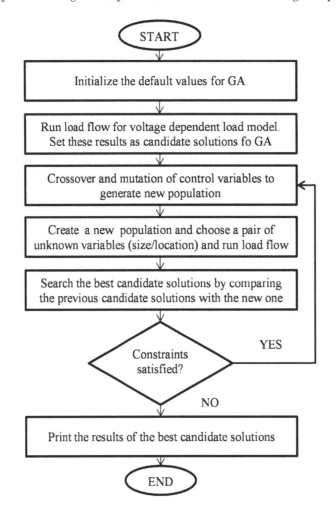

SIMULATION RESULTS

From the seasonal Mean (kW/m^2) and the Standard Deviation (kW/m^2) of the historical solar irradiance data, the values for seasonal beta (β) & alpha (α) are calculated by using equations (2) and (3) and are provided in Table 2. The hourly Probability Density Function (PDF) for the four seasons, are calculated by using equations (1) and (4) and are plotted in Figure 4.

The ambient temperature is the average of the seasonal hourly 15 years temperature data. The yearly temperature of the site is ranging in between 12 ^{0}C – 45 ^{0}C. The minimum and maximum temperature during the each season is 12 & 29 ^{0}C, 29 & 45 ^{0}C, 29 & 40 ^{0}C, and 16 & 32 ^{0}C, for Winter, Spring, Summer and Autumn, respectively.

Based on the seasonal PDF values, seasonal irradiations and seasonal ambient temperature, the expected seasonal daily solar PV outputs are calculated by using equation (5). From the expected seasonal daily solar PV outputs, it is known that this site has maximum irradiation of 907 Watts/m^2 during the months of Summer. On average, the site receives 4.4 – 6.9 peaks sunny hours (PSH).

Table 2. Summary of seasonal weather data showing alpha, beta, mean and standard deviation

Hr.No	Winter				Spring				Summer				Autumn			
	μ	σ	α	β	μ	σ	α	β	μ	σ	α	β	μ	σ	α	β
9	0.01	0.02	0.43	19.8	0.12	0.03	21.6	105	0.08	0.02	30.5	194	0.02	0.02	0.9	26.2
10	0.14	0.06	5.12	26	0.32	0.04	55.7	94.6	0.25	0.05	57.6	120	0.18	0.06	8.7	36.7
11	0.35	0.08	13	24.2	0.53	0.06	89.8	70	0.42	0.09	78.7	74.4	0.38	0.07	25.5	43.1
12	0.54	0.1	19.2	18.4	0.71	0.08	103	39.8	0.57	0.13	91.3	44.6	0.55	0.08	44	40.5
13	0.69	0.12	22.6	13.4	0.84	0.09	154	30.1	0.68	0.17	91.5	26.1	0.67	0.09	56.6	34.9
14	0.77	0.12	27.1	12.2	0.91	0.1	153	20.3	0.75	0.19	88.7	19.5	0.73	0.09	66.2	34.9
15	0.78	0.13	28.9	13.3	0.92	0.08	160	25.2	0.76	0.18	68.2	17.8	0.71	0.09	62.2	37.9
16	0.72	0.12	24.9	15.8	0.85	0.08	119	34.5	0.7	0.18	48.3	20	0.63	0.09	52.1	47.1
17	0.6	0.11	19.8	21.3	0.72	0.08	93.1	54.1	0.58	0.15	33.7	25.5	0.49	0.07	36.2	59.5
18	0.42	0.09	11.1	25.2	0.54	0.06	66.3	80.7	0.43	0.11	25.6	38.7	0.3	0.06	13.2	54.6
19	0.21	0.07	2.78	22	0.33	0.04	36	108	0.25	0.07	11.5	43.7	0.09	0.04	0.6	24.4
20	0.03	0.03	0.27	70.2	0.11	0.03	6.2	85.7	0.08	0.04	1.9	35.7	0	0	0	0

Figure 4. Probability density of solar irradiance during each season

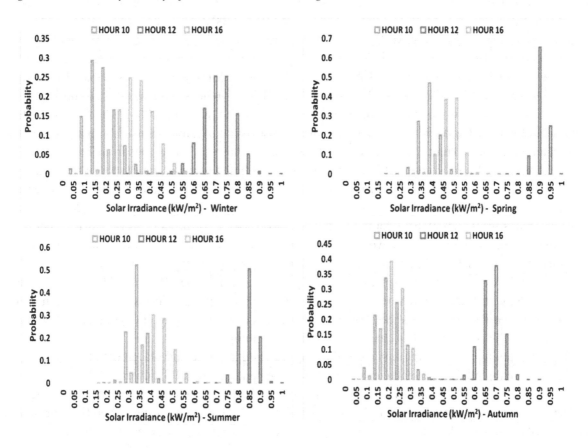

Therefore, using a PV module with following specifications, the PV module can produce 177 Watts during the months of Spring.

- Nominal operating temperature of cell (NOCT) 44 0C
- Current at maximum power point (IMPP) 8.28 A
- Voltage at maximum power point (VMPP 30.2 V
- Short-circuit Current (ISC) 8.7 A
- Open-circuit voltage (VOC) 37.6 V
- Current temperature coefficients (Ki) 0.0045 A/C
- Voltage temperature coefficients (Kv) 0.1241 V/C

Case Studies

This section consists of results of the simulation, calculated by Mixed Integer Optimization using Genetic Algorithm (MIOGA) for the optimal sizing and placement of Battery-Sourced Solar Photovoltaic (B-SSPV) plants in distribution networks. The main objective of the study is to reduce the total energy losses in distribution network by determining the optimum sizing of PV plant and battery storage, and by determining the dynamic scheduling for charging and discharging of the battery storage. The proposed algorithm is simulated and applied IEEE 33 bus and IEEE 69 bus test distribution networks. The active and reactive demands of IEEE 33 bus network are 3715 kW & 2300 kVAr, whereas, the active and reactive demands of IEEE 69 bus network are 3800 kW & 2690 kVAr. The total base case real and reactive power losses for IEEE 33 bus are 211 kW & 143 kVAr, whereas the total base case real and reactive power losses for IEEE 69 bus are 225 kW & 102 kVAr (Chang, Mithulananthan, & Saha, 2011; Hung & Mithulananthan, 2012; Naik, Khatod, & Sharma, 2013). The single line diagrams, line and load data of both distribution networks are available in (Venkatesh, Ranjan, & Gooi, 2004). The first bus in the radial distribution networks is as slack bus, and in that case, this bus cannot be used for placing the DG units. Therefore, the DG units can be considered suitable to be installed at any bus from 2 to 33 in IEEE 33 bus system and from 2 to 69 in IEEE 69 bus system. For both test cases, four types of time varying voltage-dependent load models are used. These load models include constant, industrial, residential and commercial loads. The four time varying loads are modeled by using the equations (28) and (29). The constraints for the simulations for the both test networks are kept the same as provided earlier. For investigating the impact of BESS, two cases are considered. In the first case, the simulation work is considers impact of solar PV plant in the distribution network, where the optimization takes place for determining the optimum sizes of solar PV plant only. In the second case, BESS is added in the simulation work along with the solar PV plant. In the second case, the optimization is done for determining the sizes of solar PV plant and BESS, and the optimization of the energy requirements for scheduling the timings of the charging and discharging of the battery storage.

The simulation results for the first case, showing the results of size and placement of PV plant, the reduction in real power losses, voltage deviations and the penetration of PV power in IEEE 33 bus and IEEE 69 bus test distribution networks are summarized in Table 3 and Table 4. Due to the difference of energy consumption and availability of power from the solar PV plant during a specific hour in the both distribution networks, the optimal size of PV plant is considerably different for each time varying voltage dependent load model. The optimum locations of solar PV farm in IEEE 33 is bus no.6, whereas optimum locations of solar PV farm in IEEE 69 is bus no.61. The sizes of the solar PV plants and the

Table 3. Summary of results with PV plant only in IEEE 33 bus test system

Parameters	Constant		Industrial		Residential		Commercial	
	Without	With PV	Without	With PV	Without	With PV	Without	With PV
PV size (MW)@Bus No		4.94@6		4.88@6		4.62@6		4.42@6
Real Energy Losses (MWh)	14.15	10.80	13.81	10.55	12.49	9.58	11.55	8.88
Reduction in ELoss (%)		23.67%		23.60%		23.29%		23.06%
PLDev		0.763		0.764		0.767		0.769
DG Penetration (%)		31.41		31.25		30.59		30.08
VDev	0.183	0.179	0.180	0.177	0.169	0.166	0.161	0.158

Table 4. Summary of results with PV plant only in IEEE 69 bus test system

Parameters	Constant		Industrial		Residential		Commercial	
	Without	With PV	Without	With PV	Without	With PV	Without	With PV
PV size (MW)@Bus No		3.62@61		3.45@61		3.44@61		3.26@61
Real Energy Losses (MWh)	15.06	10.28	14.65	10.02	13.10	9.05	11.99	8.37
Reduction in ELoss (%)		31.75%		31.62%		30.88%		30.22%
PLDev		0.682		0.684		0.691		0.698
DG Penetration (%)		22.44		22.05		21.62		21.57
VDev	0.173	0.170	0.171	0.167	0.160	0.157	0.151	0.149

rate of reduction in network losses in both distribution networks is linear for almost each time varying voltage-dependent load model.

The reduction in total energy losses after the addition of solar PV plant in IEEE 33 bus distribution network are 23.67%, 23.60%, 23.29% and 230.06% for the constant, the industrial, the residential and the commercial load models, respectively. On the other hand, the reduction in total energy losses after the addition of solar PV plant in IEEE 69 bus distribution network are 31.75%, 31.62%, 30.88% and 30.22% for the constant, the industrial, the residential and the commercial load models, respectively.

The simulation results for the second case, showing the results of size and placement of PV plant and BESS unit, the reduction in real power losses, voltage deviations and the penetration of (B-SSPV) plant power in IEEE 33 bus and IEEE 69 bus test distribution networks are summarized in Table 5 and Table 6.

As compared to the results in first case, the total size of PV plant due to the addition of BESS unit in both distribution networks is significantly higher than the size of PV plant for each time varying voltage dependent load model. Due to the increased sizes of PV plant in both distribution networks, the penetration levels of PV power are greatly enhanced for each time varying voltage dependent load model. In additions to the increases in PV plant sizes, the reduction in total energy losses observed in B-SSPV case is also much higher than the reduction in energy loss in first case (PV only).

The addition of BESS unit did not bring any change to the location of PV plants in both distribution networks. The optimum location of B-SSPV plant in IEEE 33 is bus no.6, and also optimum location

Table 5. Summary of results with B-SSPV for each time varying voltage dependent load model in IEEE 33 bus distribution network

Parameters	Constant		Industrial		Residential		Commercial	
	Without	With PV-BESS	Without	With PV-BESS	Without	With PV-BESS	Without	With PV-BESS
PV size (MW)@Bus No		7.22@6		7.04@6		6.44@6		6.05@6
Total BESS Size (MWh)		14.44		14.07		12.87		12.07
Real Energy Losses (MWh)	14.15	9.50	13.81	9.29	12.49	8.55	11.55	7.84
Reduction in ELoss (%)		32.85%		32.74%		31.57%		32.06%
PLDev		0.671		0.673		0.684		0.679
DG Penetration (%)		43.05		42.76		41.35		41.87
VDev	0.183	0.181	0.180	0.179	0.169	0.163	0.161	0.156

Table 6. Summary of results with B-SSPV for each time varying voltage dependent load model in IEEE 69 bus distribution network

Parameters	Constant		Industrial		Residential		Commercial	
	Without	With PV-BESS	Without	With PV-BESS	Without	With PV-BESS	Without	With PV-BESS
PV size (MW)@Bus No		5.51@61		5.64@61		5.07@61		4.59@61
Total BESS Size (MWh)		11.02		11.28		10.14		9.08
Real Energy Losses (MWh)	15.06	8.33	14.65	8.21	13.10	7.38	11.99	6.90
Reduction in ELoss (%)		44.67%		43.98%		43.68%		42.50%
PLDev		0.553		0.560		0.563		0.575
DG Penetration (%)		32.04		32.95		31.77		30.56
VDev	0.173	0.166	0.171	0.164	0.160	0.154	0.151	0.146

of B-SSPV plant in IEEE 69 is bus no.61. The sizes of the PV plants and the BESS units and the rate of reduction in network losses in both distribution networks is also found linear for almost each time varying voltage-dependent load model.

The sizes of PV plant and BESS unit in IEEE 33 bus distribution network are 7.22 MW & 14.44 MWh, 7.04 MW & 14.07 MWh, 6.44 MW & 12.87 MWh and 6.05 MW & 12.07 MWh for the constant, the industrial, the residential and the commercial load models, respectively. After the addition of B-SSPV plant, the reduction in total energy in IEEE 33 bus distribution network are 32.85%, 32.74%, 31.57% and 32.06% for the constant, the industrial, the residential and the commercial load models, respectively.

The hourly active power demand, actual power output from PV plant and optimally scheduled output power from B-SSPV plant in IEEE 33 bus distribution network for the constant, the industrial, the residential and the commercial load models are plotted in Figure 5.

The scheduling of output power from B-SSPV plant in each load model is based on optimum scheduling of charging and discharging of battery storage. The optimization of scheduling of charging and discharging of battery storage during the simulation actually is done to achieving the main objective function; which is the reduction in the total energy losses in the network.

Figure 5. Network demand, actual PV plant power and optimally scheduled power from B-SSPV plant in IEEE 33 bus distribution network for each load model

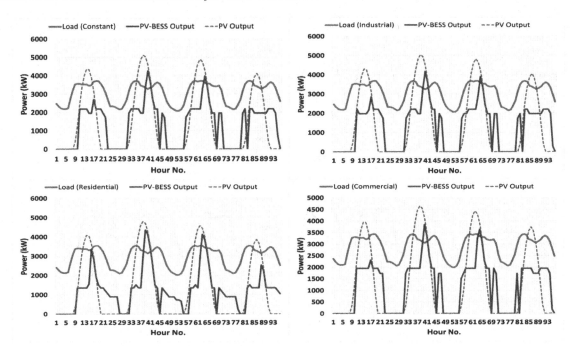

On the other hand, the sizes PV plant and BESS unit in IEEE 69 bus distribution network are 5.51 MW & 11.02 MWh, 5.64 MW & 11.28 MWh, 5.07 MW & 10.14 MWh and 4.59 MW & 9.08 MWh for the constant, the industrial, the residential and the commercial load models, respectively. After the addition of B-SSPV plant, the reduction in total energy in IEEE 33 bus distribution network are 44.67%, 43.98%, 43.68% and 42.50% for the constant, the industrial, the residential and the commercial load models, respectively.

The hourly active power demand, actual power output from PV plant and optimally scheduled output power from B-SSPV plant in IEEE 69 bus test distribution network for the constant, the industrial, the residential and the commercial load models are plotted in Figure 6. Further the impact of adding the BESS unit in the distribution network was investigated by comparing the results of B-SSPV with the results of first case (PV only). The comparison of the two cases was made in terms of the reduction in network losses, improvements in bus voltage deviations and penetrations levels in each time varying voltage dependent load model. The comparison of hourly power losses in base case, with PV only and with B-SSPV plant for each time varying voltage dependent load model in IEEE 33 and IEEE 69 bus distribution networks are plotted in Figure 7 and Figure 8.

The summary of the total energy losses in base case, with PV only and with B-SSPV plant for constant & industrial load models, and residential & commercial load models, in IEEE 33 and IEEE 69 bus distribution networks are provided in Table 7 and Table 8, respectively. From the results it is known that BESS units have greatly contributed in reducing the amount of the total energy losses for each time varying voltage dependent load model in both distribution networks. The introduction of BESS units in each time varying voltage dependent load model caused an additional reduction in total energy losses of about 8% - 9% in IEEE 33 bus and about 12% - 13% in IEEE 69 bus distribution networks.

Figure 6. Network demand, actual PV plant power and optimally scheduled power from B-SSPV plant in IEEE 69 bus distribution network for each load model

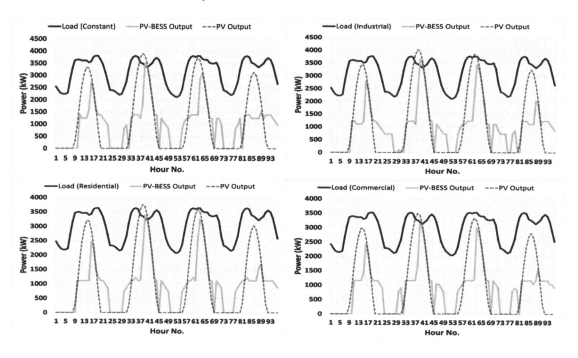

Figure 7. The comparison of hourly power losses for base case, PV only and B-SSPV for each time varying voltage dependent load model in IEEE 33bus distribution network

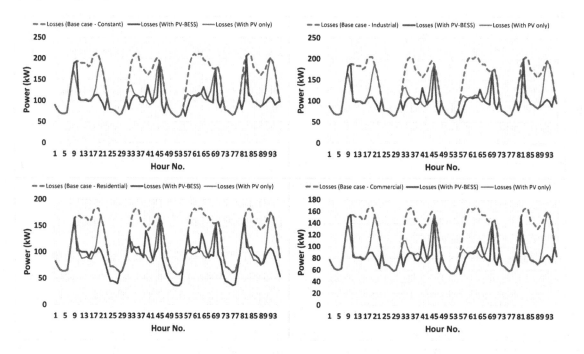

Figure 8. The comparison of hourly power losses for base case, PV only and B-SSPV for each time varying voltage dependent load model in IEEE 69bus distribution network

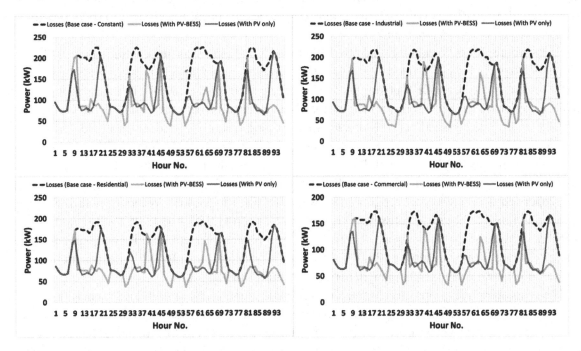

Table 7. Summary of the total energy losses (MWh) in base case, with PV only and with B-SSPV plant for constant & industrial load models

Parameters	Constant			Industrial		
	Without	With PV only	With PV-BESS	Without	With PV only	With PV-BESS
33 Bus network	14.15	10.80	9.50	13.81	10.55	9.29
69 Bus network	15.06	10.28	8.33	14.65	10.02	8.21

Table 8. Summary of the total energy losses (MWh) in base case, with PV only and with B-SSPV plant for residential & commercial load models

Parameters	Residential			Commercial		
	Without	With PV only	With PV-BESS	Without	With PV only	With PV-BESS
33 Bus network	12.49	9.58	8.55	11.55	8.88	7.84
69 Bus network	13.10	9.05	7.38	11.99	8.37	6.90

In comparison to the PV only, the addition of BESS units brought more enhancements to bus voltage profiles in both distribution networks. The voltage magnitudes of weakest bus in the base case, with PV only and with B-SSPV plant in each time varying voltage dependent load model for both distribution networks are plotted in Figure 9 and Figure 10.

Furthermore, B-SSPV plan is found favorable than PV only in terms on penetration levels. The size of the PV plants in both distribution networks was increased due to the addition of BESS units. Due to the increment in the sizes of PV plants, the total energy produced in B-SSPV plant was higher than the total energy produced in PV only, which ultimately helped to increase the plant penetration levels of B-SSPV plant. The penetration levels of each time varying voltage dependent load model in IEEE 33 bus and IEEE 69 bus distribution network are plotted in Figure 11 and Figure 12. The comparison of PV penetration of B-SSPV plant with PV only in IEEE 33 bus distribution network

With PV only, the penetration levels in IEEE 33 bus distribution network for different time varying load dependent load models are ranging in between 30.08% – to 31.40%. Whereas, with B-SSPV, the penetration levels for the same network are ranging in between 41.35% – to 43.05%. Also, with PV only in IEEE 69 bus distribution network, the penetration levels for different time varying load dependent load models are ranging in between 21.01% – to 22.44%. Whereas, with B-SSPV, the penetration levels for the same network are then ranging in between 30.56% – to 32.95%.

The sizes of PV plants and BESS unit, and their penetration levels of each load models in both distribution networks are seen varying from each other. From this, it is determined that electrical network design and types of load play an important role in determining the sizes of PV plants and battery storage. The specific requirements of different time varying load models necessitate toward the development of dynamic models for the sizing of PV plants and battery storages, as proposed in this research study.

Figure 9. The voltage magnitudes of weakest in the base case, with PV only and with B-SSPV plant in IEEE 69 bus distribution network

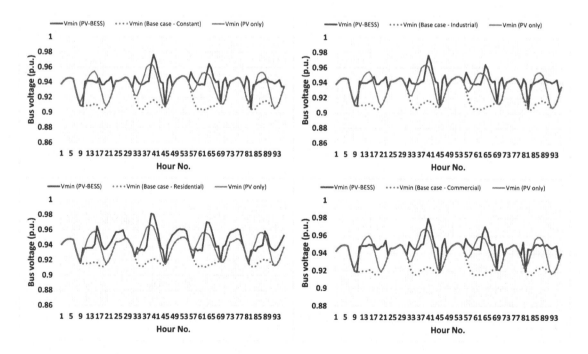

Figure 10. The voltage magnitudes of weakest in the base case, with PV only and with B-SSPV plant in IEEE 69 bus distribution network

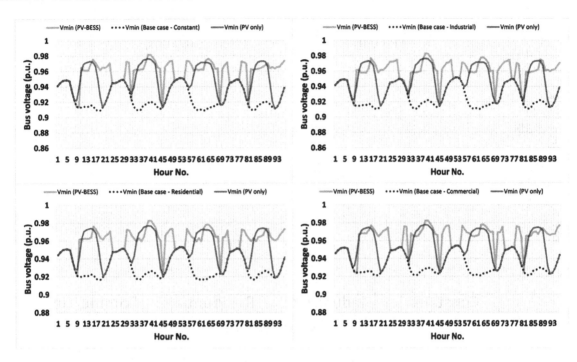

Figure 11. The comparison of PV penetration of B-SSPV plant with PV only in IEEE 33 bus distribution network

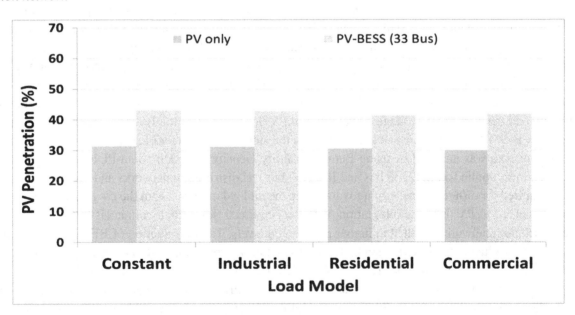

Figure 12. The comparison of PV penetration of B-SSPV plant with PV only in IEEE 69 bus distribution network

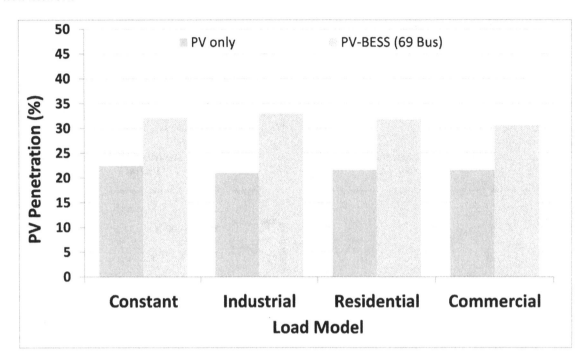

CONCLUSION

In this chapter, a Mixed Integer Optimization using Genetic Algorithm (MIOGA) was proposed for determining the optimum sizes and placements of Batter-Sourced Photovoltaic (B-SSPV) plants to reduce the total energy losses in distribution networks. The optimization framework was developed in such a way that the sizes of the PV plant and the battery storage, and the optimum levels of energy requirements for the scheduling of the charging and discharging of the battery storage, were determined dynamically. Total Energy Loss Index (TELI) was formulated as the main objective function for the optimization problem and meanwhile bus voltage deviations and PV penetrations of the Battery-Sourced Solar Photovoltaic (B-SSPV) plants were calculated. To deal the stochastic behavior of solar irradiance, 15 years of weather data was modeled by using Beta Probability Density Function (Beta-PDF). The proposed algorithm was applied on IEEE 33 bus and IEEE 69 bus test distribution networks and optimum results were acquired for different time varying voltage dependent load models. From the results, it was known that, compared to PV only, the integration of Battery-Sourced Solar Photovoltaic (B-SSPV) plants in the distribution networks resulted in higher penetration levels. The introduction of BESS units in each time varying voltage dependent load model caused an additional reduction in total energy losses of about 8% - 9% in IEEE 33 bus and about 12% - 13% in IEEE 69 bus distribution networks. With PV only, the penetration levels in IEEE 33 bus distribution network for different time varying load dependent load models were ranging in between 30.08% – to 31.40%. Whereas, with B-SSPV, the penetration levels for the same network were ranging in between 41.35% – to 43.05%. Also, with PV only in IEEE 69 bus distribution network, the penetration levels for different time varying load dependent load models were ranging in between 21.01% – to 22.44%. Whereas, with B-SSPV, the penetration levels for the same network were then ranging in between 30.56% – to 32.95%. As compared to bus voltage profiles in base case and in PV only, the improvements in the voltage deviation due to addition of battery storage was significant. The proposed algorithm was very effective in reducing total energy loss in different types and sizes of distribution networks by determining the sizes of the PV plant and the battery storage, and by determining the optimum levels of energy requirements for scheduling the charging and discharging of the battery storage.

REFERENCES

Acharya, N., Mahat, P., & Mithulananthan, N. (2006). An analytical approach for DG allocation in primary distribution network. *International Journal of Electrical Power & Energy Systems*, *28*(10), 669–678. doi:10.1016/j.ijepes.2006.02.013

Al Riza, D. F., & Gilani, S. I.-H. (2014). Standalone Photovoltaic System Sizing using Peak Sun Hour Method and Evaluation by TRNSYS Simulation. *International Journal of Renewable Energy Research*, *4*(1), 109–114.

Aman, M., Solangi, K., Hossain, M., Badarudin, A., Jasmon, G., Mokhlis, H., & Kazi, S. et al. (2015). A review of Safety, Health and Environmental (SHE) issues of solar energy system. *Renewable & Sustainable Energy Reviews*, *41*, 1190–1204. doi:10.1016/j.rser.2014.08.086

Atwa, Y., El-Saadany, E., Salama, M., & Seethapathy, R. (2010). Optimal renewable resources mix for distribution system energy loss minimization. *IEEE Transactions on Power Systems*, *25*(1), 360–370. doi:10.1109/TPWRS.2009.2030276

Bazilian, M., Mai, T., Baldwin, S., Arent, D., Miller, M., & Logan, J. (2014). Decision-making for high renewable electricity futures in the United States. *Energy Strategy Reviews*, *2*(3), 326–328. doi:10.1016/j.esr.2013.11.001

Bhargava, B., & Dishaw, G. (1998). Application of an energy source power system stabilizer on the 10 MW battery energy storage system at Chino substation. Power Systems. *IEEE Transactions on*, *13*(1), 145–151.

Bompard, E., Carpaneto, E., Chicco, G., & Napoli, R. (2000). Convergence of the backward/forward sweep method for the load-flow analysis of radial distribution systems. *International Journal of Electrical Power & Energy Systems*, *22*(7), 521–530. doi:10.1016/S0142-0615(00)00009-0

Boor, Z., & Hosseini, S. M. (2012). Optimal Placement of DG to Improve the Reliability of Distribution Systems Considering Time Varying Loads using Genetic Algorithm. *Majlesi Journal of Electrical Engineering*, *7*(1).

Calderon, M., Calderon, A., Ramiro, A., Gonzalez, J., & Gonzalez, I. (2011). Evaluation of a hybrid photovoltaic-wind system with hydrogen storage performance using exergy analysis. *International Journal of Hydrogen Energy*, *36*(10), 5751–5762. doi:10.1016/j.ijhydene.2011.02.055

Chairman, P., Bhavaraju, M., & Biggerstaff, B. (1979). IEEE reliability test system: A report prepared by the Reliability Test System Task Force of the Application of Probability Methods Subcommittee. *IEEE Transactions on Power Apparatus and Systems, 98*(6), 2047–2054.

Chang, R., Mithulananthan, N., & Saha, T. (2011). *Novel mixed-integer method to optimize distributed generation mix in primary distribution systems.* Paper presented at the Universities Power Engineering Conference (AUPEC), 2011 21st Australasian.

Chen, B., Kwan, K. H., & Tan, R. (2014). *Battery capacity planning for grid-connected solar photovoltaic systems.* Paper presented at the Signal and Information Processing Association Annual Summit and Conference (APSIPA), 2014 Asia-Pacific.

Daud, M. Z., Mohamed, A., & Hannan, M. (2013). An improved control method of battery energy storage system for hourly dispatch of photovoltaic power sources. *Energy Conversion and Management, 73*, 256–270. doi:10.1016/j.enconman.2013.04.013

Devabhaktuni, V., Alam, M., Depuru, S. S. S. R., Green, R. C., Nims, D., & Near, C. (2013). Solar energy: Trends and enabling technologies. *Renewable & Sustainable Energy Reviews, 19*, 555–564. doi:10.1016/j.rser.2012.11.024

Fan, M., Vittal, V., Heydt, G. T., & Ayyanar, R. (2012). Probabilistic power flow studies for transmission systems with photovoltaic generation using cumulants. *IEEE Transactions on Power Systems, 27*(4), 2251–2261. doi:10.1109/TPWRS.2012.2190533

Georgilakis, P. S., & Hatziargyriou, N. D. (2013). Optimal distributed generation placement in power distribution networks: Models, methods, and future research. *IEEE Transactions on Power Systems, 28*(3), 3420–3428. doi:10.1109/TPWRS.2012.2237043

Gökçek, M., Bayülken, A., & Bekdemir, Ş. (2007). Investigation of wind characteristics and wind energy potential in Kirklareli, Turkey. *Renewable Energy, 32*(10), 1739–1752. doi:10.1016/j.renene.2006.11.017

Hayter, A. (2012). *Probability and statistics for engineers and scientists.* Nelson Education.

Holland, J. H. (1968). *Hierarchical descriptions, universal spaces and adaptive systems.* DTIC Document.

Hung, D. Q., & Mithulananthan, N. (2012). *An optimal operating strategy of DG unit for power loss reduction in distribution systems.* Paper presented at the Industrial and Information Systems (ICIIS), 2012 7th IEEE International Conference on. doi:10.1109/ICIInfS.2012.6304773

Hung, D. Q., Mithulananthan, N., & Bansal, R. (2013). Analytical strategies for renewable distributed generation integration considering energy loss minimization. *Applied Energy, 105*, 75–85. doi:10.1016/j.apenergy.2012.12.023

Hung, D. Q., Mithulananthan, N., & Bansal, R. C. (2014). An optimal investment planning framework for multiple distributed generation units in industrial distribution systems. *Applied Energy, 124*, 62–72. doi:10.1016/j.apenergy.2014.03.005

Hung, D. Q., Mithulananthan, N., & Lee, K. Y. (2014). Determining PV penetration for distribution systems with time-varying load models. *IEEE Transactions on Power Systems, 29*(6), 3048–3057. doi:10.1109/TPWRS.2014.2314133

Jamali, A., Nor, N., & Ibrahim, T. (2015). *Energy storage systems and their sizing techniques in power system—A review.* Paper presented at the Energy Conversion (CENCON), 2015 IEEE Conference on.

Jamali, A., Nor, N., Ibrahim, T., & Romlie, M. F. (2016). *An analytical approach for the sizing and siting of battery-sourced inverters in distribution networks.* Paper presented at the Intelligent and Advanced Systems (ICIAS), 2016 6th International Conference on. doi:10.1109/ICIAS.2016.7824086

Jamil, M., & Anees, A. S. (2016). Optimal sizing and location of SPV (solar photovoltaic) based MLDG (multiple location distributed generator) in distribution system for loss reduction, voltage profile improvement with economical benefits. *Energy, 103*, 231–239. doi:10.1016/j.energy.2016.02.095

Khatod, D. K., Pant, V., & Sharma, J. (2013). Evolutionary programming based optimal placement of renewable distributed generators. *IEEE Transactions on Power Systems, 28*(2), 683–695. doi:10.1109/TPWRS.2012.2211044

Kothari, D., & Nagrath, I. (2008). *Power system engineering.* McGraw-Hill.

Kowsalya, M. (2014). Optimal size and siting of multiple distributed generators in distribution system using bacterial foraging optimization. *Swarm and Evolutionary Computation, 15*, 58–65. doi:10.1016/j.swevo.2013.12.001

Lee, A., Zinaman, O., Logan, J., Bazilian, M., Arent, D., & Newmark, R. L. (2012). Interactions, complementarities and tensions at the nexus of natural gas and renewable energy. *The Electricity Journal, 25*(10), 38–48. doi:10.1016/j.tej.2012.10.021

Liu, Y.-h., Wu, Z.-q., Tu, Y.-q., Huang, Q.-y., & Lou, H.-w. (2008). A Survey on Distributed Generation and Its Networking Technology. *Power System Technology, 15*, 20.

Matlab. (2015). *MathWorks R2015a.* Retrieved February 23, 2017, from https://www.mathworks.com/products/new_products/release2015a.html

Mekhilef, S., Saidur, R., & Safari, A. (2011). A review on solar energy use in industries. *Renewable & Sustainable Energy Reviews, 15*(4), 1777–1790. doi:10.1016/j.rser.2010.12.018

Monteiro, V., Pinto, J. G., Exposto, B., Gonçalves, H., Ferreira, J. C., Couto, C., & Afonso, J. L. (2012). *Assessment of a battery charger for Electric Vehicles with reactive power control.* Paper presented at the IECON 2012 - 38th Annual Conference on IEEE Industrial Electronics Society.

Moradi, M. H., & Abedini, M. (2012). A combination of genetic algorithm and particle swarm optimization for optimal DG location and sizing in distribution systems. *International Journal of Electrical Power & Energy Systems, 34*(1), 66–74. doi:10.1016/j.ijepes.2011.08.023

Naik, S., Khatod, D., & Sharma, M. (2013). *Sizing and siting of distributed generation in distribution networks for real power loss minimization using analytical approach.* Paper presented at the Power, Energy and Control (ICPEC), 2013 International Conference on. doi:10.1109/ICPEC.2013.6527753

NSRDB. (2016). *National Solar Radiation Data Base.* Retrieved March 15, 2016, from http://rredc.nrel.gov/solar/old_data/nsrdb/

Panasonic. (2015). *Panasonic Eco Solutions*. Retrieved February 23, 2017, from http://news.panasonic. co.uk/pressreleases/panasonic-debuts-high-powered-photovoltaic-module-hit-r-n330-for-uk-and-european-markets-sets-new-module-efficiency-record-1229674

Passey, R., Spooner, T., MacGill, I., Watt, M., & Syngellakis, K. (2011). The potential impacts of grid-connected distributed generation and how to address them: A review of technical and non-technical factors. *Energy Policy*, *39*(10), 6280–6290. doi:10.1016/j.enpol.2011.07.027

Plebmann, G., Erdmann, M., Hlusiak, M., & Breyer, C. (2014). Global energy storage demand for a 100% renewable electricity supply. *Energy Procedia*, *46*, 22–31. doi:10.1016/j.egypro.2014.01.154

Prabha, D. R., & Jayabarathi, T. (2016). Optimal placement and sizing of multiple distributed generating units in distribution networks by invasive weed optimization algorithm. *Ain Shams Engineering Journal*, *7*(2), 683–694. doi:10.1016/j.asej.2015.05.014

Price, W., Casper, S., Nwankpa, C., Bradish, R., Chiang, H., Concordia, C., & Wu, G. et al. (1995). Bibliography on load models for power flow and dynamic performance simulation. *IEEE Power Engineering Review*, *15*(2), 70.

Rao, R. S., Ravindra, K., Satish, K., & Narasimham, S. (2013). Power loss minimization in distribution system using network reconfiguration in the presence of distributed generation. *IEEE Transactions on Power Systems*, *28*(1), 317–325. doi:10.1109/TPWRS.2012.2197227

Shaker, H., Zareipour, H., & Wood, D. (2016). Impacts of large-scale wind and solar power integration on California's net electrical load. *Renewable & Sustainable Energy Reviews*, *58*, 761–774. doi:10.1016/j.rser.2015.12.287

Singh, D., Misra, R., & Singh, D. (2007). Effect of load models in distributed generation planning. *IEEE Transactions on Power Systems*, *22*(4), 2204–2212. doi:10.1109/TPWRS.2007.907582

Singh, D., & Verma, K. (2009). Multiobjective optimization for DG planning with load models. *IEEE Transactions on Power Systems*, *24*(1), 427–436. doi:10.1109/TPWRS.2008.2009483

SMA. (2016). *Solar Technology AG Sunny Boy TL-US series*. Retrieved February 23, 2017, from http://files.sma.de/dl/10707/SUNNYBOY6-11TLUS-DUS144518W.PDF

Tan, W.-S., Hassan, M. Y., Majid, M. S., & Rahman, H. A. (2013). Optimal distributed renewable generation planning: A review of different approaches. *Renewable & Sustainable Energy Reviews*, *18*, 626–645. doi:10.1016/j.rser.2012.10.039

Teleke, S., Baran, M. E., Bhattacharya, S., & Huang, A. Q. (2010). Rule-based control of battery energy storage for dispatching intermittent renewable sources. *IEEE Transactions on Sustainable Energy*, *1*(3), 117–124. doi:10.1109/TSTE.2010.2061880

Teng, J.-H., Luan, S.-W., Lee, D.-J., & Huang, Y.-Q. (2013). Optimal charging/discharging scheduling of battery storage systems for distribution systems interconnected with sizeable PV generation systems. *IEEE Transactions on Power Systems*, *28*(2), 1425–1433. doi:10.1109/TPWRS.2012.2230276

Tyagi, V., Rahim, N. A., Rahim, N., Jeyraj, A., & Selvaraj, L. (2013). Progress in solar PV technology: Research and achievement. *Renewable & Sustainable Energy Reviews, 20*, 443–461. doi:10.1016/j. rser.2012.09.028

Venkatesh, B., Ranjan, R., & Gooi, H. (2004). Optimal reconfiguration of radial distribution systems to maximize loadability. Power Systems. *IEEE Transactions on, 19*(1), 260–266.

Waseem, I., Pipattanasomporn, M., & Rahman, S. (2009). *Reliability benefits of distributed generation as a backup source.* Paper presented at the Power & Energy Society General Meeting, 2009. PES'09. IEEE. doi:10.1109/PES.2009.5275233

Whitley, D. (1994). A genetic algorithm tutorial. *Statistics and Computing, 4*(2), 65–85. doi:10.1007/ BF00175354

Zhu, J. (2015). *Optimization of power system operation* (Vol. 47). John Wiley & Sons.

Chapter 12
Fast Chaotic Encryption Using Circuits for Mobile and Cloud Computing:
Investigations Under the Umbrella of Cryptography

Shalini Stalin
Aisect University, India

Priti Maheshwary
Aisect University, India

Piyush Kumar Shukla
University Instituter of Technology RGPV, India

Akhilesh Tiwari
Madhav Institute of Technology, India

Ankur Khare
M. K. Ponda College of Business and Management, India

ABSTRACT

In last few decades, a lot of work has been done in the field of cryptography; it is being considered one of the safe methods to protect data. It was first used to protect communication by individuals, armies, and organizational companies. With the help encryption method, anyone can protect their data from a third-party attack. Images are used in various areas like biometric authentication, medical science, military, etc., where they are being stored or transferred over the network and the safety of such images are very important. The newest movement in encryption is chaos-based, which is a better encryption technique than AES, DES, RSA, etc. It consists of different property such as sensitive independence on original situation, non-periodicity, non-convergence, etc. In recent times, many chaos-based image encryption algorithms have been proposed, but most of them are not sufficient to provide full protection to data. In this chapter, a survey of different chaos-based image encryption techniques is discussed.

DOI: 10.4018/978-1-5225-3531-7.ch012

INTRODUCTION

A clandestine distribution plan (Abirami,2005; Elshamy, 2003; Orue, 2002) is a convention to share a mystery among members such that just specified subsets of members can recoup the mystery. In considering the security ideas of mystery sharing plans, a few creators have published ideas of security for mystery sharing plans taking into account diverse data measures. These data measures incorporate four imperative data measures: Shannon entropy, min entropy, Renyi entropy and Kolmogorov multifaceted nature. Shannon entropy is the most broadly utilized data measure, which is utilized to demonstrate limits on the offer size and on the data rate in mystery sharing plans (Fitwi, 2011; Akhvan, 2013; Pande, 2011; Soleymani,2014). As of late, min and Renyi entropies are additionally utilized as a part of investigation of the security of mystery sharing plans (Cristina, 2014; Pande, 2011).Picture stowing is a type of steganography that works by inserting information into a computerized media with the end goal of ID, annotation, and copyrighting. This paper presents a novel picture steganography framework, which implants (RGB) mystery picture inside (RGB) spread picture picked by an improved flexible back engendering neural system. The proposed framework incorporates inserting and extraction stages. Three principle stages are incorporated inside the inserting stage, which are; best cover picture determination and handling stage, mystery picture choice and preparing stage and best implanting limit choice stage separately. Best cover picture is performed utilizing SOM and ERBP calculations. Mystery picture is handled by isolating it into (Red, Green, and Blue) shading layers and DWT is then connected. The shading layers are then changed over to bit streams; altered FLFSR in turns will be utilized to scramble these streams to get more secure framework. ERBP is again used to choose the best implanting edge values. The execution has been assessed amid inserting and extraction stages considering utilizing a few spread and mystery pictures and considering a few sizes (Bakhache, 2011; Khare & Shukla, 2015).

A few scientists used ordinary cryptosystems to straight forwardly encoding pictures. However, this is not prudent because of huge information size and continuous imperatives of picture information. Ordinary cryptosystems oblige a great deal of time to specifically encode a large number of picture pixels esteem. Then again, not at all like literary information, an unscrambled picture is generally satisfactory regardless of the fact that it contains little levels of contortion. For all the afore mentioned reasons, the calculations that capacity well for printed information may not be suitable for media information (Palacios & Juarez, 2002). Numerous studies have been performed on the utilization of printed encryption calculations for pictures by altering the calculations to adjust with picture attributes. One such alternative for encoding a picture is to consider a 2D variety of picture pixels esteem as a 1D information stream and to then scramble this stream with any customary cryptosystem (Bakhache, 2012; Mondal, 2016). This would be viewed as an innocent methodology and more often than not is suitable for content and event associate for little pictures records that are to be transmitted more than an armada devoted channel (Xia & Song, 2013). Subramanyan (2011) states that a picture encryption calculation in light of AES-128 in which the encryption procedure is a bitwise XOR operation on an arrangement of picture pixels. This system utilizes a starting 128-bit key and an AES key extension transform that progressions the key for each arrangement of pixels. The mystery keys are produced freely at both the sender and the collector sides in light of the AES key development process. In this manner, the introductory key alone is shared instead of the entire arrangement of keys (Bakhache, 2011).

Sensors are basic, little, modest gadgets for catching tactile information. A gathering of these sensors cooperating shape a sensor system. Sensor hubs are intended to self-sort out into a system after sending.

Remote sensors have constrained assets as far as capacity, handling, memory, battery force, and transmission range. Remote Sensor Networks (WSNs) have an expansive scope of uses in assorted situations. At times the sensors hubs can be conveyed physically, for example, along the border of a building, or along an electrical cables or fiber optic links and so forth. However as a rule it is infeasible to convey the sensor hubs physically because of one or a greater amount of the few conceivable reasons, for example, the expansive size of the sensor system or its scope range, hard to get to landscape, perilous or hazardous environment and so forth. These elements can build the arrangement cost and time and considerably jeopardize the well being and life of faculty sending the sensors. Samples of such environment would be amazing climate conditions, for example, ice or volcanic districts and regions hit by common catastrophes like surges and seismic tremors, hard to get to landscape, for example, mountains, backwoods, forsakes and remote ocean, risky environment, for example, danger of presentation to atomic radiation, unsafe chemicals, and biohazard. In such situations, the sensor hubs can be conveyed helpfully from a sheltered separation, for instance, from an air ship. Because of the way of utilizations and sending environment of the WSNs, they may have strict security necessities. Such WSNs would incorporate those that are intended for interloper discovery, checking of regular assets, security of national landmarks and resources, observation of fringes and other such applications intended to bolster and help the exercises of law authorization and recognize and upset unlawful exercises. Such WSNs have stringent security necessities on the grounds that knaves may attempt to damage, penetrate, assault, and upset the system and take or change the information being transmitted. In WSNs security procurement is muddled by the way that there may be no supervisory body, the medium of correspondence is remote, sensor hubs have restricted assets and the system topology is composed post organization. Encryption is utilized for shielding information from unapproved get to and altering. Of the two noteworthy sorts of encryption calculations, that are open key calculations and mystery key calculations, the mystery key calculations are a well known decision. This is because of the way that, open key calculations are more processor serious and oblige longer keys accordingly costly as far as vitality utilization and capacity. They are additionally inclined to man-in-the-center assault without a commonly trusted outsider (Song & Qiao, 2015).

CRYPTOLOGY

It is the statistical learning of cryptographic techniques and cryptanalysis. Secret and confidential information can be protected by using cryptology against stealing. There are several application areas of cryptology (Khare, 2015).

CRYPTOGRAPHY

Cryptography (from Greek "hidden, mystery") is the practice and investigation of systems for secure correspondence in the vicinity of outsiders (called adversaries). it is about developing and examining conventions that square adversaries; different angles in data security, for example, information classifiedness, information uprightness, confirmation, and non-repudiation are vital to advanced cryptography(Khare & Shukla, 2015).

Figure 1.

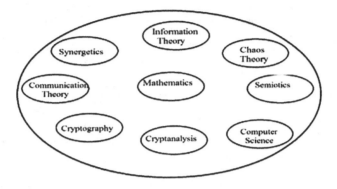

Figure 2.

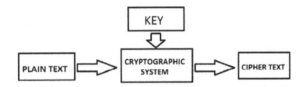

CRYPTANALYSIS

Cryptanalytic attacks are for the most part arranged into six classes that recognize the sort of data the cryptanalyst has accessible to mount an assault. The classifications of assault are recorded here generally in expanding request of the nature of data accessible to the cryptanalyst, or, proportionately, in diminishing request of the level of trouble to the cryptanalyst. The goal of the cryptanalyst in all cases is to have the capacity to unscramble new bits of cipher text without extra data. The perfect for a cryptanalyst is to remove the mystery key.

A *cipher text-just attack* is one in which the cryptanalyst acquires a specimen of cipher text, without the plaintext connected with it. This information is moderately simple to acquire in numerous situations, yet an effective cipher text-just assault is by and large troublesome, and obliges a substantial cipher text test. A known-plaintext assault is one in which the cryptanalyst gets an example of cipher text and the comparing plaintext too.

A *picked plaintext attack* is one in which the cryptanalyst has the capacity pick an amount of plaintext and after that acquire the comparing encoded cipher text.

A *versatile picked plaintext attack* is an uncommon instance of picked plaintext assault in which the cryptanalyst has the capacity pick plaintext tests progressively, and modify his or her decisions taking into account the aftereffects of past encryptions.

A *picked cipher text attack* is one in which cryptanalyst may pick a bit of cipher text and endeavor to acquire the comparing decoded plaintext. This kind of assault is by and large most appropriate to open key cryptosystems.

Table 1. Different Attacks

Type	Available Text	Attack on	After Effects	Prevention
Cipher text-just attack (Xia, Song, Shi, Yan, 2013)	Encrypted message	Cipher text	Unable to read plain text	
known plain text attack (Khare, Shukla, Silakari, 2014)	Plain text and cipher text	Plain text	Effects the big portion of plain text	
chosen picked plaintext attack (Khare, Shukla, Silakari, 2014; Bakhache, Ahmad, Assad, 2011)	Target encryption device.	Plain text	Affects the plain text and modifies it.	
chosen cipher text attack (Khare, Shukla, Silakari, 2014; Bakhache, Ahmad, & Assad, 2011)	Decrypted plain text	Cipher text	Picks a part of cipher text and decodes the plain text.	
Man-in-the-middle attacks (Song & Qiao, 2015)	Key exchange protocol	attacker is able to position himself to intercept the key exchange between two parties	attacker performs his own key exchange	Use of hash function by both sender and receiver.
Side channel attacks (Gentry, 2014)	timing, power, and radiation emissions.	Implementation details.	Changes the key.	Both sender and receiver should keep the track of time.
Brute force attacks (Khare, Shukla, Silakari, 2014)	Plain text	Plain text by trying all keys.		Key length should be bigger.
Birthday attacks (Kumar, 2015)	It is class of brute force attack	Hash function	Changes the value of hash function	

CHAOTIC SYSTEM AND THEORY

Chaotic system is an intercession between strict constancy and unpredictability based on possibility (Figure 3) (Khare & Shukla, 2015).

Chaos can be defined by some special uniqueness (Bakhache & Ahmad, 2011; Bakhache, Ahmad & Assad, 2011).

- **Nonlinearity:** It means that the changes in any element at a time not predict the changement in the same or a different element at a later time.
- **Determinism:** It has not probabilistic which is governed by precise and proper rules with none of the element of optional.

Figure 3.

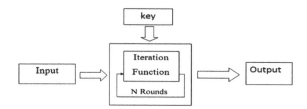

- **Sensitivity to Initial Condition:** Minor changes in its initial state can provide entirely different final state.
- **Irregularity:** It means "categorize in confusion".
- **Long Term Prediction:** It provides abandoned long term forecast due to sensitivity to initial conditions.
- **The Logistic Map:** The chaos uses one dimensional logistic map which gives the scalars for encryption system.

$$Xn+1 = A * Xn (Xn - 1)$$

APPLICATION AREAS OF CHAOS (BAKHACHE & AHMAD, 2011)

The chaos is used in many applications of mathematics, physics, information and social science in starting. There are numerous types of commercial and industrial applications based on chaos which are shown in Table 2 (Bakhache & Ahmad, 2011).

CHAOS AND CRYPTOGRAPHY (BAKHACHE & AHMAD, 2011)

Chaos and cryptography have several similar features shown in Figure 4:

1. Both chaotic and encryption system are not depended on probability.
2. Both are unpredictable with higher complexity. Any external observer cannot understand the random behaviour of the system without knowing it.
3. A chaotic system is perceptive to its initial condition means minor changes of any element can be fully changed the final state. Cryptography is a key based confusion and diffusion system, *means* updating of one bit of plain text or key could modify all bits of the cipher text with 50% possibility.

In arithmetic, a confused guide is a guide (= advancement work) that displays some kind of tumultuous conduct. Maps may be parameterized by a discrete-time or a nonstop time parameter. Discrete maps for the most part take the type of iterated capacities. Disorderly maps regularly happen in the investigation of dynamical frameworks.

Table 2. Chaos based applications

Category	Applications
Control	Control of asymmetrical activities in strategy and systems.
Synchronization	Safe connections, chaotic broad band radio, and cryptography
Information Processing	Encoding, decoding, and pattern recognition of neural networks.
Engineering	Lasers, chemical reaction, and power grids
Computers	Circuit and packet switching, robotic systems, cryptology
Communications	Image compression, network design and management

Figure 4. Relations between Chaos and Cryptography

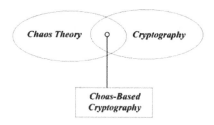

Disorderly maps regularly produce fractals. In spite of the fact that a fractal may be built by an iterative methodology, a few fractals are mulled over all by themselves, as sets as opposed to as far as the guide that produces them. This is frequently in light of the fact that there are a few distinctive iterative techniques to create the same fractal.

BLOCK AND STREAM CIPHERS

Block Cipher

Block cipher is an encryption method that divides input plaintext into blocks of equal lengths and then encrypts one block of data using the secret key at a time (Akhvan,2013). In another words, block cipher is a transformation function that maps units of plaintext bits to cipher text bits of the same unit size using secret key. In similar way, the decryption method divides the input cipher text into blocks of equal length and then applies the decryption algorithm to each block using the same shared secret key (Bakhache & Ahmad, 2011). In general, the decryption process is the reverse process of the encryption. The lengths of both the plaintext block and the corresponding cipher text block are equal as per good cipher text theory. Many modes of operations are performed if the size of input message is longer than the block size.

Block Cipher Evaluation

The following fields are used to evaluate block ciphers (Cristina, 2014; Bakhache, 2011; Xia, 2013)

1. **Key Size:** Longer key size is provided better security than shorter key size, but this will enhance the cost of creation, storage, and communication transmission.
2. **Block Size:** Block size affects the security, complexity and performance of algorithm. In general, longer block size will be provided high security but implementation cost will not be low
3. **Algorithm Complexity:** A more complex algorithm increases the implementation cost and reduces the algorithm's performance.
4. **Throughput:** The complexity of algorithm and the implementation flexibility directly concern the throughput.
5. **Security Level:** Normally, the confidence level of security increases the longer the algorithm is analyzed by cryptanalysis without any successful attacks.

6. **Data Expansion:** Expansion function increases the size of encryption data by processing it.
7. **Error Propagation:** The error bits may affect the cipher text of current and succeeding blocks of data. Some error propagation properties can be tolerated in some applications

Stream Cipher

A stream cipher is asymmetric key cipher in which digits of plaintext are combined with a pseudorandom cipher digit stream (key stream). Each digit of plaintext is encrypted one by one with the corresponding digit of the key stream in a stream cipher, to generate a digit of the cipher text stream. It is also known as state cipher where the encryption of each digit is dependent on the current state only. In general, a digit is typically a bit and the encrypting operation an exclusive-or (XOR) (Elshamy,2013; Guo,2015).

The pseudorandom key stream is typically generated serially from a random bit generator. The value serves as the cryptographic key stream for encrypting and decrypting the cipher text stream.

Types of Stream Cipher

A stream cipher gives successive bits of the key stream based on an internal state. This state is modified in basically two ways: if the state changes independently of the plaintext or cipher text information, the cipher is known as a synchronous stream cipher. By contrast, self-synchronizing stream ciphers modify their state based on previous digits of cipher text (Xia,2013; Gentry,2014).

Synchronous Stream Ciphers

In a synchronous stream cipher a stream of pseudo-random digits is generated separately of the plaintext and cipher text, and then combined with the plaintext (for encryption) or the cipher text (for decryption). Binary digits are used (bits) for processing, and the key stream is combined with the plaintext using the exclusive or operation (XOR). This is called a binary additive stream cipher.

In a synchronous stream cipher, the sender and receiver must be accurately in step for encrypting and decryption to be successful. If digits are added or deleted from the message during transmission, synchronization is lost. To re-establish synchronization, various offsets can be applied systematically to obtain the correct decryption. Another way is to tag the cipher text with markers at regular points in the output text (Lambic, 2014; Solak, 2010).

If, however, a digit is ruined in transmission, rather than added or deleted, only a single digit in the plaintext is affected and the error does not propagate to other parts of the text message. This feature is useful when the transmission error rate is high; however, it builds it less likely the error would be detected without further mechanisms. furthermore, because of this property, synchronous stream ciphers are very vulnerable to active attacks: if an attacker can alter a digit in the cipher text, he might be able to make predictable changes to the corresponding plaintext bit; for example, flipping a bit in the cipher text causes the same bit to be flipped in the plaintext (Guo, 2015; Solak, 2008).

Self-Synchronizing Stream Ciphers

Another approach uses many the previous N cipher text digits to evaluate the key stream. These schemes are known as self-synchronizing stream ciphers, asynchronous stream ciphers or cipher text auto key (CTAK). The idea of self-synchronization was patented earlier, and has the benefit that the receiver will automatically synchronize with the key stream generator after receiving N cipher text digits, making it easier to recuperate if digits are deleted or added to the message stream. Single-digit errors are restricted in their effect, affecting only up to N plaintext digits (Ozkaynak,2013).

LITERATURE SURVEY

Two-channel Lorenz chaotic cryptosystem determines the parameter by using geometrical properties to decrease the search space and minimize the average jamming noise power created by cryptosystem. System security can be extremely enhanced by using some parameters depending functions and complex keys (Orue, 2008). DNA sequence based image encryption and decryption algorithm has been used logistic map and same size grey scale image and key image. Logistic map are used to generate two chaotic sequences and scramble the elements position in DNA encoded matrix. The image quality and security has been analyzed against statistical and exhaustive attacks. XOR operation and system parameters dependent large keys are also used for encryption (Abirami, 2015). An optical image cryptosystem using Baker map and Double Random Phase Encoding (DRPE) has been proposed where Baker map is used as a pre-processing layer to enhance the security and DRPE for system utilization. Simply implemented this technique achieves good permutation and diffusion mechanisms in short time duration helpful in many real time applications (Elshamy, 2013). The multi scroll chaotic feistel structure and the substitution permutation structure publicly generated a key and pseudo random numbers for secret key encryption. The performance of this technique is analyzed using some parameters like encryption time, power consumption and compared with AES and RSA algorithms (Fitwi, 2011). A fast and secure encryption scheme is offered for encrypting images based on Arnold cat and Henon chaotic maps for medical, governmental and military applications where Arnold cat map is used for bit- and pixel-level permutations on private images, while Henon map creates private images and definite function. Security of algorithm is analyzed against chosen plaintext and brute force attack with large key size (Soleymani, 2014).

The confusion and diffusion effect is improved extensively by using high dimensional chaotic map based parallel hash function. The proposed scheme can be suitable for all features of hash function like desired statistical properties, strong collision resistance, message sensitivity and high potential and used in real world applications (Akhvan,2013). The real-time embedded systems use high potential stream cipher and simple modified logistic chaotic map which is implemented over Xilinx Virtex- 6 FPGA to provide great level of security for making the system suitable for embedded devices having real time parameters. Modified logistic map enhances the performance on the basis of higher Lyapunov exponent and uniformity of bifurcation map (Pande, 2011). The diffusion and confusion stages are combined to provide a classic bi-modular architecture for secure encryption in which the pixels of the plain image are shuffled and modified using a random permutation generator and a XOR-scheme. The performance of algorithm analyzed against statistical attacks extensively compared to the latest methodology (Cristina, 2014). The chaos based cryptosystem is mostly developed for high security, speed, complexity, cost and quality assurance over the conventional encryption algorithms used in computer engineering, communication and network security, such as robotic systems, encryption, synchronization and genetic network. An avalanche effect is the attractive property of cryptography and chaotic system which shows the minor difference in parameters of chaotic function generates completely different keys as well as cipher text. Digital circuits like XOR gate, Gray Code, are reduces the running time of algorithm and provided fast computing (khare, 2015). Chaotic Encryption is more attack-resilient and faster than other encryption techniques using properties of chaos system like avalanche effect, sensitivity to initial conditions and nonlinearity. Chaotic encryption technique using 2`s compliment gives highly secure environment against all cryptanalysis attacks and 97% better performance in terms of encryption time, throughput and power consumption (Bakhache, 2011).

Periodic switching of cryptographic keys of cyclic chaotic system is commonly enhanced the security of encryption methods in bigger networks (Palacios,2011). A high speed chaotic cryptographic technique for Wi-Fi and Zigbee networks is generated all real time requirements for secure communications in wireless industrial control and monitoring applications. Two perturbed piecewise linear chaotic map (PWLCM) is easily realized and succeeds all the statistical tests for high speed encryption and low space complexity (Bakhache, 2011). Cross coupled chaotic logistic map is generated two PRN sequences first for permutation of both gray and coloured images and second for generation of DNA sequences and Deoxyribo Nucleic Acid (DNA) is encrypted the plain images using two sets of keys. DNA sequencing is used to make the encryption process robust, imperceptible, light weight and resistant against statistical and differential attacks (Mondal, 2016). Chaotic characteristics of autonomous dynamic system of a matrix converter (MC) are studied based on the fundamental-harmonic nonlinear state equations and obtained power density spectrum and Lyapunov exponents of the MC (Xia,2013). Security of information has been done by electrocardiogram (ECG) with logistic map utilizing a portable instrument (Heart Pal) for collecting ECG signals for cryptography. Chaotic map generates the initial keys by using an intelligent algorithm and encryption is done in short time for same size of cipher text and plaintext (Chen, 2010). DNA encoding and mapping rules are introduced to encrypt the diffuse image by using Exclusive-OR operation and spatiotemporal chaos. DNA computing based image encryption demonstrates high key sensitivity, large key space and attack resiliency against differential and statistical attacks (Song, 2015). Homomorphic encryption and program obfuscation are used a delicate interference between structure and randomness by mathematicians for secure cryptography. The messages are encrypted and decrypted by using a noisy encoding and approximate ring homomorphism respectively to enhance the efficiency and computation power of technique (Gentry, 2014). The secret messages are embedded by using Reversible Watermarking based on Dierence Pair Mapping (DPM) method into a cover image and convalescing both the embedded secret message and the cover image without any deformation. The combined Dierence expansion based on predicting the pixel values and encryption algorithm based on DNA provides high embedding capacity and high security (Kumar, 2015). An improved chaotic map-based scheme is used for authentication of anonymous users to enhance reliability and security against impersonation attack and server masquerading attack in distributed networks. This scheme is validated by BAN logic (Guo, 2015). Improved version of the analyzed cryptosystem based on block cipher with dynamic S-boxes and tent map is proposed, which can eliminate the some serious design and security problems. The chosen plaintext attack and brute force attack aspire to find the elements of S-boxes (Lambic, 2014).

Multi-chaotic system for image encryption is cryptanalysed by two different attacks and weakness of cryptosystem is collected of two shuffling stages parameterized by chaotic sequences (Solak, 2010). Discretized two-dimensional chaotic maps of cryptosystem analyzed against chosen cipher text attack to show the weakness of security. The dependence among secret parameters and a smaller key space demonstrated the feasibility of cryptanalysis attacks (Solak, 2008). S-box structures used in the crypto-system play an important role in modern powerful block encryption system. A time delay chaotic system generates an S-box design algorithm fulfilling such criteria as simple and efficient implementation for theoretical and practical applications (Ozkaynak, 2013) Chaos and flexible macro block ordering (FMO) based H.264 video for region of interest (ROI) used an encryption technique to secure the video of closed circuit television (CCTV). The human face recognition for ROI and an encryption scheme is analyzed in NIST environment to show randomness and security (Peng, 2013). A stream cipher and dynamically updated look up table based secure chaotic cryptosystem is implemented using different keys to provide security against plaintext attacks. The weakness of cryptosystem is low encryption speed and lack of security which is described in this technique (Alvarez, 2004).

The cryptanalytic attacks are described the weakness of cryptosystem and key space and initial values of chaos function determines the security of cryptosystem completely (Alvarez, 2000). In recent years, a large number of discrete chaotic cryptographic algorithms have been proposed. The higher dimensional chaotic cryptographic algorithm has been appropriate for large size data encryption such as images, videos or audio data in which variables are treated as encryption keys to achieve secure transmission (Babu, 2013). The linear and differential approximation probabilities accepted various ciphers producing by exponential and chaotic maps for block encryption. The ciphers created by S-box which have been generated by chaotic maps in the Feistel network (Jakimoski, 2001). Some common framework and general guidelines for implementation, key management, and security analysis suggested for highly secure network and real time application. Basic requirements of analog chaos based secure communication such as channel noise, limited bandwidth and attenuation have been fulfilled in chaos based communication (Alvarez, 2006). The chaotic masking technique has been employed to encrypt the message with a binary sequence extracted from a chaotic map. This scheme is suitable for practical use in secure communication fulfil all the criteria as high speed, easy implementation and high security (Tang, 2004). A chaotic map based pseudo-random key stream generator is used in sequence generation and random mixing to achieve the fast throughput and facilitate hardware realization. The design of cryptosystem can enhance the randomness, speed and security (Kwok, 2007). Power and tangent function instead of linear function based Nonlinear Chaotic Algorithm used for encryption to overcome the drawback of small key space and weak security in one dimensional chaotic cryptosystem. A one-time-one password system is designed for high security and acceptable efficiency (Gao, 2006). Two or more discrete chaotic systems are combined in a complex composite discrete chaotic system (CDCS) which is analysed chaotic behaviours. Bit level permutation and pixel level diffusion is used with CDCS encryption technique to provide good performance with enhancing the privacy and reducing the time complexity (Zhu, 2016). Encryption is performed by DNA computing-splicing system and hyper-chaotic system describing the quaternary coding to provide resistance to common attacks such as statistical, differential and exhaustive attacks in the transmission applications (Niu, 2016). A new chaos based algorithm has been proposed aiming at increasing the security robustness, reliability and reduce the complexity of operations in wireless sensor networks such as ZigBee, WirelessHART and ISA100.11a. This technique fits in the low capacities of sensor motes to achieve less complexity and high efficiency (MANSOUR, 2012).

The nonlinear time-delayed feedback systems for transmitter and receiver are described using chaos shift keying modulation scheme to encode the digital signals and data recovery is done by the time delay parameter (Cuenot, 2002). The finite-state Chebyshev map, tent map, 4 dimensional torus map and 128-bit block cipher including sixteen 8×8 S-boxes are used in the public key cryptography which is performing slower operation than best conventional algorithms like RSA and AES but providing good security (Amigo, 2007). SMS (Short Message Service) is encrypted by chaos-based encryption scheme using the improved A5/1 algorithm in mobile phones. This scheme is designed to provide the chaotic logistic mapping and quantization method for getting binary sequences on FPGA environment (Qi, 2012). Pseudorandom, obit unpredictability, extreme sensitivity to initial state and structural parameter are the some important properties of chaos then non linear chaos is widely used in secure information exchange in the form of stream and block cipher over network (Luo, 2006). A novel image encryption scheme using hyper chaotic ordinary differential equation is described to generate two hyper-chaotic orbit sequences for generating initial chaotic key stream. Two rounds diffusion is introduced to generate encryption key stream related to plain image and initial chaotic key stream. Security is analysed in the form of key space analysis, histogram and correlation function (Ma, 2015). Baptista-type chaotic cryptosystem for embedding compression is determined the lookup table used for encryption adaptively based on the probability of occurrence of plaintext symbols. The compression performance is satisfactory without compromising the security (Wong, 2008). Chaotic maps has been combined the features of a skew tent map and arithmetic coding to provide a simultaneous compression and encryption scheme with two level protection of high key and plain text sensitivities approaches Shannon's entropy limit (Wong, 2010). A strong and unique biometric authentication process using templates based on hash chaos cryptography is described on biometric database to analyse the behaviour of consumer and need of loans for bank's customers (Mihailescu, 2014). A fractional-order chaotic systems based image cryptosystem has been created more complexity than integer order system against statistical attacks. An improved version of cryptosystem is used for practical applications to provide high security, consistency and attack defensibility (Ahmada, 2015). ImgFS system is designed and implemented to overcome the drawbacks of userspacefilesystem (FUSE) for digital image cryptography. ImgFS is supported full transparent file system mount, user authentication and cryptographic image files service for real time applications (KHASHAN, 2015). Chaos based cryptosystem is deployed many advantages like high security, speed and complexity for wired and wireless real time applications. There is a major problem to decide that which type of technique is used for which type of application to overcome the overheads and enhance the performance (Shukla, 2015). The discretized version of two-dimensional chaotic map is applied permutation on random numbers to maintain large key space for potential use in encryption. Random number distribution and fractal structure has been generated highly usable pseudo random numbers effectively (Lee, 2003; Beltran, 2007). Mathematical properties of chaotic dynamical systems are identified and investigated for block and stream cipher systems. Chebychev polynomials established chaotically for easy implementation of dynamic encryption systems (Schmitz, 2001). Coupled Two-dimensional Piecewise Nonlinear Chaotic Map (CTPNCM) for colour image encryption is demonstrated the number of pixel change rate (NPCR), the unified average changing intensity (UACI), and entropy can satisfy security and good performance. Masking process is provided the highly secure, sensitive and speedy encryption (Seyedzadeh, 2012)

Cloud computing is secured and authenticated by using threshold cryptography based Kerberos protocol. This method is reduced the unauthorised access, memory usage and burden of large computation (Bharill, 2013). Four cryptanalytic attacks have been shown the defects and weakness of chaotic cryptography. The improved version of chaotic cryptosystem is used to obtain high security against the four cryptanalysis attacks (Li, 2001). A nonlinear chaotic map (NCM) and XOR operation are combined to provide a new image encryption scheme. The iterative method is used to accelerated the encryption speed and high security (Wang, 2010). The size of cipher text and plain text, security, encryption speed, dynamic degradation, and virtual state space are the major drawbacks of chaos based cryptosystem. There is some open ideas are provided to use the chaotic cryptography for secure practical and real time applications (LI, 2013). Chaotic cryptography based Anti-counterfeit technique has been described for providing mutual authentication, long term security and database attacks resiliency. The intelligent identification is realized by generating the verification code and repeated queries for advance technologies (Sheng, 2012). The sensitive multimedia information is secured by image encryption method based on implementation of pixel scan, utilizing the knight's travel path and true random number. XOR operation, permutation and scrambling are used for encryption to provide resistance against statistical, differential and entropy attacks (SIVAKUMAR, 2016). Chaotic modulation, cryptography, and chaotic synchronization techniques are combined to perform secure digital communication using a Chaotic Modulator (CM), a Chaotic Secure Transmitter (CST), a Chaotic Secure Receiver (CSR) and a Chaotic Demodulator (CDM). Differential Peaks Keying (CDPK) modulation scheme is generate the analog pattern for transmission (Chien, 2005). The secret image is visually decrypted by chaotic oscillation and dynamic visual cryptography with controlled vibration of digital image surface. A harmonic, a rectangular or a piece-wise continuous waveform is oscillated the cover images with some preselected parameters (Petrauskiene, 2014). Several one dimensional chaotic maps have been interacted with each other to generate completely independent and uniform pseudo random sequences. These sequences are used as keys for block encryption by executing Exclusive-OR and shifting operations (yuan, 2009). The chaotic properties have been played a great role for selection of logistic map in different fields of engineering, physical, biological and communication (Ditto, 1995).

A fractional-order hyper chaotic encryption system is generated the cipher image by using four chaotic sequences. The colour image is encrypted by performing Exclusive-OR and shuffling operation between plain image and key. Performance of system is analyzed in detail with security, correlation, key sensitivity, attacks and histogram (Huang, 2014). Clock synchronization is combined with key agreement protocol to perform chaotic encryption which is attack resilience against man in middle and replaying attacks (Guo, 2008). Some mathematical functions like Runge-Kutta method have also been introduced in higher dimensional encryption process to enhance the performance of hyper chaotic cryptosystem. So performance of cryptosystem is exponentially increased in terms of security and complexity (Tong, 2015). Higher dimensional (4D) image encryption has been designed with large key space and some control parameters to provide highly secure and efficient real time communication (Huang, 2012).

Randomness and security has been increased by encrypting the scrambled image by pixel shifting. Scrambled image is obtained the higher resistance against exhaustive and statistical attacks than plain images (Wang, 2015). Game of life permutation and piecewise linear chaotic map (PWLCM) are combined together to generate the initial pattern by logistic map and diffuse the image to improve the speed respectively (Wang, 2012). Chaos based parallel master slave communication has been performed multiprocessing encryption decryption with PWLCM and Message Passing Interface (MPI). Large size media files are encrypted by using a client server architecture (Wang, 2013). Two dimensional rectangular transform is directly produced scrambled image dependent on pixel substitution to create confusion and diffusion simultaneously and achieve high speed and satisfactory security (Zhang, 2014). Chua's circuit is generated chaotic sequences to replace the random key sequences for one time pad encryption of images in digital secure communication. An impulsive control strategy is also introduced to synchronize the identical chaotic systems to improve the security (Li, 2013). Dual chaos with password protection is a new concept in development of cryptography for enhancing the complexity and reliability of encryption algorithms in secure communications (Zhang, 2013).

COMPARISON TABLE

The several papers are concise based on different features in Table 3.

Table 3. Comparison Table

Authors Name and Performance Comparison of Their Researches					
Features	**Orue, Fernandez, Alvareza, Pastor, Shujun, &Montoya (2008)**	**Abirami, Amutha (2015)**	**Elshamy, Rashed, Mohamed, Faragalla, Mu, Alshebeili, El-Samie, (2013)**	**Fitwi, Nouh (2011)**	**Soleymani, Nordin, & Sundararajan (2014)**	**Akhvan, Samsudin, & Akhshani (2013)**
Security	Moderately High	High	Secure Enough	Moderately High	High	High
Cipher Nature	Stream	Block	-	Stream	Stream	Block
Used Method & Platform	Chaos Synchronization &Matlab	DNA Encoding/ Decoding	Chaotic Baker Map and DRPE &Matlab	NIST & Mote Carlo Simulation	Henon& Arnold Ct Map &Matlab	High dimensional Chaotic Parallel Hash Function & NIST
Processing Speed	Slow	High	High	High	Moderate	Moderate
Efficiency & Precision	Medium	Medium	Comparable High	Medium	Medium	High
Space Complexity	Medium	Medium	Medium	High	High	High
Attacks Prevention	All four	Statistical & Exhaustive	-	Prone to Cipher & Statistical	Statistical, Brute Force & differential	Birthday & Forgery
Quality Assurance	Medium	Medium	High	Medium	Medium	High
Key Size	Large enough	Large	Large Enough	Very Large	Large	Very Large
Feasibility	Yes	No	Yes	Yes	Yes	Yes
Application Areas	Communication System	Multimedia System	Optical image Encryption	Communication System	Medical & Military Department	Real World Applications
Cost	High	Medium	High	Medium	High	Medium
Features	**Pande, Zambreno (2011)**	**Dascalescu, Boriga, & Mihailescu (2014)**	**Khare, Shukla, Silakari (2014)**	**Bakhache, Ahmad, Assad (2011a)**	**Palacios, Juarez (2002)**	**Bakhache, Ahmad, Assad (2011b)**
Security	Comparatively high	High Enough	High	High	High	High
Cipher Nature	Stream	Stream	Stream	Stream	Stream	Stream
Used Method & Platform	MLM based PRNG & XilinxVirtex-6 FPGA	PWLCM & C Language	Digital Logic & C++	Digital Logic Chaotic system & C++	Periodic switching	PWLCM & NIST Environment
Processing Speed	Enough	High	Very High	Very High	Slow	High
Efficiency & Precision	Medium	Medium	High	High	High	High
Space Complexity	High	Medium	Medium	Medium	High	Low
Attacks Prevention	Except Known Plaintext	Statistical & Differential	All Four Cryptanalysis	All Four Cryptanalysis	All four Cryptanalysis	Linear and Differential
Quality Assurance	Applicable	Moderate	High	High	High	Resemblance
Key Size	Large	Very Large	Medium	Medium	Large	Slightly Large
Feasibility	No	No	Yes	Yes	At some condition	No
Application Areas	Time Embedded Systems	Communication Systems	Military & Govt. Systems	Communication & Govt. Systems	Communication System No	Industrial Control Slightly
Cost	High	High	Low	Medium	Medium	Low

continued on following page

Table 3. Continued

Features	Mondal, Mandal (2016)	Xia, Song, Shi, & Yan (2013)	Chen, Lin (2010)	Song, Qiao (2015)	Gentry (2014)	Kumar (2015)
	\multicolumn{6}{c}{**Authors Name and Performance Comparison of Their Researches**}					
Security	**High**	High	Comparatively high	High	Medium	High
Cipher Nature	Stream	Stream	Stream and Block	Block	Stream and Block	Stream
Used Method & Platform	DNA Sequences	Matrix Converter &Matlab	ECG Circuit	DNA Encoding	Homomorphic Encryption	DPM & DNA Encoding
Processing Speed	Average	Medium	Acceptable	High	Medium	Medium
Efficiency & Precision	Medium	High	Medium	High	Medium	High
Space Complexity	High	Medium	Enough High	Medium	High	High
Attacks Prevention	Statistical & Differential	-	Brute Force Attack	Brute Force, Differential, Statistical	Brute Force	Statistical& Exhaustive
Quality Assurance	Medium	Medium	Applicable	Medium	Applicable	Medium
Key Size	Large	Moderate	Enough Large	Large	Large	Moderate
Feasibility	Yes	No	Reasonable	Yes	No	Yes
Application Areas	Medical Systems	Communication Systems	Real World Applications	Medical & Communication System	Communication System	Medical Applications
Cost	Medium	Medium	Slightly High	High	High	Medium
Features	Guo, Wen, Li, Zhang, & Jin (2015)	Lambi'c (2014)	Solak, Rhouma, & Belghith (2010)	Solak & Cokal (2008)	Özkaynak, Yavuz (2013)	Peng, Zhu, & Long (2013)
Security	**Medium**	Medium	Medium	Secure enough	Medium	High
Cipher Nature	-	Block	Stream	Block	Block	Block
Used Method & Platform	Dynamic ID authentication & ban Logic	Dynamic S- Boxes & Tent Map	Discrete Time Chaotic System	TDCM System	S-Boxes	ROI and FMO in H.264 & NIST Environment
Processing Speed	Medium	Medium	Comparatively High	Medium	Medium	Acceptable
Efficiency & Precision	High	High	Medium	Comparatively High	High	High
Space Complexity	High	Medium	Medium	High	Low	Enough High
Attacks Prevention	Impersonation & Server Masquerading	Chosen Plain Text Attacks	Known and Chosen Plaintext	Chosen Cipher text	Known And chosen Plain Text	Known And chosen Plain Text
Quality Assurance	Average	Medium	Resemblance	Medium	Average	Applicable
Key Size	Large	Large Enough	Large Enough	Short	Large	Enough Large
Feasibility	No	Yes	At Some Condition	Yes	No	Reasonable
Application Areas	Communication System	Communication System	Communication System	Communication System	Neural Network	CCTV in Airport and Bank
Cost	Medium	Medium	Medium	High	Medium	Slightly High

continued on following page

Table 3. Continued

	Authors Name and Performance Comparison of Their Researches					
Features	**Alvarez, Montoya, Romera, Pastor (2004)**	**Alvarez, Montoya, Romera, Pastor (2000)**	**Babu, Ilango (2013)**	**Jakimoski, Kocarev (2001)**	**Alvarez, Li (2006)**	**Tang, Liao, Xiao, Li (2004)**
Security	Low	High	High	Secure enough	Medium	Reasonable
Cipher Nature	Stream	Block	Stream and Block	Block	Block	Block
Used Method & Platform	Baptista System	Non Linear Dynamic System	Discrete Time Chaotic System	Block Encryption Cipher &Feistel Network	Chaotic Masking and Switching	Chaotic Masking
Processing Speed	High	Medium	Low	Comparatively High	Medium	High
Efficiency & Precision	Medium	Medium	High	Medium	Comparatively High	High
Space Complexity	High	High	High	Medium	Enough High	Medium
Attacks Prevention	Chosen Plain & Cipher Text	Known Plain and Chosen Cipher Text	Chosen and Known Plain Text	Chosen & Known Plain Text	Linear and Differential	Chosen Cipher Text
Quality Assurance	Medium	Applicable	Medium	Resemblance	Medium	Applicable
Key Size	Large	Large Enough	Large	Large Enough	Large	Large
Feasibility	Yes	No	Slightly	At Some Condition	Yes	Reasonable
Application Areas	Communication Systems	Communication System	Internet Banking	Communication System	Telecommunication System	Communication System
Cost	Medium	Medium	High	Medium	High	Slightly High
Features	**Kwok & Tang (2007)**	**Gao, Zhang, Liang, Li (2006)**	**Zhu, Zhang, Yu, Zhao, & Zhu (2016)**	**Niu, Zhou, Wang, Zheng, & Zhou (2016)**	**Mansour, Chalhoub, Bakhache (2012)**	**Cuenot, Larger, Goedebuer & Rhodes (2001)**
Security	High	Medium	High	High	High	Medium
Cipher Nature	Stream	Stream	Stream &Block	Block	Stream	-
Used Method & Platform	Fixed Point Arithmetic	Non Linear Chaotic System	CDCS Permutation & NIST	DNA Computing & Splicing Model	PWLCM and LFSR &TelosB and Matlab	Chaos Shift Keying Modulation
Processing Speed	Medium	Medium	Medium	High	High	Medium
Efficiency & Precision	High	Medium	High	Medium	High	Medium
Space Complexity	High	High	High	High	Low	High
Attacks Prevention		-	Known\ Chosen Plain Text & Differential	Exhaustive & Statistical	Except Brute Force	-
Quality Assurance	Reasonable	Medium	Medium	High	Applicable	Reasonable
Key Size	Large	Medium	Large Enough	Very Large	Large	Medium
Feasibility	Yes	No	Yes	No	Yes	No
Application Areas	Communication System	Mobile Communication	Medical Image Encryption	Transmission Systems	Industrial and Military	Communication System
Cost	Medium	Medium	High	High	High	Medium

continued on following page

Table 3. Continued

Features	Amigó, Kocarev, & Szczepanski (2007)	Pan, Ding, Qi (2012)	Luo, Shi (2006)	Ma, Ye (2015)	Wong, Yuen (2008)	Wong, Lin, Chen (2010)
Authors Name and Performance Comparison of Their Researches						
Security	Medium	Secure enough	Medium	Medium	Secure Enough	Medium
Cipher Nature	Stream and Block	Stream	Stream	Block	Block	Block
Used Method & Platform	AM, CSK, TCC and ME &Chebyshev Map	A5/1 Algorithm & GSM and FPGA System	Nonlinear Dynamic System	Hyper Chaotic Differential Systems	Huffman Coding &Baptista Map	Shannon Coding & NIST Environment
Processing Speed	Medium	Low	Low	Medium	High	High
Efficiency & Precision	High	Medium	Medium	High	Medium	Medium
Space Complexity	Enough High	Medium	High	High	High	High
Attacks Prevention	Known Plain Text & Chosen Cipher Text	-	-	Statistical & Differential	Except Known Plain Text	Known Plain Text
Quality Assurance	Medium	Medium	Resemblance	High	Medium	Applicable
Key Size	Large	Large Enough	Large Enough	Large	Large Enough	Large
Feasibility	Yes	At Some Condition	Slightly	No	Yes	Slightly
Application Areas	Industrial and Communication System	Mobile System	Multimedia System	Secure Image Communication	Commercial Field	Image and Audio Encryption System
Cost	High	Medium	Medium	High	High	High
Features	**Mihailescu (2014)**	**Ahmad, Shamsib, Khanb (2015)**	**Khasan, Zin, Sundararajan (2015)**	**Shukla, Khare, Rizivi, Stalin, & Kumar (2015)**	**Lee, Pei, Chen (2003)**	**Beltran (2007)**
Security	High	Medium	High	High	Medium	High
Cipher Nature	Block	Stream	-	Stream & Block	Stream	Block
Used Method & Platform	Biometric Templates	Fractional Order Chaotic Systems	FUSE &ImgFS& Linux	Chaotic Digital & C++	Chaotic Dynamic System	Three-level Periodic Perturbation Scheme
Processing Speed	Medium	High	Medium	High	Medium	High
Efficiency & Precision	High	Medium	High	High	Medium	High
Space Complexity	High	High	Medium	Medium	High	High
Attacks Prevention	-	Chosen Plain text Attacks	-	Known Plain Text & Chosen Cipher Text	-	Brute Force Attack
Quality Assurance	High	Reasonable	High	Medium	Reasonable	Medium
Key Size	Large	Medium	Large	Medium	Large Enough	Large
Feasibility	Yes	No	Yes	Yes	No	No
Application Areas	Banking System	Communication systems	Real Time Systems	Communication Systems	Medical Image Encryption	Real Time Multimedia Applications
Cost	High	Medium	Medium	Medium	High	High

continued on following page

Table 3. Continued

	Authors Name and Performance Comparison of Their Researches					
Features	**Schmitz (2001)**	**Sevedzadeh, Mirzakuchaki, (2012)**	**Bharill, Hamsapriva, Lalwani (2013)**	**Li, Mou, Cai (2001)**	**Xu, Wang (2010)**	**Li, Mou, Yang, Ji, & Zhang (2003)**
Security	Medium	High	High	High	Medium	Medium
Cipher Nature	Block and Stream	Block	Stream	Block	Block	-
Used Method & Platform	Chaotic Dynamic System	CTPNCM & Masking Process & NIST	Kerberos using Threshold Cryptography	Bernoulli Probabilistic System	Non Linear Map & Permutation	Probabilistic Symmetric Chaotic Cipher System
Processing Speed	Low	High	Medium	High	Medium	High
Efficiency & Precision	Desirable	Medium	High	Medium	Reasonable	Medium
Space Complexity	Medium	High	High	Medium	Medium	High
Attacks Prevention	-	Differential & Brute Force	Statistical & Differential	Brute Force & Chosen Plain Text	Known/ Chosen Plaintext & Brute Force	Chosen Plain & Cipher Text
Quality Assurance	Desirable	Medium	High	Applicable	Medium	Medium
Key Size	Large Enough	Large	Medium	Large	Large	Large
Feasibility	No	Yes	Yes	Reasonable	No	Yes
Application Areas	Communication System	Real Time Application	Railway Systems	Distributed System	Data Communication System	Communication Systems
Cost	Medium	High	High	Medium	Medium	Medium
Features	**Sheng, Wu (2012)**	**Sivakumar & Venkatesan (2016)**	**Chien, Liao (2005)**	**Petrauskiene, Palivonaite, Aleksa, & Ragulskis (2013)**	**Xing-Yuan, Qing (2009)**	**Ditto & Munakata (1995)**
Security	High	Medium	High	High	Secure Enough	High
Cipher Nature	Stream	Block	Stream	Block	Block	Stream and Block
Used Method & Platform	Digital Anticounterfeiting Technique & C# Environment	Knight's Travel Path &Matlab	CM, CST, CDR, CDM & CDPK	Dynamic Visual Cryptography & Moiré Grating	Dynamic Chaotic System	Synthesized Chaos System
Processing Speed	High	Medium	High	High	High	Medium
Efficiency & Precision	High	High	Moderate	Medium	High	High
Space Complexity	Enough High	High	Medium	Medium	Medium	Low
Attacks Prevention	Message Recovery Attack	Statistical & Entropy Attacks	Brute Force & Chosen Cipher Text	-	Brute Force & Chosen Plain Text	Brute Force & Chosen Cipher Text
Quality Assurance	Reasonable	High	Applicable	Medium	High	High
Key Size	Large Enough	Medium	Large	Large	Large Enough	Large Enough
Feasibility	Yes	No	No	Yes	Yes	Yes
Application Areas	Mutual Authentication System	Multimedia Communication System	Communication System	Visual Communication	Communication System	Chemical and Physical Application
Cost	High	Medium	High	Medium	Slightly High	High

continued on following page

Table 3. Continued

Features	Huang, Sun, Li, Liang (2015)	Guo & Zhang (2008)	Tong, Liu, Zhang, Xu, &Wang (2015)	Huang (2012)	Wang, Gu, & Zhang (2015)	
Security	High	High	High	Medium	Medium	
Cipher Nature	Block	Stream	Block	Block		
Used Method & Platform	Fractional Order Hyper Chaotic System	Han Chang's Schemes	Ravinovich System &RungeKutta Method &Matlab& NIST	4D Chaotic System	Cycle Shift & Chaotic System	
Processing Speed	High	High	High	High	Medium	
Efficiency & Precision	Medium	Medium	Medium	Medium	High	
Space Complexity	High	High	Medium	High	Medium	
Attacks Prevention	Statistical & Differential	Replaying attack	Brute Force Attack	Chosen & Known Plain Text	Exhaustive and Statistical	
Quality Assurance	Moderate	Medium	High	Applicable	Reasonable	
Key Size	Large	Large	Large Enough	Large	Large	
Feasibility	Yes	No	Yes	No	Yes	
Application Areas	Colour Image Communication	Watermarking and Communication Systems	Communication Systems	Real Time Systems	Transmission systems	
Cost	Medium	High	High	Medium	High	
Features	Wang & Jin (2012)	Wang & Chen (2013)	Zhang, Fan, Wang, & Zhao (2014)	Li, Li, Wen, & Soh (2003)	Zhang, Niu, Wang, & Liu (2013)	
Security	High	High	Medium	Secure Enough	Medium	
Cipher Nature	Block	Block	Block	Stream	Block	
Used Method & Platform	PWLCM & Game of Life Permutation	PWLCM & MPI	2D Rectangular Transform & Microsoft VC++	Chua's Circuit	Dual Chaos System &Matlab	
Processing Speed	Medium	High	High	Medium	High	
Efficiency & Precision	High	Medium	Medium	High	Medium	
Space Complexity	High	Medium	High	High	Medium	
Attacks Prevention	Differential	-	Known & Chosen Plain Text	Cipher Text Only	Statistical	
Quality Assurance	Reasonable	Applicable	Medium	High	High	
Key Size	Large Enough	Large	Medium	Large Enough	Large	
Feasibility	Yes	No	Yes	Yes	No	
Application Areas	Communication System	Multimedia System	Transmission System	Wireless and Video Phones System	Communication System	
Cost	High	Medium	High	Slightly High	Medium	

SUMMARY

Two-channel Lorenz chaotic cryptosystem and Feistel structure determine permutation structure and the parameter by using geometrical properties to enhance the security and minimize the average jamming noise power created by cryptosystem. The confusion and diffusion effect is enhanced the performance of hash function potentially for real world applications (Orue, 2008; Fitwi, 2011; Akhvan,2013; Jakimoski, 2001). A fast and secure encryption scheme is published for encrypting images based on Arnold cat, Baker and Henon chaotic maps for medical and military applications to improve the confusion and diffusion mechanism. The performance is analyzed against different cryptanalysis attacks and better throughput in real time systems. Digital circuits like XOR gate, Gray Code are reduces the time complexity of execution of algorithm and perform fast computing (Elshamy,2013; Soleymani, 2015; Cristina, 2014; Khare, 2015; Bakhache, 2011; Alvarez, 2000).

The Lyapunov exponents are improved by using matrix converter and modified logistic map with suitable level of security for embedded devices. Periodic switching and a one-time-one password system is introduced to provide higher randomness and message passing interface (Pande, 2011; Palacios, 2002; Xia, 2013; Gao, 2006). Piecewise linear chaotic map (PWLCM) is combined with different mechanism like permutation, message passing interface, masking etc to perform highly secure, fast and efficient encryption for multiple applications. The number of pixel change. rate (NPCR), the unified average changing intensity (UACI), and entropy are decided the high performance of encryption (Bakhache, 2011; Seyedzadeh, 2012; Wang, 2012; Wang, 2013).

DNA sequence is another important method for encryption and decryption which is combined with logistic maps and spatiotemporal chaos to enhance the robustness and resistance of techniques. DNA is provided large key space to resist against differential and statistical attacks (Abirami,2015; Mondal, 2016; Song, 2015;Kumar, 2015; Niu, 2016; Ahmada, 2015). Electrocardiogram (ECG) with logistic map is utilizing a portable instrument (Heart Pal) for encryption in Zigbee and wireless network to achieve high efficiency in short time. Homomorphic encryption and program obfuscation are used a noisy encoding and provided a high computational and efficient interfacing between plain text and cipher text (Chen, 2010; Gentry, 2014; MANSOUR,2012). An improved chaotic map-based scheme is used on block cipher with dynamic S-boxes for authentication of anonymous users to enhance reliability and security against brute force and chosen plain text attacks (Guo, 2015; Lambic, 2014; Solak, 2010; Ozkaynak, 2013).

The discretized version of two-dimensional chaotic map is applied permutation on random numbers to maintain large key space for potential use in encryption. Random number distribution and fractal structure has been generated highly usable pseudo random numbers effectively (Solak, 2008; Lee, 2003; Beltran, 2007). The finite-state Chebyshev map and tent map established chaotically for public key cryptography for stream and block cipher to perform fast operation with providing good security (Lee, 2003; Schmitz, 2001). Two or more discrete chaotic systems like Baptista-type chaotic cryptosystem and tent map are combined with look up table in a complex composite discrete chaotic system (CDCS) to provide bit level permutation for enhancing the privacy and reducing the time. Stream cipher is generated by using flexible macro block ordering (FMO) for region of interest (ROI) in NIST environment (Peng, 2013; Alvarez, 2015; Zhu, 2016; Wong, 2008; Wong, 2010).

Analog and discrete chaotic cryptography have been appropriate for large size data encryption in real time application. Basic requirements like channel noise, limited bandwidth have been overcome by using chaotic systems. Hardware realization and chaotic masking technique are facilitated fast throughput, random mixing and secure easy implementation for practical applications (Babu, 2013; Alvarez, 2006; Tang, 2004; Kwok, 2007).

A fractional-order chaotic systems and hyper chaotic ordinary differential equation are introduced to improve the performance and efficiency of image cryptosystem. Key space analysis, histogram and correlation function have been described the practical use of technique with consistent performance (Ma, 2015; Ahmada, 2015; Huang, 2014). Kerberos protocol is used in threshold encryption to secure operation on Cloud computing. Chaos has been many advantages like high security, speed and complexity then chaos is used to improve the performance and to overcome all the overheads of networks. All cryptanalysis attacks are shown the weakness and defects of networks so chaotic system has been efficiently introduced in cryptography for attacks resiliency (Luo, 2016; Shukla, 2015; Bharill, 2013; Li, 2001; LI, 2003). A nonlinear chaotic map (NCM) and XOR operation are combined with chaos shift keying modulation to encode the digital signals to accelerate the encryption speed. The permutation and scrambling are used to utilize the knight's travel path for sensitive multimedia information encryption and anti counterfeit technique has been described for providing mutual authentication by generating verification code (Cuenot, 2002; Wang, 2010; Sheng, 2012; SIVAKUMAR, 2016).

Higher dimensional (2D & 4D) image encryption has been described with some mathematical function like RungeKutta method to control the security and performance parameters in real time communication. Confusion and diffusion are directly produced pixel substitution based scrambled image to achieve high speed and higher resistance against statistical and brute force attacks (Ditto, 1995; Tong, 2015; Huang, 2012; Wang, 2015; Zhang, 2014).

Chaotic modulation, cryptography, and chaotic synchronization techniques are combined to perform analog signal based encryption and decryption of multimedia images. Several one dimensional chaotic maps have also been interacted to generate random sequences for keys and chaotic oscillation is used to decrypt the images visually (Chien, 2005; Petrauskiene, 2014; yuan, 2009; Li,2003).

Dual chaos with password protection and biometric chaotic authentication are new ways to deploy the practical use of secure and fast cryptography in real time systems like banking, railways systems. Clock synchronization is also used with key agreement protocol to improve the performance and attacks resiliency against replaying and statistical attacks (Mihailescu, 2014; Guo, 2008; Zhang, 2013). Digital image cryptography has been described by using ImgFS and FUSE systems to provide user transparency and authentication in mobile systems. SMS (Short Message Service) is encrypted by A5/1 algorithm in FPGA environment (Qi, 2012; KHASHAN, 2015).

CONCLUSION

From last may years many efforts have been done to maintain the security of data while transmission. This review shows how many algorithms and models have been made to achieve this. In this review four-dimensional hyper chaotic framework has been discussed which is being added to Rabinovich framework for better levels of encryption and thus make the transmission of data secure. Encryption algorithm and stenography method is being combined to protect the data. Pseudorandom sequence generator based on the Chen chaotic system has been discussed. Turbulent cryptography has been discussed and its results are remark able. Four-dimensional chaotic system has been discussed which broken down by method for Lyapunov. Equation for hyper chaos is also discussed to provide secure measures. A new four-dimensional hyper chaotic Lorenz system and its adaptive control are also being discussed. A novel image encryption scheme based on improved hyperchaotic sequences has shown very good results in protecting a data. An Enhanced Image Steganography System based on Discrete Wavelet Transformation and Resilient Back-Propagation has also been discussed. A Chaotic Cryptosystem for Images Based on Henon and Arnold Cat Map, A survey on principal aspects of secure image transmission, Image encryption for secure internet multimedia applications, Implementation IDEA algorithm for image encryption, Multimedia Encryption and Watermarking, Image encryption based on AES key expansion, Post Deployment Encryption Key Generation for a Fully Connected and Secure Wireless Sensor Network, A Novel Image Encryption Scheme based on a Nonlinear Chaotic Map, Key Management for Multiple Multicast Groups in Wireless Networks, A Novel Image Encryption Scheme Based on Multi-orbit Hybrid of Discrete Dynamical System and Implementing public-key cryptography on passive RFID tags is practical is being discussed here.

REFERENCES

Abirami, A., & Amutha, R. (2015). "Image encryption based on DNA sequence coding and Logistic map", Advances in Natural and Applied Sciences. *American-Eurasian Network for Scientific Information, 9*(9), 55–62.

Ahmada, M., Shamsib, U., & Khanb, I. R. (2015). An Enhanced Image Encryption Algorithm Using Fractional Chaotic Systems. *Procedia Computer Science, 57,* 852–859. doi:10.1016/j.procs.2015.07.494

Akhvan, A., Samsudin, A., & Akhshani, A. (2013). A novel parallel hash function based on 3D chaotic map. *EURASIP Journal on Advances in Signal Processing*, 1-12.

Alvarez, G., & Li, S. (2006). Some Basic Cryptographic Requirements for Chaos-Based Cryptosystems. *International Journal of Bifurcation and Chaos, 16*(8), 2129-2151.

Alvarez, G., Montoya, F., Romera, M., & Pastor, G. (2000). Cryptanalysis of A Chaotic Encryption System. *Physics Letters, 276,* 191-196.

Álvarez, G., Montoya, F., Romera, M., & Pastor, G. (2004). Cryptanalysis of Dynamic Look-Up Table Based Chaotic Cryptosystems. *Physics Letters A, 326,* 211–218.

Amigó, J.M., Kocarev, L., & Szczepanski, J. (2007). Theory and practice of chaotic cryptography. *Physics Letters A, 366,* 211–216.

Babu, G. S., & Ilango, P. (2013). Higher Dimensional Chaos for Audio Encryption. *Proceedings of the IEEE Symposium on Computational Intelligence in Cyber Security CICS,* 52–58.

Bakhache, B., Ahmad, K., & Assad, S., (2011b). *Chaos based improvement of the security of ZigBee and Wi-Fi networks used for industrial controls*. IEEE.

Bakhache, B., Ahmad, K., & el Assad, S. (2011a). Chaos Based Improvement of the Security of Zig-Bee and Wi-Fi Networks Used for Industrial Controls. *Proceedings of the International Conference on Information Society (i-Society),* 139–145.

Beltran, R.H. (2007). A Generalized Chaotic Encryption System of Multimedia Applications. *Revista Mexicana De Fisica, 53*(5), 332-336.

Bharill, S., Hamsapriya, T., Lalwani,P., (2013). A Secure Key for Cloud using Threshold Cryptography in Kerberos. *International Journal of Computer Applications, 79*(7), 35-41.

Chen, C. K., & Lin, C. L. (2010). Text Encryption Using ECG signals with Chaotic Logistic Map. *Proceedings of the the 5th Conference on Industrial Electronics and Applications (ICIEA) IEEE*, 1741–1746. doi:10.1109/ICIEA.2010.5515285

Chien, T., & Liao, T., (2005). Design of secure digital communication systems using chaotic modulation, cryptography and chaotic synchronization. *Chaos, Solitons and Fractals, 24*, 241–255.

Cuenot, J.B., Larger, L., Goedgebuer, J.P., & Rhodes, W.T. (2001). Chaos Shift Keying with an Optoelectronic Encryption System Using Chaos in Wavelength. *IEEE Journal of Quantum Electronics, 37*(7), 849-855.

Dascalescu, A. C., Boriga, R., & Mihailescu, M. I. (2014). A Novel Chaos-Based Image Encryption Scheme. *Annals of the University of Craiova, Mathematics and Computer Science Series, 41*(1), 47–58.

Ditto, W., & Munakata, T. (1995). Principles and Applications of Chaotic Systems. Communications of the ACM, 38(11), 96-102.

Elshamy, A. M., Rashed, A. N. Z., Mohamed, A. E. A., Faragalla, O. S., Mu, Y., Alshebeili, S. A., & El-Samie, F. E. (2013). Optical Image Encryption Based on Chaotic Baker Map and Double Random Phase Encoding. *Journal of Lightwave Technology, 31*(15), 2533–2539. doi:10.1109/JLT.2013.2267891

Fitwi A. H. & Nouh, S. (2011). Performance Analysis of Chaotic Encryption using a Shared Image as a Key. *Journal of the European Economic Association, 28*, 1-23.

Gao, H., Zhang, Y., Liang, S. & Li, D. (2006). A new chaotic algorithm for image encryption. *Chaos, Solitons and Fractals, 29*, 393–399.

Gentry, C. (2014). *Computing on the edge of chaos: Structure and randomness in encrypted computation.* Electronic Colloquium on Computational Complexity, Report No. 106.

Guo, D., Wen, Q., Li, W., Zhang, H., & Jin, Z. (2015). Key Agreement Scheme. *Wireless Personal Communication*, 1-15.

Guo, X., & Zhang, J. (2008). Cryptanalysis of the Chaotic-Based Key Agreement Protocols. *Proceedings of the International Symposium on Biometrics and Security Technologies (ISBAST)*, 1–3.

Huang, X. (2012). A New Digital Image Encryption Algorithm Based on 4D Chaotic System. *International Journal of Pure and Applied Mathematics, 80*(4), 609-616.

Huang, X., Sun, T., Li, Y., & Liang, J. (2015). A Color Image Encryption Algorithm Based on a Fractional-Order Hyperchaotic System. *Entropy, 17,* 28-38.

Jakimoski, G., & Kocarev, L. (2001). Chaos and Cryptography: Block Encryption Ciphers Based on Chaotic Maps. *IEEE Transactions on Circuits and Systems-I, Fundamental Theory and Applications, 48*(2), 163-169.

Khare, A.A., Shukla, P.B., & Silakari, S.C. (2014). Secure and Fast Chaos based Encryption System using Digital Logic Circuit. *International Journal of Computer Network and Information Security, 6*, 25-33.

Khashan, O.A.,. Zin, A.M, & Sundararajan, E.A. (2015). ImgFS: A Transparent Cryptography for Stored Images Using a Filesystem in Userspace. *Frontiers of Information Technology & Electronic Engineering, 16*(1), 28-42.

Kumar, C.V., (2015). Secured Patient Information Transmission Using Reversible Watermarking and DNA Encrytion for Medical Images. *Applied Mathematical Sciences, 9*(48), 2381 – 2391.

Kwok, H.S., & Tang, W.K.S. (2007). A Fast Image Encryption System Based on Chaotic Maps With Finite Precision Representation. *Chaos, Solitons and Fractals, Elsevier, 32*, 1518–1529.

Lambi´c, D. (2014). Security Analysis and Improvement of a Block Cipher With Dynamic S-Boxes Based on Tent Map. *Nonlinear Dynamics*, 1-9.

Lee, P., Pei, S., & Chen, Y., (2003). Generating Chaotic Stream Ciphers Using Chaotic Systems. *Chinese Journal of Physics, 41*(6), 559-581.

Li, S., Mou, X., & Cai, Y., (2001). Improving Security of a Chaotic Encryption Approach. *Physics Letters A, 290*, 127-133.

Li, S., Mou, X., Yang, B.L., Ji, Z., & Zhang, J. (2003). Problems With a Probabilistic Encryption Scheme Based on Chaotic Systems. *International Journal of Bifurcation and Chaos, 13*(10), 3063-3077.

Li, Z., Li, K., Wen, C., & Soh, Y. C. (2003). A New Chaotic Secure Communication System. IEEE Transactions on Communications, 51(8), 1306-1312.

Luo, J., & Shi, H. (2006). Research of Chaos Encryption Algorithm Based on Logistic Mapping. *Proceedings of the International Conference on Intelligent Information Hiding and Multimedia Signal*, 1–3. doi:10.1109/IIH-MSP.2006.265022

Ma, J., & Ye, R. (2015). An Image Encryption Scheme Based on Hybrid Orbit of Hyper-chaotic Systems. *International Journal of Computer Network and Information Security, 5*, 25-33.

Mansour, I., Chalhoub, G., & Bakhache, B. (2012). Evaluation of a Fast Symmetric Cryptographic Algorithm Based on the Chaos Theory for Wireless Sensor Networks. *IEEE 11th International Conference on Trust, Security and Privacy in Computing and Communications*, 913-919. doi:10.1109/TrustCom.2012.154

Mihailescu, M. I. (2014). New Enrollment Scheme for Biometric Template using Hash Chaos-Based Cryptography. *Procedia Engineering, 69*, 1459 – 1468. doi:10.1016/j.proeng.2014.03.142

Mondal, B., Mandal, T., (2016). A light weight secure image encryption scheme based on chaos & DNA computing. *Journal of King Saud University – Computer and Information Sciences*, 1-6.

Niu, H., Zhou, C., Wang, B., Zheng, X., & Zhou, S. (2016). Splicing Model and Hyper–Chaotic System For Image Encryption. *Journal of Electrical Engineering, 67*(2), 78–86.

Orue, A. B., Fernandez, V., Alvareza, G., Pastor, G., Shujun, M. L., & Montoya, F. (2008). Determination of the Parameters for a Lorenz System and Application to Break the Security of Two-channel Chaotic Cryptosystems. *Physics Letters, 372*(34), 5588–5592. doi:10.1016/j.physleta.2008.06.066

Özkaynak, F., Yavuz, S. (2013). Designing chaotic S-boxes based on time-delay chaoticsystem. *Nonlinear Dynamics, 74*, 551–557.

Palacios, A., & Juarez, H. (2002). Cryptography With Cycling Chaos. *Physics Letters*, *303*(5-6), 345–351. doi:10.1016/S0375-9601(02)01323-3

Pan, J., Ding, Q., & Qi, N. (2012). The Research of Chaos-Based SMS Encryption in Mobile Phone. *Second International Conference on Instrumentation & Measurement, Computer, Communication and Control*, 501-504. doi:10.1109/IMCCC.2012.124

Pande, A., & Zambreno, J. (2011). A Chaotic Encryption Scheme for Real-Time Embedded Systems: Design and Implementation. *Telecommunication System, Springer*, *52*, 551–561.

Peng, F., Zhu, X., & Long, M. (2013). An ROI Privacy Protection Scheme for H.264 Video Based on FMO and Chaos. IEEE Transactions on Information Forensics and Security, 8(10), 1688-1699.

Petrauskiene, V., Palivonaite, R., Aleksa, A., & Ragulskis, M., (2013). Dynamic visual cryptography based on chaotic oscillations. *Communication in Nonlinear Science and Numerical Simulation*, 1-9.

Schmitz, R., (2001). Use of Chaotic Dynamical Systems in Cryptography. *Journal of the Franklin Institute*, *338*, 429–441.

Seyedzadeh, S.M., & Mirzakuchaki, S. (2012). A fast color image encryption algorithm based on coupled two-dimensional piecewise chaotic map. *Signal Processing, 92*, 1202–1215.

Sheng, S., & Wu, X. (2012). A New Digital Anti-Counterfeiting Scheme Based on Chaotic Cryptography. *International Conference on ICT Convergence (ICTC)*, 687-691. doi:10.1109/ICTC.2012.6387119

Shukla, P.K., Khare, A., Rizvi, M.A., Stalin, S., & Kumar, S. (2015). Applied Cryptography Using Chaos Function for Fast Digital Logic-Based Systems in Ubiquitous Computing. *Entropy, 17*, 1387-1410.

Sivakumar, T., & Venkatesan, R., (2016). A New Image Encryption Method Basedon Knight's Travel Path and True Random Number. *Journal of Information Science and Engineering*, *32*, 133-152.

Solak, E., & Cokal, C. (2008). Cryptanalysis of a Cryptosystem Based on discretized Two-Dimensional Chaotic Maps. *Physics Letters A*, *372*, 6922–6924.

Solak, E., Rhouma, R., & Belghith, S. (2010). Cryptanalysis of a Multi-Chaotic Systems Based Image Cryptosystem. *Optics Communications, 283*, 232–236.

Soleymani, A., Nordin, J., & Sundararajan, E. (2014). A Chaotic Cryptosystem for Images based on Henon and Arnold Cat Map. *The Scientific World Journal*, *10*, 1–21.

Song, C., & Qiao, Y. (2015). A Novel Image Encryption Algorithm Based on DNA Encoding and Spatiotemporal Chaos. *Entropy, 17,* 6954-6968.

Subramanyan, B., Chhabria, V. M., & Sankar Babu, T. G. (2011). Image Encryption Based on AES Key Expansion. *Proceedings of the 2nd International Conference on Emerging Applications of Information Technology (EAIT '11)*, 217–220. doi:10.1109/EAIT.2011.60

Tang, G., Liao, X., Xiao, D., & Li, C. (2004). A Secure Communication Scheme Based on Symbolic Dynamics. *Proceedings of the 2004 International Conference on Communications, Circuits and Systems*, 13–17. doi:10.1109/ICCCAS.2004.1345929

Tong, X., Liu, Y., Zhang, M., Xu, H., & Wang, Z. (2015). An Image Encryption Scheme Based on Hyperchaotic Rabinovich and Exponential Chaos Maps. *Entropy, 17,* 181-196.

Wang, X., & Chen, D., (2013). A Parallel Encryption Algorithm Based on Piecewise Linear Chaotic Map. *Mathematical Problems in Engineering, 13,* 1-7.

Wang, X., Gu, S., & Zhang, Y. (2015). Novel Image Encryption Algorithm Based on Cycle Shift and Chaotic System. *Optics and Lasers in Engineering, 68,* 126–134.

Wang, X., & Jin, C. (2012). Image Encryption Using Game of Life Permutation and PWLCM Chaotic System. *Optics Communications, 285,* 412–417.

Wong, K., Lin, Q., & Chen, J. (2010). Simultaneous Arithmetic Coding and Encryption Using Chaotic Maps. IEEE Transactions on Circuits and Systems—II: Express Briefs, 57(2), 146-150.

Wong, K., & Yuen, C. (2008). Embedding Compression in Chaos-Based Cryptography. IEEE Transactions on Circuits and Systems—II: Express Briefs, 55(11), 1193-1197.

Xia, C., Song, P., Shi, T., & Yan, Y. (2013). Chaotic Dynamics Characteristic Analysisfor Matrix Converter. *IEEE Transactions on Industrial Electronics*, 60(1), 78-87.

Xing-yuan, W., & Qing, Y., (2009). A block Encryption Algorithm Based on Dynamic Sequences of Multiple Chaotic Systems. *Communications in Nonlinear Science and Numerical Simulation, 14,* 574–581.

Xuand, S., & Wang, Y. (2010). A Novel Image Encryption Scheme based on a Nonlinear Chaotic Map. *International Journal of Image, Graphics and Signal Processing, 1,* 61-68.

Zhang, X., Fan, X., Wang, J., & Zhao, Z. (2014). A Chaos-Based Image Encryption Scheme Using 2D Rectangular Transform and Dependent Substitution. In *Multimedia Tools Application* (pp. 1–19). New York: Springer Science & Business Media.

Zhang, Z., Niu, X., Wang, H., & Liu, K. (2013). Characteristics Analysis and Application of The Encryption Algorithm Based on Dual-Chaos Theory. *International Conference on Sensor Network Security Technology and Privacy Communication System (SNS & PCS),* 1-4. doi:10.1109/SNS-PCS.2013.6553850

Zhu, H., Zhang, X., Yu, H., Zhao, C., & Zhu, Z. (2016). A Novel Image Encryption Scheme Using the Composite Discrete Chaotic System. *Entropy,* 18(276), 1-27.

Chapter 13
Detection of Stator and Rotor Faults in Asynchronous Motor Using Artificial Intelligence Method

K. Vinoth Kumar
Karunya University, India

Prawin Angel Michael
Karunya University, India

ABSTRACT

This chapter deals with the implementation of a PC-based monitoring and fault identification scheme for a three-phase induction motor using artificial neural networks (ANNs). To accomplish the task, a hardware system is designed and built to acquire three phase voltages and currents from a 3.3KW squirrel-cage, three-phase induction motor. A software program is written to read the voltages and currents, which are first used to train a feed-forward neural network structure. The trained network is placed in a Lab VIEW-based program formula node that monitors the voltages and currents online and displays the fault conditions and turns the motor. The complete system is successfully tested in real time by creating different faults on the motor.

INTRODUCTION

A three phase induction motor consists of stator and a rotor. The stator is fabricated from laminated sheet steel stampings having slots on the inner periphery. The rotor may squirrel cage or wound rotor. A squirrel cage or (simply) cage rotor has a number of conducting bars housed in slots on the outer surface of rotor core (Acosta, Verucchi, Gelso, 2004). These bars are short circuited at both ends by conducting end rings. The three-phase squirrel-cage induction motor is frequently used, owing to its ruggedness, robust construction, and low cost, it can however show defects. The flow of phase currents in the stator winding produces a rotating magnetic field. This magnetic field has a constant amplitude and rotate at

DOI: 10.4018/978-1-5225-3531-7.ch013

synchronous speed assume that the rotor is initially stand still. The rotating stator field induces an EMF in the rotor conductors (Benbouzid 2000).

Since the rotor circuit is closed (either because of the end rings in cage rotor or because the slip rings are short circuited in a wound rotor), a current flows in the rotor circuits. This rotor creates a rotor field. The interaction of stator on rotor produces a torque which causes the rotation of rotor in the direction of stator rotating field. The three-phase induction motor is a workhorse of the manufacturing industry. They can come either from stator, rotor or a mechanical problem. Knowing that industrial constraints are even stronger, reliability and a safe operating system have to be considered. As a matter of fact, the stresses of induction motor generally bring about a breakdown with a range of few minutes to several days in industrial processes (Blodt, Chabert, Regnier, Faucher, 2006).

It is well known that many defects come from a rotor problem. A broken rotor bar is an example. The brazen connection between the end ring and the rotor bars, induced by several consecutive start up, is another one. Moreover, some defects can come from an eccentricity of the rotor which can be static or even dynamic. These ones are incipient, and they, slowly but surely, induce some perturbations like an increase of vibrations of the motor process, the appearance of torque ripples, and/or an increase of the temperature of the induction motor. These types of defects can lead to dismantling. A predictive maintenance cunningly allows one to avoid expensive repair due to damages.

Consequently, monitoring and fault severity have been focused on for some decades. The most popular approach is the monitoring of the induction motor, owing to the spectral analysis of the stator line current absorbed by the induction motor, this paper is devoted to the monitoring and fault detection of an induction motor drive using two current sensors. The diagnostic approach we propose in this paper is based on fuzzy fault detection, owing to human knowledge of the process. The main goal of this approach is to inform an operator of symptoms by means of indicator lights. It could be the presence (or not) of an incipient rotor defect or the presence of one rotor broken bar. This motor may encounter several fault conditions, which can damage the motor. These conditions include overload, unbalanced supply voltage, locked rotor, single phasing, under-voltage, and overvoltage. A 3.3 kW squirrel-cage, three-phase induction motor is used for this purpose (Casimir, Boutleux, Clerc, Yahoui, 2006; Calis, Cakir 2007).

ANN STRUCTURE AND FAILURE MODES

Stator Winding Failure

NNS is a simulator for artificial neural networks (ANN). This simulator is designed with a new graphical user interface. In this technique, Feed Forward Neural Network (FFNN) structure is used with back propagation algorithm is shown in figure 1. This ANN involves with one input layer and one output layer. In this technique, five neurons are used in the hidden layer. The Activation function used in hidden layer and output layer is Log Sigmoid function.

The ANN structure is trained through momentum coefficient (α) and learning coefficient (η) with 0.1 to 0.9 values and the best results obtained for momentum coefficient (α) and learning coefficient (η) is found to be 0.2. With the momentum coefficient (α) and learning coefficient (η) of 0.2, the error graph and log file is obtained. In this proposed work, Neural Network Simulator is used to diagnosis the condition of stator and rotor of a three phase squirrel cage induction motor. For training first open the NNS program, then choose create / layer from the tool menu (Didier, Ternisien, Caspary, Razik, 2007).

Figure 1. Measurement of Sequence Component

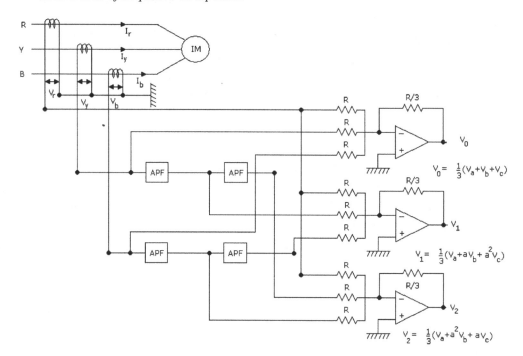

Here choose the number of neurons in the input, hidden and output layer and also select activation function, then choose feed forward connection to create a network. After that load a pattern set. Then open a control panel in tool menu. Here, one can choose the learning function, set its parameters, number of learning cycles and finally perform network initialization and learning. During training error graph displays the error curve and similarly that error can be written on log file.

In this technique, NNS (ANN) structure is trained with the derived positive and negative sequence component for normal and known faults condition of the machine. Total of 10 input patterns corresponding to different faults and normal condition as described in Table 1, are used to train ANN to predict the stator condition. Figure 2 (a). Illustrate the ANN structure trained with the data sets obtained from R phase stator winding short circuited by a low resistance between turns. After training, weights and bias values are stored in log file. Figure 2 (b) illustrates the Error graph and log file of the trained ANN to identify the stator condition. For stator inter turn fault, total of 10 patterns considered.

Rotor Failure

Motor Current Signature Analysis (MCSA) is well known tool to identify the different fault in the electrical system as well as in the machines. The types of faults using MCSA are normally analyzed through the amplitude difference between the line frequency amplitude in dB and amplitude of the first pole pass side band below the line frequency in dB. To diagnose the rotor condition Motor current signal spectrum is captured in terms of amplitude in dB versus frequency spectrum in Hz and the amplitude difference between line frequency amplitude in dB and the amplitude of the first pole pass sideband below line frequency in dB is measured by using Tektronix TDS 2014 power analyzer as in Figure 3. In this technique, Artificial neural network structure is trained with measured amplitude difference be-

Figure 2. (a) Trained ANN Structure for R-Phase Stator Winding Short Identification (b) Error Graph and Log File

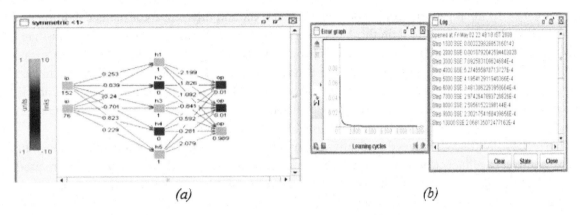

(a)   *(b)*

Table 1. Input and desired output for a stator inter turn fault

Input		Desired output	Conditions
Positive sequence magnitude in mA	Negative sequence magnitude in mA		
438	84	0 0 0	Normal Case
152	76	0 0 1	R phase short
160	120	0 1 0	Y phase short

Figure 3. MCSA Arrangement in Induction Motor

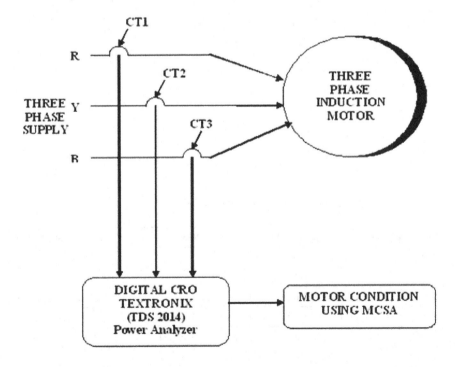

tween the line frequency amplitude in dB and amplitude of the first pole pass side band below the line frequency in dB values for good rotor, rotor bar with one crack and rotor bar with two crack condition.

A total of 10 input patterns corresponding to good rotor and different rotor faults condition as described in table 2. Are used to train the ANN to predict the rotor condition. Figure 4 (a). Illustrate the ANN structure trained with the data sets obtai4 (b). Illustrates the error graph and log file of a trained ANN to identify the rotor condition. Trained network weights and bias values from NNS and the necessary inputs for identify the particular faults are placed in LABVIEW Formula Node. Then a LabVIEW program is designed to monitors the machine condition. In figure.5 illustrates how the induction motor condition can be identified using LabVIEW (Jung, Lee, Kwon, 2006).

LabVIEW Program is designed to identify Stator inter turn condition and rotor bar condition of three phase squirrel cage induction motor. Sequence component and side band frequency values are used as input. First calculate the net value, by sum of the weighted input (input × weight) and the bias (b) which is obtained from NNS program .it is placed in LabVIEW formula node in order to calculate the activation function for hidden layer using sigmoid function.

Output from hidden layer is used as input to output layer. Once again calculate the activation function for output layer in similar method. The output goes to one if fault condition exits, otherwise it is zero. LED display the status of a machine whether it is fault or not (Bouzid & Champenois, 2008).

Figure 4. (a) Trained ANN Structure for Single cracked (broken) rotor bar using NNS (b) Error Graph and Log File

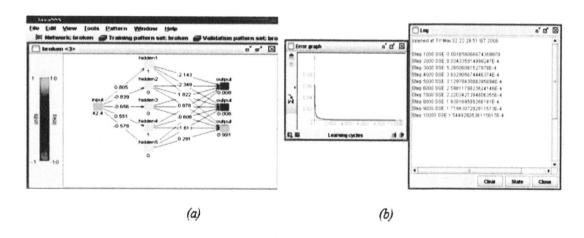

(a)   *(b)*

Table 2. Input and desired output for a broken rotor bar fault

Amplitude Difference in dB	Desired Output	Rotor condition (With at least 75% of rated load)
54-60	0 0 0	Good
48-54	0 1 0	Moderate
42-48	0 0 1	Bar crack may be developing or high resistance joints
36-42	0 1 1	Two bars may be broken or high resistance joints likely
30-36	1 1 1	Multiple broken or open bars or end ring probable

RESULTS AND DISCUSSIONS

Finally the online monitoring results for stator Inter turn fault and broken rotor bar fault is compared with the ANN desired output shown in Table 3 and Table 4. This proposed work reported that the method of identifying the stator turn and rotor bar condition in three phase induction motor and the results are shown in table 3 and table 4 respectively. It is observed that artificial neural network approach using NNS is very efficient in monitoring the faults.

CONCLUSION

This work concluded the implementation and testing of a real time based fault identification scheme for a three-phase induction motor using the ANN. To accomplish this, a hardware system was designed and built to acquire three-phase voltages and currents from an induction motor. A 1/3 HP squirrel-cage three-phase induction motor was used to create faults and collect data for training and testing the ANN based system. The LabVIEW program was written that read the voltages and voltage representation of the currents. NNS and LabVIEW have been used as soft computing tools to identify the Induction Motor faults. Feed Forward Neural Network where the Input data's are obtained from the positive and negative

Figure 5. Overall Block Diagram of ANN based Induction motor fault detection

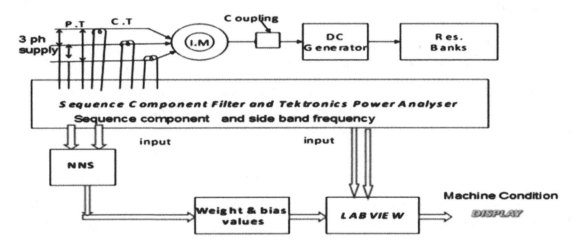

Table 3. Comparison of ANN and LabVIEW of stator inter turn fault identification

Name of the Fault	Desired output			ANN output			LabVIEW output		
Healthy case	0	0	0	0.007	0.007	0.007	0.055	0.041	0.053
R phase short	0	0	1	0.008	0.008	0.991	0.061	0.069	0.964
Y phase short	0	1	0	0.001	0.989	0.001	0.056	0.965	0.076

Table 4. Comparison of ANN and LabVIEW of Broken rotor bar fault identification

Fault	Desired output			ANN output			LabVIEW output		
Good rotor	0	0	0	0.007	0.007	0.007	0.007	0.089	0.056
Moderate rotor	0	1	0	0.007	0.992	0.007	0.039	0.945	0.041
Single cracked	0	0	1	0.008	0.008	0.991	0.045	0.044	0.921
Double cracked	0	1	1	0.007	0.992	0.992	0.080	0.981	0.966
Multi cracked	1	1	1	0.992	0.989	0.991	0.943	0.949	0.945

Sequence Component derived from Hardware circuit to identify the stator fault. The side band frequency of input motor current is obtained from Power analyser is used to identify the rotor fault. The result thus obtained is compared with the conventional technique results and have been found much more accurate in identifying the machine internal condition.

ACKNOWLEDGMENT

Authors may acknowledge to Karunya University, India that supported to any part of study.

REFERENCES

Acosta, G. G., Verucchi, C. J., & Gelso, E. R. (2004). A current monitoring system for diagnosing electrical failures in induction motors. *Mechanical Systems and Signal Processing*, *20*(1), 953–965.

Ayhan, B., Trussell, H. J., Chow, M. Y., & Song, M. H. (2008). On the use of a lower sampling rate for broken rotor bar detection with DTFT and AR-based spectrum methods. *IEEE Transactions on Industrial Electronics*, *55*(3), 1421–1434. doi:10.1109/TIE.2007.896522

Benbouzid, M. E. H. (2000). A Review of induction motors signature analysis as a medium for faults detection. *IEEE Transactions on Industrial Electronics*, *47*(5), 984–993. doi:10.1109/41.873206

Blodt, M., Chabert, M., Regnier, J., & Faucher, J. (2006). Mechanical Load Fault Detection in Induction Motors by Stator Current Time-Frequency Analysis. *IEEE Transactions on Industry Applications*, *42*(6), 1454–1463. doi:10.1109/TIA.2006.882631

Bouzid, M. B. K., & Champenois, G. (2008). New expressions of symmetrical components of the induction motor under stator faults. *IEEE Transactions on Industrial Electronics*, *60*(9), 4093–4102. doi:10.1109/TIE.2012.2235392

Çalis, H., & Çakir, A. (2007). Rotor bar fault diagnosis in three phase induction motors by monitoring fluctuations of motor current zero crossing instants. *Electric Power Systems Research*, *77*(5), 385–392. doi:10.1016/j.epsr.2006.03.017

Casimir, R., Boutleux, E., Clerc, G., & Yahoui, A. (2006). The use of features selection and nearest neighbours rule for faults diagnostic in induction motors. *Engineering Applications of Artificial Intelligence*, *19*(2), 169–177. doi:10.1016/j.engappai.2005.07.004

Didier, G., Ternisien, E., Caspary, O., & Razik, H. (2007). A new approach to detect broken rotor bars in induction machines by current spectrum analysis. *Mechanical Systems and Signal Processing*, *21*(2), 1127–1142. doi:10.1016/j.ymssp.2006.03.002

Drif, M., & Marques Cardoso, A. J. (2013). Airgap-eccentricity fault diagnosis in three-phase induction motors by the complex apparent power signature analysis. *IEEE Transactions on Industrial Electronics*, *55*(3), 1404–1410. doi:10.1109/TIE.2007.909076

Jung, J. H., Lee, J. J., & Kwon, B. H. (2006). Online diagnosis of induction motors using MCSA. *IEEE Transactions on Industrial Electronics*, *53*(6), 1842–1852. doi:10.1109/TIE.2006.885131

Rezig, A., Mekideche, M. R., & Ikhlef, N. (2014). Effect of rotor eccentricity on magnetic noise generation in induction motors. *Journal of Electrical Engineering*, *3*(4), 200–208.

Robinson, J., Whelan, C. D., & Haggerty, N. K. (2004). Trends in advanced motor protection and monitoring. *IEEE Transactions on Industry Applications*, *40*(3), 853–860. doi:10.1109/TIA.2004.827472

Robinson, J., Whelan, C. D., & Haggerty, N. K. (2004). Trends in advanced motor protection and monitoring. *IEEE Transactions on Industry Applications*, *40*(3), 853–860. doi:10.1109/TIA.2004.827472

Thakur, A., Wadhwani, S., & Sondhiya, V. (2013). Health monitoring of rotating electrical machine using soft computing techniques: A Review. *International Journal of Scientific and Research Publications*, *3*(11), 1–3.

Zhen, D., Wang, T., Gu, F., & Ball, A. D. (2013). Fault diagnosis of motor drives using stator current signal analysis based on dynamic time warping. *Mechanical Systems and Signal Processing*, *34*(1), 191–202. doi:10.1016/j.ymssp.2012.07.018

Chapter 14
Soft Computing Approaches for Image Segmentation

Siddharth Singh Chouhan
Shri Mata Vaishno Devi University, India

Utkarsh Sharma
G. L. A. University, India

Uday Pratap Singh
Madhav Institute of Technology and Science, India

ABSTRACT

In this chapter a review is done on the image segmentation techniques by using both traditional approaches and soft computing approaches. This chapter will figure out some soft computing approaches that can be used to solve the problem of identification of objects. Some traditional approaches for the extraction of objects are discussed along with their comparison with soft computing approaches. The chapter discusses various applications of image segmentation. The soft computing approaches are then analyzed and their performance is compared with the others by identifying the advantages and disadvantages of all.

INTRODUCTION

The idea to present in this chapter is to help researchers towards extraction or information of high level features from image using soft computing approaches. Soft computing methods are adaptive and robust, therefore capabilities of these approaches gives higher efficiency in finding out object from an image has been already a area of interest in today's era. There are many applications in the area of medical, forensic and economics etc. where identification of object does an image contains is an important task. In this chapter we will figure out some soft computing approaches which can be used to solve the problem of identification of objects. Along with it some traditional approaches which being already have been applied for the extraction of objects has been discussed along with their comparison with soft computing approaches. At last will discuss various applications of image segmentation.

DOI: 10.4018/978-1-5225-3531-7.ch014

Figure 1. Image Processing

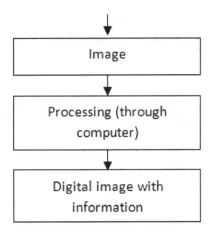

IMAGE SEGMENTATION

As the computer technology is growing day by day the inference of images in daily life has been seen quite often. The tremendous growth of internet has also incorporate use of images. With the number of applications such as social networking, banking, graphical password and so on the images are used everywhere thus incorporates image processing. The images present around us are digital in nature and thus processed by using computer or other smart devices compatible with computers. So when a digital image has been processed by computer to obtain some useful information, enhance image quality, manipulate or analyze something from the given image is known as image processing or simply it can be stated that converting an image into the digital form for getting some information from it.

To incorporate images and process it through the computer becomes a challenging and most important task as the frequency of images are used growing rapidly. The most important task in an image is to detect what it contains for example consider an image shown in figure 2 let us suppose that a computer is given with the same image and a man is given with the same image to recognize the contents of the image, the man by looking at the image can easily find out that the image contains fruits but computer cannot recognize it so not only making image processed through the computer system to be in digital manner but also make the processing meaningful by detecting the contents is also a major issue. Convenient application of image segmentation range from medical application (locate tumors, breast cancer, computer guided surgery, treatment planning, measure tissue volumes etc), locate objects in satellite images (water, forest, roads, buildings, etc), Face recognition, Finger print recognition, Plant diseases recognition etc.

Image segmentation or object extraction is the method by which the contents of a digital image are recognized by the computer. Image segmentation is the process of breaking the image into very small parts so that the objects can be identified and some useful information can be generated. So in the given image figure 2 when its segmentation has been done than it could recognize the objects and thus stated that the image given to the computer contains fruit.

Object extraction (locate, identify, boundaries detection) from the image is the vital topic in the field of digital image processing. The main purpose of image segmentation is to segregate the image into necessary regions with respect to the appropriate locations which are visually distinct and uniform in accordance to some property such as texture, colour or gray level so, as to make image into something that

Figure 2. Object extraction

is more meaningful and easier to analyze. Moreover segmentation of an image depends on the problem domain or application. Image segmentation can be defined as follows:

Image segmentation is the process of dividing image in its consequent sub parts in order to achieve some useful information from the given image.

or

Object extraction is the process of getting useful information by analyzing and manipulation of the image by dividing it into subparts.

When a image has been divided into multiple segments which are identified as super pixels. The property of pixel in an image and information of pixels near to that pixel are two basic parameters for any image segmentation algorithm. Image engineering can be defined as that which contains three layers as:

1. Image processing
2. Image analysis
3. Image understanding

Furthermore image segmentation can also be used to differentiate different objects in the image, because our image is divided into foreground and background, the role of image segmentation is to divide these two regions from one another which categorizes the region of interest that is foreground from rest of region that is background.

To understand the process of segmentation from the computer point of view here we shows that how an image has been segmentated using matlab.

Figure 3. Foreground and background separation

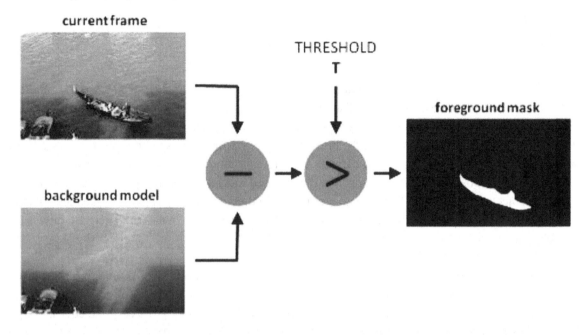

Figure 4. Image segmentation using Matlab

Despite the fact that diverse segmentation procedures are within reach, each strategy is not similarly proper for a specific sort of picture. Accordingly the algorithm which is suitable for one category of picture may not be appropriate for another categories of pictures. Subsequently, there is no consistently upheld strategy for image segmentation for all classes of pictures and therefore it remains a test in image processing and computer vision (Kuruvilla J., et al., 2016).

We can classify the segmentation in following classes:

- Threshold
- Feature Based Clustering
- Region Based
- Edge Based

Region Based

Pixels which are associated and have some comparable properties form a region. Region based division is a methodology of breaking an image into regions. Translation of pictures can be done by regions. A region may identify with particular challenge or differing parts of an object. Region based systems are overall better in large pictures (where edges are difficult to recognize). Sensible precision levels are offered in region based procedures.

Edge Based

Algorithms for image segmentations all around rely on upon intensity values which are irregular and relative values of intensities. In case of discontinuous intensity values, the approach is to section the image in perspective of unforeseen changes in intensity, for instance, edges in an image. Division in perspective of Edge Detection suggests the breaking points where there is an unforeseen change in the intensity or estimation of brightness of the image. Edge identification is the issue of basic values in image analysis. As far as possible signify the edges of the required image. Accordingly by the revelation of its edges, the object can be divided from the image. The yield that is gotten by applying edge identification proof calculation is a binary picture. Edge based methods are instinctive in nature . There are three basic steps in identification of edges.

- **Enhancement and Filtering:** Keeping as a top priority the ultimate objective to empower the edge recognition, it is fundamental to control however much noise as could sensibly be normal and choose changes in intensity in the region of a point, without wrecking the certified edges.
- **Discovery of Edge Points:** Figure out which edge pixels should be discarded as noise and which should be held (for the most part, thresholding gives the manage used to identification).
- **Localization of Edge:** Not most of the points in an image are edges for a particular application. Edge control choose the right range of an edge. Diminishing of edge and associating are ordinarily required in this progression.(Kuruvilla J., et al.,2016).

Threshold

Image segmentation by thresholding is a basic and intense procedure for fragmenting pictures having objects which are light on comparatively shady foundation. The operation of thresholding changes over a multi level image into a binary image by selecting an appropriate cutoff T and partition image pixels into a couple of parts and objects are separated from the background. The segment of the objects from the given background is generally done by picking a regard T. Dependent upon the thresholding regard there are two systems. global thresholding and local thresholding (Muller H.,et. al., 2004). Exactly when T is reliable, the approach is called global thresholding otherwise it is termed as local thresholding. If the brightening of the background is uneven then the global thresholding method advance toward getting to be failed. Regardless, these uneven lightening effects are reimbursed in local thresholding methodology by using distinctive edges.

If the constrain of any pixel (x,y) is more noticeable than or comparable to the threshold regard, then it is considered as a bit of the concern else it has a place with background. Impenetrability to noise is less when we grasp this technique.

Feature Based Clustering

Clustering is the way toward gathering together of objects in view of some comparative properties so that each group contains comparative items which are not at all like the objects of different groups.

Clustering is a procedure which can be performed by various calculations utilizing diverse techniques for figuring or finding the group. The nature of the great grouping techniques delivers low inter-cluster and high intra-cluster similitudes. A general way to deal with picture clustering includes tending to the accompanying issues:

1. Representation of image.
2. Organization of data.
3. Classification of an image in to an suitable cluster.

The Clustering techniques are characterized into Fuzzy C- Means[FCM] Algorithm, K mean clustering and so forth. K-means is one of the quick, strong, least difficult unsupervised learning algorithm that tackle the notable issue of clustering. The technique is to characterize the given informational collection through a specific number of k clusters that are settled from the earlier. K-means algorithms for clustering gives ideal outcome when data set are different.

Fuzzy Clustering is a strategy which enable the objects to have a place with more than one clustering with various membership. This is the one of the viable technique for recognition of patterns. Most normally utilized algorithm for fuzzy clustering is the Fuzzy C-Mean(Patil A. J, et al.,2015). By utilizing FCM we can hold data of the informational data set. In FCM, membership is assigned to the data point for each center of cluster accordingly of which information indicate may have a place more than one centre of cluster.

SOFT COMPUTING

Soft computing strategies have different elements which can be utilized as a part of digital image processing which helps in better comprehension of picture. Detail survey of different soft computing procedures utilized for edge recognition is analyzed.

Fuzzy Logic

Fuzzy logic assists in managing instabilities in logical thinking . It has been connected to processing of images in numerous viewpoints (Berzins V., 1984). Picture Segmentation points is to partition pixels into comparable area i.e. crisp sets (Senthilkumaran N., et al., 2008). Fuzzy segmentation thus isolates pixels into fuzzy sets i.e. every pixel may have a place mostly with many sets and regions of picture (Mehrara H., et al., 2009; Mettam GR, et al., 1999).

Artificial Neural Networks

Artificial neural network is propelled by the way data is handled in the nervous system. Learning capacity of neural system helps in image handling operations. The system "learns" by changing the interconnection of the layers. At the point when the system is satisfactorily prepared, it can sum up pertinent yield for an set of data as input. A significant property of neural systems is that of generalization. A neural network which is trained can give a right coordinating as yield information for an arrangement of input data which is unseen. Learning regularly happens by case through training, where the algorithm for training iteratively changes the association weights (Senthilkumaran N., et al., 2008; Zhang L., et. al.,2009).

Genetic Algorithms

Genetic algorithms get from the evolution hypothesis has been in given by John Holland in 1975. Theory of evolution expected that for a given populace just those people who all around adjusted to the environment can survive and transmit their components to their next generation.GA has been utilized to take care of different issues in digital image processing, including segmentation of image (Borji An., et. al., 2007).

Particle Swarm Optimization

Particle Swarm Optimization was presented by James Kennedy and Russell Eberhart in 1995.This method depends on winged creature rushing conduct given by scholar Frank Heppner. This approach is generally utilized for those issues whose arrangements can be spoken to as a point in a n-dimensional solution space. Instate the space and haphazardly skims number of particles into movement (Setayesh M., et. al., 2009). Watching "wellness" of every molecule in every cycle with their neighbors and "imitate" effective neighbors (those whose present position speaks to a superior answer for the issue than theirs) by moving towards them. In view of various plans for gathering the particles into rivalries, semi-autonomous groups can be utilized.

Ant Colony Optimization

Ant colony optimization (ACO) is one of most well known method for optimization. It is propelled by the characteristic conduct of species of ants. Ants store their pheromone on the ground to manage their rummaging. It is for the most part valuable for tackling complex computational issues. The goal of ants is to discover best way for their goal (Patil A. J., et al., 2015).ACO adjusts this marvel of nature of ants to shapes fake ants which speak to it as a product specialist to discover ideal answers for a given optimization issue.

Adaptive Neuro Fuzzy Inference System(ANFIS)

Adaptive Neuro Fuzzy Inference System(ANFIS) is utilized to distinguish edges. It is a crossover strategy in light of Fuzzy logic and neural network (Abdallah An., Alshennawy and Ayman A. Aly, 2009). ANFIS take favorable circumstances to develop Fuzzy inference framework by utilizing test data sets. It utilizes key elements of both the procedure, for example, if there should arise an occurrence of Neural network gives the adaptability though the fuzzy logic manages imprecision and vulnerability of the framework. Generally speaking the Fuzzy logic inferred the model and after that neural network give adjusting to the principles of beginning fuzzy model to deliver last ANFIS model.

TRADITIONAL APPROACHES

Several algorithms and techniques have been formulated for segmentation of image. Some of the traditional techniques are discussed in this chapter.

Classification of traditional approaches is shown in Figure 5.

Region Growing

It is the simplest form of the image segmentation. Region in an image are a group of connected pixels with similar properties. The selection of image subset or region is based on some criteria can be gray level or texture and this region is denoted by R. It is also termed as similarity based segmentation. In each and every step at least one pixel is bound or related with region and is acquire into consideration. The vector is created after identifying the change in the texture and color. This process is repeated for each boundary pixel in the region. From this the edge are detected for further segmentation. There are two types of region based segmentation

Region Growing Methods

This method works on some predefined criteria that groups sub regions or pixels into a larger region. It starts with a seed point and by growing appending the nearer pixels that have same attributes like color, texture, gray scale, shape etc.

Region Splitting and Merging

Region splitting differs region merging in the sense that in the first one complete image is considered as a single region and then region is split into disjoint regions which are different. Whereas on the other hand the second one starts with small region and merges the region based on some similarities such as color, texture, gray scale etc and it has been done once the splitting has been done.

The working of region growing algorithm using Euclidean distance to measure pixel homogeneity is as follows. Consider the two pixels p1 and p2 with the given RGB values as shown in figure 6. We plot a scatter diagram for the given values into the RGB color space model. You can see the pixels p1 and pixel p2 in the color spaces. We are going to use Euclidean distance to measure whether the given pixels are homogeneous or not homogeneous.

So for doing it the following method is used:

$$d_{p1,p2} = \sqrt{(R_1-R_2)^2 + (G_1-G_2)^2 + (B_1-B_2)^2}$$

Figure 5. Traditional Segmentation approaches

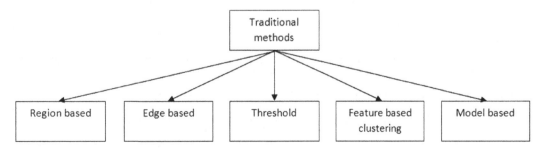

Figure 6. Example 1

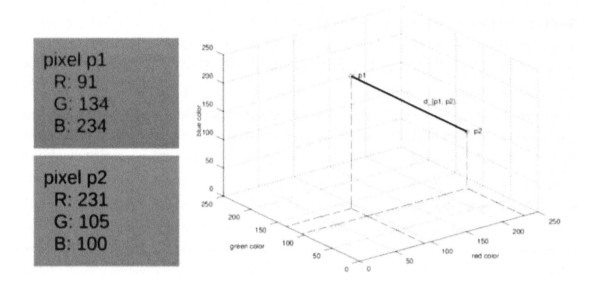

$$d_{p1,p2} = \sqrt{(91\text{-}231)^2 + (134\text{-}105)^2 + (234\text{-}100)^2}$$

$$d_{p1,p2} \approx 195.951$$

So after calculation we got the Euclidean distance between the two pixels is 195.951. Now for getting the result about homogeneity the user must define a homogeneity threshold (T) between the pixels given by

$$d_{p1,p2} \leq T \rightarrow \text{pixels are homogeneous}$$

$$d_{p1,p2} > T \rightarrow \text{pixels are } not \text{ homogeneous}$$

If the value of Euclidean distance is less than or equal to the threshold value than the pixels are homogenous and if the value of Euclidean distance is greater than the threshold value than the pixels are not homogenous.

Advantages

1. It is one of the better segmentation algorithms when compared with others.
2. When proper seed is selected than gives accurate result.
3. It flows from inner region to outer region gives clear boundaries of an object.
4. It has interactive and automatic technique for image segmentation gives user to choose from the two.
5. Has a tendency to work well for the images having higher contrast.

Disadvantages

1. Works on single operator which does not suit on all images.
2. It is difficult to assign stopping criteria for what level the segmentation has to be done.
3. This method is sequential in manner.
4. It is expensive both in terms of time and memory.

Watershed Algorithm

Morphological watersheds show an integral way to deal with the image segmentation. It is particularly valuable for dividing objects that are touching each other. To compute watersheds there are lots of techniques have been developed. The basic idea of watershed id using a geographical terminology begins with piercing the regional minima of the surface. Then slowly immerse the image into the lake. The water continuously floods the basins corresponding to the various minima we erect a dam (line) to prevent the merging of two different water from different minima. For the kind of separation shown in figure 7 where boundaries of two different object touches each other this algorithm is best suited for.

Algorithm

Consider the topographic surface shown in figure 8. Water would gather in one of the two catchment bowls. Water falling on the watershed edge line isolating the two bowls would probably gather into both of the two catchment bowls and the edge lines in a picture.

Figure 7. Watershed algorithm

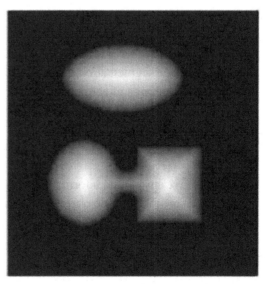

Figure 8. Watershed algorithm working

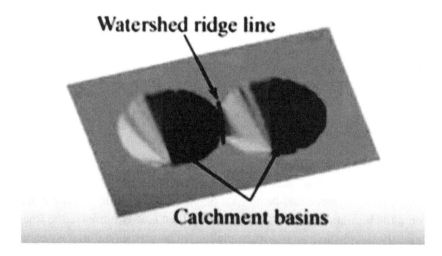

Working

Assume a gap is punched at each local minimum which is regional and the total geography is overwhelmed from beneath by giving the water a chance to increment through the openings at a predictable rate. Pixels underneath the water level at a predefined time are set apart as overflowed. When we raise the water level incrementally, the overwhelmed areas will bring up in size. In the long run, the water will ascend to a level where two overflowed regions from part catchment bowls will combine. At the point when this happens, the calculation develops a one-pixel wide dam that isolates the two areas. The flooding keeps anticipating the whole picture is fragmented into two separate catchment bowls partitioned by watershed edge lines.

Advantages

1.   This method is considerable in terms of accuracy.
2.   It speed of image segmentation is fast.
3.   It is moderate in terms of automaticity.
4.   It region continuity is also reasonable.

Disadvantages

1.   It does not give any spatial information.
2.   It is not suitable for multiple object detection.
3.   It is not resistance to noise.

Edge Detection

Edges are the spots in the picture where very quickly the intensity is changing out. Edges are noteworthy neighborhood changes in the picture and are critical elements for examining pictures. Edges for the most

Figure 9. Edge detection

part happen on the limit between two distinct regions in a picture. Edge discovery is every now and again the initial phase in recuperating data from pictures. Because of its significance, edge identification keeps on being a dynamic research territory. Edge detection is a picture handling procedure for finding the limits of objects inside pictures. It works by distinguishing discontinuities in image brightness. Edge recognition is utilized for image segmentation and information extraction in fields, for example, computer vision, image processing and machine vision. A portion of the edge detection algorithms include Laplacian, Sobel, Canny, Robinson, Roberts, Prewitt, Krisch and fuzzy logic methods. Essentially there are three sorts of edges in a picture slanting, horizontal and vertical. Presently the question emerges that why to recognize edges, the edges encased the vast majority of the shape data so by utilizing these channels or edge recognition calculations and afterward upgrading those territories by enhancing sharpness edge of a picture can be distinguished.

An edge in a picture is a key local change in the intensity of image, normally related with a irregularity in also the intensity of image or the principal subsidiary of the intensity of image. Discontinuities in the intensity of the image can be likewise (1) step discontinuities, where the intensity of image unexpectedly adjusts from one incentive on one side of the intermittent to an alternate on the contrasting side, or (2) line discontinuities, where the intensity of image rapidly changes esteem yet then comes back to the beginning with some minor distances . Be that as it may, step and line edges are uncommon in natural pictures. In view of components of low-frequency or the smoothing presented by most detecting gadgets, sharp discontinuities once in a while be in genuine signs. Step edges progress toward becoming slope edges and line edges move toward becoming rooftop edges, where power differ are not prompt but rather happen over a limited separation. Delineations of these edge profiles are appeared in Figure 10.

It is likewise doable for an edge to have both line and step attributes. For instance, a surface that changes orientation with one level surface then onto the next will make a step edge; yet in the event that the surface has a specular piece of reflectance and if the surface curve is adjusted, there can be a highlight because of the specular segment as the orientation of surface of the adjusted corner sidestep the correct plot for specular reflection. The edge diagram created by such a circumstance resembles a step edge with a line edge as superimposed. There are likewise edges related with changes in the main subsidiary of the picture power. For instance, common reflection from the sides of an inward corner

Figure 10. Types of edges

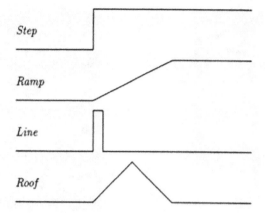

produces rooftop edges. Edges arc basic picturc highlights since they may compare to critical elements of objects in the prospect. For instance, the limit of a question more often than not delivers step edges in light of the fact that the intensity of image of the object is unique in relation to the intensity of the image of the background.

There are 3 steps in edge detection (Lakshmi S., Sankaranarayanan V., 2010)

1. Filtering
2. Enhancement
3. Detection

Some methods for edge detection are as follows:

1. Roberts Edge Detection.
2. Prewitt Edge Detection.
3. Sobel Edge Detection.
4. Canny Edge Detection.
5. Laplacian Edge Detection.
6. Gradient Edge Detection.

Thresholding Method

Thresholding otherwise called segmentation based on intensity by and large originates from edge based segmentation of image. It is one of the generally utilized strategies. It is valuable in segregating forefront from the background. By choosing a satisfactory value of threshold as T, the images which are in gray-level can be converted in to images of binary nature. The image which is binary ought to hold the greater part of the basic data with respect to the position and state of the objects of significance (foreground). The advantage of acquiring initial as a binary image is that it facilitates the multifaceted nature of the information and rearranges the method of acknowledgment and characterization. The most successive approach to change over a gray-level picture to a binary picture is to pick a solitary threshold esteem (T). At that point all the gray level values beneath this T will be sort as black(0), and those above T will be white (1). The division situation winds up noticeably one of choosing the best possible incentive for the limit T. An intermittent technique used to choose T is by breaking down the histograms of the kind of pictures that craving to be segmented. The perfect case is the point at which the histogram shows just two prevailing modes and an unmistakable valley (bimodal). For this situation the estimation of T is picked as the valley point between the two modes. In genuine applications histograms are more composite, with many pinnacles and not clear valleys, and it is not generally simple to pick the estimation of T.

Thresholding can be of two sorts Local Thresholding and Global Thresholding: When there is single esteem distinction amongst closer view and foundation question of a picture then it is limit by global by and large utilized by Otsu, Entropy technique. Furthermore, picture is sub isolated into different parts or regions and limit an incentive for every subpart is picked then this strategy is known as local.

Threshold Techniques

- Mean Technique
- P-Tile Technique
- Optimal Technique
- Histogram Dependent Technique (HDT)
- Edge maximization technique (EMT) Technique
- Visual Technique

Figure 11. Thresholded image

Advantages

1. No need to have prior information of an image.
2. Implementation is easy and fast.
3. It can be applied in real time application.
4. In terms of computational it is inexpensive.

Disadvantages

1. Highly sensitive to noise.
2. Selection of threshold value is very important.
3. Does not work well for flat or broad valley images.
4. Does not give any spatial information of an image.
5. Cost of segmentation is high.

K-Means Clustering and Hierarchical Clustering

Clustering means to make group of data points. K means algorithm is the most popular and most widely used clustering algorithm. It is an iterative algorithm. It can be best explained by the pictorial explanation however working of the algorithm is also given but we will discuss it through examples. Let us suppose that some points are given as shown in figure 12(i) and it has to be into two clusters X an Y. It does two things firstly it divides the data pints into two groups that is X and Y and than secondly it rearranges the data points after getting the mean values of the cluster and again rearranges them again and continues the process till clusters are arranged. So you can see in the figure 12(i1) after final arrangement the cluster is shown.

Working

1. No of cluster must be known to be k.
2. K no of cluster centers such that they are farthest apart from each other.
3. Consider each data point and assign it to the cluster which is closest.
4. Recalculate cluster centers by finding mean of data points belonging to the same cluster.
5. Repeat step 3 and 4 till shifting of cluster centers are observed.

Advantages

1. Small value of k higher the computational efficiency.
2. Numbers of homogenous regions are large.
3. Can remove noise spots.
4. Reduces false blobs.

Figure 12. Clustering of points

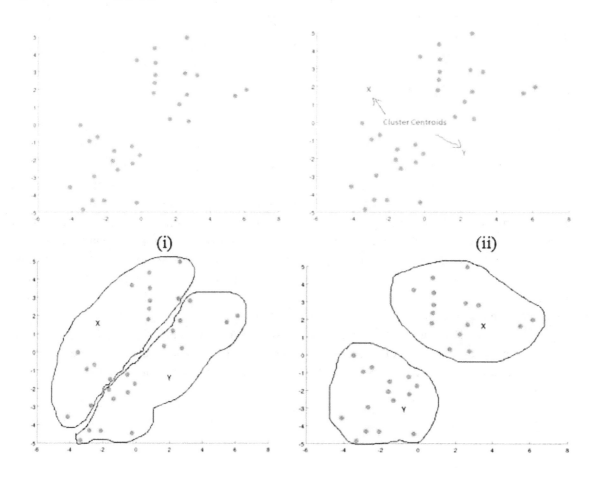

(i)   (ii)

Disadvantages

1. Sometimes difficult to predict k with number of clusters are fixed.
2. With non globular cluster does not work well.
3. Expensive in terms of computational ability.
4. For initialization of cluster number and center it is sensitive.

Model Based Segmentation

The approaches based on Model assumes that certain pattern is found in the objects in an image. This type of segmentation is also known as Markov Random field. This is a color segmentation technique which uses inbuilt region smoothness constraint which already exists in MRF. For further processing components of the color pixels tuple are considered as independent random variables. This technique is used in finding edges accurately with the help of edge detection algorithm. MRF considers the area relationship which makes it appealing for displaying surface and contexture of pictures. MRF likewise utilizes expectation maximization (EM) for extraction of objects. This calculation is very unpredictable regarding its scientific definition and profoundly computational. This calculation has pulled in specialists to utilize it in picture division of its capacity to integrate spatial, spectral and textural properties of a picture.

SOFT COMPUTING APPROACHES

Genetic Algorithm (GA)

With the use of color images the quality of segmentation is also increased, but along with it also increases the complexity of problem. Genetic algorithm is a way to handle this complexity. Genetic algorithm is a technique for optimization used in segmentation of images. It's the more favorite choice other than the traditional methods because of its gracefulness and usefulness of solving problems. Functioning of GA is based on the mechanics of natural selection, natural genetics and evolution of organisms allowing an algorithm to adapt. GA prevents from trapping into locally optimal solutions, because most often it's a global searching technique making it to deal with hard combinatorial search problems efficiently. For better solutions GA applies 'survival of the fittest' strategy in their search for better solutions to manipulate and maintain a family, or population, of solutions.

Segmentation based on knowledge, object recognition, Feature extraction and classification of images are the regions in processing of image where, genetic algorithms can be effectively been utilized for. The genetic algorithm trademark is their adequacy and vigor in taking care of noise, insufficient data and uncertainty.

GA performs on the basis of three noteworthy operations

1. Selection
2. Crossover
3. Mutation

These operators, which depend on guidelines of probability, are connected to the populace, and progressive generations are delivered.

The first step in Producing populace of chromosomes is the finding of an ideal solution. With the assistance of operators for each generation will have another arrangement of chromosomes. An objective, or fitness function is characterized by the issue. The parent choice process guarantees that the fittest individuals from the populace have most elevated likelihood of getting to be parents, with the expectation that their posterity will join alluring components, and have unrivaled wellness, to both. The calculation ends either when an arrangement of generation number is come to, or the wellness has come to an "acceptable" level. Arrangements are spoken to by a populace of individual chromosomes, normally portrayed as binary strings. Form genes chromosomes are created, each of which can characterize a particular characteristic. The efficiency in how well a problem is solved a fitness score will be assigned on the basis of performance to each individual. Which in turns on the basis of higher the fitness scores higher the probability of breeding and through crossover and mutation breeding creates next generation. This will be creating a new generation unlike either of parents with crossover uniting chromosomes of two Mutation of individuals which happen only a few percent of the time randomly modify chromosomes of a novel individual.

The use of a genetic algorithm requires the determination of six fundamental issues: (1) chromosome representation, (2) selection function, (3) creation of the initial population, (4) genetic operators making up the reproduction function, (5) fitness function, and (6) termination criteria.

The Genetic Algorithm consists of the following steps:

1. Generate the initial population.
2. Evaluate the fitness of the each individual according to a fitness function.
3. Select the fittest individual for mating.
4. Apply reproductive operators (e.g. crossover, mutation) to create offspring.
5. Evaluate the fitness of the offspring and select the fit individuals from the current generation and the offspring. They form the population of the next generation.
6. Stop if stopping criterion is met, else goes to step 3.

Particle Swarm Optimization

PSO is proposed by James Kennedy and Russell Eberhart in 1995. It's a population based optimization combines self experience with social behavior inspired by birds and fishes. A swarm is an obviously not organized aggregation (populace) of moving element that tends to group together while every individual is by all accounts moving in an irregular heading. The principle of particle swarm optimization is it uses a number of particles that constitute a swarm moving around in the space looking for the best optimal

Figure 13. Genetic algorithm workflow

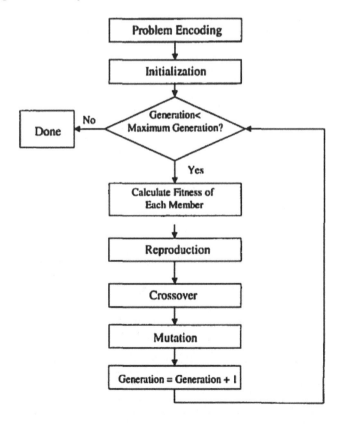

solution. Each particle in search space regulates its flying according to its own flying experience as well as the flying experience of the other particles.PSO is identified with evolutionary calculation, a few similitudes to evolution strategies and genetic algorithms. Every particle is traversed through the space of search, having its location balanced in view of its separation from its very own best position and the separation from the best molecule of the swarm. For every particle the performance is measured by using a function of fitness which relies upon the issues of streamlining. Every i^{th} particle flies through the search space which is n-dimensional Rn and keeps up the accompanying data:

1. x_i, the present position of the molecule i(x-vector).
2. p_i, the individual best position of the molecule i(p-vector).
3. v_i, the present speed of the molecule i(v-vector).

Populaces introduced by allocating irregular positions and speeds potential arrangements are flown through hyperspace. Every molecule monitors its "best" (most astounding wellness) position in hyperspace.

1.   This is termed as "pbest" for an individual molecule.
2.   It is known as "gbest" for the best in the populace.
3.   It is termed as "lbest" for the best in a characterized territory.

Figure 14. Particle swarm optimization workflow

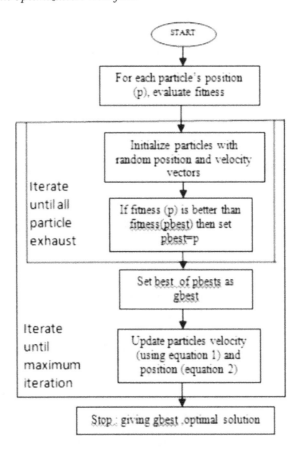

Advantages

1. Concept is simple.
2. Implementation is easy.
3. Efficient in computation.
4. Effectiveness on a vast category of problems.

Fuzzy Logic

Number of strategies utilized for segmentation of images utilizes fuzzy method. Segmentation of image using fuzzy is developing in fame on account of quick expansion of fuzzy set hypothesis, the improvement of different fuzzy set based scientific displaying blends of fuzzy, neural system and genetic algorithm. Fuzzy procedure has its effective and reasonable application in computer vision system, image processing and pattern recognition. Fuzzy grouping includes the undertaking of partitioning information into homogeneous classes or bunch so that things in a similar class are as comparative as could reasonably be expected and things in various classes are as various as likely. Grouping can likewise be considered as a type of compression of data, where a substantial number of tests are changed over into few delegate bunches or models. Contingent upon the information and sort of utilization, distinctive sorts of similitude measures might be utilized to distinguish classes, where the closeness measure controls how the groups are made. A few instances of qualities that can be utilized as comparability list incorporates separation, network and intensity. In non fuzzy or hard grouping, information is separated into fresh bunches, where every information indicate has a place precisely one group.

The objective of bunching is to isolate the given arrangement of information or articles into groups which speaks to subsets or a gathering. The parcel has two properties.

1. Homogeneity (inside the bunch): the information which have a place with one group ought to be as comparative as could be expected under the circumstances.
2. Heterogeneity (between the groups): the information which have a place with various bunch ought to be as various as could reasonably be expected.

Fuzzy nature of the bunching makes it conceivable to beat the obvious way of pattern descriptions, regardless of the possibility that the picked descriptors are not best ones, the calculation may at present be strong to this decision, in some cases issues in deciding the outskirts of the distinctive structures. In this manner it is reasonable to characterize membership, for which an enormous esteem demonstrates expanded certainty that a pixel fit into a specific structure. Finally, it is plausible to incorporate some human expert information all the while, keeping in mind the end goal to diminish the perplexity near the edges of coronal structure.

Edge detection strategies based on fuzzy are widely utilized for segmentation of image. Capable fuzzy strategy based edge discovery strategy which would yield great division comes about on demand of some edge tracking procedures and once in a while even without use of edge tracking strategies. The regular set hypothesis depends on a membership valued as binary, which suggests that a specific component in addition has a place with a specific set or it doesn't fit into it. A crisp set is characterized as one whose components completely fit into the set and they have all around characterized normal traits, which can be measured quantitatively. In a crisp set the continuous attributes are similarly shared by every one of the components of the set. On the other hand, in fuzzy sets the level of enrollment of a component to the set is shown by values of membership, which signify the level to which the component has a place with the set. The membership esteem lies in the vicinity of 0 and 1, with participation "0" demonstrating no enrollment and "1" showing full enrollment of the component. In a crisp set, the enrollment estimations of its components are whichever 0 or 1. The enrollment of a component z in a fuzzy set is gained utilizing a participation work $\mu(x)$ that maps every component having a place with the fuzzy set XF to the interval [0, 1].

Image Processing by fuzzy methods is the gathering of all methodologies that comprehend, processing and representation of images; their features and segments as fuzzy set. There are two huge reasons on the utilization of fuzzy methods in processing of image. (i) Fuzzy procedures are powerful apparatuses for representation and processing of knowledge. (ii) Fuzzy procedures can deal with the in-clearness and vagueness proficiently. The in-clearness in picture processing is owed to ambiguity in grayness, uncertain data, and geometrical fuzziness. A case of vagueness is the pixel's brightness (Ambiguity in grayness), the edge of the segments (geometrical fuzziness) and finding a vehicle in the picture (knowledge uncertainty). The fuzzy methodologies for extraction of objects are isolated into four methodologies as sketched out in. The methodologies are 'Division by means of thresholding', 'Division through grouping', 'Segmentation based on Rules' and 'Supervised Segmentation' .

Fuzzy C Means Algorithm (FCM)

The method of classifying objects in such a way that samples of the same group are similar to one another than to the other different groups is known as clustering. There are many clustering techniques which can be divided into hard clustering and fuzzy clustering scheme each of them having their own properties. In conventional or hard clustering technique each data set point is being restricted to exactly one cluster which results segmentation to be very crisp in nature that is every pixel is just belonging to one class only. Because of this limitation it creates issues in many real life situations such as poor contrast, limited spatial resolution, overlapping intensities, noise etc making difficult for hard clustering. This limitation of hard clustering is overcome by fuzzy clustering methods which with the help of membership function produces the ides of partial membership belonging. Fuzzy c means is the commonly used and studied unsupervised classification method used for image segmentation. FCM also can also retain much more information as compared to other traditional methods and it does have robust characteristics for ambiguity. This technique along with its derivates has been used for image segmentation, data mining, classification and pattern recognition. FCM mainly works on noise free images because of its limitation to convey any information about spatial context. Fuzzy clustering method can also be used for modeling and image data analysis. Clustering is the technique which requires high volume of computation and is been used for pattern recognition in image processing. And due to the high computational this method require frequent disk access causing inefficiency in the system. So to reduce this some parallel algorithms can be used for increasing the efficiency and performance of such systems.

Fuzzy C – means method proposed by Y. Yang

Advantages

1.   It gives better performance than K-means.
2.   It converges very well and it's an unsupervised technique.

Disadvantages

1. It is sensitive to noise.
2. It is computationally expensive.
3. Determination of fuzzy membership is difficult.

Active Contours or Snake

The theory of active contours models was primarily introduced in 1987. Segmentation of images or extraction of objects with the help of active contours model (Snakes) was initiated by Kass. An active contour is an energy limiting procedure that identifies determined elements inside a picture. It is an adaptable surface which can be progressively adjusted to required edges or it can be utilized to programmed objects extraction. It comprises of an arrangement of control focuses joined by straight lines. The dynamic form is depicted by the quantity of control focuses and also progression of each other. Fitting dynamic forms to shapes in pictures is an intelligent system. The client must suggest an underlying form, which is very near the proposed shape. The shape will then be pulled in to highlights in the picture removed by interior vitality producing an attractor picture.

Active contour models (snakes) target is to apply division strategy to a picture by doing distortion to the contours initially towards the limit of the interest of object. This is finished by distorting an underlying contour to limiting the function for energy which characterized on contours. There are two segments in the energy (i)the interior energy of deformation which is little when the contour is smooth. (ii) potential energy: which is little when the counter is adjusted to the edges of the picture. Both parts are shape integrals regarding a parameter of contour. The fundamental favorable position of snake models is the capacity of snakes to give a straight depiction of the protest amid the season of merging without including additional preparing. Snakes can be spoken to by two models (i) models based on edge (ii) region based models. The traits of the picture decides the model we ought to pick.

The idea behind deformable models, or active contours, for extraction of object is very basic. The client indicates an early figure for the contour, which is then moved by picture driven powers to the limits of the yearning objects. In such models, two sorts of powers are considered - the inward strengths, characterized inside the curve, are proposed to keep the model smooth amid the deformation procedure, while the external forces, which are ascertained from the hidden picture information, are planned to push the model toward an object limit or other wanted components inside the picture. One method for depicting this curve is by utilizing an explicit parametric form, which is the approach utilized as a part of snakes. This causes issues when the curves need to experience part or converging, amid their development to the coveted shape. To address this many-sided quality, the certain dynamic form approach, rather than expressly taking after the moving interface itself, takes the novel interface and inserts it in higher dimensional scalar capacity, particular over the total picture. The utilization of level set process has given greater adaptability and comfort in the usage of active contours.

Preferences

1. Snakes have demonstrated helpful for intelligent detail of image contours.
2. The snake demonstrate give a brought together treatment to a gathering of visual issues that have been treated diversely before.

3. The snakes gives various generally isolated neighborhood minima to further levels of processing.

Disadvantage

1. Requires strong image gradients.

Neural Network

The aftereffect of picture segmentation is an arrangement of contours removed from the picture that on the whole cover the entire picture. An artificial neural system is a recreation of a real sensory system. It comprises in various neurons that opposite with each other. This artificial computational model of a real sensory system was suggest in 1943 by McCulloch and Pitts. Since 1990, ANN has come to be utilized as an alternate approach for picture segmentation. Their benefits, for example, elegant degradation within the sight of noise, their ability to be utilized as a part of real-time applications and the simplicity of executing them with VLSI processors, prompted a prospering of ANN-based strategies for segmentation. All sorts of neural systems have been connected with an alternate level of achievement. The for the most part utilized being Kohonen and Hopfield ANNs.

The NN-based picture segmentation procedures can for the most part be partitioned into two classes: unsupervised and supervised techniques. Supervised strategies require master human contribution for segmentation. Generally this implies human experts are painstakingly choosing the training information that is then utilized to form sections of pictures. Unsupervised procedures are incompletely or completely frequent. Client intercession may be important sooner or later in the system to enhance execution of the techniques, yet the results ought to be pretty much human free. An unsupervised division method consequently partitions the pictures without administrator mediation.

Working

With the end goal of extraction of objects at first, the feed forward neural systems are introduced and prepared with quick back-propogation calculation. In the wake of preparing, these systems are reproduced. The different components take out from the picture are appointed as the input examples to the ANNs. As the system is two layered, two enactment capacities are utilized. For preparing the system, imperatives, for example, sum squared mistake performance function which is utilized to process the execution of the system amid preparing at whatever point prepare is called. It is best to prepare the system on both noisy and perfect vectors, with the goal that system can hold noisy information vectors. Until system has low total squared mistake it has been prepared on perfect vectors. All preparation is done utilizing back-propagation with both versatile learning rate and stimulus with the function prepare box. A discretionary parameter is characterized to set the quantity of epochs among input amid preparing. At last a prepared system is made and this prepared system is additionally mimicked and include extraction is done utilizing wavelets.

Most of the techniques require sample data and a priori knowledge. This problem can be solved by using another method of artificial intelligence – genetic algorithms (GAs). In classical methods like thresholding, edge detection and texture segmentation genetic algorithm have been already used. Neural network is another approach for removing the necessity of predefined knowledge with the use of PCNN and LEGION. They have a high efficiency in terms of their flexibility and lack of a priori information. There is no general applicable framework or method has been found for image segmentation or object segmentation, even though some results in that course are promising.

Advantages

1. It is generally used for medical image segmentation.
2. Its main advantage is not dependent on the probability density distribution function.

Disadvantages

1. It is computationally complex.
2. It cost and memory is also high.
3. Overtraining of nodes should be avoided.

CONCLUSION

The segmentation of image using diverse methods, for instance, genetic algorithms, fuzzy logic and competitive neural network have been discussed conversely with the ordinary strategies. By differentiating fuzzy and neural system, segmentation of image using neural framework (Competitive)is better approach when stood out from fuzzy grouping methodologies. The genetic algorithms in segmentation of image in like manner thought to be exchange approach. Genetic Algorithm are used to lessen the multifaceted nature of the issue. In segmentation of image Genetic algorithms are used for the adjustment of the parameters in existing segment counts and are viewed as optimizing agents for functions. Genetic algorithms are instruments on probabilistic and misfortune, not by any stretch of the imagination they will have a comparable kind of headway when associated with a comparative issue. Fuzzy logic and ANN strategies required more information seeing system and more math as appear differently in relation to Gas. Picture division has a couple of uses in various consistent fields like Satellite imaging, Map confirmation, Medical imaging, et cetera. Sensitive Computing system shows more consistency and its trustworthiness over traditional techniques.

In spite of many years of research, there is no inside and out recognized picture segmentation system since picture segmentation is affected by groups of components, for instance, kind of image, shading, noise level, intensity, etc. In this way there is no single calculation that is correlated on an extensive variety of pictures and nature of issue. As a result of each and every above segment, picture division still remains a noteworthy pending issue in the regions of picture processing. Methods that are specific to particular applications much of the time fulfill better execution and the assurance of proper approach to manage a division issue can be a troublesome issue. A singular approach to manage parcel all grouping of pictures may be in every practical sense unfeasible. The past data on the picture can give better results and gives customer the choice to pick appropriate system to segment the image.

REFERENCES

Alshennawy, A. A., & Aly, A. A. (2009). Edge Detection In Digital Images Using Fuzzy Logic Technique. *World Academy of Science, Engineering and Technology, 51*, 178–186.

Berzins, V. (1984). Accuracy of laplacian edge detectors. *Accuracy of Laplacian Edge Detector Computer Vision, Graphics, and Image Processing, 27*(2), 195–210. doi:10.1016/S0734-189X(84)80043-2

Borji, A., & Hamidi, M. (2007). Evolving a Fuzzy Rule-Base for Image Segmentation. *International Journal of Intelligent Systems and Technologies*, 178-183.

Kuruvilla, J., Sankar, A., & Sukumaran, D. (n.d.). A Study on image analysis of Myristica fragrans for Automatic Harvesting. *IOSR Journal of Computer Engineering*.

Lakshmi, S., & Sankaranarayanan, V. (2010). *A study of Edge Detection Techniques for Segmentation Computing Approaches. IJCA*.

Mehrara, H., Zahedinejad, M., & Pourmohammad, A. (2009). Novel Edge Detection Using BP Neural Network Based on Threshold Binarization. *Second International Conference on Computer and Electrical Engineering*, 408-412.

Mettam, G. R., & Adams, L. B. (1999). How to prepare an electronic version of your article. In B. S. Jones & R. Z. Smith (Eds.), *Introduction to the electronicage* (pp. 281–304). New York: E-Publishing Inc.

Muller, H., Michoux, N., Bandon, D., & Geissbuhler, A. (2004). A review of content based image retrieval systems in medical applications clinical benefits and future directions. *International Journal of Medical Informatics, 73*(1), 1–23. doi:10.1016/j.ijmedinf.2003.11.024 PMID:15036075

Patil, A.J., Patil, C.S., Karhe, R.R., & Aher, M.H. (n.d.). Comparative Study of Different Clustering Algorithms. *International Journal of Advanced Research in Electrical, Electronics and Instrumentation Energy*.

Senthilkumaran, N., & Rajesh, R. (2008). Edge Detection Techniques for Image Segmentation - A Survey. *Proceedings of the International Conference on ManagingN ext Generation Software Applications*, 749-760.

Setayesh, M., Zang, M., & Jonhnton, M. (2009). A new homogeneity-based approach to edge detection using PSO. *Proc. 24th International Conference Image and Vision Computing*, 231-236. doi:10.1109/IVCNZ.2009.5378404

Zhang, L., Xiao, M., Ma, J., & Song, H. (2009). Edge Detection by Adaptive Neuro-Fuzzy Inference System. *2nd International Congress on Image and Signal Processing, CISP '09*. doi:10.1109/CISP.2009.5304595

Chapter 15
An Innovative Design of RF Energy Harvester for Wireless Sensor Devices

Pankaj Agrawal
Mahatma Gandhi Chitrakoot Gramodaya Vishwavidyalaya, India

Akhilesh Tiwari
Madhav Institute of Technology and Science, India

Uday Pratap Singh
Madhav Institute of Technology and Science, India

ABSTRACT

Due to growing demand of energy, green technologies are highly attractive among researchers because of their non-conventional nature. Energy harvesting is one of their best parts. Very low cost of maintenance and non-polluting nature are major reasons behind their growing demand. However, for ultra-low power applications, such as in wireless sensor devices, the energy scavenging from RF signal is another alternative. In the last few years, a great interest has been seen in microwave power scavenging for charging wireless devices. This chapter presents a RF energy harvesting circuit with tuned π-matching network that resonates at desired incident RF frequency to boost these signals. Various computer intelligent techniques have been used to optimize parameters value of matching circuit. The designed circuit has been analyzed for input power range from -30 dBm to 0 dBm. Approximately 80% maximum PCE is achieved at RF input of 0 dBm with 4 KΩ load. It is also demonstrated that better output power is produced for power range -15 dBm to 0 dBm at higher load values.

INTRODUCTION

Energy harvesting is the most prominent solution to increase efficiency and battery life span of low power wireless devices. In the past few decades the application of wireless devices operated from ultra low power sources have drastically increased in wireless communication system. With technological advance-

DOI: 10.4018/978-1-5225-3531-7.ch015

ment, power requirement of various electrical and electronic devices has decreased, which encouraged researchers to move towards energy harvester to provide continuous power supply for ultra low power devices like wireless sensors. The process of energy harvesting is to collect amounts of radiations from number of available natural and human made energy sources, converting them in to usable electrical energy and store it for charging up wireless sensor devices. Energy is available everywhere in the ambient around us. Table 1 estimate the amount of power hich can be harvested from various energy sources.

From these available energy, RF power is present everywhere whether indoor or outdoor locations. This energy is useful for harvesting purpose in ultra low power applications especially in wireless sensor devices. Radio frequency (RF) signals are the electromagnetic waves lie in the frequency band of 30 MHz to 300 GHz. These waves are being used in wireless information communication like FM radio, AM radio, Digital TV, Wi-Fi, GSM mobile and UHF or microwave communication.

Wireless transmission of energy by electromagnetic waves is very first demonstrated by Heinrich Hertz (Brown, 1984). He represented the generation of RF signal by employing a system having gap with very high potential difference across it. These signals were detected by using another gap in metal ring at receiver point. This work is further carried out by Nikola Tesla for RF power transmission in 1989 at Colorado. Another attempt of wireless power transmission using RF waves is carried out by H. V. Noble during early 1930's in the Westinghouse Laboratory by using identical 100 MHz dipoles as transmitter and receiver both. He got success to transfer hundred watts of power. After the development of microwave generators and waveguides in late 1950's, wireless transmission increases rapidly. Different wireless devices like FM Radio, DTH receiver, Cellular mobile phone and Wi-Fi work with different frequency and power levels. They continuously receive RF signal from large number of transmitters for their operation (Khalfi, Hamdaoui, Ghorbel, Guizani & Zhang, 2016). Limited battery life span of such wireless devices is major motivation behind the companies and research groups to encourage them to develop new technologies which enable them to operate for an enhanced period of time. It is also possible to energise battery of these devices with freely available RF signals received by them, called RF energy harvesting or power scavenging. Now days, energy harvesting from low power Radio frequency (RF) signal is an attractive and very promising field. It holds a promising future for generating a required amount of electrical energy for operating wireless communicating electronics devices. In wireless sensor networks, low power consumption is a major challenge. From the point of view of system cost and

Table 1. Estimation of harvested energy (Nintanavongsa et. al., 2012)

Energy Sources	Harvested Power Density
1. Light energy (a) Indoor (b) Outdoor	10 µw / cm^2 10 mw / cm^2
2. Temperature difference (a) Human (b) Industry	25 µw / cm^2 1 - 10 mw / cm^2
3. Vibration energy (a) Human (b) Industry	4 µw / cm^2 100 µw / cm^2
4. RF energy (a) GSM network (b) WiFi network	0.1 µw / cm^2 1 µw / cm^2

lifetime, energy dissipation in wireless sensor networks has become an emerging and active research field. In last decades the size and amount of power supply has been drastically reduced for many devices which require very less amount of power to recharge the battery (Al-Lawati, Al-Busaidi & Nadir, 2012). Wireless sensor networks (WSN) used in environment, agriculture and structures application demands continuous availability of power sources with long lifetime. With emerging growth of wireless communication system, massive amount of RF energy broadcasted through huge number of public service signal sources like cell phone towers, handheld radios, Wi-Fi networks and television (T.V.) or radio broadcast stations (Olgun, Chen & Volakis, 2012). Hence it is very useful to collect this energy and may provide to different wireless devices such as wearable medical sensors, headsets, microcontrollers, cell phones and so on, which may increase their battery life or even may avoid the requirement of battery through this technique. Since huge amount of ambient RF energy is available, spread over several frequency bands according to their application areas. Table 2 represents the amount of power transmitted by various RF sources (Arrawatia, Baghini & Kumar, 2011).

From table 2 it is clear that ample amount of energy is available in environment for harvesting applications. Hence it is possible to receive them in combined form and converted into equivalent electrical energy by employing appropriate circuit. It is an alternate way to provide energy solution for ultra low power wireless sensor devices or circuits which operate on microwatts, which is the form of renewable energy. In this process freely available high frequency environmental energy is transformed into applicable electrical energy with the help of non linear Schottky diodes.

Since signal transmission takes place from mobile phone towers throughout the day, they work as perpetual sources of accessible energy. Received signal power from RF sources may be estimated by Friis transmission equation as given by equation 1.

$$\mathrm{P}_r = \frac{P_t G_t G_r}{\left(\frac{4\pi d}{\lambda}\right)^2} \cdot \mathrm{P}_r = \frac{P_t G_t G_r}{\left(\frac{4\pi d}{\lambda}\right)^2} \cdot \tag{1}$$

Where

P_r = Power received at receiver

Table 2. Power Delivered by different RF signal transmitter

Source	Frequency	Available Power
FM Radio system	88 – 108 MHz	Tens of Kwatt
TV Transmitter	180 – 220 MHz	Tens of Kwatt
Cell Tower	869–890 MHz (CDMA) 930–960 MHz (GSM 900) 1810–1880 MHz (GSM 1800) 2110–2170 MHz (GSM 3G) 18550–1990 MHz (GSM 4G LTE)	10 to 20 Kwatt
Wi-Fi Network	2.45–5.8 GHz	Few watt

P_t = Power transmitted

G_t = Gain of transmitter antenna

G_r = Gain of receiver antenna

d = Distance between the transmitter and receiver

λ = Wavelength of received signal

Although it is very small because most of the power is dissipated as heat or absorbed by other materials. Eqn. 1 reveals that power intercepted at receiver is a function of both frequency and distance from RF transmitter. Variation in received power with distance from cell tower (GSM 900 band) is analysed in (Arrawatia, Diddi, Kochar, Baghini & Kumar, 2012) by considering transmitter antenna gain 17 dB and receiver antenna gain 9 dB at 950 MHz signal frequency. Received signal power was -9 dBm, -3 dBm, 8 dBm and 17 dBm at 200 m, 100 m, 50 m and 10 m respectively from transmitter. This observation proves that as distance from cell tower increases received signal strength going to decrease exponentially. Hence tiny amount of RF power is received at wireless devices. A study on cell tower radiation is done in (Kumar, 2010) which demonstrate the variation of RF signal strength at different places. Measurement of radiations from cell phone tower was carried out at various locations in Delhi, Gurgaon and Mumbai which are given in Table 3.

The measured power is maximum upto 0 dBm at Delhi-Gurgaon Highway after Toll Naka because there were 3 cell towers near the highway which increased the received power. Whereas in residential areas measured power is very less which proves requirement of highly efficient system design for RF energy harvesting. In this manuscript authors have reviewed the various radio frequency (RF) energy harvester circuits which utilized different rectifier and voltage boosting circuit. Operation of energy harvester is explored. An innovative design of RF energy harvesting circuit for wireless sensor network devices is presented with π-matching network whose parameters value are optimized to provide better matching and enhanced circuit power conversion efficiency. Effect of variation in input signal power, signal frequency and variable load on output voltage and conversion efficiency have been analysed and discussed.

RF ENERGY HARVESTING SYSTEM

Fundamental block diagram of RF energy harvester is shown in fig. 1 which depicts the hardware requirements of designed system. It describes the process of energy harvesting involved in designed system.

It consist of receiving antenna, rectifier circuit and storage device to provide continuous DC output.

Receiving Antenna

An antenna is essential element for RF energy harvesting. It captures the incident RF signal power at the receiver and transport it to the connected sensor node. It is a metallic rod or piece of wire which can transmit or receive RF signal. It is a means of transition between free space and guided device. The

Table 3. Measurement of received RF power and power density (Kumar, 2010)

Location	Measured Power in dBm	Power Density in μW/m²
Delhi-Gurgaon Highway, near Toll Naka	0	70686
Khar Bridge, Mumbai	0	70686
Worli Naka	-4	28274
Tilak Bridge, Dadar	-4	28274
Bandra Bridge	-6	17756
Airport Bridge	-6	17756
Near Hub mall, Goregaon	-10	7069
IIT Bombay, Main Building	-10	7069
JK Cement group, Worli	-12	4460
Ustav Chowk, Kharghar	-12	4460
Siddhivinayak Temple	-14	2814
Race Course, Haji Ali	-14	2814
Powai Plaza	-14	2814
Vile Parle	-16	1776
Peddar Road (Punjab National Bank)	-16	1776
Poddar Medical College	-16	1776
Vashi Highway, near Turbhe	-18	1120
Andheri Bridge	-18	1120
Nerul Bridge	-20	707
Vivero pre School	-22	446
Powai police station	-22	446
L&T Bridge	-24	281.4
Rajeev Gandhi nagar	-26	177
On road near Evita	-28	112
D-Mart, Hiranandani, Powai	-34	28
Poddar Road, opposite Mukesh Ambani Residence	-36	17.8

Figure 1. Fundamental block diagram of RF energy harvester

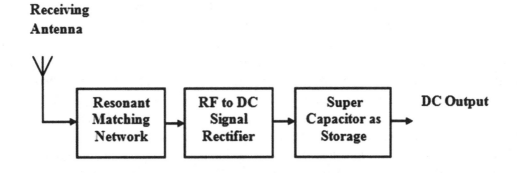

guided device may in the form of coaxial cable, parallel wire line or hollow waveguide which transport electromagnetic energy between transmitter and receiver. Receiving antenna intercepts RF radiations incident from different sources (Ramesh & Rajan, 2014) and convert it in to equivalent electrical signal through electromagnetic induction process. A typical antenna may be considered as series combination of AC voltage source and impedance. Variation of magnetic field in RF signal induces electric potential across the antenna conductors which produces alternating current equivalent to incident RF signal. Hence antenna works as a transducer (Masotti, Costanzo & Adami, 2013) which converts electromagnetic radiation in to electrical energy. Power delivered by antenna is very much affected by effective antenna aperture and its directive gain. It is the amount of maximum power density provides by actual antenna in particular direction compared to reference antenna. Other key parameters which affect the received power are polarisation, path loss, antenna efficiency and directivity. According to requirement antenna may be single, dual or multiband (Shrestha, Noh & Choi, 2013; Zhao, Xu, Yin, Lu, Vue, Gong, Wei & Wang, 2015; Uzun, 2015; Raj, 2016). Since different cell operator transmit signal at different frequencies, hence it is more favourable to use multiband antenna with wide band width (Sun, Guo, He & Zhong, 2013). When the impedance of connected load is equal to the antenna impedance, it supplies maximum power to the connected circuit, called matching condition. Under matched condition the developed voltage from antenna to connected load is given by equation 2.

$$V_{L} = 2\sqrt{2P_{in}R_{a}} \ \frac{R_{L}}{R_{a} + R_{L}} \cdot \ V_{L} = 2\sqrt{2P_{in}R_{a}} \ \frac{R_{L}}{R_{a} + R_{L}} \tag{2}$$

Where

R_{L} = Load resistance

R_{a} = Radiation resistance of antenna

P_{in} = Available maximum RF input power at antenna

Equation 2 indicates that antenna with higher antenna radiation resistance provides more output voltage.

Resonant Matching Network

It is a resonant voltage boosting network which maximizes the signal power supplied from antenna to rectifier circuit. One of the major issues of harvesting circuit is to transfer received power completely from antenna to rectifier or voltage multiplier circuit without any loss. This is possible only with appropriately designed matching network having optimized components. Impedance of rectifier circuit is non linear function of incoming signal frequency and power, so broadband matching network is necessary for efficient power transfer. If harvesting circuit does not have proper matching, RF power will get reflected from rectifier circuit which give rise to formation of standing waves in the harvester between antenna and rectifier. These standing waves comprise maxima and minima depending on relative phase of incident and reflected wave. Matching network works on the principle of maximum power transfer condition (Beh, Imura & Hori, 2010). According to this principle to transfer maximum power from source to load, impedance of source network must be equal to complex conjugate value of load impedance. Hence this network matches antenna impedance with rectifier impedance to minimize reflection losses.

Various types of matching network topologies may be used such as resistive matching, transformer matching and lumped element matching network. In resistive matching topology matching is achieved through resistive element. Here circuit becomes matched but most of the power will be dissipated as heat in resistive part. So it is not good option. Transformer matching works on the mutual induction phenomenon in which source voltage and current values transformed to other values at load end. But transformer matching can match only real part of source and load impedance, whereas rectifier or voltage multiplier circuit consist of both real and imaginary part in its impedance. So transformer matching does not provide complete solution of matching because it does not provide matching for imaginary part which is a major cause of energy reflection from load. Lumped element matching network may be classified as L-type and π-type matching network comprises inductor and capacitor elements. The L-type matching circuit configuration consist of single L-C network as series inductor with shunt capacitor or series capacitor with shunt inductor depending on the load impedance as shown in figure 2. The bandwidth of single L-C matching circuit can be increased by employing another lumped parameter with existing network. It provides controllable quality factor with improved impedance matching.

RF to DC Signal Rectifier

To charge the batteries of wireless devices, DC voltage is required (Kamalinejad, Keikhosravy, Mirabbasi & Leung, 2013). Hence boosted RF signal delivered from matching circuit is converted into applicable DC signal by using RF to DC signal rectifier circuit (Nimo, Beckedahl, Ostertag & Reindl, 2015; Karolak, Taris, Thierry, Deval, Begueret & Mariano, 2012). Schottky diodes and MOSFET transistors are mostly used to design rectifier circuit. These devices may be used in three different configurations as half wave rectifier, full wave bridge rectifier and voltage multiplier. The performance of rectifier circuit is estimated by the saturation current, device junction capacitance and forward resistance of the diode. It determines the power conversion efficiency of rectifier circuit. The received signal power is affected by separation between transmitter and receiver antenna, transmitted power and frequency, antenna configuration and polarization as described by Friss transmission equation. Due to which rectifier circuit produces small DC output. To increase DC voltage at output it is more appropriate to use zero bias schottky diode (Theilmann, Presti, Kelly & Asbeck, 2010; Zbitou, Latrac & Toutain, 2006) to build rectifier circuit. These alleviate RF to DC conversion efficiency at small input power. These diodes may be used in half wave or full wave bridge rectifier configuration. Later is more suitable because it gives high output. Such configuration using schottky diodes and diode connected n-type MOSFET is shown in figure 3.

N-type or P-type MOSFET (metal oxide semiconductor field effect transistor) with low threshold voltage may be used in place of schottky diodes because they increase voltage sensitivity of the rectifier,

Figure 2. L-type matching network configuration

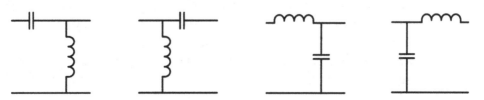

Figure 3. Full wave bridge rectifier for RF to DC conversion

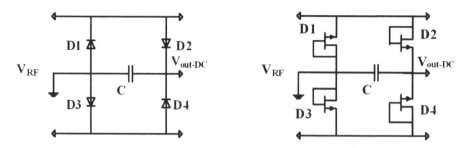

but having high substrate losses. The operation of full wave bridge rectifier can be understood in two half cycle. First is positive half cycle where RF input is positive and other is negative half cycle in which RF input is negative. Let V_{th} is threshold voltage of the diode and V_{RF} is amplitude of input RF signal. During positive half cycle of the RF input, diode D2 and D3 conduct, whereas D1 and D4 remain in reverse bias. In the negative half cycle of the RF input, diode D1 and D4 conduct whereas diode D2 and D3 remain in reverse bias. In both cycle flow of current in load capacitor C takes place in same direction, hence the output DC voltage across capacitor becomes equal to $V_{RF} - 2*V_{th}$. To start rectifying operation, it is required that the value of input RF signal must be greater than the twice of threshold voltage of diode. To increase DC output, voltage multiplier circuit with significant number of stage may be used in place of full wave rectifier because it works as charge pump and gives high efficiency. Charge pump rectifiers are most widely used in ultra low power energy harvesting circuit.

LITERATURE REVIEW

In the past several design style of RF energy harvester have been proposed but all of them are not executable for energy scavenging from available ambient energy. It is common practise to use HSMS or SMS Skywork hot carrier diodes to build RF energy harvesting system. These diodes having metal semiconductor junction due to which there threshold voltage is approximately zero and they can efficiently respond to microwave frequency. Various RF to DC signal rectifier design implementation topologies using schottky diodes used in literature are shown in figure 4. Full wave RF to DC converter may be designed by using Villard or Dickson voltage multiplier circuit (Kadupitiya, Abeythunga, Ranathunga & De Silva, 2015; Uzun, 2016).

These circuits perform voltage multiplication action to improve output DC voltage. The authors in (Younus, Hegde, Prabhakar & Vinoy, 2016) designed a RF energy harvester chip using 180nm CMOS technology. The designed circuit having capability to harvest energy from minimum -12 dBm input power level. Designed circuit employs two stage voltage doubler for RF to DC conversion. To enhance output voltage such five stages are connected in cascade. They achieved 0.5 volt output at -10 dBm input power level and 0.4 volt at -12 dBm input power with conversion efficiency of 30% at 865 – 868 MHz signals. An RF energy harvester using HSMS – 2852 Schottky diode to harvest energy from GSM – 900 MHz band signal is designed in (Uzun, 2016). Circuit is fabricated using two stage Dickson voltage multiplier with L-matching network and achieved maximum 45% conversion efficiency at input power level of 0dBm. In (Agrawal, 2016) researcher presented a half wave rectifier using HSMS – 2852 Schottky diode with

Figure 4. (a) Half Wave Rectifier (b) Villard or Cockcraft-Walton or Grienacher Voltage Multiplier (c) Dickson Voltage Multiplier (d) Modified Villard or Cockcraft-Walton or Grienacher Voltage Multiplier

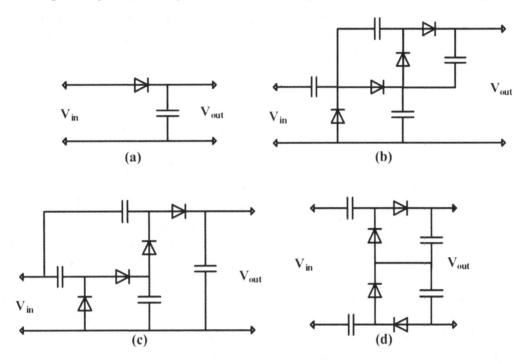

L – matching network and achieved 0.5 volt output with -10 dBm input power level at 900 MHz signal. To increase RF to DC conversion efficiency, a triple band RF energy harvester employing number of voltage multiplier circuit at DTV (Digital Television) 575 MHz, GSM 900 MHz and 2.45 GHz Wi-Fi frequency bands was designed in (Uzun, 2015). The authors achieved average 43% conversion efficiency for individual system and maximum 68% efficiency with triple band harvesting system. A dual band RF energy scavenging circuit using HSMS – 2820 Schottky diode is presented in (Shariati, Rowe, Scott & Ghorbani, 2015). The authors achieved 54.3% effective efficiency with 72.8 mV output at -10 dBm input power level for 490 & 860 MHz dual frequency band. Harvesting circuit is prepared by connecting Schottky diode in Dickson voltage doubler configuration with optimized matching circuit parameters.

A low power RF energy harvesting circuit integrated in 65 nm CMOS process is presented in (Liu, Mu, Ma, Tu, Zhu & Yang, 2015). A 10 stage rectifier is designed in association with 2nd order threshold compensation and low power management unit which comprises a voltage limiter, voltage sensor and a capacitor less LDO (Low Dropout regulator). This harvester works in two modes, one is charge mode and other is burst mode. Second order compensation technique removes the body effect in standard CMOS circuit. Since the received RF energy is very much small to run the whole system continuously, therefore designed system works discontinuously in charge and burst mode. In the charge mode designed circuit consume only 97 nA with -21.4 dBm (7.24 µWatt) RF signal and provide maximum 10 mA current to load at 1 Volt output.

Carbon nanotube field effect transistor (CNFET) based RF energy harvesting circuit is developed in (Kumar & Islam, 2015). A voltage multiplier circuit is developed by employing diode connected CNFET in 8 – stage voltage doubler configuration. The designed circuit is optimized to work with 60 mV AC input signal and after AC to DC conversion it provides 389 mV DC output. Maximum conversion ratio greater than 6 is achieved at input frequency of 900 MHz. To wirelessly charge passive deep brain simulation devices (DBS), a rectenna based RF energy harvesting circuit is presented in (Hosain, Kouzani, Tye, Kaynak & Berk, 2015). The authors formed RF to DC converter circuit operates at 915 MHz signal using 4 different techniques which are Delon doubler, Greinacher voltage tripler, Delon voltage quadrupler and two stage charge pumped architectures using HSMS – 285C Schottky diode. They achieved maximum 78%, 73% and 76% conversion efficiency respectively from given architecture at -5 dBm input RF power for varying R_{Load} from 5 to 15 KΩ. It is observed that charge pump based rectifier produces best result and provide 3.24 volt DC output at -5 dBm input power level with 76% conversion efficiency.

Villard voltage doubler architecture based RF energy harvester is investigated in (Kadupitiya, Abeythunga, Ranathunga & De Silva, 2015). A seven stage voltage multiplier circuit is designed using HSMS – 2850 Schottky diode, operated with designed patch antenna. Maximum 2.5 volt DC output is achieved at 900 MHz RF energy signal. Since Schottky diode is a nonlinear device whose input impedance varies with input power level. Some diode work efficiently on high input power whereas some on low input power. Hence to harvest energy efficiently from both low and high input power a combined rectifier circuit is developed (Abdallah, Costantine, Ramadan, Tawk, Ayoub, Christodoulou & Kabalan, 2015) using HSMS – 2860 and HSMS – 2852 Schottky diode. Former is used for high power whereas later is for low input power level. Maximum 50% conversion efficiency is achieved for -10 dBm input RF signal and 81% PCE for 6 dBm input operated at 2.1 GHz.

A 90 – nm CMOS technology based 5 stage cross coupled differential RF to DC rectifier with 7 – bit binary weighted capacitor bank is fabricated in (Stoopman, Keyrouz, Visser, Philips & Serdijn 2014). The authors achieved 1 volt DC output at -27dBm input sensitivity. Power conversion efficiency of 40% is reported at -17 dBm, 868 MHz RF input signal. A rectenna employing SMS – 7630 Schottky diode rectifier is designed and fabricated in (Pham & Pham, 2013). Output power of 11.6 μwatt for 1μwatt/cm³ input power density at 915 MHz and 65.5 μwatt output at 2.45 GHz is achieved. Open circuit output voltage of 1.4 volt is produced at 6μw/m² input power density with 915 MHz RF signal. Another five stage charge pump RF to DC converter using skywork SMS 7630 Schottky diode is reported in (Kim, Vyas, Bito, Niotaki, Collado, Georgiadis & Tentzeris, 2014). It produced 1.8 volt for -15 dBm RF input signal with 19.5% power conversion efficiency for digital TV band 512 – 566 MHz.

For very low input RF signal, an RF to DC converter employing 90 – nm CMOS technology is designed in (Parihar, Kumar, Jha & Sharma, 2014). Authors investigated Villard voltage multiplier circuit and achieved 10% power conversion efficiency at -19 dBm input RF signal with 1 volt DC output at 900 MHz frequency band.

To take advantage of low leakage current and high power conversion efficiency, heterojunction tunnel FET (HTFET) based RF to DC converter have been investigated in (Liu, Li, Vaddi, Ma, Datta & Narayanan, 2014) as shown in figure 5 and 6. Authors evaluated 2-transistor, 4-transistor complementary HTFET and n-type HTFET design with optimized parameters. Maximum 84% power conversion efficiency (PCE) with 4-transistor n-type HTFET and 85% with 4-transistor cross coupled HTFET rectifier is produced at -33.7 dBm and -34.5 dBm input power respectively. They showed maximum 0.5 volt DC output at 0.3 volt input. It has been observed that 2-transistor HTFET rectifier gives low V_{DC} output for low RF input power as compared to 4-transistor HTFET rectifier because of increased leakage power

Figure 5. Two transistor HTFET rectifier

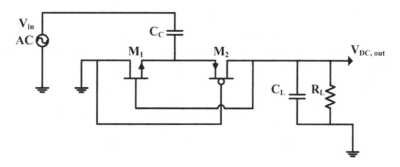

Figure 6. Four transistor HTFET rectifier

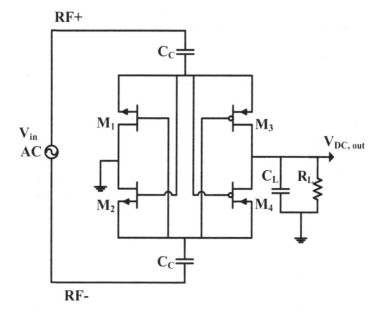

loss. At power higher than -25 dBm 2-transistor HTFET rectifier gives increased V_{DC} output than others due to reduction in power loss because of less and smaller transistor dimension. At more RF input power, due to high V_{RF} input the transistor power dissipation is decreased while other power losses increase. 4-transistor HTFET rectifier gives high power conversion efficiency.

Bridge rectifier based RF to DC converter is presented in (Hosain, Kouzani, Samad & Tye, 2015). A rectifier circuit using HSMS-285C Schottky diode with L – matching network is designed. Maximum 61.55% power conversion efficiency and 1 volt DC output for -10 dBm RF input power of 915 MHz is achieved. Measured bandwidth was 18 MHz from 910 to 928 MHz. Five stage Dickson voltage multiplier based dual band RF to DC converter is investigated in (Saraiva, Borges, Pinho, Goncalves, Santiago, Barroca, Tavares, Gouveia, Carvalho, Balasingham, Velez, Loss & Salvado, 2014) for 900 & 1800 MHz GSM frequency bands. For 0 dBm RF input 22% conversion efficiency and for -4 dBm input 3 volt output with 20% conversion efficiency is produced.

As a new approach, spin diode based RF energy harvester is analysed in (Hemour, Zhao, Lorenz, Houssameddine, Gui, Hu & Wu, 2014).It has been observed that spin diode may increase RF to DC rectification efficiency at very small power. Spin diode is magnetic tuned junction diode having two ferromagnetic electrodes known as reference layer and free layer which are kept apart by insulating layer of MgO (magnesium oxide). Relative alignment of magnetization of free and reference layer after resistance of spin diode. This structure has two stable states at zero volts. One is low resistance when two layer having parallel (P) magnetization and other is high resistance when layers having antiparallel (AP) magnetization. These states may be changed by applying external magnetic field or external voltage due to spin transfer torque. These diodes are mainly used in read heads of hard disk and in magnetic random access memory (MRAM).

As the input impedance of zero bias Schottky diode is non linear and varies with input power, so designing of matching network for different input power level having different element value for efficient RF to DC conversion. Hence dynamic impedance matching network based RF energy harvester is proposed in (Felini, Merenda & Corte, 2014). A control loop is designed by using control unit and variable matching capacitance as shown in figure 7.

Control unit estimates the power level of input RF signal to circuit and varies the capacitance to optimum value for best impedance matching from the set of available discrete capacitance. The input power is estimated from output voltage of rectifier applied to control unit. Circuit is designed with HSMS – 2850 Schottky diode and maximum 21% power conversion efficiency with 1.2 volt DC output at -10 dBm, 868 MHz RF input power is achieved.

To demonstrate the effect of variable threshold voltage of MOSFET on rectifier performance a dynamic threshold MOS (DTMOS) based RF to DC rectifier is developed in (Chouhan & Halonen, 2014). In forward bias, device has low threshold voltage provide high output and in reverse bias, device has high threshold voltage to ensure low leakage loss. A circuit with 180 – nm CMOS technology is fabricated and maximum 23% power conversion efficiency is achieved for -10 dBm, 433 MHz RF input power at load of 10 KΩ.

Voltage doubler type Latour architecture based RF to DC rectifier circuit using parasitic element and microstrip line as matching network is presented in (Mabrouki, Latrach & Lorrain, 2014). Author achieved 38% and 21% power conversion efficiency at -10 dBm & -20 dBm input RF signal respectively with load resistance of 10 KΩ at 850 MHz frequency. A dual band half wave rectifier works on 1800 MHz and 2100 MHz is reported in (Sun, Guo, He & Zhong, 2013). This rectifier used microstrip line

Figure 7. Dynamic impedance matching network

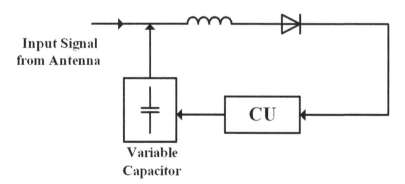

as matching network, HSMS – 2852 Schottky diode as rectifying device and achieved maximum 40% power conversion efficiency with DC output voltage varies between 300 mV to 400 mV for 455 µW/m² input power density.

Threshold self compensation technique based RF to DC rectifier is proposed in (Hameed & Moez, 2013). It consist number of PMOS transistor in cascade in which gate terminal is connected to previous node instead of later node. This scheme induced threshold voltage and provides increased output voltage. Circuit is designed using IBM – 130 nm CMOS process. Author achieved 1 volt DC output for -22 dBm RF input at 915 MHz with 1 MΩ load. A self calibrating cross connected bridge RF to DC rectifier is developed in (Stoopman, Keyrouz, Visser, Philips & Serdijn, 2013) using 90 nm standard CMOS process. Maximum 31.5% conversion efficiency and 1 volt DC output is achieved for -26.3 dBm RF input power at 868 MHz. A comparison of various reported CMOS based RF energy harvester is given in table 4.

Table 4. Comparison of CMOS based RF energy harvesting circuit

RF Input Power	Frequency Used (MHz)	Technology Used	Output Voltage	Peak Conversion Efficiency	Source
-10 dBm	865 - 868	180 nm CMOS	0.5 V	30%	(Younus et. al., 2016)
-27 dBm	868	90 nm CMOS	1 V	40%	(Stoopman et. al., 2014)
-19 dBm	900	90 nm CMOS	1V	10%	(Parihar et. al., 2014)
-10 dBm	433	180 nm CMOS	NA	23%	(Chouhan et. al.,2014)
-22 dBm	915	130 nm CMOS	1V	NA	(Hameed et. al., 2013)
-26.3 dBm	868	90 nm CMOS	1V	31.5%	(Stoopman et. al., 2013)
-19 dBm	900	130 nm CMOS	1V	9%	(Li et. al., 2013)
-19 dBm	950	130 nm CMOS	0.6 V	54%	(Popovic et. al., 2013)
50 µW	915	20 nm HTFET	0.2 V	98%	(Liu et. al., 2013)
-14 dBm	900	130 nm CMOS	2 V	32%	(Scorcioni et. al., 2012)
-17 dBm	915	130 nm CMOS	1.7 V	1%	(Scorcioni et. al., 2012)
-10 dBm	2400	130 nm CMOS	1 V	10%	(Masuch et. al., 2012)
-20 dBm	900	130 nm CMOS	1.2 V	63%	(Karolak et. al., 2012)
-10 dBm	900	180 nm CMOS	2.6 V	46%	(Lin et. al., 2012)
-11 dBm	950	180 nm CMOS	0.84 V	40%	(Arrawatia et. al., 2012)
-19 dBm	915	90 nm CMOS	1.2 V	2%	(Papotto et. al., 2011)
-10 dBm	915	0.25 µm Silicon on Sapphire CMOS	NA	60%	(Theilmann et. al., 2010)
-15 dBm	900	0.35 µm CMOS	1.5 V	13%	(Yao et. al., 2009)
-25 dBm	2200	130 nm CMOS	1 V	NA	(Salter et. al., 2009)
-12 dBm	953	180 nm CMOS	1.2 V	67.5%	(Kotani et. al., 2009)
-22.6 dBm	960	250 nm CMOS	1 V	60%	(Le et. al., 2008)
-11 dBm	900	180 nm CMOS	1.75 V	26.5%	(Yi et. al., 2008)
-14 dBm	920	180 nm CMOS	1 V	5%	(Shameli et. al., 2007)

By employing HSMS – 285C Schottky diode, a half wave rectifier for RF to DC converter is reported in (Singh, Ponnaganti, Prabhakar & Vinoy, 2013). Author established 1.03 volt DC output and maximum 35% conversion efficiency for -10 dBm RF input at 960 MHz. A dual band CMOS RF to DC rectifier using voltage boosting network is reported in (Li, Shao, Shahshahan, Goldsman, Salter & Metze, 2013) with 130 nm CMOS process. Conversion efficiency of 9% and 1 volt DC output is produced for 900 MHz & 1900 MHz bands at -19 dBm RF input signal.

Photo voltaic (PV) cell connected highly efficient CMOS RF to DC converter was developed in (Kotani, 2013). Photo voltaic cell compensates the threshold voltage of MOSFET and improves the RF to DC conversion efficiency. Maximum 30% conversion efficiency at -20dBm RF input power is achieved for 920MHz. RF to DC rectifier using Cockcraft Walton voltage multiplier architecture was reported in (Kanaya, Tsukamoto, Hirabaru, Kanemoto, Pokharel & Yoshida, 2013) as shown in figure 8.

Circuit is designed with HSMS – 286Y Schottky diode and achieved 2.5 volt DC output and maximum 44% PCE for 100 mV, 900 MHz input signal with 10 MΩ load. To receive energy from different frequency band, a triple band highly efficient RF to DC rectifier is reported in (Pham & Pham, 2013). It works on 900 MHz, 1900 MHz and 2.4 GHz (WiFi) frequency band. Proposed circuit is shown in figure 9. There are three inductors L_2, L_3 and L_4 for three matching frequencies. Inductor L_2 provides matching for 900 MHz, L_3 provides matching for 1900 MHz and L_4 for 2.4 GHz. By selecting appropriate value of these inductors, impedance matching for different desired frequency bands may be achieved and these

Figure 8. Four – stage Cockcraft Walton voltage multiplier

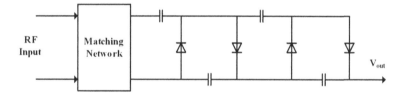

Figure 9. Triple RF to DC rectifier

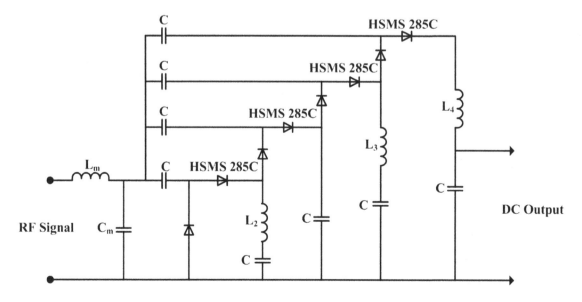

frequencies can be controlled independently. Achieved maximum efficiency was 80% at 940 MHz with RF input power of 10 dBm, 47% at 1950 MHz with 8 dBm RF input and 43% at 2.44 GHz with 16 dBm RF input power. Output DC voltage of 302 mV and 30% PCE is produced when energy is harvested simultaneously for all these three bands with 10 dBm input RF power. Received power was 7.06 μW which was 3.4 times higher than the addition of all power at these three single bands.

Optimized design of RF to DC rectifier using bulk modulation and voltage boosting network is presented in (Zulkifli, Sampe, Islam, Mohamed & Wahab, 2015). Achieved output was 400 mV higher compared to conventional design of existing full wave rectifier using diode connected MOSFET. Voltage across source and bulk V_{sb} of CMOS determines its threshold voltage V_{th}. By employing bulk modulation, threshold voltage V_{th} decreases so that efficiency and output voltage show improvement. A comparison of various reported RF energy harvester based on Schottky diodes is given in table 5.

Antenna also plays a major role in energy harvesting system (Costanzo, Fabiani, Romani, Masotti & Rizzoli, 2010). Design of an antenna for RF energy harvesting having vital role to decide system reliability and overall conversion efficiency (Zeng, Siden, Wang & Nilsson, 2007). General receiving antenna must be so designed that it could deliver maximum RF power to harvester circuit (Ukkonen, Schaffrath, Sydanheimo & Kivikoski, 2006). High gain antenna provides highly efficient harvester. Microstrip patch antenna is an attractive option for RF energy harvesting operation because it has low profile, less bulky and planar structure (Ramesh & Rajan, 2014).

A microstrip antenna (Sim, Shuttleworth, Alexander & Grieve, 2010) consists of a very thin metallic patch placed over a ground plane (Weigand, 2005). The radiating microstrip patch and metallic ground plane are separated by a dielectric material known as substrate as shown in figure 10. Several methods to design high frequency patch antenna is presented in (Ramesh & Rajan 2014) for RF energy harvesting application. The authors achieved 9.815 dB return loss, VSWR of 1.95 and 7.97 dB gain with efficient design. Comparison of various size and design style of microstrip patch antenna used for RF energy harvesting application is explored in (Shrestha, Noh & Choi, 2013).

Figure 10. Three-dimensional view of rectangular patch antenna

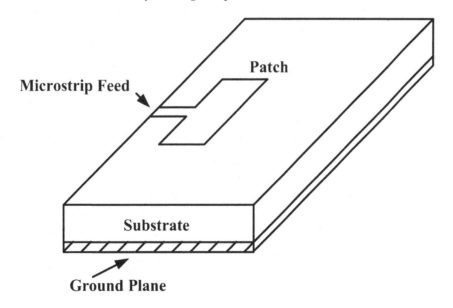

Table 5. Comparison of Schottky diode based RF energy harvesting circuit

RF Input Power	Frequency Used (MHz)	Technology Used	Output Voltage	Peak Conversion Efficiency	Source
-10 dBm	900	Avago HSMS – 2852 HWR	0.5 V	NA	(Agrawal, 2016)
-10 dBm	490 & 860 Dual band	Avago HSMS – 2820	72.8 mV	54.3%	(Shariati et. al., 2015
-10 dBm	915	Avago HSMS – 285C	1 V	61.55%	(Hosain et. al., 2015)
-15 dBm	512 – 566 DTV Band	Skywork SMS – 7630	1.8 V	19.5%	(Kim et. al., 2014
-10 dBm	868	Avago HSMS – 2850	1.2 V	21%	(Felini et. al., 2014)
-10 dBm	960	Avago HSMS – 285C	1.03 V	35%	(Singh et. al., 2013)
-10 dBm	900	Avago HSMS – 286Y	2.5 V	44%	(Kanaya et. al., 2013)
-10 dBm	2400	Avago HSMS – 2850	50 µW	NA	(Alam et. al., 2013)
-10 dBm	900	Avago HSMS – 2852	1.08 V	NA	(Thierry et. al., 2012)
-10 dBm	915	Avago HSMS – 2852	1 V	NA	(Nintanavongsa et. al., 2012)
-15 dBm	550	Schottky Diode	134 mV	18%	(Mikeka et. al., 2011)
-10 dBm	900	Schottky Diode	0.21 V	NA	(Arrawatia et. al., 2011)
-15 dBm	2450	Avago HSMS – 2852	1 V	47%	(Olgun et. al., 2010)
-10 dBm	2450	Skywork SMS – 7630	100 mV	42%	(Vera et. al., 2010)
-10 dBm	2450	Avago HSMS – 2860	NA	34%	(Riviere et. al., 2010)
-10 dBm	900	Avago HSMS – 2850	0.2 V	NA	(Jabbar et. al., 2010)
1.5 µW/cm²	2400	Skywork SMS – 7630	100 mV	38%	(Georgiadis et. al., 2010)

The optimization of antenna designs for metallic and non metallic objects using genetic algorithm (GA) is presented in (Kim & Chung, 2006). GA optimizes the dimension and return loss of designed RF antenna. Different innovative design of RF receiving antenna is proposed in (Stupf, Mittra, Yeo & Mosig, 2006) which provide higher efficiency compare to existing one. A dual band antenna for RF energy harvesting is developed in (Bakkali, Pelegri-Sebastia, Sogorb, Llario, & Bou-Escriva, 2016) which give 25 dB and 13.5 dB return loss at 2.4 GHz and 5 GHz respectively. SMS – 7630 Schottky diode based RF to DC rectifier also designed which produces 1.3 volt DC output for 10 dBm RF input power at 60 cm distance from intended signal generator. SMS – 7630 Schottky diode was selected because of low substrate losses, low forward voltage and very fast switching. For continuous and uninterrupted operation of a glucose sensor implanted in a human body, a dual band antenna have been proposed in (Mouris, Soliman, Ali, Eshrah & Badawi, 2016), which was integrated together with rectifying circuit to provide enough harvested power. A capacitively loaded printed inverted antenna was fabricated on a flexible thin liquid crystal polymer rogers substrate because of its easiness to be implanted in human body. Proposed antenna produces radiation efficiency of 73% and 85% at 1.6 GHz and 2.4 GHz respectively. By employing HSMS – 282P Schottky diode, single stage voltage multiplier was developed. In combination with band pass filter it provides 81% conversion efficiency at 2.4 GHz and 71% at 1.6 GHz RF signal. A frame work on data and energy transfer optimization for charging up mobile device from RF energy harvesting system is reported in (Khalfi, Hamdaoui, Ghorbel, Guizani & Zhang, 2016). Methods for optimized power allocation in multicarrier communication system between base station and mobile devices for communicated data and power available for energy harvesting are proposed. To capture outdoor RF energy and convert it into usable form, two different patch antennas were designed in (Le, Fong & Luong, 2010). First design was a low profile folded shorted patch antenna with small ground plane and wide bandwidth whereas in second design there were four pair of slot embedded in ground plane. The achieved antenna gain was about 3.9 dBi, 5.9 dBi and 6.3 dBi at 867 MHz, 915 MHz and 953 MHz respectively. A 64 element spiral rectenna array with dual circular polarization is proposed in (Hagerty, Helmbrecht, McCalpin, Zane & Popovic, 2004). It works in frequency of 2 to 18 GHz with incident wave of single and multiple frequencies.

A multi band RF energy harvesting for wireless sensing devices by using MEMS switches is investigated in (Raj, 2016). Radio frequency MEMS components may be used as tunable capacitors and inductor in matching network as switches in VCO (voltage controlled oscillator) and resonators. MEMS switches also used in duplexers, band mode selection and to provide time delay in phased arrays and reconfigurable antennas. This technology provide on chip switches with negligible power loss in the range of nano joule level, high quality varactors and oscillators which generate several MHz to GHz frequency signals.

To deliver maximum power a wireless sensor receiver detection system has been presented in (Yang, Chen, Huang, Lu & Chung, 2015). A 915 MHz RF signal generator has been designed using 2×2 patch antenna array and reflection type phase shifters. High gain differential microstrip antenna for RF power harvesting application is proposed in (Arrawatia, Baghini, & Kumar, 2015). Achieved gain was 8.5 dBi at center frequency with VSWR less than 2 for frequency band 870 MHz to 1050 MHz and antenna efficiency was 80%. Complete RF energy harvester used with this antenna has 65.3% maximum conversion efficiency with 3 KΩ load.

A dual band patch antenna for high efficiency RF to DC rectifier is designed in (Zhao, Xu, Yin, Lu, Vue, Gong, Wei & Wang, 2015) for RF energy harvesting application. It radiates effectively at 920 MHz and 2.4 GHz. Lower resonant frequency and higher output current is presented by using meander slot and shorting probe. Return loss of -20.67 dB at 920MHz & -22.53 dB at 2.45 GHz has achieved with 0.2dBi antenna gain at 920MHz. High efficiency four stage voltage doubler as rectifier as also designed using HSMS – 286C, which provide78% conversion efficiency at dual frequency band in association with patch antenna. Produced output voltage was 7.62 volt at input power level of 15 dBm. Compact circularly polarized microstrip antenna (CMPA) with slits is reported in (Nasimuddin, Qing & Chen, 2009) for RFID application. To reduce antenna size, slits are diagonally cut onto the square shaped patch having circular polarization operation. Achieved bandwidth was 4 MHz at 920 MHz center frequency.

To increase efficiency of RF energy harvester, the authors in (Henrique, Lorenz, Hemour, Li, Xie, Gauthier, Fay & Wu, 2015) used backward tunnel diode in RF to DC rectifier. They demonstrated good conversion efficiency at 1μW input power range because it has low parasitic junction capacitance. They produced 3.8% conversion efficiency at -40 dBm input and 18.2% for -30 dBm input power at 2.35 GHz RF signal. The authors reported 25.3% increment in efficiency as compared to ideal Schottky diode of same junction resistance and approximately 10 times higher efficiency compared to real HSMS – 285B Schottky diode. Backward tunnel diode produced improved results because it has less parasitic losses and higher intrinsic current responsivity.

A hybrid rectifier circuit which can efficiently harvest energy from combination of RF signal and low frequency PZT (piezoelectric) signal is presented in (Trung, Feng, Haftiger & Chakrabartty, 2014). The piezoelectric signal is used to provide biasing for cross coupled differential rectifier chain which reduces its threshold voltage. So that low amplitude RF signal can be efficiently harvested. The designed harvester circuit was operated with 10 MHz RF signal and 1 KHz PZT signal. The designed chip was fabricated using 0.5μm CMOS process. A power management circuit for charging up a thin film battery is developed in (Popovic, Korhummel, Dunbar, Scheeler, Dolgov, Zane, Falkenstein & Hagerty, (2014). It consists of low power microcontroller which optimizes function of connected transceiver and power reception circuit to achieve increase system conversion efficiency. It works in the power range of 20 – 200 μW/cm^2 input power density with 1.9 GHz cellular and 2.4 GHz ISM frequency bands. Microcontroller unit communicates with sensor and transceiver, reduces passive components and dissipated power. It maintains balance of energy distribution from input RF energy to available stored energy and energy required by sensor and transceiver for their efficient operation.

An efficient design of rectenna for RF energy harvesting application is reported in (Moon, Cho, Kim & Jung, 2013). It consists of broadband dipole antenna and rectangular ground plane supported by two ground walls. These ground walls have function of supporting and harvesting energy from back radiation of proposed rectenna. The amount of harvested energy was 1.74% of input power. A triple band antenna which may be used to harvest energy from 900, 1900 MHz and 2.4 GHz WiFi sources is proposed in (Masotti, Costanzo & Adami, 2013). This antenna is developed by using composite right left hand (CRLH) transmission line with different design techniques. Also an efficient multiband RF to DC rectifier is designed by modifying Dickson voltage doubler structure. The authors have achieved 80%, 46% and 42% conversion efficiency at 940 MHz, 1950 MHz and 2440MHz respectively. Designed system have collected 6.6 times more power compared to single 900 MHz and 3.4 times more than combined individual bands.

RF power harvesting circuit energized through dual power source as from digital TV (DTV) signal and RF signal is implemented in (Mikeka & Arai, 2011). The authors used single pole double through (SPDT) switches for channel selection. Designed system produced 1.5 volt DC with 24 mA nominal current in 80 minute with -5 dBm input power. To enhance chip area utilization, a rectenna with 130 nm CMOS based differential full wave rectifier is reported in (Le, Fong & Luong, 2010). At the perimeter of chip, loop antenna is placed while remaining area is occupied by other circuitries. This scheme increases area efficiency of designed rectenna chip. The author achieved 0.5 μW output power from 20dBm, 4 GHz RF signal.

To increase efficiency of CMOS rectifier used in RF energy harvesting application, different biasing scheme is proposed in (Bakhtiar, Jalali & Mirabbasi, 2010). These biasing schemes enable the rectifier to adjust according to the input power levels to achieve maximum power conversion efficiency. The proposed circuit is designed in 130 nm standard CMOS process.

Use of quartz crystal resonator as matching device between receiving antenna and RF to DC rectifier is presented in (Ungan, Polozecv, Walker & Reindi, 2009). The resonance frequency of quartz crystal was 24 MHz. The authors achieved 1volt DC output with 22% PCE for -30 dBm input signal power. Dickson voltage multiplier based RF to DC rectifier using CMOS technology is presented in (Facen & Boni, 2006). To provide compatibility with digital CMOS technology, a low threshold differential rectifier is proposed.

ENERGY HARVESTING CIRCUIT WITH RESONATOR

Generally RF signal to DC voltage rectifier contains two main parts, one is impedance matching circuit and other is voltage multiplier circuit. In given circuit Dickson voltage multiplier as charge pump was used as the RF to DC converter because of its easiness in analysis. The Avago HSMS – 2820 Schottky diode was selected as rectifying element due to approximately zero threshold voltage (www.avagotech.com/docs/AV02-1320EN) and fast switching operation. To produce maximum DC output from the circuit, π – network as impedance matching circuit is also used. All the simulations were carried out with the help of Agilent Advanced Design System (ADS) software. Figure 11 shows the designed RF energy harvesting circuit. A filter circuit may be applied at the output of converter to produce smooth DC output but due to this, circuit will become bulky and costly.

Incident RF signals are alternating in nature having very small amplitude level of its power and voltage. The charge pump circuit increases the output voltage and convert alternating voltage to DC output. There are number of voltage multiplier configurations are possible but Dickson charge pump configuration is used in proposed circuit. This circuit having two Schottky diodes and two capacitors in each stage. In given circuit single stage of voltage multiplier called voltage doubler is used because of its smaller circuit size and low internal losses. The selection of diodes has significant section in the RF energy harvesting circuit design. The diodes must have small forward voltage drop, low threshold voltage, small junction capacitance and higher switching speed to provide efficient output at ultra low input power levels. Hence Avago HSMS – 2820 Schottky diodes were used because their forward voltage drop is 340 mV, junction capacitance is 0.7 pF and series resistance is 6 Ω. This diode is used for both analog and digital circuit. It may be used in number of analog and digital applications like mixing, detecting, switching, sampling, clamping and wave shaping. It having low series resistance, better RF characteristics and can be used as surface mounted devices which helps in reducing circuit size and cost. The input impedance of a diode is a function of junction capacitance, series resistance and the value of connected load. The equivalent linear circuit model of used Schottky diode is shown in figure 12. It having parallel combination of junction capacitance and junction resistance with series resistance R_S. Hence effective impedance of equivalent circuit model of figure 11 can be represented as follows:

Figure 11. Proposed RF energy harvester

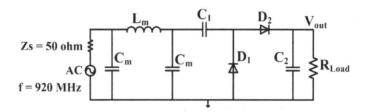

Figure 12. Linear equivalent circuit model of the Schottky diode

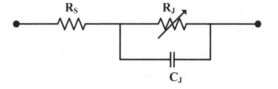

$$Z_{Diode=} R_S + \frac{R_J}{1 + J\omega R_J C_J} \cdot Z_{Diode=} R_S + \frac{R_J}{1 + J\omega R_J C_J} - \tag{3}$$

Where Z_{Diode} is equivalent input impedance of the diode, C_J is junction capacitance, R_J is junction resistance and R_S is series resistance.

Junction resistance is expressed as

$$R_J = \frac{8.33 \times 10^{-5} \, nT}{I_b + I_s} \cdot R_J = \frac{8.33 \times 10^{-5} \, nT}{I_b + I_s} - \tag{4}$$

Where

I_b = Externally applied bias current in μA

I_s = Saturation current in μA

T = Temperature in ^{0}K

n = Ideality factor

Saturation current I_s is a function of junction barrier potential of diode and can vary from picoamps for high barrier potential diode to μamps in low barrier potential diode. Impedance of diode is a non linear function of junction temperature and saturation current. As junction temperature is a function of input RF power hence impedance of diode also varies with applied power which affects the conversion efficiency. Variation of input impedance of Schottky diode with frequency of input signal is shown in figure 13.

From impedance curve it is obvious that HSMS – 2820 Schottky diode has negative value of its reactance. As frequency increases imaginary part of input impedance approaches to zero value which provides more matched condition. Because deviation of imaginary part of impedance from zero values gives reflection and shows mismatched condition.

To provide efficient power transfer from antenna to multiplier circuit, matching network is used between antenna and charge pump circuit for maximum power scavenging from RF signals, whose parameters value is optimized by estimating approximate RF signal frequency and applied power levels. There are number of matching network configuration is available for such purpose. In this work π – matching network is used because of its simplicity and more bandwidth. A small change in its parameter values may affect the frequency at which system produces maximum conversion efficiency. Used matching network consists of series inductor with two parallel capacitors. Components value of this circuit is determined by using software with applying different optimization techniques. This circuit matches the antenna impedance of 50 Ω with impedance of voltage multiplier circuit. Presented harvesting circuit can be used at single frequency band for designed matching network whose value is determined by scattering parameter curve. S-parameter values of designed harvesting circuit with Smith chart are shown in figure 14.

From S – parameter graph it is obvious that the lowest return loss is achieved at 920 MHz which shows appropriate matching. Hence resonant frequency of the system is also 920 MHz which is the

Figure 13. Real and imaginary values of input impedance of Schottky diode

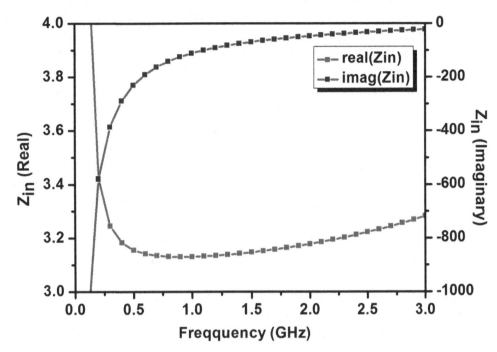

Figure 14. Simulated S – parameter with Smith chart of harvester circuit

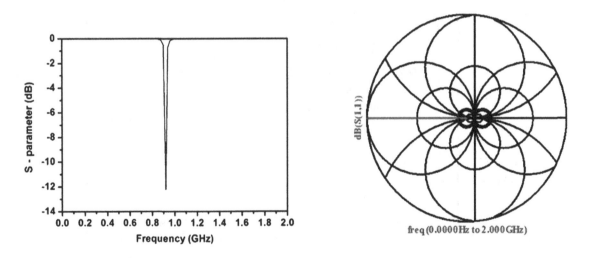

input signal frequency to this circuit. Designed energy harvester circuit shown in figure 10 consists of Schottky diodes, capacitors, matching inductor and load resistance. Analysis is start by first applying negative phase of input signal. During negative half cycle of input, diode D_1 is in forward bias condition and hence flows current while diode D_2 is in reverse bias condition remains cut off. At the peak value of negative input, voltage across capacitor C_1 is $V_{RF} - V_{th}$, where V_{RF} is the amplitude of input RF signal and V_{th} is threshold voltage of schottky diode. During positive half cycle of input signal diode D_1 become reverse biased and the right plate of capacitor C_1 is charged up to voltage value $2\times . \times (_F - V_{th})$. Diode D_2 becomes turn on and charge stored on capacitor C_1 is transferred to capacitor C_2. Hence at the end of positive phase voltage across capacitor C_2 is expressed as $V_{out} = 2\times . \times (_F - V_{th})$. High value of load resistance is applied at the output to provide more output voltage at very low current level.

The output behaviour of the system is perceived by varying different parameters of the circuit like load resistance, input signal frequency and RF input power. Variation of output voltage with load resistance for different input power level is shown in figure 15. The transient analysis performed on the harvester circuit to compute its time response is given in figure 16. The output voltage value becomes 1.57 V within 5 µSec with load resistance of value 100 KΩ. It is observed that output voltage level is more for higher input power. Increment of output voltage is better for input power greater than -15 dBm, because used Schottky diode work more efficiently for higher input power level. It is also noticed that output level is more for large load resistance. Hence load resistance plays a major role in RF energy harvesting circuit to produce better output. So value of load resistance connected to the circuit must be known.

If the load resistance does not match the circuit impedance for maximization of power transfer, another matching circuit may be used in harvesting circuit. This circuit improves output voltage and power conversion efficiency.

Output power and power conversion efficiency variation with load resistance for different input power level is presented in figure 17 and 18 respectively. Analysis is done for input power from -30 dBm to 0 dBm and load resistance value between 0 KΩ to 100 KΩ. Applied frequency is kept constant at 920

Figure 15. Output load voltage variation versus RF input power for different R_L

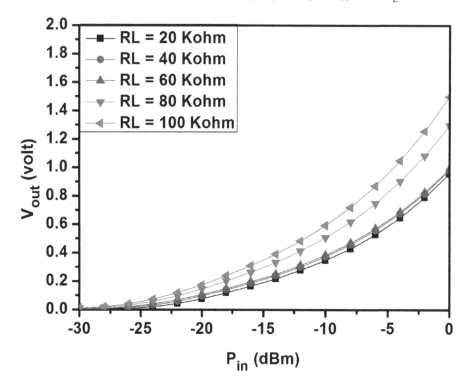

Figure 16. Variation of output voltage with simulation time

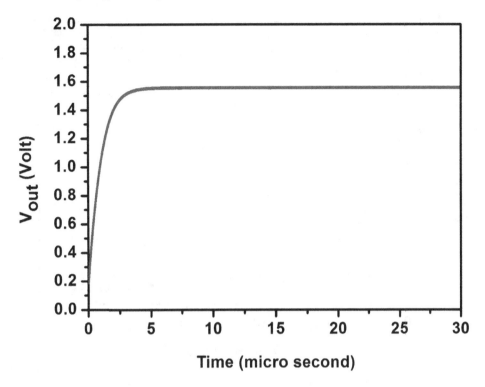

Figure 17. Variation of output power versus RF input power for different R_L

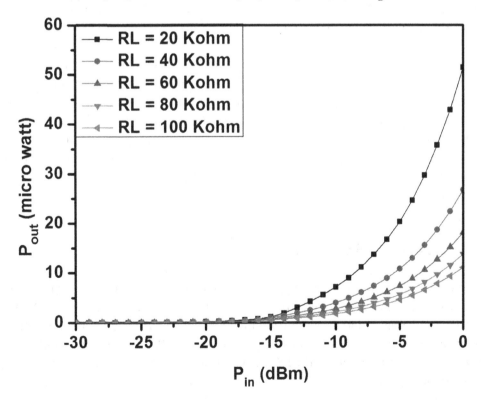

Figure 18. Variation of power conversion efficiency versus load R_L for different input power level

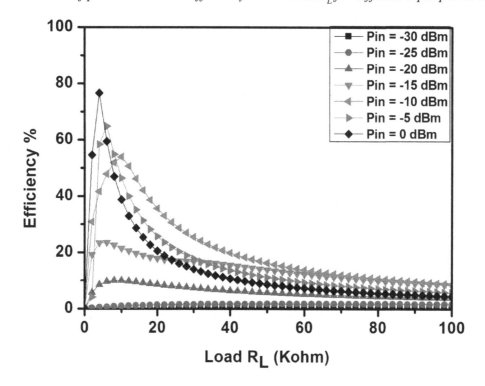

MHz and input is swept form -30 dBm to 0 dBm in simulation. It can be observed that there is sever change in RF to DC conversion efficiency with increasing load resistance value. First it increases and then decreases at higher value of load resistance. Circuit attains maximum 76.5% conversion efficiency for load value of 4 KΩ.

Conversion efficiency is increase with input power level because used Schottky diodes were designed for high RF power values. The efficiency of the circuit shows increment until reverse voltage across the diode is less than the breakdown voltage. When reverse voltage becomes higher than this limit the efficiency decreases significantly because some part of the input power is dissipated as heat in the diode. Since circuit efficiency is better at high RF power levels hence in the environment of ultra low RF power level two or more energy harvester may be used to provide efficient output. The 920 MHz working frequency were selected in the simulation because most of the GSM network operating around this frequency band.

FUTURE RESEARCH DIRECTIONS

RF power captured at the receiver is inversely proportional to the square of distance between transmitter and receiver. Also it is very much affected by antenna gain and directivity of receiver. So to increase efficiency of RF energy harvester, development of a high gain antenna is an immerging research area. There are large numbers of cell phone operator which work on different operating frequency with different bandwidth. So to produce substantial DC output from RF energy harvesting circuit it is require to capture all of these signals and convert them in to electrical energy. For this development of a multiband antenna with wide bandwidth is another major research topic. Impedance of Schottky diode varies with input RF power level and frequency. This creates a problem in impedance matching between receiver antenna and harvester circuit. It is necessary to design a matching circuit whose parameters value dynamically adjusted according to input RF power and frequency to provide optimum impedance matching and enables harvester circuit to produce improved DC output. To reduce energy loss at energy harvester, it must be placed in line of sight with RF transmitter. Mobility of cell devices also reduces level of received RF power. Therefore RF energy source must be located such that it could support number of RF energy receivers to be energised.

CONCLUSION

Chemical batteries are mostly used to charge up low power electronic devices but RF energy harvester may replace them and provides a viable power system for these devices. These systems are not affected by environmental conditions compared to other charging systems. The proposed system has been simulated with variable power supply and load resistance. Input RF power is the most significant parameter to decide produced output DC power. It has been observed that power conversion efficiency is low at small RF input power. The designed system can be used up to the power level higher than -25 dBm. The other factors which decide the system efficiency are input signal frequency, value of circuit components and quality of impedance matching network and voltage multiplier circuit. The proposed system can enables the wireless devices to operate without batteries or it can enhance the life span of battery of the devices. A comprehensive review of RF energy harvesting circuit with their implementation techniques, output characteristics and possible applications is presented. Then operation and characteristics of designed system is discussed in detail. Subsequently output features of proposed system have been explored. Finally the future research directions and design challenges in implementing RF energy harvesting circuit are presented.

REFERENCES

Abdallah, M., Costantine, J., Ramadan, A. H., Tawk, Y., Ayoub, F., Christodoulou, C. G., & Kabalan, K. Y. (2015). Wide power range RF energy harvesting circuit. *International Symposium on Antennas and Propagation & USNC/URSI National Radio Science Meeting*. 1296–1297. doi:10.1109/APS.2015.7305037

Agrawal, P. (2016). Effect of matching network on ambient RF energy harvesting circuit for wireless sensor networks. *International Journal of Current Engineering & Scientific Research*, 3(1), 82–88.

Al-Lawati, M., Al-Busaidi, M., & Nadir, Z. (2012). RF energy harvesting system design for wireless sensors. *International Multi Conference on Systems, Signals and Devices*, 1 – 4. doi:10.1109/SSD.2012.6197969

Alam, S. B., Ullah, M. S., & Moury, S. (2013). Design of a low power 2.45 GHz RF energy harvesting circuit for rectenna. *International Conference on Informatics, Electronics & Vision (ICIEV)*, 1 – 4. doi:10.1109/ICIEV.2013.6572628

Arrawatia, M., Baghini, M. S., & Kumar, G. (2011). RF energy harvesting system from cell tower in 900 Mhz band. *National Conference on Communications (NCC)*, 1 – 5.

Arrawatia, M., Baghini, M. S., & Kumar, G. (2015). Differential microstrip antenna for RF energy harvesting. *IEEE Transactions on Antennas and Propagation, 63*(4), 1581–1588. doi:10.1109/TAP.2015.2399939

Arrawatia, M., Diddi, V., Kochar, H., Baghini, M. S., & Kumar, G. (2012). An integrated CMOS RF energy harvester with differential microstrip antenna and on-chip charger. *International Conference on VLSI Design*, 209 – 214. doi:10.1109/VLSID.2012.72

Bakhtiar, A. S., Jalali, M. S., & Mirabbasi, S. (2010). A high-efficiency CMOS rectifier for low-power RFID tags. *International Conference on RFID*, 83 – 88. doi:10.1109/RFID.2010.5467271

Bakkali, A., Pelegri-Sebastia, J., Sogorb, T., Llario, V., & Bou-Escriva, A. (2016). A dual-band antenna for rf energy harvesting systems in wireless sensor networks. *Journal of Sensors, 2016*, 1–8. doi:10.1155/2016/5725836

Beh, T. C., Imura, T., & Hori, M. K. Y. (2010). Basic study of improving efficiency of wireless power transfer via magnetic resonance coupling based on impedance matching. *International Symposium on Industrial Electronics*, 2011 – 2016.

Brown, W. C. (1984). The history of power transmission by radio waves. *IEEE Transactions on Microwave Theory and Techniques, 32*(9), 1230–1242. doi:10.1109/TMTT.1984.1132833

Chouhan, S. S., & Halonen, K. (2014). The design and implementation of DTMOS biased all PMOS rectifier for RF Energy Harvesting. *New Circuits and Systems Conference (NEWCAS)*, 444 – 447. doi:10.1109/NEWCAS.2014.6934078

Costanzo, A., Fabiani, M., Romani, A., Masotti, D., & Rizzoli, V. (2010). Co-design of ultra-low power RF/Microwave receivers and converters for RFID and energy harvesting applications. *IEEE MTT-S International Microwave Symposium Digest (MTT)*, 856 – 859.

Facen, A., & Boni, A. (2006). Power supply generation in CMOS passive UHF RFID tags. *International Conference on Research in Microelectronics and Electronics*, 33 – 36. doi:10.1109/RME.2006.1689889

Felini, C., Merenda, M., & Corte, F. G. D. (2014). Dynamic impedance matching network for RF energy harvesting systems. *IEEE RFID Technology and Applications Conference (RFID-TA)*. 86 – 90. doi:10.1109/RFID-TA.2014.6934206

Georgiadis, A., Andia, G., & Collado, A. (2010). Rectenna design and optimization using reciprocity theory and harmonic balance analysis for electromagnetic (EM) energy harvesting. *IEEE Antennas and Wireless Propagation Letters, 9*(1), 444–446. doi:10.1109/LAWP.2010.2050131

Hagerty, J. A., Helmbrecht, F. B., McCalpin, W. H., Zane, R., & Popovic, Z. B. (2004). Recycling ambient microwave energy with broad band rectenna arrays. *IEEE Transactions on Microwave Theory and Techniques, 52*(3), 1014–1024. doi:10.1109/TMTT.2004.823585

Hameed, Z., & Moez, K. (2013). Fully-integrated passive threshold-compensated PMOS rectifier for RF energy harvesting. *International Midwest Symposium on Circuits and Systems (MWSCAS)*, 129 – 132. doi:10.1109/MWSCAS.2013.6674602

Hemour, S., Zhao, Y., Lorenz, C. H. P., Houssameddine, D., Gui, Y., Hu, C. M., & Wu, K. (2014). Towards low-power high-efficiency RF and microwave energy harvesting. IEEE Transactions on Microwave Theory and Techniques, 62(4), 965 – 976.

Henrique, C., Lorenz, P., Hemour, S., Li, W., Xie, Y., Gauthier, J., & Wu, K. et al. (2015). Breaking the efficiency barrier for ambient microwave power harvesting with heterojunction backward tunnel diodes. *IEEE Transactions on Microwave Theory and Techniques, 63*(12), 4544–4555. doi:10.1109/TMTT.2015.2495356

Hosain, M. K., Kouzani, A. Z., Samad, M. F., & Tye, S. J. (2015). A miniature energy harvesting rectenna for operating a head-mountable deep brain stimulation device. *IEEE Access on Special Section on Bio-Compatible Materials and Bio-Electromagnetics for Bio-Medical Applications, 3*(1), 223–234.

Hosain, M. K., Kouzani, A. Z., Tye, S., Kaynak, A., & Berk, M. (2015). RF rectifiers for EM power harvesting in a deep brain stimulating device. *Australasian Physical & Engineering Sciences in Medicine*, 1–16. PMID:25600671

Jabbar, H., Song, Y. S., & Jeong, T. T. (2010). RF energy harvesting system and circuits for charging of mobile devices. *IEEE Transactions on Consumer Electronics, 56*(1), 247–252. doi:10.1109/TCE.2010.5439152

Kadupitiya, J. C. S., Abeythunga, T. N., Ranathunga, P. D. M. T., & De Silva, D. S. (2015). Optimizing RF energy harvester design for low power applications by integrating multi stage voltage doubler on patch antenna. *International Conference on Ubi-Media Computing (UMEDIA).* 335 – 338. doi:10.1109/UMEDIA.2015.7297481

Kamalinejad, P., Keikhosravy, K., Mirabbasi, S., & Leung, V. C. M. (2013). An efficiency enhancement technique for CMOS rectifiers with low start-up voltage for UHF RFID tags. *International Green Computing Conference (IGCC)*, 1 – 6. doi:10.1109/IGCC.2013.6604483

Kanaya, H., Tsukamoto, S., Hirabaru, T., Kanemoto, D., Pokharel, R. K., & Yoshida, K. (2013). Energy harvesting circuit on a one sided directional flexible antenna. *IEEE Microwave and Wireless Components Letters, 23*(3), 164–166. doi:10.1109/LMWC.2013.2246779

Karolak, D., Taris, Thierry, Deval, Y., Begueret, J. B., & Mariano, A. (2012). Design comparison of low-power rectifiers dedicated to RF energy harvesting. *International Conference on Electronics, Circuits and Systems (ICECS)*, 524 – 527. doi:10.1109/ICECS.2012.6463693

Khalfi, B., Hamdaoui, B., Ghorbel, M. B., Guizani, M., & Zhang, X. (2016). Joint data and power transfer optimization for energy harvesting wireless networks. *IEEE Conference on Computer Communications Workshops*, 1-6. doi:10.1109/INFCOMW.2016.7562175

Kim, G., & Chung, Y. C. (2006). Optimization of UHF RFID tag antennas using a genetic algorithm. *Antennas and Propagation Society International Symposium*, 2087 – 2090.

Kim, S., Vyas, R., Bito, J., Niotaki, K., Collado, A., Georgiadis, A., & Tentzeris, M. M. (2014). Ambient RF energy harvesting technologies for self-sustainable standalone wireless sensor platforms. *Proceedings of the IEEE, 102*(11), 1649–1666. doi:10.1109/JPROC.2014.2357031

Kotani, K. (2013). Highly efficient CMOS rectifier assisted by symmetric and voltage-boost PV-cell structures for synergistic ambient energy harvesting. *Custom Integrated Circuits Conference (CICC)*, 1 – 4. doi:10.1109/CICC.2013.6658515

Kotani, K., Sasaki, A., & Ito, T. (2009). High efficiency differential drive CMOS rectifier for UHF RFIDs. *IEEE Journal of Solid-State Circuits*, *44*(11), 3011–3018. doi:10.1109/JSSC.2009.2028955

Kumar, G. (2010). Report on cell tower radiation. Electrical Engineering Department, IIT Bombay, Powai, Mumbai.

Kumar, V., & Islam, A. (2015). CNFET based voltage multiplier circuit for rf energy harvesting applications. *International Conference on Communication Systems and Network Technologies (ICCSNT)*, 789 – 791. doi:10.1109/CSNT.2015.59

Le, H., Fong, N., & Luong, H. C. (2010). RF energy harvesting circuit with on-chip antenna for biomedical applications. *International Conference on Communications and Electronics (ICCE)*, 115 – 117.

Le, T., Mayaram, K., & Fiez, T. (2008). Efficient far-field radio frequency energy harvesting for passively powered sensor networks. *IEEE Journal of Solid-State Circuits*, *43*(5), 1287–1302. doi:10.1109/JSSC.2008.920318

Li, B., Shao, X., Shahshahan, N., Goldsman, N., Salter, T., & Metze, G. M. (2013). An antenna co-design dual band RF energy harvester. *IEEE Transactions on Circuits and Systems. I, Regular Papers*, *60*(12), 1–11. doi:10.1109/TCSI.2013.2264712

Lin, G. C., Lee, M. W., & Hsu, Y. C. (2012). An AC-DC rectifier for RF energy harvesting system. *Proceedings of Asia-Pacific Microwave Conference*, 1052 – 1054. doi:10.1109/APMC.2012.6421822

Liu, H., Datta, S., & Narayanan, V. (2013). Tunnel FET based ultra low power high sensitivity UHF RFID rectifier. *Proceedings of the International Symposium on Low Power Electronics and Design*, 157 – 162. doi:10.1109/ISLPED.2013.6629287

Liu, H., Li, X., Vaddi, R., Ma, K., Datta, S., & Narayanan, V. (2014). Tunnel FET RF rectifier design for energy harvesting applications. *IEEE Journal on Emerging and Selected Topics in Circuits and Systems.*, *4*(4), 400–411. doi:10.1109/JETCAS.2014.2361068

Liu, L. X., Mu, J. C., Ma, N., Tu, W., Zhu, Z. M., & Yang, Y. T. (2015). An Ultra-Low-Power Integrated RF Energy Harvesting System in 65-nm CMOS Process. *Circuits, Systems, and Signal Processing*, *35*(2), 42–441.

Mabrouki, A., Latrach, M., & Lorrain, V. (2014). *High efficiency low power rectifier design using zero bias schottky diodes. Faible Tension Faible Consommation (FTFC), 1 – 4*. IEEE.

Masotti, D., Costanzo, A., & Adami, S. (2013). Design and realization of a wearable multi frequency RF energy harvesting system. *Proceedings of The European Conference on Antennas and Propagation (EUCAP)*, 517 – 520.

Masuch, J., Restituto, M. D., Milosevic, D., & Baltus, P. (2012). An RF-to-DC energy harvester for co-integration in a low-power 2.4 GHz transceiver frontend. *International Symposium on Circuits and Systems (ISCAS)*, 680 – 683. doi:10.1109/ISCAS.2012.6272124

Mikeka, C., & Arai, H. (2011). Microwave tooth for sensor power supply in battery-free applications. *Proceedings of the Asia-Pacific Microwave Conference*, 1802 – 1805.

Mikeka, C., Arai, H., Georgiadis, A., & Collado, A. (2011). DTV band micropower RF energy-harvesting circuit architecture and performance analysis. *International Conference on RFID-Technologies and Applications*, 561 – 567. doi:10.1109/RFID-TA.2011.6068601

Moon, J. I., Cho, I. K., Kim, S. M., & Jung, Y. B. (2013). Design of efficient rectenna with vertical ground walls for RF energy harvesting. *Electronics Letters*, *49*(17), 1–3. doi:10.1049/el.2013.2251

Mouris, B. A., Soliman, A. M., Ali, T. A., Eshrah, I. A., & Badawi, A. (2016). Efficient dual-band energy harvesting system for implantable biosensors. *International Symposium on Antenna Technology and Applied Electromagnetics (ANTEM)*, 1-2. doi:10.1109/ANTEM.2016.7550242

Nasimuddin, Q. X., & Chen, Z. N. (2009). Compact circularly polarized microstrip antenna for RFID handheld reader applications. *Asia Pacific Microwave Conference (APMC)*, 1950 – 1953. doi:10.1109/APMC.2009.5385294

Nimo, A., Beckedahl, T., Ostertag, T., & Reindl, L. (2015). Analysis of passive RF-DC power rectification and harvesting wireless RF energy for micro-watt sensors. *AIMS Energy*, *3*(2), 184–200. doi:10.3934/energy.2015.2.184

Nintanavongsa, P., Muncuk, U., Lewis, D. R., & Chowdhury, K. R. (2012). Design optimization and implementation for RF energy harvesting circuits. *IEEE Journal on Emerging and Selected Topics in Circuits and Systems*, *2*(1), 24–33. doi:10.1109/JETCAS.2012.2187106

Olgun, U., Chen, C. C., & Volakis, J. L. (2010). Wireless power harvesting with planar rectennas for 2.45 GHz RFIDs. *URSI International Symposium on Electromagnetic Theory*, 329 – 331. doi:10.1109/URSI-EMTS.2010.5637008

Olgun, U., Chen, C. C., & Volakis, J. L. (2012). Design of an efficient ambient WiFi energy harvesting system. *IET Microwaves, Antennas & Propagation*, *6*(11), 1200–1206. doi:10.1049/iet-map.2012.0129

Papotto, G., Carrara, F., & Palmisano, G. (2011). A 90-nm CMOS threshold-compensated RF energy harvester. *IEEE Journal of Solid-State Circuits*, *46*(9), 1985–1997. doi:10.1109/JSSC.2011.2157010

Parihar, P. D., Kumar, P., Jha, C. K., & Sharma, A. (2014). Renewable battery charging method using CMOS RF energy harvesting circuit design. *International Conference on Reliability, Infocom Technologies and Optimization (ICRITO)*, 1 – 5. doi:10.1109/ICRITO.2014.7014738

Pham, B. L., & Pham, A. V. (2013). Triple bands antenna and high efficiency rectifier design for RF energy harvesting at 900, 1900 and 2400 MHz. *IEEE MTT-S International Microwave Symposium Digest*, 1 – 4. doi:10.1109/MWSYM.2013.6697364

Popovic, Z., & Falkenstein, E. A., (2013). Low-Power Far-Field Wireless Powering for Wireless Sensors. *Proceedings of the IEEE*, *101*(6), 1397 – 1409. doi:10.1109/JPROC.2013.2244053

Popovic, Z., Korhummel, S., Dunbar, S., Scheeler, R., Dolgov, A., Zane, R., & Hagerty, J. et al. (2014). Scalable RF energy harvesting. *IEEE Transactions on Microwave Theory and Techniques*, *62*(4), 1046–1056. doi:10.1109/TMTT.2014.2300840

Raj, V. A. (2016). MEMS based multi-band energy harvesting for wireless sensor network applications. *International Conference on Energy Efficient Technologies for Sustainability (ICEETS)*, 573-576. doi:10.1109/ICEETS.2016.7583819

Ramesh, G. P., & Rajan, A. (2014). microstrip antenna designs for RF energy harvesting. *International Conference on Communication and Signal Processing*, 1653 – 1657. doi:10.1109/ICCSP.2014.6950129

Riviere, S., Alicalapa, F., Douyere, A., & Lan Sun Luk, J. D. (2010). A compact rectenna device at low power level. *Progress In Electromagnetics Research C*, *16*(1), 137–146. doi:10.2528/PIERC10071604

Salter, T., Choi, K., Peckerar, M., Metze, G., & Goldsman, N. (2009). RF energy scavenging system utilising switched capacitor DC-DC converter. *Electronics Letters*, *45*(7), 1–2. doi:10.1049/el.2009.0153

Saraiva, H. M., Borges, L. M., Pinho, P., Goncalves, R., Santiago, R. C., Barroca, N., & Salvado, R. et al. (2014). Experimental characterization of wearable antennas and circuits for RF energy harvesting in WBANs. *Vehicular Technology Conference (VTC Spring)*, 1 – 5. doi:10.1109/VTCSpring.2014.7022920

Scorcioni, S., Larcher, L., & Bertacchini, A. (2012). A 868MHz CMOS RF-DC power converter with -17dBm input power sensitivity and efficiency higher than 40% over 14dB input power range. *IEEE International Conference on RFID (RFID)*, 109 – 112.

Scorcioni, S., Larcher, L., & Bertacchini, A. (2012). Optimized CMOS RF-DC converters for remote wireless powering of RFID applications. *IEEE International Conference on RFID (RFID)*, 47 – 53. doi:10.1109/RFID.2012.6193055

Shameli, A., Safarian, A., Rofougaran, A., Rofougaran, M., & Flaviis, F. D. (2007). Power harvester design for passive UHF RFID tag using a voltage boosting technique. *IEEE Transactions on Microwave Theory and Techniques*, *55*(6), 1089–1097. doi:10.1109/TMTT.2007.896819

Shariati, N., Rowe, S. T., Scott, J. R., & Ghorbani, K. (2015). Multi-Service highly sensitive rectifier for enhanced RF energy scavenging. *Nature*, *9655*, 1–9.

Shrestha, S., Noh, S. K., & Choi, D. Y. (2013). Comparative study of antenna designs for RF energy harvesting. *International Journal of Antennas and Propagation*, *2013*(1), 1 – 11.

Sim, Z. W., Shuttleworth, R., Alexander, M. J., & Grieve, B. D. (2010). Compact patch antenna design for outdoor RF energy harvesting in wireless sensor networks. *Progress in Electromagnetics Research*, *105*(1), 273–294. doi:10.2528/PIER10052509

Singh, G., Ponnaganti, R., Prabhakar, T. V., & Vinoy, K. J. (2013). A tuned rectifier for RF energy harvesting from ambient radiations. *AEÜ. International Journal of Electronics and Communications*, *67*(7), 1–6. doi:10.1016/j.aeue.2012.12.004

Stoopman, M., Keyrouz, S., Visser, H. J., Philips, K., & Serdijn, W. A. (2013). A self-calibrating RF energy harvester generating 1V at -26.3 dBm. *Symposium on VLSI Circuits Digest of Technical Papers*, 226 – 227.

Stoopman, M., Keyrouz, S., Visser, H. J., Philips, K., & Serdijn, W. A. (2014). Co-Design of a CMOS rectifier and small loop antenna for highly sensitive RF energy harvesters. *IEEE Journal of Solid-State Circuits*, *59*(3), 622–634. doi:10.1109/JSSC.2014.2302793

Stupf, M., Mittra, R., Yeo, J., & Mosig, J. R. (2006). Some novel design for RFID antennas and their performance enhancement with metamaterials. *IMP Antennas and Propagation Society International Symposium*, 1023 – 1026. doi:10.1109/APS.2006.1710707

Sun, H., Guo, Y. X., He, M., & Zhong, Z. (2013). A dual-band rectenna using broad-band yagi antenna array for ambient RF power harvesting. *IEEE Antennas and Wireless Propagation Letters*, *12*, 918–921. doi:10.1109/LAWP.2013.2272873

Theilmann, P. T., Presti, C. D., Kelly, D., & Asbeck, P. M. (2010). Near zero turn-on voltage high-efficiency UHF RFID rectifier in silicon-on-sapphire CMOS. *Radio Frequency Integrated Circuits Symposium*, 105 – 108. doi:10.1109/RFIC.2010.5477409

Thierry, T., Valerie, V., & Ludivine, F. (2012). A 900MHz RF energy harvesting module. *New Circuits and Systems Conference (NEWCAS)*, 445 – 448.

Trung, N. T., Feng, T., Haftiger, P., & Chakrabartty, S. (2014). Sub-threshold CMOS voltage-multipliers using hybrid RF piezoelectric energy scavenging. *International Conference on Communications and Electronics (ICCE)*, 304 – 308.

Ukkonen, L., Schaffrath, M., Sydanheimo, L., & Kivikoski, M. (2006). Analysis of integrated slot-type tag antennas for passive UHF RFID. *Antennas and Propagation Society International Symposium*, 1343 – 1346. doi:10.1109/APS.2006.1710794

Ungan, T., Polozecv, X. L., Walker, W., & Reindi, L. (2009). RF energy harvesting design using high Q resonators. *IEEE MTT-S International Microwave Workshop on Wireless Sensing, LocalPositioning, and RFID (IMWS)*, 1 – 4. doi:10.1109/IMWS2.2009.5307869

Uzun, Y. (2015). Design of an efficient triple band RF energy harvester. *ACES Journal*, *30*, 1286–1293.

Uzun, Y. (2016). Design and implementation of RF energy harvesting system for low-power electronic devices. *Journal of Electronic Materials*, *45*(8), 3842–3847. doi:10.1007/s11664-016-4441-5

Vera, G. A., Georgiadis, A., Collado, A., & Via, S. (2010). Design of a 2.45 GHz rectenna for electromagnetic (EM) energy scavenging. *Radio and Wireless Symposium (RWS)*, 61 – 64. doi:10.1109/RWS.2010.5434266

Weigand, S. M. (2005). Compact microstrip antenna with forward directed radiation pattern for RFID reader card. *Antennas and Propagation Society International Symposium*, 337 – 340. doi:10.1109/APS.2005.1552011

Yang, S. F., Chen, C. C., Huang, T. H., Lu, C. Y., & Chung, P. J. (2015). Design of a 2×2 antenna-array RF power emitter with object detection function for sensor location identification. *International Microwave Workshop Series on RF and Wireless Technologies for Biomedical and Healthcare Applications (IMWS-BIO)*, 65 – 66. doi:10.1109/IMWS-BIO.2015.7303779

Yao, Y., Wu, J., Shi, Y., & Dai, F. F. (2009). A fully integrated 900-MHz passive RFID transponder front end with novel zero threshold RF–DC rectifier. *IEEE Transactions on Industrial Electronics*, *56*(7), 2317–2325. doi:10.1109/TIE.2008.2010180

Yi, J., Ki, W.-H., & Tsui, C.-Y. (2008). Analysis and design strategy of UHF micro-power CMOS rectifiers for micro-sensor and RFID applications. *IEEE Transactions on Circuits and Systems. I, Regular Papers*, *54*(1), 153–166. doi:10.1109/TCSI.2006.887974

Younus, S., Hegde, B., Prabhakar, T. V., & Vinoy, K. J. (2016). RF Energy harvesting chip powered sensor node. *International Conference on Electronics, Circuits & Systems*, 1-4.

Zbitou, J., Latrac, M., & Toutain, S. (2006). Hybrid rectenna and monolithic integrated zero-bias microwave rectifier. *IEEE Transactions on Microwave Theory and Techniques*, *54*(1), 147–152. doi:10.1109/TMTT.2005.860509

Zeng, X., Siden, J., Wang, G., & Nilsson, H. E. (2007). Slots in metallic label as RFID tag antenna. *Antennas and Propagation Society International Symposium*, 1749 – 1752.

Zhao, Q., Xu, J., Yin, H., Lu, Z., Vue, L., Gong, Y., & Wang, W. et al. (2015). Dual band antenna and high efficiency rectifier for RF energy harvesting system. *International Symposium on Microwave, Antenna, Propagation, and EMC Technologies (MAPE)*, 682 – 685.

Zulkifli, F. F., Sampe, J., Islam, M. S., Mohamed, M. A., & Wahab, S. A. (2015). Optimization of RF- DC converter in micro energy harvester using voltage boosting network and bulk modulation technique for biomedical devices. *IEEE Regional Symposium on Micro and Nanoelectronics (RSM)*, 1 – 4. doi:10.1109/RSM.2015.7354975

KEY TERMS AND DEFINITIONS

Bandwidth: The range of frequency of used signal. It is also defined as gap between lower and upper 3 dB cut off frequency.

Breakdown Voltage: In any diode the minimum applied forward bias voltage below which the diode remains cut off and does not flow current.

Broadband: Wide range of operating frequency.

Conversion Efficiency: The ratio of produced output power to applied input power.

HSMS Schottky Diode: High speed metal semiconductor junction diode having very fast switching speed can operate at microwave frequency range.

RF Signal: Electromagnetic signals lie in the frequency range around 3 KHz to 300 GHz, commonly used for RADAR and wireless communication application.

S Parameter: Scattering parameter utilized for determining signal flow condition of a device used in microwave circuit. It uses matched load to determine behaviour of electrical network.

Schottky Diode: A solid state diode having metal semiconductor junction. It is also known as hot carrier diode due to its fast switching speed and very low forward voltage drop.

SMS Schottky Diode: Skywork metal semiconductor junction.

Threshold Voltage: Minimum required gate to source voltage in MOSFET devices to start conduction between drain and source terminal.

Compilation of References

Abdallah, M., Costantine, J., Ramadan, A. H., Tawk, Y., Ayoub, F., Christodoulou, C. G., & Kabalan, K. Y. (2015). Wide power range RF energy harvesting circuit. *International Symposium on Antennas and Propagation & USNC/URSI National Radio Science Meeting.* 1296 – 1297. doi:10.1109/APS.2015.7305037

Abdeddaim, M., Ounis, A., Djedoui, N., & Shrimali, M. K. (2016). Pounding hazard mitigation between adjacent planar buildings using coupling strategy. *Journal of Civil Structural Health Monitoring, 6*(3), 603–617. doi:10.1007/s13349-016-0177-4

Abdul Hasib, A., & Hew Wooi, P. (2002). Fuzzy Logic Control of a three phase Induction Motor using Field Oriented Control Method. *Society of Instrument and Control Engineers, SICE Annual Conference,* 264-267.

Abirami, A., & Amutha, R. (2015). "Image encryption based on DNA sequence coding and Logistic map", Advances in Natural and Applied Sciences. *American-Eurasian Network for Scientific Information, 9*(9), 55–62.

Acharya, N., Mahat, P., & Mithulananthan, N. (2006). An analytical approach for DG allocation in primary distribution network. *International Journal of Electrical Power & Energy Systems, 28*(10), 669–678. doi:10.1016/j.ijepes.2006.02.013

Acosta, G. G., Verucchi, C. J., & Gelso, E. R. (2004). A current monitoring system for diagnosing electrical failures in induction motors. *Mechanical Systems and Signal Processing, 20*(1), 953–965.

Afonso, J. L., F. J. (1998). Genetic Algorithm Techniques Applied to the Control of a Three-Phase Induction Motor. *UK Mechatronics Forum International Conference,* 142-146.

Agarwal, R., & Srikant, R. (1994). Fast Algorithms for Mining Association Rules in Large Databases. *VLDB '94 Proceedings of the 20th International Conference on Very Large Data Bases,* 487-499.

Agarwal, R., Imielinski, T., & Swami, A. (1993) Mining association rules between sets of items in large databases. *Proceedings of the 1993 ACM SIGMOD International Conference on Management of Data,* 207–216. doi:10.1145/170035.170072

Agrawal, P. (2016). Effect of matching network on ambient RF energy harvesting circuit for wireless sensor networks. *International Journal of Current Engineering & Scientific Research, 3*(1), 82–88.

Ahmada, M., Shamsib, U., & Khanb, I. R. (2015). An Enhanced Image Encryption Algorithm Using Fractional Chaotic Systems. *Procedia Computer Science, 57,* 852 – 859. doi:10.1016/j.procs.2015.07.494

Ahmed, A. H., & Nahla, E. Z. G. Y. (2009). Fuzzy Logic Controlled Shunt Active Power Filter for Three-phase Four-wire Systems with Balanced and Unbalanced Loads. World Academy of Science, Engineering and Technology, 58, 621-626.

Ahmed, S., Zhang, M., & Peng, L., (2012). Genetic programming for biomarker detection in mass spectrometry data. *Advances in Artificial Intelligence, 7691,* 266-278.

Ahmed, S., Zhang, M., & Peng, L. (2013). Enhanced feature selection for biomarker discovery in LC-MS data using GP. *Proceedings on IEEE Congress on Evolutionary Computation*, 584-591. doi:10.1109/CEC.2013.6557621

Ahmed, S., Zhang, M., & Peng, L. (2014). Improving feature ranking for biomarker discovery in proteomics mass spectrometry data using genetic programming. *Connection Science*, 26(3), 215–243. doi:10.1080/09540091.2014.906388

Akhvan, A., Samsudin, A., & Akhshani, A. (2013). A novel parallel hash function based on 3D chaotic map. *EURASIP Journal on Advances in Signal Processing*, 1-12.

Al Riza, D. F., & Gilani, S. I.-H. (2014). Standalone Photovoltaic System Sizing using Peak Sun Hour Method and Evaluation by TRNSYS Simulation. *International Journal of Renewable Energy Research*, 4(1), 109–114.

Alam, S. B., Ullah, M. S., & Moury, S. (2013). Design of a low power 2.45 GHz RF energy harvesting circuit for rectenna. *International Conference on Informatics, Electronics & Vision (ICIEV)*, 1 – 4. doi:10.1109/ICIEV.2013.6572628

Ali, S. F., & Ramaswamy, A. (2009). Optimal fuzzy logic control for MDOF structural systems using evolutionary algorithms. *Engineering Applications of Artificial Intelligence*, 22(3), 407–419. doi:10.1016/j.engappai.2008.09.004

Al-Lawati, M., Al-Busaidi, M., & Nadir, Z. (2012). RF energy harvesting system design for wireless sensors. *International Multi Conference on Systems, Signals and Devices*, 1 – 4. doi:10.1109/SSD.2012.6197969

Alshennawy, A. A., & Aly, A. A. (2009). Edge Detection In Digital Images Using Fuzzy Logic Technique. *World Academy of Science, Engineering and Technology*, 51, 178–186.

Alvarez, G., & Li, S. (2006). Some Basic Cryptographic Requirements for Chaos-Based Cryptosystems. *International Journal of Bifurcation and Chaos*, 16(8), 2129-2151.

Alvarez, G., Montoya, F., Romera, M., & Pastor, G. (2000). Cryptanalysis of A Chaotic Encryption System. *Physics Letters, 276*, 191-196.

Álvarez, G., Montoya, F., Romera, M., & Pastor, G. (2004). Cryptanalysis of Dynamic Look-Up Table Based Chaotic Cryptosystems. *Physics Letters A, 326*, 211–218.

Aman, M., Solangi, K., Hossain, M., Badarudin, A., Jasmon, G., Mokhlis, H., & Kazi, S. et al. (2015). A review of Safety, Health and Environmental (SHE) issues of solar energy system. *Renewable & Sustainable Energy Reviews, 41*, 1190–1204. doi:10.1016/j.rser.2014.08.086

Amigó, J.M., Kocarev, L., & Szczepanski, J. (2007). Theory and practice of chaotic cryptography. *Physics Letters A, 366*, 211–216.

Amini, F., Hazaveh, N. K., & Rad, A. A. (2013). Wavelet PSO-Based LQR Algorithm for Optimal Structural Control Using Active Tuned Mass Dampers. *Computer-Aided Civil and Infrastructure Engineering*, 28(7), 542–557. doi:10.1111/mice.12017

Anad, S. M., Dash, A., Kumar, M. S. J., & Kesarkar, A. (2011). Prediction and Classification of Thunderstorms using Artificial Neural Network. *International Journal of Engineering Science and Technology*, 3(5), 4031–4035.

Antsaklis, P. J. (1995, June). Intelligent learning control. *IEEE Control Syst.*, 15(3), 5–7. doi:10.1109/MCS.1995.594467

Arrawatia, M., Baghini, M. S., & Kumar, G. (2011). RF energy harvesting system from cell tower in 900 Mhz band. *National Conference on Communications (NCC)*, 1 – 5.

Arrawatia, M., Baghini, M. S., & Kumar, G. (2015). Differential microstrip antenna for RF energy harvesting. *IEEE Transactions on Antennas and Propagation*, 63(4), 1581–1588. doi:10.1109/TAP.2015.2399939

Arrawatia, M., Diddi, V., Kochar, H., Baghini, M. S., & Kumar, G. (2012). An integrated CMOS RF energy harvester with differential microstrip antenna and on-chip charger. *International Conference on VLSI Design*, 209 – 214. doi:10.1109/VLSID.2012.72

Aslam, M. W., Zhu, Z., & Nandi, A. K. (2013). Feature generation using genetic programming with comparative partner selection for diabetes classification. *Expert Systems with Applications*, *40*(13), 5402–5412. doi:10.1016/j.eswa.2013.04.003

Atwa, Y., El-Saadany, E., Salama, M., & Seethapathy, R. (2010). Optimal renewable resources mix for distribution system energy loss minimization. *IEEE Transactions on Power Systems*, *25*(1), 360–370. doi:10.1109/TPWRS.2009.2030276

Ayhan, B., Trussell, H. J., Chow, M. Y., & Song, M. H. (2008). On the use of a lower sampling rate for broken rotor bar detection with DTFT and AR-based spectrum methods. *IEEE Transactions on Industrial Electronics*, *55*(3), 1421–1434. doi:10.1109/TIE.2007.896522

Azar, A. T., & El-Metwally, S. M. (2013). Decision Tree classifiers for automated medical diagnoses. *Neural Computing & Applications*, *23*(7), 2387–2403. doi:10.1007/s00521-012-1196-7

Babu, G. S., & Ilango, P. (2013). Higher Dimensional Chaos for Audio Encryption. *Proceedings of the IEEE Symposium on Computational Intelligence in Cyber Security CICS*, 52–58.

Badhe, V., Thakur, R.S., & Thakur, G.S. (2015). Vague Set Theory for Profit Pattern and Decision Making in Uncertain Data. *International Journal of Advanced Computer Science and Applications*, *6*(6), 182–186. doi:10.14569/IJACSA.2015.060625

Bakhache, B., Ahmad, K., & Assad, S., (2011b). *Chaos based improvement of the security of ZigBee and Wi-Fi networks used for industrial controls*. IEEE.

Bakhache, B., Ahmad, K., & el Assad, S. (2011a). Chaos Based Improvement of the Security of ZigBee and Wi-Fi Networks Used for Industrial Controls. *Proceedings of the International Conference on Information Society (i-Society)*, 139–145.

Bakhtiar, A. S., Jalali, M. S., & Mirabbasi, S. (2010). A high-efficiency CMOS rectifier for low-power RFID tags. *International Conference on RFID*, 83 – 88. doi:10.1109/RFID.2010.5467271

Bakkali, A., Pelegri-Sebastia, J., Sogorb, T., Llario, V., & Bou-Escriva, A. (2016). A dual-band antenna for rf energy harvesting systems in wireless sensor networks. *Journal of Sensors*, *2016*, 1–8. doi:10.1155/2016/5725836

Banisheikholeslami, A., Behnamfar, F., & Ghandil, M. (2016). A beam-to-column connection with visco-elastic and hysteretic dampers for seismic damage control. *Journal of Constructional Steel Research*, *117*, 185–195. doi:10.1016/j.jcsr.2015.10.016

Basak, P., Sarkar, D., & Mukhopadhyay, A. K. (2012). Estimation of Thunderstorm Days from the Radio-sonde Observations at Kolkata (22.53⁰ N, 88.33⁰ E), India during Pre-monsoon Season: An ANN Based Approach. *Earth Science India*, *5*(4), 139–151.

Basiri, M. E., Ghasem-Aghaee, N., & Aghdam, M. H. (2008). Using ant colony optimization-based selected features for predicting post-synaptic activity in proteins. *EvoBIO, LNCS*, *4973*, 12–23.

Bazilian, M., Mai, T., Baldwin, S., Arent, D., Miller, M., & Logan, J. (2014). Decision-making for high renewable electricity futures in the United States. *Energy Strategy Reviews*, *2*(3), 326–328. doi:10.1016/j.esr.2013.11.001

Beh, T. C., Imura, T., & Hori, M. K. Y. (2010). Basic study of improving efficiency of wireless power transfer via magnetic resonance coupling based on impedance matching. *International Symposium on Industrial Electronics*, 2011 – 2016.

Beltran, R.H. (2007). A Generalized Chaotic Encryption System of Multimedia Applications. *Revista Mexicana De Fisica, 53*(5), 332-336.

Benbouzid, M. E. H. (2000). A Review of induction motors signature analysis as a medium for faults detection. *IEEE Transactions on Industrial Electronics, 47*(5), 984–993. doi:10.1109/41.873206

Berriri, M., Chevrel, P., & Lefebvre, D. (2008). Active damping of automotive powertrain oscillation by a partial torque compensator. *Control Engineering Practice, 16*(7), 874–883. doi:10.1016/j.conengprac.2007.10.010

Berzins, V. (1984). Accuracy of laplacian edge detectors. *Accuracy of Laplacian Edge Detector Computer Vision, Graphics, and Image Processing, 27*(2), 195–210. doi:10.1016/S0734-189X(84)80043-2

Bhanu, B., Lee, S., & Ming, J. (1995). Adaptive image segmentation using a genetic algorithm. *IEEE Transactions on Systems, Man, and Cybernetics, 25*(12), 1543–1567. doi:10.1109/21.478444

Bhargava, B., & Dishaw, G. (1998). Application of an energy source power system stabilizer on the 10 MW battery energy storage system at Chino substation. Power Systems. *IEEE Transactions on, 13*(1), 145–151.

Bharill, S., Hamsapriya, T., Lalwani,P., (2013). A Secure Key for Cloud using Threshold Cryptography in Kerberos. *International Journal of Computer Applications, 79*(7), 35-41.

Bhartiya, S., & Whiteley, J. R. (2001, September). Development of inferential measurements using neural networks. *ISA Transactions, 40*(4), 307–323. doi:10.1016/S0019-0578(01)00004-0 PMID:11577819

Bitaraf, M., Ozbulut, O. E., Hurlebaus, S., & Barroso, L. (2010). Application of semi-active control strategies for seismic protection of buildings with MR dampers. *Engineering Structures, 32*(10), 3040–3047. doi:10.1016/j.engstruct.2010.05.023

Blake, C., Koegh, E., & Mertz, C. J. (1999). *Repository of Machine Learning*. University of California at Irvine. Retrieved from http://www.mlearn.ics.uci.edu/MLRepository.html

Blodt, M., Chabert, M., Regnier, J., & Faucher, J. (2006). Mechanical Load Fault Detection in Induction Motors by Stator Current Time-Frequency Analysis. *IEEE Transactions on Industry Applications, 42*(6), 1454–1463. doi:10.1109/TIA.2006.882631

Blum, C. (2005). Ant colony optimization: Introduction and recent trends. *Science Direct*, 353–373.

Bompard, E., Carpaneto, E., Chicco, G., & Napoli, R. (2000). Convergence of the backward/forward sweep method for the load-flow analysis of radial distribution systems. *International Journal of Electrical Power & Energy Systems, 22*(7), 521–530. doi:10.1016/S0142-0615(00)00009-0

Boor, Z., & Hosseini, S. M. (2012). Optimal Placement of DG to Improve the Reliability of Distribution Systems Considering Time Varying Loads using Genetic Algorithm. *Majlesi Journal of Electrical Engineering, 7*(1).

Booysens, A., & Viriri, S. (2014). Detection of Lightning Pattern Changes using Machine Learning Algorithms. *Proceeding of International Conference on Communications, Signal Processing and Computers.*

Borji, A., & Hamidi, M. (2007). Evolving a Fuzzy Rule-Base for Image Segmentation. *International Journal of Intelligent Systems and Technologies*, 178-183.

Bouzid, M. B. K., & Champenois, G. (2008). New expressions of symmetrical components of the induction motor under stator faults. *IEEE Transactions on Industrial Electronics, 60*(9), 4093–4102. doi:10.1109/TIE.2012.2235392

Braz-César, M., & Barros, R. (2017). Optimization of a Fuzzy Logic Controller for MR Dampers using an Adaptive Neuro-Fuzzy Procedure. *International Journal of Structural Stability and Dynamics, 17*(05), 1740007. doi:10.1142/S0219455417400077

Brin, S., Motwani, R., Ullman, J., & Tsur, S. (1997). Dynamic Itemset Counting and Implication Rules for Market basket data. *Proceedings of the 1997 ACM SIGMOD International Conference on Management of Data*, 207-216. doi:10.1145/253260.253325

Brodersen, M. L., & Høgsberg, J. (2016). Hybrid damper with stroke amplification for damping of offshore wind turbines. *Wind Energy (Chichester, England)*, *19*(12), 2223–2238. doi:10.1002/we.1977

Brown, W. C. (1984). The history of power transmission by radio waves. *IEEE Transactions on Microwave Theory and Techniques*, *32*(9), 1230–1242. doi:10.1109/TMTT.1984.1132833

Buchmann, R., Donnet, F., Gomez, P., Faure, E., Augé, I., & Pétrit, F. (2004). *Disydent: un environnement pour la conception*. Université Paris, VI.

Calderon, M., Calderon, A., Ramiro, A., Gonzalez, J., & Gonzalez, I. (2011). Evaluation of a hybrid photovoltaic-wind system with hydrogen storage performance using exergy analysis. *International Journal of Hydrogen Energy*, *36*(10), 5751–5762. doi:10.1016/j.ijhydene.2011.02.055

Çalis, H., & Çakir, A. (2007). Rotor bar fault diagnosis in three phase induction motors by monitoring fluctuations of motor current zero crossing instants. *Electric Power Systems Research*, *77*(5), 385–392. doi:10.1016/j.epsr.2006.03.017

Canale, M., Fagiano, L., & Novara, C. (2006). Semiactive suspension control using "fast" model predictive techniques. *IEEE Transactions on Control Systems Technology*, *14*(6), 1034–1046. doi:10.1109/TCST.2006.880196

Canale, M., Fagiano, L., & Razza, V. (2010). Approximate NMPC for vehicle stability: Design, implementation and SIL testing. *Control Engineering Practice*, *18*(6), 630–639. doi:10.1016/j.conengprac.2010.03.002

Carroll, J., & Dawson, D. M. (1995). Integrator backstepping techniques for the tracking control of permanent magnet brush DC motors. *IEEE Transactions on Industry Applications*, *55*(2), 248–255. doi:10.1109/28.370270

Caruntu, C. F., Balau, A. E., Lazar, M., van den Bosch, P. P. J., & Di Cairano, S. (2011). A predictive control solution for driveline oscillations damping. In Hybrid systems: Computation and Control (pp. 181-190). Chicago, IL: Academic Press. doi:10.1145/1967701.1967728

Caruntu, C. F., & Lazar, C. (2012). Robustly stabilising model predictive control design for networked control systems with an application to direct current motors. *IET Control Theory & Applications*, *6*(7), 943–952. doi:10.1049/iet-cta.2011.0103

Caruntu, C. F., & Lazar, C. (2014). Network delay predictive compensation based on time-delay modelling as disturbance. *International Journal of Control*, *87*(10), 2012–2026.

Caruntu, C. F., Lazar, M., Di Cairano, S., Gielen, R. H., & van den Bosch, P. P. J. (2011). Horizon-1 predictive control of networked controlled vehicle drivetrains. *18th IFAC World Congress*, 3824-3830. doi:10.3182/20110828-6-IT-1002.02780

Caruntu, C. F., Lazar, M., Gielen, R. H., van den Bosch, P. P. J., & Di Cairano, S. (2013). Lyapunov based predictive control of vehicle drivetrains over CAN. *Control Engineering Practice*, *21*(12), 1881–1898. doi:10.1016/j.conengprac.2012.05.012

Casimir, R., Boutleux, E., Clerc, G., & Yahoui, A. (2006). The use of features selection and nearest neighbours rule for faults diagnostic in induction motors. *Engineering Applications of Artificial Intelligence*, *19*(2), 169–177. doi:10.1016/j.engappai.2005.07.004

Chairman, P., Bhavaraju, M., & Biggerstaff, B. (1979). IEEE reliability test system: A report prepared by the Reliability Test System Task Force of the Application of Probability Methods Subcommittee. *IEEE Transactions on Power Apparatus and Systems*, *98*(6), 2047–2054.

Chakrabarty H. & Bhattacharya S. (2014). Prediction of Severe Thundestorms Applying Neural Network using RSRW Data. *International Journal of Computer Application, 89*(16).

Chakrabarty, H., & Bhattacharya, S. (2015). Application of K-Nearest Neighbor Technique to Predict Severe Thunderstorms. *International Journal of Computer Applications, 110*(10).

Chakrabarty, H., Murthy, C. A., Bhattacharya, S., & Gupta, A. D. (2013 b). Application of Artificial Neural Network to Predict Squall-Thunderstorms using RAWIND Data. *International Journal of Scientific & Engineering Research, 4*(5), 1313–1318.

Chakrabarty, H., Murthy, C. A., & Gupta, A. D. (2013 a). Application of Pattern Recognition Techniques to Predict Severe Thunderstorms. *International Journal of Computer Theory and Engineering, 5*(6), 850–855. doi:10.7763/IJCTE.2013.V5.810

Chakraborty, Sharma, & Tewari. (2017). Application of soft computing techniques over hard computing techniques: A survey. *International Journal of Indestructible Mathematics & Computing, 1*(1), 8-17.

Chang, R., Mithulananthan, N., & Saha, T. (2011). *Novel mixed-integer method to optimize distributed generation mix in primary distribution systems.* Paper presented at the Universities Power Engineering Conference (AUPEC), 2011 21st Australasian.

Chang, Y.-H., & Chan, W.-S. (2014). Adaptive dynamic surface control for uncertain nonlinear systems with interval type-2 fuzzy neural networks. *IEEE Transactions on Cybernetics, 44*(2), 293–304. doi:10.1109/TCYB.2013.2253548 PMID:23757550

Chatterjee, D., & Chakrabarty, H. (2015). Application of Machine Learning Technique to Predict Severe Thunderstorm using upper Air Data. *International Journal of Scientific and Engineering Research, 6*(7), 1527–1530.

Chatterjee, P., Pradhan, D., & De, U. K. (2008). Simulation of Local Severe Storm by Mesoscale Model MM5. *Indian Journal of Radio & Space Physics, 37*(6), 419–433.

Chaudhari, S. (2011). A Probe for Consistency in CAPE and CINE during the Prevalence of Severe Thunderstorms: Statistical-Fuzzy Coupled Approach. *Atmospheric and Climate Science, 01*(04), 197–205. doi:10.4236/acs.2011.14022

Chaudhuri, S. (2007). Preferred Type of Cloud in the Genesis of Severe Thunderstorms- A Soft Computing Approach. *Atmospheric Research, 88*(2), 149–156. doi:10.1016/j.atmosres.2007.10.008

Chelliah, M., Sankaran, S., Prasad, S., Gopalan, N., & Sivaselvan, B. (2012, January). Routing for Wireless Mesh Networks with Multiple Constraints Using Fuzzy Logic. *The International Arab Journal of Information Technology, 9*(1).

Chen, B., Kwan, K. H., & Tan, R. (2014). *Battery capacity planning for grid-connected solar photovoltaic systems.* Paper presented at the Signal and Information Processing Association Annual Summit and Conference (APSIPA), 2014 Asia-Pacific.

Chen, Y., Li, Z., Nie, L., Hu, X., Wang, X., Chua, T. S., & Zhang, X. (2012). A Semi-Supervised Bayesian Network Model for Microblog Topic Classification. In Coling, 561-576.

Chen, C. K., & Lin, C. L. (2010). Text Encryption Using ECG signals with Chaotic Logistic Map. *Proceedings of the the 5th Conference on Industrial Electronics and Applications (ICIEA) IEEE*, 1741–1746. doi:10.1109/ICIEA.2010.5515285

Chen, C.-W., Yeh, K., Chiang, W.-L., Chen, C.-Y., & Wu, D.-J. (2007a). Modeling, Hinf Control and Stability Analysis for Structural Systems Using Takagi-Sugeno Fuzzy Model. *Journal of Vibration and Control, 13*(11), 1519–1534. doi:10.1177/1077546307073690

Chen, D., T. G. (2005). Shunt Active Power Filters Applied in the Aircraft Power Utility. In *36th Power Electronics Specialists Conference, PESC '05* (pp. 59-63). IEEE. doi:10.1109/PESC.2005.1581602

Chen, H., & Tan, C. (2012). Prediction of type- 2 diabetes based on several element levels in blood and chemo metrics. *Biological Trace Element Research, 147*(1-3), 67–74. doi:10.1007/s12011-011-9306-4 PMID:22201046

Chen, S.-H., Zheng, L.-A., & Chou, J.-H. (2007b). A Mixed Robust/Optimal Active Vibration Control for Uncertain Flexible Structural Systems with Nonlinear Actuators Using Genetic Algorithm. *Journal of Vibration and Control, 13*(2), 185–201. doi:10.1177/1077546307070228

Chen, W., & Zhang, Z. (2010). Globally stable adaptive backstepping fuzzy control for output-feedback systems with unknown high-frequency gain sign. *Fuzzy Sets and Systems, 161*(6), 821–836. doi:10.1016/j.fss.2009.10.026

Chien, T., & Liao, T., (2005). Design of secure digital communication systems using chaotic modulation, cryptography and chaotic synchronization. *Chaos, Solitons and Fractals, 24*, 241–255.

Chiewchitboon, T., Soonthomphisaj, & Piyarat. (2003). Speed Control of Three-phase Induction Motor Online Tuning by Genetic Algorithm. *Fifth International Conference on Power Electronics and Drive Systems, PEDS 2003*, 184-188. doi:10.1109/PEDS.2003.1282751

Choi, K.-M., Cho, S.-W., Kim, D.-O., & Lee, I.-W. (2005). Active control for seismic response reduction using modal-fuzzy approach. *International Journal of Solids and Structures, 42*(16-17), 4779–4794. doi:10.1016/j.ijsolstr.2005.01.018

Choubey & Paul. (2015). GA_J48graft DT: A Hybrid Intelligent System for Diabetes Disease Diagnosis. *International Journal of Bio-Science and Bio-Technology, 7*(5), 135–150.

Choubey, & Paul. (2016). Classification Techniques for Diagnosis of Diabetes Disease: A Review. *International Journal of Biomedical Engineering and Technology, 21*(1), 15–39.

Choubey & Paul. (2016). GA_MLP NN: A Hybrid Intelligent System for Diabetes Disease Diagnosis. *International Journal of Intelligent Systems and Applications, 8*(1), 49-59.

Choubey, & Paul. (2017). GA_RBF NN: A Classification System for Diabetes. *International Journal of Biomedical Engineering and Technology, 23*(1), 71–93.

Choubey, D. K., & Paul, S. (2017). GA_SVM-A Classification System for Diagnosis of Diabetes. In Handbook of Research on Nature Inspired Soft Computing and Algorithms. IGI Global.

Choubey, Paul, & Bhattacharjee. (2014). Soft Computing Approaches for Diabetes Disease Diagnosis: A Survey. *International Journal of Applied Engineering Research, 9*, 11715-11726.

Choubey, D. K., Paul, S., Kuamr, S., & Kumar, S. (2017). Classification of Pima Indian Diabetes Dataset using Naive Bayes with Genetic Algorithm as an Attribute Selection. *Proceedings of the International Conference on Communication and Computing Systems (ICCCS 2016)*, 451-455.

Chouhan, S. S., & Halonen, K. (2014). The design and implementation of DTMOS biased all PMOS rectifier for RF Energy Harvesting. *New Circuits and Systems Conference (NEWCAS)*, 444 – 447. doi:10.1109/NEWCAS.2014.6934078

Cintineo, J. L., Pavolonis, M. J., Sieglaff, J. M., & Lindsey, D. T. (2012). Probabilistic Nowcasting of Severe Convection. *National Weather Association Annual Meeting*, Madison, WI.

Cloosterman, M. B. G., Hetel, L., van de Wouw, N., Heemels, W. P. M. H., Daafouz, J., & Nijmeijer, H. (2010). Controller synthesis for networked control systems. *Automatica, 46*(10), 1584–1594. doi:10.1016/j.automatica.2010.06.017

Cloosterman, M. B. G., van de Wouw, N., Heemels, W. P. M. H., & Nijmeijer, H. (2009). Stability of networked control systems with uncertain time-varying delays. *IEEE Transactions on Automatic Control, 54*(7), 1575–1580. doi:10.1109/TAC.2009.2015543

Collins, W., & Tissot, P. (n.d.). Use of an Artificial Neural Network to Forecast Thunderstorm Location. *NOAA*.

Colquhoun, J. R. (1987). A Decision Tree Method of Forecasting Thunderstorms, Severe Thunderstorms and Tornadoes. American Meteorological Society.

Costanzo, A., Fabiani, M., Romani, A., Masotti, D., & Rizzoli, V. (2010). Co-design of ultra-low power RF/Microwave receivers and converters for RFID and energy harvesting applications. *IEEE MTT-S International Microwave Symposium Digest (MTT)*, 856 – 859.

Cuenot, J.B., Larger, L., Goedgebuer, J.P., & Rhodes, W.T. (2001). Chaos Shift Keying with an Optoelectronic Encryption System Using Chaos in Wavelength. *IEEE Journal of Quantum Electronics, 37*(7), 849-855.

Dai, S.-L., Wang, C., & Wang, M. (2014, January). Dynamic learning from adaptive neural network control of a class of nonaffine nonlinear systems. *IEEE Transactions on Neural Networks and Learning Systems, 25*(1), 111–123. doi:10.1109/TNNLS.2013.2257843 PMID:24806648

Dangor, M. (2014). *Dynamic neural network-based feedback linearization of electrohydraulic suspension systems* (Doctoral dissertation).

Dangor, M., Dahunsi, O. A., Pedro, J. O., & Ali, M. M. (2014). Evolutionary algorithm-based PID controller tuning for nonlinear quarter-car electrohydraulic vehicle suspensions. *Nonlinear Dynamics, 78*(4), 2795–2810. doi:10.1007/s11071-014-1626-4

Dascalescu, A. C., Boriga, R., & Mihailescu, M. I. (2014). A Novel Chaos-Based Image Encryption Scheme. *Annals of the University of Craiova, Mathematics and Computer Science Series, 41*(1), 47–58.

Dasgupta, S., & De, U. K. (2004). A Logistic Regression Model for Prediction of Premonsoon Convective Development over Kolkata. *Indian Journal of Radio & Space Physics, 33*, 252–255.

Daud, M. Z., Mohamed, A., & Hannan, M. (2013). An improved control method of battery energy storage system for hourly dispatch of photovoltaic power sources. *Energy Conversion and Management, 73*, 256–270. doi:10.1016/j.enconman.2013.04.013

Davis, R. A., Charlton, A. J., Oehlschlager, S., & Wilson, J. C. (2006). Novel feature selection method for genetic programming using metabolomic ^{1}H NMR data. *Chemometrics and Intelligent Laboratory Systems, 81*(1), 50–59. doi:10.1016/j.chemolab.2005.09.006

Deepa, S. N., & Sivanandam. (2007). *Principles of Soft Computing*. John Wiley & Sons India Pvt. Ltd.

Deepa, S., & Kalimuthu, M. (2012). An Optimization of Association Rule Mining Algorithm using Weighted Quantum behaved PSO. *International Journal of Power Control Signal and Computation, 3*(1), 80-85.

Devabhaktuni, V., Alam, M., Depuru, S. S. S. R., Green, R. C., Nims, D., & Near, C. (2013). Solar energy: Trends and enabling technologies. *Renewable & Sustainable Energy Reviews, 19*, 555–564. doi:10.1016/j.rser.2012.11.024

Dhankot, M. A., & Soni, D. P. (2017). Behaviour of Triple Friction Pendulum isolator under forward directivity and fling step effect. *KSCE Journal of Civil Engineering, 21*(3), 872–881. doi:10.1007/s12205-016-0690-3

Di Cairano, S., Yanakiev, D., Bemporad, A., Kolmanovsky, I., & Hrovat, D. (2010). Model predictive powertrain control: An application to idle speed regulation. In L. del Re et al. (Eds.), Automotive Model Predictive Control (pp. 183-194). Springer-Verlag Berlin Heidelberg.

Di Cairano, S., Bemporad, A., Kolmanovsky, I. V., & Hrovat, D. (2007). Model predictive control of magnetically actuated mass spring dampers for automotive applications. *International Journal of Control, 80*(11), 1701–1716. doi:10.1080/00207170701379804

Didier, G., Ternisien, E., Caspary, O., & Razik, H. (2007). A new approach to detect broken rotor bars in induction machines by current spectrum analysis. *Mechanical Systems and Signal Processing, 21*(2), 1127–1142. doi:10.1016/j.ymssp.2006.03.002

Ding, J., Sun, X., Zhang, L., & Xie, J. (2017). *Optimization of Fuzzy Control for Magnetorheological Damping Structures*. Shock and Vibration.

Ditto, W., & Munakata, T. (1995). Principles and Applications of Chaotic Systems. Communications of the ACM, 38(11), 96-102.

Dorigo, M., & Stutzle, T. (2004). *Ant Colony Optimization*. MIT Press.

Drif, M., & Marques Cardoso, A. J. (2013). Airgap-eccentricity fault diagnosis in three-phase induction motors by the complex apparent power signature analysis. *IEEE Transactions on Industrial Electronics, 55*(3), 1404–1410. doi:10.1109/TIE.2007.909076

Dufour, P., Bhartiya, S., Dhurjati, P. S., & Doyle, F. J. III. (2005). Neural network-based software sensor: Training set design and application to a continuous pulp digester. *Control Engineering Practice, 13*(2), 135–143. doi:10.1016/j.conengprac.2004.02.013

Dugan, R. C. M. F. (1996). Electrical Power Systems Quality. New York: McGraw-Hill.

Dyke, S. J., Spencer, B. F., Jr., Sain, M. K., & Carlson, J. D. (1996). Experimental verification of semi-active structural control strategies using acceleration feedback. *Proceedings of the 3rd International Conference on Motion and Vibration Control.*

Eberhart, R., & Kennedy, J. (1995). A new optimizer using particle swarm theory. *Micro Machine and Human Science, 1995. MHS'95, Proceedings of the Sixth International Symposium*, 39-43. doi:10.1109/MHS.1995.494215

Ehrlich, P., & Radke, S. (2013). Energy-aware software development for embeddedsystems in HW/SW co-design. *IEEE 16th International Symposium on Design and Diagnostics of Electronic Circuits & Systems (DDECS).*

Eid, A., El-Kishky, H., Abdel-Salam, M., & El-Mohandes, T. (2010). VSCF Aircraft Electric Power System Performance with Active Power Filters. *42nd South Eastern Symposium on System Theory University of Texas at Tyler*, 182-187. doi:10.1109/SSST.2010.5442838

Elshamy, A. M., Rashed, A. N. Z., Mohamed, A. E. A., Faragalla, O. S., Mu, Y., Alshebeili, S. A., & El-Samie, F. E. (2013). Optical Image Encryption Based on Chaotic Baker Map and Double Random Phase Encoding. *Journal of Lightwave Technology, 31*(15), 2533–2539. doi:10.1109/JLT.2013.2267891

Emamghoreishi, S. A., Moini, R., & Sadeghi, S. H. H. (2001). *A Modular Neural Network Approach for Locating Cloud-To-Ground Lightning Strokes*. IEEE. doi:10.1109/ISEMC.2001.950547

Emmanouilidis, C., Hunter, A., Maclntyre, J., & Cox, C. (1999). Multiple-criteria genetic algorithms for feature selection in neuro-fuzzy modeling. *International Joint Conference on Neural Networks (IJCNN'99)*, *6*, 4387-4392. doi:10.1109/IJCNN.1999.830875

Erguzel, T. T., Ozekes, S., Gultekin, S., & Tarhan, N. (2014). Ant Colony Optimization Based Feature Selection Method for QEEG Data Classification. *Psychiatry Investigation*, *11*(3), 243–250. doi:10.4306/pi.2014.11.3.243 PMID:25110496

Estevez, P. A., & Caballero, R. E. (1998) A niching genetic algorithm for selecting features for neural classifiers. *Proceedings of 8th International Conference on Artificial Neural Networks*, 311-316. doi:10.1007/978-1-4471-1599-1_45

Eswaran, M., Athul, S., Niraj, P., Reddy, G. R., & Ramesh, M. R. (2017). Tuned liquid dampers for multi-storey structure: Numerical simulation using a partitioned FSI algorithm and experimental validation. *Sadhana*, *42*(4), 449–465.

Facen, A., & Boni, A. (2006). Power supply generation in CMOS passive UHF RFID tags. *International Conference on Research in Microelectronics and Electronics*, 33 – 36. doi:10.1109/RME.2006.1689889

Fan, M., Vittal, V., Heydt, G. T., & Ayyanar, R. (2012). Probabilistic power flow studies for transmission systems with photovoltaic generation using cumulants. *IEEE Transactions on Power Systems*, *27*(4), 2251–2261. doi:10.1109/TPWRS.2012.2190533

Farrell, J. A. (1998, September). Stability and approximator convergence in nonparametric nonlinear adaptive control. *IEEE Transactions on Neural Networks*, *9*(5), 1008–1020. doi:10.1109/72.712182 PMID:18255784

Farrell, J. A., & Polycarpou, M. M. (2006). *Adaptive Approximation Based Control: Unifying Neural, Fuzzy and Traditional Adaptive Approximation Approaches*. Hoboken, NJ: Wiley. doi:10.1002/0471781819

Felini, C., Merenda, M., & Corte, F. G. D. (2014). Dynamic impedance matching network for RF energy harvesting systems. *IEEE RFID Technology and Applications Conference (RFID-TA)*. 86 – 90. doi:10.1109/RFID-TA.2014.6934206

Filip-Vacarescu, N., Vulcu, C., & Dubina, D. (2016). Numerical Model of a Hybrid Damping System Composed of a Buckling Restrained Brace with a Magneto Rheological Damper. *Mathematical Modelling in Civil Engineering*, *12*(1), 13–22.

Fitwi A. H. & Nouh, S. (2011). Performance Analysis of Chaotic Encryption using a Shared Image as a Key. *Journal of the European Economic Association*, *28*, 1-23.

Flatau, A. B., Hall, D. L., & Schlesselman, J. M. (1993). Magnetostrictive Vibration Control Systems. *Journal of Intelligent Material Systems and Structures*, *4*(4), 560–565. doi:10.1177/1045389X9300400419

Fock, E. (2014, August). Global sensitivity analysis approach for input selection and system identification purposes—A new framework for feedforward neural networks. *IEEE Transactions on Neural Networks and Learning Systems*, *25*(8), 1484–1495. doi:10.1109/TNNLS.2013.2294437 PMID:25050946

Gao, H., Zhang, Y., Liang, S. & Li, D. (2006). A new chaotic algorithm for image encryption. *Chaos, Solitons and Fractals*, *29*, 393–399.

Gawande, R. P., & Ghuse, N. D. (2015). An Efficient Approach towards Thunderstorm Detection using Saliency Map. *International Journal of Computer Science and Information Technologies*, *6*(3), 2429–2434.

Gentry, C. (2014). *Computing on the edge of chaos: Structure and randomness in encrypted computation*. Electronic Colloquium on Computational Complexity, Report No. 106.

Georgiadis, A., Andia, G., & Collado, A. (2010). Rectenna design and optimization using reciprocity theory and harmonic balance analysis for electromagnetic (EM) energy harvesting. *IEEE Antennas and Wireless Propagation Letters*, *9*(1), 444–446. doi:10.1109/LAWP.2010.2050131

Georgilakis, P. S., & Hatziargyriou, N. D. (2013). Optimal distributed generation placement in power distribution networks: Models, methods, and future research. *IEEE Transactions on Power Systems*, *28*(3), 3420–3428. doi:10.1109/TPWRS.2012.2237043

Ghamarian, A. H., Stuijk, S., Basten, T., Geilen, M. G. W., & Theelen, B. D. (2007). *Latency Minimization for Synchronous Data Flow Graphs*. Digital System Design Architectures, Methods and Tools.

Ghosh, A., & Ledwich, G. (2002). *Power Quality Enhancement Using Custom Power Devices*. Boston, MA: Kluwer. doi:10.1007/978-1-4615-1153-3

Ghosh, S., Sen, P. K., & De, U. K. (1999). Identification of Significant Parameters for the Prediction of Pre-monsoon Thunderstorms at Calcutta, India. *International Journal of Climatology*, *19*(6), 673–681. doi:10.1002/(SICI)1097-0088(199905)19:6<673::AID-JOC384>3.0.CO;2-O

Gidaris, I., & Taflanidis, A. A. (2015). Performance assessment and optimization of fluid viscous dampers through life-cycle cost criteria and comparison to alternative design approaches. *Bulletin of Earthquake Engineering*, *13*(4), 1003–1028. doi:10.1007/s10518-014-9646-5

Gielen, R. H., & Lazar, M. (2009a). Stabilization of networked control systems via non-monotone control Lyapunov functions. In *48th IEEE Conference on Decision and Control* (pp. 7942-7948). Shanghai, China: IEEE. doi:10.1109/CDC.2009.5400139

Gielen, R. H., & Lazar, M. (2011). Stabilization of polytopic delay difference inclusions via the Razumikhin approach. *Automatica*, *47*(12), 2562–2570. doi:10.1016/j.automatica.2011.08.046

Gielen, R. H., Olaru, S., Lazar, M., Heemels, W. P. M. H., van de Wouw, N., & Niculescu, S.-I. (2010). On polytopic inclusions as a modeling framework for systems with time-varying delays. *Automatica*, *46*(3), 615–619. doi:10.1016/j.automatica.2010.01.002

Giri, P. K. (2012). A Survey on Soft Computing Techniques for Multi-Constrained QoS Routing in MANET. *IJCIT*, *3*(2).

Gökçek, M., Bayülken, A., & Bekdemir, Ş. (2007). Investigation of wind characteristics and wind energy potential in Kirklareli, Turkey. *Renewable Energy*, *32*(10), 1739–1752. doi:10.1016/j.renene.2006.11.017

Gokila, D., & Rajalakshmi, S. (2014). Weighted Quantum Particle Swarm Optimization To Association Rule Mining And PSO To Clustering. *Journal of Theoretical and Applied Information Technology*, *65*(3), 680–686.

Goldberg, D. E. (1989). *Genetic Algorithms in Search, Optimization, and Machine Learning*. Reading, MA: Addison-Wesley Professional.

Gorinevsky, D. (1995, September). On the persistency of excitation in radial basis function network identification of nonlinear systems. *IEEE Transactions on Neural Networks*, *6*(5), 1237–1244. doi:10.1109/72.410365 PMID:18263411

Grzymala Busse, J. W. (1997). A new version of the rule induction system. *Fundamenta Informaticae*, *31*, 27–39.

Guclu, R., & Yazici, H. (2007). Fuzzy Logic Control of a Non-linear Structural System against Earthquake Induced Vibration. *Journal of Vibration and Control*, *13*(11), 1535–1551. doi:10.1177/1077546307077663

Guillermin, P. (1996). Fuzzy logic Applied to Motor Control. *IEEE Transactions on Industry Applications, 32*(1), 51–56. doi:10.1109/28.485812

Guo, D., Wen, Q., Li, W., Zhang, H., & Jin, Z. (2015). Key Agreement Scheme. *Wireless Personal Communication*, 1-15.

Guo, X., & Zhang, J. (2008). Cryptanalysis of the Chaotic-Based Key Agreement Protocols. *Proceedings of the International Symposium on Biometrics and Security Technologies (ISBAST)*, 1–3.

Hagerty, J. A., Helmbrecht, F. B., McCalpin, W. H., Zane, R., & Popovic, Z. B. (2004). Recycling ambient microwave energy with broad band rectenna arrays. *IEEE Transactions on Microwave Theory and Techniques, 52*(3), 1014–1024. doi:10.1109/TMTT.2004.823585

Haldulakar, R., & Agrawal, J. (2011). Optimization of Association Rule Mining through Genetic Algorithm. *International Journal on Computer Science and Engineering, 3*(3), 1252-1259.

Hameed, Z., & Moez, K. (2013). Fully-integrated passive threshold-compensated PMOS rectifier for RF energy harvesting. *International Midwest Symposium on Circuits and Systems (MWSCAS)*, 129–132. doi:10.1109/MWSCAS.2013.6674602

Han, J., & Kamber, M. (2006). Data Mining: Concepts and Techniques. Morgan Kaufmann.

Hanlon, C. J., Young, G. S., Verlinde, J., Small, A. A., & Bose, S. (2014). Probabilistic Forecasting for Isolated Thunderstorms using a Genetic Algorithm: The DC3 Campaign. *Journal of Geophysical Research, D, Atmospheres, 119*(1), 65–74. doi:10.1002/2013JD020195

Hashemi, S. M. A., Haji Kazemi, H., & Karamodin, A. (2016). Localized genetically optimized wavelet neural network for semi-active control of buildings subjected to earthquake. *Structural Control and Health Monitoring, 23*(8), 1074–1087. doi:10.1002/stc.1823

Haykin, S. (1994). *Neural Networks: A Comprehensive Foundation*. Upper Saddle River, NJ: Prentice-Hall.

Hayter, A. (2012). *Probability and statistics for engineers and scientists*. Nelson Education.

Heemels, W. P. M. H., Teel, A. R., van de Wouw, N., & Nesic, D. (2010). Networked control systems with communication constraints: Tradeoffs between transmission intervals, delays and performance. *IEEE Transactions on Automatic Control, 55*(8), 1781–1796. doi:10.1109/TAC.2010.2042352

Hemour, S., Zhao, Y., Lorenz, C. H. P., Houssameddine, D., Gui, Y., Hu, C. M., & Wu, K. (2014). Towards low-power high-efficiency RF and microwave energy harvesting. IEEE Transactions on Microwave Theory and Techniques, 62(4), 965 – 976.

Henrique, C., Lorenz, P., Hemour, S., Li, W., Xie, Y., Gauthier, J., & Wu, K. et al. (2015). Breaking the efficiency barrier for ambient microwave power harvesting with heterojunction backward tunnel diodes. *IEEE Transactions on Microwave Theory and Techniques, 63*(12), 4544–4555. doi:10.1109/TMTT.2015.2495356

Heo, G., Kim, C., Jeon, S., Seo, S., & Jeon, J. (2016). Research on Hybrid Seismic Response Control System for Motion Control of Two Span Bridge. *Journal of Physics: Conference Series, 744*(1), 1–12.

Hermans, R. M., Lazar, M., Di Cairano, S., & Kolmanovsky, I. V. (2009). Low complexity model predictive control of electromagnetic actuators with a stability guarantee. In *28th American Control Conference* (pp. 2708-2713). St. Louis, MO: Academic Press. doi:10.1109/ACC.2009.5160328

Herpel, T., Hielscher, K. S., Klehmet, U., & German, R. (2009). Stochastic and deterministic performance evaluation of automotive CAN communication. *Computer Networks, 53*(8), 1171–1185. doi:10.1016/j.comnet.2009.02.008

Hespanha, J., Naghshtabrizi, P., & Xu, Y. (2007). A survey of recent results in networked control systems. *Proceedings of the IEEE - Special Issue on Technology of Networked Control Systems, 95*(1), 138-162. doi:10.1109/JPROC.2006.887288

Hickey, S. J. (2013). Naive Bayes Classification of Public Health Data with Greedy Feature Selection. *Communications of the IIMA, 13*(2), 87–97.

Hiemenz, G. J., & Wereley, N. M. (1999). Seismic Response of Civil Structures Utilizing Semi-Active MR and ER Bracing Systems. *Journal of Intelligent Material Systems and Structures, 10*(8), 646–651. doi:10.1106/TTXP-20DM-G861-HU0M

Hocine, R., Kalla, H., Kalla, S., & Arar, C. (2012). A methodology for verification of embedded systems based on systemc. *International Conference on Complex Systems (ICCS)*. doi:10.1109/ICoCS.2012.6458557

Holland, J. H. (1968). *Hierarchical descriptions, universal spaces and adaptive systems*. DTIC Document.

Holland, J. H. (1975). *Adaptation in Natural and Artificial Systems: an introductory analysis with applications to biology, control, and artificial intelligence*. University of Michigan Press.

Hong, S.-R., & Choi, S.-B. (2005). Vibration Control of a Structural System Using Magneto-Rheological Fluid Mount. *Journal of Intelligent Material Systems and Structures, 16*(11-12), 931–936. doi:10.1177/1045389X05053917

Hosain, M. K., Kouzani, A. Z., Samad, M. F., & Tye, S. J. (2015). A miniature energy harvesting rectenna for operating a head-mountable deep brain stimulation device. *IEEE Access on Special Section on Bio-Compatible Materials and Bio-Electromagnetics for Bio-Medical Applications, 3*(1), 223–234.

Hosain, M. K., Kouzani, A. Z., Tye, S., Kaynak, A., & Berk, M. (2015). RF rectifiers for EM power harvesting in a deep brain stimulating device. *Australasian Physical & Engineering Sciences in Medicine*, 1–16. PMID:25600671

Hrovat, D., Asgari, J., & Fodor, M. (2000). Automotive mechatronic systems. In C. T. Leondes (Ed.), *Mechatronic Systems Techniques and Applications* (Vol. 2, pp. 1–98). CRC Press.

Hsu, C.-F. (2013, April). Adaptive neural complementary sliding-mode control via functional-linked wavelet neural network. *Engineering Applications of Artificial Intelligence, 26*(4), 1221–1229. doi:10.1016/j.engappai.2012.11.012

Huang, J., Raabe, A., Hu, B. C., & Knoll, A. (2013). *A framework for reliability-aware design exploration on MPSoC based systems*. Springer Science and Business Media.

Huang, X. (2012). A New Digital Image Encryption Algorithm Based on 4D Chaotic System. *International Journal of Pure and Applied Mathematics, 80*(4), 609-616.

Huang, X., Sun, T., Li, Y., & Liang, J. (2015). A Color Image Encryption Algorithm Based on a Fractional-Order Hyperchaotic System. *Entropy, 17,* 28-38.

Huang, C., Bai, Y., & Liu, X. (2010). H-infinity state feedback control for a class of networked cascade control systems with uncertain delay. *IEEE Transactions on Industrial Informatics, 6*(1), 62–72. doi:10.1109/TII.2009.2033589

Hung, D. Q., & Mithulananthan, N. (2012). *An optimal operating strategy of DG unit for power loss reduction in distribution systems*. Paper presented at the Industrial and Information Systems (ICIIS), 2012 7th IEEE International Conference on. doi:10.1109/ICIInfS.2012.6304773

Hung, D. Q., Mithulananthan, N., & Bansal, R. (2013). Analytical strategies for renewable distributed generation integration considering energy loss minimization. *Applied Energy, 105,* 75–85. doi:10.1016/j.apenergy.2012.12.023

Hung, D. Q., Mithulananthan, N., & Bansal, R. C. (2014). An optimal investment planning framework for multiple distributed generation units in industrial distribution systems. *Applied Energy, 124,* 62–72. doi:10.1016/j.apenergy.2014.03.005

Hung, D. Q., Mithulananthan, N., & Lee, K. Y. (2014). Determining PV penetration for distribution systems with time-varying load models. *IEEE Transactions on Power Systems*, *29*(6), 3048–3057. doi:10.1109/TPWRS.2014.2314133

IEEE(1992*IEEE Recommended Practices and Requirements for Harmonic Control in Electrical Power Systems, IEEE Standard 519-1992*. IEEE.

Inbarani, H. H., Azar, A. T., & Jothi, G. (2014). Supervised hybrid feature selection based on PSO and Rough sets for medical diagnosis. *Computer Methods and Programs in Biomedicine*, *113*(1), 175–185. doi:10.1016/j.cmpb.2013.10.007 PMID:24210167

Ismail, B., Abdeldjebar, H., Abdelkrim, B., Mazari, B., & Rahli, M. (2008). Optimal Fuzzy Self-Tuning of PI Controller Using Genetic Algorithm for Induction Motor Speed Control. *International Journal of Automotive Technology*, *2*(2), 85–95. doi:10.20965/ijat.2008.p0085

Jabbar, H., Song, Y. S., & Jeong, T. T. (2010). RF energy harvesting system and circuits for charging of mobile devices. *IEEE Transactions on Consumer Electronics*, *56*(1), 247–252. doi:10.1109/TCE.2010.5439152

Jafarzadeh, H., & Sadeghzadeh, M. (2014). Improved Apriori algorithm using fuzzy logic. *IJARCSSE*, *4*(6), 439-447.

Jain, S., Agrawal, P., & Gupta, H. (2002). Fuzzy logic controlled shunt active power filter for power quality improvement. *IEE Proceedings. Electric Power Applications*, *149*(5), 317–328. doi:10.1049/ip-epa:20020511

Jakimoski, G., & Kocarev, L. (2001). Chaos and Cryptography: Block Encryption Ciphers Based on Chaotic Maps. *IEEE Transactions on Circuits and Systems-I, Fundamental Theory and Applications*, *48*(2), 163-169.

Jamali, A., Nor, N., & Ibrahim, T. (2015). *Energy storage systems and their sizing techniques in power system—A review*. Paper presented at the Energy Conversion (CENCON), 2015 IEEE Conference on.

Jamali, A., Nor, N., Ibrahim, T., & Romlie, M. F. (2016). *An analytical approach for the sizing and siting of battery-sourced inverters in distribution networks*. Paper presented at the Intelligent and Advanced Systems (ICIAS), 2016 6th International Conference on. doi:10.1109/ICIAS.2016.7824086

Jamil, M., & Anees, A. S. (2016). Optimal sizing and location of SPV (solar photovoltaic) based MLDG (multiple location distributed generator) in distribution system for loss reduction, voltage profile improvement with economical benefits. *Energy*, *103*, 231–239. doi:10.1016/j.energy.2016.02.095

Jamshidi, M., & Chang, C. C. (2017) A new self-powered electromagnetic damper for structural vibration control. *Proceedings SPIE Sensors and Smart Structures Technologies for Civil, Mechanical, and Aerospace Systems*.

Jayaram, I., & Purdy, C. (2012). Using constraint graphs to improve embedded systemsdesign. *IEEE 55th International Midwest Symposium on Circuits and Systems (MWSCAS)*.

Jiang, Z. P., & Wang, Y. (2001). Input-to-state stability for discrete-time nonlinear systems. *Automatica*, *37*(6), 857–869. doi:10.1016/S0005-1098(01)00028-0

Jing, C., Youlin, X., Weilian, Q., & Zhtlun, W. (2004). Seismic response control of a complex structure using multiple MR dampers: Experimental investigation. *Earthquake Engineering and Engineering Vibration*, *3*(2), 181–193. doi:10.1007/BF02858233

Joe, P., Koppert, H. J., & Heizenreder, D. (n.d.). *Severe Weather Forecasting Tool in the Ninjo Workstation*. Meteorological Service of Canada.

Johari, D., Rahman, T. K. A., & Musirin, I. (2007). Artificial Neural Network based Technique for Lightning Prediction. In *Proceeding of Student Conference on Research and Development*. IEEE.

Johnson, J. G., Pantelides, C. P., & Reaveley, L. D. (2015). Nonlinear rooftop tuned mass damper frame for the seismic retrofit of buildings. *Earthquake Engineering & Structural Dynamics*, *44*(2), 299–316. doi:10.1002/eqe.2473

Jordans, R., Siyoum, F., Stuijk, S., Kumar, A., & Corpal, H. (2011). *An Automated Flow to Map Throughput Constrained Application to a MPSoC*. Academic Press.

Jung, J. H., Lee, J. J., & Kwon, B. H. (2006). Online diagnosis of induction motors using MCSA. *IEEE Transactions on Industrial Electronics*, *53*(6), 1842–1852. doi:10.1109/TIE.2006.885131

Juntian, G., Shanqiang, G., Wanxing, F., Han, Z., & Yue, C. (2014). A Movement Prediction Method of CG Flashes based on Lightning and Convective Clouds Clustering and Tracking Technology. In *Proceeding of International Conference on Lightning Protection* (ICLP) (pp. 555-559). IEEE.

Juntian, G., Shanqiang, G., & Wanxing, F. (2011). A Lightning Motion Prediction Technology based on Spatial Clustering Method. In *Proceeding of International Conference on Lightning*. IEEE. doi:10.1109/APL.2011.6110234

Kadupitiya, J. C. S., Abeythunga, T. N., Ranathunga, P. D. M. T., & De Silva, D. S. (2015). Optimizing RF energy harvester design for low power applications by integrating multi stage voltage doubler on patch antenna. *International Conference on Ubi-Media Computing (UMEDIA)*. 335 – 338. doi:10.1109/UMEDIA.2015.7297481

Kahn, G. (1974). The semantics of a simple language for parallel programming. *Information Processing*, *74*, 471-475. doi:10.1109/MDSO.2007.28

Kamalinejad, P., Keikhosravy, K., Mirabbasi, S., & Leung, V. C. M. (2013). An efficiency enhancement technique for CMOS rectifiers with low start-up voltage for UHF RFID tags. *International Green Computing Conference (IGCC)*, 1 – 6. doi:10.1109/IGCC.2013.6604483

Kanaya, H., Tsukamoto, S., Hirabaru, T., Kanemoto, D., Pokharel, R. K., & Yoshida, K. (2013). Energy harvesting circuit on a one sided directional flexible antenna. *IEEE Microwave and Wireless Components Letters*, *23*(3), 164–166. doi:10.1109/LMWC.2013.2246779

Karan, S., Major, B., & Sally, A. M. (2009). Real Time Power Estimation and Thread Scheduling via Performance Counters. *SIGARCH Computer Architecture News*, *37*.

Karlik, B., & Oztoprak, E. (2012). Personalized cancer treatment by using Naïve Bayes Classifier. *International Journal of Machine Learning and Computing*, *2*(3), 339–344. doi:10.7763/IJMLC.2012.V2.141

Karolak, D., Taris, Thierry, Deval, Y., Begueret, J. B., & Mariano, A. (2012). Design comparison of low-power rectifiers dedicated to RF energy harvesting. *International Conference on Electronics, Circuits and Systems (ICECS)*, 524 – 527. doi:10.1109/ICECS.2012.6463693

Kawai, T. (1977). New Element Models in Discrete Structural Analysis. *Journal of the Society of Naval Architects of Japan*, *141*(141), 174–180. doi:10.2534/jjasnaoe1968.1977.174

Kazmierska, J., & Malicki, J. (2008). Application of the Naïve Bayesian Classifier to optimize treatment decisions. *Radiotherapy and Oncology: Journal of the European Society for Therapeutic Radiology and Oncology*, *86*(2), 211–216. doi:10.1016/j.radonc.2007.10.019 PMID:18022719

Kelly, T. E. (2001). *In-Structure Damping and Energy Dissipation Design Guidelines*. Holmes Consulting Group. Available on www.holmesgroup.com

Kelly, J. M., Leitmann, G., & Soldatos, A. G. (1987). Robust Control of Base-Isolated Structures under Earthquake Excitation. *Journal of Optimization Theory and Applications*, *53*(2), 159–180. doi:10.1007/BF00939213

Kensaku, K., Caitlin, A., Houlihan, E., Andrew, B., & David, F. L. (2005). Improving clinical practice using clinical decision support systems: a systematic review of trials to identify features critical to success. *BMJ (Clinical Research Ed.), 330*(7494), 765.

Khalfi, B., Hamdaoui, B., Ghorbel, M. B., Guizani, M., & Zhang, X. (2016). Joint data and power transfer optimization for energy harvesting wireless networks. *IEEE Conference on Computer Communications Workshops*, 1-6. doi:10.1109/INFCOMW.2016.7562175

Khalid, S. N. (2009). Application of Power Electronics to Power System. New Delhi: University Science Press.

Khalid, S., & Dwivedi, B. (2007). A Review of State of Art Techniques in Active Power Filters and Reactive Power Compensation. *National Journal of Technology, 3*(1), 10–18.

Khalid, S., & Dwivedi, B. (2013). Power quality improvement of constant frequency aircraft electric power system using Fuzzy Logic, Genetic Algorithm and Neural network control based control scheme. *International Electrical Engineering Journal, 4*(3), 1098–1104.

Khalil. (2002). *Nonlinear Systems* (3rd ed.). Upper Saddle River, NJ: Prentice-Hall.

Khare, A.A., Shukla, P.B., & Silakari, S.C. (2014). Secure and Fast Chaos based Encryption System using Digital Logic Circuit. *International Journal of Computer Network and Information Security, 6*, 25-33.

Khashan, O.A.,. Zin, A.M, & Sundararajan, E.A. (2015). ImgFS: A Transparent Cryptography for Stored Images Using a Filesystem in Userspace. *Frontiers of Information Technology & Electronic Engineering, 16*(1), 28-42.

Khatod, D. K., Pant, V., & Sharma, J. (2013). Evolutionary programming based optimal placement of renewable distributed generators. *IEEE Transactions on Power Systems, 28*(2), 683–695. doi:10.1109/TPWRS.2012.2211044

Khemaissia, S., & Morris, A. (1998, June). Use of an artificial neuroadaptive robot model to describe adaptive and learning motor mechanisms in the central nervous system. *IEEE Transactions on Systems, Man, and Cybernetics. Part B, Cybernetics, 28*(3), 404–416. doi:10.1109/3477.678635 PMID:18255956

Khodabandolehlou, H., Pekcan, G., Fadali, M. S., & Salem, M. (2017). Active neural predictive control of seismically isolated structures. *Structural Control and Health Monitoring*, e2061. doi:10.1002/stc.2061

Kiencke, U., & Nielsen, L. (2005). *Automotive control systems: For engine, driveline, and vehicle.* Springer-Verlag Berlin. doi:10.1007/b137654

Kim, G., & Chung, Y. C. (2006). Optimization of UHF RFID tag antennas using a genetic algorithm. *Antennas and Propagation Society International Symposium*, 2087 – 2090.

Kim, H.-S., & Roschke, P. N. (2006). Design of fuzzy logic controller for smart base isolation system using genetic algorithm. *Engineering Structures, 28*(1), 84–96. doi:10.1016/j.engstruct.2005.07.006

Kim, H.-S., & Roschke, P. N. (2007). GA-fuzzy control of smart base isolated benchmark building using supervisory control technique. *Advances in Engineering Software, 38*(7), 453–465. doi:10.1016/j.advengsoft.2006.10.004

Kim, S., Vyas, R., Bito, J., Niotaki, K., Collado, A., Georgiadis, A., & Tentzeris, M. M. (2014). Ambient RF energy harvesting technologies for self-sustainable standalone wireless sensor platforms. *Proceedings of the IEEE, 102*(11), 1649–1666. doi:10.1109/JPROC.2014.2357031

Kobori, T. (1990). Technology Development and Forecast of Dynamical Intelligent Building (D.I.B). *Journal of Intelligent Material Systems and Structures, 1*(4), 391–407. doi:10.1177/1045389X9000100402

Komorowski, J., & Ohrn, A. (1999). Modelling prognostic power of cardiac tests using rough sets. *Artificial Intelligence in Medicine, 15*(2), 167–191. doi:10.1016/S0933-3657(98)00051-7 PMID:10082180

Kotani, K. (2013). Highly efficient CMOS rectifier assisted by symmetric and voltage-boost PV-cell structures for synergistic ambient energy harvesting. *Custom Integrated Circuits Conference (CICC)*, 1–4. doi:10.1109/CICC.2013.6658515

Kotani, K., Sasaki, A., & Ito, T. (2009). High efficiency differential drive CMOS rectifier for UHF RFIDs. *IEEE Journal of Solid-State Circuits, 44*(11), 3011–3018. doi:10.1109/JSSC.2009.2028955

Kothari, D., & Nagrath, I. (2008). *Power system engineering*. McGraw-Hill.

Kowsalya, M. (2014). Optimal size and siting of multiple distributed generators in distribution system using bacterial foraging optimization. *Swarm and Evolutionary Computation, 15*, 58–65. doi:10.1016/j.swevo.2013.12.001

Koza, J. R. (1992). *Genetic Programming: On the Programming of Computers by Means of Natural Selection*. Cambridge, MA: MIT Press.

Kumar, A. (2017). Intelligent and efficient routing for manet: A soft computing technique. *International Journal of Research in Computer Applications and Robotics, 5*(1).

Kumar, C.V., (2015). Secured Patient Information Transmission Using Reversible Watermarking and DNA Encrytion for Medical Images. *Applied Mathematical Sciences, 9*(48), 2381 – 2391.

Kumar, G. (2010). Report on cell tower radiation. Electrical Engineering Department, IIT Bombay, Powai, Mumbai.

Kumar, P., & Mahajan, A. (2009). Soft Computing Techniques for the Control of an Active Power Filter. *IEEE Transactions on Power Delivery, 24*(1), 452–461. doi:10.1109/TPWRD.2008.2005881

Kumar, S. (2003). On Packet Switched Networks for on-Chip Communication. In *Networks on Chip*. Kluwer Academic.

Kumar, V., & Islam, A. (2015). CNFET based voltage multiplier circuit for rf energy harvesting applications. *International Conference on Communication Systems and Network Technologies (ICCSNT)*, 789 – 791. doi:10.1109/CSNT.2015.59

Kurdila, A. J., Narcowich, F. J., & Ward, J. D. (1995, March). Persistency of excitation in identification using radial basis function approximants. *SIAM Journal on Control and Optimization, 33*(2), 625–642. doi:10.1137/S0363012992232555

Kuruvilla, J., Sankar, A., & Sukumaran, D. (n.d.). A Study on image analysis of Myristica fragrans for Automatic Harvesting. *IOSR Journal of Computer Engineering*.

Kwok, H.S., & Tang, W.K.S. (2007). A Fast Image Encryption System Based on Chaotic Maps With Finite Precision Representation. *Chaos, Solitons and Fractals, Elsevier, 32*, 1518–1529.

Lakhani, M. T., & Soni, D. P. (2017). Comparative Study of Smart Base-Isolation Using Fuzzy Control and Neural Network. *Procedia Engineering, 173*, 1825–1832. doi:10.1016/j.proeng.2016.12.227

Lakshmanan, V., & Stumpf, G. J. (n.d.). A Real-Time Learning Technique to Predict Cloud -to- Ground Lightning. *NOAA*.

Lakshmi, S., & Sankaranarayanan, V. (2010). *A study of Edge Detection Techniques for Segmentation Computing Approaches. IJCA*.

Lambi´c, D. (2014). Security Analysis and Improvement of a Block Cipher With Dynamic S-Boxes Based on Tent Map. *Nonlinear Dynamics*, 1-9.

Lam, T., Anderschitz, M., & Dietz, V. (2006, February). Contribution of feedback and feedforward strategies to locomotor adaptations. *Journal of Neurophysiology, 95*(2), 766–773. doi:10.1152/jn.00473.2005 PMID:16424453

Landi, L., Grazi, G., & Diotallevi, P. P. (2016). Comparison of different models for friction pendulum isolators in structures subjected to horizontal and vertical ground motions. *Soil Dynamics and Earthquake Engineering*, *81*, 75–83. doi:10.1016/j.soildyn.2015.10.016

Lavopa, E., Zanchetta, P., Sumner, M., & Cupertino, F. (2009). Real-time estimation of Fundamental Frequency and harmonics for active shunt power filters in aircraft Electrical Systems. *IEEE Transactions on Industrial Electronics*, *56*(8), 412–416. doi:10.1109/TIE.2009.2015292

Lazar, M. (2006). *Model predictive control of hybrid systems: Stability and robustness* (PhD thesis). Eindhoven University of Technology, The Netherlands.

Lazar, M. (2009). Flexible control Lyapunov functions. In *28th American Control Conference* (pp. 102-107). St. Louis, MO: Academic Press.

Lazar, M., & Heemels, W. P. M. H. (2008). Optimized input-to-state stabilization of discrete-time nonlinear systems with bounded inputs. In *27th American Control Conference* (pp. 2310-2315). Seattle, WA: Academic Press. doi:10.1109/ACC.2008.4586836

Lazar, M., Heemels, W. P. M. H., Weiland, S., & Bemporad, A. (2006). Stabilizing model predictive control of hybrid systems. *IEEE Transactions on Automatic Control*, *51*(11), 1813–1818. doi:10.1109/TAC.2006.883059

Le Boudec, J.-Y., & Thiran, P. (2001). *Network calculus*. Springer-Verlag Berlin. doi:10.1007/3-540-45318-0

Lee, P., Pei, S., & Chen, Y., (2003). Generating Chaotic Stream Ciphers Using Chaotic Systems. *Chinese Journal of Physics*, *41*(6), 559-581.

Lee, A., Zinaman, O., Logan, J., Bazilian, M., Arent, D., & Newmark, R. L. (2012). Interactions, complementarities and tensions at the nexus of natural gas and renewable energy. *The Electricity Journal*, *25*(10), 38–48. doi:10.1016/j.tej.2012.10.021

Lee, R. R., & Passner, J. E. (1993). *The Development and Verification of TIPS: An Expert System to Forecast Thunderstorm Occurrence*. Academic Press.

Lee, S.-H., & Terzopoulos, D. (2006, July). Heads up! Biomechanical modeling and neuromuscular control of the neck. *ACM Transactions on Graphics*, *25*(3), 1188–1198. doi:10.1145/1141911.1142013

Le, H., Fong, N., & Luong, H. C. (2010). RF energy harvesting circuit with on-chip antenna for biomedical applications. *International Conference on Communications and Electronics (ICCE)*, 115 – 117.

Lekkas, S., & Mikhailov, L. (2010). Evolving fuzzy medical diagnosis of Pima Indians diabetes and of dermatological disease. *Artificial Intelligence in Medicine*, *50*(2), 117–126. doi:10.1016/j.artmed.2010.05.007 PMID:20566274

Leonhard, W. (1985). *Control of electrical drives*. New York: Springer-Verlag. doi:10.1007/978-3-662-11371-4

Le, T., Mayaram, K., & Fiez, T. (2008). Efficient far-field radio frequency energy harvesting for passively powered sensor networks. *IEEE Journal of Solid-State Circuits*, *43*(5), 1287–1302. doi:10.1109/JSSC.2008.920318

Li, S., Mou, X., & Cai, Y., (2001). Improving Security of a Chaotic Encryption Approach. *Physics Letters A*, *290*, 127-133.

Li, S., Mou, X., Yang, B.L., Ji, Z., & Zhang, J. (2003). Problems With a Probabilistic Encryption Scheme Based on Chaotic Systems. *International Journal of Bifurcation and Chaos*, *13*(10), 3063-3077.

Li, Z., Li, K., Wen, C., & Soh, Y. C. (2003). A New Chaotic Secure Communication System. IEEE Transactions on Communications, 51(8), 1306-1312.

Li, B., Shao, X., Shahshahan, N., Goldsman, N., Salter, T., & Metze, G. M. (2013). An antenna co-design dual band RF energy harvester. *IEEE Transactions on Circuits and Systems. I, Regular Papers*, *60*(12), 1–11. doi:10.1109/TCSI.2013.2264712

Li, H. N., Jia, Y., & Wang, S. Y. (2004). Theoretical and Experimental Studies on Reduction for Multi-Model Seismic Responses of High-Rise Structures by Tuned Liquid Dampers. *Journal of Vibration and Control*, *10*, 1041–1056.

Li, H., & Shi, Y. (2013). Output feedback predictive control for constrained linear systems with intermittent measurements. *Systems & Control Letters*, *62*(4), 345–354. doi:10.1016/j.sysconle.2013.01.003

Li, H., Sun, Z., Liu, H., & Chow, M. Y. (2008). Predictive observer-based control for networked control systems with network-induced delay and packet dropout. *Asian Journal of Control*, *10*(6), 638–650. doi:10.1002/asjc.65

Lin, C.-C., Lu, L.-Y., Lin, G.-L., & Yang, T.-W. (2010). Vibration control of seismic structures using semi-active friction multiple tuned mass dampers. *Engineering Structures*, *32*(10), 3404–3417. doi:10.1016/j.engstruct.2010.07.014

Lin, C.-K. (2006). Nonsingular terminal sliding mode control of robot manipulators using fuzzy wavelet networks. *IEEE Transactions on Fuzzy Systems*, *14*(6), 849–859. doi:10.1109/TFUZZ.2006.879982

Lin, G. C., Lee, M. W., & Hsu, Y. C. (2012). An AC-DC rectifier for RF energy harvesting system. *Proceedings of Asia-Pacific Microwave Conference*, 1052 – 1054. doi:10.1109/APMC.2012.6421822

Li, T.-S., Tong, S.-C., & Feng, G. (2010a). A novel robust adaptive-fuzzy-tracking control for a class of nonlinear multi-input/multi-output systems. *IEEE Transactions on Fuzzy Systems*, *18*(1), 150–160. doi:10.1109/TFUZZ.2009.2038277

Li, T.-S., Wang, D., Feng, G., & Tong, S.-C. (2010b). A DSC approach to robust adaptive NN tracking control for strict-feedback nonlinear systems. *IEEE Transactions on Systems, Man, and Cybernetics. Part B, Cybernetics*, *40*(3), 915–927. doi:10.1109/TSMCB.2009.2033563 PMID:19887321

Litta, A. J., Idicula, S. M., & Francis, C. N. (2012). Artificial Neural Network for the Prediction of Thunderstorms over Kolkata. *International Journal of Computers and Applications*, *50*(11), 50–55. doi:10.5120/7819-1135

Liu, Y.-h., Wu, Z.-q., Tu, Y.-q., Huang, Q.-y., & Lou, H.-w. (2008). A Survey on Distributed Generation and Its Networking Technology. *Power System Technology, 15*, 20.

Liu, D., Wang, D., & Li, H. (2014, February). Decentralized stabilization for a class of continuous-time nonlinear interconnected systems using online learning optimal control approach. *IEEE Transactions on Neural Networks and Learning Systems*, *25*(2), 418–428. doi:10.1109/TNNLS.2013.2280013 PMID:24807039

Liu, G. P. (2001). *Nonlinear Identification and Control: A Neural Network Approach*. London, UK: Springer. doi:10.1007/978-1-4471-0345-5

Liu, G. P., Xia, Y., Chen, J., Rees, D., & Hu, W. (2007). Networked predictive control of systems with random network delays in both forward and feedback channels. *IEEE Transactions on Industrial Electronics*, *54*(3), 1282–1297. doi:10.1109/TIE.2007.893073

Liu, H., Datta, S., & Narayanan, V. (2013). Tunnel FET based ultra low power high sensitivity UHF RFID rectifier. *Proceedings of the International Symposium on Low Power Electronics and Design*, 157 – 162. doi:10.1109/ISLPED.2013.6629287

Liu, H., Li, X., Vaddi, R., Ma, K., Datta, S., & Narayanan, V. (2014). Tunnel FET RF rectifier design for energy harvesting applications. *IEEE Journal on Emerging and Selected Topics in Circuits and Systems.*, *4*(4), 400–411. doi:10.1109/JETCAS.2014.2361068

Liu, L. X., Mu, J. C., Ma, N., Tu, W., Zhu, Z. M., & Yang, Y. T. (2015). An Ultra-Low-Power Integrated RF Energy Harvesting System in 65-nm CMOS Process. *Circuits, Systems, and Signal Processing*, *35*(2), 42–441.

Liu, T., Wang, C., & Hill, D. J. (2009, September). Learning from neural control of nonlinear systems in normal form. *Systems & Control Letters*, *58*(9), 633–638. doi:10.1016/j.sysconle.2009.04.001

Liut, D. A., Matheu, E. E., Singh, M. P., & Mook, D. T. (2000). A Modified Gradient-Search Training Technique for Neural-Network Structural Control. *Journal of Vibration and Control*, *6*(8), 1243–1268. doi:10.1177/107754630000600807

Liu, X., Lu, R., Ma, J., Chen, L., & Qin, B. (2016). Privacy-preserving patient centric clinical decision support system on naïve Bayesian classification. *IEEE Journal of Biomedical and Health Informatics*, *20*(2), 655–668. doi:10.1109/JBHI.2015.2407157 PMID:26960216

Liu, X., Xia, Y., Mahmoud, M. S., & Deng, Z. (2010). Modeling and stabilization of MIMO networked control systems with network constraints. *International Journal of Innovative Computing, Information, & Control*, *6*(10), 4409–4419.

Liu, Y.-J., Gao, Y., Tong, S., & Li, Y. (2016, February). Fuzzy approximation-based adaptive backstepping optimal control for a class of nonlinear discretetime systems with dead-zone. *IEEE Transactions on Fuzzy Systems*, *24*(1), 16–28. doi:10.1109/TFUZZ.2015.2418000

Liu, Y.-J., & Tong, S. (2014, October). Adaptive fuzzy control for a class of nonlinear discrete-time systems with backlash. *IEEE Transactions on Fuzzy Systems*, *22*(5), 1359–1365. doi:10.1109/TFUZZ.2013.2286837

Liu, Y.-J., Tong, S., & Chen, C. P. (2013). Adaptive fuzzy control via observer design for uncertain nonlinear systems with unmodeled dynamics. *IEEE Transactions on Fuzzy Systems*, *21*(2), 275–288. doi:10.1109/TFUZZ.2012.2212200

Li, Y., Tong, S., & Li, T. (2015). Adaptive fuzzy output feedback dynamic surface control of interconnected nonlinear pure-feedback systems. *IEEE Transactions on Cybernetics*, *45*(1), 138–149. doi:10.1109/TCYB.2014.2333738 PMID:25051573

Loussifi, H., Nourim, K., & Braiek, N. B. (2016). A new efficient hybrid intelligent method for nonlinear dynamical systems identification: The Wavelet Kernel Fuzzy Neural Network. *Communications in Nonlinear Science and Numerical Simulation*, *32*, 10–30. doi:10.1016/j.cnsns.2015.08.010

Lu, A., Ke, Y., Cheng, J., & Ng, W. (2007). *Mining Vague Association Rules*. Springer.

Lu, C.-H. (2011). Wavelet fuzzy neural networks for identification and predictive control of dynamic systems. *IEEE Transactions on Industrial Electronics*, *58*(7), 3046–3058. doi:10.1109/TIE.2010.2076415

Lu, L.-Y., Lin, G.-L., & Kuo, T.-C. (2008). Stiffness controllable isolation system for near-fault seismic isolation. *Engineering Structures*, *30*(3), 747–765. doi:10.1016/j.engstruct.2007.05.022

Luo, Y. Z. C. (2011). A cascaded shunt active power filter with high performance for aircraft electric power system. In Energy Conversion Congress and Exposition (ECCE) (pp. 1143 – 1149). IEEE.

Luo, J., & Shi, H. (2006). Research of Chaos Encryption Algorithm Based on Logistic Mapping. *Proceedings of the International Conference on Intelligent Information Hiding and Multimedia Signal*, 1–3. doi:10.1109/IIH-MSP.2006.265022

Lu, S., & Ba¸sar, T. (1998, May). Robust nonlinear system identification using neuralnetwork models. *IEEE Transactions on Neural Networks*, *9*(3), 407–429. doi:10.1109/72.668883 PMID:18252465

M, A., Sudhanshu, S., Kumar, A., & Ghose, M.K. (2009). Optimized association rule mining using genetic algorithm. *Advances in Information Mining*, *1*(2), 01-04.

Ma, J., & Ye, R. (2015). An Image Encryption Scheme Based on Hybrid Orbit of Hyper-chaotic Systems. *International Journal of Computer Network and Information Security*, *5*, 25-33.

Mabrouki, A., Latrach, M., & Lorrain, V. (2014). *High efficiency low power rectifier design using zero bias schottky diodes. Faible Tension Faible Consommation (FTFC)*, *1 – 4*. IEEE.

Maciejowski, J. M. (2002). *Predictive control with constraints*. Harlow: Prentice Hall.

Mangalampalli, A. (2009). *Pudi, Vikram*. Fuzzy Association Rule Mining Algorithm for Fast and Efficient Performance on Very Large Datasets.

Mansour, I., Chalhoub, G., & Bakhache, B. (2012). Evaluation of a Fast Symmetric Cryptographic Algorithm Based on the Chaos Theory for Wireless Sensor Networks. *IEEE 11th International Conference on Trust, Security and Privacy in Computing and Communications*, 913-919. doi:10.1109/TrustCom.2012.154

Masotti, D., Costanzo, A., & Adami, S. (2013). Design and realization of a wearable multi frequency RF energy harvesting system. *Proceedings of The European Conference on Antennas and Propagation (EUCAP)*, 517 – 520.

Masuch, J., Restituto, M. D., Milosevic, D., & Baltus, P. (2012). An RF-to-DC energy harvester for co-integration in a low-power 2.4 GHz transceiver frontend. *International Symposium on Circuits and Systems (ISCAS)*, 680 – 683. doi:10.1109/ISCAS.2012.6272124

Matlab. (2015). *MathWorks R2015a*. Retrieved February 23, 2017, from https://www.mathworks.com/products/new_products/release2015a.html

Matsui, K., Suganami, Y., & Kosugi, Y. (1999). Feature selection by genetic algorithm for MRI segmentation. *Systems and Computers in Japan*, *30*(7), 69–78. doi:10.1002/(SICI)1520-684X(19990630)30:7<69::AID-SCJ8>3.0.CO;2-U

Maulik, U. (2009). Medical image segmentation using genetic algorithms. *IEEE Transactions on Information Technology in Biomedicine*, *13*(2), 166–173. doi:10.1109/TITB.2008.2007301 PMID:19272859

Mauricio Aredes, J. H. (1997). Three-Phase Four-Wire Shunt Active Filter Control Strategies. *IEEE Transactions on Power Electronics*, *12*(2), 311–318. doi:10.1109/63.558748

Ma, X., Chou, C.-A., Sayama, H., & Chaovalitwongse, W. A. (2016). Brain response pattern identification of fMRI data using a particle swarm optimization-based approach. *Brain Informatics*, *3*(3), 181–192. doi:10.1007/s40708-016-0049-z PMID:27747594

Mehrara, H., Zahedinejad, M., & Pourmohammad, A. (2009). Novel Edge Detection Using BP Neural Network Based on Threshold Binarization. *Second International Conference on Computer and Electrical Engineering*, 408-412.

Mekhilef, S., Saidur, R., & Safari, A. (2011). A review on solar energy use in industries. *Renewable & Sustainable Energy Reviews*, *15*(4), 1777–1790. doi:10.1016/j.rser.2010.12.018

Melingui, A., Lakhal, O., Daachi, B., Mbede, J. B., & Merzouki, R. (2015, December). andR.Merzouki,"Adaptive neural network control of a compact bionic handling arm. *IEEE/ASME Transactions on Mechatronics*, *20*(6), 2862–2875. doi:10.1109/TMECH.2015.2396114

Mendonca, L. F., Farinha, G. J., & Sousa, J. M. C. (2013). Modified binary PSO for feature selection using SVM applied to mortality prediction of septic patients. *Applied Soft Computing*, *13*(8), 3494–3504. doi:10.1016/j.asoc.2013.03.021

Mettam, G. R., & Adams, L. B. (1999). How to prepare an electronic version of your article. In B. S. Jones & R. Z. Smith (Eds.), *Introduction to the electronicage* (pp. 281–304). New York: E-Publishing Inc.

Mihailescu, M. I. (2014). New Enrollment Scheme for Biometric Template using Hash Chaos-Based Cryptography. *Procedia Engineering, 69*, 1459 – 1468. doi:10.1016/j.proeng.2014.03.142

Mikeka, C., & Arai, H. (2011). Microwave tooth for sensor power supply in battery-free applications. *Proceedings of the Asia-Pacific Microwave Conference*, 1802 – 1805.

Mikeka, C., Arai, H., Georgiadis, A., & Collado, A. (2011). DTV band micropower RF energy-harvesting circuit architecture and performance analysis. *International Conference on RFID-Technologies and Applications*, 561 – 567. doi:10.1109/RFID-TA.2011.6068601

Mishra, G., Ananth, V., Shelke, K., Sehgal, D., & Valadi, J. (2016). Classification of anti- hepatitis peptides using Support Vector Machine with hybrid Ant Colony Optimization: The Luxembourg database of trichothecene type B *F. graminearum* and *F. culmorum producers. Bioinformation, 12*(1), 12–14. doi:10.6026/97320630012012 PMID:27212838

Modares, H., Lewis, F. L., & Naghibi Sistani, M.-B. (2013, October). Adaptive optimal control of unknown constrained-input systems using policy iteration and neural networks. *IEEE Transactions on Neural Networks and Learning Systems, 24*(10), 1513–1525. doi:10.1109/TNNLS.2013.2276571 PMID:24808590

Mondal, B., Mandal, T., (2016). A light weight secure image encryption scheme based on chaos & DNA computing. *Journal of King Saud University – Computer and Information Sciences*, 1-6.

Monteiro, V., Pinto, J. G., Exposto, B., Gonçalves, H., Ferreira, J. C., Couto, C., & Afonso, J. L. (2012). *Assessment of a battery charger for Electric Vehicles with reactive power control*. Paper presented at the IECON 2012 - 38th Annual Conference on IEEE Industrial Electronics Society.

Moon, J. I., Cho, I. K., Kim, S. M., & Jung, Y. B. (2013). Design of efficient rectenna with vertical ground walls for RF energy harvesting. *Electronics Letters, 49*(17), 1–3. doi:10.1049/el.2013.2251

Moradi, M. H., & Abedini, M. (2012). A combination of genetic algorithm and particle swarm optimization for optimal DG location and sizing in distribution systems. *International Journal of Electrical Power & Energy Systems, 34*(1), 66–74. doi:10.1016/j.ijepes.2011.08.023

Mouris, B. A., Soliman, A. M., Ali, T. A., Eshrah, I. A., & Badawi, A. (2016). Efficient dual-band energy harvesting system for implantable biosensors. *International Symposium on Antenna Technology and Applied Electromagnetics (ANTEM)*, 1-2. doi:10.1109/ANTEM.2016.7550242

Mousavi, S. H., Noroozi, N., Safavi, A. A., & Ebadat, A. (2011). Modeling and control of nonlinear systems using novel fuzzy wavelet networks: The output adaptive control approach. *Communications in Nonlinear Science and Numerical Simulation, 16*(9), 3798–3814. doi:10.1016/j.cnsns.2010.12.041

Muller, H., Michoux, N., Bandon, D., & Geissbuhler, A. (2004). A review of content based image retrieval systems in medical applications clinical benefits and future directions. *International Journal of Medical Informatics, 73*(1), 1–23. doi:10.1016/j.ijmedinf.2003.11.024 PMID:15036075

Munoz de la Pena, D., & Christofides, P. D. (2008). Lyapunov-based model predictive control of nonlinear systems subject to data losses. *IEEE Transactions on Automatic Control, 53*(9), 2076–2089. doi:10.1109/TAC.2008.929401

Murakami, Y., & Mizuguchi, K. (2010). Applying the Naïve Bayes classifier with kernel density estimation to the prediction of protein-protein interaction sites. *Bioinformatics (Oxford, England), 26*(15), 1841–1848. doi:10.1093/bioinformatics/btq302 PMID:20529890

Naik, S., Khatod, D., & Sharma, M. (2013). *Sizing and siting of distributed generation in distribution networks for real power loss minimization using analytical approach*. Paper presented at the Power, Energy and Control (ICPEC), 2013 International Conference on. doi:10.1109/ICPEC.2013.6527753

Narasingarao, M., Manda, R., Sridhar, G., Madhu, K., & Rao, A. (2009). A clinical decision support system using multilayer perceptron neural network to assess well-being in diabetes. *The Journal of the Association of Physicians of India*, *57*, 127–133. PMID:19582980

Narendra, K. S. (1996, October). Neural networks for control theory and practice. *Proceedings of the IEEE*, *84*(10), 1385–1406. doi:10.1109/5.537106

Nasimuddin, Q. X., & Chen, Z. N. (2009). Compact circularly polarized microstrip antenna for RFID handheld reader applications. *Asia Pacific Microwave Conference (APMC)*, 1950 – 1953. doi:10.1109/APMC.2009.5385294

Natori, K., Oboe, R., & Ohnishi, K. (2008). Stability analysis and practical design procedure of time delayed control systems with communication disturbance observer. *IEEE Transactions on Industrial Informatics*, *4*(3), 185–197. doi:10.1109/TII.2008.2002705

Naus, G. (2010). *Model-based control for automotive applications* (PhD Thesis). Eindhoven University of Technology, The Netherlands.

Neelakantan, V. A., & Washington, G. N. (2008). Vibration Control of Structural Systems using MR dampers and a Modified Sliding Mode Control Technique. *Journal of Intelligent Material Systems and Structures*, *19*(2), 211–223. doi:10.1177/1045389X06074509

Neill-Carrillo, E. O., Arroyo, J., Rosado, J., Santiago, J., & Jimenez, I. (2002). The Atmospheric Phenomena Laboratory: Connecting Electrical and Computer Engineering Through Undergraduate Research. In *Proceeding of 32nd ASEE Frontiers in Education Conference*. IEEE doi:10.1109/FIE.2002.1158725

Neshatian, K., & Zhang, M. (2009). Dimensionality reduction in face detection: A genetic programming approach. *Proc. 24th International Conference Image Vis. Comput. New Zealand (IVCNZ)*, 391-396.

Nimo, A., Beckedahl, T., Ostertag, T., & Reindl, L. (2015). Analysis of passive RF-DC power rectification and harvesting wireless RF energy for micro-watt sensors. *AIMS Energy*, *3*(2), 184–200. doi:10.3934/energy.2015.2.184

Nintanavongsa, P., Muncuk, U., Lewis, D. R., & Chowdhury, K. R. (2012). Design optimization and implementation for RF energy harvesting circuits. *IEEE Journal on Emerging and Selected Topics in Circuits and Systems*, *2*(1), 24–33. doi:10.1109/JETCAS.2012.2187106

Nishimura, I., Abdel-Ghaffar, A. M., Masri, S. F., Miller, R. K., Beck, J. L., Caughey, T. K., & Iwan, W. D. (1992). An Experimental Study of the Active Control of a Building Model. *Journal of Intelligent Material Systems and Structures*, *3*(1), 134–165. doi:10.1177/1045389X9200300108

Niu, H., Zhou, C., Wang, B., Zheng, X., & Zhou, S. (2016). Splicing Model and Hyper–Chaotic System For Image Encryption. *Journal of Electrical Engineering*, *67*(2), 78–86.

Norman, M., Samsul, B., Mohd, N., & Jasronita, J., & B., O. S. (2004). A Fuzzy logic Controller for an Indirect vector Controlled Three Phase Induction. *Proceedings of Analog And Digital Techniques In Electrical Engineering*, 1–4.

Novo, T., Varum, H., Teixeira-Dias, F., Rodrigues, H., Silva, M. F., Costa, A. C., & Guerreiro, L. (2014). Tuned liquid dampers simulation for earthquake response control of buildings. *Bulletin of Earthquake Engineering*, *12*(2), 1007–1024. doi:10.1007/s10518-013-9528-2

NSRDB. (2016). *National Solar Radiation Data Base*. Retrieved March 15, 2016, from http://rredc.nrel.gov/solar/old_data/nsrdb/

O'Dwyer, A. (2006). *Handbook of PI and PID controller tuning rules*. London: Imperial College Press. doi:10.1142/p424

Oates, W. S., & Smith, R. C. (2008). Nonlinear Optimal Control Techniques for Vibration Attenuation Using Magnetostrictive Actuators. *Journal of Intelligent Material Systems and Structures*, *19*(2), 193–209. doi:10.1177/1045389X06074159

Olgun, U., Chen, C. C., & Volakis, J. L. (2010). Wireless power harvesting with planar rectennas for 2.45 GHz RFIDs. *URSI International Symposium on Electromagnetic Theory*, 329 – 331. doi:10.1109/URSI-EMTS.2010.5637008

Olgun, U., Chen, C. C., & Volakis, J. L. (2012). Design of an efficient ambient WiFi energy harvesting system. *IET Microwaves, Antennas & Propagation*, *6*(11), 1200–1206. doi:10.1049/iet-map.2012.0129

Omar, M. A., Hassan, M. K., Soh, A. Ch., & Kadir, M. Z. A. (2013). Lightning Severity Classification Utilizing the Meteorological Parameters: A Neural Network Approach. In *Proceeding of International Conference on Control System, Computing and Engineering*, (pp. 111-116). IEEE.

Onat, A., Naskali, A. T., & Parlakay, E. (2008). Model based predictive networked control systems. In *17th IFAC World Congress* (pp. 13000-13005). Seoul, Korea: Academic Press.

Orue, A. B., Fernandez, V., Alvareza, G., Pastor, G., Shujun, M. L., & Montoya, F. (2008). Determination of the Parameters for a Lorenz System and Application to Break the Security of Two-channel Chaotic Cryptosystems. *Physics Letters*, *372*(34), 5588–5592. doi:10.1016/j.physleta.2008.06.066

Otani, S. (2004). Earthquake Resistant Design of Reinforced Concrete Buildings. *Journal of Advanced Concrete Technology*, *2*(1), 3–24. doi:10.3151/jact.2.3

Ozbulut, O. E., & Hurlebaus, S. (2010). Fuzzy control of piezoelectric friction dampers for seismic protection of smart base isolated buildings. *Bulletin of Earthquake Engineering*, *8*(6), 1435–1455. doi:10.1007/s10518-010-9187-5

Özkaynak, F., Yavuz, S. (2013). Designing chaotic S-boxes based on time-delay chaoticsystem. *Nonlinear Dynamics*, *74*, 551–557.

P, P. J., K, B. B., & Eduardo, B. d. (2001). A Stator-Flux-Oriented Vector-Controlled Induction Motor Drive with Space-Vector PWM and Flux-Vector Synthesis by Neural Networks. *IEEE Transaction on Industry Applications, 37*(5), 1308-1318.

Palacios, A., & Juarez, H. (2002). Cryptography With Cycling Chaos. *Physics Letters*, *303*(5-6), 345–351. doi:10.1016/S0375-9601(02)01323-3

Pan, J., Ding, Q., & Qi, N. (2012). The Research of Chaos-Based SMS Encryption in Mobile Phone. *Second International Conference on Instrumentation & Measurement, Computer, Communication and Control*, 501-504. doi:10.1109/IMCCC.2012.124

Pan, Y., & Yu, H. (2014). Biomimetic hybrid feedback feedforword adaptive neural control of robotic arms. *Proc. IEEE Symp. Comput. Intell. Control Autom.*, 1–7. doi:10.1109/CICA.2014.7013254

Panasonic. (2015). *Panasonic Eco Solutions*. Retrieved February 23, 2017, from http://news.panasonic.co.uk/pressreleases/panasonic-debuts-high-powered-photovoltaic-module-hit-r-n330-for-uk-and-european-markets-sets-new-module-efficiency-record-1229674

Pande, A., & Zambreno, J. (2011). A Chaotic Encryption Scheme for Real-Time Embedded Systems: Design and Implementation. *Telecommunication System, Springer*, *52*, 551–561.

Pandey, A., & Pardasani, K. R. (2013). A Model for Vague Association Rule Mining in Temporal Databases. *Journal of Information and Computer Science*, *8*(1), 63–74.

Pandey, A., & Pardasani, K. R. (2012). A Model for Mining Course Information using Vague Association Rule. *International Journal of Computers and Applications*, *58*(20), 1–5. doi:10.5120/9395-7825

Pan, Y., Liu, Y., Xu, B., & Yu, H. (2016, April). Hybrid feedback feedforward: An efficient design of adaptive neural network control. *Neural Networks*, *76*, 122–134. doi:10.1016/j.neunet.2015.12.009 PMID:26890657

Pan, Y., Sun, T., & Yu, H. (2015, December). Peaking-free output-feedback adaptive neural control under a non-separation principle. *IEEE Transactions on Neural Networks and Learning Systems*, *26*(12), 3097–3108. doi:10.1109/TNNLS.2015.2403712 PMID:25794400

Pan, Y., Zhou, Y., Sun, T., & Er, M. J. (2013, January). Composite adaptive fuzzy H∞ tracking control of uncertain nonlinear systems. *Neurocomputing*, *99*(1), 15–24. doi:10.1016/j.neucom.2012.05.011

Papotto, G., Carrara, F., & Palmisano, G. (2011). A 90-nm CMOS threshold-compensated RF energy harvester. *IEEE Journal of Solid-State Circuits*, *46*(9), 1985–1997. doi:10.1109/JSSC.2011.2157010

Parihar, P. D., Kumar, P., Jha, C. K., & Sharma, A. (2014). Renewable battery charging method using CMOS RF energy harvesting circuit design. *International Conference on Reliability, Infocom Technologies and Optimization (ICRITO)*,1 – 5. doi:10.1109/ICRITO.2014.7014738

Park, J. S., Chen, & Yu, P. S. (1995). An Effective Hash-Based Algorithm for Mining Association Rule. *Proceedings of the 1995 ACM SIGMOD International Conference on Management of Data*, 175-186. doi:10.1145/223784.223813

Park, K.-S., Koh, H.-M., & Ok, S.-Y. (2002). Active control of earthquake excited structures using fuzzy supervisory technique. *Advances in Engineering Software*, *33*(11-12), 761–768. doi:10.1016/S0965-9978(02)00044-3

Park, K.-S., Koh, H.-M., & Seo, C.-W. (2004). Independent modal space fuzzy control of earthquake-excited structures. *Engineering Structures*, *26*(2), 279–289. doi:10.1016/j.engstruct.2003.10.005

Passey, R., Spooner, T., MacGill, I., Watt, M., & Syngellakis, K. (2011). The potential impacts of grid-connected distributed generation and how to address them: A review of technical and non-technical factors. *Energy Policy*, *39*(10), 6280–6290. doi:10.1016/j.enpol.2011.07.027

Patearia. (2011). Performance analysis of dynamic routing protocol in mobile ad hoc network. *Journal of Global Research in Computer Science*, *2*(10).

Patel, B., Chaudhari, V. K., Karan, R. K., & Rana, Y. K. (2011). Optimization of Association Rule Mining Apriori Algorithm Using ACO. *International Journal of Soft Computing and Engineering*, *1*(1), 24–26.

Patil, A.J., Patil, C.S., Karhe, R.R., & Aher, M.H. (n.d.). Comparative Study of Different Clustering Algorithms. *International Journal of Advanced Research in Electrical, Electronics and Instrumentation Energy*.

Patrascu, M. (2011). *Advanced Techniques for Seismic Vibration Control* (PhD Thesis). Department of Automatic Control and Systems Engineering, University Politehnica of Bucharest.

Patrascu, M., & Ion, A. (2015b). *GAOT-ECM Seismic Vibration Case Study*. Available online: http://www.mathworks.com/matlabcentral/fileexchange/51131-gaot-ecm-seismic-vibration-case-study

Patrascu, M. (2015). Genetically enhanced modal controller design for seismic vibration in nonlinear multi-damper configuration. *Proceedings of the Institution of Mechanical Engineers. Part I, Journal of Systems and Control Engineering*, *229*(2), 158–168. doi:10.1177/0959651814550540

Patrascu, M., Dumitrache, I., & Patrut, P. (2012). A Comparative Study for Advanced Seismic Vibration Control Algorithms. *U.P.B. Scientific Bulletin, Series C*, *74*(4), 3–16.

Patrascu, M., & Ion, A. (2015a). *Seismic Vibration Control with Semi-Active Dampers*. Bucharest: MatrixRom.

Patrascu, M., & Ion, A. (2016). Evolutionary Modeling of Industrial Plants and Design of PID Controllers. In *Nature-Inspired Computing for Control Systems* (pp. 73–119). Springer International Publishing. doi:10.1007/978-3-319-26230-7_4

Patrascu, M., Patrascu, A., & Beres, I. (2017). An immune evolution mechanism for the study of stress factors in supervised and controlled systems. In *IEEE Evolving and Adaptive Intelligent Systems* (pp. 1–8). EAIS. doi:10.1109/EAIS.2017.7954823

Pawlak, Z. (1982). Rough Sets. *International Journal of. Computer and Information Sciences, 11*(5), 341–356. doi:10.1007/BF01001956

Pawlak, Z., Grazymala-Busse, J. W., Slowinski, R., & Ziarko, W. (1995). Rough sets. *Communications of the ACM, 38*(11), 88–95. doi:10.1145/219717.219791

Pedro, J. O., Dangor, M., Dahunsi, O. A., & Ali, M. M. (2014). Intelligent feedback linearization control of nonlinear electrohydraulic suspension systems using particle swarm optimization. *Applied Soft Computing, 24*, 50–62. doi:10.1016/j.asoc.2014.05.013

Peng, F., Zhu, X., & Long, M. (2013). An ROI Privacy Protection Scheme for H.264 Video Based on FMO and Chaos. IEEE Transactions on Information Forensics and Security, 8(10), 1688-1699.

Petrauskiene, V., Palivonaite, R., Aleksa, A., & Ragulskis, M., (2013). Dynamic visual cryptography based on chaotic oscillations. *Communication in Nonlinear Science and Numerical Simulation*, 1-9.

Pettersson, M. (1997). *Driveline modeling and control* (PhD Thesis). Linkoping University, Sweden.

Pham, B. L., & Pham, A. V. (2013). Triple bands antenna and high efficiency rectifier design for RF energy harvesting at 900, 1900 and 2400 MHz. *IEEE MTT-S International Microwave Symposium Digest*, 1 – 4. doi:10.1109/MWSYM.2013.6697364

Philippe, J.M., Carbon, A., Brousse, O., & Paindavoine, M. (2015). Exploration and design of embedded systems including neural algorithms. *Design, Automation & Test in Europe Conference & Exhibition (DATE)*.

Philippe, M., Essick, R., Dullerud, G. E., & Jungers, R. M. (2016). Stability of discrete-time switching systems with constrained switching sequences. *Automatica, 72*, 242–250. doi:10.1016/j.automatica.2016.05.015

Ping, L., Tao-rong, Q., & Yu-yuan, L. (2013). The Study on the Model of Thunderstorm Forecast Based on RS-SVM. *Journal of Convergence Information Technology, 8*(10), 66–74. doi:10.4156/jcit.vol8.issue10.9

Plebmann, G., Erdmann, M., Hlusiak, M., & Breyer, C. (2014). Global energy storage demand for a 100% renewable electricity supply. *Energy Procedia, 46*, 22–31. doi:10.1016/j.egypro.2014.01.154

Popovic, Z., & Falkenstein, E. A., (2013). Low-Power Far-Field Wireless Powering for Wireless Sensors. *Proceedings of the IEEE, 101*(6), 1397 – 1409. doi:10.1109/JPROC.2013.2244053

Popovic, Z., Korhummel, S., Dunbar, S., Scheeler, R., Dolgov, A., Zane, R., & Hagerty, J. et al. (2014). Scalable RF energy harvesting. *IEEE Transactions on Microwave Theory and Techniques, 62*(4), 1046–1056. doi:10.1109/TMTT.2014.2300840

Pozo, F., Ikhouane, F., Pujol, G., & Rodellar, J. (2006). Adaptive Backstepping Control of Hysteretic Base-Isolated Structures. *Journal of Vibration and Control, 12*(4), 373–393. doi:10.1177/1077546306063254

Prabha, D. R., & Jayabarathi, T. (2016). Optimal placement and sizing of multiple distributed generating units in distribution networks by invasive weed optimization algorithm. *Ain Shams Engineering Journal, 7*(2), 683–694. doi:10.1016/j.asej.2015.05.014

Preumont, A., Voltan, M., Sangiovanni, A., Mokrani, B., & Alaluf, D. (2016). Active tendon control of suspension bridges. *Smart Structures and Systems*, *18*(1), 31–52. doi:10.12989/sss.2016.18.1.031

Price, W., Casper, S., Nwankpa, C., Bradish, R., Chiang, H., Concordia, C., & Wu, G. et al. (1995). Bibliography on load models for power flow and dynamic performance simulation. *IEEE Power Engineering Review*, *15*(2), 70.

Prost-Boucle, A., Muller, O., & Rousseau, F. (2014). A Fast and Stand-alone HLS Methodology for Hardware Accelerator Generation Under Resource Constraints. *Journal of Systems Architecture*.

Putra, A. W., & Lursinsap, C. (2014). *Cumulonimbus Prediction using Artificial Neural Network Back Propagation with Radiosonde Indeces*. Academic Press.

Qiu, T., Zhang, S., Zhou, H., Bai, X., & Liu, P. (2013). Application Study of Machine Learning in Lightning Forecasting. *Information Technology Journal*, *12*(21), 6031–6037. doi:10.3923/itj.2013.6031.6037

Rajasekaran, S. P. (2005). *Neural Networks, Fuzzy Logic and Genetic Algorithm: Synthesis and Applications*. New Delhi: Prentice Hall of India.

Raj, V. A. (2016). MEMS based multi-band energy harvesting for wireless sensor network applications. *International Conference on Energy Efficient Technologies for Sustainability (ICEETS)*, 573-576. doi:10.1109/ICEETS.2016.7583819

Ramesh, G. P., & Rajan, A. (2014). microstrip antenna designs for RF energy harvesting. *International Conference on Communication and Signal Processing*, 1653 – 1657. doi:10.1109/ICCSP.2014.6950129

Rani, A., Singh, V., & Gupta, J. R. P. (2013). Development of soft sensor for neural network based control of distillation column. *ISA Transactions*, *52*(3), 438–449. doi:10.1016/j.isatra.2012.12.009 PMID:23375672

Rao, M. M., & Datta, T. K. (2005). Predictive Active Control of Building Frames with a Solo Neurocontroller. *Journal of Vibration and Control*, *11*, 627–641.

Rao, R. S., Ravindra, K., Satish, K., & Narasimham, S. (2013). Power loss minimization in distribution system using network reconfiguration in the presence of distributed generation. *IEEE Transactions on Power Systems*, *28*(1), 317–325. doi:10.1109/TPWRS.2012.2197227

Rawlings, J. B., & Mayne, D. Q. (2009). *Model predictive control: Theory and design*. Nob Hill Publishing.

Reddy, C. Anisha, P. R., & Prasad, L. V. (2014). *Detection of Thunderstorms using Data Mining and Image Processing*. Academic Press.

Renzi, E., & De Angelis, M. (2005). Optimal Semi-active Control and Non-linear Dynamic Response of Variable Stiffness Structures. *Journal of Vibration and Control*, *11*, 1253–1289.

Renzi, E., & Serino, G. (2003). Testing and modelling a semi-actively controlled steel frame structure equipped with MR dampers. *Structural Control and Health Monitoring*, *11*(3), 189–221. doi:10.1002/stc.36

Rew, K.-H., Han, J.-H., & Lee, I. (2002). Multi-Modal Vibration Control Using Adaptive Positive Position Feedback. *Journal of Intelligent Material Systems and Structures*, *13*(1), 13–22. doi:10.1177/1045389X02013001866

Rezig, A., Mekideche, M. R., & Ikhlef, N. (2014). Effect of rotor eccentricity on magnetic noise generation in induction motors. *Journal of Electrical Engineering*, *3*(4), 200–208.

Ribakov, Y. (2009). Semi-active Pneumatic Devices for Control of MDOF Structures. *The Open Construction and Building Technology Journal*, *3*(1), 141–145. doi:10.2174/1874836800903010141

Riviere, S., Alicalapa, F., Douyere, A., & Lan Sun Luk, J. D. (2010). A compact rectenna device at low power level. *Progress In Electromagnetics Research C, 16*(1), 137–146. doi:10.2528/PIERC10071604

Robbins, K. R., Zhang, W., & Bertrand, J. K. (2008). The Ant Colony Algorithm for Feature Selection in High-Dimension Gene Expression Data for Disease Classification. *Journal of Mathematical Medicine and Biology*, 1-14.

Robinson, J., Whelan, C. D., & Haggerty, N. K. (2004). Trends in advanced motor protection and monitoring. *IEEE Transactions on Industry Applications, 40*(3), 853–860. doi:10.1109/TIA.2004.827472

Rojas, R. (1996). *Neural Network- A Systematic Introduction*. Berlin: Spriger-Verlag.

Rossi, P. J., Hasu, V., Koistinen, J., Moisseev, D., Makela, A., & Saltikoff, E. (2014). Analysis of a Statistically Initialized Fuzzy Logic Scheme for Classifying the Severity of Convective Storms in Finland. Royal Meteorological Society.

Rostalski, P., Besselmann, T., Maric, M., Van Belsen, F., & Morari, M. (2007). A hybrid approach to modelling control and state estimation of mechanical, systems with backlash. *International Journal of Control, 80*(11), 1729–1740. doi:10.1080/00207170701493985

Rousseau, F., Sasongko, A., & Jerraya, A. (2005). *Shortening SoC Design Time with New Prototyping Flow on Reconfigurable Platform*. IEEE-NEWCAS Conference.

Rubió-Massegú, J., Rossell, J. M., & Karimi, H. R. (2016). Vibration control strategy for large-scale structures with incomplete multi-actuator system and neighbouring state information. *IET Control Theory & Applications, 10*(4), 407–416. doi:10.1049/iet-cta.2015.0737

Saerens, B., Diehl, M., Swevers, J., & Van den Bulck, E. (2008). Model predictive control of automotive powertrains—First experimental results. In *47th IEEE Conference on Decision and Control* (pp. 5692-5697). Cancun, Mexico: Academic Press. doi:10.1109/CDC.2008.4738740

Saggar, M., Agrawal, A., & Lad, A. (2004). Optimization of Association Rule Mining using Improved Genetic Algorithms. *IEEE International Conference on Systems, Man and Cybernetics*. doi:10.1109/ICSMC.2004.1400923

Sahab, M. G., Toropov, V. V., & Gandomi, A. H. (2013) A review on traditional and modern structural optimization: problems and techniques. *Metaheuristic Applications in Structures and Infrastructures*, 25-47.

Saifullah Khalid, B. D. (2013). Application of AI techniques in implementing Shunt APF in Aircraft Supply System. In *SOCROPROS Conference on Dec 26-28* (pp. 333-341). Roorkee, India: Springer Lecture Notes.

Saifullah Khalid, B. D. (2013). Comparative critical analysis of SAF using soft computing and conventional control techniques for high frequency (400 Hz) aircraft system. In *IEEE 1st International Conference on Condition Assessment Techniques in Electrical Systems (CATCON)* (pp. 100-110). Kolkata, India: IEEE.

Saifullah Khalid, B. D. (2010). Power Quality: An Important Aspect. *International Journal of Engineering Science and Technology, 2*(11), 6485–6490.

Saifullah Khalid, B. D. (2011). Power Quality Issues, Problems, Standards & their Effects in Industry with Corrective Means. *International Journal of Advances in Engineering and Technology, 1*(2), 1–11.

Saifullah Khalid, B. D. (2013). Comparison of Control Strategies for Shunt Active Power Filter under balanced, unbalanced and distorted supply conditions. *IEEE Sponsored National Conference on Advances in Electrical Power and Energy Systems (AEPES-2013)*, 37-41.

Saifullah, K., & Bharti, D. (2014). Comparative Evaluation of Various Control Strategies forShunt Active Power Filters in Aircraft Power Utility of 400 Hz. *Majlesi Journal of Mechatronic Systems, 3*(2), 1–5.

Salehi, M., & Ejlali, A. (2015). A Hardware Platform for Evaluating Low-Energy Multiprocessor Embedded Systems Based on COTS Devices. *Industrial Electronics, IEEE Transactions.*

Salter, T., Choi, K., Peckerar, M., Metze, G., & Goldsman, N. (2009). RF energy scavenging system utilising switched capacitor DC-DC converter. *Electronics Letters, 45*(7), 1–2. doi:10.1049/el.2009.0153

Samanta, A., & Banerji, P. (2010). Structural vibration control using modified tuned liquid dampers. *The IES Journal Part A: Civil & Structural Engineering, 3*(1), 14–27.

Saraiva, H. M., Borges, L. M., Pinho, P., Goncalves, R., Santiago, R. C., Barroca, N., & Salvado, R. et al. (2014). Experimental characterization of wearable antennas and circuits for RF energy harvesting in WBANs. *Vehicular Technology Conference (VTC Spring)*, 1 – 5. doi:10.1109/VTCSpring.2014.7022920

Sastry, S., & Bodson, M. (1989). *Adaptive Control: Stability, Convergence and Robustness*. Englewood Cliffs, NJ: Prentice-Hall.

Savasere, A., Omiecinski, E., & Navathe, S. (1995). An Efficient Algorithm for Mining Association Rules in Large Databases. *Proceedings of the 21st VLDB Conference*, 432-444.

Schmitz, R., (2001). Use of Chaotic Dynamical Systems in Cryptography. *Journal of the Franklin Institute, 338*, 429–441.

Scorcioni, S., Larcher, L., & Bertacchini, A. (2012). A 868MHz CMOS RF-DC power converter with -17dBm input power sensitivity and efficiency higher than 40% over 14dB input power range. *IEEE International Conference on RFID (RFID)*, 109 – 112.

Scorcioni, S., Larcher, L., & Bertacchini, A. (2012). Optimized CMOS RF-DC converters for remote wireless powering of RFID applications. *IEEE International Conference on RFID (RFID)*, 47 – 53. doi:10.1109/RFID.2012.6193055

Senouci, B., Bouchhima, A., Rousseau, F., Petrot, F., & Jerraya, A. (2007). *Prototyping Multiprocessor System-on-Chip Applications: A Platform-Based Approach*. IEEE Distributed Systems Online.

Senthilkumaran, N., & Rajesh, R. (2008). Edge Detection Techniques for Image Segmentation - A Survey. *Proceedings of the International Conference on ManagingN ext Generation Software Applications*, 749-760.

Seong-Hwan, K., & Tae-Sik, P. (2001). Speed-Sensorless Vector Control of an Induction Motor Using Neural Network Speed Estimation. *IEEE Transactions on Industrial Electronics, 48*(3), 609–614. doi:10.1109/41.925588

Sergio, C. A., Antonio, M. Á., Felipe, R., Francisco, R. P., & Hipólito, G. M., & Aguirre. (2011). Soft core based embedded Systems in critical aerospace applications. *Journal of Systems Architecture.*

Setayesh, M., Zang, M., & Jonhnton, M. (2009). A new homogeneity-based approach to edge detection using PSO. *Proc. 24th International Conference Image and Vision Computing*, 231-236. doi:10.1109/IVCNZ.2009.5378404

Seyedzadeh, S.M., & Mirzakuchaki, S. (2012). A fast color image encryption algorithm based on coupled two-dimensional piecewise chaotic map. *Signal Processing, 92*, 1202–1215.

Shahriari-kahkeshi, M., & Sheikholeslam, F. (2014). Adaptive fuzzy wavelet network for robust fault detection and diagnosis in non-linear systems. *IET Control Theory & Applications, 8*(15), 1487–1498. doi:10.1049/iet-cta.2013.0960

Shaker, H., Zareipour, H., & Wood, D. (2016). Impacts of large-scale wind and solar power integration on California's net electrical load. *Renewable & Sustainable Energy Reviews, 58*, 761–774. doi:10.1016/j.rser.2015.12.287

Shameli, A., Safarian, A., Rofougaran, A., Rofougaran, M., & Flaviis, F. D. (2007). Power harvester design for passive UHF RFID tag using a voltage boosting technique. *IEEE Transactions on Microwave Theory and Techniques, 55*(6), 1089–1097. doi:10.1109/TMTT.2007.896819

Shanker, M. S. (1996). Using neural networks to predict the onset of diabetes mellitus. *Journal of Chemical Information and Computer Sciences*, *36*(1), 35–41. doi:10.1021/ci950063e PMID:8576289

Sharawi, M., Elmahdy, H., & Emary, E. (n.d.). *Routing Wireless Sensor Networks based on Soft Computing Paradigms: Survey*. Retrieved from https://www.researchgate.net/publication/255754336

Sharawi, Saroit, El-Mahdy, & Emary. (2013). Routing wireless sensor networks based on soft computing paradigms: Survey. *International Journal on Soft Computing, Artificial Intelligence and Applications, 2*(4).

Shariati, N., Rowe, S. T., Scott, J. R., & Ghorbani, K. (2015). Multi-Service highly sensitive rectifier for enhanced RF energy scavenging. *Nature*, *9655*, 1–9.

Sharma, S., Kumar, S., & Singh, B. (2014). Hybrid Intelligent Routing in Wireless Mesh Networks: Soft Computing Based Approaches. *Intelligent Systems and Applications, 1*, 45-57. Retrieved from http://www.mecs -press.org/

Sheng, S., & Wu, X. (2012). A New Digital Anti-Counterfeiting Scheme Based on Chaotic Cryptography. *International Conference on ICT Convergence (ICTC)*, 687-691. doi:10.1109/ICTC.2012.6387119

Shi, Y., & Yu, B. (2011). Robust mixed *H2/H∞* control of networked control systems with random time delays in both forward and backward communication links. *Automatica*, *47*(4), 754–760. doi:10.1016/j.automatica.2011.01.022

Shojaei, K. (2015, July). Neural adaptive robust output feedback control of wheeled mobile robots with saturating actuators. *International Journal of Adaptive Control and Signal Processing*, *29*(7), 855–876. doi:10.1002/acs.2509

Shook, D. A., Roschke, P. N., Lin, P.-Y., & Loh, C.-H. (2008). GA-optimized fuzzy logic control of a large-scale building for seismic loads. *Engineering Structures*, *30*(2), 436–449. doi:10.1016/j.engstruct.2007.04.008

Shrestha, S., Noh, S. K., & Choi, D. Y. (2013). Comparative study of antenna designs for RF energy harvesting. *International Journal of Antennas and Propagation*, *2013*(1), 1 – 11.

Shrivastava, S., & Rajput, V. (2015). Particle Swarm Optimization Based Association Rule Mining. *International Journal of Computers and Applications*, *5*(5), 105–114.

Shukla, P.K., Khare, A., Rizvi, M.A., Stalin, S., & Kumar, S. (2015). Applied Cryptography Using Chaos Function for Fast Digital Logic-Based Systems in Ubiquitous Computing. *Entropy, 17*, 1387-1410.

Siddesh, Muralidhara, & Harihar. (n.d.). Routing in Ad Hoc Wireless Networks using Soft Computing techniques and performance evaluation using Hypernet simulator. *International Journal of Soft Computing and Engineering*.

Sim, Z. W., Shuttleworth, R., Alexander, M. J., & Grieve, B. D. (2010). Compact patch antenna design for outdoor RF energy harvesting in wireless sensor networks. *Progress in Electromagnetics Research*, *105*(1), 273–294. doi:10.2528/PIER10052509

Singh, D., Misra, R., & Singh, D. (2007). Effect of load models in distributed generation planning. *IEEE Transactions on Power Systems*, *22*(4), 2204–2212. doi:10.1109/TPWRS.2007.907582

Singh, D., & Verma, K. (2009). Multiobjective optimization for DG planning with load models. *IEEE Transactions on Power Systems*, *24*(1), 427–436. doi:10.1109/TPWRS.2008.2009483

Singh, G., Ponnaganti, R., Prabhakar, T. V., & Vinoy, K. J. (2013). A tuned rectifier for RF energy harvesting from ambient radiations. *AEÜ. International Journal of Electronics and Communications*, *67*(7), 1–6. doi:10.1016/j.aeue.2012.12.004

Sivakumar, T., & Venkatesan, R., (2016). A New Image Encryption Method Basedon Knight's Travel Path and True Random Number. *Journal of Information Science and Engineering*, *32*, 133-152.

Slimani, T. (2013). Class Association Rules Mining based Rough Set Method. *International Journal of Computer Science & Network Solutions, 1*(3), 1-10.

SMA. (2016). *Solar Technology AG Sunny Boy TL-US series*. Retrieved February 23, 2017, from http://files.sma.de/dl/10707/SUNNYBOY6-11TLUS-DUS144518W.PDF

Smiri, K., & Jemai, A. (2011). NoC-MPSoC Performance Estimation with Synchronous Data Flow (SDF) Graphs. Autonomous and Intelligent Systems (AIS'2011), 406-415. doi:10.1007/978-3-642-21538-4_40

Smiri, K., Ben Fadhel, A., Jemai, A., & Ammari, A-C. (2011). Automatic Generation of Software-Hardware Migration in MPSoC Systems. *Journal of Computer Technology and Application.*

Smiri, K., Jemai, A., & Ammari, A-C. (2008). Evaluation of the Disydent Co-design Flow for an MJPEG Case Study. *International Review on Computers and Software.*

Smiri, K., & Jemai, A. (2009). *Migration Methodology in MPSoC Based on Performance Analysis via SDF Graph.* Advances in Computational Sciences and Technology.

Solak, E., & Cokal, C. (2008). Cryptanalysis of a Cryptosystem Based on discretized Two-Dimensional Chaotic Maps. *Physics Letters A, 372,* 6922–6924.

Solak, E., Rhouma, R., & Belghith, S. (2010). Cryptanalysis of a Multi-Chaotic Systems Based Image Cryptosystem. *Optics Communications, 283,* 232–236.

Soleymani, A., Nordin, J., & Sundararajan, E. (2014). A Chaotic Cryptosystem for Images based on Henon and Arnold Cat Map. *The Scientific World Journal, 10,* 1–21.

Song, C., & Qiao, Y. (2015). A Novel Image Encryption Algorithm Based on DNA Encoding and Spatiotemporal Chaos. *Entropy, 17,* 6954-6968.

Sontag, E. D., & Wang, Y. (1995). On characterizations of the input-to-state stability property. *Systems & Control Letters, 24*(5), 351–359. doi:10.1016/0167-6911(94)00050-6

Sousa, L., Antao, S., & Germano, J. (2013). A Lab Project on the Design and Implementation of Programmable and Configurable Embedded Systems. *IEEE Transaction.*

Spencer, B. F., Jr., & Sain, M. K. (1997). Controlling Buildings: A New Frontier in Feedback. IEEE Control Systems Magazine, 17(6), 19-35.

Srimani, P.K. & Koti, M.S. (2012). Cost sensitivity analysis and the prediction of optimal rules for medical data by using rough set theory. *International Journal of Industrial and Manufacturing Engineering*, 74-80.

Stern, H. (n.d.). *Using a Knowledge-Based System to Predict Thunderstorm.* Bureau of Meteorology, Australia.

Stewart, P., Zavala, J., & Flemming, P. (2005). Automotive drive by wire controller design by multi-objectives techniques. *Control Engineering Practice, 13*(2), 257–264. doi:10.1016/j.conengprac.2004.03.010

Stoopman, M., Keyrouz, S., Visser, H. J., Philips, K., & Serdijn, W. A. (2013). A self-calibrating RF energy harvester generating 1V at -26.3 dBm. *Symposium on VLSI Circuits Digest of Technical Papers,* 226 – 227.

Stoopman, M., Keyrouz, S., Visser, H. J., Philips, K., & Serdijn, W. A. (2014). Co-Design of a CMOS rectifier and small loop antenna for highly sensitive RF energy harvesters. *IEEE Journal of Solid-State Circuits, 59*(3), 622–634. doi:10.1109/JSSC.2014.2302793

Stupf, M., Mittra, R., Yeo, J., & Mosig, J. R. (2006). Some novel design for RFID antennas and their performance enhancement with metamaterials. *IMP Antennas and Propagation Society International Symposium*, 1023 – 1026. doi:10.1109/APS.2006.1710707

Subramanyan, B., Chhabria, V. M., & Sankar Babu, T. G. (2011). Image Encryption Based on AES Key Expansion. *Proceedings of the 2nd International Conference on Emerging Applications of Information Technology (EAIT '11)*, 217–220. doi:10.1109/EAIT.2011.60

Sun, G., Wang, D., Li, T., Peng, Z., & Wang, H. (2013). Single neural network approximation based adaptive control for a class of uncertain strict-feedback nonlinear systems. *Nonlinear Dynamics*, *72*(1-2), 175–184. doi:10.1007/s11071-012-0701-y

Sun, H., Guo, Y. X., He, M., & Zhong, Z. (2013). A dual-band rectenna using broad-band yagi antenna array for ambient RF power harvesting. *IEEE Antennas and Wireless Propagation Letters*, *12*, 918–921. doi:10.1109/LAWP.2013.2272873

Swaroop, D., Hedrick, J. K., Yip, P. P., & Gerdes, J. C. (2000). Dynamic surface control for a class of nonlinear systems. *IEEE Transactions on Automatic Control*, *45*(10), 1893–1899. doi:10.1109/TAC.2000.880994

Symans, M. D., & Constantinou, M. C. (1997a). Experimental Testing and Analytical modeling of Semi-Active Fluid Dampers for Seismic Protection. *Journal of Intelligent Material Systems and Structures*, *8*(8), 644–657. doi:10.1177/1045389X9700800802

Symans, M. D., & Costantinou, M. C. (1997b). Seismic testing of a building structure with a semiactive fluid damper control system. *Earthquake Engineering & Structural Dynamics*, *26*(7), 759–777. doi:10.1002/(SICI)1096-9845(199707)26:7<759::AID-EQE675>3.0.CO;2-E

Symans, M. D., Madden, G. J., & Wongprasert, N. (1999). Semi-Active Hybrid Seismic Isolation Systems: Addressing the Limitations of Passive Isolation Systems. *Proc. of Structures Congress 1999*.

Tang, X., Zhuang, L., & Gao, Y. (2011). Support Vector Based on Chaos Particle Swarm Optimization for Lightning Prediction. *CSISE*, 727-733.

Tang, G., Liao, X., Xiao, D., & Li, C. (2004). A Secure Communication Scheme Based on Symbolic Dynamics. *Proceedings of the 2004 International Conference on Communications, Circuits and Systems*, 13–17. doi:10.1109/ICCCAS.2004.1345929

Tan, W.-S., Hassan, M. Y., Majid, M. S., & Rahman, H. A. (2013). Optimal distributed renewable generation planning: A review of different approaches. *Renewable & Sustainable Energy Reviews*, *18*, 626–645. doi:10.1016/j.rser.2012.10.039

Tanwani, A. K., & Farooq, M. (2009). The role of biomedical dataset in classification. *Conference on Artificial Intelligence in Medicine in Europe*, 370-374. doi:10.1007/978-3-642-02976-9_51

Teleke, S., Baran, M. E., Bhattacharya, S., & Huang, A. Q. (2010). Rule-based control of battery energy storage for dispatching intermittent renewable sources. *IEEE Transactions on Sustainable Energy*, *1*(3), 117–124. doi:10.1109/TSTE.2010.2061880

Templin, P. (2008). Simultaneous estimation of driveline dynamics and backlash size for control design. In *IEEE International Conference on Control Applications* (pp. 13-18). San Antonio, TX: IEEE. doi:10.1109/CCA.2008.4629642

Temurtas, H., Yumusak, N., & Temurtas, F. (2009). A comparative study on diabetes disease diagnosis using neural networks. *Expert Systems with Applications*, *36*(4), 8610–8615. doi:10.1016/j.eswa.2008.10.032

Teng, J.-H., Luan, S.-W., Lee, D.-J., & Huang, Y.-Q. (2013). Optimal charging/discharging scheduling of battery storage systems for distribution systems interconnected with sizeable PV generation systems. *IEEE Transactions on Power Systems, 28*(2), 1425–1433. doi:10.1109/TPWRS.2012.2230276

Teng, J., Xing, H. B., Lu, W., Li, Z. H., & Chen, C. J. (2016). Influence analysis of time delay to active mass damper control system using pole assignment method. *Mechanical Systems and Signal Processing, 80*, 99–116. doi:10.1016/j.ymssp.2016.04.008

Thakur, A., Wadhwani, S., & Sondhiya, V. (2013). Health monitoring of rotating electrical machine using soft computing techniques: A Review. *International Journal of Scientific and Research Publications, 3*(11), 1–3.

Thangaraj, R., Thanga, R. C., Pant, M., Ajit, A., & Grosan, C. (2010). Optimal gain tuning of PI speed controller in induction motor drives using particle swarm optimization. *Logic Journal of IGPL Advance Access*, 1-4.

Theilmann, P. T., Presti, C. D., Kelly, D., & Asbeck, P. M. (2010). Near zero turn-on voltage high-efficiency UHF RFID rectifier in silicon-on-sapphire CMOS. *Radio Frequency Integrated Circuits Symposium*, 105 – 108. doi:10.1109/RFIC.2010.5477409

Thierry, T., Valerie, V., & Ludivine, F. (2012). A 900MHz RF energy harvesting module. *New Circuits and Systems Conference (NEWCAS)*, 445 – 448.

Toivonen, H. (1996) Sampling large databases for Association rules. *Proceedings of the 22nd VLDB Conference*, 134-145.

Tong, X., Liu, Y., Zhang, M., Xu, H., & Wang, Z. (2015). An Image Encryption Scheme Based on Hyperchaotic Rabinovich and Exponential Chaos Maps. *Entropy, 17*, 181-196.

Tong, S.-C., Li, Y.-M., Feng, G., & Li, T.-S. (2011a). Observer-based adaptive fuzzy backstepping dynamic surface control for a class of MIMO nonlinear systems. *IEEE Transactions on Systems, Man, and Cybernetics. Part B, Cybernetics, 41*(4), 1124–1135. doi:10.1109/TSMCB.2011.2108283 PMID:21317084

Tong, S., Li, C., & Li, Y. (2009). Fuzzy adaptive observer backstepping control for MIMO nonlinear systems. *Fuzzy Sets and Systems, 160*, 2755–2775. doi:10.1016/j.fss.2008.09.004

Tong, S., Li, Yu., & Li, Y. (2011b). Observer-based adaptive fuzzy backstepping control for a class of stochastic nonlinear strict-feedback systems. *IEEE Transactions on Systems, Man, and Cybernetics. Part B, Cybernetics, 41*(6), 1693–1704. doi:10.1109/TSMCB.2011.2159264 PMID:21788195

Trung, N. T., Feng, T., Haftiger, P., & Chakrabartty, S. (2014). Sub-threshold CMOS voltage-multipliers using hybrid RF piezoelectric energy scavenging. *International Conference on Communications and Electronics (ICCE)*, 304 – 308.

Tubaldi, E., Ragni, L., & Dall'Asta, A. (2015). Probabilistic seismic response assessment of linear systems equipped with nonlinear viscous dampers. *Earthquake Engineering & Structural Dynamics, 44*(1), 101–120. doi:10.1002/eqe.2461

Tyagi, V., Rahim, N. A., Rahim, N., Jeyraj, A., & Selvaraj, L. (2013). Progress in solar PV technology: Research and achievement. *Renewable & Sustainable Energy Reviews, 20*, 443–461. doi:10.1016/j.rser.2012.09.028

Ukkonen, L., Schaffrath, M., Sydanheimo, L., & Kivikoski, M. (2006). Analysis of integrated slot-type tag antennas for passive UHF RFID. *Antennas and Propagation Society International Symposium*, 1343 – 1346. doi:10.1109/APS.2006.1710794

Ungan, T., Polozecv, X. L., Walker, W., & Reindi, L. (2009). RF energy harvesting design using high Q resonators. *IEEE MTT-S International Microwave Workshop on Wireless Sensing, LocalPositioning, and RFID (IMWS)*, 1 – 4. doi:10.1109/IMWS2.2009.5307869

Uz, M. E., & Hadi, M. N. (2014). Optimal design of semi active control for adjacent buildings connected by MR damper based on integrated fuzzy logic and multi-objective genetic algorithm. *Engineering Structures, 69,* 135–148. doi:10.1016/j.engstruct.2014.03.006

Uzun, Y. (2015). Design of an efficient triple band RF energy harvester. *ACES Journal, 30,* 1286–1293.

Uzun, Y. (2016). Design and implementation of RF energy harvesting system for low-power electronic devices. *Journal of Electronic Materials, 45*(8), 3842–3847. doi:10.1007/s11664-016-4441-5

Van Der Heijden, A., Serrarens, F., Camlibel, M., & Nijmeijer, H. (2007). Hybrid optimal control of dry clutch engagement. *International Journal of Control, 80*(11), 1717–1728. doi:10.1080/00207170701473995

Vasconcellos, C. A., Beneti, C., Sato, F., Pinheiro, L. C., & Curotto, C. L. (2006). Electrical Thunderstorm Nowcasting using Lightning Data Mining. *Proceeding of International Lightning Detection Conference.* doi:10.2495/DATA060161

Venkatesh, B., Ranjan, R., & Gooi, H. (2004). Optimal reconfiguration of radial distribution systems to maximize loadability. Power Systems. *IEEE Transactions on, 19*(1), 260–266.

Vera, G. A., Georgiadis, A., Collado, A., & Via, S. (2010). Design of a 2.45 GHz rectenna for electromagnetic (EM) energy scavenging. *Radio and Wireless Symposium (RWS),* 61 – 64. doi:10.1109/RWS.2010.5434266

Verlinde, H., De Cock, M., & Boute, R. (2006). Fuzzy Versus Quantitative Association Rules: A Fair Data-Driven Comparison. *IEEE Transactions on Systems, Man, and Cybernetics, 36*(3), 679–683. doi:10.1109/TSMCB.2005.860134 PMID:16761820

Wagner, M. J., & Smith, M. A. (2008, October). Shared internal models for feedforward and feedback control. *The Journal of Neuroscience, 28*(42), 10663–10673. doi:10.1523/JNEUROSCI.5479-07.2008 PMID:18923042

Wang, G., & Zhang, M., XinheXu, & Jiang, C. (2006). Optimization of Controller Parameters based on the Improved Genetic Algorithms. *IEEE Proceedings of the 6th World Congress on Intelligent Control and Automation,* 3695-3698.

Wang, X., & Chen, D., (2013). A Parallel Encryption Algorithm Based on Piecewise Linear Chaotic Map. *Mathematical Problems in Engineering, 13,* 1-7.

Wang, X., & Jin, C. (2012). Image Encryption Using Game of Life Permutation and PWLCM Chaotic System. *Optics Communications, 285,* 412–417.

Wang, X., Gu, S., & Zhang, Y. (2015). Novel Image Encryption Algorithm Based on Cycle Shift and Chaotic System. *Optics and Lasers in Engineering, 68,* 126–134.

Wang, C., & Hill, D. J. (2006, January). Learning from neural control. *IEEE Transactions on Neural Networks, 17*(1), 130–146. doi:10.1109/TNN.2005.860843 PMID:16526482

Wang, C., Wang, M., Liu, T., & Hill, D. J. (2012, October). Learning from ISS-modular adaptive NN control of nonlinear strict-feedback systems. *IEEE Transactions on Neural Networks and Learning Systems, 23*(10), 1539–1550. doi:10.1109/TNNLS.2012.2205702 PMID:24808000

Wang, D. H., & Liao, W. H. (2005). Semiactive Controllers for Magnetorheological Fluid Dampers. *Journal of Intelligent Material Systems and Structures, 16*(11-12), 983–993. doi:10.1177/1045389X05055281

Wang, D., & Huang, J. (2005). Neural network-based adaptive dynamic surface control for a class of uncertain nonlinear systems in strict-feedback form. *IEEE Transactions on Neural Networks, 16*(1), 195–202. doi:10.1109/TNN.2004.839354 PMID:15732399

Wang, F., Liu, Z., Zhang, Y., Chen, X., & Chen, C. L. P. (2015). Adaptive fuzzy dynamic surface control for a class of nonlinear systems with fuzzy dead zone and dynamic uncertainties. *Nonlinear Dynamics*, *79*(3), 1693–1709. doi:10.1007/s11071-014-1768-4

Wang, H., Wang, D., & Peng, Z. (2014). Neural network based adaptive dynamic surface control for cooperative path following of marine surface vehicles via state and output feedback. *Neurocomputing*, *133*, 170–178. doi:10.1016/j.neucom.2013.11.019

Wang, M., Chen, B., & Dai, S.-L. (2007). Direct adaptive fuzzy tracking control for a class of perturbed stric-feedback nonlinear systems. *Fuzzy Sets and Systems*, *158*(24), 2655–2670. doi:10.1016/j.fss.2007.06.001

Wang, M., Wang, C., & Liu, X. (2014, September). Dynamic learning from adaptive neural control with predefined performance for a class of nonlinear systems. *Inf. Sci.*, *279*, 874–888. doi:10.1016/j.ins.2014.04.038

Wang, Q., & Fan, W. (2011). Application of PSO in Thunderstorms Forecast. *Advanced Materials Research*, *171-172*, 536–539. doi:10.4028/www.scientific.net/AMR.171-172.536

Wang, Y.-C., Chien, C.-J., Chi, R., & Hou, Z. (2015, September). A fuzzy-neural adaptive terminal iterative learning control for fed-batch fermentation processes. *International Journal of Fuzzy Systems*, *17*(3), 423–433. doi:10.1007/s40815-015-0059-7

Waseem, I., Pipattanasomporn, M., & Rahman, S. (2009). *Reliability benefits of distributed generation as a backup source.* Paper presented at the Power & Energy Society General Meeting, 2009. PES'09. IEEE. doi:10.1109/PES.2009.5275233

Website Ptolemy. (2013). *Ptolemy project heterogeneous modeling and design.* Retrieved from http://www.ptolemy.eecs.berkeley.edu

Website SoCLib. (2017). Retrieved from http://www.soclib.fr

Weigand, S. M. (2005). Compact microstrip antenna with forward directed radiation pattern for RFID reader card. *Antennas and Propagation Society International Symposium*, 337 – 340. doi:10.1109/APS.2005.1552011

Weng, L. Y., Omar, J. B., Siah, Y. K., Ahmed, S. K., Abidin, I. B. Z., & Abdullah, N. (2010). Lightning Forecasting using ANN-BP & Radiosonde. In *Proceedings of International Conference on Intelligent Computing and Cognitive Informatics*. IEEE.

Whitley, D. (1994). A genetic algorithm tutorial. *Statistics and Computing*, *4*(2), 65–85. doi:10.1007/BF00175354

Wilson, C. M. D., & Abdullah, M. M. (2010). Structural vibration reduction using self-tuning fuzzy control of magnetorheological dampers. *Bulletin of Earthquake Engineering*, *8*(4), 1037–1054. doi:10.1007/s10518-010-9177-7

Wong, K., & Yuen, C. (2008). Embedding Compression in Chaos-Based Cryptography. IEEE Transactions on Circuits and Systems—II: Express Briefs, 55(11), 1193-1197.

Wong, K., Lin, Q., & Chen, J. (2010). Simultaneous Arithmetic Coding and Encryption Using Chaotic Maps. IEEE Transactions on Circuits and Systems—II: Express Briefs, 57(2), 146-150.

Woods, E. J. (1990). Aircraft Electrical System computer Simulation. *Proceedings of the 25th Intersociety Energy Conversion Engineering Conference, IECEC-90*, 84-89. doi:10.1109/IECEC.1990.716551

Xia, C., Song, P., Shi, T., & Yan, Y. (2013). Chaotic Dynamics Characteristic Analysisfor Matrix Converter. *IEEE Transactions on Industrial Electronics, 60*(1), 78-87.

Xing-yuan, W., & Qing, Y., (2009). A block Encryption Algorithm Based on Dynamic Sequences of Multiple Chaotic Systems. *Communications in Nonlinear Science and Numerical Simulation, 14*, 574–581.

Xiong, J., Lam, J., Shu, Z., & Mao, X. (2014). Stability analysis of continuous-time switched systems with a random switching signal. *IEEE Transactions on Automatic Control, 59*(1), 180–186. doi:10.1109/TAC.2013.2266751

Xuand, S., & Wang, Y. (2010). A Novel Image Encryption Scheme based on a Nonlinear Chaotic Map. *International Journal of Image, Graphics and Signal Processing, 1*, 61-68.

Xu, B., Shi, Z., Yang, C., & Sun, F. (2014). Composite neural dynamic surface control of a class of uncertain nonlinear systems in strict-feedback form. *IEEE Transactions on Cybernetics, 44*(12), 2626–2634. doi:10.1109/TCYB.2014.2311824 PMID:24718583

Xu, B., Yang, C., & Shi, Z. (2014, March). Reinforcement learning output feedback NN control using deterministic learning technique. *IEEE Transactions on Neural Networks and Learning Systems, 25*(3), 635–641. doi:10.1109/TNNLS.2013.2292704 PMID:24807456

Yan, G., & Zhou, L. L. (2006). Integrated fuzzy logic and genetic algorithms for multi-objective control of structures using MR dampers. *Journal of Sound and Vibration, 296*(1-2), 368–382. doi:10.1016/j.jsv.2006.03.011

Yang, S. F., Chen, C. C., Huang, T. H., Lu, C. Y., & Chung, P. J. (2015). Design of a 2×2 antenna-array RF power emitter with object detection function for sensor location identification. *International Microwave Workshop Series on RF and Wireless Technologies for Biomedical and Healthcare Applications (IMWS-BIO), 65 – 66*. doi:10.1109/IMWS-BIO.2015.7303779

Yang, S. M., Chen, C. J., & Huang, W. L. (2006). Structural Vibration Suppression by a Neural-Network Controller with a Mass-Damper Actuator. *Journal of Vibration and Control, 12*(5), 495–508. doi:10.1177/1077546306064269

Yang, X. S., Bekdaş, G., & Nigdeli, S. M. (2016). Review and applications of metaheuristic algorithms in civil engineering. In *Metaheuristics and Optimization in Civil Engineering* (pp. 1–24). Springer International Publishing. doi:10.1007/978-3-319-26245-1_1

Yang, Y., Feng, G., & Ren, J. (2004). A combined backstepping and small-gain approach to robust adaptive fuzzy control for strict-feedback nonlinear systems. *IEEE Transactions on Systems, Man, and Cybernetics. Part A, Systems and Humans, 34*(3), 406–420. doi:10.1109/TSMCA.2004.824870

Yang, Y., & Zhou, C. (2005). Adaptive fuzzy H_∞ stabilization for strict-feedback canonical nonlinear systems via backstepping and small-gain approach. *IEEE Transactions on Fuzzy Systems, 13*(1), 104–112. doi:10.1109/TFUZZ.2004.839663

Yan, W. (2012, July). Toward automatic time-series forecasting using neural networks. *IEEE Transactions on Neural Networks and Learning Systems, 23*(7), 1028–1039. doi:10.1109/TNNLS.2012.2198074 PMID:24807130

Yao, Y., Wu, J., Shi, Y., & Dai, F. F. (2009). A fully integrated 900-MHz passive RFID transponder front end with novel zero threshold RF–DC rectifier. *IEEE Transactions on Industrial Electronics, 56*(7), 2317–2325. doi:10.1109/TIE.2008.2010180

Ye, C. Z., Yang, J., Geng, D. Y., Zhou, Y., & Chen, N. Y. (2002). Fuzzy rules to predict degree of malignancy in brain glioma. *Medical & Biological Engineering & Computing, 40*(2), 145–152. doi:10.1007/BF02348118 PMID:12043794

Yi, J., Ki, W.-H., & Tsui, C.-Y. (2008). Analysis and design strategy of UHF micro-power CMOS rectifiers for micro-sensor and RFID applications. *IEEE Transactions on Circuits and Systems. I, Regular Papers, 54*(1), 153–166. doi:10.1109/TCSI.2006.887974

Yoo, D. K., & Wang, L. (2007). Model based wheel slip control via constrained optimal algorithm. In *IEEE International Conference on Control Applications* (pp. 1239-1246). Singapore: IEEE.

Younus, S., Hegde, B., Prabhakar, T. V., & Vinoy, K. J. (2016). RF Energy harvesting chip powered sensor node. *International Conference on Electronics, Circuits & Systems*, 1-4.

Youssef, A., & Zergainoh, N. E. (2007). Simulink-based MPSoC Design: New Approach to Bridge the Gap between Algorithm and Architecture Design. *IEEE Computer Society Annual Symposium.*

Yu, B., Shi, Y., & Huang, J. (2011). Modified generalized predictive control of networked systems with application to a hydraulic position control system. *ASME Journal of Dynamic Systems, Measurement, and Control, 133*(3), 031009-1, 031009–9. doi:10.1115/1.4003385

Yue, D., Tian, E., Zhang, Y., & Peng, C. (2009). Delay-distribution-dependent robust stability of uncertain systems with time-varying delay. *International Journal of Robust and Nonlinear Control, 19*(4), 377–393. doi:10.1002/rnc.1314

Yu, J., Shi, P., Dong, W., Chen, B., & Lin, C. (2015). Neural network-based adaptive dynamic surface control for permanent magnet synchronous motors. *IEEE Transactions on Neural Networks and Learning Systems, 26*(3), 640–645. doi:10.1109/TNNLS.2014.2316289 PMID:25720014

Yves, S. (2014). *The AAA methodology and syndex.* Retrieved from http://www.syndex.org

Zafarani, M. M., Halabian, A. M., & Behbahani, S. (2016). Optimal coupled and uncoupled fuzzy logic control for magneto-rheological damper-equipped plan-asymmetric structural systems considering structural nonlinearities. *Journal of Vibration and Control.* doi:10.1177/1077546316660030

Zamani, A. A., Tavakoli, S., & Etedali, S. (2017). Control of piezoelectric friction dampers in smart base-isolated structures using self-tuning and adaptive fuzzy proportional–derivative controllers. *Journal of Intelligent Material Systems and Structures, 28*(10), 1287–1302. doi:10.1177/1045389X16667561

Zargarzadeh, Dierks, & Jagannathan. (2014). Adaptive neural network-based optimal control of nonlinear continuous-time systems in strict-feedback form. *Int. J. Adapt. Control Signal Process, 28*(3-5), 305–324.

Zbitou, J., Latrac, M., & Toutain, S. (2006). Hybrid rectenna and monolithic integrated zero-bias microwave rectifier. *IEEE Transactions on Microwave Theory and Techniques, 54*(1), 147–152. doi:10.1109/TMTT.2005.860509

Zekri, M., Sheikholeslam, F., & Sadri, S. (2008). Adaptive fuzzy wavelet network control design for nonlinear systems. *Fuzzy Sets and Systems, 159*(20), 2668–2695. doi:10.1016/j.fss.2008.02.008

Zeng, X., Siden, J., Wang, G., & Nilsson, H. E. (2007). Slots in metallic label as RFID tag antenna. *Antennas and Propagation Society International Symposium*, 1749 – 1752.

Zepka, G. S., & Pinto, O., Jr. (2008). A Forecast Cloud- to- Ground Lightning System Based on a Neural Network-Preliminary Results. *Proceedings of 20th International Lightning Detection Conference & 2nd International Lightning Meteorology Conference.*

Zepka, G. S., Pinto, O. Jr, & Saraiva, A. C. V. (2014). Lightning Forecasting in Southeastern Brazil using the WRF model. *Atmospheric Research, 135-136*, 344–362. doi:10.1016/j.atmosres.2013.01.008

Zerikat, M., & Chekroun, S. (2008). Adaptation Learning Speed Control for a High-Performance Induction Motor using Neural Networks. Proceedings of World Academy of Science, Engineering and Technology, 294-299.

Zhang, Z., Niu, X., Wang, H., & Liu, K. (2013). Characteristics Analysis and Application of The Encryption Algorithm Based on Dual-Chaos Theory. *International Conference on Sensor Network Security Technology and Privacy Communication System (SNS & PCS)*, 1-4. doi:10.1109/SNS-PCS.2013.6553850

Zhang, H., Wang, E., Zhang, N., Min, F., Subash, R., & Su, C. (2015). Semi-active sliding mode control of vehicle suspension with magneto-rheological damper. *Chinese Journal of Mechanical Engineering*, 28(1), 63–75. doi:10.3901/CJME.2014.0918.152

Zhang, J. (1999). Inferential estimation of polymer quality using bootstrap aggregated neural networks. *Neural Networks*, 12(6), 927–938. doi:10.1016/S0893-6080(99)00037-4 PMID:12662667

Zhang, L., Xiao, M., Ma, J., & Song, H. (2009). Edge Detection by Adaptive Neuro-Fuzzy Inference System. *2nd International Congress on Image and Signal Processing, CISP '09*. doi:10.1109/CISP.2009.5304595

Zhang, T. P., & Ge, S. S. (2008). Adaptive dynamic surface control of nonlinear systems with unknown dead zone in pure feedback form. *Automatica*, 44(7), 1895–1903. doi:10.1016/j.automatica.2007.11.025

Zhang, X., Fan, X., Wang, J., & Zhao, Z. (2014). A Chaos-Based Image Encryption Scheme Using 2D Rectangular Transform and Dependent Substitution. In *Multimedia Tools Application* (pp. 1–19). New York: Springer Science & Business Media.

Zhang, Y., Alleyne, A. G., & Zheng, D. (2005). A hybrid control strategy for active vibration isolation with electrohydraulic actuators. *Control Engineering Practice*, 13(3), 279–289. doi:10.1016/j.conengprac.2004.03.009

Zhao, D., & Li, Y. (2015). Fuzzy control for seismic protection of semiactive base-isolated structures subjected to near-fault earthquakes. *Mathematical Problems in Engineering*.

Zhao, Q., Xu, J., Yin, H., Lu, Z., Vue, L., Gong, Y., & Wang, W. et al. (2015). Dual band antenna and high efficiency rectifier for RF energy harvesting system. *International Symposium on Microwave, Antenna, Propagation, and EMC Technologies (MAPE)*, 682 – 685.

Zhao, Y. B., Liu, G. P., & Rees, D. (2010). Packet-based dead-band control for internet-based networked control systems. *IEEE Transactions on Control Systems Technology*, 18(5), 1057–1067. doi:10.1109/TCST.2009.2033118

Zhen, D., Wang, T., Gu, F., & Ball, A. D. (2013). Fault diagnosis of motor drives using stator current signal analysis based on dynamic time warping. *Mechanical Systems and Signal Processing*, 34(1), 191–202. doi:10.1016/j.ymssp.2012.07.018

Zhong Chen, Y. L., Yingpeng Luo, , & Miao Chen, . (2012). Control and Performance of a Cascaded Shunt Active Power Filter for Aircraft Electric Power System. *IEEE Transactions on Industrial Electronics*, 59(9), 3614–3623. doi:10.1109/TIE.2011.2166231

Zhou, H., Sun, L., & Xing, F. (2014). Damping of full-scale stay cable with viscous damper: Experiment and analysis. *Advances in Structural Engineering*, 17(2), 265–274. doi:10.1260/1369-4332.17.2.265

Zhu, H., Zhang, X., Yu, H., Zhao, C., & Zhu, Z. (2016). A Novel Image Encryption Scheme Using the Composite Discrete Chaotic System. *Entropy*, 18(276), 1-27.

Zhu, J. (2015). *Optimization of power system operation* (Vol. 47). John Wiley & Sons.

Zulkifli, F. F., Sampe, J., Islam, M. S., Mohamed, M. A., & Wahab, S. A. (2015). Optimization of RF- DC converter in micro energy harvester using voltage boosting network and bulk modulation technique for biomedical devices. *IEEE Regional Symposium on Micro and Nanoelectronics (RSM)*, 1 – 4. doi:10.1109/RSM.2015.7354975

About the Contributors

Uday Pratap Singh was born on February 6, 1979 in Sultanpur, U.P., India. He is currently working as an Assistant Professor in the Department of Applied Mathematics, Madhav Institute of Technology & Science, Gwalior, India. He completed B.Sc. at the K.N.I.P.S.S., Sultanpur, U.P., M.Sc. at the Indian Institute of Technology, Guwahati, India, and received Ph.D. in Computer Science from Barkatullah University, Bhopal. He has published/presented about 30 research papers in International/ National Journals and at Conferences on Soft Computing, Image Processing, etc. His areas of research include Computational Intelligence, Soft Computing, Image Processing etc. He has also qualified from CSIR (NET). He is a life member of the Computer Society of India.

Akhilesh Tiwari has received Ph.D. degree in Information Technology from Rajiv Gandhi Technological University, Bhopal, India. He is currently working as Associate Professor in the department of CSE & IT, Madhav Institute of Technology & Science, Gwalior, M.P. (India). His area of current research includes knowledge discovery in databases & data mining, and wireless Networks. He is also acting as a reviewer & member in editorial board of various international journals. He is having the memberships of various Academic/ Scientific societies including IETE, CSI, GAMS, IACSIT, and IAENG.

* * *

Pankaj Agrawal received his Master's degree from ABV-IIITM Gwalior, India in 2006. Currently he is pursuing Ph. D. from Mahatma Gandhi Chitrakoot Gramodaya Vishwavidyalaya (MGCGV) Chitrakoot, Satna, India. His research area is RF energy harvesting and its application for wireless sensor devices.

Abid Ali received the BSc. (Hons) in Electronics from University of Sindh, Jamshoro, Pakistan, in 2007, and Master of Engineering in Electrical Power from Universiti Teknologi Malaysia (UTM), Skudai, Johor Bahru, Malayisa, in 2012. In 2012, he joined Osmani & Co., Pakistan, and worked for the development of 50 MW wind and 40 MW solar PV plants for the first smart city of Pakistan. He is currently pursuing the Ph.D. degree at Electrical and Electronic Engineering Department, Universiti Teknologi Petronas (UTP), Perak, Malaysia. His current research interests include the integration of battery storage for the utility-scale photovoltaic plants.

Sowkarthika B is currently pursuing the M. tech. degree in computer science and engineering from CSE/IT department, MITS Gwalior (M.P), India. She has received B.E. degree from College of Engineering, Guindy, Tamilnadu, India. Her areas of interest are data mining, Association rule mining, frequent pattern mining, vague set, Intelligent techniques and their applications.

Kanchan Bala did her Bachelors in Engineering in Computer Science and Engineering from Rajasthan University, followed by Master of Technology in Computer science and pursuing Ph.D from Birla Institute of Technology, Mesra in 2005, 2009 and 2015 respectively . She is currently the Research Scholar in Department of Computer Science and Engineering, Birla Institute of Technology, Mesra, Jharkhand, India. She has 4 research publications in international journals, book and conference proceedings to her credit. She has been the member of CSI. Her research interests include soft computing, data mining, Big Data.

Kishore Bingi received the B.Tech. (Hons.) degree in Electrical & Electronics Engineering from Bapatla Engineering College (BEC), Bapatla, Andhra Pradesh, India, in 2012, and the M.Tech (Hons.) degree in Instrumentation and Control Systems from National Institute of Technology (NIT) Calicut, Calicut, Kerala, India, in 2014. He worked with TATA consultancy service as an Assistant systems Engineer from 2015 to 2016. He is currently pursuing the Ph.D. degree with the Electrical and Electronic Engineering Department, Universiti Teknologi Petronas (UTP), Perak, Malaysia. His current research interests include process modeling, control and optimization.

Constantin Florin Caruntu received his Ph.D. degree in Systems Engineering from the Gheorghe Asachi Technical University of Iasi, Romania, November 2011. He is currently an associate professor in the Department of Automatic Control and Applied Informatics at the same university, Faculty of Automatic Control and Computer Engineering. His current research interests include model predictive control, networked control systems, automotive control systems and vehicle platooning.

Dilip Kumar Choubey received his M.Tech degree in Computer Science and Engineering from Oriental College of Technology (O.C.T), Bhopal, India in 2012 and has B.E. degree in Information Technology from Bansal Institute of Science and Technology (B.I.S.T), Bhopal, India in 2010. Currently, He is Pursuing Ph.D since March 2014 from Birla Institue of Technology (B.I.T), Mesra, Ranchi, India. He worked as an Asst. Prof. in Lakshmi Narain College of Technology (L.N.C.T), Bhopal, India and Oriental College of Technology (O.C.T), Bhopal, India. He has more than 6 years of teaching and research experience. He is a author of 1 book and has more than 13 research publications in international journals, book chapters and conference proceedings to his credit. He has been the member of the organizing and technical program committees of some conferences and Workshop. He has been attended so many workshop's/Seminar's/Conference's. He is the lifetime members of several professional bodies such as The International Association of Engineers (IAENG), The Internet Society Switzerland (ISOC), The Society of Digital Information and Wireless Communications (SDIWC), Universal Association of Computers and Electronics Engineers (UACEE), Associate Member (till 4 May, 2019), Computer Science Teachers Association (CSTA), Member (Individual III, till 11/08/2016), etc. His research interests include Machine Learning, Soft Computing, Bioinformatics, Data Mining, Pattern Recognition, and Database Management System, etc.

Siddharth Singh Chouhan received B.E. degree in 2010 and M.Tech in 2012 in Computer Science and Engineering from RGPV University, Bhopal, India. He is currently pursuing Ph.D. Degree form Department of Computer Science and Engineering at Shri Mata Vaishno Devi University Katra, Jammu and Kashmir. His area of interest is soft computing, image processing. He had authored several research papers published at reputed journals and conferences.

Deepanshu Dubey was born on 24 June 1992 in Gwalior Madhya Pradesh India. He has completed his schooling from Kendriya Vidhyalya in 2010 and completed his bachelor of engineering in electronics and communication branch from RGPV Bhopal in year of 2014. Currently he is pursuing his PGDFM (equivalent to MBA) from Indian Institute of Forest Management, Bhopal M.P Area of Interest: PLC, SKADA and Embedded System.

Deepika Dubey has completed her Bachelor of Engineering and Master of Engineering from RGPV University, Bhopal, India. At present, she is perusing Ph.D. from Uttrakhand Technical University, Dehradun, India. Her area of interest are Image Processing, Computer Vision, and networking.

Taib Ibrahim was born in Kedah, Malaysia in 1972. He received the B.Eng (Hons) in electrical and electronics engineering, MSc. in electrical power engineering and PhD in electrical machine design from Coventry University, U.K. in 1996, University of Strathclyde, UK in 2000 and University of Sheffield, UK in 2009, respectively. His employment experience includes Airod (M) Sdn Bhd and Universiti Teknologi PETRONAS (UTP). Currently, he is cluster leader for power, control and instrumentation in UTP. His research interests range from electrical machines developments to their associated drives.

Amit Kumar is currently a research scholar at the Department of Computer Sc. and Engg., BIT Mesra, Ranchi, India. He received M.Tech degree in Computer Science from BIT Mesra, Ranchi, India and M.C.A from U.P.Technical University, Lucknow,India. With more than 7 years of teaching experience, he published many research articles. His main areas of research interest are machine learning, data mining and soft computing.

K. Vinoth Kumar was born on 30th April 1984, in Vellore, Tamil Nadu, India. He received his Undergraduate degree in Electrical and Electronics Engineering from Anna University, Chennai, India in the year 2006 and Post Graduate degree specializing in Power Electronics and Drives from VIT University, Vellore, India in the year 2008. He is currently Assistant Professor in the Department of Electrical Sciences at Karunya University, Coimbatore, India. His research interests include Fault diagnosis in industrial drives, Neuro Fuzzy computing and Power Electronics & Drives. He has been actively involved in the Internal Quality Assurance Cell at Karunya University. His contribution in setting up the experiments for the Power Electronics Laboratory is also commendable. He published research papers in both international and national journals as well as in conferences. He is authored the Book titled "Basic Electrical and Electronics Engineering" published by John Wiley & Sons India in 2014 and Neural Networks, Soft Computing textbooks in 2012. He has delivered lectures on Energy Conservation inn Industries, New techniques for Energy auditing and other related areas in various workshop and seminars as well as guided 14 UG and 14 PG Student projects and One International student project.

Prawin Angel Michael's research interests include Fault diagnosis in industrial drives, Neuro Fuzzy computing and Power Electronics & Drives. She has been actively involved in the Placement Cell at Karunya University. His contribution in setting up the experiments for the Power Electronics Laboratory is also commendable.

Deepika Singh Kushwah was born in 22 October 1989. She has completed her M.Tech from Jaypee University of Engineering & Technology, Guna in 2013 her thesis on wired networks and that of on RFD of BGP. At present she is working as HOD of CSE Department in ShriRam Institute of Information & Technology, Banmore, Madhya Pradesh. Her areas of interests are Computer Networks, Databases & software engineering.

Mili Ghosh Nee Lala did her M.Tech in Remote Sensing from Birla Institute of Technology, Mesra in 2002 and Ph.D in Geomatics from Indian Institute of Technology, Roorkee in 2009.She is currently the Assistant Professor in Department of Remote Sensing, Birla Institute of Technology, Mesra, Jharkhand, India. Her research interests include Environmental Modeling and Planetary Remote Sensing. She has 24 research publications in international journals, book chapters and conference proceedings to her credit.

Priti Maheshwary is working as Associate Professor in Dept. of CSE in AISECT University since 2015. She got her PhD in Computer Application from MANIT Bhopal. She has more than 20 papers published in journals of repute.

Nursyarizal Mohd Nor received his PhD. in Electrical Power Engineering from Universiti Teknologi PETRONAS (UTP), Perak, Malaysia, in 2009. Currently he is a committed Associate Professors with over 16 years of research and academic experience as a part of the Electrical and Electronics Engineering Department in UTP. At UTP, he has developed numerous projects on national and international level in frames of Electrical Protection Box, Portable Thermoelectric Generator, Health Monitoring System, Portable Solar Generator and etc. His research interests include specialization in Power Economics Operation and Control, Power System Analysis and Power System State Estimation. He has successfully published numerous research articles in peer reviewed international journals, book chapters, conferences and symposiums.

Monica Patrascu received a PhD in Systems Engineering from University Politehnica of Bucharest in 2012, an MSc in Intelligent Control Systems and a BSc in Control Engineering from the Faculty of Automatic Control and Computer Science, University Politehnica of Bucharest, Romania. Dr. Patrascu is an Associate Professor at the Department of Automatic Control and Systems Engineering, University Politehnica of Bucharest. Research interests include intelligent control systems, evolutionary computing, large scale systems, heuristic optimization, emergent systems, multi-agent systems, and complex systems.

Sanchita Paul did her Bachelors in Engineering in Computer Science and Engineering from Burdwan University, followed by Master of Engineering in Software Engineering and Ph.D from Birla Institute of Technology, Mesra in 2004, 2006 and 2012 respectively . She is currently the Assistant Professor in Department of Computer Science and Engineering, Birla Institute of Technology, Mesra, Jharkhand, India. She is a co-author of 1 book and has 48 research publications in international journals, book chapters and conference proceedings to her credit. She has been the member of the organizing and technical program committees of several International conferences and Workshop. She has also acted as Principal Investigator in an AICTE funded project.

Mohd Fakhizan Romlie graduated with a BEng. (Hons) in Electrical & Electronic from Universiti Teknologi PETRONAS in 2004, MEng. in Power System Engineering from the University of Western Australia in 2006 and PhD in Electrical Engineering from University of Nottingham, UK in 2014. Currently, he is a lecturer at the Universiti Teknologi PETRONAS. His research interests include smart grid, renewable energy and wireless power transfer.

Bikash Kanti Sarkar is currently a Faculty at the Department of Computer Sc. and Engg., BIT Mesra, Ranchi, India. A Ph.D. in Computer Science from Jadavpur University (Kolkata). He did his M.Phil.(C.S.) from Annamalai University, MCA from BESU (Howrah) and M.Sc. (Mathematics) from IIT Kharagpur. With more than 17 years of teaching experience, he published many research articles and books.

Utkarsh Sharma is currently working as an asst. prof. In CSE Dept. at G.L.A University, Mathura (U.P.). He had worked on various domains like Cloud computing, parallel algorithms, with specialization in evolutionary algorithms. He received his M.tech in CSE from Jaypee University Noida, (U.P.). He had authored several research papers, published at reputed conferences and journals including IEEE.

Kamel Smiri was born in Tunis, Tunisia, on December 02, 1976. He received an engineering degree from the National School of Engineering in Monastir (ENIM), Tunisia in 2001 and the Master degrees from the University of MANAR II, Faculty of Science of Tunis (FST), Tunisia, in 2005. In 2012, I obtained PhD in computer sciences on Performance evaluation and MPSOC design flow based of performance estimation. Since 2007, he has been an assistant professor of computer engineering at the Faculty of Science of Tunis (FST) in Tunis, Tunisia.

Index

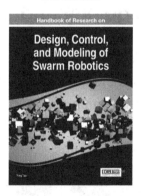

Stay Current on the Latest Emerging Research Developments

Become an IGI Global Reviewer for Authored Book Projects

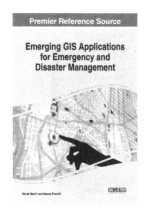

The overall success of an authored book project is dependent on quality and timely reviews.

In this competitive age of scholarly publishing, constructive and timely feedback significantly decreases the turnaround time of manuscripts from submission to acceptance, allowing the publication and discovery of progressive research at a much more expeditious rate. Several IGI Global authored book projects are currently seeking highly qualified experts in the field to fill vacancies on their respective editorial review boards:

Applications may be sent to:
development@igi-global.com

Applicants must have a doctorate (or an equivalent degree) as well as publishing and reviewing experience. Reviewers are asked to write reviews in a timely, collegial, and constructive manner. All reviewers will begin their role on an ad-hoc basis for a period of one year, and upon successful completion of this term can be considered for full editorial review board status, with the potential for a subsequent promotion to Associate Editor.

If you have a colleague that may be interested in this opportunity,
we encourage you to share this information with them.

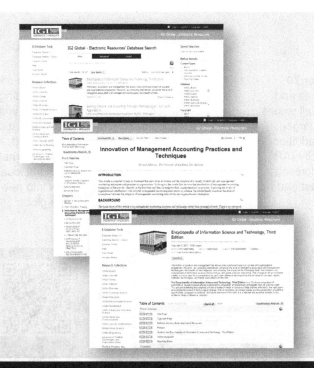

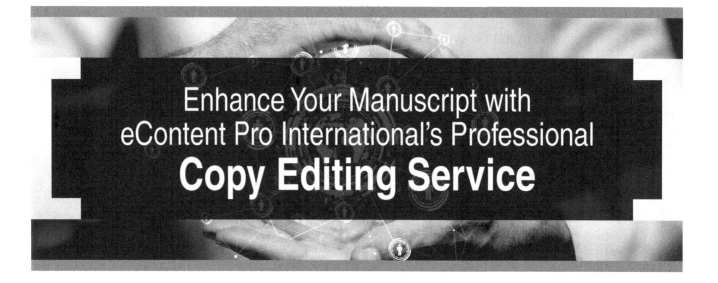

Information Resources Management Association

Advancing the Concepts & Practices of Information Resources
Management in Modern Organizations

Become an IRMA Member

Members of the **Information Resources Management Association (IRMA)** understand the importance of community within their field of study. The Information Resources Management Association is an ideal venue through which professionals, students, and academicians can convene and share the latest industry innovations and scholarly research that is changing the field of information science and technology. Become a member today and enjoy the benefits of membership as well as the opportunity to collaborate and network with fellow experts in the field.

IRMA Membership Benefits:

- **One FREE Journal Subscription**
- **30% Off Additional
  Journal Subscriptions**
- **20% Off Book Purchases**
- Updates on the latest events and research on Information Resources Management through the IRMA-L listserv.
- Updates on new open access and downloadable content added to Research IRM.
- A copy of the Information Technology Management Newsletter twice a year.
- A certificate of membership.

IRMA Membership $195

Scan code or visit **irma-international.org** and begin by selecting your free journal subscription.

Membership is good for one full year.

Printed in the United States
By Bookmasters